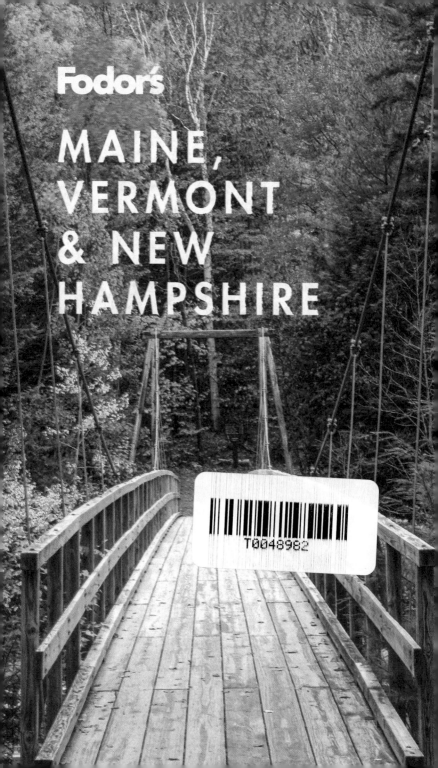

Fodor's

MAINE, VERMONT & NEW HAMPSHIRE

T0048982

Welcome to Maine, Vermont, and New Hampshire

Maine, Vermont, and New Hampshire are quintessential New England, with the quaint towns, brilliant fall foliage, and picturesque landscapes the region is famous for. It's easy to enjoy the outdoors by hiking a section of the Appalachian Trail, skiing the Green Mountains, or taking a scenic drive in Acadia National Park. Smaller cities offer their own pleasures: boutiques and galleries, dockside lobster shacks, and colonial architecture. As you plan your upcoming travels, please confirm that places are still open and let us know when we need to make updates by writing to us at editors@fodors.com.

TOP REASONS TO GO

★ **Fall foliage:** Leaf peepers gather for the country's best festival of colors.

★ **Regional food:** Vermont maple syrup and cheese, Maine lobster and blueberries.

★ **Outdoor fun:** Hiking, boating, biking, or simply taking in a magnificent view.

★ **Small towns:** A perfect day includes strolling a town green and locavore dining.

★ **Fantastic skiing:** All three states have wonderful winter retreats with superb slopes.

★ **The Coast:** Historic lighthouses and harbors, plus whale-watching and sailing.

Contents

Fodor's Features

MAPS

Chapter 1

EXPERIENCE MAINE, VERMONT, AND NEW HAMPSHIRE

15 ULTIMATE EXPERIENCES

Maine, Vermont, and New Hampshire offer terrific experiences that should be on every traveler's list. Here are Fodor's top picks for a memorable trip.

1 Count Covered Bridges

There are 54 of these American symbols still in use in New Hampshire. In fact, the Cornish-Windsor Bridge (1866) is New England's only covered bridge that connects two states, the country's longest wooden bridge, and the world's longest two-span covered bridge. (Ch. 5)

2 Get Away from It All

You won't find high-rises or neon lights in Rangeley Lakes, just peace and quiet, panoramic vistas, beautiful sunsets, and a brilliant night sky. *(Ch. 6)*

3 Boating on Lake Champlain

The 107-mile-long lake is hugely popular for recreation— you can rent numerous types of vessels, take lessons, or, cruise aboard *Spirit of Ethan Allen*. *(Ch. 4)*

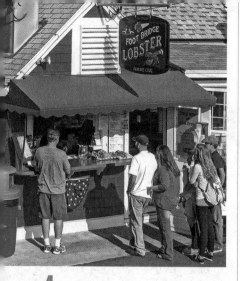

4 Have a Maine Lobster

A trip to Maine isn't complete without a meal featuring the official state crustacean. Whether it's a classic lobster dinner, a bowl of lobster stew, or a lobster roll, bring your appetite. *(Ch. 7)*

5 Boating on Lake Winnipesaukee

You won't run out of space or adventures at New Hampshire's largest lake. Rentals are available to explore more than 250 islands, and there are numerous waterfront restaurants. *(Ch. 5)*

6 Hike Mt. Monadnock

At 3,165 feet, Mt. Monadnock looms over southwestern New Hampshire. The only way to reach the summit is by foot, and the miles of trails attract well over 120,000 hikers each year. *(Ch. 5)*

7 Visit a Working Farm

Several Vermont farmers welcome visitors for a day, overnight, or a few days. Guests can help with chores like collecting eggs, milking cows, feeding sheep, picking veggies, or baking bread. *(Ch. 4)*

8 Explore Acadia National Park

At New England's only national park, drive or bike the 27-mile Park Loop Road, climb the summit of Cadillac Mountain, or explore miles of trails and carriage roads. *(Ch. 7)*

9 Historic and Hip Portland

Old Port has eclectic restaurants and boutiques, while the Arts District has the Portland Museum of Art. The Eastern Promenade has a 2-mile paved waterside trail. *(Ch. 7)*

10 Cruise on a Windjammer

Pretty Camden Harbor and nearby Rockland are home ports for a fleet of owner-operated schooners that take guests on voyages around Maine's rugged coast, peninsulas, and islands. *(Ch. 7)*

11 Ski Vermont

Snuggled in and around Vermont's Green Mountains are nearly two dozen major ski resorts, including Sugarbush, Snow, Stratton, and Stowe. *(Ch. 4)*

12 Walk around Portsmouth

This port city is more than just boats. Great restaurants, galleries, and nightlife coexist with historic sites and cultural venues all within walking distance of each other. *(Ch. 5)*

13 Vermont Sugar Shacks

There are about 1,500 sugarhouses in Vermont. These shacks produce about 2.5 million gallons of syrup annually, or about half of all maple syrup consumed in the United States. *(Ch. 4)*

14 Wend Your Way through the White Mountains

Mt. Washington (6,288 feet) is the highest peak in New Hampshire and the northeastern U.S. There are great views, but it's cold and windy even in midsummer. *(Ch. 5)*

15 Treat Yo'self at Ben & Jerry's

At the Ben & Jerry's Factory in Waterbury, take the half-hour guided factory tour to watch ice cream being made, then mosey over to the Scoop Shop for a treat. *(Ch. 4)*

WHAT'S WHERE

1 Vermont. Vermont has farms, freshly starched towns and small cities, quiet country lanes, and bustling ski resorts. The Green Mountain state is synonymous with cheese and maple syrup, and its billboard-free back roads may be the most scenic in the region.

2 New Hampshire. Portsmouth is the star of the state's 18-mile coastline. The Lakes Region is a popular summertime escape, and the White Mountains' dramatic vistas attract photographers and adventurous hikers farther north.

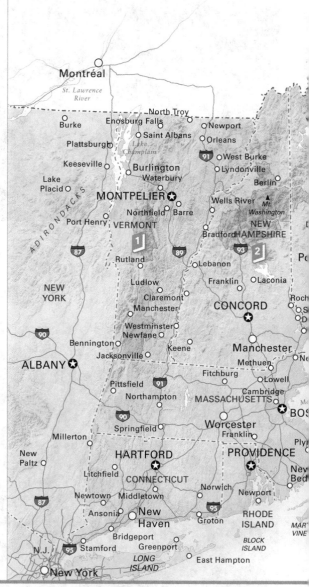

3 **Inland Maine.** The largest New England state's rugged interior—including the Western Lakes and vast North Woods regions—attracts skiers, hikers, campers, anglers, and other outdoors enthusiasts.

4 **The Maine Coast.** Classic villages, rocky shorelines, and picturesque Main Streets draw thousands of vacationers to Maine.

5 **Acadia National Park.** Acadia National Park is where majestic mountains meet the coast; Bar Harbor is the park's gateway town.

Maine's Best Seafood Shacks

BITE INTO MAINE, CAPE ELIZABETH, ME

This spot serves high-quality lobster rolls from a cart near Portland Head Light and has additional locations in Portland and Scarborough. The contemporary twists make the trip worth it, and the LBT (Lobster, Bacon and Tomato) sandwich is sheer heaven.

SHANNON'S UNSHELLED, BOOTHBAY HARBOR, ME

The namesake of this shack first got the idea to set up shop when her father posed the simple question: "Where can you buy a quick lobster roll in Boothbay Harbor?" The shack is now beloved for its grilled and buttered buns stuffed with whole lobsters and served with a side of garlicky, sea-salted drawn butter.

MUSCONGUS BAY LOBSTER, MUSCONGUS, ME

Locals and summer folks chow down on delicious seafood straight from the sea; if you can, grab a table on the deck overlooking the expansive bay. It's BYOB for now (a bar is planned for the future), so bring appropriate provisions. And, there's a kids' menu.

BOB'S CLAM HUT, KITTERY, ME

With fresh (never frozen) shellfish and a cheery, old-school vibe, Bob's also serves up scrumptious, homemade sauces, including their tangy Moxie BBQ sauce, to smother over golden fried clams, alongside some of the creamiest New England clam chowder around.

THE LOBSTER SHACK, OGUNQUIT, ME

A fixture since 1947 in Ogunquit's bustling Perkins Cove, this cozy weathered-shingle lobster pound is just across from the oft-photographed footbridge. Choose from a 1/4- to a whopping 1-pound lobster roll, or try the delicious roll with hand-picked Maine crab meat.

FIVE ISLANDS LOBSTER COMPANY, GEORGETOWN, ME
Located on a lively working wharf overlooking Sheepscot Bay, this cheerful spot welcomes hungry folks with its delicious seafood and stunning views. The family-friendly atmosphere extends to the menu, which also has plenty of "not from the sea" options.

THE HIGHROLLER LOBSTER CO., PORTLAND, ME
What many consider to be Portland's top lobster shop has plenty going for it, from the friendly service to the creative (try the lime-jalapeño mayo) takes on traditional lobster rolls. Be sure to give the tantalizing lobby pop—lobster tail on a stick—a try.

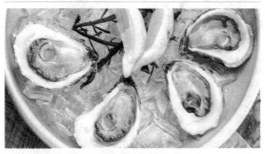

THE SHUCK STATION, NEWCASTLE, ME
There's a lobster roll on the menu, but here it's all about oysters—fried oysters, fried oyster tacos, oysters Rockefeller, oyster po'boys, BBQ oysters, and of course, raw oysters. This laid-back and family-friendly joint has a kids' menu and lots of local beers on tap.

THE CLAM SHACK, KENNEBUNKPORT, ME
For more than a half century, this shack has been known for speedy service and great takeout fare, like its traditional boiled lobster dinners and lobster rolls on freshly baked buns. Eat at one of several wooden picnic tables that overlook the Kennebunk River. There's even a lemonade stand to complete the experience.

RED'S EATS, WISCASSET, ME
It's not uncommon to see hungry customers forming long lines outside this famous red shack, which opened in 1938. The lobster roll (served with local butter) is a huge draw, but the menu features other staples like fried clams, shrimp, and scallops. Hot dogs, hamburgers, and grilled cheese round out the options.

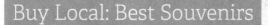

Buy Local: Best Souvenirs

JAMS AND PRESERVES
Pick up strawberry preserves, apple butter, cranberry sauce, or blueberry jam at farmers' markets or country stores like Old Country Store & Museum (NH), East Boothbay General Store (ME), or the Vermont Country Store.

ANTIQUES AND COLLECTIBLES
Collectibles and antiques abound from cities like Portland (Old Port District) to towns like Chester, VT; Littleton, NH; and Wells, ME. In Vermont, Route 100 winds from Wilmington to Stowe past craft studios and general stores. Along the coast, Maine's Route 1 has Colonial furniture and architectural antiques shops, as well as quirky galleries.

MOCCASINS
Maine shoemakers craft some of the best moccasins, and Quoddy, known for its custom, made-to-order moccasins, deck shoes, and boots, is one of the best. Reach out when you're Down East or back home; the wait for shoes is worth it. Ditto for Wassookeag, another great Maine maker of bespoke footwear.

CANVAS BAGS
Nothing says durability like canvas; nothing says coastal New England like sailing. Portland-based Sea Bags has creative, rope-handled totes made from recycled sails. Port Canvas in Arundel, Maine, also hand-crafts sporty, custom-izable canvas totes and duffels—perfect for lugging your souvenirs home.

MAPLE SYRUP
Each spring, sugarhouses tap their maple trees and boil the resultant sap down into syrup. Although it takes about 40 gallons of sap to make 1 gallon of syrup, locally made varieties are readily avail-able—Grades A and B and in light, medium, and dark (for baking only) shades of amber. The best-known states are New Hampshire and Vermont.

TOYS

Vermont Teddy Bears are guaranteed for life; there's even a hospital for Teddy emergencies! Vermont's Real Good Toys makes finely crafted dollhouses and miniature accessories. New Hampshire's Annalee Dolls are distinctive, cute, and collectible—especially the holiday ones.

YARN AND KNITWEAR

The wares of independent spinners and knitters can be found throughout the region. Noteworthy companies include Bartlettyarns, Inc., which has been in Maine since 1821; New Hampshire's Harrisville Designs, and Maine's Swans Island Company.

FLANNEL WOOLENS

New England's textile industry declined in the 1920s and '30s, but Vermont's Johnson Woolen Mills is still going strong. The warm, soft, and often boldly checked flannel shirts, jackets, capes, wraps, scarves, and hats sold in its factory store and elsewhere are splurge-worthy classics.

CRAFT BEER AND CIDER

New England has a long brewing history, but it's the region's newer, trendier operations that are most interesting, like New Hampshire's Schilling Beer Co. and Vermont's Hill Farmstead Brewery. There's a small brewery (or cidery) in almost every city and small town. Notable ciders include Maine's Urban Farm Fermentory and Vermont's family-friendly Cold Hollow.

LOBSTER

Seafood markets, lobster pounds, and even some independent lobstermen sell lobster to-go. You have 48 hours (max) from purchase to cook them, and lobsters must be kept lightly chilled but alive, with claws rubber-banded, until then. Ask about shipping or look into online retailers like Maine Lobster Now, The Lobster Guy, and Lobsters New England.

Most Picturesque Towns in Maine, Vermont, and New Hampshire

WOODSTOCK, VT

This quintessential Vermont town is ridiculously, wonderfully picturesque—classic covered bridges, local cheese makers, cider mills, working farms and orchards, sugar shacks, meandering brick streets, and a town center that is straight out of a Norman Rockwell painting.

EASTPORT, ME

Down East Maine is more than worth the hike, if only to pay a visit to Eastport, a picturesque seaside town with historic architecture situated on pristine Moose Island. A world apart, Eastport prides itself on its fishing and lobstering industries, excellent local arts scene, and vibrant indigenous community.

JACKSON, NH

With a village green reached via a covered bridge and a slew of charming country inns, farm-to-table eateries, and ruggedly scenic trails for hiking and cross-country skiing, this peaceful hamlet lies in the heart of the White Mountains.

CAMDEN, ME

With its brick architecture and Victorian mansions, Maine doesn't get any more picturesque than this village. Situated in the heart of the Mid-Coast, the charming town with its restaurants, galleries, and boutiques is surrounded by a working harbor.

KEENE, NH

Stunning brick streets, charming maple farms, quaint storefronts, classic covered bridges, and a college town vibe combine to create the quintessential New England experience. The darling of the state's southwestern Monadnock Region even has a white clapboard church with a soaring spire.

TAMWORTH, NH

The town is home to the often photographed Chocorua Lake and Mt. Chocorua. A clutch of villages—Tamworth, Chocorua, South Tamworth, Wonalancet, and Whittier—and six historic churches lie within its borders. It's also home to Barnstormers Theatre, the country's oldest repertory theatre.

WESTON, VT

A little less than 12 miles south of Okemo Mountain Resort, this little village really lives up to its much advertised charm and quaintness. The picture-perfect hamlet is home to the Weston Playhouse Theatre Company, a classic town green with Victorian bandstand, and an assortment of shops.

Camden, ME

MONHEGAN, ME
Artists have flocked to Monhegan Island since at least the mid-19th century to relish both its isolated location and staggeringly beautiful terrain. The island's dramatic cliffs overlook some of the most stunning coastal landscapes in Maine where puffin, seals, porpoises, and whales mingle among the bevy of smaller, rocky islands surrounding it.

STOWE, VT
The rolling hills and valleys beneath Mt. Mansfield, Vermont's highest peak, create the tiny village of Stowe. Here you'll find a few blocks of shops and restaurants clustered around a picture-perfect white church with a lofty steeple—not far from Stowe's fabled slopes.

DORSET, VT
Surrounded by mountains and anchored by a village green that's bordered by white clapboard homes and inns, Dorset has a solid claim to the title of Vermont's most picture-perfect town. Dorset West Road, a beautiful residential road west of the town green, and the marble Dorset Church with its two Tiffany stained-glass windows, add to the charm.

WOLFEBORO, NH
Known as the country's oldest summer resort, Wolfeboro is nestled along the shores of Lake Winnipesaukee. The downtown boasts boutiques and eateries, while the resident prep school, Brewster Academy, adds to the charm with its century-old, white clapboard buildings.

DAMARISCOTTA, ME
Just north of Wiscasset, this often overlooked village is surrounded by salt marsh preserves and oyster beds. The village's historic brick architecture and quaint but vibrant Main Street overlooks the harbor where the annual and delightfully oddball Pumpkinfest and Regatta takes place.

Maine, Vermont, and New Hampshire's Best Beaches

FOOTBRIDGE BEACH, OGUNQUIT, ME

This spot offers excellent swimming, beach combing, and bodysurfing opportunities, as well as a boat launch for kayaks, small boats, and standup paddleboards. Typically less crowded than neighboring Ogunquit Beach, it's reached by crossing a footbridge that runs over the Ogunquit River.

ROQUE BLUFFS STATE PARK, ROQUE BLUFFS, ME

Largely sandy, with some pebbly spots thrown in for good measure, this half-mile crescent beach offers bracing Atlantic Ocean swims as well as temperate dips in a 60-acre pond that backs up to the beach.

GOOSE ROCKS BEACH, KENNEBUNKPORT, ME

A wildly popular beach in warmer months, Goose Rocks Beach is treasured for its long stretch of clean sand and close proximity to town. Parking can be tough and permits are required, but it's well worth the headache to get up early and snatch a spot.

WALLIS SANDS STATE BEACH, RYE, NH

This family-friendly swimmers' beach near Portsmouth has bright white sand, a picnic area, a store, and beautiful views of the Isles of Shoals.

SAND BAR STATE PARK, MILTON, VT

Vermont is not known for its beaches, but its plethora of lakes means that there are actually quite a few worth checking out. This 2,000-foot-long beach remains shallow well out from shore, making it a perfect spot for families with young kids.

PEMAQUID BEACH, NEW HARBOR, ME

Pemaquid Beach is a draw for families and couples looking for a quintessential beach day complete with an umbrella, sand bucket, and ice cream, all of which can be rented or purchased from the kiosk near the changing facilities and community center.

MT. SUNAPEE STATE PARK, NEWBURY, NH

One of the prettiest and most relaxing of New Hampshire's many noteworthy freshwater beaches, this family-welcoming stretch of sand in the shadows of one of the state's favorite ski mountains is lovely for swimming, or renting kayaks, canoes, and stand-up paddleboards.

NORTH BEACH, BURLINGTON, VT

Located on Lake Champlain, the area's largest beach is also the

Sand Beach, Acadia, ME

only one with lifeguards during the summer. There's a grassy picnic area, a snack bar, and a playground, as well as kayak, canoe, and standup paddleboard rentals.

JASPER BEACH, MACHIASPORT, ME

Named after the many deep red pebbles scattered across its shore, this pocket beach tucked away in Howard Cove is definitely off the beaten path. Beach combers come to seek out the rare jasper stones among the equally red, volcanic rhyolite pebbles, while those seeking solitude find it in the salt marsh and fresh and saltwater lagoons.

SAND BEACH, ACADIA, ME

What this sandy beach lacks in size is well compensated by its commanding view of the mountains and craggy shores that draw millions of people to Mount Desert Island each year. Several trail heads dot the beach and lead up the surrounding cliffs, where you'll be rewarded with spectacular panoramas of the shore and beach below.

MOWRY BEACH, LUBEC, ME

On the U.S.-Canadian border, this majestic beach has dramatic tides which produce excellent clamming conditions and superb beach runs at low tide. A small boardwalk leads through a heady mess of fragrant rose bushes out to the shore from where you can spy Lubec's famous lighthouse, as well as its Canadian neighbors.

REID STATE PARK BEACH, GEORGETOWN, ME

One of the Pine Tree State's rare sandy beaches, Reid State Park is a surfer's and sunbather's paradise. Rarely crowded, even in summer, the beach stretches a mile and a half along the Atlantic, with large, undulating sand dunes and essential nesting areas for some of the state's endangered birds.

Historical Sites in Maine, Vermont, and New Hampshire

PORTLAND HEAD LIGHT, CAPE ELIZABETH, ME
Built in 1791, this 80-foot lighthouse is one of New England's most picturesque in any season. The keeper's quarters (operational 1891–1989) house a seasonally open museum and gift shop; surrounding Fort William Park, site of an army fort between 1872 and 1964, is open year-round.

MAINE MARITIME MUSEUM, BATH, ME
The museum's permanent exhibits cover it all from Bath Iron Works's role in building the nation's navy to a collection of more than 100 small wooden water crafts. In warmer months, board the 1906 schooner, the *Mary E.*, for sails with docents.

STRAWBERY BANKE, PORTSMOUTH, NH
Located in Colonial downtown Portsmouth, the seasonal, 10-acre living-history complex has docents in period garb portraying tavern keepers, merchants, artisans, and other everyday folk, and more than 40 structures dating from the 17th to 20th centuries.

CANTERBURY SHAKER VILLAGE, LACONIA, NH
Established in 1792, this village practiced equality of the sexes and races, common ownership, celibacy, and pacifism; the last member of the community passed away in 1992. Engaging guided tours—you can explore on your own—pass through some of the 694-acre property's more than 25 restored buildings, many of them with original furnishings, and there are daily crafts demonstrations.

BILLINGS FARM AND MUSEUM, WOODSTOCK, VT
Founded in 1871, this is one of the country's oldest operating dairy farms. In addition to watching the herds of Jersey cows, horses, and other farm animals at work and play, you can tour the restored 1890 farmhouse, and learn about 19th-century farming and domestic life. Pick up some raw-milk cheddar while you're here.

CHARLESTOWN, NH
Charlestown boasts one of New Hampshire's largest historic districts, with about 60 homes—all handsome examples of Federal, Greek Revival, and Gothic Revival architecture (and 10 built before 1800)—clustered about the town center. Several merchants on the main street distribute interesting walking tour brochures of the district.

Canterbury Shaker Village, Laconia, NH

HILDENE, MANCHESTER, VT

Built in 1905, this 24-room Georgian Revival mansion was the summer home of Abraham Lincoln's son Robert. It provides insight into the lives of the Lincoln family, as well as an introduction to the lavish Manchester life of the early 1900s. It's the centerpiece of a beautifully preserved 412-acre estate, which also contains Hildene Farm and elaborate formal gardens.

BRETTON WOODS, NH

Even if you're not staying at the dramatic Omni Mount Washington Hotel, it's worth visiting as not only is it breathtaking but it was the site of the 1944 United Nations conference that created the International Monetary Fund and the International Bank for Reconstruction and Development (and the birth of many conspiracy theories). The area is also known for one of the state's most beloved attractions, the Mount Washington Cog Railway, which was built in 1858.

MONTPELIER, VT

The country's smallest capital city has a quaint, historic downtown that's home to the Vermont History Museum; its Vermont-focused collection (everything from a catamount [the now-extinct local cougar] to Ethan Allen's shoe buckles) began in 1838. A few doors away, the country's oldest legislative chambers still in their original condition are found in the Vermont State House. Self-guided tours are available year-round, but free guided tours run from late June to October.

SHELBURNE MUSEUM, SHELBURNE, VT

Nothing says "Vermont" like a big red barn, and the museum has two really big, really red barns that house American fine, folk, and decorative art as well as vintage toys, hats, decoys, firearms, a vintage carousel, miniature circus-parade figurines, and more than 200 horse-drawn vehicles.

Outdoor Activities in Maine, Vermont, and New Hampshire

SKI VERMONT AND NEW HAMPSHIRE

Not far from the U.S.-Canadian border, some of New England's best ski slopes (and top-notch resorts) can be found in Vermont's Green Mountains (Jay Peak and Stowe) and New Hampshire's White Mountains (Bretton Woods and Cannon Mountain).

CRUISING MAINE'S COAST

Experience Maine's 3,478 miles of coastline from the water. Charter a boat, big or small, in any of the state's harbors; a popular option is on a schooner ship. It can be chilly on the sea, even in summer, so you'll need to layer and bring rain gear.

MILES OF BIKE TRAILS

Many of the region's top ski resorts have become four-season destinations offering challenging mountain biking trails over the once snow-covered slopes. There's also the 110-mile Kingdom Trails in Vermont and more than 500 miles of trails in New Hampshire.

PADDLE LAKE CHAMPLAIN

Leaf peeping and Vermont are virtually synonymous, but most visitors don't think about taking in the Green Mountain State's stunning fall foliage from out on the water. Best accessed from Burlington, you can rent a standup paddleboard or kayak to explore the lake while surrounded by majestic mountains covered in thick forests that put on a colorful display.

HIKE THE APPALACHIAN TRAIL

Tackling the entire length of America's most notorious hiking trail is a commitment. You can always explore some of its most scenic stretches, however, many of them set along the 161-mile leg through New Hampshire. Featuring more miles above treeline than any other state, this is one of the route's most challenging and rewarding sections, with steep inclines leading to stunning alpine tundra and breathtaking views.

BOATING ON THE ALLAGASH WILDERNESS WATERWAY

The 92-mile-long series of rivers, streams, ponds, and lakes that comprises this northern Maine waterway ribbon their way through the delicate, tundralike landscape of the Northern Woods. The waterway remains fairly rustic with limited resources along the route, which seems to be one of the major reasons it attracts fans of canoeing and kayaking.

Go on a leaf peeping bicycle tour along the Stowe Bike Path, VT.

LEAF PEEPING IN VERMONT

With its many nature preserves, green spaces, and hiking trails, Vermont shines in every season, but autumn may be its finest. You'd be hard-pressed to find a lovelier stroll through an autumnal Vermont landscape than in the charming village of Stowe, which is home to the Stowe Recreational Path, a paved, 5½-mile greenway that leads you to picture-perfect village and mountain views.

HIT THE LINKS IN MAINE AND NEW HAMPSHIRE

Coastal Maine and New Hampshire's mountains have some stunning, beautifully maintained golf courses that reward players with great challenges and magnificent scenery. The course at Rockport's Samoset Resort ranks among the best in coastal New England, while Crotched Mountain in the Monadnocks and Waukewan near Lake Winnipesaukee are top courses in New Hampshire.

EXPERIENCE A SCENIC BYWAY

Kancamagus Highway ("The Kanc"), a 34.5-mile scenic byway that crosses New Hampshire from Lincoln near the Vermont border to Conway near Maine, passes through the White Mountains National Forest—a beautiful ride that's truly magnificent in autumn. Stop along the way to admire the White Mountains Presidential Range or take a hike into the forest.

EXPLORE ACADIA NATIONAL PARK

Boasting around 160 miles of pristine coastal hiking trails and meandering carriage roads peppered with charming stone bridges, America's oldest national park east of the Mississippi River offers bountiful opportunities to experience Maine's raw, natural beauty.

Maine, Vermont, and New Hampshire with Kids

Favorite destinations for family vacations in the region include Vermont's Lake Champlain, New Hampshire's White Mountains, and coastal Maine—but, in general, the entire region has plenty to offer families. Throughout New England, you'll have no problem finding reasonably priced, kid-friendly hotels and family-style restaurants, as well as museums, beaches, parks, planetariums, and lighthouses.

LODGING

New England has many family-oriented resorts with lively children's programs. Farms that accept guests can be great fun for children. Rental houses and apartments abound, particularly around ski areas. In the off-season, these can be especially economical, because most have kitchens—saving you the expense of restaurant dining for some or all meals.

VERMONT

ECHO Leahy Center for Lake Champlain, Burlington. Lots of activities and hands-on exhibits make learning about the geology and ecology of Lake Champlain an engaging experience.

Montshire Museum of Science, Norwich. This interactive museum uses more than 60 hands-on exhibits to explore nature and technology. The building sits amid 110 acres of nature trails and woodlands, where animals roam freely.

Shelburne Farms, Shelburne. This working dairy farm is also an educational and cultural resource center. Visitors can watch artisans make the farm's famous cheddar cheese from the milk of more than 100 purebred and registered Brown Swiss cows. A children's farmyard and walking trails round out the experience.

NEW HAMPSHIRE

Lost River Gorge and Whale's Tale Waterpark, Lincoln and North Woodstock. Kids can scramble through boulder caves in Lost River Gorge, and float on inner tubes and bodysurf in a giant wave pool at one of New England's biggest water parks. More family fun is nearby at Franconia Notch State Park.

Lake Winnipesaukee, Weirs Beach. The largest lake in the state, Lake Winnipesaukee provides plenty of family-friendly fun. Base yourself in the Laconia community of Weirs Beach, where kids can swim, play arcade games, cruise the lake, take a scenic railroad along the shoreline, and even see a drive-in movie.

SEE Science Center, Manchester. For kids who love LEGO, the models of old Manchester and the mill yard are sure to impress. There are also rotating exhibits and science demonstrations.

MAINE

Acadia National Park, Mount Desert Island. Head out on a whale- and puffin-watching trip from Bar Harbor, drive up scenic Cadillac Mountain, swim at Echo Lake Beach, hike one of the many easy trails, and don't forget to sample some wild blueberry pie.

Maine Narrow Gauge Railroad Museum, Portland. For train fans, check out the scenic rides on these narrow-gauge trains. In the winter, they have Polar Express theme trips.

Coastal Maine Botanical Garden, Boothbay. The "children's garden" is a wonderland of stone sculptures, rope bridges, small teahouse-like structures with grass roofs, and even a hedge maze. Children and adults alike adore the separate woodland fairy area.

Maine, Vermont, and New Hampshire Today

MAINE

In recent decades, Maine's congressional delegation has hovered around 50/50—half Democrat and Republican, and half male and female, which somewhat resembles the makeup of the state. Voters legalized recreational marijuana in 2016, and the state now has nearly 100 retail pot shops. Since 2000, Somali immigration has generated both tensions and welcome cultural diversity in Lewiston and Portland. As paper mills shutter, farming is on the upswing, while the billion-dollar tourism industry struggles to find enough workers yet fuels rising real estate prices and rents in popular destinations.

VERMONT

Few states are more proud of its rugged, independent, and liberal spirit than Vermont. From Ethan Allen to Bernie Sanders, Vermonters have never been afraid to follow a different drumbeat and be outspoken about it. This is perhaps never more on display than in the state's long-standing protection of the environment that borders on obsession. It's one of only four states that ban billboards (Maine is the only other in New England), and strict regulations on land use and development makes many towns and villages appear as if pulled from Norman Rockwell paintings. During fall, the peak tourist season, the landscape literally takes your breath away with an array of fiery reds, golds, oranges, and bronze bursting from the hills and valleys. Cities are few and far between, with Burlington topping out at just 45,200 people, but a robust cultural and arts scene thrives throughout the state, thanks to the abundance of colleges, collectives, and individual artists that continually draw inspiration from the Vermont spirit and beauty. Locals and tourists do the same on the ski slopes, hiking trails, bike paths, and swimming holes, and there's plenty for all.

NEW HAMPSHIRE

With its state motto of "Live Free or Die" and a long-running political reputation as one of the nation's swingiest—albeit *slightly* left of center—states, New Hampshire marches to its own drummer. The fifth smallest—and 10th least populous—state in America maintains a fierce libertarian streak, collects neither sales tax nor income tax, and each presidential year holds the country's first primary (at least as of this writing—Nevada has made a bid to hold its primary earlier in 2024). Like the rest of northern New England, ruggedly mountainous New Hampshire is characterized by a mostly rural, heavily wooded topography that gives way to more densely populated small cities and suburbs only in its southeastern corner. Relatively prosperous, with the eighth-highest median household income in the country, New Hampshire has also enjoyed slow but steady growth in recent years, lagging behind only Massachusetts in population growth since 2010 among New England's six states.

What to Read and Watch

LOBSTERMAN

Dahlov Ipcar, a native New Englander, is best remembered as a writer and illustrator of children's books, many of which took place in her home state of Maine. One such classic is *Lobsterman,* which portrays the day in the life of a lobsterman and his son as they work along the coast of Maine.

IT

You won't find Derry, Maine on any map, but you can visit it via a number of chilling tales courtesy of horror writer Stephen King, including his 1986 novel *It,* which follows a group of friends who try to kill a monster that terrorizes their town; a film by the same name was made in 2017.

WE HAVE ALWAYS LIVED IN THE CASTLE

Shirley Jackson's novel follows Merricat Blackwood, who lives in isolation on her family's Vermont estate with her sister Constance and their infirm Uncle Julian. When an estranged cousin arrives, the already uneasy state of the Blackwood home is thrown into disarray.

THE CIDER HOUSE RULES

This 1999 screen adaptation of a 1985 novel by John Irving was set in 1940s Maine and filmed in Maine, New Hampshire and Vermont (and Massachusetts, too). Featuring an all-star cast including Kathy Baker, Michael Caine, and Tobey Maguire, the film depicts the father-son-like relationship between an orphan (Maguire), and the orphanage's doctor (Caine), who takes him under his wing.

THE SECRET HISTORY

In Donna Tartt's 1992 novel, Richard leaves his working-class, California home behind in order to attend a liberal arts college in Vermont. Once there he falls in with a privileged group of classics students, but beneath the group's veneer of charm and sophistication is a dark, violent secret.

ON GOLDEN POND

Big Squam and Little Squam lakes in central New Hampshire had starring roles in this 1981 film. So did the lakes' loons that greeted lead actors Katharine Hepburn and Henry Fonda, who played an aging (and somewhat cranky) couple returning once more to a beloved family summer retreat. It was the last role played by Fonda, whose movie daughter was played by his actual daughter, Jane Fonda.

THE IRON GIANT

This charming animated film tells the story of Hogarth, a young boy who befriends a giant robot after it crashes in Maine. When a paranoid government agent tries to destroy the giant, Hogarth enlists help to save the gentle-hearted automaton.

THE HOTEL NEW HAMPSHIRE

This coming-of-age novel by John Irving, published in 1981, features a New Hampshire family whose parents met as teens while working together at a Maine summer resort. The book has a better reputation than the film adaptation that was released a few years later.

STRANGLEHOLD

This podcast series, produced by NPR, examines how New Hampshire outperforms its small stature on the nation's presidential primary stage, where it looms large in influence and attention.

WHITE CHRISTMAS

This holiday classic follows a song and dance team and a pair of performing sisters as they travel to a Vermont inn where they've been booked to perform over Christmas. The inn, owned by their old army commander, is on the verge of failure, so they stage a nationally televised yuletide extravaganza in order to save it.

TRAVEL SMART

2

★ CAPITALS
Augusta, ME; Concord, NH; Montpelier, VT

⸬ POPULATION
6,367,000

💬 LANGUAGE
English

$ CURRENCY
U.S. dollar

☎ AREA CODES
ME: 207; NH: 603; VT: 802

⚠ EMERGENCIES
911

🚗 DRIVING
On the right

⚡ ELECTRICITY
120–240 v/60 cycles; plugs have two or three rectangular prongs

⏱ TIME
Eastern Time (same as New York)

🌐 WEB RESOURCES
visitmaine.com
www.visitnh.gov
www.vermontvacation.com

CANADA
U.S.
QUÉBEC

NEW BRUNSWICK

MAINE

Baxter State Park
Mt. Katahdin

Lake Champlain

VERMONT

Montpelier ✪

Mt. Washington

Augusta ✪

Acadia National Park

NOVA SCOTIA

NEW HAMPSHIRE

Concord ✪

NEW YORK

MASSACHUSETTS

Boston ✪

Cape Cod National Seashore

Hartford ✪

Providence ✪

CONNECTICUT

RHODE ISLAND

Martha's Vineyard

Nantucket

Atlantic Ocean

N.J.

Know Before You Go

Maine, Vermont, and New Hampshire have their share of regional character, color, and flavor—not to mention a few geographical and seasonal challenges. Here are some tips that will enrich your trip and ease your travels.

IT'S WICKED GOOD TO LEARN SOME LINGO.

To avoid seeming like a "chowdah-head" (aka chowder head, aka idiot), brush up on some basic dialect. Want a big, long sandwich? Order a grinder, not a sub or a hero, and wash it down with a frappe or a tonic, not a milkshake or soda. At the hotel, grab the "clickah" (clicker) to change the TV station. At the supermarket, grab a carriage to shop for picnic sundries. If people direct you to a rotary, they mean traffic circle. And, even if you're traveling north toward, say, Bar Harbor, you're headed Down East.

YOU CAN'T ALWAYS GET THEAH FROM HEAH.

The shortest distance between two points isn't always a straight—or single—line. Finding the real Maine, Vermont, or New Hampshire means driving (and getting lost on) its scenic byways. And GPS and cell-phone service will be disrupted, especially up north, so pack road maps or an atlas. There are a few places where you won't need a car, though. Cities have great public transit options to, within, and around them. You'll have to take a ferry—few take cars—to access the numerous islands off Maine's coast, but most are bike friendly so plan accordingly. In Acadia National Park, you'll have to trade your car for hiking boots, a bike, or a carriage (an actual horse and buggy, not a shopping cart).

DON'T FORGET THE DRAMAMINE.

Elevations aren't as dramatic as those out west, but car sickness is possible on drives through White Mountain National Forest, on the Kancamagus Scenic Byway, or even the North Woods' Golden Roads. Roads ribbon up, down, and around—just as they do along rugged, often-precipitous stretches of Atlantic coast.

SMALL TOWNS RULE.

You might have to dig a little deeper to sightsee here, but it's worth it. Most villages have a Colonial- or Revolutionary-era homestead or site, small museum or historical society, and time-honored tavern or country store. Photo-worthy commons (open spaces once used for grazing livestock and around which towns were built) are worth seeking out and can be found in many small towns, from Woodstock, Vermont, to Bethel, Maine.

EVEN THE BIG CITIES HERE ARE RELATIVELY SMALL.

Manchester, New Hampshire, the region's largest city, has just about 112,658 people. The next biggest, Portland, Maine, has 66,218 people, followed by Burlington, Vermont, which has just over 42,545. Despite their small size, most cities have thriving cultural scenes; several are major university towns (Brunswick and Hanover) and/or are steeped in history (Portland). Regardless, you can allow less time for urban explorations and more time for losing yourself in the bucolic settings.

THE BEST FOODS ARE WHOLESOME, HEARTY BASICS.

Field- or fishing-boat-totable is the norm, with abundant local produce and seafood that includes lobster; quahogs or other clams; bay or sea scallops; and pollack, hake, haddock, or cod (the latter two might appear on local menus as "scrod"). In Maine, lobster-roll meat is lightly dressed in mayonnaise; though you may also find it drizzled with melted butter. Chowder is creamy and may contain bacon.

Everywhere, though, maple syrup adorns shaved ice (or snow!) and ice cream as well as pancakes; breakfast home fries are griddled and seasoned just so; and craft beer and cider pair well with boiled dinners and Yankee pot roast. Be sure to try a Moxie, an "energizing," regionally unique tonic (aka soda).

IN THE LAND OF THE COUNTRY INN, IT'S BEST TO BOOK AHEAD.

Although there are abundant chain hotels and several large, notable Victorians—seaside and near the slopes—smaller inns, often historical and privately owned, are among the best lodgings. Loads of charm and lower room counts make booking ahead essential, especially during peak seasons, when there might also be a two-night minimum. And "peak seasons" vary. Leaf-peeping season is roughly late September to mid-October in Maine, New Hampshire, and Vermont. At the region's ski areas, the season might be November through April or even May.

THE WATER IS COLD UP HERE.

Even in late August, ocean temperatures off Maine and New Hampshire only climb to the upper 50s or lower 60s—still limb-numbingly chilly. Wet suits (and water shoes for rockier shores) are musts for surfing and standup paddleboarding. Obviously, the farther north you go, the shorter the beach season, with some properties reducing their hours or shuttering entirely between Labor Day and Memorial Day or July Fourth. The lakes may be a bit warmer with water temps hovering around the 70s, but once the sun goes down it gets wicked chilly.

WHEN IT COMES TO PARKLAND, THE STATES HAVE IT.

Although much of New England is woodsy, the entire region has only one national park (Acadia) and just two national forests (Green Mountain and White Mountain). That said, there are plenty of opportunities to hike, canoe, kayak, mountain bike, camp, and otherwise embrace the outdoors in the plethora of park or recreation/wilderness areas overseen by each state.

SOME OF THE FLIES BITE.

First, it's the black flies, whose bites leave red, itchy welts. May through June is the season, which is particularly notorious in Maine. Then, in July, it's the deer flies. Summer also sees greenhead flies (aka saltmarsh greenheads) in some coastal areas. On hikes, use insect repellent and wear clothing that covers your arms and legs. And don't forget to check for ticks. The disease they're known to carry was named after a New England town: Lyme, Connecticut.

THE PEOPLE ARE WARM AND WELCOMING

The idea of the self-reliant, thrifty, and often stoic New England Yankee has taken on almost mythic proportions in American folklore, but in some parts of New England—especially in rural Maine, New Hampshire, and Vermont—there still is some truth to this image, which shouldn't come as a surprise. You need to be independent if you farm an isolated field, live in the middle of a vast

forest, or work a fishing boat miles off the coast. As in any part of the country, there are stark differences between the city mice and the country mice of New England. Both, however, are usually well educated and fiercely proud of the region, its rugged beauty, and its contributions to the nation.

SPORTS IS A RELIGION

This is Sox and Pats country. New England fans follow Massachusetts's sports teams as if they were their own. Boston is home to three of the region's four major sports teams—Red Sox baseball, Bruins hockey, and Celtics basketball. The New England Patriots (football) play in the small suburb of Foxboro, about 30 miles southwest of Downtown Boston. The city is also home to the Boston Marathon, New England's largest sporting event and the world's oldest annual marathon.

KNOW THE DO'S AND DON'TS OF BUYING CANNABIS

If you're age 21 or older you can purchase cannabis—in smoking and in edible forms—for recreational use in Maine and Vermont. Do buy only from a dispensary licensed to sell adult-use cannabis. Legally, you can only use cannabis on private property, not in public places, and especially not in hotel rooms.

Getting Here and Around

Air

Most travelers visiting the area use a major gateway, such as Boston, Providence, Hartford, Manchester, Portland, or even Albany, and then rent a car to explore the region. Most destinations are no more than six hours apart by car, which is good because it's costly and generally impractical to fly within Maine, Vermont, and New Hampshire, unless you're going to some of the more remote parts of Inland Maine.

AIRPORTS

The main gateway to New England is Boston's Logan International Airport (BOS). New Hampshire's Manchester Boston Regional Airport (MHT), Maine's Portland International Jetport (PWM), and Vermont's Burlington International Airport (BTV) are other major airports.

Other convenient airports are Albany International Airport (ALB) in Albany, New York, near Vermont, and Bangor International Airport (BGR) in Bangor, Maine.

FLIGHTS

Boston's Logan Airport has direct flights arriving from all over North America and abroad. Some sample flying times to Boston are: 2½ hours from Chicago, 6½ hours from London, and 6 hours from Los Angeles. Times from other U.S. cities are similar, if slightly shorter, to Albany and Hartford, assuming you can find direct flights.

American, Delta, Frontier, JetBlue, Southwest, and United serve airports in Albany, Boston, Manchester, and Portland. Alaska, Allegiant, Boutique Air, Hawaiian, Spirit, and Sun Country fly into Boston. Cape Air, a regional carrier, serves various New England airports in Maine, New Hampshire, and Vermont.

Boat

A number of ferries, some seasonal and some passenger-only, operate along the coast. Maine State Ferry Service provides ferry service to the islands of Mantinicus, Vinalhaven, North Haven, Islesboro, Swans Island, and Frenchboro. You can bring your car on the ferries to Islesboro, Vinalhaven, North Haven, and Mantinicus.

The CAT is a seasonal car ferry that travels between Yarmouth, Nova Scotia, and Bar Harbor, Maine. The trip takes about 3½ hours.

Casco Bay Lines connects the city of Portland with the islands of Casco Bay.

Bus

Buses are a practical way to get to a major entry-point in northern New England, but you can't explore the smaller towns in any practical way through bus service.

Concord Coach buses connect Boston with several cities in New Hampshire and Maine; the company also operates a route between New York City and Portland. Dartmouth Coach runs buses from both Boston and New York City to Hanover and Lebanon, in New Hampshire's Upper Valley. C&J buses (with Wi-Fi) serve Dover (near Durham) and Portsmouth, New Hampshire, and Ogunquit, Maine; C&J also provides service to New York City. Both Concord and C&J leave from Boston's South Station, which is connected to the Amtrak rail station, and from Logan Airport.

Megabus also offers low fares, and its buses (with free Wi-Fi) serve New York City and many other East Coast cities. Both use Boston's South Station; Megabus stops in Portland, Montpelier, and Burlington.

With extremely low fares, FlixBus buses equipped with Wi-Fi and electrical outlets connect Boston to several destinations in Vermont, as well as Portsmouth and Portland.

🚗 Car

As public transportation options are limited in this area, a car is almost essential. Interstate 95 enters New England at the New York border, follows the Connecticut shoreline, and then heads north to Providence, Boston, and Portland before ending at the Canadian border in Calais, Maine.

CAR RENTAL

Major airports serving the region all have on-site car-rental agencies. A few train or bus stations have one or two car-rental agencies on-site, as well.

Rates at Boston's Logan Airport begin at around $50 per day and $300 per week for an economy car with air-conditioning, automatic transmission, and unlimited mileage. The same car might go for around $60 per day and $175 per week at a smaller airport. These rates do not include state tax on car rentals, which varies depending on the airport but generally runs 12%–15%. It usually costs less to rent a car away from an airport, but be sure to consider how easy or difficult it may be to get to that off-airport location with luggage.

Most agencies won't rent to drivers under the age of 21, and several major agencies won't rent to anyone under 25 or over the age of 75. When picking up a rental car, non-U.S. residents need a

Getting Here and Around

voucher for any prepaid reservation made in their home country, a passport, a driver's license, and a travel policy that covers each driver. Logan Airport is spread out and usually congested; if returning a rental vehicle there, allow plenty of time to do so before heading to your flight.

GASOLINE

Gas stations are easy to find throughout the region, but prices vary from station to station. The majority have self-serve pumps that accept credit or debit cards.

PARKING

Finding street parking in Portland, Maine, or any resort or seaside town, can be a pain in the summer. Park in a garage or lot if it's an option. Always pay attention to signs: some streets or lots may be reserved for residents only.

ROAD CONDITIONS

Major state and U.S. routes are generally well maintained, with snowplows at the ready during the winter to salt and plow. Secondary state routes and rural roads can be a mixed bag; Route 1, for example, is well maintained; but traffic is stop-and-go and can get tied up in even the smallest coastal towns.

ROADSIDE EMERGENCIES

Call ☏ 911 for any travel emergency. For breakdowns, dial a towing service.

RULES OF THE ROAD

Throughout the region, you're permitted to make a right turn on a red light except where posted. Be alert for one-way streets and rotaries (aka traffic circles). Cars entering traffic circles must yield to cars that are already in the circle.

🚆 Train

Amtrak offers frequent daily service along its Northeast Corridor route from Washington, D.C., Philadelphia, and New York to Boston, with stops in Connecticut and Rhode Island. Amtrak's high-speed Acela trains link Boston and Washington, with stops at New York, Philadelphia, and other cities along the way. The Downeaster connects Boston and Brunswick, Maine, with stops in coastal New Hampshire and Portland.

Other Amtrak services include the Vermonter between Washington, D.C., and St. Albans, Vermont and the Ethan Allen Express between New York and Rutland, Vermont.

Essentials

🍴 Dining

Although certain ingredients and preparations are common to the region as a whole, New England's cuisine varies greatly from place to place. Urban centers like Burlington and Portland, and upscale resort areas have stellar restaurants, many of them with culinary luminaries at the helm and a reputation for creative—and occasionally daring—menus.

Elsewhere, restaurant food tends more toward the simple, traditional, and conservative. Towns and cities have a variety of international restaurants, especially excellent Italian, French, Japanese, Indian, and Thai eateries. There are also many diners serving burgers and other comfort food—a few serve breakfast all day.

The proximity to the ocean accounts for the abundance of very fresh seafood, and the area's numerous boutique dairy, meat, and vegetable suppliers account for other choice ingredients. Menus in the more upscale and tourism-driven communities often note which Vermont dairy or Maine farm a particular goat cheese or heirloom tomato came from.

MEALS AND MEALTIMES

For an early breakfast, pick places that cater to a working clientele. City, town, and roadside establishments specializing in breakfast for early workers often open their doors at 5 or 6 am. At country inns, breakfast is seldom served before 8 am; if you need to get an earlier start, ask ahead of time. Lunch generally runs 11 am–2:30 pm; dinner is usually served 6–9 pm, with early-bird specials sometimes beginning at 5. Only in larger cities will you find dinner available much later than 9 pm. Many restaurants in New England close Monday and sometimes Sunday or Tuesday, although this is never true in resort areas during high season.

However, resort-town eateries often shut down completely in the off-season.

Unless otherwise noted, the restaurants listed are open daily for lunch and dinner.

RESERVATIONS AND DRESS

It's a good idea to make a reservation if you can. We only mention them specifically when reservations are essential—there's no other way you'll ever get a table—or when they are not accepted. For popular restaurants, book as far ahead as you can, and reconfirm as soon as you arrive. Large parties should always call ahead to check the reservations policy. We mention dress only when men are required to wear a jacket or a jacket and tie.

WINE, BEER, AND SPIRITS

New England is no stranger to microbrews. Offering hearty English-style ales and special seasonal brews are breweries such as Vermont's Long Trail, Maine's Shipyard, and New Hampshire's Smuttynose Brewing Co. Green Mountain Cidery makes Woodchuck hard cider in Middlebury, Vermont.

New England is beginning to earn some respect as a wine-producing region. Cabernet Franc, Vidal, Riesling, and other grape varieties capable of withstanding the region's harsher winters and relatively shorter growing season compared to California and other leading areas have been the basis of promising enterprises. Even Vermont is getting into the act with the Snow Farm Vineyard in the Lake Champlain Islands and Boyden Valley Winery in Cambridge.

Although a patchwork of state and local regulations affect the hours and locations of places that sell alcoholic beverages, New England licensing laws are fairly liberal. State-owned or franchised stores sell hard liquor in New Hampshire, Maine, and Vermont. Many travelers

Essentials

have found that New Hampshire offers the region's lowest prices due to the lack of a sales tax; look for state-run liquor "supermarkets" on interstates in the southern part of the state—but keep in mind that it's illegal to take untaxed liquor across state lines. A bottle or two isn't a problem, but undercover cops are on the lookout for anyone transporting a huge stash.

⊕ Health and Safety

Lyme disease, so named for its having been first reported in the town of Lyme, Connecticut, is a potentially debilitating disease carried by deer ticks. They thrive in dry, brush-covered areas, particularly in coastal areas. Always use insect repellent: the potential for outbreaks of Lyme disease makes it imperative that you protect yourself from ticks from early spring through summer and into fall. To prevent bites, wear light-color clothing and tuck pant legs into socks. Look for black ticks about the size of a pinhead around hairlines and the warmest parts of the body. If you have been bitten, consult a physician—especially if you see the telltale bull's-eye bite pattern. Flu-like symptoms often accompany a Lyme infection. Early treatment is imperative.

New England's most annoying insect pests are black flies and mosquitoes. The former are a phenomenon of late spring and early summer and are generally a problem only in densely wooded areas of the far north. Mosquitoes, however, are a nuisance just about everywhere. The best protection against both pests is repellent containing DEET; if you're camping in the woods during black fly season, you'll also want to use fine mesh screening in eating and sleeping areas and even wear mesh headgear. One pest particular to coastal areas, especially salt marshes, is the greenhead fly, which has a nasty bite and is hard to kill. It is best repelled by a liberal application of Avon Skin So Soft or a similar product.

Coastal waters attract seafood lovers who enjoy harvesting their own clams, mussels, and even lobsters; permits are required, and casual harvesting of lobsters is strictly forbidden. Amateur clammers should be aware that New England shellfish beds are periodically visited by red tides, during which microorganisms can render shellfish poisonous. To keep abreast of the situation, inquire when you apply for a license (usually at town halls or police stations) and pay attention to red tide postings as you travel.

Rural New England is one of the country's safest regions. In cities—Portland, for example—observe the usual precautions: avoid out-of-the-way or poorly lit areas at night; don't let handbags out of your sight; and be on your guard, not only during the deserted wee hours but also in crowds, when pickpockets may be at work. Keep your valuables in the hotel or room safe. When using an ATM, choose a busy, well-lit place such as an enclosed bank lobby.

If your vehicle breaks down in a rural area, pull as far off the road as possible, tie a handkerchief to your radio antenna (use flares at night—check if your rental agency can provide them), and stay in your car with the doors locked until help arrives. Don't pick up hitchhikers. If you're planning to leave a car overnight to make use of off-road trails or camping facilities, look for a supervised parking area whenever possible. Cars left at trailhead parking lots are a target for theft or vandalism.

COVID-19

Almost all restrictions, including vaccination and masking requirements, have been lifted across the United States except in healthcare facilities and nursing homes. Some travelers may still wish to wear a mask in confined spaces, including on airplanes, on public transportation, and at large indoor gatherings, but that is increasingly a personal choice. Be aware that where local mandates still exist, they should be followed.

🏠 Lodging

In New England you can bed down in a basic chain hotel or a luxurious grande dame, but unless you're staying in a city, this is really bed-and-breakfast land. Charming—and sometimes historic— inns, small hotels, and B&Bs dot the region and provide a glimpse of local life.

Hotel prices are the lowest cost of a standard double room in high season.

HOUSE AND APARTMENT RENTALS

You are most likely to find a house, apartment, or condo rental in areas of New England where ownership of second homes is common, such as beach resorts and ski country. Home-exchange directories sometimes list rentals alongside exchanges. Another good bet is to contact real-estate agents in the area in which you are interested, or check VRBO or Airbnb.

BED-AND-BREAKFASTS

In many less touristy areas, B&Bs offer an affordable, homey alternative to chain properties. In most major towns, expect to pay about the same or more for a historic inn. Many of the region's finest restaurants are attached to country inns, so you often don't have to go far for the best meal in town. Quite a few inns serve substantial breakfasts.

HOTELS

Major hotel and motel chains are amply represented in New England. The region is also liberally supplied with small, independent motels.

Reservations are always a good idea, particularly in summer and winter resort areas; at college towns in September and at graduation time in spring; and at areas renowned for autumn foliage. Most hotels and motels will hold your reservation until 6 pm; call ahead if you plan to arrive late. All will hold a late reservation for you if you guarantee it with your credit card.

In Vermont all hotels are no-smoking by state law. All lodgings listed have private baths unless otherwise noted.

💲 Money

It costs a bit more to travel in most of New England than it does in the rest of the country, the most costly areas being Portland and coastal resort towns. You'll also find some posh inns and restaurants in parts of Vermont and New Hampshire. ATMs are plentiful, and large-denomination bills (as well as credit cards) are readily accepted in tourist destinations during the high season.

CREDIT CARDS

Major credit cards are readily accepted throughout New England, though in rural areas you may encounter difficulties or the acceptance of only MasterCard or Visa. If you'll be making an excursion into Canada, be aware that many outlets there accept Visa but not MasterCard.

Essentials

Tipping Guidelines for New England

Bartender	$1 to $5 per round of drinks, depending on the number of drinks
Bellhop	$1 or $2 per bag, depending on the level of the hotel
Hotel concierge	$5 or more, if they perform a service for you
Hotel doorman	$1 or $2 if they help you get a cab
Hotel maid	$2 to $5 a day depending on the level of the hotel, either daily or at the end of your stay, in cash
Hotel room-service waiter	$2 to $5 per delivery, even if a service charge has been added
Porter at airport or train Station	$1 per bag
Skycap at airport	$2 or $3 per bag checked
Taxi driver	15% to 20%, but round up the fare to the next dollar amount
Tour guide	15% of the cost of the tour
Valet parking attendant	$3 to $5, but only when you get your car
Waiter	15% to 20%, with 20% being the norm at high-end restaurants; nothing additional if a service charge is added to the bill
Other attendants	Restroom attendants in expensive restaurants expect some small change or $1. Tip coat-check personnel at least $1 or $2 per item checked unless there is a fee, then nothing.

Packing

The principal rule of weather in New England is that there are no rules. A cold, foggy spring morning often warms to a bright, 60°F afternoon. A summer breeze can suddenly turn chilly, and rain often appears with little warning. Thus, the best advice on how to dress is to layer your clothing; that way, you can peel off or add garments as needed for comfort. Even in summer you should bring long pants, a sweater or two, and a water-proof windbreaker, for evenings are often chilly, and sea spray can make things cool. Showers are frequent, so pack a raincoat and umbrella.

Casual sportswear—walking shoes and jeans or khakis—will take you almost everywhere, but swimsuits and bare feet will not: shirts and shoes are required attire at even the most casual venues. Dress in restaurants is generally casual, except at some of the distinguished restaurants in Maine coast towns such as Kennebunkport, and a few inns. Upscale resorts, at the very least, will require men to wear collared shirts at dinner, and jeans are often frowned upon.

In summer, bring a hat and sunscreen. You can bring or buy insect repellent. If you find yourself walking in wooded areas, near brush, or around foliage from early spring through fall, be sure to check your body for ticks, which can cause Lyme disease if not removed.

Did You Know?

Lake Winnipesaukee, in the foothills of the White Mountains, is the largest lake in New Hampshire and a major tourist destination.

Great Itineraries

New Hampshire and Maine, 7 Days

Revel in the coastlines of two New England states—New Hampshire and Maine—on the path from the region's smallest shoreline to its highest peak, Mt. Washington. An assortment of New England's coastal treasures are at your fingertips as you pilot the ins and outs of the jagged northeastern coastline, before ascending the heights of the White Mountains. Plenty of fascinating towns and villages will vie for your attention with charming shops, seafood restaurants, and picture-perfect views.

Fly in: Manchester-Boston Regional Airport (MHT), Manchester, New Hampshire.

Fly out: Manchester-Boston Regional Airport (MHT), Manchester, New Hampshire.

DAY 1: NEW HAMPSHIRE COAST
Kick off your trek in the southeastern corner of the Granite State. New Hampshire fronts the Atlantic for a scant 18 miles, but its coastal landmarks range from honky-tonk **Hampton Beach** to quiet **Odiorne Point State Park** in Rye and pretty **Portsmouth,** where the cream of pre-Revolutionary society built Georgian- and Federal-style mansions—visit a few at the **Strawbery Banke Museum.** Stay the night in **Portsmouth** at the centrally located **Ale House Inn.**

DAY 2: THE YORKS
Much of the appeal of the Maine Coast lies in its geographical contrasts, from its long stretches of swimming and walking beaches in the south to the cliff-edged, rugged, rocky coasts in the north. And not unlike the physical differences of the shoreline, each town along the way reveals a slightly different character, starting with **York.**

In **York Village** take a leisurely stroll through the seven buildings of the **Museums of Old York,** getting a glimpse of 18th-century life in this gentrified town. Spend time wandering amid the shops or walking the nature trails and beaches around **York Harbor.** There are several grand lodging options here, most with views of the harbor. If you prefer a livelier pace, continue on to **York Beach,** a haven for families with plenty of entertainment venues. Stop at **Fox's Lobster House** after visiting **Nubble Light** for a seaside lunch or dinner.

Logistics: 10 miles; via I–95 N; 15 minutes, starting in Portsmouth.

DAY 3: OGUNQUIT AND THE KENNEBUNKS
For well over a century, **Ogunquit** has been a favorite vacation spot for those looking to combine the natural beauty of the ocean with a sophisticated environment. Take a morning walk along the **Marginal Way** to see the waves crashing on the rocks. In **Perkins Cove,** have lunch, stroll the shopping areas, or sign on with a lobster-boat cruise to learn about Maine's most important fishery—the state's lobster industry supplies more than 90% of the world's lobster intake. See the extraordinary collection at the **Ogunquit Museum of American Art,** take in a performance at one of the several theater venues, or just spend time on the beach.

Head north to the Kennebunks, allowing at least two hours to wander through the shops and historic homes of **Dock Square** in **Kennebunkport.** This is an ideal place to rent a bike and amble around the backstreets, to head out on Ocean Avenue to view the large mansions, or ride to one of the several beaches to relax awhile. Spend your third night in Kennebunkport.

Logistics: 22 miles; via I–95 N; 30 minutes, starting in York.

DAYS 4 AND 5: PORTLAND

If you have time, you can easily spend several days in Maine's largest city, exploring its historic neighborhoods, shopping and eating in the **Old Port,** or visiting one of several excellent museums. A brief side trip to **Cape Elizabeth** takes you to **Portland Head Light,** Maine's first lighthouse, which was commissioned by George Washington in 1787. The lighthouse is on the grounds of **Fort Williams Park** and is an excellent place to bring a picnic. Be sure to spend some time wandering the ample grounds. There are also excellent walking trails (and views) at nearby **Two Lights State Park.** If you want to take a boat tour while in Portland, get a ticket for Casco Bay Lines and see some of the islands that dot the bay. Spend two nights in Portland.

Logistics: 28 miles; via I–95 N; 40 minutes, staring in Kennebunkport.

DAY 6: BRETTON WOODS

Wake up early and drive to Bretton Woods, where you will spend nights six and seven. The driving time from Portland to Bretton Woods is approximately three hours, due to two-lane, steep mountain roads.

■ **TIP→ Be sure to drive a four-wheel-drive vehicle in winter.**

Drive northwest along U.S. 302 toward **Sebago Lake,** a popular water-sports area in the summer, and continue on toward the time-honored New England towns of Naples and Bridgton. Just 15 miles from the border of New Hampshire, and nearing Crawford Notch, U.S. 302 begins to thread through New Hampshire's **White Mountains,** passing beneath brooding **Mt. Washington** before arriving in Bretton Woods. ⸱

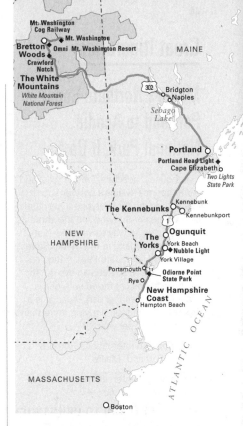

Logistics: 98 miles; via ME 113 N and U.S. 302 W; 3 hours, starting in Portland.

DAY 7: THE WHITE MOUNTAINS

In Bretton Woods, the **Mt. Washington Cog Railway** still chugs to the summit, and the **Omni Mount Washington Resort** recalls the glory days of White Mountain resorts. Beloved winter activities here include snowshoeing and skiing on the grounds of the Mount Washington Resort. You can even zipline here in winter. Afterward, defrost with a cup of steaming hot cider while checking out vintage photos of the International Monetary Conference, held here in 1944, or head to the Cave, a prohibition-era speakeasy, for a drink.

Great Itineraries

Maine's Northern Coast: Portland to Acadia National Park, 6 Days

Lighthouses, beaches, lobster rolls, and water sports—Maine's northern coast has something for everyone. Quaint seaside villages and towns line the shore as U.S. 1 winds its way toward the easternmost swath of land in the United States at Quoddy Head State Park. Antiquing is a major draw, so keep an eye out for roadside shops crammed with gems. Maine's only national park, Acadia, is a highlight of the tour, drawing more than 2 million visitors per year.

Fly in: Portland International Jetport (PWM), Portland, Maine.

Fly out: Bangor International Airport, (BGR), Bangor, Maine.

DAY 1: PORTLAND TO BRUNSWICK
Use Maine's maritime capital as your jumping-off point to head farther up the Maine Coast, or, as Mainers call it, "Down East." Plan to spend half of your first day in Portland, then head to Brunswick for the night.

Portland shows off its restored waterfront at the **Old Port.** From there, before you depart, you can grab a bite at either of two classic Maine eateries: **Gilbert's Chowder House** or **Becky's Diner,** or check out what's new in the buzzy restaurant scene here. For a peek at the freshest catch of the day, wander over to the **Harbor Fish Market,** a Portland institution since 1968, and gaze upon Maine lobsters and other delectable seafood. Two lighthouses on nearby **Cape Elizabeth, Two Lights** and **Portland Head,** still stand vigil.

Following U.S. 1, travel northeast along the ragged, island-strewn coast of Down East Maine and make your first stop at the retail outlets of **Freeport,** home of **L.L. Bean.** Almost 3 million people visit the massive flagship store every year, where you can find everything from outerwear to camping equipment. Just 10 miles north of Freeport on U.S. 1, **Brunswick** is home to the campus of **Bowdoin College,** the superb **Bowdoin College Museum of Art,** and also features a superb coastline for kayaking. Plan for dinner and an overnight in Bath.

Logistics: 30 miles; via U.S. 1 N; 30 minutes from Portland airport.

DAY 2: BATH
In **Bath,** Maine's shipbuilding capital, tour the **Maine Maritime Museum,** stopping for lunch on the waterfront. Check out the boutiques and antiques shops, or take in the plenitude of beautiful homes. From here it's a 30-minute detour down Route 127 to Georgetown Island and Reid State Park, where you will find a quiet beach lining Sheepscot Bay—and maybe even a sand dollar or two to take home, if you arrive at low tide. For a stunning vista, make your way to Griffith Head.

Drive north and reconnect with U.S. 1. Continue through the towns of **Wiscasset** and **Damariscotta,** where you may find yourself pulling over to stop at the outdoor flea markets and intriguing antiques shops that line the road. Another hour from here is **Rockland,** where you'll spend your second night.

Logistics: 52 miles; via U.S. 1 N; 1 hour 15 minutes, starting in Brunswick.

DAY 3: ROCKLAND, CAMDEN, AND CASTINE
From Rockland, spend the day cruising on a majestic schooner or reserve a tee time at Somerset Resorts' 18-hole

championship course that overlooks Rockland Harbor. If you're an art lover, save some time for Rockland's **Farnsworth Art Museum,** the **Wyeth Center,** and the **Maine Center for Contemporary Art.**

In **Camden** and **Castine,** exquisite inns occupy homes built from inland Maine's golden timber. Camden is an ideal place to stay overnight as you make your way closer to Acadia National Park; it is a beautiful seaside town with hundreds of boats bobbing in the harbor, immaculately kept antique homes, streets lined with boutiques and specialty stores, and restaurants serving lobster at every turn. The modest hills (by Maine standards, anyway) of nearby Mt. Battie offer good hiking and a great spot from which to picnic and view the surrounding area. It is also one of the hubs for the beloved and historic windjammer fleet—there is no better way to see the area than from the deck of one of these graceful beauties.

Logistics: 62 miles; via U.S. 1 N and Rte. 166 S; 1½ hours, starting in Rockland.

DAYS 4 AND 5: MOUNT DESERT ISLAND AND ACADIA NATIONAL PARK
On Day 4, head out early for **Bar Harbor** and plan to spend two nights here, using the bustling village as jumping-off point

for the park—Bar Harbor is less than 5 miles from the entrance to **Mount Desert Island's** 27-mile Park Loop Road. Spend at least a day exploring **Acadia National Park,** Maine's only national park and its most popular tourist destination. Enjoy the island's natural beauty by kayaking its coast, biking the 45-mile, historic, unpaved, carriage-road system, and driving to the summit of **Cadillac Mountain** for a stunning panorama.

Logistics: 52 miles; via Rte. 166 N, U.S. 1 N and Rte. 3 E; 1¼ hours, starting in Castine.

DAY 6: BAR HARBOR TO QUODDY HEAD STATE PARK
About 100 miles farther along U.S. 1 and "Way Down East" is Quoddy Head State Park in Lubec, Maine. Here, on the easternmost tip of land in the United States, sits the **West Quoddy Head Light,** one of 60 lighthouses that dot Maine's rugged coastline. Depending on the time of year (and your willingness to get up very early), you may be lucky enough to catch the East Coast's first sunrise here.

Logistics: 103 miles; via U.S. 1 N; 2½ hours, starting in Bar Harbor. From the park, it is 119 miles (2½ hours) to the Bangor airport via Rte. 9 W.

Great Itineraries

Best of Vermont, 7 Days

Following roads that weave through the Green Mountains and charming towns, this 200-mile journey is ideal at any time of year and covers Vermont from top to bottom.

Fly in: Bradley International Airport (BDL), Hartford, Connecticut.

Fly out: Burlington International Airport (BTV), Burlington, Vermont.

DAY 1: BRATTLEBORO

Artsy **Brattleboro** is the perfect place to begin a tour of Vermont, and it's worth taking a day to do some shopping and exploring. Catch a movie at the art deco **Latchis Theatre,** browse in a bookstore, or simply grab a cup of joe and people-watch. For dinner, make a reservation well in advance at tiny **T.J. Buckley's,** one of the best restaurants in the state. Spend your first night in Brattleboro.

Logistics: 78 miles; via I–91 N; 1 hour and 15 minutes from Bradley airport.

DAYS 2-4: KILLINGTON

Depart Brattleboro heading west on Route 9 and link up with Route 100 in Wilmington. As you travel north along the eastern edge of **Green Mountain National Forest,** you'll pass a plethora of panoramic overlooks and delightful ski towns. Stop to snap a photo, or take a moment to peruse the selection at a funky general store, as you make your way toward gigantic Killington Peak. Spend the next three nights in **Killington,** the largest ski resort in Vermont, and an outdoor playground year-round. A tip for skiers: one of the closest places to the slopes to stay is **The Mountain Top Inn & Resort.**

Wake up early to carve the mountain's fresh powder in winter. Nonskiers can still enjoy the snow, whether at the tubing park, on a snowmobile adventure, or in snowshoes on one of several trails. In summer, long after the ground has thawed, those trails are opened to mountain bikers and hikers. For a more leisurely activity, try your hand at the 18-hole disc-golf course. The excellent Grand Spa is also a lovely way to spend the day.

Logistics: 94 miles; via Rte. 9 W, Rte. 100 N, 2½ hours, starting in Brattleboro.

DAY 5: KILLINGTON TO BURLINGTON

Continue on Route 100 north until you reach Hancock, then head west on Route 125. Welcome to the land of poet Robert Frost, who spent almost 40 years living in Vermont, summering in the nearby tiny mountain town of Ripton, where he wrote numerous poems. Plaques along the 1.2-mile **Robert Frost Interpretive Trail,** a quiet woodland walk that takes about 30 minutes, display commemorative quotes from his poems, including his classic, "The Road Not Taken." After your stroll, head north on U.S. 7 until you hit Burlington.

Burlington, Vermont's largest city and home to the **University of Vermont,** is located on the eastern shore of Lake Champlain. Bustling in the summer and fall, the **Burlington Farmers' Market** is filled with everything from organic meats and cheeses to freshly cut flowers and maple syrup. Spend the night in Burlington. In the evening, check out **Nectar's,** where the band Phish played their first bar gig, or wander into any of the many other pubs and cafés that attract local musicians.

Logistics: 84 miles; via Rte. 100 N, Rte. 125 W, and U.S. 7 N; 2½ hours, starting in Killington.

DAY 6: SHELBURNE AND LAKE CHAMPLAIN

On your second day in Burlington, you can take a day trip south to the **Magic Hat Brewing Company**; established in 1994, it was at the forefront of Vermont's micro-brewery explosion. Take a free half-hour guided or self-guided tour of the Artifactory (even dogs are welcome), and fill a growler from one of the 48 taps pumping out year-round, seasonal, and experimental brews. A stone's throw down U.S. 7, in **Shelburne,** is family-friendly **Shelburne Farms.** Watch the process of making cheese from start to finish, or wander the gorgeous 1,400-acre estate designed by Frederick Law Olmsted, co-designer of New York's Central Park. The grounds overlook beautiful **Lake Champlain** and make the perfect setting for a picnic. In winter Shelburne Farms offers sleigh rides and other themed activities; if you're visiting in late July, don't miss the **Vermont Cheesemakers Festival,** showcasing more than 200 varieties of cheese crafted by 40 local purveyors. If you can't get enough, you can opt to spend the night here.

Logistics: 3.6 miles, via U.S. 7 to Magic Hat; another 3.4 miles to Shelburne Farms; 40 minutes round-trip altogether.

DAY 7: STOWE

A 30-minute drive down Interstate 89 from Burlington reunites you with Route 100 in the town of Waterbury. Head north in the direction of Stowe, and in under 2 miles you can make the obligatory pit stop at **Ben & Jerry's Ice Cream Factory.** The factory tour offers a lively behind-the-scenes look at how their ice cream is made; at the end of the tour, you get to taste limited-release creations only available at the factory before voting on your favorites.

Next, set out for the village of **Stowe.** Its proximity to Mt. Mansfield (Vermont's highest peak at 4,395 feet) has made Stowe a popular ski destination since the 1930s. If there's snow on the ground, hit the slopes, hitch a ride on a one-horse open sleigh, or simply put your feet up by the fire and enjoy a Heady Topper (an unfiltered, hoppy, American Double IPA beloved by beer aficionados the world over). In warmer weather, pop into the cute shops and art galleries that line the town's main street and sample some of the finest cheddar cheese and maple syrup that Vermont has to offer. Rejuvenate yourself at **Topnotch Resort,** which offers more than 100 different treatments. Spend your final night here.

Logistics: 36 miles; via I–89 S and Rte. 100 N; 45 minutes, starting in Burlington. From Stowe to the Burlington airport: 33 miles; via Rte. 100 and I–89 N; 41 minutes.

On the Calendar

January

NH Sanctioned & Jackson Invitational Snow Sculpting Competition, Jackson, NH. Started in 2000, the free event takes place at Black Mountain Ski and features more than 12 teams carving intricate snow sculptures. ⊕ *jacksonnh.com*.

February

Winter Carnival, Hanover, NH. Started in 1911, Dartmouth's winter festival celebrates the season with races, polar bear plunges, and snow sculpture contests. ⊕ *students.dartmouth.edu/collis/ events/winter-carnival*.

Winter Brew Fest, Burlington, Vermont. Breweries, cideries, and distilleries are all represented at the event in the Champlain Valley Exposition. ⊕ *www.winter-brewfestvt.com*.

March

Maine Maple Sunday Weekend. Participating sugarhouses, all members of the Maine Maple Producers Association, offer tours, demonstrations, activities, and free samples. ⊕ *mainemapleproducers.com*.

New Hampshire Maple Weekend. Participating sugarhouses throughout the state offer tours, behind-the-scenes access, and sometimes, breakfast. ⊕ *nhmapleproducers.com/maple-weekend-2*.

April

Patriot's Day. A Maine state holiday celebrated on the third Monday in April, it marks the anniversary of the first battles of the American Revolution.

Vermont Maple Festival, St. Albans, VT. This weekend is all about syrup. There's a pancake breakfast, a carnival and parade, and, of course, plenty of yummy maple treats. ⊕ *www.facebook.com/ VermontMapleFestival*.

May

Down East Spring Birding Festival, Cobscook Bay. America's easternmost birding festival occurs during spring migration and nesting season. There are guided hikes, sightseeing boat rides, sunset cruises, and speakers. ⊕ *cobscookinstitute.org/ birdfest*.

Wildquack Duck River Festival, Jackson, New Hampshire. This zany event features 3,500 yellow rubber ducks racing downstream. Pick the winning ducks and get rewarded with prizes that range from vacation stays to gift baskets. ⊕ *jacksonnh.com*.

June

Quechee Hot Air Balloon Festival, Quechee, Vermont. See 20 hot air balloons take to the skies over the Upper Valley of Vermont and New Hampshire. Admission includes live music, a kids' area, balloon glows, and access to more than 60 art and food booths. ⊕ *www.quecheeballoonfestival.com*.

Windjammer Days, Boothbay Harbor. In late June and early July, check out this seaside town's fleet of historic ships over a week that also includes a boat parade, shipyard tours, and a pancake breakfast. ⊕ *www.boothbayharborwindjammerdays.org*.

August

Champlain Valley Fair, Essex Junction, Vermont. The state's biggest single event has exhibits on Vermont's livestock and produce, carnival rides and games, and live entertainment. Did we mention the deep-fried cheesecake? ⊕ *www.champlainvalleyfair. org.*

Maine Antiques Festival, Union. Maine's largest antiques fair generally takes place in early or mid-August near Camden and Rockland. ⊕ *www.maineantiquesfestival.com.*

Maine Lobster Festival, Rockland. Stuff your face with lobster tails and claws during this three-day "lobstravaganza" that puts almost 20,000 pounds of delicious crustacean at your fingertips. ⊕ *mainelobsterfestival.com.*

Vermont Cheesemakers Festival, Shelburne, VT. Artisanal cheeses and local beer and wine highlight this daylong festival that features samples of more than 200 cheese varieties from 40 artisan cheese makers. ⊕ *vtcheesefest.com.*

Machias Wild Blueberry Festival, Machias. Savor the state's tart-sweet berries with a blueberry-pancake breakfast, and attend a kids' parade and a fish fry during this fruit-filled, three-day celebration. ⊕ *www.machiasblueberry.com.*

September

Camden Windjammer Festival. Held Labor Day weekend, the region's fleet sails into the harbor and is open for tours. ⊕ *www.facebook.com/WindjammerFestival.*

New Hampshire Highland Games & Festival, Lincoln, New Hampshire. Three-day celebration of Scottish music, food and drink, athletics, dance, and culture that takes place at Loon Mountain Resort. ⊕ *nhscot.org.*

October

Harvest on the Harbor, Portland. The state's top food-and-wine fest, held over a weekend late in October, is a great place to sample the latest creations of dozens of acclaimed chefs. ⊕ *harvestontheharbor.com.*

New Hampshire Pumpkin Festival, Laconia, NH. This family-friendly gathering near Lake Winnipesaukee tries to outdo itself each October by featuring the most lit pumpkins. ⊕ *www.nhpumpkinfestival.com.*

November

Billings Farm Thanksgiving Weekend, Woodstock, Vermont. Experience Thanksgiving—preparations, menu, and entertainment—as it was celebrated in the 1890s. There are holiday food activities, events in the house, and horse-drawn wagon rides. ⊕ *billingsfarm.org.*

Christmas Prelude, Kennebunkport. Take part in the hat parade, shop at the crafts fair, see the fireworks, or watch for Santa arriving on a lobster boat—these are just a few of the activities at this 10-day annual event. ⊕ *www.christmasprelude.com.*

Lighting of the Nubble, York, Maine. The famous coastal Maine lighthouse gets all dressed up for the holidays in late November, and stays light through New Years Day.

December

Inn to Inn Holiday Cookie Tour, White Mountains, NH. This self-guided tour includes sweet treats, copious Christmas decorations, and charming winter scenes. ⊕ *www.countryinnsinthewhitemountains.com.*

Winter Wassail Weekend, Woodstock, VT. The annual fete features a parade with holiday-costume clad horses and riders, live music, house tours, kids' activities, and a Wassail Feast. ⊕ *www.woodstockvt.com.*

Contacts

✈ Air

AIRPORTS Bangor International Airport. (*BGR*). ✉ *287 Godfrey Blvd., Bangor* ☎ *207/992–4600* ⊕ *www. flybangor.com.* **Burlington International Airport.** ✉ *South Burlington* ☎ *802/863–2874* ⊕ *www.btv.aero.* **Logan International Airport.** ✉ *Boston* ☎ *800/235–6426* ⊕ *www.massport. com* Ⓜ *Blue, Silver lines.* **Manchester-Boston Regional Airport.** ✉ *Manchester* ☎ *603/624–6539* ⊕ *www.flymanchester. com.* **Portland International Jetport.** (*PWM*). ✉ *1001 Westbrook St., Portland* ☎ *207/774–7301* ⊕ *www. portlandjetport.org.* **Albany International Airport.** ✉ *Albany* ☎ *518/242–2222* ⊕ *www.albanyairport.com.*

🚌 Bus

INFORMATION C&J. ☎ *603/430–1100* ⊕ *www. ridecj.com.* **Concord Coach Lines.** ✉ *Thompsons Point Rd., Portland* ☎ *800/639–3317* ⊕ *www.concordcoachlines.com.* **Dartmouth Coach.** ☎ *800/637–0123* ⊕ *dartmouthcoach.com.* **FlixBus.** ☎ *855/626–8585* ⊕ *www.flixbus.com.*

🚆 Train

INFORMATION Amtrak. ☎ *800/872–7245* ⊕ *www. amtrak.com.*

🧭 Tours

BIKING VBT Bicycling and Walking Vacations. ✉ *Williston* ☎ *855/335–9225* ⊕ *www.vbt.com.*

GENERAL INTEREST New England Vacation Tours. ☎ *800/742–7669* ⊕ *www. newenglandvacationtours. com.* **Northeast Unlimited Tours.** ☎ *800/759–6820* ⊕ *www.newenglandtours. com.* **Wolfe Tours & Adventures.** ☎ *978/255–1645* ⊕ *www.wolfetours.com.*

MOOSE TOURS Pemi Valley Moose Tours. ✉ *136 Main St., Lincoln* ☎ *603/745–2744* ⊕ *www.moosetoursnh.com.*

SKIING Inn to Inn. ✉ *52 Park St., Brandon* ☎ *802/247–3300* ⊕ *www. inntoinn.com.*

📍 Visitor Information

CONTACTS Maine Office of Tourism. ☎ *888/624–6345* ⊕ *www.visitmaine.com.* **New Hampshire Division of Travel and Tourism Development.** ☎ *800/386–4664* ⊕ *www.visitnh.gov.* **Vermont Department of Tourism and Marketing.** ☎ *800/837–6668* ⊕ *www. vermontvacation.com.*

ONLINE RESOURCES Visit New England. ⊕ *www. visitnewengland.com.* **Yankee Magazine.** ⊕ *www. newengland.com.*

Chapter 3

BEST FALL FOLIAGE DRIVES AND ROAD TRIPS

A CELEBRATION

Picture this: one scarlet maple offset by the stark white spire of a country church, a whole hillside of brilliant foliage foregrounded by a vintage barn, or perhaps a covered bridge straddling a cobalt river. Such iconic scenes have launched a thousand Instagram posts and turned New England into the ultimate fall destination for leaf peepers.

OF COLOR

Above, Vermont's Green Mountains are multicolored in the fall (and often white in winter).

Mother Nature, of course, puts on an annual autumn performance elsewhere, but this one is a showstopper. Like the landscape, the mix of deciduous (leaf-shedding) trees is remarkably varied here and creates a broader than usual palette. New England's abundant evergreens lend contrast, making the display even more vivid. Every September and October, leaf peepers arrive to cruise along country lanes, join outdoor adventures, or simply stroll on town greens.

Did you know the brilliant shades actually lurk in the leaves all year long? Leaves contain three pigments. The green chlorophyll, so dominant in summer that it obscures the red anthocyanins and orangey-yellow carotenoids, decreases in fall and reveals a crayon box of color.

PREDICTING THE PEAK

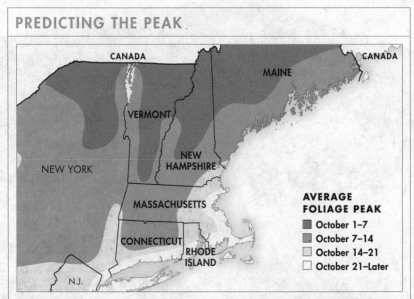

AVERAGE FOLIAGE PEAK
- October 1–7
- October 7–14
- October 14–21
- October 21–Later

LOCATION

Pinning down precisely when colors will appear remains an inexact science, although location plays a major role. Typically, the transformation begins in the highest and northernmost parts of New England in mid-September, then moves steadily into lower altitudes and southern sectors throughout October.

For trip planning, think in terms of regions rather than states. In Maine (a huge state that runs north–south) leaf color can peak anytime from the fourth week of September to the third week of October, depending on the locale.

WEATHER

Early September weather is another deciding factor. From the foliage aficionado's perspective, the ideal scenario is calm, temperate days capped by nights that are cool but still above freezing. If the weather is too warm, it delays the onset of the season. If it's too dry or windy, the leaves shrivel up or blow off.

COLOR CHECK RESOURCES

Curious about current conditions? In season, most states maintain websites reporting on foliage conditions. Weather Channel has peak viewing maps and Foliage Network uses a network of spotters to chart changes.

- **Connecticut:** www.ct.gov/dep
- **Foliage Network:** www.foliagenetwork.com
- **Maine:** www.mainefoliage.com
- **Massachusetts:** www.massvacation.com
- **New Hampshire:** www.visitnh.gov
- **Rhode Island:** www.visitrhodeisland.com
- **Vermont:** www.vermontvacation.com
- **Weather Channel:** www.weather.com

TOP TREES FOR COLOR

A AMERICAN BEECH. This tree's smooth, steel-gray trunk is crowned with gold, copper, and bronze-tinted leaves in autumn, giving it a metallic sheen. Though the elliptical leaves sometimes hang on all winter, its "fruit" goes fast because beechnuts are a popular snack for birds, squirrels, and even bears.

B NORTHERN RED OAK. The upside of oaks is that they retain their fall shading until late in the season—the downside is that, for most species, that color is a boring brown. Happily, the northern red isn't like other members of the oak family. Its elongated, flame-shaped leaves turn fiery crimson and incandescent orange.

C QUAKING ASPEN. Eyes and ears both prove useful when identifying this aspen. Look for small, ovate leaves that usually become almost flaxen. Or listen for the leaves' quake: a sound, audible in even a gentle breeze, which the U.S. Forest Service likens to that made by "thousands of fluttering butterfly wings."

D SUGAR MAPLE. The leaf of the largest North American maple species is so lovely that Canada put it on its national flag. Each generally has five multi-pointed lobes—plus enough anthocyanin to produce a deep red color. The tree itself produces plentiful sap and is the cornerstone of New England's syrup industry.

E WHITE ASH. This tall tree typically grows to between 65 to 100 feet. Baseball enthusiasts admire the wood (which is used to craft bats); while foliage fans admire the compound leaves, each consisting of five to nine slightly serrated, tapering leaflets. They range in hue from burgundy and purple to amber.

F WHITE BIRCH. A papery, light, bright bark makes this slender hardwood easily recognizable. Centuries ago, Native Americans used birch wood to make everything from canoes to medicinal teas. Today's photographers know the bark also makes great pictures since it provides a sharp contrast to the tree's vibrant yellow leaves.

FANTASTIC FALL ITINERARY

The Berkshires

Fall is the perfect time to visit New England—country roads wind through dense forests exploding into reds, oranges, yellows, and purples. For inspiration, here is an itinerary for the truly ambitious that links the most stunning foliage areas; choose a section to explore more closely. Like autumn itself, this route works its way south from northern Vermont into Connecticut, with one or two days in each area.

VERMONT

NORTHWEST VERMONT

In Burlington, the elms will be turning colors on the University of Vermont campus. You can ride the ferry across Lake Champlain for great views of Vermont's Green Mountains and New York's Adirondacks. After visiting the resort town of Stowe, detour off Route 100 beneath the cliffs of Smugglers' Notch. The north country's palette unfolds in Newport, where the blue waters of Lake Memphremagog reflect the foliage.

NORTHEAST KINGDOM

After a side trip along Lake Willoughby, explore St. Johnsbury, where the Fairbanks Museum and St. Johnsbury Athenaeum reveal Victorian tastes in art and natural-history collecting. In Peacham, stock up for a picnic at the Peacham Store.

NEW HAMPSHIRE

WHITE MOUNTAINS AND LAKES REGION

Interstate 93 narrows as it winds through craggy Franconia Notch. Get off the interstate for the sinuous Kancamagus Highway portion of Route 112 that passes through the mountains to Conway. In Center Harbor, in the Lakes Region, you can ride the MS *Mount Washington* for views of the Lake Winnipesaukee shoreline, or ascend to Moultonborough's Castle in the Clouds for a falcon's-eye look at the colors.

MT. MONADNOCK

In Hanover, stroll around the Dartmouth College campus, then head south around Lake Sunapee. Several trails climb Mt. Monadnock, near Peterborough, and colorful vistas extend as far as Boston.

⇨ For local drives perfect for an afternoon, also see our Fall Foliage Drive Spotlights.

THE MOOSE IS LOOSE!

Take "Moose Crossing" signs seriously, because things won't end well if you hit an animal that stands 6 feet tall and weighs 1,200 pounds. Some 40,000 reside in northern New England. To search out these ungainly creatures in the wild, consider an organized moose safari in northern New Hampshire or Maine.

MASSACHUSETTS

THE MOHAWK TRAIL

In Shelburne Falls, the Bridge of Flowers displays the last of autumn's blossoms. Follow the Mohawk Trail section of Route 2 as it ascends into the Berkshire Hills—and stop to take in the view at the hairpin turn just east of North Adams (or drive up Mt. Greylock, the tallest peak in Massachusetts, for more stunning vistas). In Williamstown, the Clark Art Institute has gorgeous grounds and houses a collection of impressionist works.

THE BERKSHIRES

The scenery around Lenox, Stockbridge, and Great Barrington has long attracted the talented and the wealthy. Near U.S. 7, you can visit the homes of novelist Edith Wharton (the Mount, in Lenox), sculptor Daniel Chester French (Chesterwood, in Stockbridge), and diplomat Joseph Choate (Naumkeag, in Stockbridge).

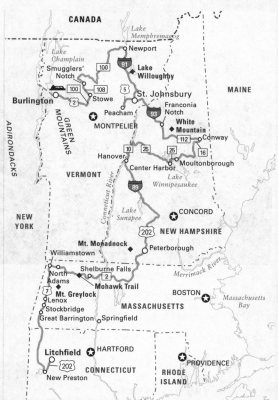

CONNECTICUT

THE LITCHFIELD HILLS

This area of Connecticut combines the feel of upcountry New England with exclusive urban polish. The wooded shores of Lake Waramaug are home to the striking Hopkins Inn and Hopkins Vineyard. Litchfield has a perfect village green—a quintessential New England town center.

FOLIAGE PHOTO HINT

Don't just snap the big panoramic views. Look for single, brilliantly colored trees with interesting elements nearby, like a weathered gray stone wall or a freshly painted white church. These images are often more evocative than big blobs of color or panoramic shots.

LEAF PEEPER PLANNER

Hot-air balloons and ski-lift rides give a different perspective on fall's color.

Enjoying fall doesn't necessarily require a multistate road trip. If you are short on time (or energy), a simple autumnal stroll might be just the ticket: many state parks even offer free short ranger-led rambles.

HIKE AND BIKE ON A TOUR

You can sign on for foliage-focused hiking holidays with **Country Walkers** (☎ 855/445–5603 ⊕ www.country-walkers.com) and **Boundless Journeys** (☎ 800/941–8010 ⊕ www.boundless-journeys.com); or cycling ones with **Discovery Bicycle Tours** (☎ 800/257–2226 ⊕ www.discoverybicycletours.com) and **VBT Bicycling Vacations** (☎ 855/202–2251 ⊕ www.vbt.com). Individual state tourism boards list similar operators elsewhere.

SOAR ABOVE THE CROWDS

New Hampshire's Cannon Mountain (☎ 603/823–8800 ⊕ www.cannonmt.com) is only one of several New England ski resorts that provides gondola or aerial tram rides during foliage season. Area hot-air balloon operators, like **Above Reality Hot Air Balloon Rides** (☎ 802/373–4007 ⊕ www.balloonvermont.com), help you take it in from the top.

ROOM AT THE INN?

Accommodations fill quickly in autumn. Vermont's top lodgings sell out months in advance for the first two weeks in October. So book early and expect a two-night minimum stay requirement. If you can't find a quaint inn, try basing yourself at an Airbnb or off-season ski resort. Also, be prepared for some sticker shock; if you can travel midweek, you'll often save quite a bit.

RIDE THE RAILS OR THE CURRENT

Board the **Essex Steam Train** for a ride through the Connecticut countryside (☎ 800/377–3987 ⊕ www.essexsteam-train.com) or float through northern Rhode Island on the **Blackstone Valley Explorer** riverboat (☎ 401/724–2200 ⊕ www.rivertourblackstone.com).

VERMONT FALL FOLIAGE DRIVE

Nearly 80% of Vermont is forested, with cities few and far between. The state's interior is a rural playground for leaf peepers, and it's widely considered to exhibit the most intense range of colors anywhere on the continent. Its tiny towns and hamlets—the few distractions from the dark reds, yellows, oranges, and russets—are as pristine as nature itself.

Begin this drive in Manchester Village, along the old-fashioned, well-to-do homes lining Main Street, and continue south to Arlington, North Bennington, and Old Bennington. Stop just a mile south along Route 7A at **Hildene.** The 412 acres of explorable grounds at the estate of Abraham Lincoln's son are ablaze with color, and the views over the Battenkill Valley are as good as any you can find. Drive south another mile along 7A to the **Equinox Valley Nursery,** where you can sample delicious apple cider and doughnuts amid views of the arresting countryside. A few more miles south along 7A is the small town of Arlington.

BEST TIME TO GO
Late September and early October are the times to go, with the southern area peaking about a week later than the north. Remember to book hotels in advance. The state has a Fall Foliage Hotline and an online interactive map (☎ 802/828–3239 ⊕ www.foliage-vermont.com).

PLANNING YOUR TIME
The drive from Manchester to Bennington outlined here takes just 30 minutes, but a relaxed pace is best suited to taking in all the sights.

From Route 7A in Arlington you can take two adventurous and stunning detours. One is pure foliage: follow Route 313 west a few miles to the New York State border for more beautiful views. Or head east 1 mile to East Arlington, where there's a delightful chocolate emporium. (You can continue even farther east from this spot to Kelly Stand Road leading into the Green Mountains—a little-known route that can't be beat.) Back on 7A South in Arlington, stop at the delightful **Arlington Dairy Bar** for a Vermont creemee.

Farther south in Shaftsbury is **Clear Brook Farm,** a brilliant place for fresh produce and pumpkins. Robert Frost spent much of his life in South Shaftsbury, and you can learn about his life at his former home, the **Stone House.** From South Shaftsbury take Route 67 through North Bennington and continue on to Route 67A in Old Bennington. Ride the elevator up the 306-foot-high **Bennington Battle Monument** to survey the season's progress across four states. Back down from the clouds, walk a few serene blocks to the cemetery of the **Old First Church,** where Robert Frost is buried, and contemplate his autumnal poem, "Nothing Gold Can Stay."

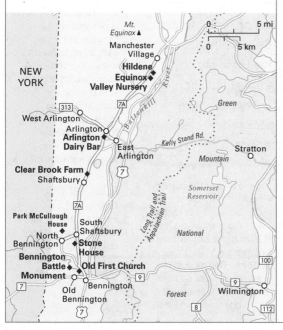

3

Best Fall Foliage Drives and Road Trips

VERMONT FALL FOLIAGE DRIVE

NEED A BREAK?

Arlington Dairy Bar. Along 7A waits a big red dairy barn surrounded on all sides by Vermont's color-changing landscape. There are few greater ways to enjoy fall foliage than leaning on the hood of your car with a double scoop of local pumpkin and maple walnut ice cream, or a chocolate-dipped Vermont creemee. ⊠ *3158 Rte. 7A, Arlington* ☎ *802/375–2546* ⊕ *www.facebook.com/ ArlingtonDairyBar.*

Clear Brook Farm. This 25-acre certified organic farm sells its own produce, in addition to plants, baked goods, and other seasonal treats. ⊠ *47 Hidden Valley Rd., Manchester* ☎ *802/442– 4273* ⊕ *www.clearbrook- farm.com.*

Equinox Valley Nursery. This nursery carries fresh produce, seasonal snacks, and cider doughnuts. There's family-friendly fall activities—a corn maze, hayrides, and pumpkin carving—as well as the property's 300-odd scarecrows. ⊠ *1158 Main St., Manchester* ☎ *802/362–2610* ⊕ *www. equinoxvalleynursery. com* ⊠ *Free.*

NEW HAMPSHIRE FALL FOLIAGE DRIVE

Quaint villages graced with green commons, white town halls, and covered bridges: southwestern New Hampshire is dominated by the imposing rocky summit of Mt. Monadnock and the brilliant colors of autumn. Kancamagus Highway is another classic foliage route, but for more solitude and less traffic, try this more accessible route that peaks a few weeks later than the state's far north.

The Granite State is the second-most-forested state in the nation; by mid-October the colors of the leaves of its maple, birch, elm, oak, beech, and ash trees range from green to gold, purple to red, and orange to auburn. Routes 12, 101, 124, and U.S. 202 form a loop around **Mt. Monadnock.** Start on the picturesque Main Street in Keene with a stop for coffee at Prime Roast Café; for New Hampshire–made products, take a walk on Main Street or detour west on Route 9 to reach **Stonewall Farm**, a lovely spot for a stroll or to buy fresh produce.

BEST TIME TO GO
The best time to view foliage in southern New Hampshire is generally early October, but it can vary by up to four weeks. For updates about leaf changes, visit the Foliage Tracker page on the website of **Visit New Hampshire** (☎ 603/271–2665 ⊕ *www.visitnh. gov*).

PLANNING YOUR TIME
Expect to travel about 55 miles. The journey can take up to a full day if you stop to explore along the way.

From Keene, travel east on Route 101 through Dublin. In **Peterborough**, browse the local boutiques as well as the superb **Mariposa Museum,** which exhibits a colorful collection of costumes and musical instruments from every corner of the globe. If you need a bite to eat before continuing on your journey or later for dinner, stop by **Harlow's Pub,** a convivial spot in Peterborough's scenic downtown.

Then turn south on U.S. 202 toward Jaffrey Village. Just west on Route 124, in historic Jaffrey Center, be sure to visit the **Meeting House Cemetery,** where author Willa Cather is buried. One side-trip, 4 miles south on U.S. 202, leads to the majestic **Cathedral of the Pines** in Rindge, one of the best places in the region for foliage viewing because evergreens offset the brilliant shades of red.

Heading west on Route 124, you can take Dublin Road to the main entrance of **Monadnock State Park** or continue along to the Old Toll Road parking area for one of the most popular routes up the mountain, the **Old Halfway House Trail.** All the hiking trails have great views, including the area's many lakes. Continuing on U.S. 124, head southwest on Fitzwilliam Road to Fitzwilliam. If you have time, pop into **Bloomin' Antiques** to browse their selection of fine art and unusual antiques.

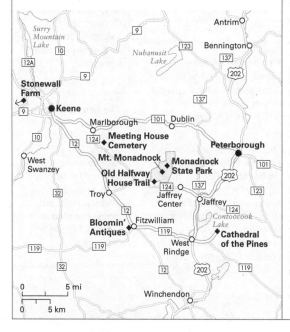

3

Best Fall Foliage Drives and Road Trips NEW HAMPSHIRE FALL FOLIAGE DRIVE

NEED A BREAK?

Bloomin' Antiques. Make a stop here to hunt for fine art and unusual antiques. ✉ *3 Templeton Tpke., Fitzwilliam* ☎ *800/386–4664* ⊕ *bloominantiques.com.*

Harlow's Pub. Open for lunch, dinner, and Sunday brunch, this friendly tavern with a patio overlooking Peterborough's scenic village center serves creative comfort fare and local craft beer. ✉ *3 School St., Peterborough* ☎ *603/924–6365* ⊕ *www. harlowspub.com.*

Stonewall Farm. A working dairy farm with a dramatic setting amid fields and forests, Stonewall is open daily and presents an active schedule of events, including maple sugaring and seasonal horse-drawn hayrides. Walking and snowshoeing trails lace the property, and a farm shop sells organic produce, gourmet snacks, and the farm's own luscious Frisky Cow Gelato. Young children love the discovery room, and the interactive greenhouse is geared for all ages. ✉ *242 Chesterfield Rd., Keene* ☎ *603/357–7278* ⊕ *www.stonewallfarm. org.*

INLAND MAINE FALL FOLIAGE DRIVE

Swaths of pine, spruce, and fir trees offset the red, orange, and yellow of maples and birches along this popular foliage drive through western Maine's mountains.

Wending its way to the four-season resort town of Rangeley, near its northern terminus, the route passes stunning overlooks, forest-lined lakes, waterfalls, hiking trails, and a state park. Mountain vistas are reflected in the many (often connected) lakes, ponds, rivers, and streams.

Route 17 heads north past old homesteads and fields along the Swift River Valley before making a mountainous switchback ascent to **Height of Land,** the drive's literal pinnacle. The must-stop overlook here has off-road parking, interpretive panels, stone seating, and a short path to the **Appalachian Trail.** On a clear day, you can look west to mountains on the New Hampshire border. **Mooselookmeguntic Lake** and **Upper Richardson Lake** seem to float amid the forestland below. A few miles north of here is an overlook for Rangeley Lake, also with interpretive panels.

BEST TIME TO GO
Fall color usually peaks in the first or second week of October. Get fall foliage updates at ⊕ *www.mainefoliage.com.*

PLANNING YOUR TIME
The Rangeley Lakes National Scenic Byway and a state byway (⊕ *www.exploremaine.org/byways*) make up most of this 58-mile drive (1½ hours without stops), but plan for a relaxed, full day of exploring.

In tiny, welcoming Oquossoc, where Routes 17 and 4 meet, enjoy a burger or wood-fired pizza with one of the many Maine craft brews on tap at **Portage Tap House.** The hamlet is also home to the **Outdoor Heritage Museum,** where you can learn why visitors have come here to fish, hunt, and enjoy the outdoors since the mid-1800s. The trailhead for **Bald Mountain,** a popular hike, is just outside the village.

Rangeley, 7 miles east on Route 4, has restaurants, inns, a waterfront park, and outdoorsy shops. The countryside sweeps into view along public hiking trails at the 175-acre **Wilhelm Reich Museum.** There's also hiking at Rangeley Lakes Trail Center on Saddleback Mountain.

The road to **Rangeley Lake State Park** is accessible from both Routes 4 and 17, as is the **Appalachian Trail.** Overhanging foliage frames waterfalls at the scenic rest areas at each end of the drive: at Coos Canyon on Route 17 en route to Height of Land, and at Smalls Falls on Route 4 near Madrid, the terminus. Both spots have swimming holes, several falls, and paths with views of their drops. Coos Canyon is along the Swift River, a destination for recreational gold panning. You can rent or buy panning equipment at **Coos Canyon Rock and Gift,** across from its namesake. The seasonal shop also sells premade sandwiches, ice cream, and snacks.

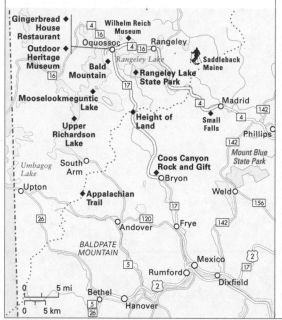

NEED A BREAK?

Coos Canyon Rock and Gift. Along with prospecting equipment, the seasonal shop sells souvenirs, to-go foods, and ice cream. ⊠ 472 Swift River Rd. (Rte. 17), Byron ☎ 207/364–4900 ⊕ www. cooscanyonrockandgift. com.

Rangeley Lakes Heritage Trust. The trust protects 14,000 acres of land in the Rangeley Lakes area. Both online and at its Rangeley office, the trust has maps and descriptions of its 35 miles of recreational trails and access roads, along with information about fishing, hunting, snowmobiling, picnicking, and other outdoor activities. ⊠ 2424 Main St., Rangeley ☎ 207/864–7311 ⊕ www.rlht.org.

Wilhelm Reich Museum. This seasonal museum showcases the life and work of controversial physician-scientist Wilhelm Reich (1897–1957). Open year-round, the 175-acre property has great trails and an observatory with magnificent views. ⊠ 19 Orgonon Circle, off Rte. 4, Rangeley ☎ 207/864–3443 ⊕ www. wilhelmreichmuseum. org ⊴ Museum $10, grounds free.

3

Best Fall Foliage Drives and Road Trips INLAND MAINE FALL FOLIAGE DRIVE

Chapter 4

VERMONT

Updated by
Jordan Barry
and Jessica Kelly

◉ Sights	🍴 Restaurants	🛏 Hotels	⬤ Shopping	🍸 Nightlife
★★★★★	★★★★☆	★★★★☆	★★★☆☆	★★☆☆☆

WELCOME TO VERMONT

TOP REASONS TO GO

★ **Small-Town Charm:** Vermont rolls out a seemingly never-ending supply of tiny towns replete with white-steepled churches, town greens, red barns, general stores, and bed-and-breakfasts.

★ **Ski Resorts:** The East's best skiing can be found in well-managed, modern facilities with great views and lots and lots of powdery, fresh snow.

★ **Fall Foliage:** Perhaps the most vivid colors in North America wave from the trees in September and October.

★ **Gorgeous Landscapes:** This sparsely populated, heavily forested state is an ideal place to find peace and quiet amid the mountains, valleys, and lakes.

★ **Vibrant Local Eats:** The rich soil, and an emphasis on the state's maker-artisan culture, has led to great dairies, orchards, vineyards, specialty stores, and farm-to-table restaurants. Even the world-famous beer scene is known to highlight state-grown hops and locally made malt.

1 Brattleboro. A hippie enclave with an artistic and activist disposition.

2 Wilmington. The hub of Mt. Snow Valley.

3 Bennington. The economic center of southwest Vermont.

4 Arlington. Once the home of painter Norman Rockwell.

5 Manchester. Sophisticated with upscale shopping.

6 Dorset. Home to two of the state's best and oldest general stores.

7 Stratton. It's all about Stratton Mountain Resort.

8 Weston. Home to the Vermont Country Store.

9 Ludlow. Okemo Mountain Resort's home.

10 Grafton. Both a town and a museum.

11 Norwich. One of the most picturesque towns.

12 Quechee. Restaurants and shops in old mills.

13 Woodstock. Upscale shops and the venerable Woodstock Inn.

14 Killington. The East Coast's largest ski resort.

15 Rutland. Slowly gaining traction as a foodie town.

16 Brandon. Artists Guild and the Basin Bluegrass Festival.

17 Middlebury. Restaurants, shops, and Middlebury College.

18 Waitsfield and Warren. The ski meccas of Mad River Glen and Sugarbush.

19 Montpelier. The state's capital.

20 Stowe. Quintessential eastern ski town.

21 Jeffersonville. The four-season Smugglers' Notch Resort.

22 Burlington. Vermont's most populous city with a lively food scene.

23 Shelburne. Shelburne Farms and Shelburne Museum.

24 Lake Champlain Islands. Numerous islands including Isle La Motte, North Hero, Grand Isle, and South Hero.

25 Montgomery and Jay. Small village near the Jay Peak ski resort and the Canadian border.

26 Lake Willoughby. Home to the world-renowned Bread and Puppet Theater museum.

27 Greensboro. Home to one of the world's best breweries.

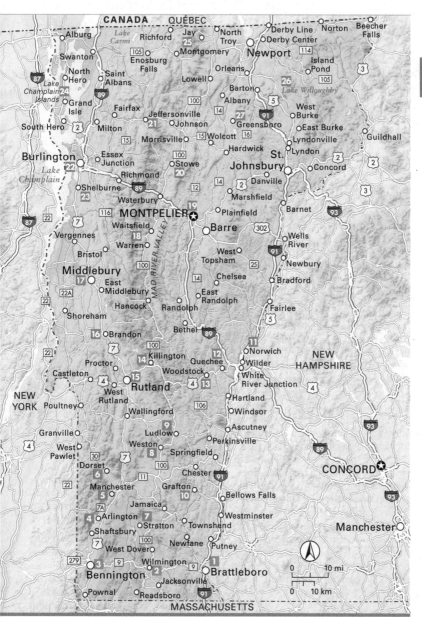

Vermont's a land of hidden treasures and unspoiled scenery. Wander anywhere in the state—nearly 80% is forest—and you'll find pristine countryside dotted with farms and framed by mountains. Tiny towns with picturesque church steeples, village greens, and covered bridges are perfect for exploring.

Sprawl has no place here. Highways are devoid of billboards by law, and on some roads cows still stop traffic twice a day en route to and from pasture. In spring, sap boils in sugarhouses, some built generations ago, while up the road a chef trained at the now-closed New England Culinary Institute in Montpelier might use the syrup to glaze a pork tenderloin.

It's the landscape, for the most part, that attracts people to Vermont. Rolling hills belie rugged terrain underneath the green canopy of forest growth. In summer, clear lakes and streams provide ample opportunities for swimming, boating, and fishing; hills attract hikers and mountain bikers. The more than 14,000 miles of roads, many of them only intermittently traveled by cars, are great for biking. In fall the leaves have their last hurrah, painting the mountainsides in vibrant yellow, gold, red, and orange. Vermont has the best ski resorts in the eastern United States, centered on the spine of the Green Mountains running north to south; and the traditional heart of skiing here is the town of Stowe. Almost anywhere you go, no matter what time of year, the Vermont countryside will make you reach for your camera.

Although Vermont may seem locked in time, technological sophistication appears where you least expect it: wireless Internet access in a 19th-century farmhouse-turned-inn and cell phone coverage from the state's highest peaks. Like an old farmhouse under renovation, though, the state's historic exterior is still the main attraction.

MAJOR REGIONS

Vermont can be divided into three regions: **Southern Vermont, Central Vermont,** and **Northern Vermont.**

Most people's introduction to the state is **Southern Vermont,** a relatively short drive from New York and Boston. As elsewhere across the state, you'll find unspoiled towns, romantic B&Bs, lush farms, and pristine forests. The area is flanked by **Bennington** on the west and **Brattleboro** on the east. There are charming towns like **Wilmington, Arlington, Manchester, Dorset, Weston, Grafton,** and **Townshend**, as well as ski destinations like **Stratton** and **Ludlow** (home to Okemo Resort).

Central Vermont is characterized by the rugged Green Mountains, which run north–south through the center of the state, and the gently rolling dairy lands east of Lake Champlain. It's home to the state's capital, **Montpelier,** the former mill towns of **Quechee** and **Middlebury**, artist enclaves like **Brandon**, and beautiful towns like **Norwich** and **Woodstock**, and plucky **Rutland**. Ski buffs flock to **Killington** and **Waitsfield** and **Warren** (for Mad River Glen and Sugarbush).

Northern Vermont is a place of contrasts. It's where you'll find the area known as the Northeast Kingdom, a refuge for nature lovers and those who love getting away from it all, as well as the state's largest city, **Burlington**, which has dramatic views of Lake Champlain and the Adirondacks, and it's neighboring Winooski. There's plenty of skiing in **Stowe, Jeffersonville** (Smugglers' Notch Resort), and **Jay** (Jay Peak) as well as outdoor adventures in **Lake Willoughby** and East Burke. And postcard-perfect scenery oozes in **Shelburne**, Charlotte, **Montgomery**, and the **Lake Champlain Islands**.

Planning

There are many ways to take advantage of Vermont's beauty: skiing or hiking its mountains, biking or driving its back roads, fishing or sailing its waters, shopping for local products, visiting museums and sights, or simply finding the perfect inn and never leaving the front porch.

Getting Here and Around

Distances are relatively short, yet the mountains and back roads will slow a traveler's pace. You can see a representative north–south cross section of Vermont in a few days; if you have up to a week, you can really hit the highlights.

AIR
American, Delta, JetBlue, Porter, and United fly into Burlington International Airport. Rutland State Airport has daily service to and from Boston on Cape Air.

CAR
Vermont is divided by a mountainous north–south middle, with a main highway on either side: scenic U.S. 7 on the western side and Interstate 91 (which begins in New Haven, Connecticut, and runs through Hartford, central Massachusetts, and along the Connecticut River in Vermont to the Canadian border) on the east. Interstate 89 runs from New Hampshire across central Vermont from White River Junction to Burlington and up to the Canadian border. For current road conditions, check New England 511's website.

New England 511
☎ *511* ⊕ *newengland511.org.*

FERRY
This company operates ferries on three routes between Vermont and New York: from Grand Isle, Vermont to Plattsburgh, New York; Burlington to Port Kent, New York; and Charlotte, Vermont to Essex, New York.

TRAIN
Amtrak has daytime service on the *Vermonter*, linking Washington, D.C. and New York City with Brattleboro, Bellows Falls, Windsor, White River Junction, Randolph, Montpelier, Waterbury, Essex Junction, and St. Albans.

Other Amtrak services include the *Ethan Allen Express*, which connects New York City with Castleton, Rutland, Middlebury, Vergennes, and Burlington.

Amtrak
☎ *800/872–7245* ⊕ *www.amtrak.com.*

Hotels

Vermont's relatively rare large chain hotels are mostly found in Burlington, Manchester, and Rutland; elsewhere it's primarily inns, B&Bs, and small motels. The inns and B&Bs, some of them quite luxurious, provide what many visitors consider the quintessential Vermont

4

Vermont PLANNING

lodging experience. Most areas have traditional ski-base condos; at these you sacrifice charm for ski-and-stay deals and proximity to the lifts. Lodging rates are highest during foliage season, late September–mid-October, and lowest in late spring and November, although many properties close during these times. Winter is high season at ski resorts.

Hotel reviews have been shortened. For full reviews visit Fodors.com.

Restaurants

Everything that makes Vermont good and wholesome is distilled in its restaurants. Many of them belong to the **Vermont Fresh Network** (⊕ www.vermontfresh.net), a partnership that encourages chefs to create menus emphasizing Vermont's wonderful bounty; especially in summer and early fall, the produce and meats are impeccable.

Great chefs come to Vermont for the quality of life, and the Montpelier-based New England Culinary Institute was until recently a recruiting ground for new talent. Seasonal menus use local fresh herbs and vegetables along with native game. Look for imaginative approaches to New England foods like maple syrup (Vermont is the largest U.S. producer); dairy products (cheese in particular); native fruits and berries; heritage apples (explore the ever-growing cider scene); and regional game like venison, quail, and pheasant. Small-batch goods, from salsa to caramels, are made with Vermont ingredients. Beer has become yet another claim to fame in Vermont, thanks to more breweries per capita than any other state and recognition far and wide. Indeed, craft brewers as far away as Poland are now producing "Vermont-style" IPAs, and Hill Farmstead in Greensboro has been dubbed the best brewery in the world seven times by RateBeer, a brew-review website, since opening doors in 2010.

Creemee vs. Soft-Serve

A creemee is Vermont's answer to soft-serve ice cream. It often has a higher fat content than typical soft-serve—thanks in part to state specialties like local dairy and maple syrup—making it especially rich, silky and, well, creamy. (Hence the name.)

Your chances of finding a table for dinner vary with the season: lengthy waits are common in tourist centers at peak times—a reservation is always advisable.

Restaurant reviews have been shortened. For full reviews visit Fodors.com.

What It Costs in U.S. Dollars			
$	$$	$$$	$$$$
RESTAURANTS			
under $18	$18–$24	$25–$35	over $35
HOTELS			
under $200	$200–$299	$300–$399	over $399

Tours

Inn to Inn
SPECIAL-INTEREST TOURS | This company arranges guided and self-guided hiking, skiing, snowshoeing, and biking trips from inn to inn in Vermont. ⊠ *52 Park St., Brandon* ☎ *802/247–3300* ⊕ *www.inntoinn.com* ⊗ *Closed Nov.–mid-May.*

VBT Bicycling and Walking Vacations
BICYCLE TOURS | This global guide company leads bike tours in Vermont as well as Maine and Massachusetts. The Vermont itineraries included a self-guided tour of the Middlebury countryside and the Lake Champlain coast and a guided tour of

Burlington, the Champlain Islands, and surrounding country villages. ⊠ *Williston* ☎ *855/335–9225* ⊕ *www.vbt.com* ✉ *From $1795.*

Visitor Information

CONTACTS Ski Vermont/Vermont Ski Areas Association. ⊠ *Montpelier* ☎ *802/223–2439* ⊕ *www.skivermont.com*. **Vermont Department of Tourism and Marketing.** ⊠ *Montpelier* ☎ *800/837–6668* ⊕ *www. vermontvacation.com*. **Vermont's Northeast Kingdom.** ☎ *802/626–8511* ⊕ *getnekedvt. com*.

When to Go

In summer Vermont is lush and green, and in winter the hills and towns are blanketed white with snow, inspiring skiers to challenge the peaks at Stowe and elsewhere. Fall, however, is always the most amazing time to come. If you have never seen the state's kaleidoscope of autumn colors, it's well worth braving the slow-moving traffic and shelling out a few extra bucks for lodging. The only time things really slow down is during "stick season" in November, when the leaves have fallen but there's no snow yet, and "mud season" in late spring, when even innkeepers counsel guests to come another time. Activities in the Champlain Islands essentially come to a halt in the winter, except for ice fishing and snowmobiling, and two of the biggest attractions, Shelburne Farms and the Shelburne Museum, are closed mid-October–April. Otherwise, Vermont is open for business year-round.

Brattleboro

60 miles south of White River Junction.

Brattleboro has drawn political activists and earnest counterculturists since the 1960s. The arts-oriented town and

environs (population 12,000) remains politically and culturally active; after Burlington, this is Vermont's most offbeat locale.

GETTING HERE AND AROUND
Brattleboro is near the intersection of Route 9, the principal east–west highway also known as the Molly Stark Byway, and Interstate 91. For downtown, take Exit 2 from Interstate 91.

ESSENTIALS
VISITOR INFORMATION Brattleboro Area Chamber of Commerce. ⊠ *Brattleboro* ☎ *802/254–4565, 877/254–4565* ⊕ *www. brattleborochamber.org.*

◉ Sights

Brattleboro Museum and Art Center
ART MUSEUM | Downtown is the hub of Brattleboro's art scene, at the forefront of which is this museum in historic Union Station. It presents changing exhibitions of works by local, national, and international artists, and hosts lectures, readings, and musical performances. ⊠ *10 Vernon St., Brattleboro* ☎ *802/257–0124* ⊕ *www. brattleboromuseum.org* ✉ *$10 suggested donation* ⏱ *Closed Mon. and Tues.*

Putney
TOWN | Nine miles upriver, this town of fewer than 3,000 residents—the country cousin of bustling Brattleboro—is a haven for writers and fine-craft artists. There are many pottery studios to visit, the requisite general store, and a few orchards. Each November during the Putney Craft Tour, dozens of artisans open their studios and homes for live demonstrations and plenty of fun. ⊠ *Putney.*

◍ Restaurants

Cai's Dim Sum Catering
$ | CHINESE | The sourcing and gathering of local ingredients at the heart of chef-owner Cai Xi Silver's cooking is inspired by the food memories of her childhood in Chongqing, China. Her

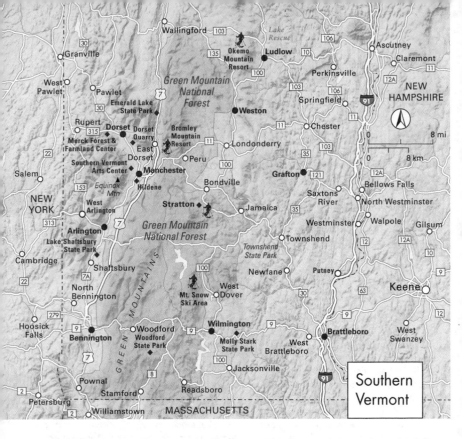

family's Sichuan and Shanghai influences come to life in a to-go menu that includes delicate steamed buns, perfect dumplings, and abundance boxes highlighting regional home cooking backed by Vermont ingredients. **Known for:** steamed buns; assorted seasonal dumplings; abundance boxes with local vegetables, rice, chicken, or tofu. $ *Average main: $15* ✉ *814 Western Ave., Brattleboro* ☎ 802/257–7898 ⊕ *dimsumvt.com* ⊙ *Closed Tues and for in-room dining; take-out/delivery only.*

★ Peter Havens

$$$ | **AMERICAN** | A longtime Brattleboro favorite helmed since 2012 by chef Zachary Corbin, this chic little bistro is known for impeccably presented cuisine that draws heavily on local sources. One room is painted a warm red, another in sage, and a changing lineup of contemporary paintings adorns the walls of both rooms. **Known for:** pan-roasted duck breast; cocktail and wine list; vanilla bean crème brûlée. $ *Average main: $30* ✉ *32 Elliot St., Brattleboro* ☎ 802/257–3333 ⊕ *www.peterhavens.com* ⊙ *Closed Mon. and Tues. No lunch Sun., Wed., and Thurs.*

Top of the Hill Grill

$ | **BARBECUE** | **FAMILY** | Don't let the diminutive size of this roadside smokehouse deceive you. The place produces big flavors locals line up for: hickory-smoked ribs, apple-smoked turkey, beef brisket, and pulled pork, to name a few. **Known for:** "burnt ends" (brisket burnt ends); excellent view of West River; outdoor deck. $ *Average main: $15* ✉ *632 Putney Rd., Brattleboro* ☎ 802/258–9178 ⊕ *www.topofthehillgrill.com* ⊙ *Closed Nov.–Mar.*

Whetstone Station Restaurant and Brewery
$ | **INTERNATIONAL** | One of Brattleboro's most happening hangouts is this nano-brewery and restaurant perched over the Connecticut River. The beer and classic American comfort food are good, but it's the view of the river and its forested banks that drops jaws. **Known for:** rooftop beer garden; "Big 'Stoner" imperial IPA; poutine and steak tips. [$] *Average main: $16* ✉ *36 Bridge St., Brattleboro* ☎ *802/490–2354* 🌐 *www.whetstonestation.com.*

Coffee and Quick Bites

★ Chelsea Royal Diner
$ | **DINER** | **FAMILY** | Built into a vintage 1938 Worcester diner, one of the few remaining in the country, the Chelsea Royal Diner serves all-day breakfast and Blue Plate specials from produce (eggs included) sourced from their backyard farm. Save room for homemade ice cream made with local milk and cream from the St. Albans Co-op Creamery—flavors range from VT Maple Cream to Blueberry, Pumpkin, and Mocha Malted Milk Ball. **Known for:** homemade ice cream and soft serve; all-day breakfast; Blue Plate Specials, like Friday Fish Fry and Sunday Yankee Pot Roast. [$] *Average main: $13* ✉ *487 Marlboro Rd., Brattleboro* ☎ *802/254–8399* 🌐 *www.chelsearoyaldiner.com.*

Mocha Joe's Cafe
$ | **CAFÉ** | The team at this spot for coffee and conversation takes great pride in sourcing direct-trade beans from places like Kenya, Ethiopia, and Guatemala, and pairs them with an assortment of cookies, cakes, and muffins. This is ground zero for Brattleboro's bohemian contingent and fellow travelers. **Known for:** socially conscious coffee; maple latte; trendy clientele. [$] *Average main: $5* ✉ *82 Main St., at Elliot St., Brattleboro* ☎ *802/257–7794* 🌐 *www.mochajoes.com.*

Hotels

★ The Inn on Putney Road
$$ | **B&B/INN** | Thoughtful and comforting details abound in this 1931 French-style manse such as the mini-refrigerator and basket stocked with complimentary soda, water, granola bars, and snacks, as well as gas fireplaces in several guest rooms. **Pros:** lovely breakfast room; nice blend of traditional and modern design; pottery by artist Steven Procter scattered throughout. **Cons:** tight parking; outside downtown; rooms in front sometimes suffer traffic noise. [$] *Rooms from: $239* ✉ *192 Putney Rd., Brattleboro* ☎ *802/536–4780* 🌐 *www.innonputney-road.com* 🛏 *6 rooms* 🍴 *Free Breakfast.*

Latchis Hotel
$ | **HOTEL** | Though not lavish, the guest rooms in this 1938 art deco building have the original sinks and tiling in the bathrooms, and many overlook Main Street, with New Hampshire's mountains in the background. **Pros:** heart-of-town location; lots of personality; reasonable rates. **Cons:** limited breakfast; sound-masking machines sometimes required; few parking spots. [$] *Rooms from: $130* ✉ *50 Main St., Brattleboro* ☎ *802/254–6300, 800/798–6301* 🌐 *www.latchishotel.com* 🛏 *33 rooms* 🍴 *Free Breakfast.*

Performing Arts

Latchis Theatre
THEMED ENTERTAINMENT | This movie theater's architecture represents a singular blending of art deco and Greek Revival style, complete with statues, columns, and 1938 murals by Louis Jambor (1884–1955), a noted artist and children's book illustrator. The Latchis hosts art exhibits, streams live events, and has four screening rooms. For a sense of the theater's original grandeur, buy a ticket for whatever is showing on the big screen. Though the space may not be a state-of-the-art cinema, watching a film here is far more memorable than at

any multiplex. ⊠ *50 Main St., Brattleboro* ☎ *802/254–6300, 800/798–6301* ⊕ *www. latchis.com.*

🛍 Shopping

ART GALLERIES

Gallery Art Walk

ART GALLERIES | On this walk, you'll pass more than 30 galleries and other venues downtown and nearby that exhibit art; it takes place 5:30–8:30 pm on the first Friday evening of the month. ☎ *802/257–2616* ⊕ *www.gallerywalk.org.*

Gallery in the Woods

ART GALLERIES | This funky trilevel store sells art, jewelry, and light fixtures from around the world. Rotating shows take place in the upstairs and downstairs galleries. ⊠ *145 Main St., Brattleboro* ☎ *802/257–4777* ⊕ *www.galleryinthe-woods.com.*

Vermont Artisan Designs

ART GALLERIES | Artworks and functional items in ceramic, glass, wood, fiber, and other media created by more than 300 artists are on display at this gallery. ⊠ *106 Main St., Brattleboro* ☎ *802/257–7044* ⊕ *www.vtart.com.*

Vermont Center for Photography

ART GALLERIES | The center exhibits works by American photographers. Opening receptions are held on the first Friday evening of the month. ⊠ *49 Flat St., Brattleboro* ☎ *802/251–6051* ⊕ *www. vcphoto.org.*

BOOKS

Brattleboro Books

BOOKS | Bibliophiles will love hunting for buried treasure in this mini labyrinth of used books. ⊠ *36 Elliot St., Brattleboro* ☎ *802/257–7777* ⊕ *www.brattleboro-books.com.*

🏃 Activities

BIKING

Brattleboro Bicycle Shop

BIKING | This shop rents hybrid bikes (call ahead to reserve one), does repair work, and sells maps and equipment. ⊠ *165 Main St., Brattleboro* ☎ *802/254–8644, 800/272–8245* ⊕ *www.bratbike.com.*

CANOEING AND KAYAKING

Vermont Canoe Touring Center

CANOEING & ROWING | Canoes and kayaks are available for rent here. Payment is by cash or check only. ⊠ *451 Putney Rd., Brattleboro* ☎ *802/257–5008* ⊕ *www. vermontcanoetouringcenter.com.*

HIKING

Fort Dummer State Park

HIKING & WALKING | You can hike and camp within the 217 acres of forest at this state park, the location of the first permanent European settlement in Vermont. That site is now submerged beneath the Connecticut River, but it is viewable from the northernmost scenic vista on Sunrise Trail. ⊠ *517 Old Guilford Rd., Brattleboro* ☎ *802/254–2610* ⊕ *www.vtstateparks. com/fortdummer.html* 🎫 *$5* ⊗ *Facilities closed early Sept.–late May.*

MULTISPORT OUTFITTERS

Burrows Specialized Sports

BIKING | This full-service sporting goods store rents and sells bicycles, snowboards, skis, and snowshoes, and has a repair shop. ⊠ *105 Main St., Brattleboro* ☎ *802/254–9430* ⊕ *www.burrowssports. com.*

Sam's Outdoor Outfitters

LOCAL SPORTS | At this labyrinthine two-story sports emporium you can find outerwear, shoes, and gear for all seasons and activities. Grab a bag of free popcorn while you're shopping. ⊠ *74 Main St., Brattleboro* ☎ *802/254–2933* ⊕ *www.samsoutfitters.com.*

Wilmington

18 miles west of Brattleboro.

The village of Wilmington, with its classic Main Street lined with 18th- and 19th-century buildings, anchors the Mt. Snow Valley. Most of the valley's lodging and dining establishments, however, can be found along Route 100, which travels 5 miles north to West Dover and Mt. Snow, where skiers flock on winter weekends. The area abounds with cultural activity from concerts to art exhibits year-round.

GETTING HERE AND AROUND

Wilmington is at the junction of Route 9 and Route 100. West Dover and Mount Snow are a few miles to the north along Route 100.

ESSENTIALS

VISITOR INFORMATION Southern Vermont Deerfield Valley Chamber of Commerce. ✉ *Wilmington* ☎ *802/464–8092, 877/887–6884* 🌐 *www.visitvermont.com.*

👁 Sights

Molly Stark State Park

STATE/PROVINCIAL PARK | FAMILY | The park is known for its great camping (there are two loops) and popular snowshoe trails, and there's a picnic pavilion. The Molly Stark Heritage Trail runs through this area, known as a scenic bypass. There is a 1.7-mile loop hike to the fire tower atop Mt. Olga that culminates in a 360-degree view of southern Vermont and northern Massachusetts. ✉ *705 Rte. 9 E, Wilmington* ☎ *802/464–5460* 🌐 *www.vtstateparks.com/mollystark.html.*

Who Was Molly Stark? 👁

In the heart of Wilmington beside the Crafts Inn stands a sculpture in honor of Molly Stark, the wife of the Revolutionary War general John Stark. The general was said to have roused his troops in the Battle of Bennington, vowing victory over the British: "They are ours, or this night Molly Stark sleeps a widow!" He lived, and hence the victory path across Vermont (now Route 9) is called the Molly Stark Trail (or Byway).

🍴 Restaurants

Dot's Restaurant

$ | DINER | FAMILY | Under the classic red neon sign at the main corner in downtown Wilmington, Dot's remains a local landmark and a reminder of diners of yore. Residents and skiers pack the tables and counter for American comfort food classics, starting at 5:30 am with the Berry-Berry pancake breakfast, with four kinds of berries. **Known for:** convivial community hangout; river-view seating; Dot's "jailhouse" chili. [$] *Average main: $10* ✉ *3 W. Main St., Wilmington* ☎ *802/464–7284* 🌐 *www.facebook.com/DotsofVermont.*

La Casita Taqueria y Mas

$ | MEXICAN | FAMILY | Hidden away in the back of a parking lot behind The Anchor, La Casita is a favorite haunt for Mexican fare, including homemade bottled hot sauces, shatteringly crisp flautas, and loaded burritos. The drink menu is no slouch either, with a variety of local beers and seasonal margaritas on hand to wash down platters of tacos and sizzling fajitas. **Known for:** sizzling fajita platters; warm, friendly atmosphere; cooked-to-order carne asada. $ *Average main: $16* ✉ *14 S. Main St., Wilmington* ☎ *802/464–8500.*

The Village Roost

$ | **INTERNATIONAL** | This bigger-on-the-inside café and lunch joint comes with ample space, especially in the barn-chic back room that serves resting travelers, gaming locals, and conferring coworkers. Keeping them oiled is a menu of organic, non-GMO, locally sourced sandwiches, burgers, soups, and salads. **Known for:** large stone fireplace in the back; quality coffee and tea; hangout space. $ *Average main: $11* ✉ *20 W. Main St., Wilmington* ☎ *802/464–3344* 🌐 *www.villageroost.com* 🕒 *No dinner.*

Coffee and Quick Bites

Butter Mountain Bakery

$ | **BAKERY** | Chewy homemade bagels, craggy loaves of sourdough, and brown butter maple cookies are just a handful of the offerings waiting at this tucked-away hidden gem, but remember to preorder as walk-ins aren't usually accommodated. Keep an eye out for seasonal specials like fresh fruit galettes and walnut-studded chocolate brownies—the menu is always changing. **Known for:** crusty loaves of sourdough; seasonal galettes, like strawberry-basil; snickerdoodle cookies. $ *Average main: $5* ✉ *1 School St., Wilmington* ☎ *802/780–0232* 🌐 *www.buttermountainbakery.com/* 🕒 *Closed Sun.–Thurs.*

1a Coffee Roasters

$ | **CAFÉ** | This great new addition to Vermont's coffee scene has some of the best cold brew in the state. Mainly solar-powered, it recently got a sustainability grant from Oatly, and serves its iced drinks in sleek glass jars; pastries come from nearby Starfire Bakery. **Known for:** great outdoor patio; cold brew coffee; solar-powered coffee roaster. $ *Average main: $5* ✉ *123 W Main St., Wilmington* ☎ *802/265–0284* 🌐 *www.1acoffee.com* 🕒 *Closed Mon.–Tues. No dinner.*

Hotels

Deerhill Inn

$ | **B&B/INN** | The restaurant at this quintessential New England inn is among the best in town. **Pros:** complimentary house-baked cookies; some rooms have whirlpool tubs; toiletries by L'Occitane. **Cons:** must drive to Mount Snow and town; traditional flowered wallpaper and upholstery in spots; two-night minimum required for weekends. $ *Rooms from: $165* ✉ *14 Valley View Rd., West Dover* ☎ *802/464–3100, 800/993–3379* 🌐 *www.deerhillinn.com* 🛏 *13 rooms* 🍴 *Free Breakfast.*

Grand Summit Hotel

$$$ | **RESORT** | **FAMILY** | Mount Snow's comfortable main hotel is an easy choice for skiers whose main priority is getting on the slopes as quickly as possible. **Pros:** easy ski access; lots of children's activities; fitness center. **Cons:** somewhat bland decor; can be busy and crowded; resort fee. $ *Rooms from: $380* ✉ *39 Mt. Snow Rd., West Dover* ☎ *800/451–4211* 🌐 *www.mountsnow.com* 🛏 *196 rooms* 🍴 *No Meals.*

Activities

Molly Stark State Park is home to some of the state's most popular snowshoe trails. Mount Olga Trail is a relatively easy 1.7-mile loop culminating in a 360-degree view of southern Vermont and northern Massachusetts.

SKIING

Mount Snow

SKIING & SNOWBOARDING | The closest major ski area to all of the Northeast's big cities, Mount Snow prides itself on its hundreds of snowmaking fan guns—more than any other resort in North America. There are four major downhill areas. The main mountain comprises

The poet Robert Frost is buried in Bennington at the Old First Church.

mostly intermediate runs, while the north face has the majority of expert runs. The south face, Sunbrook, has wide, sunny trails. It connects to Carinthia, which is dedicated to terrain parks and glade skiing. In summer, the 600-acre resort has an 18-hole golf course, 11.3 miles of lift-serviced mountain-bike trails, and an extensive network of hiking trails. In 2018, the resort debuted a brand-new, $22 million, 42,000-square-foot Carinthia Base Lodge, five times the size of the previous lodge. **Facilities:** 86 trails; 600 acres; 1,700-foot vertical drop; 20 lifts. ⊠ *39 Mt. Snow Rd., West Dover* ☎ *802/464–3333, 802/464–2151 for snow conditions, 800/245–7669* ⊕ *www. mountsnow.com* ⊠ *Lift ticket: $149.*

Timber Creek

SKIING & SNOWBOARDING | North of Mount Snow, this appealingly small cross-country skiing and snowshoeing center has 4½ miles of groomed loops. You can rent equipment and take lessons here. ⊠ *13 Tanglewood Rd., at Rte. 100, West Dover* ☎ *802/464–0999* ⊕ *www.timbercreekxc. com* ⊠ *$25.*

Bennington

21 miles west of Wilmington.

Bennington is the commercial focus of Vermont's southwest corner and home to Bennington College. It's really three towns in one: Downtown Bennington, Old Bennington, and North Bennington. Downtown has retained much of the industrial character it developed in the 19th century, when paper mills, gristmills, and potteries formed the city's economic base. The outskirts of town are commercial and not worth a stop, so make your way right into Downtown and Old Bennington to appreciate the area's true charm.

GETTING HERE AND AROUND

The heart of modern Bennington is the intersection of U.S. 7 and Route 9. Old Bennington is a couple of miles west on Route 9, at Monument Avenue. North Bennington is a few miles north on Route 67A.

ESSENTIALS

VISITOR INFORMATION Bennington Area Chamber of Commerce. ✉ *Bennington* ☎ *802/447–3311* ⊕ *www.bennington. com.*

◉ Sights

Bennington Battle Monument

MONUMENT | FAMILY | This 306-foot stone obelisk with an elevator to the top commemorates General John Stark's Revolutionary War victory over the British, who attempted to capture Bennington's stockpile of supplies. Inside the monument you can learn all about the battle, which took place near Walloomsac Heights in New York State on August 16, 1777, and helped bring about the surrender of British commander "Gentleman Johnny" Burgoyne two months later. The top of the tower affords commanding views of the Massachusetts Berkshires, the New York Adirondacks, and the Vermont Green Mountains. ✉ *15 Monument Circle, Old Bennington* ☎ *802/447–0550* ⊕ *www. benningtonbattlemonument.com* 💰 *$5* ⊘ *Closed Wed. and Nov.–Apr.*

Bennington College

COLLEGE | Contemporary stone sculpture and white-frame neo-Colonial dorms surrounded by acres of cornfields punctuate the green meadows of the placid campus of Bennington College. ✉ *1 College Dr., off U.S. 7, North Bennington* ☎ *802/442–5401* ⊕ *www.bennington.edu.*

★ Bennington Museum

HISTORY MUSEUM | The rich collections here feature military artifacts, early tools, dolls, and the Bennington Flag, one of the oldest of the Stars and Stripes in existence. Other areas of interest include early Bennington pottery, the Gilded Age in Vermont, mid-20th-century modernist painters who worked in or near Bennington, glass and metalwork by Lewis Comfort Tiffany, and photography, watercolors, and other works on paper. The highlight for many visitors, though, is the largest public collection of works by Grandma Moses (1860–1961), the popular self-taught artist who lived and painted in the area. ✉ *75 Main St., Old Bennington* ☎ *802/447–1571* ⊕ *www.benningtonmuseum.org* 💰 *$12* ⊘ *Closed Jan.–Mar.*

Lake Shaftsbury State Park

STATE/PROVINCIAL PARK | FAMILY | You'll find a swimming beach, nature trails, boat and canoe rentals, and a snack bar at this pretty park. ✉ *262 Shaftsbury State Park Rd., 10½ miles north of Bennington, Bennington* ☎ *802/375–9978* ⊕ *www. vtstateparks.com/shaftsbury.html* ⊘ *Facilities closed early Sept.–mid-May.*

Old Bennington

HISTORIC DISTRICT | West of downtown, this National Register Historic District is well endowed with stately Colonial and Victorian mansions. The site of the Catamount Tavern, where Ethan Allen organized the Green Mountain Boys to capture Ft. Ticonderoga in 1775, is marked by a bronze statue of Vermont's indigenous mountain lion, now extinct. ✉ *Monument Ave., Old Bennington.*

The Old First Church

CEMETERY | In the graveyard of this church, the tombstone of the poet Robert Frost proclaims, "I had a lover's quarrel with the world." ✉ *1 Monument Circle, at Monument Ave., Old Bennington* ☎ *802/447–1223* ⊕ *www. oldfirstchurchbenn.org* 💰 *Free.*

Park-McCullough House

HISTORIC HOME | The architecturally significant Park-McCullough House is a 35-room classic French Empire–style mansion, built in 1865 and furnished with period pieces. Several restored flower gardens grace the landscaped grounds, and a barn holds some antique carriages. Guided tours happen on the hour while the house is open. The grounds are open daily year-round. ✉ *1 Park St., at West St., North Bennington* ☎ *802/442–5441* ⊕ *www.parkmccullough.org* 💰 *$15* ⊘ *Closed Oct.–May.*

Robert Frost Stone House Museum
HISTORIC HOME | Robert Frost came to Shaftsbury in 1920, he wrote, "to plant a new Garden of Eden with a thousand apple trees of some unforbidden variety." The museum, now part of Bennington College, tells the story of the poet's life and highlights the nine years (1920–29) he spent living in the house with his wife and four children. It was here that he penned "Stopping by Woods on a Snowy Evening" and published two books of poetry. You can wander 7 of the Frost family's original 80 acres. Among the apple boughs you just might find inspiration of your own. ✉ *121 Historic Rte. 7A, Shaftsbury* ☎ *802/447–6200* 🌐 *www.bennington.edu* 🎟 *$10* 🕒 *Closed Tues. and Wed.*

Woodford State Park
STATE/PROVINCIAL PARK | **FAMILY** | At 2,400 feet, this has the highest state campground in Vermont. Adams Reservoir is the dominant feature and focus of activities, with swimming, fishing, and boating, including canoes, kayaks, and paddleboards for rent. A nature trail also circles the reservoir. ✉ *142 State Park Rd., Bennington* ✥ *10 miles east of Bennington* ☎ *802/447–7169* 🌐 *www.vtstateparks.com/woodford.html* 🕒 *Facilities closed mid-Oct.–mid-May.*

🍴 Restaurants

Harvest Brewing
$ | **MEXICAN FUSION** | This nanobrewery in the heart of downtown Bennington is a haven of craft beers with English-style porters and inventive brews like Melon Grab fruited IPA. All of these beers become the perfect palate cleansers for good pub fare like loaded nachos and deep fried chimichangas. **Known for:** hazy IPAs; hearty Mexican-inspired pub fare; seasonal brews from smooth stouts to crisp lagers. [$] *Average main: $8* ✉ *201 South St., Bennington* ☎ *802/430–9915* 🌐 *www.harvestbrewing.net.*

Madison Brewing Company
$$ | **BURGER** | Since opening in the 1990s as the area's first brewpub, this enclave of exposed brick and bubbling brewing tanks has become a watering hole for fresh IPAs and stacked burgers. A full bar and myriad pub fare offer plenty of reasons to elbow up to the wraparound bar. **Known for:** craft beer on draft; classic New England–style pub fare; gourmet burgers. [$] *Average main: $21* ✉ *428 Main St., Bennington* ☎ *802/442–7397* 🌐 *www.madisonbrewingco.com.*

Village Garage Distillery
$ | **ECLECTIC** | An old highway equipment garage is now filled with a shiny copper still and barrels of aging spirits, visible through big windows from the attached tasting room; cocktails made with the distillery's gin, vodka, rye, and bourbon are twists on the classics, detailed in blueprint-like sketches on the menu. The food is surprisingly inventive for tasting room fare, including chicken and waffles, bowls of ramen, and a burger made from cattle fed the distillery's spent grain, served on a spent grain bun. **Known for:** local grain in the distillery; live music; Village Bonfire whiskey with smoked maple syrup. [$] *Average main: $17* ✉ *107 Depot St., Bennington* ☎ *802/447–7663* 🌐 *villagegarage.com* 🕒 *Closed Mon.–Tues.*

🛏 Hotels

The Eddington House Inn
$ | **B&B/INN** | In the heart of North Bennington, just around the corner from three covered bridges and Bennington College, this impeccably maintained, 18th-century three-bedroom house is a great value. **Pros:** budget prices for a great B&B; "endless desserts" in dining room 24 hours a day; summer guest passes to Lake Paran. **Cons:** slightly off usual tourist track; only three rooms so it fills up fast; no front desk or after-hours reception. [$] *Rooms from: $159* ✉ *21 Main St., North Bennington*

☎ *802/442–1511* 🌐 *www.eddington-houseinn.com* 🛏 *3 suites* 🍴 *Free Breakfast.*

★ Four Chimneys Inn
$ | **B&B/INN** | This exquisite, three-story, neo-Georgian (circa 1915) looks out over a substantial lawn and a wonderful old stone wall. **Pros:** walking distance to several Bennington sights; a complimentary full country breakfast; extremely well kept. **Cons:** dinner only offered for special events; no coffee or tea in rooms; a bit stuffy. [$] *Rooms from: $189* ✉ *21 West Rd., Old Bennington* ☎ *802/447–3500* 🌐 *www.fourchimneys.com* 🛏 *11 rooms* 🍴 *Free Breakfast.*

The Hardwood Hill
$ | **HOTEL** | Built in 1937, this fully renovated roadside motel has been given a distinct artsy, boutique upgrade by a foursome of new owners, three of whom are working artists, which translates into a sculpture garden out front, regular workshops by a resident artist, and performances on the red stage on the vast, hammock-dappled back lawn. **Pros:** excellent restaurant right next door; good value for cost; "arts package" includes tickets and discounts at local sights. **Cons:** must drive to town; rooms somewhat small; no restaurant or dining area. [$] *Rooms from: $99* ✉ *864 Harwood Hill Rd., Bennington* ☎ *802/442–6278* 🌐 *www.harwoodhillmotel.com* 🛏 *17 rooms* 🍴 *Free Breakfast.*

South Shire Inn
$$ | **B&B/INN** | Originally built for banker Louis A. Graves, this beautiful Victorian is a cozy and intimate bed and breakfast that looks like a regular house from the outside. **Pros:** set back from crowds; plenty of character; breakfast included. **Cons:** small-scale property; not within walking distance of much; no on-site restaurant. [$] *Rooms from: $200* ✉ *124 Elm St., Bennington* ☎ *802/447–3839* 🌐 *southshire.com* 🛏 *9 rooms* 🍴 *Free Breakfast.*

Billboardless Vermont

Did you know that there are no billboards in Vermont? The state banned them in 1967 (similar laws exist in Maine, Alaska, and Hawaii), and the last one came down in 1975, so when you look out your window, you see trees and other scenery—not advertisements.

Performing Arts

Basement Music Series
MUSIC | The Vermont Arts Exchange sponsors this fun and funky contemporary music series at the downtown Masonic Lodge. Some performances sell out, so it's wise to purchase tickets in advance. ✉ *504 Main St., Bennington* ☎ *800/838–3006 for ticket hotline* 🌐 *www.vtartx-change.org/music.*

Oldcastle Theatre Company
MUSIC | This fine regional theater company focuses on American classics and crowd-pleasing musicals. The group's venue also hosts occasional concerts. ✉ *331 Main St., Bennington* ☎ *802/447–0564* 🌐 *www.oldcastletheatre.org* 🕓 *Closed Dec.–Mar.*

Shopping

The Apple Barn & Country Bake Shop
MARKET | **FAMILY** | Homemade baked goods, fresh cider, Vermont cheeses, maple syrup, and around a dozen varieties of apples are among the treats for sale here. There's berry picking in season, for a fun family stop, and on weekends you can watch the bakers make cider doughnuts. ✉ *604 Rte. 7S, 1½ miles south of downtown Bennington, Bennington* ☎ *802/447–7780* 🌐 *www.theapplebarn.com.*

Vermont Maple Syrup

Vermont is the country's largest producer of maple syrup. A visit to a maple farm is a great way to learn all about sugaring, the process of extracting maple tree sap and making syrup. Sap is stored in a sugar maple tree's roots in the winter, and in the spring when conditions are just right, the sap runs up and can be tapped. Sugaring season runs March to April, which is when all maple syrup in the state is produced.

One of the best parts of visiting a maple farm is getting to taste and compare the four grades of syrup. As the sugaring season goes on and days become warmer, the sap becomes progressively darker and stronger in flavor. Grades are defined by color, clarity, density, and flavor. Is one grade better than another? Nope, it's just a question of taste. Sap drawn early in the season produces the lightest color, and has the most delicate flavor: this is called golden. Amber has a mellow flavor. Dark is much more robust, and Very Dark is the most flavorful, making it often the favorite of first-time tasters.

When visiting a maple farm, make sure they make their own syrup, as opposed to just bottling or selling someone else's. You'll learn more about the entire process that way. **Vermont Maple Syrup** (☎ 802/858–9444; ⊕ www.vermontmaple.org), a great resource, has a map of maple farms that host tours, a directory of producers open year-round, and a list of places from which you can order maple syrup by mail. You can also get the lowdown on events such as the annual Maple Open House Weekend, when sugarhouses throughout the state open their doors to visitors.

4

Vermont ARLINGTON

The Bennington Bookshop
BOOKS | The state's oldest independent bookstore sells the latest new releases and hosts weekly readings, signings, and lectures. ✉ 467 Main St., Bennington ☎ 802/442–5059 ⊕ www.benningtonbookshop.com.

Now And Then Books
BOOKS | This labyrinthine second-story bookstore stocks nearly 45,000 secondhand volumes. ✉ 439 Main St., Bennington ☎ 802/442–5566 ⊕ www.nowandthenbooksvt.com.

 Activities

HIKING
Long Trail
HIKING & WALKING | Four miles east of Bennington, the Long Trail crosses Route 9 and runs south to the top of Harmon Hill. Allot two or three hours for this steep hike. ✉ Bennington.

Arlington

15 miles north of Bennington.

Smaller than Bennington and more down-to-earth than upper-crust Manchester to the north, Arlington exudes a certain Rockwellian folksiness, and it should: the illustrator Norman Rockwell lived here from 1939 to 1953, and many neighbors served as models for his portraits of small-town life.

GETTING HERE AND AROUND
Arlington is at the intersection of Route 313 and Route 7A. Take Route 313 West to reach West Arlington.

Sights

West Arlington

TOWN | Norman Rockwell once lived in this place with a quaint town green. If you follow Route 313 west from Arlington, you'll pass by the Wayside Country Store, a slightly rickety charmer where you can pick up sandwiches and chat with locals. The store carries everything from ammo and sporting goods to toys, teas, and maple syrup. Continue on, and cross West Arlington's red covered bridge, which leads to the town green. To loop back to Route 7A, take River Road along the south side of the Battenkill River, a scenic drive. ✉ *West Arlington.*

Coffee and Quick Bites

Arlington Dairy Bar

$ | **AMERICAN** | **FAMILY** | The big red barn with a sprawling lawn and walk-up ice cream window is a quintessential summer snack shack. It's where paper boats holding cheeseburgers, loaded hot dogs, and lobster rolls make way for soft-serve sundaes, stacked ice-cream cones, and root beer floats. **Known for:** nostalgic snack bar atmosphere; ice-cream cones and sundaes; cheeseburgers and hot dogs. [$] *Average main: $5* ✉ *3158 Rte. 7A, Arlington* ☎ *802/375–2546.*

Wayside Country Store

$ | **AMERICAN** | **FAMILY** | The motto of Arlington's one-stop-shop says it all: "If we don't have it, you don't need it!" This charming country store is known for carrying anything from toilet paper to boxed cocoa mix and boasts a popular deli complete with build-your-own sandwiches, prepared foods, and house-made specials like freshly baked biscuits. **Known for:** locally made goods; deli wraps and sandwiches; specialty prepared foods, from stuffed peppers to roasted chicken legs. [$] *Average main: $7* ✉ *3307 Rte. 313 W, Arlington* ☎ *802/375–2792.*

Hotels

The Arlington Inn & Spa

$ | **B&B/INN** | The Greek Revival columns of this 1847 home lend it an imposing presence in the middle of town, but the atmosphere within is friendly and old-fashioned. **Pros:** heart-of-town location; breakfast included for guests; on site massages available for guests. **Cons:** no dinner service; elegant but old-fashioned decor; no tea or coffee in rooms. [$] *Rooms from: $199* ✉ *3904 Rte. 7A, Arlington* ☎ *802/375–6532* 🌐 *www.arlingtoninn.com* 🛏 *17 rooms* 🍴 *Free Breakfast.*

★ Hill Farm Inn

$$ | **B&B/INN** | **FAMILY** | Few hotels or inns in Vermont can match the sumptuous views of Mt. Equinox and surrounding hillscape of this former dairy farm built in 1830, whether seen from the large wraparound porch, the fire pit (where you can roast s'mores), or the outdoor hot tub. **Pros:** outdoor pool and hot tub; perfect Vermont wedding setting; Vermont Castings stoves in many rooms. **Cons:** books up on weekends with weddings; bringing alcohol not allowed; can be buggy in summer, like all Vermont. [$] *Rooms from: $235* ✉ *458 Hill Farm Rd., off Rte. 7A, Sunderland* ☎ *802/375–2269* 🌐 *www.hillfarminn.com* 🛏 *12 rooms* 🍴 *Free Breakfast.*

West Mountain Inn

$$ | **B&B/INN** | **FAMILY** | This 1810 farmhouse sits on 150 mountainside acres with hiking trails and easy access to the Battenkill River, where you can canoe or go tubing; in winter, guests can sled down a former ski slope or borrow snowshoes or cross-country skis. **Pros:** atmospheric Colonial dining room; lots of activities; wood-panel dining room with fireplace. **Cons:** dining room not ideal for kids; dirt road to property uneven and pitted; tiny bathrooms in some rooms. [$] *Rooms from: $205* ✉ *144 W. Mountain Inn Rd., at Rte. 313, Arlington*

☎ *802/375–6516* ⊕ *www.westmountain-inn.com* 🛏 *20 rooms* 🍴 *Free Breakfast.*

🛍 Shopping

Village Peddler

SOUVENIRS | FAMILY | This shop has a "chocolatorium," where you can learn all about cocoa. It sells fudge and other candies and stocks a large collection of teddy bears, one of whom is giant and made of chocolate. ⊠ *261 Old Mill Rd., East Arlington* ☎ *802/375–6037* ⊕ *www. villagepeddlervt.com.*

Manchester

9 miles northeast of Arlington.

Well-to-do Manchester has been a popular summer retreat since the mid-19th century, when city dwellers traveled north to take in the cool, clean air at the base of 3,840-foot Mt. Equinox. Manchester Village's tree-shaded marble sidewalks and stately old homes—Main Street here could hardly be more pic-ture-perfect—reflect the luxurious resort lifestyle of more than a century ago. A mile north on Route 7A, Manchester Center is the commercial twin to Colonial Manchester Village; it's also where you'll find the town's famed upscale factory outlets doing business in attractive faux-Colonial shops.

Manchester Village houses the world head-quarters of Orvis, the outdoor-goods brand that was founded here in the 19th century and has greatly influenced the town ever since. The complex includes a fly-fishing school featuring lessons given in its casting ponds and the Battenkill River.

GETTING HERE AND AROUND

Manchester is the main town for the ski resorts of Stratton (a half-hour drive on Route 30) and Bromley (15 minutes to the northeast on Route 11). It's 15 minutes north of Arlington along scenic Route 7A.

ESSENTIALS

VISITOR INFORMATION Green Mountain National Forest Visitor Center. ⊠ *2538 Depot St., Manchester* ☎ *802/362–2307* ⊕ *www.fs.usda.gov/main/gmfl.* **Manchester Visitor Center.** ⊠ *4826 Main St., Manchester* ⊕ *www.manchestervermont.com.*

👁 Sights

American Museum of Fly Fishing

OTHER MUSEUM | This museum houses the world's largest collection of angling art and angling-related objects—more than 1,500 rods, 800 reels, 30,000 flies, including the tackle of Winslow Homer, Babe Ruth, Jimmy Carter, and other nota-bles. Every August, vendors sell antique equipment at the museum's fly-fishing festival. You can also practice your casting out back. ⊠ *4070 Main St., Manchester* ☎ *802/362–3300* ⊕ *www.amff.org* 💲 *$5* 🕐 *Closed Mon.-Wed.*

★ Hildene

GARDEN | FAMILY | A twofold treat, the summer home of Abraham Lincoln's son Robert provides insight into the lives of the Lincoln family, as well as an introduction to the lavish Manchester life of the early 1900s. In 1905, Robert built a 24-room Georgian Revival mansion where he and his descendants lived until 1975. It's the centerpiece of a beautifully preserved 412-acre estate and holds many of the family's prized possessions, including one of three surviving stovepipe hats owned by Abraham and a Lincoln Bible. When the 1,000-pipe Aeolian organ is played, the music reverberates as though from the mansion's very bones.

Rising from a 10-acre meadow, Hildene Farm is magnificent. The agriculture center is built in a traditional style—post-and-beam construction of timber felled and milled on the estate, and you can watch goat cheese being made.

The highlight, though, may be the elab-orate formal gardens, where a thousand

The formal gardens and mansion at Robert Todd Lincoln's Hildene are a far cry from his father's log cabin.

peonies bloom every June. There is also a teaching greenhouse, restored 1903 Pullman car, a 600-foot floating boardwalk across the Battenkill wetlands, and more than 12 miles of walking trails. When conditions permit, you can cross-country ski and snowshoe on the property. ✉ *1005 Hildene Rd., at Rte. 7A, Manchester* ☎ *802/362–1788, 800/578–1788* 🌐 *www.hildene.org* 🎟 *$23.*

★ Southern Vermont Arts Center

ARTS CENTER | At the end of a long, winding driveway, this center has a permanent collection of more than 800 19th- and 20th-century American artworks and presents temporary exhibitions. The original building, a Georgian mansion set on 100 acres, contains 12 galleries with works by more than 600 artists, many from Vermont. The center also hosts concerts, performances, and film screenings. In summer and fall, the views from the café at lunchtime are magnificent. ✉ *930 SVAC Dr., West Rd., Manchester* ☎ *802/362–1405* 🌐 *www.svac.org* 🎟 *$10* 🕒 *Closed Mon. Nov.–May.*

🍴 Restaurants

The Crooked Ram

$ | **WINE BAR** | Originally a tiny bottle shop when it opened doors in 2017, the Crooked Ram has since transformed into a cozy beer-and-wine bar with an excellent restaurant and spacious summertime backyard serving wood-fired pizzas. It's now a destination for hyperlocal drafts, seasonal small plates, and brimming Vermont cheese boards, plus a thoughtful stock of unique ciders and natural wines to-go. **Known for:** drafts of local craft beer in stemmed beer glasses; award-winning Vermont cheeses and charcuterie; seasonal patio seating. [$] *Average main: $15* ✉ *4026 Main St., Manchester* ☎ *802/231–1315* 🌐 *thecrookedramvt.com* 🕒 *Closed Mon.-Wed.*

Mistral's at Toll Gate

$$$$ | **FRENCH** | This classic French restaurant is tucked in a grotto on the climb to Bromley Mountain. The two dining rooms are perched over the Bromley Brook, and at night a small waterfall is magically illuminated—ask for a window table. **Known for:** chateaubriand béarnaise; crispy sweetbreads Dijonnaise; wine list. [$] *Average main: $36* ✉ *10 Toll Gate Rd., off Rte. 11/30, Manchester* ☎ *802/362–1779* 🌐 *www.mistralsattollgate.com* ⏲ *Closed Mon.-Wed. No lunch.*

★ Moonwink

$ | BURMESE | May and Wes Stannard opened this counter-service spot in 2018, spotlighting May's native Burmese cooking in Wes's childhood hometown. In one of the best stops for Burmese fare on the East Coast, you'll find vibrant noodle bowls like *Nan Gyi Thoke* (thick round rice noodles with chicken curry), fermented tea leaf salad, and "Burma Bowls" with sprouted peas and chicken curry. **Known for:** oh no kuo swel (creamy coconut broth with vegetables or chicken served over egg noodles); la phat thok (Moonwink's take on the Burmese fermented tea leaf salad); mo hinga (a special fish stew with noodles served on Friday and Saturday only). [$] *Average main: $13* ✉ *4479 Main St., Manchester* ☎ *802/768–8671.*

★ Mystic Cafe & Wine Bar

$$ | ECLECTIC | This spacious, brand-new, Euro-chic restaurant is earning plenty of local praise for its gussied-up takes on international cuisines with a Vermont-farmhouse accent. That means plenty of kale, butternut squash, sweet potato, and cheddar in the salads, sandwiches, and tapas-style shared plates. **Known for:** paella with Israeli couscous; French toast; wine list. [$] *Average main: $20* ✉ *4928 Main St., Manchester Center* ☎ *802/768–8086* 🌐 *www.mysticcafeandwinebar.com* ⏲ *Closed Sun. and Mon.*

The Reluctant Panther Inn & Restaurant

$$$$ | AMERICAN | The dining room at this luxurious inn is a large, modern space where rich woods and high ceilings meld into a kind of "nouveau Vermont" aesthetic. The contemporary American cuisine emphasizes farm-to-table ingredients and has earned the restaurant "Gold Barn" honors from the Vermont Fresh Network. **Known for:** wine list; chef of the year award by the Vermont Chamber of Commerce; lobster-and-Brie fondue. [$] *Average main: $37* ✉ *39 West Rd., Manchester* ☎ *800/822–2331, 802/362–2568* 🌐 *www.reluctantpanther.com* ⏲ *Closed Sun. and Mon.*

★ The Silver Fork at the Old Library

$$$ | ECLECTIC | This intimate, elegant bistro is owned by husband-and-wife team Mark and Melody French, who spent years in Puerto Rico absorbing the flavors of the island that are reflected in the eclectic international menu. After nine years in their original space on Main Street, in 2020 the couple moved their restaurant into the newly renovated, 123-year-old Skinner Library, fashioning a bartop from the 1897 wooden shelving. **Known for:** shrimp mofongo (with mashed plantains); wine and cocktail list; special occasions. [$] *Average main: $30* ✉ *48 West Rd., Manchester* ☎ *802/768–8444* 🌐 *www.thesilverforkvt.com* ⏲ *Closed Sun. and Mon. No lunch.*

Ye Olde Tavern

$$$ | AMERICAN | This circa-1790 Colonial inn dishes up Yankee favorites along with plenty of New England charm, made all the more intimate by the candlelight. To learn more about the colorful history of the building, simply ask the manager, who makes a regular appearance at tables. **Known for:** cheddar-and-ale onion soup; traditional pot roast; 1790 Taproom Ale (custom brew by Long Trail). [$] *Average main: $26* ✉ *5183 Main St., Manchester* ☎ *802/362–0611* 🌐 *www.yeoldetavern.net.*

☕ Coffee and Quick Bites

★ Willoughby's Depot Eatery

$ | BAKERY | FAMILY | Home of the World Famous Mrs. Murphy's Donuts, this beloved shop turns out fresh doughnuts daily from its small, white-clapboard storefront. Old-fashioned doughnuts come hot from the fryer in the wee hours of the morning, so arrive early for the best selection of flavors like cinnamon, maple cream, and cakey cider doughnuts loaded with warming spices. **Known for:** cinnamon raised; cider cake; sugar-dusted crullers. [$] *Average main: $3* ✉ *374 Depot St., Manchester* ☎ *802/362–1874* 🌐 *www.willoughbysdepoteatery.com.*

Hotels

Barnstead Inn
$$ | **B&B/INN** | This boutique inn has created its own little oasis, taking 1830s farmhouse lodging to the next level by pairing New England charm with luxury amenities. **Pros:** modern amenities; walking distance to the downtown area; soaking tubs and special touches in the rooms. **Cons:** no pet friendly rooms; not a class country inn in terms of decor; no children under 12 (thought some might find this a "pro"). [$] *Rooms from: $299* ✉ *349 Bonnet St., Manchester* 🌐 *www.barnsteadinn.com* 🛏 *23 rooms* 🍴 *Free Breakfast.*

Equinox
$$$ | **RESORT** | In Manchester Village, nearly all life revolves around the historic Equinox Inn, whose fame and service have carved it into the Mt. Rushmore of accommodation in Vermont. **Pros:** on-site spa, fitness center, and pool; excellent steak house on-site; newly redesigned 18 hole golf course, tennis courts, extensive network of walking trails and close proximity to several major ski mountains. **Cons:** somewhat corporate feel; lines at reception can make checking in and out take long; lots of weddings can sometimes overcrowd. [$] *Rooms from: $391* ✉ *3567 Main St., Manchester* ☎ *802/362–4700, 866/837–4219* 🌐 *www.equinoxresort.com* 🛏 *147 rooms* 🍴 *No Meals.*

Inn at Manchester
$$ | **B&B/INN** | Located between the Taconic and Green Mountains just a short distance from Manchester's main strip, the Inn at Manchester has a variety of comfortable rooms, all slightly different from the next. **Pros:** free, homemade breakfast; pub on-site; pool and fireplaces. **Cons:** no-frill rooms; the decor could be consider dated and old school; 15 minutes' walk to the village center. [$] *Rooms from: $200* ✉ *3967 Main St., Manchester* ☎ *802/362–1793* 🌐 *innatmanchester.com* 🛏 *21 rooms* 🍴 *Free Breakfast.*

Taconic Hotel
$$$ | **HOTEL** | Vermont's only Kimpton, which opened in 2015, attempts to walk the fine line between its corporate boutique design and a Vermont flavor—the latter of which is distilled, quite literally, in The Copper Grouse, the hotel's on-site enclave of seasonal plates and craft cocktails. **Pros:** locally handmade walking sticks from Manchester Woodcraft in rooms; no additional fee for pets; the house restaurant, the Copper Grouse, does a good turn on American bistro cuisine, cocktails included. **Cons:** not very Vermonty experience; only chain's rewards members get free high-speed Internet/Wi-Fi; tiny pool. [$] *Rooms from: $339* ✉ *3835 Main St., Manchester* ☎ *802/362–0147* 🌐 *www.taconichotel.com* 🛏 *87 rooms* 🍴 *No Meals.*

Nightlife

Falcon Bar
LIVE MUSIC | This sophisticated bar has live music on weekends. In summer, don't miss the wonderful outdoor deck. In winter, the place to be is around the giant Vermont slate firepit. ✉ *Equinox Resort, 3567 Main St., Manchester* ☎ *800/362–4747* 🌐 *www.equinoxresort.com.*

Union Underground

BARS | One of Manchester's hot spots, this part underground, part aboveground pub and restaurant offers lots of space, a sleek green-marble bar, craft beer, a pool table, and tasty classics with all the fixings. ✉ *4928 Main St., Manchester Center* ☎ *802/367–3951.*

🛍 Shopping

ART AND ANTIQUES

Long Ago & Far Away

ANTIQUES & COLLECTIBLES | This store specializes in fine Indigenous artwork, including Inuit stone sculpture. ✉ *Green Mountain Village Shops, 4963 Main St., Manchester* ☎ *802/362–3435* ⊕ *www.longagoandfaraway.com.*

Manchester Woodcraft

CRAFTS | The millions of trees in the Green Mountains make Vermont a wood-carver's dreamscape. The saws, planes, and scrapers of the woodshop here turn out a range of handsome household goods, plus a wide selection of pieces and parts for DIY fans. ✉ *175 Depot St., Manchester Center* ☎ *802/362–5770* ⊕ *www.manchesterwoodcraft.com.*

Tilting at Windmills Gallery

ANTIQUES & COLLECTIBLES | This large gallery displays the paintings and sculptures of nationally known artists. ✉ *24 Highland Ave., Manchester Center* ☎ *802/362–3022* ⊕ *www.tilting.com.*

BOOKS

Northshire Bookstore

BOOKS | FAMILY | The heart of Manchester Center, this bookstore is adored by visitors and residents alike for its ambience, selection, and service. Up the iron staircase is a second floor dedicated to children's books, toys, and clothes. ✉ *4869 Main St., Manchester* ☎ *802/362–2200, 800/437–3700* ⊕ *www.northshire.com.*

CLOTHING

Manchester Designer Outlets

SHOPPING CENTER | This is the most upscale collection of stores in northern New England—and every store is a discount outlet. The architecture reflects the surrounding homes, so the place looks a bit like a Colonial village. The long list of famous-brand clothiers here includes Kate Spade, Yves Delorme, Michael Kors, Ann Taylor, Tumi, BCBG, Armani, Coach, Polo Ralph Lauren, Brooks Brothers, and Theory. ✉ *97 Depot St., Manchester* ☎ *802/362–3736, 800/955–7467* ⊕ *www.manchesterdesigneroutlets.com.*

Orvis Flagship Store

OTHER SPECIALTY STORE | The lodgelike Orvis store carries the company's latest clothing, fly-fishing gear, and pet supplies—there's even a trout pond. At this required shopping destination for many visitors—the Orvis name is pure Manchester—there are demonstrations of how fly rods are constructed and tested. You can attend fly-fishing school across the street. ✉ *4180 Main St., Manchester* ☎ *802/362–3750* ⊕ *www.orvis.com.*

🏃 Activities

BIKING

Battenkill Bicycles

BIKING | This shop rents, sells, and repairs bikes and provides maps and route suggestions. ✉ *99 Bonnet St., Manchester* ☎ *802/362–2734* ⊕ *battenkillbicycles.com.*

FISHING

Trico Unlimited

FISHING | Teaching the art and science of fly-fishing, Trico Unlimited offers lessons for all different age groups and experience levels. They are an Orvis Endorsed Fly-Fishing Guide operator. ✉ *Manchester* ☎ *802/379–2005* ⊕ *www.tricounlimited.com.*

HIKING

There are bountiful hiking trails in the Green Mountain National Forest. Shorter hikes begin at the Equinox Resort, which owns about 1,000 acres of forest and has a great trail system open to the public.

Equinox Preserve

HIKING & WALKING | A multitude of well-groomed walking trails for all abilities thread the 914 acres on the slopes of Mt. Equinox, including a trail to the summit. ⊠ *Multiple trailheads, End of West Union St., Manchester* ☎ *802/366–1400 Equinox Preservation Trust* ⊕ *www.equinox-preservationtrust.org.*

Long Trail

HIKING & WALKING | One of the most popular segments of Vermont's Long Trail leads to the top of Bromley Mountain. The strenuous 5.4-mile round-trip takes about four hours. ⊠ *Rte. 11/30, Manchester* ⊕ *www.greenmountainclub.org.*

Lye Brook Falls

HIKING & WALKING | This 4.6-mile hike starts off Glen Road and ends at Vermont's most impressive cataract, Lye Brook Falls. The moderately strenuous journey takes four hours. ⊠ *Off Glen Rd., south from E. Manchester Rd. just east of U.S. 7, Manchester* ⊕ *www.green-mountainclub.org.*

Mountain Goat

HIKING & WALKING | Stop here for hiking, cross-country-skiing, and snowshoeing equipment (some of which is available to rent), as well as a good selection of warm clothing. ⊠ *4886 Main St., Manchester* ☎ *802/362–5159* ⊕ *www.mountaingoat.com.*

SPAS

Spa at Equinox

SPAS | Some of Vermont's best spa treatments are found behind the mahogany doors and beadboard wainscoting of the Equinox Spa and are well worth the splurge. At one end are an indoor pool and outdoor hot tub; at the other end are the treatment rooms. The signature 100-minute Spirit of Vermont combines Reiki, reflexology, and massage, and will leave you feeling like a whole, complete person. The locker rooms feature steam rooms

and saunas. Day passes are available for all ages. ⊠ *Equinox Resort, 3567 Rte. 7A, Manchester* ☎ *802/362–4700, 800/362–4747* ⊕ *www.equinoxresort.com.*

Dorset

7 miles north of Manchester.

Lying at the foot of many mountains and with a village green surrounded by white clapboard homes and inns, Dorset has a solid claim to the title of Vermont's most picture-perfect town. Dorset has just 2,000 residents, but two of the state's best and oldest general stores.

The country's first commercial marble quarry opened here in 1785. Dozens more opened, providing the marble for the main research branch of the New York Public Library and many 5th Avenue mansions, among other notable landmarks, as well as the sidewalks here and in Manchester. A remarkable private home made entirely of marble can be seen on Dorset West Road, a beautiful residential road west of the town green. The marble Dorset Church on the green has two Tiffany stained-glass windows.

◉ Sights

★ Dorset Quarry

BODY OF WATER | FAMILY | On hot summer days the sight of dozens of families jumping, swimming, and basking in the sun around this massive 60-foot-deep swimming hole makes it one of the most wholesome and picturesque recreational spots in the region. First mined in 1785, the stone from the country's oldest commercial marble quarry was used to build the main branch of the New York Public Library and the Montreal Museum of Fine Arts. ⊠ *Rte. 30, Dorset* ☎ ⛱ *Free.*

Emerald Lake State Park

STATE/PROVINCIAL PARK | This park has a well-marked nature trail, a small beach, boat rentals, and a snack bar.

✉ *65 Emerald Lake La., East Dorset* ☎ *802/362–1655* ⊕ *www.vtstateparks. com/emerald.html* 💲 *$5* ⊙ *Facilities closed mid-Oct.–mid-May.*

Merck Forest & Farmland Center

FARM/RANCH | **FAMILY** | This 3,162-acre educational center has 30 miles of nature trails for hiking, cross-country skiing, snowshoeing, horseback riding, and rustic camping. You can visit the 62-acre farm, which grows organic fruit and vegetables (sold at the visitor center), and check out the horses, sheep, pigs, and chickens while you're there—you're even welcome to help out with the chores. ✉ *3270 Rte. 315, Rupert* ☎ *802/394– 7836* ⊕ *www.merckforest.org* 💲 *Free.*

Restaurants

The Dorset Inn

$$$ | **AMERICAN** | Built in 1796, this inn has been continuously operating ever since, and the comfortable tavern and formal dining room serve a Colonial-influenced bistro menu. A member of the Vermont Fresh Network, the restaurant benefits greatly from its strong connections with local farmers. **Known for:** wine list; Vermont's oldest continually operating inn; whiskey and bourbon menu. 💲 *Average main: $27* ✉ *Dorset Green, 8 Church St., Dorset* ☎ *802/867–5500* ⊕ *www.dorset-inn.com* ⊙ *No lunch.*

🛏 Hotels

Barrows House

$$ | **HOTEL** | This renovated 19th-century manse, once the residence of the town's pastor, incorporates a modern boutique aesthetic into the traditional-style inn, especially in the attached gastropub, which features a long, polished metal bar and backlighted marble. **Pros:** good bar and restaurant; chintz-free decor; large gardens. **Cons:** rooms can become drafty in cold weather; robes only in

luxury suites; no coffee or tea in rooms. 💲 *Rooms from: $275* ✉ *3156 Rte. 30, Dorset* ☎ *802/867–4455* ⊕ *www. barrowshouse.com* 🛏 *27 rooms* ⦿ *Free Breakfast.*

Squire House Bed & Breakfast

$$ | **B&B/INN** | On a wonderfully quiet road, this inn, built in 1918, has guest rooms that combine modern comforts and antique fixtures. **Pros:** big estate feels like your own; wood-burning fireplace in two rooms; crème brûlée French toast at breakfast. **Cons:** basic bathrooms; two-night minimum required for peak periods; one-night reservation costs additional $60 fee in some periods. 💲 *Rooms from: $210* ✉ *3395 Dorset West Rd., Dorset* ☎ *802/867–0281* ⊕ *www.squirehouse. com* 🛏 *4 rooms* ⦿ *Free Breakfast.*

🎭 Performing Arts

Dorset Players

THEATER | The prestigious summer theater troupe presents the annual Dorset Theater Festival. Plays are staged in a wonderful converted pre-Revolutionary War barn. ✉ *Dorset Playhouse, 104 Cheney Rd., Dorset* ☎ *802/867–5570* ⊕ *www.dorsetplayers.org.*

👜 Shopping

Dorset Union Store

GENERAL STORE | Dating to 1816, this 200-year-old general store is the oldest continuously operating country store in Vermont. Under the reins of co-owners Cindy Laudenslager and Gretchen Schmidt, it has great prepared dinners, a full deli, delicious homemade baked goods, and a big wine selection. It also sells interesting gifts, and houses its own soft-serve ice-cream machine. ✉ *Dorset Green, 31 Church St., Dorset* ☎ *802/867– 4400* ⊕ *www.dorsetunionstore.com.*

Stratton

26 miles southeast of Dorset.

Stratton is really Stratton Mountain Resort, a mountaintop ski resort with a self-contained "town center" of shops, restaurants, and lodgings clustered at the base of the slopes. When the snow melts, golf, tennis, and a host of other summer activities are big attractions, but the ski village remains quiet.

GETTING HERE AND AROUND

From Manchester or U.S. 7, follow Route 11/30 east until they split. Route 11 continues past Bromley ski mountain, and Route 30 turns south 10 minutes toward Bondville, the town at the base of the mountain. At the junction of Routes 30 and 100 is the village of Jamaica, with its own cluster of inns and restaurants on the eastern side of the mountain.

🍴 Restaurants

J.J. Hapgood General Store and Eatery
$ | **AMERICAN** | **FAMILY** | You won't find a better meal at any other general store in the state. This is really more of a classic American restaurant, serving farm-to-table breakfast, lunch, and dinner, than a place to pick up the essentials, but like any good general store, it's a friendly and relaxed gathering spot for locals. **Known for:** buttermilk biscuits; outdoor patio; wood-fired pizzas. [$] *Average main: $12* ✉ *305 Main St., Peru* ☎ *802/824–4800* 🌐 *www.jjhapgood.com* 🕒 *No dinner Mon. and Tues.*

🛏 Hotels

Long Trail House
$$ | **APARTMENT** | Directly across the street from the ski village, this condo complex is one of the closest to the slopes. **Pros:** across the street from ski lift; views of the mountain; outdoor heated pool and hot tub. **Cons:** 4:30 check-in later than most in Vermont; two-night stay required on weekends; busy tourist center in season. [$] *Rooms from: $230* ✉ *759–787 Stratton Mountain Access Rd., Stratton* ☎ *802/297–4000, 800/787–2886* 🌐 *www.stratton.com* 🛏 *145 rooms* 🍽 *No Meals.*

★ **Three Mountain Inn**
$$ | **B&B/INN** | A 1780s tavern, this romantic inn in downtown Jamaica feels authentically Colonial, from the wide-plank paneling to the low ceilings. **Pros:** romantic setting; well-kept rooms; enchanting dinners alongside wood-burning fireplaces. **Cons:** 15-minute drive to skiing; two-night reservations requested for weekends and peak foliage; deposit equal to 50% of the reserved stay required. [$] *Rooms from: $234* ✉ *30 Depot St., Jamaica* ✥ *10 miles northeast of Stratton* ☎ *802/874–4140* 🌐 *www.threemountaininn.com* 🛏 *10 rooms* 🍽 *Free Breakfast.*

🍸 Nightlife

Mulligans
PUBS | Popular Mulligans hosts bands and DJs in the downstairs Green Door Pub on weekends. Upstairs, cozy up beside the fireplace with ribs, steak, and traditional fish-and-chips, or opt for tempura plates and sushi bowls from Mulligans' newest in-house offshoot, Snowfish Sushi. ✉ *Village Sq., Stratton Mountain, Stratton* ☎ *802/297–9293* 🌐 *www.mulligansstratton.com.*

🏃 Activities

SKIING

Bromley Mountain Resort
SKIING & SNOWBOARDING | **FAMILY** | About 20 minutes from Stratton, Bromley is a favorite with families thanks to a child-care center for kids ages six weeks–six years and programs for ages 2½ to 17. The trails are evenly split among beginner, intermediate, and advanced, with nothing too challenging. Beginning skiers and snowboarders have expanded access to terrain-based training in the

dedicated Learning Zone, and everyone can unwind in the base lodge and "village." An added bonus: trails face south, making for glorious spring skiing and warm winter days. **Facilities:** 47 trails; 300 acres; 1,334-foot vertical drop; 9 lifts. ✉ *3984 Rte. 11, Peru* ☎ *802/824–5522, 866/856–2201 for snow conditions* ⊕ *www.bromley.com* ✉ *Lift ticket: $96.*

Stratton Mountain

SKIING & SNOWBOARDING | About 25 minutes from Manchester, and featuring an entire faux Swiss village at its base, Stratton Mountain draws families and young professionals. Beginners will find more than 40% of the mountain accessible to them, but that doesn't mean there aren't some great steeps for the experts. The resort prides itself on its immaculate grooming and excellent cruising on all trails. An on-site day-care center takes children ages six weeks–five years for indoor activities and outdoor excursions. Children also love careening down one of four groomed lift-serviced lanes at the resort's Coca Cola Tube Park. Stratton has 11 miles of cross-country skiing, and in summer there are 15 outdoor clay tennis courts, 27 holes of golf, and hiking trails accessed by a gondola. The sports complex (open year-round) has a 75-foot indoor saltwater pool, sauna, indoor tennis courts, and a fitness center. **Facilities:** 97 trails; 670 acres; 2,003-foot vertical drop; 11 lifts. ✉ *5 Village Lodge Rd., Bondville* ☎ *802/297–4211 for snow conditions, 800/787–2886* ⊕ *www.stratton.com* ✉ *Lift ticket: $180.*

Weston

17 miles north of Stratton.

Best known as the home of the Vermont Country Store, Weston was one of the first Vermont towns to discover its own intrinsic loveliness—and marketability. With its summer theater, classic town green with Victorian bandstand, and an assortment of shops, the little village really lives up to its vaunted image.

🎭 Performing Arts

Weston Playhouse

THEATER | The oldest professional theater in Vermont produces plays, musicals, and other works. The season runs mid-June–late October. ✉ *703 Main St., off Rte. 100, Weston* ☎ *802/824–5288* ⊕ *www.westonplayhouse.org.*

🛍 Shopping

The Vermont Country Store

GENERAL STORE | This store opened in 1946 and is still run by the Orton family, though it has become something of an empire, with a large catalog and online business. One room is set aside for Vermont Common Crackers and bins of fudge and copious candy. In others you'll find nearly forgotten items such as Lilac Vegetol aftershave, as well as practical items like sturdy outdoor clothing. Nostalgia-evoking implements dangle from the rafters. The associated Mildred's Grill restaurant next door serves casual meals and, if you can't get enough, there's a second store on Route 103 in Rockingham. ✉ *657 Main St., Weston* ☎ *802/824–3184* ⊕ *www.vermontcountrystore.com.*

Ludlow

9 miles northeast of Weston.

Ludlow, once a largely nondescript industrial town, is a budding hub of inns, restaurants, and cafés beside Okemo, one of Vermont's largest and most popular ski resorts.

GETTING HERE AND AROUND

Routes 100 and 103 join in northern Ludlow, separating about 2 miles south in the small downtown, where Route 103 becomes Main Street.

🍴 Restaurants

★ **The Downtown Grocery**

$$$ | **BISTRO** | There's a cozy romance to this oasis of seasonal and local cooking, with its corner seats, tea lights, intimate bar, and chalkboard menu. It was the area's first farm-to-table restaurant when co-owners Abby and Rogan Lechthaler opened doors in 2010, and it has continued to be a mainstay thanks to excellent hospitality, warm-spirited creativity, and nightly-changing specials. **Known for:** seasonal cocktails; small-producer-focused wine list; schedule changes month-to-month with limited seating. [$] *Average main: $30* ✉ *41 Depot St., Ludlow* ☎ *802/228–7566* 🌐 *thedowntowngrocery.com* 🕒 *Closed Tues.-Thurs. and Sunday.*

Goodman's American Pie

$ | **PIZZA** | **FAMILY** | This place has the best wood-fired pizza in town. It also has character to spare: sit in chairs from old ski lifts and step up to the counter fashioned from a vintage VW bus to design your pie from 29 ingredients. **Known for:** arcade games and pool table in the back; pizza by the slice; outdoor deck. [$] *Average main: $17* ✉ *5 Lamere Sq., Ludlow* ☎ *802/228–4271* 🌐 *www.goodmansamericanpie.com.*

★ **The Hidden Kitchen at The Inn at Weathersfield**

$$$ | **FRENCH FUSION** | So many Vermont restaurants claim the farm-to-table, local-sourcing, organic approach to cooking, but the chef at the Inn at Weathersfield is more passionate and rigorous than most, with more than 75% of ingredients coming from within a 25-mile radius in season. Enjoy the exquisite French-influenced regional dishes inside the inn itself, on its back patio, or in the separate "Hidden Kitchen" at the back of the property, where monthly cooking workshops and tastings take place. **Known for:** wine list; charcuterie and cheese boards; atmospheric inside and out. [$] *Average main: $28* ✉ *1342 Rte. 106, Perkinsville* ✣ *15 miles east of Ludlow* ☎ *802/263–9217* 🌐 *www.weathersfieldinn.com.*

Mojo Cafe

$ | **FUSION** | In 2014, Jodi and John Seward opened this funky, casual watering hole fusing Mexican and Cajun cooking. Tacos, burritos, bowls, and po' boys frequently feature Vermont meats and produce, while craft beers and specialty cocktails continue to highlight the state's bounty in local beer and spirits. **Known for:** limited seating and no reservations; alligator and andouille gumbo; funky burritos like the "Betty," with tequila-citrus tofu and avocado sauce. [$] *Average main: $10* ✉ *106 Main St., Ludlow* ☎ *802/228–6656.*

☕ Coffee and Quick Bites

★ **Green Mountain Sugar House**

$ | **ICE CREAM** | **FAMILY** | This red-roofed sugarhouse on the edge of Lake Rescue has one of the best maple creemees in the state of Vermont. Locals Ann and Doug Rose have owned the sugaring house since 1985, and almost four decades later continue to uphold their destination-worthy reputation for award-winning maple syrup. **Known for:** Vermont maple creemees; award-winning maple syrup; maple brittle and fudge. [$] *Average main: $5* ✉ *820 Rte. 100 N, Ludlow* ☎ *800/643–9338* 🌐 *www.gmsh.com.*

🛏 Hotels

Inn at Water's Edge

$ | **B&B/INN** | Former Long Islanders Bruce and Tina Verdrager converted their old ski house and barns into this comfortably refined haven, perfect for those who want to ski but not stay in town. **Pros:** bucolic setting on a lakefront, with swimming access; two canoes for guest use; golf and spa packages are available. **Cons:** ordinary rooms; lots of flowered

Vermont Artisanal Cheese 🍴

Vermont is the artisanal cheese capital of the country, with several dozen creameries open to the public churning out hundreds of different cheeses. Many creameries are "farmstead" operations, meaning that the animals whose milk is made into cheese are kept on-site. If you eat enough cheese during your time in the state, you may be able to differentiate between the many types of milk (cow, goat, sheep, or even water buffalo) and make associations between the geography and climate of where you are and the taste of the local cheeses.

This is one of the reasons that taking a walk around a dairy is a great idea: you can see the process in action, from grazing to aging to eating. The **Vermont Cheese Trail map,** which you can view or download on the website of the Vermont Cheese Council (☎866/261–8595; 🌐www.vtcheese.com), has a comprehensive list of dairies, many of which you can visit. Though hours are given for some, it's generally recommended that you still call ahead.

At the **Vermont Cheesemakers Festival** (☎802/261–8595; 🌐www.vtcheesefest.com), which takes place in July or August in Shelburne, cheesemakers gather to sell their various cheeses. Beer and wine are served to wash it all down.

wallpaper and upholstery; no sights within walking distance. [$] *Rooms from: $175* ✉ *45 Kingdom Rd., Ludlow* ✥ *5 miles north of Ludlow* ☎ *802/228–8143, 888/706–9736* 🌐 *www.innatwatersedge.com* 🛏 *11 rooms* 🍴 *Free Breakfast.*

★ Inn at Weathersfield

$$ | **B&B/INN** | Set far back from the road, this 1792 home built by a Revolutionary War veteran is a world unto itself, and an Eden-esque one at that, with flowering gardens, croaking frog pond, and extensive forest on its 21 acres. **Pros:** dynamite restaurant and tavern; ideal for weddings; monthly cooking classes. **Cons:** 15-mile drive from the Okemo slopes; no sights within walking distance; no coffee or tea in rooms. [$] *Rooms from: $219* ✉ *1342 Rte. 106, Perkinsville* ☎ *802/263–9217* 🌐 *www.weathersfieldinn.com* 🕒 *Closed 1st 2 wks in Nov.* 🛏 *12 rooms* 🍴 *Free Breakfast.*

Activities

SKIING

Okemo Mountain Resort

SKIING & SNOWBOARDING | **FAMILY** | Family fun is the focus of southern Vermont's highest vertical ski resort, which has dozens of beginner trails, some wide intermediate runs, terrain parks throughout, a tubing facility, a nursery, an ice rink, indoor basketball and tennis courts, and a children's pool with slides. There's even a Kids' Night Out child-care program on Saturday evening during the regular season, so parents can have date nights. The Okemo Valley Nordic Center has miles of cross-country and snowshoeing trails. Summer diversions include golfing, mountain biking, and activities and rides in the Adventure Zone. The newer Jackson Gore base features the latest (and fanciest) venues the resort has to offer. **Facilities:** 121 trails; 667 acres; 2,200-foot vertical drop; 20 lifts. ✉ *77 Okemo Ridge Rd., Ludlow* ☎ *802/228–1600 resort services, 802/228–5222 for snow* *conditions, 800/786–5366 🌐 www.okemo.com 🎟 Lift ticket: $155.*

Grafton

20 miles south of Ludlow.

Out-of-the-way Grafton is as much a historical museum as a town. During its heyday, citizens grazed 10,000 sheep and spun their wool into sturdy yarn for locally woven fabric. As the wool market declined, so did Grafton. In 1963 the Windham Foundation—Vermont's second-largest private foundation—commenced the town's rehabilitation. The Old Tavern (now called the Grafton Inn) was preserved, along with many other commercial and residential structures.

GETTING HERE AND AROUND

Routes 11, 35, and 103 intersect in Grafton.

👁 Sights

Historical Society Museum

HISTORY MUSEUM | This endearingly cluttered museum documents the town's history with photographs, soapstone displays, quilts, musical instruments, furniture, tools, and other artifacts. ✉ *147 Main St., Grafton* ☎ *802/843–2584* 🌐 *www.graftonhistoricalsociety.com* 🎟 *$5* 🕒 *Closed Tues. and Wed. Memorial Day–Columbus Day, and Tues., Wed., and weekends Columbus Day–Memorial Day.*

🍴 Restaurants

Phelps Barn Pub at The Grafton Village Inn

$$ | **BURGER** | This wood-clad restaurant with a second-floor loft, hanging tea lights, and Vermont-inspired pub fare was originally a carriage house for the guests' horses at The Grafton Village Inn. Today, it's a beautiful and rustic spot for eating local, from crispy skinned local duck breast to seasonal vegetable risotto to a Vermont beef burger capped with Grafton cheddar cheese. **Known for:** rustic interiors with a sense of history; the Phelps burger with local beef and Grafton cheddar; local ingredients as a member of the Vermont Fresh Network. [$] *Average main: $24* ✉ *92 Main St., Grafton* ☎ *802/843–2248* 🌐 *www.graftoninnvermont.com* 🕒 *Closed Sun. and Mon.*

☕ Coffee and Quick Bites

MKT: Grafton

$ | **CAFÉ** | **FAMILY** | When the 19th-century Grafton Village Store shuttered 174 years after opening, locals June Lupiani and Alexandra Hartman decided to revive the abandoned building and give it new life. Their modern, newly renovated general store opened doors in 2015, and quickly became a meeting spot for locals and travelers seeking groceries, deli sandwiches, prepared foods, and homemade pastries. **Known for:** scratch-made pastries; local groceries; deli sandwiches and salads. [$] *Average main: $10* ✉ *162 Main St., Grafton* ☎ *802/843–2255.*

🛏 Hotels

The Grafton Inn

$ | **B&B/INN** | This 1801 classic encourages you to linger on its wraparound porches, in its authentically Colonial common rooms, or with a book by the fire in its old-fashioned library, but those who want to get outside can access the nearby Grafton Ponds Outdoor Center and its 2,000 acres of trails, forests, and fields. **Pros:** handsome historic building; seasonal swim pond; game room with pool table and Ping-Pong; two dining options—the Old Tavern and Phelps Barn Pub—serve American fare. **Cons:** lots of flowered upholstery and wallpaper; resort fee; no tea or coffee in rooms. [$] *Rooms from: $189* ✉ *92 Main St., Grafton* ☎ *802/234–8718, 800/843–1801* 🌐 *www.graftoninnvermont.com* 🛏 *45 rooms* 🍴 *Free Breakfast.*

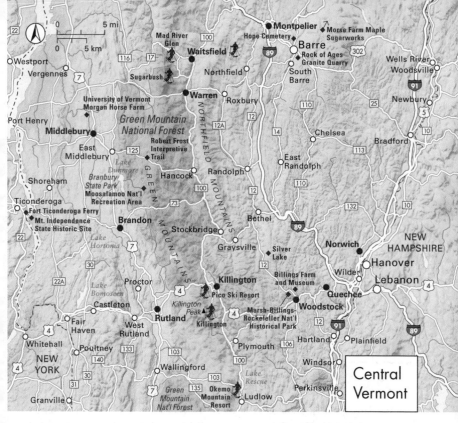

Central Vermont

Norwich

6 miles north of White River Junction.

On the bank of the Connecticut River, Norwich is graced with beautifully maintained 18th- and 19th-century homes set about a handsome green. Norwich is the Vermont sister town to sophisticated Hanover, New Hampshire (home of Dartmouth College), across the river.

GETTING HERE AND AROUND

Most attractions are off Interstate 91; the town sits a mile to the west.

⊙ Sights

★ Montshire Museum of Science

SCIENCE MUSEUM | FAMILY | Numerous hands-on exhibits at this 100-acre science museum explore nature and technology.

Kids can make giant bubbles, watch marine life swim in aquariums, construct working hot air balloons, and explore a maze of outdoor trails by the river. Adults will happily join the fun. An ideal destination for a rainy day, this is one of the finest museums in New England. ⊠ *1 Montshire Rd., Norwich* ☎ *802/649–2200* ⊕ *www. montshire.org* ⊠ *$18.*

☕ Coffee and Quick Bites

King Arthur Flour Baker's Store

$ | BAKERY | The café at King Arthur Flour is a fine spot for both the pit-stop sandwich and the leisurely pastry and latte. The adjacent shop and market area is a must-see for those who love bread; the shelves are stocked with all the ingredients and tools in the company's Baker's Catalogue, including flours, mixes, and local jams, and syrups. **Known for:** croissants, cookies, and brownies; freshly baked loaves of bread; goods to-go, such as local butter, housemade granola, and cheesy crackers. [$] *Average main: $12* ✉ *105 U.S. 5 S, Norwich* ☎ *802/649–3361* 🌐 *www.kingarthurflour.com.*

Activities

Lake Morey Ice Skating Trail

ICE SKATING | For the most fun you can have on skates, head to America's longest ice-skating trail. From January to March, the frozen lake is groomed for ice-skating, providing a magical 4½-mile route amid forested hillsides. Bring your own skates or rent them at the Lake Morey Resort, which maintains the trail. ✉ *1 Clubhouse Rd., Fairlee* ☎ *800/423–1211* 🌐 *www.lakemoreyresort.com.*

Quechee

11 miles southwest of Norwich, 6 miles west of White River Junction.

A historic mill town, Quechee sits just upriver from its namesake gorge, an impressive 165-foot-deep canyon cut by the Ottauquechee River. Most people view the gorge from U.S. 4. To escape the crowds, hike along the gorge or scramble down one of several trails to the river.

Sights

★ **Simon Pearce**

FACTORY | **FAMILY** | A restored woolen mill by a waterfall holds Quechee's main attraction: this marvelous glass-blowing factory, store, and restaurant. Water power still drives the factory's furnace. Take a free self-guided tour of the downstairs factory floor, and see the amazing glassblowers at work. The store sells beautifully crafted contemporary glass and ceramic tableware. An excellent, sophisticated restaurant with outstanding views of the falls uses Simon Pearce glassware and is justifiably popular. ✉ *The Mill, 1760 Quechee Main St., Quechee* ☎ *802/295–2711* 🌐 *www.simonpearce.com.*

Vermont Institute of Natural Science Nature Center

COLLEGE | **FAMILY** | Next to Quechee Gorge, this science center has 17 raptor exhibits, including bald eagles, peregrine falcons, and owls. All caged birds were found injured and are unable to survive in the wild. In summer, experience "Raptors Up Close," a 30-minute live bird program that happens three times a day. ✉ *149 Natures Way, Quechee* ☎ *802/359–5000* 🌐 *www.vinsweb.org* 🎟 *$18.*

Restaurants

★ **The Mill at Simon Pearce**

$$$ | **AMERICAN** | Sparkling glassware from the studio downstairs, exposed brick, flickering candles, and large windows overlooking the falls of the roaring Ottauquechee River create an ideal setting for contemporary American cuisine—the food alone is worth the pilgrimage. The wine cellar holds several hundred labels. **Known for:** romantic atmosphere; Simon Pearce glassware and pottery; complimentary house-made potato chips. [$] *Average main: $28* ✉ *1760 Main St., Quechee* ☎ *802/295–1470* 🌐 *www.simonpearce.com.*

Hotels

Quechee Inn at Marshland Farm

$$ | **B&B/INN** | Each room in this handsomely restored 1793 country home has Queen Anne–style furnishings and period antiques. **Pros:** home of Colonel Joseph Marsh, Vermont's first lieutenant governor; spacious grounds; fresh baked cookies every afternoon. **Cons:** some bathrooms are dated; fills up with weddings; lots of flowered upholstery and wallpaper. [$] *Rooms from: $287* ✉ *1119 Main St., Quechee* ☎ *802/295–3133, 800/235–3133* 🌐 *www.quecheeinn.com* 🔑 *25 rooms* 🍴 *Free Breakfast.*

Simon Pearce is a glassblowing factory, store, and restaurant; the factory's furnace is still powered by hydroelectricity from Quechee Falls.

Woodstock

4 miles west of Quechee.

Woodstock is a Currier & Ives print come to life. Well-maintained Federal-style houses surround the tree-lined village green, across the street from a covered bridge. The town owes much of its pristine appearance to the Rockefeller family's interest in historic preservation and land conservation and to native George Perkins Marsh, a congressman, diplomat, and conservationist who wrote the pioneering book *Man and Nature* (1864) about humanity's use and abuse of the land. Only busy U.S. 4 mars the tableau.

ESSENTIALS

VISITOR INFORMATION Woodstock Vermont Area Chamber of Commerce. ⊠ *Woodstock* ☎ *802/457–3555, 888/496–6378* ⊕ *www.woodstockvt.com.*

👁 Sights

Billings Farm and Museum

FARM/RANCH | FAMILY | Founded by Frederick H. Billings in 1871, this is one of the oldest operating dairy farms in the country. In addition to watching the herds of Jersey cows, horses, and other farm animals at work and play, you can tour the restored 1890 farmhouse, and in the adjacent barns learn about 19th-century farming and domestic life. The biggest takeaway, however, is a renewed belief in sustainable agriculture and stewardship of the land. Pick up some raw-milk cheddar while you're here. ⊠ *69 Old River Rd., Woodstock* ✛ *½ mile north of Woodstock* ☎ *802/457–2355* ⊕ *www.billingsfarm.org* 🎫 *$17.*

Marsh-Billings-Rockefeller National Historical Park

HISTORIC HOME | Vermont's only national park is the nation's first to focus on conserving natural resources. The pristine 555-acre spread includes the mansion, gardens, and carriage roads of Frederick H. Billings (1823–90), a financier and the president of the Northern Pacific Railway. The entire property was the gift of Laurance S. Rockefeller (1910–2004), who lived here with his wife, Mary (Billings's granddaughter). You can learn more at the visitor center, tour the residential complex with a guide every hour on the hour, and explore the 20 miles of trails and old carriage roads that climb Mt. Tom. ⊠ *54 Elm St., Woodstock* ☎ *802/457-3368* ⊕ *www. nps.gov/mabi* ⊠ *Tour $9.*

Silver Lake

BODY OF WATER | Vermont lakes don't get more picturesque than this gem across the street from the Barnard General Store. Plus, it's open for swimming, boating, fishing, and camping. ⊠ *20 State Park Beach Rd., Barnard* ☎ *802/234-9451* ⊕ *www.vtstateparks.com/silver.html.*

🍴 Restaurants

Angkor Wat Restaurant

$$ | **CAMBODIAN** | Chef Chy Tuckerman was raised in Cambodia, Thailand, Oregon, and New Hampshire until moving to Woodstock in 1997 to continue learning the art of baking at local Mountain Creamery. A decade later, he opened his sunny, BYOB restaurant just off Route 4, where he fuses the Cambodian and Thai cooking of his heritage into mouthwatering dishes like ginger chicken stir fry, Khmer curry soup, and traditional luk lok made with beef from nearby Cloudland Farm. **Known for:** cozy atmosphere and BYOB dining; house-made desserts; dishes fusing traditional Khmer and Thai cooking. ⓢ *Average main: $18* ⊠ *61 Pleasant St., Woodstock* ☎ *802/457-9029* ⊕ *www. angkorwatvt.com* ⊗ *Closed Mon.*

Barnard Inn Restaurant and Max's Tavern

$$$$ | **AMERICAN** | The dining room in this 1796 brick farmhouse exudes 18th-century charm, but the food is decidedly 21st century. Former San Francisco restaurant chef-owner Will Dodson creates inventive three- and four-course prix-fixe menus with international flavors, or more casual

versions at Max's Tavern, also on-site. **Known for:** device-free restaurant; popular for weddings; pond and perennial gardens. ⓢ *Average main: $60* ⊠ *5518 Rte. 12, 8 miles north of Woodstock, Barnard* ☎ *802/234-9961* ⊕ *www.barnardinn.com* ⊗ *Closed Sun. and Mon. No lunch.*

Cloudland Farm

$$$$ | **AMERICAN** | With the table literally on the farm, this restaurant delivers a unique farm-to-table experience that makes it worth the short drive from Woodstock. All ingredients for the seasonal prix-fixe menus come fresh from the farm or local growers, especially Cloudland's own pork, beef, chicken, and turkey. **Known for:** large fireplace in dining room; homemade carrot cake with red wine caramel and carrot jam; bring your own wine or beer. ⓢ *Average main: $45* ⊠ *1101 Cloudland Rd., North Pomfret* ☎ *802/457-2599* ⊕ *www.cloudlandfarm. com* ⊗ *No lunch Fri. and Sat.*

★ Mountain Creamery

$ | **AMERICAN** | **FAMILY** | This locally beloved diner in the town center sources most of its ingredients from their own farm in Killington. "Mile High Apple Pie," ice cream made with local dairy, and daily blue plate specials are only a handful of reasons Mountain Creamery is a Woodstock mainstay. **Known for:** homemade ice cream made with local dairy; farm-sourced diner fare; blue plate specials. ⓢ *Average main: $12* ⊠ *33 Central St., Woodstock* ☎ *802/457-1715* ⊕ *www. mountaincreameryvt.com.*

The Prince and the Pauper

$$ | **FRENCH** | Modern French and American fare with a Vermont accent is the focus of this candlelit Colonial restaurant off the town green. Three-course prix-fixe meals cost $53, but a less expensive bistro menu is available in the lounge. **Known for:** artwork for sale; complimentary cinema tickets; wine list. ⓢ *Average main: $24* ⊠ *24 Elm St., Woodstock* ☎ *802/457-1818* ⊕ *www.princeandpauper.com* ⊗ *Closed Sun. and Mon.*

Ransom Tavern

$$$ | ITALIAN | Arrive early for a seat at the wraparound bar and a perfectly made negroni. The wood-fired, Neapolitan-style pizzas are excellent, as is the inventive cocktail list and the plentiful supply of local beers on draft. **Known for:** wood-fired pizza; craft cocktail and local drafts; farm-fresh ingredients. $ *Average main: $30* ✉ *Kedron Valley Inn, 4778 South Rd., South Woodstock* ☎ *802/457–1473* ⊕ *www.kedronvalleyinn.com* ⊗ *Closed Mon. and Tues.*

★ Worthy Kitchen

$ | AMERICAN | FAMILY | One of Woodstock's liveliest and most popular places to eat, this upscale pub and bistro remains buzzing through most evenings. The chalkboard on the wall lists the hearty menu of American comfort classics given farm-to-table twists, and the craft beer selection is excellent. **Known for:** beer list; social hot spot; burgers with Wagyu beef patties. $ *Average main: $14* ✉ *442 Woodstock Rd., Woodstock* ☎ *802/457–7281* ⊕ *www.worthyvermont.com* ⊗ *No lunch weekdays.*

☕ Coffee and Quick Bites

Mont Vert Cafe

$ | CAFÉ | This charming two-story café in the center of Woodstock sources most of its ingredients in state. It's the perfect stop for a Vermont maple latte with local dairy, produce-laden salads, and wraps or egg sandwiches worthy of a long line. **Known for:** espresso drinks; breakfast sandwiches; seasonal specials. $ *Average main: $12* ✉ *28 Central St., Woodstock* ☎ *802/457–7143* ⊕ *www.monvertcafe.com* ⊗ *Closed Thurs.*

Village Butcher

This emporium of Vermont edibles has great sandwiches, cheeses, local beers, and delicious baked goods—perfect for a picnic or for lunch on the go. **Known for:** great sandwiches; on-site butcher; daily sides and salads. $ *Average main: $* ✉ *18 Elm St., Woodstock* ☎ *802/457–2756* ⊕ *www.villagebutchervt.com* ⊗ *Closed Sun.–Mon. No dinner.*

🛏 Hotels

★ The Fan House Bed and Breakfast

$$ | B&B/INN | This charming inn dating to 1840 is as authentic as it gets in Vermont. **Pros:** 300-plus-thread-count linens and down comforters; walking distance to Silver Lake and general store; library nook. **Cons:** no major sights in walking distance; on busy main road; set back and difficult to see from road. $ *Rooms from: $200* ✉ *6297 Rte. 12 N, Woodstock* ☎ *802/234–6704* ⊕ *www.thefanhouse.com* ▤ *No credit cards* ⊗ *Closed Apr.* ⤢ *3 rooms* ⌹ *Free Breakfast.*

506 On the River

$ | HOTEL | FAMILY | Behind a somewhat bland prefab exterior lies an eclectic boutique experience, thanks in large part to the virtual curiosity cabinet of exotic (or faux exotic) knickknacks stuffed throughout the premises, brought by the Africa-based owners. **Pros:** impressive cocktail menu in bar; patio dining with view of river; lots of activities and space for families. **Cons:** 5 miles west of Woodstock; child-friendly means lots of children; a bit buggy. $ *Rooms from: $199* ✉ *1653 W. Woodstock Rd., Burlington* ☎ *802/457–5000* ⊕ *www.ontheriverwoodstock.com* ⤢ *45 rooms* ⌹ *Free Breakfast.*

Kedron Valley Inn

$ | B&B/INN | You're likely to fall in love at first sight with the main 1828 three-story brick building here, the centerpiece of this 15-acre retreat, but wait until you see the spring-fed pond, which has a white sand beach with toys for kids. **Pros:** on-site restaurant with a great wine list; historic facade with modern interiors and amenities; next door to South Woodstock Country Store. **Cons:** 5 miles south of Woodstock; limited cell service; no sights within walking distance. $ *Rooms from:*

The upscale Woodstock area is known as Vermont's horse country.

$199 ✉ 4778 South Rd., South Woodstock ☎ 802/457–1473, 800/836–1193 🌐 www.kedronvalleyinn.com ⏲ Closed Apr. 🛏 16 rooms 🍴 Free Breakfast.

The Shire Riverview Motel
$ | **HOTEL** | Many rooms in this immaculate motel have decks, and most have fabulous views of Ottauquechee River, which runs right along the building. **Pros:** within walking distance of Woodstock's green and shops; sweeping river views; discounted access to Woodstock Recreation Center pool and fitness center. **Cons:** basic rooms; unexciting exterior; not all rooms have river views. [$] *Rooms from: $198 ✉ 46 Pleasant St., Woodstock ☎ 802/457–2211 🌐 shirewoodstock.com 🛏 42 rooms 🍴 No Meals.*

★ **Twin Farms**
$$$$ | **RESORT** | Let's just get it out there: Twin Farms is the best lodging in Vermont, and the most expensive, but it's worth it. **Pros:** luxury fit for A-list Hollywood stars, including Oprah Winfrey and Tom Cruise; Japanese furo in woods; on-site spa. **Cons:** steep prices; no children allowed; minimum stays during peak periods and many weekends. [$] *Rooms from: $1,900 ✉ 452 Royalton Tpke., Barnard ☎ 802/234–9999 🌐 www.twinfarms.com 🛏 20 rooms 🍴 All-Inclusive.*

★ **The Woodstock Inn and Resort**
$$$ | **RESORT** | **FAMILY** | A night at the Woodstock Inn, one of Vermont's premier accommodations, is an experience in itself, with a location on Woodstock's gorgeous green that's hard to beat. **Pros:** historic property; perfect central location; one of the best spas in Vermont. **Cons:** posh ambience not for everyone; slightly slick and corporate; very expensive for Vermont. [$] *Rooms from: $339 ✉ 14 The Green, Woodstock ☎ 802/332–6853, 888/338–2745 🌐 www.woodstockinn.com 🛏 142 rooms 🍴 No Meals.*

🛍 Shopping

ART GALLERIES

Gallery on the Green

ART GALLERIES | This corner gallery in one of Woodstock's oldest buildings showcases paintings by New England artists depicting regional landscapes. ⊠ *1 The Green, Woodstock* ☎ *802/457–4956* ⊕ *www.galleryonthegreen.com.*

CRAFTS

Andrew Pearce Bowls

CRAFTS | Son of Simon Pearce, Andrew is making a name in his own right with his expertly and elegantly carved wood bowls, cutting boards, furniture, and artwork. Visitors can watch the carvers at work through windows into the production room. ⊠ *59 Woodstock Rd., Taftsville* ☎ *802/735–1884* ⊕ *www.andrewpearce-bowls.com.*

Collective

CRAFTS | This funky and attractive shop sells local jewelry, glass, pottery, and clothing from numerous local artisans. ⊠ *47 Central St., Woodstock* ☎ *802/457–1298* ⊕ *www.collective-theartofcraft.com.*

★ Farmhouse Pottery

CERAMICS | More and more of James and Zoe Zilian's "studio pottery" is showing up in luxury establishments around the country, even earning the Oprah seal of approval. A visit to the home shop just west of Woodstock shows why, with a rustic but elegant range of stoneware pitchers, enamel jars, linen oven mitts, and beehive salt cellars. Visitors can watch the potters in action through large windows into the production room. ⊠ *1837 W. Woodstock Rd., Woodstock* ☎ *802/457–7486* ⊕ *www.farmhousepot-tery.com.*

FOOD

Sugarbush Farm

MARKET | **FAMILY** | Take the Taftsville Covered Bridge to this farm, where you can learn how maple sugar is made and sample as much maple syrup as you'd like. The farm also makes excellent cheeses. ⊠ *591 Sugarbush Farm Rd., off U.S. 4, Woodstock* ☎ *802/457–1757, 800/281–1757* ⊕ *www.sugarbushfarm.com.*

Woodstock Farmers' Market

MARKET | **FAMILY** | The indoor market is a year-round buffet of local produce, fresh fish, and excellent sandwiches and pastries. The hot lunch and dinner embrace classic American comfort food. ⊠ *979 Woodstock Rd., aka U.S. 4, Woodstock* ☎ *802/457–3658* ⊕ *www.woodstock-farmersmarket.com.*

🏃 Activities

GOLF

Woodstock Inn and Resort Golf Club

GOLF | Robert Trent Jones Sr. designed the resort's challenging course. ⊠ *76 South St., Woodstock* ☎ *802/457–6674, 888/338–2745* ⊕ *www.woodstockinn.com/golf-club* 🏌 *Non-Peak (Mon.–Thurs.) $115, Peak (Fri.–Sun.) $155* ⚑. *18 holes, 6001 yards, par 70.*

SKIING

Tubbs Snowshoes & Fischer Nordic Adventure Center

SKIING & SNOWBOARDING | The Woodstock Inn's Nordic complex has nearly 25 miles of picturesque groomed cross-country ski trails around Mt. Tom and Mt. Peg. Equipment and lessons are available. ⊠ *76 South St., Woodstock* ☎ *802/457–6674* ⊕ *www.woodstockinn.com* 🎿 *Trail pass: $35.*

SPAS

The Bridge House Spa at Twin Farms

SPAS | A visit to Twin Farms is a trip to another world, and a spa treatment here completes the getaway. The spa at the luxury lodging expounds a philosophy of wellness that goes beyond the realm of massages and skin treatments. Employing an organic product line by Vermont-based Tata Harper and Lunaroma, the spa offers facials, polishes, aromatherapy, massages, and mud wraps that administer a heavenly reboot to your skin and muscles. ✉ *Twin Farms, 452 Royalton Tpke., Barnard* ☎ *802/234–9999* ⊕ *www.twinfarms.com.*

Spa at the Woodstock Inn and Resort

SPAS | A mesmerizing, 10,000-square-foot, nature-inspired facility, this LEED-certified spa is a world unto itself, with 10 treatment rooms, ultratranquil relaxation area, eucalyptus steam room, and a sophisticated shop stocked with designer bath products. Elegant, minimalist design accentuates the beautiful setting: natural light pours into sparkling dressing rooms and the firelit Great Room, and an outdoor meditation courtyard has a hot tub and a Scandinavian-style sauna. The mood is serene, the treatments varied: start with the 80-minute Himalayan Salt Stone Massage. ✉ *Woodstock Inn and Resort, 14 The Green, Woodstock* ☎ *802/457–6697, 888/338–2745* ⊕ *www.woodstockinn. com/spa.*

Killington

20 miles northwest of Woodstock.

With only a gas station, a post office, a motel, and a few shops at the intersection of U.S. 4 and Route 100, it doesn't quite feel like the East's largest ski resort is nearby. The village of Killington has suffered from unfortunate strip development along the access road to the ski resort, but the 360-degree views atop Killington Peak, accessible via the resort's gondola, make it worth the drive.

🍵 Coffee and Quick Bites

Liquid Art Coffeehouse & Eatery

$ | **CAFÉ** | This cerulean blue A-frame is a mountainside gem for morning baked goods, award-winning chilli, and specialty drinks like the Mounds latte (espresso, steamed milk, coconut, and chocolate syrup). It also doubles as a local art gallery, so you can peruse the work of Vermont artists over a pick-me-up. **Known for:** specialty lattes; cozy corner tables and free Wi-Fi; award-winning vegetarian chilli. **$** *Average main: $6* ✉ *37 Miller Brook Rd., Killington* ☎ *802/422–2787* ⊕ *www. liquidartvt.com* ⊗ *Closed Tues. and Wed.*

🛏 Hotels

Birch Ridge Inn

$ | **B&B/INN** | A slate-covered carriageway about a mile from the Killington ski resort leads to this popular off-mountain stay, a former executive retreat in two renovated A-frames. **Pros:** variety of quirky designs; five-minute drive to the slopes; near Killington nightlife. **Cons:** restaurant closed Sunday and Monday; outdated and tired style; no coffee or tea in rooms. **$** *Rooms from: $139* ✉ *37 Butler Rd., Killington* ☎ *802/422–4293, 800/435–8566* ⊕ *www.birchridge.com* ⊗ *Closed May* ⇨ *10 rooms* �‖ *Free Breakfast.*

The Mountain Top Inn & Resort

$$$ | **RESORT** | **FAMILY** | This four-season resort hosts everything from cross-country skiing and snowshoeing on 37 miles of trails in the winter to horseback riding, tennis, and swimming and boating in the 740-acre lake throughout the rest of the year. **Pros:** family-friendly vibe; three suites have fireplaces; views of mountains and lake from some rooms. **Cons:** fees for activities can add up; tea/coffeemakers only in suites; limited to no cell service. **$** *Rooms from: $325* ✉ *195 Mountain Top Rd., Chittenden* ☎ *802/483–2311* ⊕ *www.mountaintopinn.com* ⇨ *59 rooms* �‖ *No Meals.*

🍸 Nightlife

McGrath's Irish Pub

PUBS | On Friday and Saturday, listen to live Irish music and sip Guinness draft at the Inn at Long Trail's pub. ✉ *709 U.S. 4, Killington* ☎ *802/755–7181* ⊕ *www. innatlongtrail.com.*

Pickle Barrel Night Club

DANCE CLUBS | During ski season, this club has live music on Friday and Saturday. After 8, the crowd moves downstairs for dancing, sometimes to big-name bands. ⊠ *1741 Killington Rd., Killington* ☎ *802/422–3035* ⊕ *www.picklebarrel-nightclub.com.*

Activities

BIKING

True Wheels Bike Shop

BIKING | Part of the Basin Sports complex, this shop rents bicycles and has information about local routes. ⊠ *2886 Killington Rd., Killington* ☎ *802/422–3234, 877/487–9972* ⊕ *www.basinski.com/ true-wheels-bike-shop.*

FISHING

Gifford Woods State Park

FISHING | This state park's Kent Pond is a terrific fishing spot. ⊠ *34 Gifford Woods Rd., Killington* ✛ *½ mile north of U.S. 4* ☎ *802/775–5354* ⊕ *www.vtstateparks. com/gifford.html* ⊠ *$5* ☉ *Facilities closed late Oct.–mid-May.*

GOLF

Killington Golf Course

GOLF | At its namesake resort, the course has a challenging layout. ⊠ *4763 Killington Rd., Killington* ☎ *802/422– 6700* ⊕ *www.killington.com/summer/ golf_course* ⊠ *$27 for 9 holes and $47 for 18 holes, weekdays; $37 for 9 holes and $52 for 18 holes, weekends* ⚐ *18 holes, 6186 yards, par 72* ☉ *Closed mid-Oct.–mid-May.*

HIKING

Deer Leap Trail

HIKING & WALKING | This 3-mile round-trip hike begins near the Inn at Long Trail and leads to a great view overlooking Sherburne Gap and Pico Peak. ⊠ *Trailhead off U.S. 4, just east of Inn at Long Trail, Rutland.*

SKIING

★ **Killington**

SKIING & SNOWBOARDING | FAMILY | "Megamountain" aptly describes Killington. Thanks to its extensive snowmaking capacity, the resort typically opens in early November, and the lifts often run into late April or early May. Skiing includes everything from Outer Limits, the East's steepest and longest mogul trail, to the 6½-mile Great Eastern. The 18-foot Superpipe is one of the best rated in the East. There are also acres of glades. Après-ski activities are plentiful, and Killington ticket holders can also ski Pico Mountain—a shuttle connects the two areas. Summer activities at Killington–Pico include mountain biking, hiking, and golf. **Facilities:** 155 trails; 1,509 acres; 3,050-foot vertical drop; 21 lifts.

■ TIP→ **Park at the base of the Skyeship Gondola to avoid the more crowded access road.** ⊠ *4763 Killington Rd., Killington* ☎ *802/422–3261 for snow conditions, 800/734–9435* ⊕ *www.killington.com* ⊠ *Lift ticket: $165.*

Pico

SKIING & SNOWBOARDING | When weekend hordes descend upon Killington, locals head to Pico. One of Killington's "seven peaks," Pico is physically separated from its parent resort. Trails range from elevator-shaft steep to challenging intermediate runs near the summit. Easier terrain can be found near the bottom of the mountain's nearly 2,000-foot vertical drop, and the learning slope is separated from the upper mountain, so hotshots won't bomb through it. The lower express quad can get crowded, but the upper one rarely has a line. **Facilities:** 57 trails; 468 acres; 1,967-foot vertical drop; 7 lifts. ⊠ *73 Alpine Dr., Mendon* ☎ *802/422–1330, 802/422–1200 for snow conditions* ⊕ *www.picomountain.com* ⊠ *Lift ticket: $97.*

SNOWMOBILE TOURS

Snowmobile Vermont

SNOW SPORTS | Blazing down forest trails on a snowmobile is one way Vermonters embrace the winter landscapes. Rentals are available through Snowmobile Vermont at several locations, including Killington and Okemo. Both have hour-long guided tours across groomed ski trails ($99). If you're feeling more adventurous, take the two-hour backcountry tour through 25 miles of Calvin Coolidge State Forest ($159). ✉ *170 Rte. 100, Bridgewater Corners* ☎ *802/422–2121* 🌐 *www.snowmobilevermont.com.*

Rutland

15 miles southwest of Killington, 32 miles south of Middlebury.

The strip malls and seemingly endless row of traffic lights on and around U.S. 7 in Rutland are very un-Vermont. Two blocks west, however, stand the mansions of marble magnates. In Rutland you can grab a bite and see some interesting marble, and Depot Park hosts the county farmers' market Saturday 9–2. This isn't a place to spend too much time sightseeing, though.

ESSENTIALS

VISITOR INFORMATION Rutland Region Chamber of Commerce. ✉ *Rutland* ☎ *802/773–2747, 800/756–8880* 🌐 *www.rutlandvermont.com.*

Sights

Wilson Castle

HISTORIC HOME | Completed in 1867, this 32-room mansion was built over the course of eight years by a Vermonter who married a British aristocrat. Within the opulent setting are 84 stained-glass windows (one inset with 32 Australian opals), hand-painted Italian frescoes, and 13 fireplaces. The place is magnificently furnished with European and Asian objets d'art. October evenings bring haunted castle tours. ✉ *2708 West St., Proctor* ☎ *802/773–3284* 🌐 *www.wilsoncastle.com* 🎟 *$12.*

Restaurants

Roots

$$ | **MODERN AMERICAN** | Since opening in 2011, chef-owner Donald Billings has created a locavore restaurant driven by ingredients made within miles of the dining room. Humanely raised livestock and Vermont-grown produce is the inspiration behind menu favorites like laden cheese boards, braised pork belly, and homemade Parker House rolls served warm with Vermont butter. **Known for:** Vermont beers and spirits; frequently changing locavore menu; special Prime Rib Thursday. [$] *Average main: $24* ✉ *55 Washington St., Rutland* ☎ *802/747–7414* 🌐 *www.rootsrutland.com* 🕐 *Closed Sun. and Mon.*

Coffee and Quick Bites

★ **Jones' Donuts**

$ | **BAKERY** | Since 1923, Jones' has been a destination for doughnuts and baked goods made fresh each day in the earliest hours of the morning. Fill a box with cinnamon rolls, pie squares, apple turnovers, and some of the best doughnuts in the state. **Known for:** maple glazed doughnuts; crullers; sticky buns. [$] *Average main: $2* ✉ *23 West St., Rutland* ☎ *802/773–7810* 🕐 *Closed Mon. and Tues.*

Activities

BOATING

Woodard Marine

BOATING | Rent pontoon boats, speedboats, standup paddleboards, and kayaks at the Lake Bomoseen Marina. ✉ *145 Creek Rd., off Rte. 4A, Castleton, Rutland* ☎ *802/265–3690* 🌐 *www.woodardmarine.com.*

Brandon

15 miles northwest of Rutland.

Thanks to an active group of artists, tiny Brandon is making a name for itself. In 2003 the Brandon Artists Guild, led by American folk artist Warren Kimble, auctioned off 40 life-size fiberglass pigs painted by local artists. The "Really Really Pig Show" raised money for the guild, and has since brought small-town fame to this community through its annual shows. Brandon is also home to the Basin Bluegrass Festival, held in July.

ESSENTIALS

VISITOR INFORMATION Brandon
Visitor Center. ⊠ *4 Grove St., Brandon* ☎ *802/247–6401* ⊕ *www.brandon.org.*

 Sights

Brandon Artists Guild

ART GALLERY | The guild exhibits and sells affordable paintings, sculpture, and pottery by more than 30 local member artists. ⊠ *7 Center St., Brandon* ☎ *802/247–4956* ⊕ *brandonartistsguild. org* ⛬ *Free* ⊙ *Closed Mon. Dec.–Apr.*

Brandon Museum at the Stephen A. Douglas Birthplace

HISTORY MUSEUM | The famous statesman was born in this house in 1813. He left 20 years later to establish himself as a lawyer, becoming a three-time U.S. senator and arguing more cases before the U.S. Supreme Court than anyone else. This museum recounts the early Douglas years, early town history, and the antislavery movement in Vermont, the first state to abolish slavery. ⊠ *4 Grove St., at U.S. 7, Brandon* ☎ *802/247–6401* ⊕ *www. brandon.org* ⛬ *Free* ⊙ *Closed Sun. and mid-Oct.–mid-May.*

Foley Brothers Brewery

BREWERY | Though this is a bare bones tasting room—no food, no tours, just glass pours and growlers—we argue that it has great charm, unique Vermont personality, and some of the best beer in the state. There is space to sit outside in the summer months in a nearby field with beautiful views, and the brewery's golden retriever is locally beloved. ⊠ *79 Stone Mill Dam Rd., Brandon* ☎ *802/465–8413* ⊕ *foleybrothersbrewing. com* ⊙ *Closed Mon. and Tues., and Sun. Jan.–May.*

Moosalamoo National Recreation Area

NATURE PRESERVE | Covering nearly 16,000 acres of the Green Mountain National Forest, this area northeast of Brandon attracts hikers, mountain bikers, and cross-country skiers who enjoy the 70-plus miles of trails through wondrous terrain. If there is anywhere to stop and smell the flowers in Vermont, this is it. ⊠ *Off Rtes. 53 and 73, Brandon* ⊕ *www. moosalamoo.org.*

Mt. Independence State Historic Site

HISTORIC SIGHT | Mt. Independence is one of the nation's most revered Revolutionary War sites, documenting the efforts to defend New York, New England, and the battle for American liberty. This key defensive position gained its name between 1776 and 1777, when the barely dried ink of the Declaration of Independence was read to United States soldiers assembled on the rugged peninsula east of Lake Champlain. Annual events include guided nature and history hikes on the site's 6 miles of hiking trails; historical lectures; archaeological investigations; a "Soldiers Atop the Mount" living history weekend; and a yearly reading of the Declaration of Independence. ⊠ *497 Mt. Independence Rd., Orwell* ☎ *802/948–2000* ⊕ *historicsites.vermont. gov/mount-independence.*

Red Clover Ale

BREWERY | Red Clover Ale opened in Brandon's tiny town center under the reigns of two brothers and a brother-in-law. The family trio focuses on creative ales alongside skilled representations of the classics, like their pitch-perfect pilsners and stouts. Their ongoing IPA series is as special as the birds they're named after, like American Redstart and Yellow Warbler. Excellent pop-up food vendors are occasionally found on-site—otherwise, a corkboard near the entrance is covered in local takeout menus for perusing to one's liking. ✉ *43 Center St., Brandon* ☎ *802/465–8412* 🌐 *www.redcloverale.com* ⏲ *Closed Mon.–Wed.*

🍴 Restaurants

Café Provence

$$ | CAFÉ | Robert Barral, the former executive chef of the New England Culinary Institute, graces Brandon with this informal eatery one story above the main street. Flowered seat cushions, dried-flower window valences, and other hints of Barral's Provençal birthplace abound, as do his eclectic, farm-fresh dishes. **Known for:** Sunday brunch; thin tomato pie; seafood stew. [$] *Average main: $23* ✉ *11 Center St., Brandon* ☎ *802/247–9997* 🌐 *www.cafeprovencevt.com* ⏲ *Closed Mon. and Tues.*

☕ Coffee and Quick Bites

Gourmet Provence Bakery

$ | BAKERY | Next door to Café Provence, this French bakery offers coffee, pastries (yes, there are croissants and eclairs), prepared food, and specialty goods during the day. There's also a modest wine shop featuring plenty of old-world bottles. **Known for:** coffee and espresso drinks; homemade pastries; wine shop and artisanal goods. [$] *Average main: $8* ✉ *37 Center St., Brandon* ☎ *802/247–3002* 🌐 *cafeprovencevt.com* ⏲ *Closed Mon.*

🛏 Hotels

★ Blueberry Hill Inn

$$ | B&B/INN | In the Green Mountain National Forest, 5½ miles off a mountain pass on a dirt road, you'll find this secluded inn with lush gardens and a pond with a wood-fired sauna on its bank; there's lots to do if you're into nature: biking, hiking, and cross-country skiing on 43 miles of trails. **Pros:** skis and snowshoes to rent in winter; the restaurant prepares a Vermont-infused, four-course prix-fixe menu most nights; homemade cookies. **Cons:** fills up with wedding parties; no cell phone service; no coffee or tea in rooms. [$] *Rooms from: $269* ✉ *1245 Goshen–Ripton Rd., Goshen* ☎ *802/247–6735* 🌐 *www.blueberryhillinn.com* 🔑 *12 rooms* 🍴 *Free Breakfast.*

The Lilac Inn

$ | B&B/INN | The best B&B in town has cheery, comfortable guest rooms in a central setting half a block from the heart of Brandon. **Pros:** many rooms have king beds; within walking distance of town; garden gazebo for relaxation. **Cons:** busy in summer with weddings; quaint but tepid traditional design; no coffee or tea in rooms. [$] *Rooms from: $169* ✉ *53 Park St., Brandon* ☎ *802/247–5463, 800/221–0720* 🌐 *www.lilacinn.com* 🔑 *9 rooms* 🍴 *Free Breakfast.*

🏃 Activities

GOLF

Neshobe Golf Club

GOLF | This bent-grass course has terrific views of the Green Mountains. Several local inns offer golfing packages. ✉ *224 Town Farm Rd., Brandon* ☎ *802/247–3611* 🌐 *neshobe.com* 🎫 *$25 for 9 holes, $44 for 18 holes* ⛳ *18 holes, 6341 yards, par 72.*

HIKING

Branbury State Park

HIKING & WALKING | A large turnout on Route 53 marks the trailhead for a moderate hike to the Falls of Lana, a highlight of this park on the shores of Lake Dunmore near the Moosalamoo National Recreation Area. ✉ *3570 Lake Dunmore Rd., Brandon* 🌐 *www.vtstateparks.com/branbury.html* 🎫 *$5* ⏲ *Facilities closed late Oct.–late May.*

Mt. Horrid

HIKING & WALKING | For great views from a vertigo-inducing cliff, hike up the Long Trail to Mt. Horrid. The steep, hour-long hike starts at the top of Brandon Gap. ⊠ *Trailhead at Brandon Gap Rte. 73 parking lot, about 8 miles east of Brandon, Brandon* ⊕ *www.fs.usda.gov/main/gmfl.*

Trails at Mt. Independence State Historic Site

HIKING & WALKING | West of Brandon, four trails—two short ones of less than a mile each and two longer ones—lead to some abandoned Revolutionary War fortifications. ⊠ *497 Mt. Independence Rd., just west of Orwell, Orwell* ⊹ *Parking lot is at top of hill* ☏ *802/948–2000* ⊕ *historicsites.vermont.gov/mount-independence* ⌲ *$5* ⊘ *Closed mid-Oct.–late May.*

Middlebury

17 miles north of Brandon, 34 miles south of Burlington.

In the late 1800s Middlebury was the largest Vermont community west of the Green Mountains, an industrial center of river-powered wool and grain mills. This is Robert Frost country: Vermont's late poet laureate spent 23 summers at a farm east of Middlebury. Still a cultural and economic hub amid the Champlain Valley's serene pastoral patchwork—and the home of top-notch Middlebury College—the town and rolling countryside invite a day of exploration.

◉ Sights

Edgewater Gallery

ART GALLERY | This gallery sits alongside picturesque Otter Creek, and the paintings, jewelry, ceramics, and pieces of furniture inside are just as arresting. Exhibitions in the bright, airy space change regularly, demonstrating the owner's ambition to be more gallery than shop, though all pieces are for sale. A second gallery is across the

Middlebury Tasting Trail

Among Vermont's craft beer, cider, spirits, and wine explosion, the Middlebury area stands out, with a large cluster of producers with welcoming tasting rooms. Seven, all within a 10-mile radius of the city, have banded together to create the Middlebury Tasting Trail. Find full details at ⊕ *www.middtastingtrail.com.*

creek in the Battell Building. ⊠ *1 Mill St., Middlebury* ☏ *802/458–0098* ⊕ *edgewatergallery.co* ⌲ *Free.*

Fort Ticonderoga Ferry

TRANSPORTATION | Established in 1759, the Fort Ti cable ferry crosses Lake Champlain between Shoreham and Fort Ticonderoga, New York, at one of the oldest ferry crossings in North America. The trip takes seven minutes. ⊠ *4831 Rte. 74 W, Shoreham* ☏ *802/897–7999* ⊕ *www.forttiferry.com* ⌲ *Cars $12, bicycles $5, pedestrians $4* ⊘ *Closed Nov.–Apr.*

Lincoln Peak Vineyard

WINERY | Named "Winery of the Year" at the International Cold Climate Wine Competition in 2016, this vineyard —now owned by nearby Shelburne Vineyard— is enjoying the fruits of its labor, with an increase in traffic to its tasting room and shop. Enjoy the Frontenac, La Crescent, and Marquette varieties from both vineyards on the postcard-pretty porch overlooking a small pond. ⊠ *142 River Rd., Middlebury* ☏ *802/388–7368* ⊕ *www.lincolnpeakvineyard.com* ⊘ *Closed Mon. and Tues. late Oct.–Dec.; Mon.–Thurs. Jan.–late May.*

Middlebury College

COLLEGE | Founded in 1800, this college was conceived as a more godly alternative to the worldly University of Vermont, though it has no religious affiliation today. The postmodern architecture of the **Mahaney Center for the Arts,** which offers music, theater, and dance performances throughout the year, stands in provocative contrast to the early-19th-century stone buildings in the middle of town. ✉ *131 College St., Middlebury* ☎ *802/443–5000* 🌐 *www.middlebury.edu.*

Robert Frost Interpretive Trail

TRAIL | Plaques along this easy 1.2-mile wooded trail bear quotations from Frost's poems. A picnic area is across the road from the trailhead. ✉ *Trailhead on Rte. 125, 10 miles east of downtown, Middlebury* 🌐 *www.fs.usda.gov/main/gmfl.*

University of Vermont Morgan Horse Farm

FARM/RANCH | **FAMILY** | The Morgan horse, Vermont's official state animal, has an even temper, high stamina, and slightly truncated legs in proportion to its body. This farm, about 2½ miles west of Middlebury, is a breeding and training center where in summer you can tour the stables and paddocks. ✉ *74 Battell Dr., off Morgan Horse Farm Rd., Weybridge* ☎ *802/388–2011* 🌐 *www.uvm.edu/morgan* 🎫 *$8* 🕒 *Closed late Oct.–Apr.*

Vermont Folklife Center

ARTS CENTER | The redbrick center's exhibits include photography, antiques, folk paintings, manuscripts, and other artifacts and contemporary works that examine various facets of Vermont life. ✉ *88 Main St., Middlebury* ☎ *802/388–4964* 🌐 *www.vermontfolklifecenter.org* 🎫 *Donations accepted* 🕒 *Closed Sun. and Mon.*

Woodchuck Cider House

BREWERY | This cidery has come a long way since its beginnings in a two-car garage in Proctorsville in 1991, transforming into this $34 million complex that divides its space between a pub, gift shop, and factory. A self-guided tour, with informational signs, includes a look through large windows onto the production floor. ✉ *1321 Exchange St., Middlebury* ☎ *802/385–3656* 🌐 *www.woodchuck.com* 🕒 *Closed Mon. and Tues.*

🍴 Restaurants

Minifactory

$ | **CAFÉ** | Also the home of award-winning jam company V Smiley Preserves, this all-day café serves house-made pastries, biscuit sandwiches, huge salads, creative vegetable dishes and savory yogurt with crispy lentils and poached eggs. On weekends, oysters and cocktails start in the afternoon; dinner features rich soups and roast chicken with tomato jam. **Known for:** bright, spacious seating area with big windows for people watching; well-stocked grab-and-go fridge and pantry ingredients; jammy waffle (waffle with buttered nuts, syrup, and black raspberry whip). [$] *Average main: $16* ✉ *16 Main St., Bristol* ☎ *802/453–3280* 🌐 *vermontminifactory.com* 🕒 *No dinner Sun.–Thurs.*

The Tillerman

$$$ | **PIZZA** | New owners have transformed the longtime Inn at Baldwin Creek and Mary's Restaurant, giving the 1790s farmhouse a chic update from head to toe. Pizza isn't the only thing that comes out of the new wood-fired oven; locally sourced roasted vegetables and smokey meatballs complement the fire-kissed pies. **Known for:** thoughtful drink list, including nonalcoholic options; cozy dining rooms; fresh herbs and vegetables from the kitchen garden. [$] *Average main: $25* ✉ *1868 N 116 Rd., Bristol* ☎ *802/643–2237* 🌐 *www.thetillermanvt.com* 🕒 *Closed Sun.–Tues. No lunch.*

☕ Coffee and Quick Bites

★ **Haymaker Bun Co.**

$ | **BAKERY** | This sunlit café and bakery overlooking Otter Creek houses some of the best coffee and pastries in the state thanks to chef-owner Caroline Corrente, who honed her skills at pastry school in France before zeroing in on a love for brioche dough. Corrente's specialty sweet and savory buns change daily based on what is available locally—many ingredients are found within a few miles of Haymaker's doors. **Known for:** sweet and savory brioche buns; locally roasted Brio coffee and espresso; patio seating and riverside views. [$] *Average main: $6* ✉ *7 Bakery La., Middlebury* ☎ *802/989–7026* 🌐 *www.haymakerbuns.com* 🕒 *Closed Sun.*

Royal Oak Coffee

$ | **CAFÉ** | After a decade of fine-tuning their skills and tastebuds in the coffee industry, Royal Oak co-owners Alessandra and Matthew Delia-Lobo opened their own café on Seymour Street, an easy pit stop along the Middlebury Tasting Trail. The menu, featuring Vermont-based beans from Vivid Coffee Roasters, is known for shaken ice maple lattes in the summer and frothy cardamom-vanilla lattes in the winter (a seasonal special that, say the Delia-Lobos, now never leaves the menu due to popularity). **Known for:** specialty lattes using scratch-made syrups; cold brew; Gibralters, hot and iced. [$] *Average main: $5* ✉ *30 Seymour St., Middlebury* ☎ *802/349–1609* 🌐 *www.royaloakcoffee.com.*

Stone Leaf Teahouse

$ | **CAFÉ** | Partially hidden in Middlebury's historic Marble Works district, this oasis of tea is known for made-to-order spiced chai, house-roasted oolong, and loose leaf teas imported from small farmers in China, India, Nepal, Japan, and Taiwan. **Known for:** specialty teaware sold on-site; oolong roasted in-house; seasonal herbal tea blends. [$] *Average main: $5* ✉ *Marble Works, 111 Maple St., Middlebury* ☎ *802/458–0460* 🌐 *www.stoneleaftea.com.*

Hotels

Inn on the Green

$$ | **B&B/INN** | Listed on the National Register of Historic Places, this 1803 inn and its carriage house sit in the center of bucolic Middlebury near the college campus; the inn offers a delicious breakfast, bicycles you are free to use, and Adirondack chairs that are perfect for enjoying the grounds and views. **Pros:** ideal, central location; complimentary continental "breakfast-in-bed"; Aveda hair and skin-care products. **Cons:** some rooms small and close together; typical country-inn design; no coffee or tea in rooms. [$] *Rooms from: $285* ✉ *71 S. Pleasant St., Middlebury* ☎ *802/388–7512, 888/244–7512* 🌐 *www.innonthegreen.com* 🔑 *11 rooms* 🍴 *Free Breakfast.*

★ **Swift House Inn**

$$ | **B&B/INN** | The 1814 Georgian mansion channels a classic New England style into three buildings on 4 acres of lawns and gardens. **Pros:** attractive, spacious, well-kept rooms; complimentary day pass to Middlebury Fitness Club; some rooms have private decks; on-site restaurant, Jessica's, is one of the best fine-dining options in town. **Cons:** not quite in the heart of town; weak Wi-Fi in some areas; somewhat typical country-inn design. [$] *Rooms from: $245* ✉ *25 Stewart La., Middlebury* ☎ *866/388–9925* 🌐 *www.swifthouseinn.com* 🔑 *20 rooms* 🍴 *Free Breakfast.*

Nightlife

Two Brothers Tavern

PUBS | Head to this watering hole for pub food a cut above the usual, plus local microbrews on tap in the sports-friendly bar. Look closely at the dollar bills pasted to the ceiling. There's even a marriage proposal up there, along with the answer. Food is served until at least midnight. ✉ *86 Main St., Middlebury* ☎ *802/388–0002* 🌐 *www.twobrotherstavern.com.*

Waitsfield and Warren

32 miles northeast (Waitsfield) and 25 miles east (Warren) of Middlebury.

Skiers first discovered the high peaks overlooking the pastoral Mad River Valley in the 1940s. Today, this valley and its two towns, Waitsfield and Warren, attract the hip, the adventurous, and the low-key. Warren in particular is tiny and adorable, with a general store popular with tour buses. The gently carved ridges cradling the valley and the swell of pastures and fields lining the river seem to keep notions of ski-resort sprawl at bay. With a map from the Sugarbush Chamber of Commerce you can investigate back roads off Route 100 that have exhilarating valley views.

ESSENTIALS

VISITOR INFORMATION Mad River Valley Visitor Information Center. ✉ *44 Bridge St., Waitsfield* ☎ *802/496–3409* 🌐 *www.madrivervalley.com.*

🍴 Restaurants

★ American Flatbread Waitsfield
$$ | **PIZZA** | The organically grown flour and vegetables—and the wood-fired clay ovens that unite them—take the pizza here to another level. In summer, you can dine outside around fire pits in the beautiful valley. **Known for:** maple–fennel sausage pie; homemade fruit crisp with Mountain Creamery ice cream; Big Red Barn art gallery on-site. [$] *Average main: $18* ✉ *46 Lareau Rd., off Rte. 100, Waitsfield* ☎ *802/496–8856* 🌐 *www.americanflatbread.com* 🕒 *Closed Mon.–Wed. No lunch.*

The Mad Taco
$ | **MEXICAN** | Mexican cuisine rooted in Vermont ingredients makes this a go-to stop for locals and travelers alike—particularly those who just ascended the rugged incline of nearby Camel's Hump, one of the state's highest peaks. Chef-owner Joey Nagy and Georgia Von Trapp, his partner, source much of their local haul from their own Marble Hill Farm, fueling delicious cooking from carnitas and al pastor to fresh house-made salsa and slow-roasted yams in the outside smoker. **Known for:** tacos with local All Souls tortillas; Cubano sandwich with smoked Vermont meat; house-made margaritas and local craft beer. [$] *Average main: $12* ✉ *5101 Main St., Waitsfield* ☎ *802/496–3832* 🌐 *www.themadtaco.com.*

★ Peasant
$$$ | **EUROPEAN** | The menu may be short in this small, rustic-chic space serving French- and Italian-influenced country fare, but the tastiness is immense, with some of the best pasta dishes in the state. Additional warmth is added by its "peasant family" operation, too, with dad in the kitchen, mom decorating the scene, and daughter running the front of house. **Known for:** unique "Peasant's Prunes" dessert; Vermont pork Bolognese with penne and Asiago; craft cocktail and wine list. [$] *Average main: $26* ✉ *40 Bridge St., Waitsfield* ☎ *802/496–6856* 🌐 *www.peasantvt.com* 🕒 *Closed Mon.-Wed. No lunch.*

Pitcher Inn Dining Room and Tracks
$$$ | **AMERICAN** | Claiming two aesthetics and one menu, this dining experience offers a posh and pretty upstairs dining room with classic white tablecloths or a stony, subterranean "Tracks," with billiards and shuffleboard on the side. Dishes cover upscale versions of regional classics, with a few international flavors, too. **Known for:** cocktail list with Vermont spirits; duck breast; artisanal cheese board with onion chutney. [$] *Average main: $30* ✉ *275 Main St., Warren* ☎ *802/496–6350* 🌐 *www.pitcherinn.com.*

☕ Coffee and Quick Bites

Canteen Creemee Company
$ | **AMERICAN** | **FAMILY** | Stop by the takeout window of this new-wave snack shack for fried chicken, griddled burgers, and kimchi-stuffed grilled cheese. Stay for the homemade creemees, Vermont's answer to soft-serve ice cream; state classics like maple are always on offer, as are seasonal specials like ginger, cinnamon, lemon, and fresh blueberry. **Known for:** creemees and sundaes; fried chicken, griddled

burgers, and hot dogs; limited winter hours. $ *Average main: $8* ✉ *5123 Main St., Waitsfield* ☎ *802/496–6003* ⊕ *www.canteencreemee.com* ◷ *Closed Mon.–Fri.*

🛏 Hotels

★ The Inn at Round Barn Farm

$$ | **B&B/INN** | A Shaker-style round barn—one of only five in Vermont—is the centerpiece of this eminently charming B&B set among the hills of the Mad River Valley with resident ducks, squirrels, chipmunks, and songbirds that make it feel like a Disney movie. **Pros:** miles of walking and snowshoe trails; game room with billiard table and board games; gorgeous gardens with lily ponds. **Cons:** no a/c in common areas; fills up for wedding parties; no sights within walking distance. $ *Rooms from: $219* ✉ *1661 E. Warren Rd., Waitsfield* ☎ *802/496–2276* ⊕ *www.theroundbarn.com* ⇨ *12 rooms* ⦿ *Free Breakfast.*

Mad River Barn

$ | **B&B/INN** | This supposed former bunk house for the Civilian Conservation Corps in the 1930s is now one of the Mad River Valley's chicest accommodations, thanks to extensive renovations in 2013 that transformed it into a rustic farmhouse with an edge of industrial. **Pros:** multiple-sized rooms, sleeping up to six people; game room includes shuffleboard, air hockey, foosball, and more; several family suites, with bunkbeds. **Cons:** first-floor rooms can suffer noise; lots of weddings in summer can keep it busy and booked; no TVs in rooms. $ *Rooms from: $145* ✉ *2849 Mill Brook Rd., Waitsfield* ☎ *802/496–3310, 800/631–0466* ⊕ *www.madriverbarn.com* ⇨ *18 rooms* ⦿ *Free Breakfast.*

★ The Pitcher Inn

$$$$ | **B&B/INN** | One of Vermont's three Relais & Châteaux properties, the unique Pitcher Inn has it all including a supremely romantic restaurant and bubbling brook running alongside. **Pros:** exceptional and

fun design; across from Warren General Store; complimentary hybrid bikes and access to the Sugarbush Health and Racquet Club. **Cons:** two-night minimum stay on many weekends in peak period; limited no cell phone service; restaurant closed on Tuesday. $ *Rooms from: $500* ✉ *275 Main St., Warren* ☎ *802/496–6350* ⊕ *www.pitcherinn.com* ⇨ *11 rooms* ⦿ *Free Breakfast.*

🛍 Shopping

All Things Bright and Beautiful

ANTIQUES & COLLECTIBLES | This eccentric Victorian house is filled to the rafters with stuffed animals of all shapes, sizes, and colors, as well as folk art, European glass, and Christmas ornaments. ✉ *27 Bridge St., Waitsfield* ☎ *802/496–3997.*

The Warren Store

GENERAL STORE | This general store has everything you'd hope to find in tiny but sophisticated Vermont: a nice selection of local beer and wine, cheeses, baked goods, strong coffee, and delicious sandwiches and prepared foods. In summer, grab a quick lunch on the small deck by the water; in winter, warm up at the wood stove. Warm, woolly clothing and accessories can be found upstairs. ✉ *284 Main St., Warren* ☎ *802/496–3864* ⊕ *www.warrenstore.com.*

🏃 Activities

GOLF

Sugarbush Resort Golf Club

GOLF | Great views and challenging play are the hallmarks of this mountain course designed by Robert Trent Jones Sr. ✉ *Sugarbush, 1840 Sugarbush Access Rd., Warren* ☎ *802/583–6725* ⊕ *www.sugarbush.com* ⛳ *$115 for 18 holes, weekdays; $130 for 18 holes, weekends* 🏌 *18 holes, 6464 yards, par 70.*

MULTISPORT OUTFITTER

Clearwater Sports

ADVENTURE TOURS | FAMILY | This outfitter rents canoes and kayaks, and leads guided river trips in warmer months. When the weather turns cold, it offers snowshoeing and backcountry skiing tours. ⊠ 4147 Main St., Waitsfield ☎ 802/496–2708 ⊕ www.clearwatersports.com.

SKIING

Blueberry Lake Cross Country and Snowshoeing Center

SKIING & SNOWBOARDING | This ski area has 18 miles of trails through thickly wooded glades. ⊠ 424 Plunkton Rd., East Warren ☎ 802/496–6687 ⊕ www.blueberrylake-skivt.com ⊠ Daily Pass Trail Fees: $22.

Mad River Glen

SKIING & SNOWBOARDING | A pristine alpine experience, Mad River attracts rugged individualists looking for less polished terrain. The area was developed in the late 1940s and has changed relatively little since then. It remains one of only three resorts in the country that ban snowboarding, and it's one of only two in North America that still has a single-chair lift. Mad River is steep, with slopes that follow the mountain's fall lines. The terrain changes constantly on the interconnected trails of mostly natural snow (expert trails are never groomed). Telemark skiing and snowshoeing are also popular. **Facilities:** 53 trails; 115 acres; 2,037-foot vertical drop; 5 lifts. ⊠ 62 Mad River Resort Rd., off Rte. 17, Waitsfield ☎ 802/496–3551 ⊕ www.madriverglen.com ⊠ Lift ticket: $99.

Sugarbush

SKIING & SNOWBOARDING | FAMILY | A true skier's mountain, Sugarbush has plenty of steep, natural snow glades and fall-line drops. Not as rough around the edges as Mad River Glen, the resort has an extensive computer-controlled system for snowmaking and many groomed trails between its two mountain complexes. This is a great choice for intermediate skiers, who will find top-to-bottom runs all over the resort; there are fewer options for beginners. Programs for kids include the enjoyable Sugarbear Forest, a terrain garden full of fun bumps and jumps. At the base of the mountain are condominiums, restaurants, shops, bars, and a health-and-racquet club. **Facilities:** 111 trails; 484 acres; 2,600-foot vertical drop; 16 lifts. ⊠ 102 Forest Dr., Warren ✛ From Rte. 17, take German Flats Rd. south; from Rte. 100, take Sugarbush Access Rd. west ☎ 802/583–6300, 800/537–8427 ⊕ www.sugarbush.com ⊠ Lift ticket: $189.

Montpelier

38 miles southeast of Burlington, 115 miles north of Brattleboro.

With only about 8,000 residents, little Montpelier is the country's smallest capital city, but it has a youthful energy and a quirky spirit that's earned it the local nickname "Montpeculiar." The quaint, historic downtown area bustles by day with thousands of state and city workers walking to meetings and business lunches. The nightlife can't match Burlington's, but several bars, theaters, and cinemas provide ample entertainment. The city is also a springboard for exploring the great outdoors of Central Vermont.

GETTING HERE AND AROUND

Vermont's capital city is easily accessible from Interstate 89, taking about 45 minutes from Burlington by car through the heart of the Green Mountains. It's also on the main Boston–Montreal bus route. Downtown is flat and easily walkable, but exploring the surrounding hills requires a modest level of fitness as well as a solid pair of shoes or boots, especially during the winter.

Did You Know?

Vermont actually means "Green Mountains" (in French). The Long Trail, the Appalachian Trail, and many other hiking routes crisscross the namesake peaks, which are part of the Appalachian Mountain chain.

👁 Sights

★ Hope Cemetery

CEMETERY | Montpelier's regional rival, Barre, the "Granite Capital of the World," may lack the polish and pedigree of the state capital, but it's home to this gorgeous cemetery filled with superbly crafted tombstones by master stonecutters. A few embrace the avant-garde, while others take defined shapes like a race car, a biplane, and a soccer ball. ⊠ *201 Maple Ave., Barre* ☎ *802/476–6245.*

Hubbard Park

STATE/PROVINCIAL PARK | Rising behind the Vermont State House and stretching 196 acres, this heavily forested park offers locals (and their happy, leash-free dogs) miles of pretty trails and wildlife to enjoy. On its highest peak is a romantic stone tower that looks out to 360-degree views of the surrounding mountains. ⊠ *400 Parkway St., Montpelier* ☎ *802/223–7335 Montpelier Parks department* ⊕ *www. montpelier-vt.org* ✉ *Free.*

★ Morse Farm Maple Sugarworks

FACTORY | **FAMILY** | With eight generations of sugaring, the Morses may be the oldest maple family in existence, so you're sure to find an authentic experience at their farm. Burr Morse—a local legend—heads up the operation now, along with his son Tom. More than 5,000 trees produce the sap used for syrup (you can sample all the grades), candy, cream, and sugar—all sold in the gift shop. Grab a maple creemee (soft-serve ice cream), take a seat on a swing, and stay awhile. Surrounding trails offer pleasant strolls in summer and prime cross-country skiing in winter. ⊠ *1168 County Rd., Montpelier* ☎ *800/242–2740* ⊕ *www.morsefarm.com* ✉ *Free.*

Rock of Ages Granite Quarry

NATURE SIGHT | Attractions here range from the awe-inspiring (the quarry resembles the Grand Canyon in miniature) to the mildly ghoulish (you can consult a directory of tombstone dealers throughout the country) to the whimsical (an outdoor granite bowling alley). At the crafts center, skilled artisans sculpt monuments and blast stone, while at the quarries themselves, workers who clearly earn their pay cut 25-ton blocks of stone from the sheer 475-foot walls. (You may recognize these walls from a chase scene in the 2009 *Star Trek* movie.) ⊠ *558 Graniteville Rd., off I-89, Graniteville* ☎ *802/476–3119, 866/748–6877* ⊕ *www.rockofages.com* ✉ *Guided tours $7* ⊗ *Closed Sun. and mid-Oct.–mid-May.*

Vermont History Museum

HISTORY MUSEUM | The collection here, begun in 1838, focuses on all things Vermont—from a catamount (the now-extinct local cougar) to Ethan Allen's shoe buckles. The museum store stocks fine books, prints, and gifts. A second location in Barre, the Vermont History Center, has rotating exhibits with notable photographs and artifacts. ⊠ *109 State St., Montpelier* ☎ *802/828–2291* ⊕ *www. vermonthistory.org* ✉ *$7* ⊗ *Closed Sun. and Mon.*

Vermont State House

GOVERNMENT BUILDING | The regal capitol building surrounded by forest is emblematic of this proudly rural state. With a gleaming dome and columns of Barre granite measuring 6 feet in diameter, the State House is home to the country's oldest legislative chambers still in their original condition. Interior paintings and exhibits depict much of Vermont's sterling Civil War record. A self-guided tour, available year-round, takes you through the governor's office and the house and senate chambers. Free guided tours run from late June to October. ⊠ *115 State St., Montpelier* ☎ *802/828–2228* ⊕ *statehouse.vermont.gov* ✉ *Donations accepted* ⊗ *Closed Sun.; also Sat. Nov.–June.*

🍴 Restaurants

Oakes & Evelyn

$$$$ | AMERICAN | Vermont may be landlocked, but regionally sourced seafood fills the menu at this upscale farm-to-table restaurant in the state capital; the raw bar—think Cape Cod oysters and cold-smoked scallop crudo—is a particular draw. Large plates include prime strip loin with bone marrow and black-truffle raclette with local ricotta ravioletto. **Known for:** luxurious ingredients; creative cocktails, including multiple Bloody Mary options at brunch; bao buns with spiced crispy local mushrooms. [$] *Average main: $38* ✉ *52 State St., Montpelier* ☎ *802/347–9100* 🌐 *www.oakesandevelyn.com* ⏲ *Closed Mon.–Tues. No lunch.*

Pearl Street Pizza

$$ | PIZZA | The handmade Italian brick oven is the centerpiece of this hot new pizza spot, which shares a former department store building with AR Market and the curing facility for Vermont Salumi. The team cranks out perfectly blistered Neapolitan-style pizzas and thick grandma pies, with classic and weekly special toppings that range from fire-roasted mushrooms to roast pork and miso drizzle. **Known for:** Tom Cat Tiramisu made with local barrel-aged gin; housemade pasta of the week; local mozzarella and real San Marzano tomatoes. [$] *Average main: $24* ✉ *159 N. Main St., Barre* ☎ *802/622–8600* 🌐 *pearlstpizza.com* ⏲ *Closed Sun.–Tues.*

Sarducci's

$$ | ITALIAN | FAMILY | Montpelier's most popular restaurant draws its crowd less for the classic American Italian dishes than the conviviality, charm, and sizeable portions, not to mention the picturesque Winooski River flowing directly alongside the windows. The pizza comes fresh from wood-fired ovens, while the rest of the menu features your favorite pennes, Alfredos, and raviolis, with pleasing tweaks on the old formulas. **Known for:** date night; large gluten-free menu; local favorite. [$] *Average main: $18* ✉ *3 Main St., Montpelier* ☎ *802/223–0229* 🌐 *www.sarduccis.com* ⏲ *No lunch Sun.*

The Skinny Pancake

$ | CAFÉ | This dine-in crêperie makes a great stop for breakfast, lunch, or an easy dinner. The signature crepes go sweet and savory and are filled with fruit, vegetables, and meat from more than a dozen Vermont farms. **Known for:** inventive hot chocolate recipes; Locavore's Dream crepe with chicken, cran-apple chutney, spinach, and blue cheese; Pooh Bear crepe with cinnamon sugar and local honey. [$] *Average main: $9* ✉ *89 Main St., Montpelier* ☎ *802/262–2253* 🌐 *www.skinnypancake.com.*

★ Three Penny Taproom

$ | ECLECTIC | This celebrated taproom remains one of the state's best, thanks in large part to its ability to acquire beers few others in the region can. The vibe feels straight out of an artsy neighborhood in Brussels, but with the earthiness of Vermont. **Known for:** darn good burger; top happy-hour hangout in town; premier Vermont and hard-to-get brews. [$] *Average main: $15* ✉ *108 Main St., Montpelier* ☎ *802/223–8277* 🌐 *www.threepennytaproom.com.*

★ Wilaiwan's Kitchen

$ | THAI | In 2012, co-owners Wilaiwan Phonjan-Azarian and Timothy Azarian traded their locally adored street cart for a brick-and-mortar location offering some of the best Thai food in the state, if not on the East Coast. Most of the menu reflects the Laotian influence of Phonjan-Azarian's upbringing in northeast Thailand, and Vermont ingredients from eggs to chiles inspire dishes that change weekly. **Known for:** weekly changing menus featuring local ingredients; noodle specials, like khao soy and gwit diow, with homemade chili pastes; sunny interiors covered with artwork. [$] *Average main: $10* ✉ *34 State St., Montpelier* ☎ *802/613–3587* 🌐 *wilaiwanskitchen.com* ⏲ *Closed Sun.*

☕ Coffee and Quick Bites

Bohemian Bakery

$ | BAKERY | The original Bohemian Bakery began in 2010 as a Sunday-only pop-up in the home of co-owners Annie Bakst and Robert Hunt; it quickly became a weekly haunt for expertly made French pastries. The couple now roasts coffee beans in small batches and fills daily orders of rotating favorites, like buttery kougin-am-man and croissants, custard-filled Danishes, and tall slices of cornmeal cake in their shop. **Known for:** seasonal tarts with fresh fruit and pastry cream; croissants of all kinds; coffee roasted in-house. $ *Average main: $8* ⊠ *83 Main St., Montpelier* ☎ *802/461–8119* ⊕ *www. bohemianbakeryvt.com* ⊙ *Closed Mon. and Tues.*

★ Red Hen Baking Co.

$ | CAFÉ | If you're a devotee of artisanal bakeries, it'd be a mistake not to trek the 7-plus miles from Montpelier (15 from Stowe) to have lunch, pick up freshly baked bread, or sample a sweet treat at what many consider Vermont's best bakery. Red Hen supplies bread to some of the state's premier restaurants, including Hen of the Wood, and has varied offerings every day. **Known for:** breads and pastries; local hangout; soups and sandwiches. $ *Average main: $8* ⊠ *961 U.S. 2, Suite B, Middlesex* ☎ *802/223–5200* ⊕ *www.redhenbaking.com* ⊙ *No dinner.*

🛏 Hotels

Capitol Plaza Hotel

$ | HOTEL | Montpelier's only major hotel benefits much from the State House across the street, hosting many of its visiting politicians, lobbyists, and business makers, not to mention tourists seeking a certain quality of accommodation. **Pros:** easy walking distance to all local sights, including bike path; small fitness center; the resident steak house, J. Morgans, serves probably the best cuts in town. **Cons:** somewhat bland design;

slight corporate feel; street-facing room may suffer street and bell-tower noise. $ *Rooms from: $192* ⊠ *100 State St., Montpelier* ☎ *802/223–5252, 800/274–5252* ⊕ *www.capitolplaza.com* ⊅ *65 rooms* ⊙ *No Meals.*

Inn at Montpelier

$$ | B&B/INN | The capital's most charming lodging option, this lovingly tended inn dating to 1830 has rooms filled with antique four-poster beds and Windsor chairs—all have private (if small) baths. **Pros:** beautiful home; relaxed central setting means you can walk everywhere in town; amazing porch. **Cons:** some rooms are small; somewhat bland, traditional design; no tea or coffee in rooms. $ *Rooms from: $200* ⊠ *147 Main St., Montpelier* ☎ *802/223–2727* ⊕ *www. innatmontpelier.com* ⊅ *19 rooms* ⊙ *Free Breakfast.*

🛍 Shopping

AroMed

OTHER SPECIALTY STORE | Although just a small storefront in downtown Montpelier, this shop counts customers as far away as Hawaii, thanks to owner Lauren Andrew's masterful concoctions of lotions, oils, and aromatics. Her CBD- (cannabidiol-) infused versions are particularly popular. ⊠ *8 State St., Montpelier* ☎ *802/505–1405* ⊕ *www. aromedofvt.com.*

Artisans Hand

CRAFTS | For more than 30 years, this craft gallery has been celebrating and supporting Vermont's craft community. The store sells jewelry, textiles, sculptures, and paintings by many local artists. ⊠ *89 Main St., Montpelier* ☎ *802/229–9492* ⊕ *www.artisanshand.com.*

Bear Pond Books

BOOKS | FAMILY | Old-fashioned village bookstores don't get more cute and quaint than this, and locals work hard to keep it that way by actively embracing the printed word. A community hangout, the nearly 50-year-old shop hosts numerous readings by authors, workshops, and book clubs, as well as a significant section of Vermont writers. ⊠ *77 Main St., Montpelier* ☎ *892/229–0774* ⊕ *www.bearpondbooks.com.*

Vermont Creamery

FOOD | A leader in the artisanal cheese movement, this creamery invites aficionados to visit its 4,000-square-foot production facility, where goat cheeses such as Bonne Bouche—a perfectly balanced, cloudlike cheese—are made on weekdays. The creamery is in Websterville, southwest of Montpelier. ⊠ *20 Pitman Rd., Websterville* ☎ *802/479–9371, 800/884–6287* ⊕ *www.vermontcreamery.com.*

Stowe

22 miles northwest of Montpelier, 36 miles east of Burlington.

Long before skiing came to Stowe in the 1930s, the rolling hills and valleys beneath Vermont's highest peak, 4,395-foot Mt. Mansfield, attracted summer tourists looking for a reprieve from city heat. Most stayed at one of two inns in the village of Stowe. When skiing made the town a winter destination, visitors outnumbered hotel beds, so locals took them in. This spirit of hospitality continues, and many of these homes are now country inns. The village itself is tiny—just a few blocks of shops and restaurants clustered around a picture-perfect white church with a lofty steeple—but it serves as the anchor for Mountain Road, which leads north past restaurants, lodges, and shops on its way to Stowe's fabled slopes. The road to Stowe also passes through Waterbury, which is rapidly regenerating thanks to a thriving arts and dining scene.

ESSENTIALS

VISITOR INFORMATION Stowe Area Association. ⊠ *Stowe* ☎ *800/467–8693* ⊕ *www.gostowe.com.*

 Sights

★ Alchemist Brewery

BREWERY | The brewery that launched a beer revolution in Vermont with its "Heady Topper" now welcomes guests to its shop and tasting room (known here as the Beer Cafe). Intense demand still keeps stocks of beer for sale limited. Tours ($25) of the brewery last about 30 minutes and include a commemorative tasting glass and a can of beer; it's best to reserve in advance. ⊠ *100 Cottage Club Rd., Stowe* ☎ *802/882–8165* ⊕ *www.alchemistbeer.com.*

★ Ben & Jerry's Factory

OTHER ATTRACTION | **FAMILY** | The closest thing you'll get to a Willy Wonka experience in Vermont, the 30-minute tours at the famous brand's factory are unabashedly corny and only skim the surface of the behind-the-scenes goings-on, but this flaw is almost forgiven when the samples are dished out. To see the machines at work, visit on a weekday (but call ahead to confirm if they will indeed be in operation). Another highlight is the "Flavor Graveyard," where flavors of yore are given tribute with tombstones inscribed with humorous poetry. Free, family-friendly outdoor movies also play through summer on Friday. ⊠ *1281 Waterbury-Stowe Rd., Waterbury* ☎ *802/882–2047* ⊕ *www.benjerry.com* ⊠ *Tours $6.*

★ Cold Hollow Cider Mill

FARM/RANCH | **FAMILY** | You can watch apples pressed into possibly the world's best cider at this working mill and sample it right from the tank. Its store sells all the apple butter, jams and jellies, and Vermont-made handicrafts you could want, plus the legendary 75¢ cider doughnuts. Kids love watching the "doughnut robot"

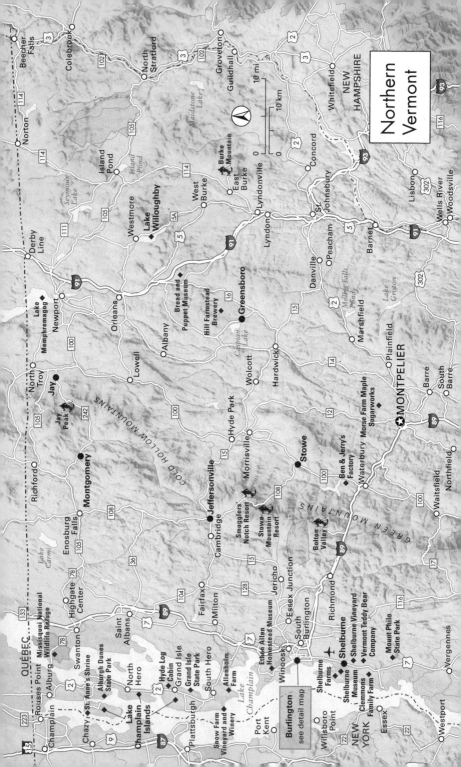

in action. The tasting room is open daily with numerous ciders on tap. ✉ *3600 Waterbury–Stowe Rd., Waterbury Center* ✥ *3 miles north of I–89* ☎ *800/327–7537* 🌐 *www.coldhollow.com.*

Vermont Ski and Snowboard Museum

HISTORY MUSEUM | The state's skiing and snowboarding history is documented here. Exhibits cover subjects such as the 10th Mountain Division of World War II, the national ski patrol, Winter Olympians, and the evolution of equipment. An early World Cup trophy is on loan, and one of the most memorable mobiles you'll ever see, made from a gondola and ski-lift chairs, hangs from the ceiling. One recent exhibit, Slope Style, focused on ski fashion from 1930 to 2014. ✉ *1 S. Main St., Stowe* ☎ *802/253–9911* 🌐 *www.vtssm.com* 🎟 *$5* 🕒 *Closed Mon.-Wed.*

🍴 Restaurants

Cork

$$ | **INTERNATIONAL** | Pursuing a mission that "the best wines are grown, not made," this natural wine bar meticulously curates an inventory of organic, biodynamic, no-additive, unfiltered, and wild-fermented vintages, either for sale in the small retail section in the front, or complementing upscale bistro dishes and boards in the classy dining room. **Known for:** mostly old-world wines, with some local labels; lots of charcuterie and shareable appetizers; in the heart of Stowe village. [$] *Average main: $23* ✉ *35 School St., Stowe* ☎ *802/760–6143* 🌐 *www.corkvt.com* 🕒 *Closed Tues. and Wed.*

Doc Ponds

$$ | **AMERICAN** | A gastropub from the folks behind the Hen of the Wood restaurant, this place has one of the best beer lists in the state. The food is excellent and the ski-lodge vibe is perfect for lunch or dinner, families or romantic two-top or solo bar seats. **Known for:** lengthy local beer list; pub fare with Vermont ingredients; log cabin atmosphere with après-ski coziness. [$] *Average main: $22* ✉ *294 Mountain Rd., Stowe* ☎ *802/760–6066* 🌐 *www.docponds.com.*

Harrison's Restaurant

$$ | **AMERICAN** | A lively locals' scene, booths by the fireplace, and creative American cuisine paired with well-chosen wines and regional brews make this place perfect for couples and families alike. The inviting bar is a good spot to dine alone or to chat with a regular. **Known for:** peanut-butter pie; wine and cocktail list; wood fireplace. [$] *Average main: $23* ✉ *25 Main St., Stowe* ☎ *802/253–7773* 🌐 *www.harrisonsstowe.com* 🕒 *No lunch.*

★ Hen of the Wood

$$$ | **ECLECTIC** | Ask Vermont's great chefs where they go for a tremendous meal, and Hen of the Wood inevitably tops the list, thanks to its sophisticated, almost artful, dishes that showcase an abundance of local produce, meat, and cheese. The utterly romantic candlelit setting is riveting: a converted 1835 gristmill beside a waterfall. **Known for:** special occasions and dates; outstanding cooking; wine and cocktail list. [$] *Average main: $28* ✉ *92 Stowe St., Waterbury* ☎ *802/244–7300* 🌐 *www.henofthewood.com* 🕒 *Closed Sun. and Mon. No lunch.*

Idletyme Brewing Company

$$$ | **AMERICAN** | In prime position on the mountain road and the Stowe Recreation Path, this brewpub's Bavarian-style lagers and Vermont IPAs are only available on-site. A solid menu of pub food, a large outdoor patio, vegetable garden, and a rich, rustic, chic design, make it a popular stop. **Known for:** "brew-ski" beer flights; ample space for large groups; outdoor Biergarten. [$] *Average main: $26* ✉ *1859 Mountain Rd., Stowe* ☎ *802/253–4765* 🌐 *www.idletymebrewing.com.*

Michael's on the Hill

$$$ | EUROPEAN | Swiss-born chef Michael Kloeti trained in Europe and New York City before opening this establishment in a 19th-century farmhouse outside Stowe. The seasonal three-course prix-fixe menus ($45 and $67) blend European cuisine with farm-to-table earthiness, exemplified by dishes such as spice-roasted duck breast and venison *navarin* (ragout). **Known for:** homemade potato gnocchi; wine list; views of Green Mountains and sunsets. $ *Average main: $34* ✉ *4182 Stowe-Waterbury Rd., 6 miles south of Stowe, Waterbury Center* ☎ *802/244–7476* ⊕ *www.michaelsonthehill.com* ◷ *Closed Tues. No lunch.*

★ Prohibition Pig

$ | AMERICAN | This restaurant and brewery in downtown Waterbury is always packed for a reason: fabulous craft beers, sandwiches, salads, and North Carolina–style barbecue served in an airy and friendly bar and dining room. If you just want a quick bite and a draft, belly up to the tasting-room bar at the brewery in the back, or pop across the street to the Craft Beer Cellar, one of the state's best beer stores. **Known for:** duck-fat fries; "craft" mac and cheese; one of the state's best draft lists and liquor collections. $ *Average main: $15* ✉ *23 S. Main St., Waterbury* ☎ *802/244–4120* ⊕ *www.prohibitionpig. com* ◷ *Closed Tues. and Wed.*

von Trapp Brewery & Bierhall

$$ | AUSTRIAN | In 2016, the Von Trapp family finally realized its long-held dream of opening a brewery making Austrian-style lagers on the grounds, and what a brewery it is. Built of thick, massive Vermont wood beams, the cavernous chalet-style space houses a rustic-chic restaurant and bar alongside the beer-making facilities serving Germanic classics, with plenty of beer to wash it down. **Known for:** Bavarian pretzels with beer-cheese dip; chicken schnitzel; Sachertorte and apple strudel. $ *Average main: $20* ✉ *1333 Luce Hill Rd., Stowe* ☎ *802/253–5750* ⊕ *www. vontrappbrewing.com.*

Zen Barn

$$ | ECLECTIC | What's more Vermont than the name "Zen Barn," especially when it includes its own yoga studio in a former hayloft? Add to that an expansive, rustic-chic interior with local art and a stage for live music, an outdoor patio looking out to green fields and mountains, and a menu of eclectic, farm-to-table fare, and the local experience is complete. **Known for:** CBD cocktails; ramen soup; live performances. $ *Average main: $18* ✉ *179 Guptil Rd., Waterbury* ☎ *802/244–8134* ⊕ *www.zenbarnvt.com.*

☕ Coffee and Quick Bites

PK Coffee

$ | CAFÉ | The inviting atmosphere of this neighborhood joint is increased by the beans they use—North Carolina–based roasters Counter Culture Coffee, known for its coffee education and sustainable sourcing. Milk comes from Sweet Rowen Farmstead, and rotating breakfast sandwiches and baked goods, like buttermilk banana bread, are made in-house. **Known for:** maple lattes; expertly made espresso and drip coffee; baked goods and breakfast sandwiches. $ *Average main: $5* ✉ *1940 Mountain Rd., Stowe* ☎ *802/760–6151* ⊕ *pkcoffee.com.*

🛏 Hotels

Field Guide Lodge

$ | HOTEL | This boutique enterprise just north of Stowe village is a whimsically stylish alternative to the town's staid resorts and cadre of inns stuck in ski-chalet mold. **Pros:** waffle kimono robes; seasonal heated pool and hot tub; Trail Suite, with a loft bedroom and view of Stowe's iconic white church. **Cons:** unique style not for everyone; no elevator; no coffee/tea in rooms. $ *Rooms from: $110* ✉ *433*

Continued on page 130

LET IT SNOW

WINTER ACTIVITIES IN VERMONT

SKIING AND SNOWBOARDING IN VERMONT

Less than 5 miles from the Canadian border, Jay Peak is Vermont's northernmost ski resort.

Ever since America's first ski tow opened in a farmer's pasture near Woodstock in January 1934, skiers have headed en masse to Vermont in winter. Today, 19 alpine and 30 nordic ski areas range in size and are spread across the state, from Mount Snow in the south to Jay Peak near the Canadian border. The snow-making equipment has also become more comprehensive over the years, with more than 80% of the trails in the state using man-made snow. Here are some of the best ski areas by various categories:

GREAT FOR KIDS Smugglers' Notch, Okemo, and **Bromley Mountain** all offer terrific kids' programs, with classes organized by age categories and by skill level. Kids as young as 3 (4 at some ski areas) can start learning. Child care, with activities like stories, singing, and arts and crafts, are available for those too young to ski; some ski areas, like Smuggler's Notch, offer babysitting with no minimum age daytime and evening.

BEST FOR BEGINNERS Beginner terrain makes up nearly half of the mountain at **Stratton**, where options include private and group lessons for first-timers. Also good are small but family-friendly **Bolton Valley** and **Bromley Mountains,** which both designate a third of their slopes for beginners.

EXPERT TERRAIN The slopes at **Jay Peak** and massive **Killington** are most notable for their steepness and pockets of glades. About 40% of the runs at these two resorts are advanced or expert. Due to its far north location, Jay Peak tends to get the most snow, making it ideal for powder days. Another favorite with advanced skiers is Central Vermont's **Mad River Glen,** where many slopes are ungroomed (natural) and the motto is "Ski it if you can." In addition, **Sugarbush, Stowe,** and **Smugglers' Notch** are all revered for their challenging untamed side country.

Mount Mansfield is better known as Stowe.   Stratton Mountain clocktower

NIGHT SKIING Come late afternoon, **Bolton Valley** is hopping. That's because it's the only location in Vermont for night skiing. Ski and ride under the lights from 4 until 8 Wednesday through Saturday, followed by a later après-ski scene.

APRÈS-SKI The social scenes at **Killington, Sugarbush,** and **Stowe** are the most noteworthy (and crowded). Stop by Stowe's Doc Ponds for one of the best beer lists around. For live music, try Castlerock Pub in Sugarbush or the Matterhorn Bar in Stowe.

SNOWBOARDING Boarders (and some skiers) will love the latest features for freestyle tricks in Vermont. **Stratton** has four terrain parks for all abilities, one of which features a boarder cross course. **Mount Snow's** Carinthia Peak is an all-terrain park–dedicated mountain, the only of its kind in New England. Head to **Killington** for Burton Stash, another beautiful all-natural features terrain park. **Okemo** has

a superpipe and eight terrain parks and a gladed park with all-natural features. Note that snowboarding is not allowed at skiing cooperative **Mad River Glen.**

CROSS-COUNTRY To experience the best of cross-country skiing in the state, simply follow the Catamount Trail, a 300-mile nordic route from southern Vermont to Canada. **The Trapp Family Lodge** in Stowe has 37 miles of groomed cross-country trails and 62 miles of back-country trails. Another top option is **The Mountain Top Inn & Resort,** just outside of Killington. Its Nordic Ski and Snowshoe Center provides instruction for newcomers, along with hot drinks and lunches when it is time to take a break and warm up.

TELEMARK Ungroomed snow and tree skiing are a natural fit with free-heel skiing at **Mad River Glen. Bromley** and **Jay Peak** also have telemark rentals and instruction.

MOUNTAIN-RESORT TRIP PLANNER

TIMING

Snow Season. Winter sports time is typically from Thanksgiving through April, weather permitting. Holidays are the most crowded.

March Madness. Most of the season's snow tends to come in March, so that's the time to go if you want to ski on fresh, nature-made powder. To increase your odds, choose a ski area in the northern part of the state.

Summer Scene. During summertime, many ski resorts reinvent themselves as prime destinations for golfers, zipline and canopy tours, mountain bikers, and weddings. Other summer visitors come to the mountains to enjoy hiking trails, climbing walls, aquatic centers, chairlift and horseback rides, or a variety of festivals.

Avoid Long Lift Lines. Try to hit the slopes early—many lifts start at 8 or 9 am, with ticket windows opening a half-hour earlier. Then take a mid-morning break as lines start to get longer and head out again when others come in for lunch.

SAVINGS TIPS

Choose a Condo. Especially if you're planning to stay for a week, save money on food by opting for a condominum unit with a kitchen. You can shop at the supermarket and cook breakfast and dinner.

Rent Smart. Consider ski rental options in the villages rather than those at the mountain. Renting right at the ski area may be more convenient, but it may also cost more.

Discount Lift Tickets. Online tickets are often the least expensive; multi-day discounts and and ski-and-stay packages will also lower your costs. Good for those who can plan ahead, early-bird tickets often go on sale before the ski season even starts.

Hit the Peaks Off-peak. In order to secure the best deals at the most competitive rates, avoid booking during school holidays. President's Week in February is the busiest, because that's when Northeastern schools have their spring break.

Top left, Killington's six mountains make up the largest ski area in Vermont. Top right, Stratton has a Snowboard-cross course.

THINK WARM THOUGHTS

It can get cold on the slopes, so be prepared. Consider proper face warmth and smart layering, plus ski-specific socks, or purchase a pair each of inexpensive hand and feet warmers that fit easily in your gloves and boots. Helmets, which can also be rented, provide not only added safety but warmth.

VERMONT SKI AREAS BY THE NUMBERS

Okemo's wide slopes attract snowbirds to Ludlow in Central Vermont.

Numbers are a helpful way to compare mountains, but remember that each resort has a distinct personality. This list is composed of ski areas in Vermont with at least 100 skiable acres. For more information, see individual resort listings.

SKI AREA	Vertical Drop	Skiable Acres	# of Trails & Lifts	Terrain Type ○	■	◆/◆◆	Snowboarding Options
Bolton Valley	1704	300	70/6	36%	37%	27%	Terrain Park
Bromley Mountain	1334	178	47/9	30%	36%	34%	Terrain Park
Burke Mountain	2011	270	50/6	10%	44%	46%	Terrain Park
Jay Peak Resort	2153	385	78/22	22%	39%	41%	Terrain Park
Killington Resort	3050	1509	155/21	17%	40%	43%	Terrain Park, Halfpipe
Mad River Glen	2037	115	52/5	30%	30%	40%	Snowboarding Not Allowed
Magic Mountain	1500	205	50/6	26%	30%	44%	Terrain Park
Mount Snow Resort	1700	588	80/20	14%	73%	13%	Terrain Park, Halfpipe
Okemo	2200	655	120/19	31%	38%	31%	Terrain Park, Superpipe, TerrainCross Park
Pico Mountain	1967	468	58/7	18%	46%	36%	Triple Slope, Terrain Park
Smugglers' Notch Resort	2610	311	78/8	19%	50%	31%	Terrain Park
Stowe Mountain Resort	2160	485	116/13	16%	59%	25%	Terrain Park
Stratton Mountain Resort	2003	670	99/11	40%	30%	25%	Terrain Park, Halfpipe, SnowboardCross Course
Sugarbush Resort	2600	578	111/16	20%	45%	30%	Terrain Park
Suicide Six	650	100	24/3	30%	40%	30%	Terrain Park

CONTACT THE EXPERTS

Ski Vermont (☎ *802/223-2439* ⊕ *www. skivermont.com*), a non-profit association in Montpelier, Vermont, and **Vermont Department of Tourism** (⊕ *www.vermontvacation. com*) are great resources for travelers planning a wintertime trip to Vermont.

KNOW YOUR SIGNS

On trail maps and the mountains, trails are rated and marked:

● Beginner   ◆ Advanced

■ Intermediate   ◆◆ Expert

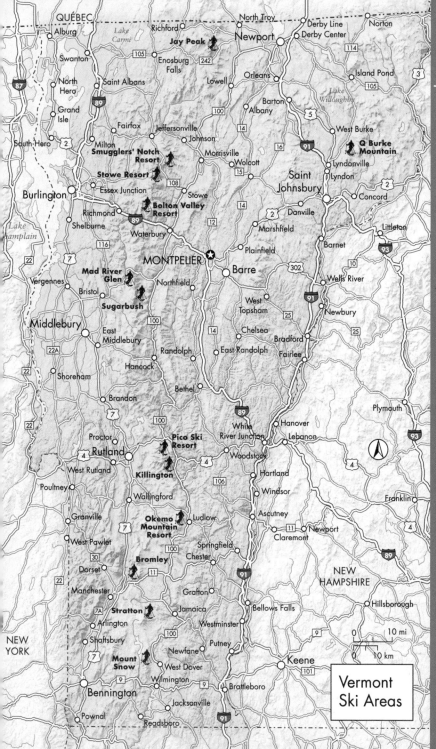

QUÉBEC

Alburg

Richford
North Troy
Newport
Derby Line
Derby Center
Norton

Swanton
Jay Peak
Enosburg Falls

105

242

North Hero

Saint Albans

87

89

Lowell
Orleans

Barton
Albany

West Burke

Island Pond

105

3

Grand Isle

Fairfax
Jeffersonville
Johnson
Morrisville
Wolcott

100

14

16

91

5

Lake Willoughby

Q Burke Mountain

South Hero

Milton
Smugglers' Notch Resort

2

15

Lyndonville

Lyndon

2

Burlington

Essex Junction
Stowe Resort

108

Stowe

Saint Johnsbury

Concord

Richmond
Bolton Valley Resort

89

Waterbury

14

12

2

Danville

Marshfield

Barnet

Littleton

93

Shelburne

Lake Champlain

116

7

MONTPELIER

Plainfield

302

10

Wells River

91

22

Mad River Glen

Northfield

Barre

West Topsham

Newbury

25

Vergennes

Bristol

Sugarbush

25

Middlebury

East Middlebury

100

14

Chelsea

Bradford

Fairlee

22A

Randolph
East Randolph

7

Shoreham

Hancock

Bethel

Plymouth

22

Brandon

7

100

89

Proctor

Pico Ski Resort

White River Junction

Hanover

Lebanon

93

Rutland

Woodstock

4

West Rutland

4

Killington

106

Hartland

4

Poultney

Wallingford

Windsor

Franklin

Granville

7

Okemo Mountain Resort

Ludlow

Ascutney

11

Newport

4

West Pawlet

30

100

Springfield
Chester

Claremont

Dorset

Bromley

11

Grafton

NEW HAMPSHIRE

Manchester

22

Stratton

Jamaica

Bellows Falls

Hillsborough

7A

Arlington

Westminster

Shaftsbury

100

Putney

9

NEW YORK

7

Mount Snow

Newfane

Keene

West Dover

101

Bennington

9

Wilmington

9

Brattleboro

Jacksonville

Pownal

91

Readsboro

0 ——— 10 mi

0 ——— 10 km

Vermont Ski Areas

Mountain Rd., Stowe ☎ 802/253–8088 🌐 https://www.larkhotels.com/hotels/field-guide-lodge 🛏 30 rooms 🍴 Free Breakfast.

Green Mountain Inn

$ | **B&B/INN** | Smack-dab in the center of Stowe Village, this classic redbrick inn has been welcoming guests since 1833; rooms in the main building and the annex feel like a country inn, while the newer buildings refine with added luxury and space. **Pros:** easy walking distance to entire village and main sights; luxury rooms include large Jacuzzis; 300-thread-count Egyptian cotton bedding and Frette bathrobes. **Cons:** farther from skiing than other area hotels; road noise in front of building; no tea in rooms. [$] *Rooms from: $169 ✉ 18 Main St., Stowe ☎ 802/253–7301, 800/253–7302 🌐 www.greenmountaininn.com 🛏 104 rooms 🍴 No Meals.*

Stone Hill Inn

$$$ | **B&B/INN** | A contemporary, romance-inducing bed-and-breakfast where classical music plays in the hallways, Stone Hill has guest rooms with two-sink vanities and two-person whirlpools in front of double-sided fireplaces. **Pros:** perennial gardens with stream; complimentary toboggan and snowshoes; Gilchrist & Soames bathroom amenities. **Cons:** possibly depressing for single people; two-night minimum on weekends and in peak period; no children allowed. [$] *Rooms from: $309 ✉ 89 Houston Farm Rd., Stowe ☎ 802/253–6282 🌐 www.stonehillinn.com 🛏 9 rooms 🍴 Free Breakfast.*

Stowe Motel & Snowdrift

$ | **HOTEL** | **FAMILY** | The accommodations at this family-owned motel on 14 acres range from studios with small kitchenettes and modern two-bedroom suites warmed by their own fireplaces to rental houses that can sleep 10 or more people. **Pros:** good value for cost; complimentary bikes; 16 acres of landscaped grounds next to river. **Cons:** basic motel-style accommodations; design and furnishings could use an update; occasional road noise. [$] *Rooms from: $149 ✉ 2043 Mountain Rd., Stowe ☎ 802/253–7629, 800/829–7629 🌐 www.stowemotel.com 🛏 62 rooms 🍴 Free Breakfast.*

★ **Spruce Peak**

$$ | **RESORT** | At the base of Mount Mansfield and Spruce Peak, this lodge would be king of the hill for its location alone, but a stay here also affords many perks including dining outposts like Tipsy Trout and Alpine Hall and rustic-meets-contemporary accommodations that run the gamut from studios and four-bedroom penthouse units to modern slopeside condos. **Pros:** mountain views; lots of children's activities; many shops supply all needs. **Cons:** somewhat sterile feel; no separate kids' pool; expensive breakfast. [$] *Rooms from: $269 ✉ 7412 Mountain Rd., Stowe ☎ 802/253–3560, 888/478–6938 reservations 🌐 www.sprucepeak.com 🛏 300 rooms 🍴 No Meals.*

Stoweflake Mountain Resort and Spa

$ | **RESORT** | With one of the largest spas in the area, Stoweflake lets you enjoy an herb-and-flower labyrinth, a fitness center reached via a covered bridge, and a hydrotherapy waterfall that cascades into a hot tub. **Pros:** walking distances to many restaurants; wide range of rooms; across the street from the recreation path. **Cons:** mazelike layout can make rooms a bit hard to find; uninspired room design; no tea in rooms. [$] *Rooms from: $198 ✉ 1746 Mountain Rd., Stowe ☎ 800/253–2232 🌐 www.stoweflake.com 🛏 180 rooms 🍴 No Meals.*

Sun & Ski Inn and Suites

$ | **HOTEL** | Not many hotels can boast having a bowling alley, but this part-new, part-renovated inn can top even that, adding an 18-hole minigolf course, an indoor pool, and small fitness center. **Pros:** close to the slopes; the family-friendly restaurant is open daily for lunch and dinner; tea/coffeemakers in rooms. **Cons:** not very Vermonty; family friendly can mean lots of children; often two-night minimum stay. $ Rooms from: $189 ☒ 1613 Mountain Rd., Stowe ☎ 802/253–7159, 800/448–5223 ⊕ www.sunandskiinn.com ➴ 39 rooms ⦿ Free Breakfast.

★ Topnotch Resort

$$$ | RESORT | FAMILY | On 120 acres overlooking Mt. Mansfield, this posh property has a contemporary look, excellent dining options, and one of the best spas in Vermont, which combine to create a world unto itself. **Pros:** ski shuttle will take you directly to the slopes; complimentary tea and cookies every afternoon; American bistro cuisine at the intimate Flannel or tuned-up bar bites at the Roost, the lively lobby bar. **Cons:** boutique style may not be for everyone; no tea in rooms; room rates fluctuate wildly. $ Rooms from: $350 ☒ 4000 Mountain Rd., Stowe ☎ 800/451–8686, 802/253–8585 ⊕ www. topnotchresort.com ➴ 91 rooms ⦿ No Meals.

★ Trapp Family Lodge

$$ | RESORT | FAMILY | Built by the Von Trapp family (of The Sound of Music fame), this Tyrolean lodge is surrounded by some of the best mountain views in Vermont and abundant romantic ambience, making it a favorite for weddings. **Pros:** alive with the sound of music; excellent beer brewed on-site; concert series and festivals in warm weather. **Cons:** some sections appear tired and in need of updating; overrun by tourists, especially on weekends; if not an active person, you'll miss half the amenities. $ Rooms from: $225 ☒ 700 Trapp Hill Rd., Stowe ☎ 802/253–8511, 800/826–7000 ⊕ www.trappfamily. com ➴ 214 rooms ⦿ No Meals.

🎭 Performing Arts

The Current

ARTS CENTERS | Above the local library, Stowe's premier art center hosts impressive rotating exhibitions of contemporary and local art throughout the year, as well as film screenings. It also provides art education to adults and children alike through workshops, lectures, events, and courses. ☒ 90 Pond St., Stowe ☎ 802/253–8358 ⊕ www.helenday.com.

Spruce Peak Performing Arts Center

CONCERTS | Part of the Spruce Peak complex, this state-of-the-art space hosts theater, music, and dance performances. ☒ 122 Hourglass Dr., Stowe ☎ 802/760–4634 ⊕ www.sprucepeakarts.org.

🛍 Shopping

CRAFTS

Jeremy Ayers Pottery

CERAMICS | One of Vermont's most skilled and distinctive potters welcomes visitors to his shop and studio in downtown Waterbury. Keep an eye out for his Waterbury Breakfast Club, which adds food trucks and artists every other Sunday, June–September. A few apartments are also available to rent in the guesthouse; the on-site venue space, 18 Elm, is open for dinner parties and special occasion events. ☒ 18 Elm St., Waterbury ☎ 802/363–3592 ⊕ www. jeremyayerspottery.com.

FOOD

Cabot Cheese Annex Store

FOOD | In addition to shelves of Vermont-made jams, mustards, crackers, and maple products, the store features a long central table with samples of a dozen Cabot cheeses. ☒ 2657 Waterbury–Stowe Rd., 2½ miles north of I-89, Stowe ☎ 802/244–6334 ⊕ www. cabotcheese.coop.

🏃 Activities

CANOEING AND KAYAKING

Umiak Outdoor Outfitters

CANOEING & ROWING | This full-service outfitter rents canoes and kayaks, organizes tours, and sells equipment. It has seasonal outposts at the Waterbury Reservoir and at North Beach in Burlington. ☒ 849 S. Main St., Stowe ☎ 802/253–2317 ⊕ www.umiak.com.

FISHING

The Fly Rod Shop

FISHING | This shop provides a guide service, offers introductory classes, and rents tackle and other equipment. ✉ *2703 Waterbury Rd., 1½ miles south of Stowe, Stowe* ☎ *802/253–7346* ⊕ *www.flyrodshop.com.*

HIKING

Moss Glen Falls

HIKING & WALKING | Four miles outside of town, this short hike leads to a stupendous 125-foot waterfall that makes a great way to cool down in summer. ✉ *615 Moss Glen Falls Rd., Stowe* ☎ *888/409–7579 Vermont State Parks* ⊕ *www.vtstateparks.com.*

Mt. Mansfield

HIKING & WALKING | Ascending Mt. Mansfield, Vermont's highest mountain, makes for a challenging day hike. Trails lead from Mountain Road to the summit, where they meet the north–south Long Trail. Views encompass New Hampshire's White Mountains, New York's Adirondacks, and southern Québec. The Green Mountain Club publishes a trail guide. ✉ *Trailheads along Mountain Rd., Stowe* ☎ *802/244–7037* ⊕ *www.greenmountainclub.org.*

★ Stowe Recreation Path

HIKING & WALKING | An immaculately maintained, paved recreation path begins behind the Community Church in town and meanders about 5 miles along the river valley, with many entry points along the way. Whether you're on foot, skis, bike, or in-line skates, it's a tranquil spot to enjoy the outdoors. In autumn, there's a corn maze, and at least four shops along the path rent bikes. ✉ *Stowe* ⊕ *www.stowerec.org.*

SKIING

Stowe Mountain Resort

SKIING & SNOWBOARDING | The name of the village is Stowe, and the name of the mountain is Mt. Mansfield—but to generations of skiers, it's all just plain "Stowe." The area's mystique attracts as many serious skiers as social ones. Stowe is a giant among Eastern ski mountains with intimidating expert runs, but its symmetrical shape allows skiers of all abilities to enjoy long, satisfying runs from the summit. Improved snowmaking capacity, new lifts, and free shuttle buses that gather skiers along Mountain Road have made it all much more convenient. Yet the traditions remain, like the Winter Carnival in January and the Sugar Slalom in April, to name two. Spruce Peak, where you'll find the Adventure Center and the Mountain Lodge, is separate from the main mountain; the peak has a teaching hill and offers a pleasant experience for intermediates and beginners. In the summer, there's a Tree Top Adventure course and an awe-inspiring zipline that extends from the top of the gondola to the bottom in three breathtaking runs. **Facilities:** 116 trails; 485 acres; 2,160-foot vertical drop; 13 lifts. ✉ *5781 Mountain Rd., Stowe* ☎ *802/253–3000, 802/253–3600 for snow conditions* ⊕ *www.stowe.com* 🎟 *Lift ticket: $199.*

SPAS

Spa and Wellness Center at Spruce Peak

SPAS | This 21,000-square-foot facility has 18 private treatment rooms, a fitness center, and a year-round outdoor pool and hot tub. In addition to the usual array of facials, scrubs, and massages for adults, the spa offers a separate program for kids. ✉ *Spruce Peak, 7412 Mountain Rd., Stowe* ☎ *802/760–4782* ⊕ *www.spruce-peak.com.*

Spa at Stoweflake

SPAS | One of the largest spas in New England, the Spa at Stoweflake features a massaging hydrotherapeutic waterfall, a Hungarian mineral pool, 30 treatment rooms, and more than 150 treatments like the Bingham Falls Renewal, named after a local waterfall. This treatment begins with a body scrub and a Vichy shower, followed by an aromatherapy oil massage. The spacious men's and women's sanctuaries have saunas, steam rooms, and whirlpool tubs. ✉ *Stoweflake Mountain Resort and Spa, 1746 Mountain Rd., Stowe* ☎ *802/760–1083* 🌐 *www.stoweflake.com.*

Spa at Topnotch

SPAS | Calm pervades the Spa at Topnotch, with its birchwood doors, natural light, and cool colors. Signature treatments include the Mt. Mansfield Saucha, a three-stage herbal body treatment, and the Little River Stone Massage, which uses the resort's own wood-spice oil. There's even Rover Reiki (really) for your canine friend. Locker areas are spacious, with saunas, steam rooms, and whirlpool tubs. The indoor pool has lots of natural light. Daily classes in tai chi, yoga, and Pilates are offered in the nearby fitness center. ✉ *Topnotch Resort and Spa, 4000 Mountain Rd., Stowe* ☎ *802/253–6463* 🌐 *www.topnotchresort.com.*

Jeffersonville

18 miles north of Stowe.

Jeffersonville is just over Smugglers' Notch from Stowe but miles away in feeling and attitude. In summer, you can drive over the notch road as it curves precipitously around boulders that have fallen from the cliffs above, then pass open meadows and old farmhouses and sugar shacks on the way down to town. Below the notch, Smugglers' Notch Ski Resort is the hub of activity year-round. Downtown Jeffersonville, once home to an artists' colony, is quiet but has excellent dining and nice art galleries.

GETTING HERE AND AROUND

Like most places in Vermont, a car is essential to explore this area. From Burlington, it's about a 45-minute drive along Route 15. Or you can cruise north on Route 108 from Stowe for 30 minutes; however, the road is closed for much of the winter.

Sights

Stella14 Wines

WINERY | Master Sommelier David Keck moved home to Vermont in 2020 and started making wine with grapes from one of the state's oldest vineyards at Boyden Valley Winery. Now, Stella14's full lineup — from effervescent, lively pet-nats to intense, serious Frontenac Noir — is poured by the glass in the cozy tasting room or out on its large back patio and lawn. Wines from other Vermont producers such as La Garagista Farm + Winery, Ellison Estate Vineyard, and Iapetus are available for side-by-side tasting, too. ✉ *105 Main St., Jeffersonville* ☎ *832/431–1301* 🌐 *www.stella14wines.com* 🕒 *Closed Sun.–Wed.*

Coffee and Quick Bites

Burger Barn

$ | **AMERICAN** | **FAMILY** | Local grass-fed burgers and handcut fries are the name of the game at this bright-green food truck. Try one of Burger Barn's more inventive offshoots, like the Nutty Goat: goat cheese, maple crushed walnuts, caramelized onions, bacon and mayo. **Known for:** grass-fed burgers; food truck atmosphere and outside dining; cash only. [$] *Average main: $8* ✉ *4968 Rte. 15, Jeffersonville* ☎ *802/730–3441* 💳 *No credit cards.*

Hotels

★ Smugglers' Notch Resort

$$$ | **RESORT** | **FAMILY** | With five giant water parks for summer fun and just about every winter activity imaginable, including the new 26,000-square-foot indoor "FunZone 2.0," this resort is ideal for families; nightly rates include lift tickets, lessons, and all resort amenities. **Pros:** great place for families to learn to ski; views of several mountains; shuttles to the slopes. **Cons:** not a romantic getaway for couples; extra cost for daily cleaning; very busy during peak season.

$ *Rooms from: $322* ✉ *4323 Rte. 108 S, Jeffersonville* ☎ *802/332–6841, 800/419–4615* ⊕ *www.smuggs.com* � *600 condominiums* ⊙| *No Meals.*

🛍 Shopping

ANTIQUES

Route 15 between Jeffersonville and Johnson is dubbed the "antiques highway."

Buggy Man

ANTIQUES & COLLECTIBLES | This store sells all sorts of collectibles, including horse-drawn vehicles. ✉ *853 Rte. 15, 7 miles east of Jeffersonville, Johnson* ☎ *802/635–2110.*

CLOTHING

★ **Johnson Woolen Mills**

SHOPPING CENTER | This factory store has great deals on woolen blankets, household goods, and the famous Johnson outerwear. ✉ *51 Lower Main St. E, 9 miles east of Jeffersonville, Johnson* ☎ *802/635–2271* ⊕ *www.johnsonwoolenmills.com.*

🏃 Activities

KAYAKING

Vermont Canoe and Kayak

KAYAKING | This outfitter rents canoes and kayaks for use on the Lamoille River, and leads guided canoe trips to Boyden Valley Winery. ✉ *4805 Rte. 15, behind the Family Table, Jeffersonville* ☎ *802/644–8336* ⊕ *vtcanoeandkayak.com* ⊙ *Closed mid-Sept.–late May.*

TOURS

Northern Vermont Llama Co.

SPECIAL-INTEREST TOURS | These llamas carry everything, including snacks and lunches, for half-day treks along the trails of Smugglers' Notch. Reservations are essential. ✉ *766 Lapland Rd., Waterville* ☎ *802/644–2257* ⊕ *www.northernvermontllamaco.com* ➣ *$60* ⊙ *Closed early Sept.–late May.*

SKIING

Smugglers' Notch

SKIING & SNOWBOARDING | FAMILY |
The "granddaddy of all family resorts," Smugglers' Notch (or "Smuggs") receives consistent praise for its family programs. Its children's ski school is one of the best in the country—possibly *the* best—and there are challenges for skiers of all levels, spread over three separate areas. There's ice-skating, tubing, seven terrain parks, Nordic skiing, snowshoe trails, and a snowboarding area for kids ages 2½–6. Summer brings waterslides, treetop courses, ziplines, and crafts workshops—in other words, something for everyone. **Facilities:** 78 trails; 300 acres; 2,610-foot vertical drop; 8 lifts. ✉ *4323 Rte. 108 S, Jeffersonville* ☎ *802/332–6854, 800/419–4615* ⊕ *www.smuggs.com* ➣ *Lift ticket: $85.*

Burlington

31 miles southwest of Jeffersonville, 76 miles south of Montréal, 349 miles north of New York City, 223 miles northwest of Boston.

As you drive along Main Street toward downtown Burlington, it's easy to see why this three-college city is often called one of the most livable small cities in the United States. Downtown Burlington is filled with hip restaurants and bars, art galleries, and vinyl-record shops. At the heart is the Church Street Marketplace, a bustling pedestrian mall with trendy shops, crafts vendors, street performers, and sidewalk cafés. To the west, Lake Champlain shimmers beneath the towering Adirondacks on the New York shore and provides the best sunsets in the state. The revitalized Burlington waterfront teems with outdoors enthusiasts who bike or stroll along its recreation path, picnic on the grass, and ply the waters in sailboats and motor craft in summer.

To the north, the eclectic enclave of Winooski, a newly refurbished former mill town, houses its own cadre of interesting bars, cafés, shops, and eateries.

◉ Sights

★ Burlington Farmers Market
MARKET | Burlington's Saturday farmers' market is an absolute must-see when visiting in summer or fall. Set up in a spacious lot in the city's South End, the market is jam-packed with local farmers selling a colorful array of organic produce, flowers, baked goods, maple syrup, meats, cheeses, and prepared foods. Local artisans also sell their wares, and there's live music. ✉ *345 Pine St., Burlington* ☎ *802/310–5172* ⊕ *www. burlingtonfarmersmarket.org* 🖃 *Free.*

★ Church Street Marketplace
MARKET | **FAMILY** | For nearly 40 years, this pedestrian-only thoroughfare has served as Burlington's center of commerce, dining, and entertainment, with boutiques, cafés, restaurants, and street vendors the focus by day, and a lively bar and music scene at night. On sunny days, there are few better places to be in Burlington. ✉ *2 Church St., Burlington* ☎ *802/863–1648* ⊕ *www.churchstmarketplace.com.*

ECHO Leahy Center for Lake Champlain
SCIENCE MUSEUM | **FAMILY** | Kids and adults can explore the geology and ecology of the Lake Champlain region through the center's more than 100 interactive exhibits, including the newest additions at the Action Lab. The lab's 3D Water Projection Sandbox manages to make learning about watersheds exciting. You can also get an up-close look at 70 species of indigenous animals, or immerse digitally in the natural world at the 3D theater, which presents science and nature films every day. ✉ *1 College St., Burlington* ☎ *802/864–1848* ⊕ *www.echovermont. org* 🖃 *$18.*

Ethan Allen Homestead Museum
HISTORY MUSEUM | When Vermont hero Ethan Allen retired from his Revolutionary activities, he purchased 350 acres along the Winooski River and built this modest cabin in 1787. The original structure is a real slice of 18th-century life, including such frontier hallmarks as saw-cut boards and an open hearth for cooking. The kitchen garden resembles the one the Allens would have had. There's also a visitor center and miles of biking and hiking trails. In warmer months, climb Ethan Allen Tower at the south end of neighboring Ethan Allen Park for stupendous views of Lake Champlain and the Green Mountains.

■ **TIP→ Don't forget mosquito repellent.**
✉ *1 Ethan Allen Homestead, off Rte. 127, Burlington* ☎ *802/865–4556* ⊕ *www.ethanallenhomestead.org* 🖃 *$15* ⊙ *Closed Nov.–Apr.*

★ Foam Brewers
BREWERY | Co-founder and acclaimed brewer Todd Haire spent 13 years at Magic Hat Brewing and another two years at Switchback before opening his own Burlington operation alongside fellow co-founders Bobby Grim, Sam Keane, Jon Farmer, and Dani Casey in 2016. Since then, Foam has gained international praise, including a spot as one of the world's 10 best new breweries—bestowed by BeerAdvocate—the year they opened. Snack boards and food truck pit-stops compliment their sought-after drafts, also available at the attached sister restaurant, Deep City. An outdoor patio faces the stunning views of the Lake Champlain Waterfront. ✉ *112 Lake St., Burlington* ☎ *802/399–2511* ⊕ *www.foambrewers.com.*

Green Mountain Audubon Nature Center
SCIENCE MUSEUM | **FAMILY** | This is a wonderful place to discover Vermont's outdoor wonders. The center's 255 acres of diverse habitats are a sanctuary for all things wild, and the 5 miles of trails provide an opportunity to explore the

4

Vermont BURLINGTON

workings of differing natural communities. Events include bird-monitoring walks, wildflower rambles, nature workshops, and educational activities for children and adults. ✉ *255 Sherman Hollow Rd., 18 miles southeast of Burlington, Huntington* ☎ *802/434–3068* ⊕ *vt. audubon.org* 🗺 *Donations accepted.*

Pine Street

NEIGHBORHOOD | A once-abandoned relic of the Industrial Revolution, Pine Street is the heartbeat of Burlington's recently revamped South End Arts District, an enclave of bars, restaurants, breweries, art galleries, and eateries. Start at the intersection of Pine and Maple Street and begin walking south to find a treasure trove of all things art, music, food, and drink. Dedalus Wine Market & Bar has one of the most expansive selections of natural wine on the East Coast. Myers Bagels has been turning out wood-fired, Montréal-style bagels for over twenty years. The S.P.A.C.E Gallery and Conant Metal & Light attract artists from within state borders and far beyond, and the popular restaurant and performance venue ArtsRiot hosts weekly food truck celebrations in the warmer months. Make sure to stop by The Soda Plant, a small business incubator with over thirty local artisans, artists, and makers inside a newly refurbished 19th-century industrial soda factory, including nationally acclaimed Brio Coffeeworks. ✉ *Pine St., between Maple and Flynn, Burlington.*

Switchback Brewing Co.

BREWERY | Switchback may not get as much press as other more famous craft Vermont beers, but it's a solid, respected brew that's well worth exploring at the brewery and taproom in Burlington's buzzing South End. In addition to superfresh beer right from the tap and a short but savory menu of bar bites, the space hosts regular events and live music throughout the year. ✉ *160 Flynn Ave., Burlington* ☎ *802/651–4114* ⊕ *www. switchbackvt.com.*

University of Vermont

COLLEGE | Crowning the hilltop above Burlington is the University of Vermont, known as UVM for the abbreviation of its Latin name, Universitas Viridis Montis, meaning the University of the Green Mountains. With nearly 12,000 students, this is the state's principal institution of higher learning. The most architecturally impressive buildings face the main campus green and have gorgeous lake views, as does the statue of founder Ira Allen, Ethan's brother. ✉ *85 S. Prospect St., Burlington* ☎ *802/656–3131* ⊕ *www. uvm.edu.*

★ Waterfront Park

CITY PARK | This formerly derelict industrial district and railroad depot underwent a remarkable transformation in the late '80s and early '90s into a gorgeous stretch of green, with a boardwalk lapped by the lake. It's also a linchpin for a number of sights and facilities, with the Echo Center on the south end, a bodacious skate park on the north, and the Burlington Bike Path running through it all. Sunsets are particularly popular. ✉ *10 College St., Burlington* ☎ *802/864–0123 City of Burlington Parks, Recreation & Waterfront* ⊕ *www.enjoyburlington.com* 🗺 *Free.*

Zero Gravity Beer Hall

BREWERY | What started as a single bar tap in a pizza restaurant has turned into one of Burlington's most successful and hippest beers, thanks to frothy gems like Conehead and Green State Lager. Its shiny new brewery in the South End Arts District is always buzzing—and starts that buzz first thing in the morning with coffee and waffles. Tasty complements continue throughout the day with items like bratwurst, crispy cheddar curds, and foodie-friendly bistro bites. ✉ *716 Pine St., Burlington* ☎ *802/497–0054* ⊕ *www. zerogravitybeer.com.*

Beaches

North Beach

BEACH | FAMILY | Along Burlington's "new" North End a long line of beaches stretches to the Winooski River delta, beginning with North Beach, which has a grassy picnic area, a snack bar, and boat rentals. Neighboring Leddy Park offers a more secluded beach. **Amenities:** food and drink; lifeguards; parking (fee); showers; toilets. **Best for:** partiers; swimming; walking; windsurfing. ✉ *North Beach Park, 52 Institute Rd., off North Ave., Burlington* ☎ *802/865–7247* ⊕ *www.enjoyburlington.com/venue/north-beach* 🚆 *Parking $8 (May–Oct.).*

 Restaurants

American Flatbread Burlington

$$ | PIZZA | Seating is first-come, first-served at this popular pizza spot, and the wood-fired clay dome ovens pump out delicious and amusingly named pies like "Dancing Heart" (garlic oil, Italian grana padano cheese, toasted sesame seeds) and "Power to the People" (chicken, buffalo sauce, carrots, mozzarella, and blue cheese dressing) in full view of the tables. Fresh salads topped with locally made cheese are also popular. **Known for:** beers brewed on-site; spacious outdoor seating area; many ingredients sourced from farm 2 miles away. $ *Average main: $18* ✉ *115 St. Paul St., Burlington* ☎ *802/861–2999* ⊕ *www.americanflatbread.com.*

Burlington Beer Company

$$ | AMERICAN | For craft beer and inventive pub food, head to this spacious taproom in a historic factory building where the world-renowned Lumière brothers produced films in the early 1900s. Pair your pint of Strawberry Whale Cake (strawberry cream ale) or Vaulted Blue (IPA with notes of candied citrus peel and ripe peaches) with smoked trout dip and loaded birria fries, or opt for hearty sandwiches such as shaved steak or the mushroom Philly. **Known for:** lively, spacious atmosphere filled with natural light; pub food and apps to split; seasonal and classic craft beers. $ *Average main: $20* ✉ *180 Flynn Ave., Burlington* ☎ *802/863–2337* ⊕ *www.burlingtonbeercompany.com.*

Farmhouse Tap and Grill

$$ | AMERICAN | The line out the door on a typical weekend night should tell you a lot about the local esteem for this farm-to-table restaurant. Serving only local beef, cheese, and produce in a classy but laid-back style, Farmhouse Tap and Grill provides one of the finest meals in the area. **Known for:** local cheese and charcuterie plates; downstairs taproom or the outdoor beer garden; raw bar. $ *Average main: $20* ✉ *160 Bank St., Burlington* ☎ *802/859–0888* ⊕ *www.farmhousetg.com.*

Guild Tavern

$$$ | STEAKHOUSE | Some of Vermont's best steak—all meat is sourced from local farms, dry-aged a minimum of 21 days, and cooked to absolute perfection—can be found roasting over hardwood coals in this tavern's open kitchens. The space itself is also a treat, with antique chicken feeders serving as light fixtures and a soapstone-topped bar in the center. **Known for:** steak for two combo; poutine with hand-cut fries; extensive cocktail list. $ *Average main: $25* ✉ *1633 Williston Rd., Burlington* ☎ *802/497–1207* ⊕ *www.guildtavern.com* ☯ *No lunch.*

★ Hen of the Wood Burlington

$$$ | MODERN AMERICAN | The Burlington branch of Hen of the Wood offers a slicker, more urban vibe than its original Waterbury location but serves the same inventive yet down-to-earth cuisine that sets diners' hearts aflutter and tongues wagging. Indeed, many consider this the best restaurant in Vermont, so drop your finger anywhere on the menu and you won't go wrong. **Known for:** mushroom toast; dollar oysters every night 4–5 pm; perfect date night spot. $ *Average* main: $30 ✉ 55 Cherry St., Burlington ☎ 802/540–0534 ⊕ www.henofthewood. com ☺ No lunch.

★ Honey Road
$$$$ | MEDITERRANEAN | This Church Street restaurant has garnered multiple James Beard Foundation nominations, launching it into a golden age under the helm of co-owners Allison Gibson and chef Cara Chigazola Tobin. Serving arguably the best dinner in Burlington, high expectations are satisfied thanks to creative takes on eastern Mediterranean cuisine, including a selection of sensational mezes. **Known for:** daily Honey Time happy hour with $1 chicken wings; muhammara (hot pepper) dip with house-made pita; the cutting edge of local cuisine. $ *Average main: $45* ✉ 156 Church St., Burlington ☎ 802/497–2145 ⊕ www. honeyroadrestaurant.com ☺ No lunch.

Istanbul Kebab House
$$ | TURKISH | FAMILY | The classics of Turkish cuisine are served with surprising authenticity and maximum deliciousness thanks to the culinary talents of its Istanbul-raised owners, plus locally sourced produce and meats. The open terrace upstairs offers the only rooftop dining in Burlington. **Known for:** Turkish casseroles (güveç) baked in earthenware bowls; best kebabs in Burlington, if not Vermont; lavash bread made to order. $ *Average main: $19* ✉ 175 Church St., Burlington ☎ 802/857–5091 ⊕ www.istanbulkebabhousevt.com ☺ Closed Mon.

Leunig's Bistro and Cafe
$$$ | CAFÉ | This popular café delivers alfresco bistro cuisine with a distinct French flavor, plus a friendly European-style bar and live jazz. Favorite entrées include salade niçoise, *soupe au pistou* (vegetable and white bean soup with Asiago and pesto), and beef bourguignon. **Known for:** crème brûlée; Sunday brunch; outdoor seating on Church Street. $ *Average main: $28* ✉ 115 Church St., Burlington ☎ 802/863–3759

⊕ www.leunigsbistro.com ☺ Closed Mon. and Sun.

May Day
$$ | AMERICAN | Local industry pros Mojo Hancy-Davis and Matthew Peterson launched this cozy neighborhood spot with a menu that ranges from nostalgic favorites—like a beef patty melt on rye—to delicately plated vegetable dishes, such as delicata squash with Bayley Hazen blue cheese custard and whey-braised tomatoes. Go lowbrow for drinks with a Narragansett lager, or highbrow with a bottle of grower Champagne. **Known for:** simple yet delectable desserts; adventurous natural wine list; bustling industry night on Mondays. $ *Average main: $22* ✉ 258 N. Winooski Ave., Burlington ☎ 802/540–9240 ⊕ www. maydayvt.com ☺ Closed Tues.–Thurs. No lunch.

Onion City Chicken & Oyster
$$ | AMERICAN | Laura Wade and Aaron Josinsky's new casual spot serves up fried chicken in various forms — from honey-butter wings to whole birds. Comfort-food sides include collard greens that you can add housemade bacon to, a whole grilled onion, fluffy beignets filled with cheddar, and yes, there are oysters (options change daily). **Known for:** sophisticated but fun atmosphere; lobster roll and hot dog baskets; well-made classic cocktails. $ *Average main: $20* ✉ 3 E. Allen St., Winooski ☎ 802/540–8489 ⊕ www.mlcvt.com ☺ Closed Mon.–Wed. No lunch.

Pizzeria Verita
$$$ | ITALIAN |"The truth is in the dough" is the long-standing motto of Burlington's destination for expert Neopolitan pies. The bubbled, chewy crusts are flame-kissed by live fire, and Italian-inspired ingredients are sourced mostly from local farmers like the house-made mozzarella that graces classic pies like the beautifully simple Margherita. **Known for:** excellent cocktails, especially the house negroni; wood-fired Neopolitan pizza; farm-sourced

ingredients. [$] *Average main: $30* ✉ *156 St. Paul St., Burlington* ☎ *802/489–5644* 🌐 *www.pizzeriaverita.com.*

Restaurant Poco

$$ | AMERICAN | Owners Stefano Cicirello and Susie Ely parked what was originally Dolce VT food truck in a hip space that looks straight out of Brooklyn. The menu of shared plates changes regularly but leans global, with dishes such as Kung Pao cauliflower served alongside pork Milanese and a very good burger. **Known for:** cozy atmosphere; small plates to share; walk-in only. [$] *Average main: $18* ✉ *55 Main St., Burlington* ☎ *802/497-2587* 🌐 *www.restaurantpoco.com* 🕒 *Closed Sun.–Tues. No lunch.*

A Single Pebble

$$ | CHINESE | "Gather, discover, and connect" is the slogan and theme at this intimate Chinese restaurant on the first floor of a residential row house. Traditional Cantonese- and Sichuan-style dishes are served family style, and the "mock eel" was given two chopsticks up on the Food Network's *The Best Thing I Ever Ate.* **Known for:** many vegetarian options; fire-blistered green beans wok-tossed with flecks of pork; chef's tasting menu. [$] *Average main: $22* ✉ *133 Bank St., Burlington* ☎ *802/865–5200* 🌐 *www.asinglepebble.com* 🕒 *Closed Sun.*

Trattoria Delia

$$$ | ITALIAN | If you didn't make that trip to Umbria this year, the next best thing is this Italian country eatery around the corner from City Hall Park. The secret to the ambience goes well beyond the high-quality, handmade pasta dishes to the supercozy woody interior, a transplanted sugarhouse from New Hampshire. **Known for:** excellent wine list; wood-grilled prosciutto-wrapped Vermont rabbit; primo Italian desserts. [$] *Average main: $27* ✉ *152 St. Paul St., Burlington* ☎ *802/864–5253* 🌐 *www.trattoriadelia.com* 🕒 *No lunch.*

Zabby and Elf's Stone Soup

$ | AMERICAN | The open front, woody interior, and community spirit make Stone Soup a downtown favorite for lunch, especially on warm days. The small but robust salad bar is the centerpiece, with excellent hot and cold dishes—a perfect complement to the wonderful soups and fresh sandwiches. **Known for:** vegetarian dishes; gluten-free baked goods; New York Jewish-style cooking. [$] *Average main: $13* ✉ *211 College St., Burlington* ☎ *802/862–7616* 🌐 *www.stonesoupvt.com* 🕒 *Closed Sun. and Mon.*

☕ Coffee and Quick Bites

Burlington Bay Market & Cafe

$ | AMERICAN | This may be a local hub for grabbing a quick sandwich or a case of beer, but its true fame stands with its seasonal creemee window. During the warmer months, lines snake around the corner for the café's beloved soft serve, particularly the house specialty: twisted black raspberry and maple ice cream in a cone, extra sprinkles. **Known for:** maple and black raspberry creemees; grocery staples and necessities; sandwiches, burgers, and hot dogs. [$] *Average main: $5* ✉ *125 Battery St., Burlington* ☎ *802/864–0110* 🌐 *www.burlingtonbay-cafe.com.*

Kestrel Coffee Roasters

$ | CAFÉ | Two alumni of Blue Hill at Stone Barns, one of the country's most lauded restaurants, moved to Burlington in 2017 to realize their dreams of opening a coffee shop together. The duo focus on meticulously sourced beans roasted fresh in-house, scratch-made baked goods, and a frequently changing menu of farm-sourced sandwiches. **Known for:** small-batch roasted coffee beans; homemade baked goods; maple lattes. [$] *Average main: $5* ✉ *47 Maple St., Burlington* ☎ *802/391–0081* 🌐 *www.kestrelcoffees.com* 🕒 *Closed Sun.*

Onyx Tonics

$ | **CAFÉ** | This coffee-tasting bar would satisfy the staunchest coffee aficionado, with its rotating menu of specialty drinks designed to highlight the texture and flavor profile of distinct beans and roasters; so it's not surprising that co-founder Jason Gonzales won a top 10 spot in the 2013 World Cup Tasting Championship (the coffee Olympics). If a coffee education is what you want with your morning cup, Onyx Tonics offers it—thankfully with a friendly and inviting atmosphere—as baristas have been known to warn against adding milk to a certain drip coffee, because it would raise the acidity of the brew and alter its delicate flavor. **Known for:** coffee-tasting bar; the VT Big Easy, coffee and chicory mixed with milk and maple syrup; featured espresso and drip coffee beans. [$] *Average main: $6* ✉ *126 College St., Burlington* ☎ *802/777–2583* 🌐 *onyxtonics.com.*

Shy Guy Gelato

$ | **ITALIAN** | Some of the best gelato outside of Italy is found on St. Paul Street. Co-owner Paul Sansone was inspired by his Italian heritage to work abroad as an apprentice to some of Southern Italy's most notable gelato masters; he returned to Vermont years later to open his own scoop shop alongside one of Burlington's longtime farm-to-table restaurant owners, Tim Elliot. **Known for:** small-batch gelato and sorbet made with local ingredients; fior di latte (fresh mozzarella) gelato; vegan-friendly sorbets. [$] *Average main: $5* ✉ *198 St. Paul St., Burlington* ☎ *802/355–2320* 🌐 *shyguygelato.com* 🕒 *Closed Mon.–Wed.*

Speeder & Earl's Coffee

$ | **CAFÉ** | This family-owned coffee roaster has been turning out small-batch beans and blends since 1993, making it a well-loved local watering-hole for almost three decades. This quirky, funky café is a prime old-school spot to pick up a bag of beans or mull over the morning paper with a cup of Maple French Roast. **Known for:** small-batch coffee blends; house-roasted beans; quirky vibes in a sunny café space. [$] *Average main: $4* ✉ *412 Pine St., Burlington* ☎ *802/658–6016* 🌐 *speederandearls.com.*

Hotels

Courtyard Burlington Harbor

$$$ | **HOTEL** | A block from the lake and a five-minute walk from the heart of town, this attractive chain hotel has a pretty bar and lobby area with couches around a fireplace. **Pros:** right in downtown; some of the best lake views in town; across the street from park and lake. **Cons:** lacks local charm; a bit corporate in ambience; fee for self-parking. [$] *Rooms from: $329* ✉ *25 Cherry St., Burlington* ☎ *802/864–4700* 🌐 *www.marriott.com* 🛏 *161 rooms* 🍴 *No Meals.*

Hilton Garden Inn

$$$ | **HOTEL** | One of Burlington's newest hotels, this more playful edition of the Hilton family sits on an ideal location halfway between downtown and the lakefront, putting both in easy walking reach. **Pros:** some rooms have views of the lake; Vermont Comedy Club in the same building; well above average restaurant. **Cons:** uninspired design in rooms; surrounded by busy streets with traffic; small pool. [$] *Rooms from: $309* ✉ *101 Main St., Burlington* ☎ *802/951–0099* 🌐 *www.hiltongardeninn3.hilton.com* 🛏 *139 rooms* 🍴 *No Meals.*

★ **Hotel Vermont**

$$$ | **HOTEL** | Since opening in 2013, the Hotel Vermont has held the hospitality crown for style and cool, which is showcased in the almost magically spacious lobby, with its crackling wood fire, walls of smoky black Vermont granite, reclaimed oak floors, and local artwork. **Pros:** Juniper restaurant serves excellent cocktails; gorgeous rooms; unbelievable service. **Cons:** luxury doesn't come cheap; view of the lake often blocked by other buildings; additional fee for breakfast and

Burlington's Church Street is an open-air mall with restaurants, shops, festivals, and street performers.

self-parking. $ *Rooms from: $309* ✉ *41 Cherry St., Burlington* ☎ *802/651–0080* ⊕ *www.hotelvt.com* ⇥ *125 rooms* ¶O¶ *No Meals.*

The Lang House on Main Street

$$ | **B&B/INN** | Within walking distance of downtown in the historic hill section of town, this grand 1881 Victorian home charms completely with its period furnishings, fine woodwork, plaster detailing, stained-glass windows, and sunlit dining area. **Pros:** family-friendly vibe; interesting location; fantastic breakfast. **Cons:** no elevator; on a busy street; old-fashioned design not for everyone. $ *Rooms from: $219* ✉ *360 Main St., Burlington* ☎ *802/652–2500, 877/919–9799* ⊕ *www.langhouse.com* ⇥ *11 rooms* ¶O¶ *Free Breakfast.*

★ Made INN Vermont

$$ | **B&B/INN** | Few accommodations in Vermont find a dynamic balance between the traditional inn and trendy boutique spirit, but this eminently charming and quirky 1881 house topped with a cute cupola has done it. **Pros:** excellent location between the University of Vermont and Champlain College; vivacious and involved innkeeper; hot tub out back. **Cons:** bathrooms are private, but not en suite; rooms are modest in size; higher cost than most other inns in town. $ *Rooms from: $259* ✉ *204 S. Willard St., Burlington* ☎ *802/399–2788* ⊕ *www. madeinnvermont.com* ⇥ *4 rooms* ¶O¶ *Free Breakfast.*

🍸 Nightlife

Citizen Cider

BREWPUBS | The tiny parking lot out front gets jammed after 5 pm, as the spacious "tasting room" of this hard-cider maker fills with exuberant young, hip professionals and students. Sample cider straight or in a dozen or so cocktails. There's a full bistro menu, too. ✉ *316 Pine St., Suite 114, Burlington* ☎ *802/497–1987* ⊕ *www. citizencider.com.*

Higher Ground

LIVE MUSIC | When you feel like shaking it up to live music, come to Higher Ground—it gets the lion's share of local and national musicians. ✉ *1214 Williston Rd., South Burlington* ☎ *802/652-0777.* ⊕ *www.highergroundmusic.com.*

Mule Bar

BREWPUBS | This Winooski watering hole pours some of the best craft brews from around the state and is a must for aficionados. Outdoor seating and above-average bar bites seal the deal for its young and hip clientele. ✉ *38 Main St., Winooski* ☎ *802/399-2020* ⊕ *www. mulebarvt.com.*

Nectar's

LIVE MUSIC | Jam band Phish got its start at Nectar's, which is always jumping to the sounds of local bands, stand-up comics, and live-band karaoke and never charges a cover. Don't leave without a helping of the bar's famous fries and gravy. ✉ *188 Main St., Burlington* ☎ *802/658-4771* ⊕ *www.liveatnectars. com.*

Radio Bean

LIVE MUSIC | For some true local flavor, head to this funky place for nightly live music, an artsy vibe, and a cocktail. Performances happen every day, but Tuesday night is arguably the most fun, as the Honkey Tonk band blazes through covers of Gram Parsons, Wilco, and the like. ✉ *8 N. Winooski Ave., Burlington* ☎ *802/660-9346* ⊕ *www.radiobean.com.*

🎭 Performing Arts

★ Flynn Center for the Performing Arts

CONCERTS | It's a pleasure to see any show inside this grandiose art deco gem. In addition to being home to Vermont's largest musical theater company, it hosts the Vermont Symphony Orchestra, as well as big-name acts like Neko Case and Elvis Costello. The adjacent Flynn Space is a coveted spot for more offbeat, experimental performances. ✉ *153 Main St., Burlington* ☎ *802/863-5966* ⊕ *www. flynncenter.org.*

🛍 Shopping

With each passing year, Burlington's industrial South End attracts ever greater numbers of artists and craftspeople, who set up studios, shops, and galleries in former factories and warehouses along Pine Street. The district's annual "Art Hop" in September is the city's largest arts celebration—and a roaring good time.

FOOD

Lake Champlain Chocolates

OTHER SPECIALTY STORE | This chocolatier makes sensational truffles, caramels, candies, fudge, and hot chocolate. The chocolates are all-natural, made in Vermont, and make a great edible souvenir. Factory tours are available. A retail branch is also on Church Street. ✉ *750 Pine St., Burlington* ☎ *802/864-1807 Pine St., 802/862-5185 Church St., 800/465-5909* ⊕ *www.lakechamplainchocolates.com.*

NU Chocolat

FOOD | This European-style chocolate boutique combines Swiss-trained chocolatier, premier Belgian equipment, a minimalist's eye for detail, and a family-owned mentality. Owners Laura and Kevin Toohey and their children, co-founders Rowan and Virginia Toohey, spotlight their chocolate craftsmanship with delights like cocoa-dusted almonds, chocolate-covered candied orange peel, and uniquely beautiful seasonal truffles. ✉ *180 Battery St., Burlington* ☎ *802/540-8378* ⊕ *www.nuchocolat.com.*

SPORTING GOODS

Burton

SPORTING GOODS | The folks who started this quintessential Vermont company also helped start snowboarding. The flagship store sells equipment and clothing; a second retail branch is in downtown Burlington, on 162 College Street. ✉ *80 Industrial Pkwy., Burlington*

☎ 802/660–3200, 802/333–0400 College St. ⊕ www.burton.com.

🏃 Activities

BIKING

★ Burlington Bike Path

BIKING | FAMILY | Anyone who's put the rubber to the road on the 7½-mile Burlington Bike Path and its almost equally long northern extension on the Island Line Trail sings its praises. Along the way there are endless postcard views of Lake Champlain and the Adirondack Mountains. The northern end of the trail is slightly more rugged and windswept, so dress accordingly. ⊠ Burlington ☎ 802/864–0123 ⊕ enjoyburlington.com/place/burlington-greenway.

Ski Rack

BIKING | Burlington's one-stop shop for winter sports equipment, the Ski Rack also rents bikes and sells running gear throughout the year. ⊠ 85 Main St., Burlington ☎ 802/658–3313, 800/882–4530 ⊕ www.skirack.com.

BOATING

Burlington Community Boathouse

BOATING | This boathouse administers the city's marina as well as a summertime watering hole called Splash, one of the best places to watch the sun set over the lake. ⊠ Burlington Harbor, College St., Burlington ☎ 802/865–3377 ⊕ enjoyburlington.com.

Community Sailing Center

BOATING | FAMILY | Burlington's shiny new 22,000-square-foot Community Sailing Center has 150 watercraft to rent including kayaks, sailboats, and standup paddleboards for as little as $15 an hour. Private instruction and family lessons are available, as are floating yoga classes. ⊠ 505 Lake St., Burlington ☎ 802/864–2499 ⊕ www.communitysailingcenter.org ⊗ Closed mid-Oct.–mid-May.

Lake Champlain Shoreline Cruises

BOATING | FAMILY | The trilevel *Spirit of Ethan Allen III*, a 363-passenger vessel, offers narrated cruises, theme dinners, and sunset sails with breathtaking Adirondacks and Green Mountains views. The standard 1½-hour cruise runs four times a day; sunset cruises leave at 6:30 pm on Friday and Saturday. ⊠ Burlington Boat House, 1 College St., Burlington ☎ 802/862–8300 ⊕ www.soea.com.

True North Kayak Tours

CANOEING & ROWING | This company conducts two- and five-hour guided kayak tours of Lake Champlain that include talks about the region's natural history and customized lessons. ⊠ 25 Nash Pl., Burlington ☎ 802/238–7695 ⊕ www.vermontkayak.com.

SKIING

Bolton Valley Resort

SKIING & SNOWBOARDING | FAMILY | The closest ski resort to Burlington, about 25 miles away, Bolton Valley is a family favorite. In addition to downhill trails—more than half rated for intermediate and beginner skiers—Bolton offers 62 miles of cross-country and snowshoe trails, night skiing, and a sports center. **Facilities:** 71 trails; 300 acres; 1,704-foot vertical drop; 5 lifts. ⊠ 4302 Bolton Valley Access Rd., north off U.S. 2, Bolton ☎ 802/434–3444, 877/926–5866 ⊕ www.boltonvalley.com 🎿 Lift ticket: $89.

Shelburne

5 miles south of Burlington.

A few miles south of Burlington, the Champlain Valley gives way to fertile farmland, affording views of the rugged Adirondacks across the lake. In the middle of this farmland is the village of Shelburne, chartered in the mid-18th century and partly a bedroom community for Burlington. Shelburne Farms and the Shelburne Museum are worth at least a few hours of exploring, as are Shelburne

Vermont's African American Heritage Trail ◉

The Vermont African American Heritage Trail (⊕ vtafricanameri-canheritage.net) helps share the link between Vermont, the first state constitution to outlaw slavery, and African American residents who have lived here since the Revolutionary War. There are 22 sights throughout the state, including seven museums: Ferrisburgh's **Rokeby Museum & the Underground Railroad**; Middlebury's **Vermont Folklife Center**; the **Brandon Museum**; Manchester's **Hildene, The Lincoln Family Home**; the **Grafton History Museum**; Windsor's **Old Constitution House State Historic Site**; and Browning-ton's **Old Stone House Museum and Brownington Village.** The 148-acre **Clemmons Family Farm** in Charlotte, another stop along the heritage trail, celebrates the history, culture, arts and sciences of the African American diaspora via programs like on-site artist residencies, theater performances, literary events, and guided tours through the verdant property and its six historic buildings.

Orchards in fall, when you can pick your own apples and drink fresh cider while admiring breathtaking views of the lake and mountains beyond.

Just south of Shelburne is the beautiful, rural town of Charlotte. Expect to find open farmstands, rolling pastures and grazing cows along these serpentine roads, many of which offer hidden gems like u-pick berries and seasonal barbecues on the farm.

GETTING HERE AND AROUND

Shelburne is south of Burlington after the town of South Burlington, which is notable for its very un-Vermont traffic congestion and a commercial and fast food–laden stretch of U.S. 7. It's easy to confuse Shelburne Farms (2 miles west of town on the lake) with Shelburne Museum, which is right on U.S. 7 just south of town, but you'll want to make time for both.

◉ Sights

★ Clemmons Family Farm

FARM/RANCH | Founded in 1962 by Jackson and Lydia Clemmons, this 148-acre farm is one of a handful of Black-owned arts and culture nonprofit organizations in the state, and one of the 22 landmarks on Vermont's African American Heritage Trail. Along with acres of lush farmland, forest, meadows and ponds, six historic buildings offer space for artist residencies, art exhibits, creative studios, retreats, small performances, and community events celebrating the African diaspora. The Storytelling Room in the Barn House is a community hub for arts, sciences and culture programs, including featured exhibits and speakers' series. ✉ 2213–2122 Greenbush Rd., Charlotte ☎ 765/560–5445 ⊕ www.clemmonsfamilyfarm.org.

Fiddlehead Brewing Company

BREWERY | There isn't much to the tasting room here, but there doesn't need to be: Fiddlehead only occasionally cans its celebrated beer, making this the best place outside of a restaurant to sample it on tap (and for free). Decide which one you like best and buy a growler to go—or, better yet, take it to Folino's Pizza next door, where the pies are mighty fine. ✉ 6305 Shelburne Rd., Shelburne ☎ 802/399–2994 ⊕ www.fiddlehead-brewing.com 🎫 Free.

Mount Philo State Park

STATE/PROVINCIAL PARK | FAMILY | For many Vermont kids, this is their first hike, thanks to the relatively easy, gently rising, paved road that snakes around the sides to the top, where fabulous views of the lake and landscape await. If less inclined to walk, feel free to drive. ✉ *5425 Mt. Philo Rd., Charlotte* ☎ *802/425–2390* ⊕ *www.vtstateparks. com/philo.html* 🎫 *$5.*

★ Shelburne Farms

COLLEGE | FAMILY | Founded in the 1880s as a private estate for two very rich New Yorkers, this 1,400-acre farm is much more than an exquisite landscape: it's an educational and cultural resource center with a working dairy farm, an award-winning cheese producer, an organic market garden, and a bakery whose aroma of fresh bread and pastries is an olfactory treat. It's a brilliant place for parents to expose their kids to the dignity of farmwork and the joys of compassionate animal husbandry—indeed, children and adults alike will get a kick out of hunting for eggs in the oversize coop, milking a cow, and watching the chicken parade. There are several activities and tours daily, and a lunch cart serves up fresh-from-the-farm soups, salads, and sandwiches. Frederick Law Olmsted, the co-creator of New York City's Central Park, designed the magnificent grounds overlooking Lake Champlain; walk to Lone Tree Hill for a splendid view. If you fall in love with the scenery, arrange a romantic dinner at the lakefront mansion, or spend the night. ✉ *1611 Harbor Rd., west of U.S. 7, Shelburne* ☎ *802/985–8686* ⊕ *www. shelburnefarms.org.*

★ Shelburne Museum

HISTORY MUSEUM | FAMILY | You can trace much of New England's history simply by wandering through the 45 acres and 39 buildings of this museum. Some 25 buildings were relocated here, including an old-fashioned jail, an 1871 lighthouse, and a 220-foot steamboat,

the *Ticonderoga.* The outstanding 150,000-object collection of art, design, and Americana consists of antique furniture, fine and folk art, quilts, trade signs, and weather vanes; there are also more than 200 carriages and sleighs. The Pizzagalli Center for Art and Education is open year-round with changing exhibitions and programs for kids and adults. ✉ *6000 Shelburne Rd., Shelburne* ☎ *802/985–3346* ⊕ *www.shelburnemu-seum.org* 🎫 *$25* ⊙ *Call for hrs, which vary by season and museum.*

Shelburne Vineyard

WINERY | From U.S. 7, you'll see rows and rows of organically grown vines. Visit the attractive tasting room and learn how wine is made. Also available on-site is a Shelburne Vineyard collaboration called Iaepetus, a natural wine label from notable biodynamic winemaker Ethan Joseph. ✉ *6308 Shelburne Rd., Shelburne* ☎ *802/985–8222* ⊕ *www. shelburnevineyard.com* 🎫 *Tasting $7, tour free.*

Vermont Teddy Bear Company

FACTORY | FAMILY | On the 30-minute tour of this fun-filled factory you'll hear more puns than you ever thought possible, while learning how a few homemade bears sold from a cart on Church Street turned into a multimillion-dollar business. Patrons and children can relax, eat, and play under a large canvas tent in summer, or wander the beautiful 57-acre property. ✉ *6655 Shelburne Rd., Shelburne* ☎ *802/985–3001* ⊕ *www.vermontteddy-bear.com* 🎫 *Tour $5.*

🍴 Restaurants

Philo Ridge Farm & Market

$$$$ | AMERICAN | A leader in regenerative agriculture, two of the 400 acres of this diversified farm are dedicated to organic vegetable, flower, herb, and fruit production, which is then channeled into the market's sandwiches, salads, prepared foods, and pantry goods.

Farm-raised poultry, lamb, grass-fed beef, and heritage pork are the stars of the kitchen's elegant prix-fixe dinner menu, which changes seasonally. **Known for:** farm-raised ingredients; spectacular views; outstanding house-made buns with cultured butter. [$] *Average main: $79* ✉ *2766 Mt. Philo Rd., Charlotte* ☎ *802/539–2912* 🌐 *philoridgefarm.com* 🕒 *Closed Sun.–Tues.*

Rustic Roots

$$ | **AMERICAN** | Scuffed wood floors and chunky country tables bring the "rustic" at this converted farmhouse—but not too much. An intimate bar and maroon walls adorned with woodcrafts and art add a touch of elegance, and the French-inspired food is carefully prepared. **Known for:** coffee-maple sausage; pastrami on rye; Bloody Marys. [$] *Average main: $21* ✉ *195 Falls Rd., Shelburne* ☎ *802/985–9511* 🌐 *www.rusticrootsvt.com* 🕒 *Closed Mon. and Tues. No dinner Wed., Thurs., and Sun.*

Coffee and Quick Bites

Vermont Cookie Love

$ | **BAKERY** | The "Love Shack" on the side of VT Route 7 is known to have one of the best maple creemees in the state due to its use of Vermont maple syrup and high-butterfat dairy from Kingdom Creamery of Vermont. There are also coffee, vanilla, and chocolate creemees on offer, along with local Wilcox hard ice cream and house-made cookies made daily on-site. **Known for:** homemade cookies; maple and coffee soft serve; crushed cookie crumbles for topping cones and sundaes. [$] *Average main: $4* ✉ *6915 Rte. 7, Ferrisburgh* ☎ *802/425–8181* 🌐 *www.vermontcookielove.com* 🕒 *Creemee window closed Nov.–Mar.*

Hotels

Heart of the Village Inn

$ | **B&B/INN** | Each of the elegantly furnished rooms at this B&B in an 1886 Queen Anne Victorian provides coziness and tastefully integrated modern conveniences. **Pros:** easy walk to shops and restaurants; elegant historical building; hypoallergenic bedding and memory foam mattresses. **Cons:** near to but not within Shelburne Farms; no room service; no children under 12. [$] *Rooms from: $189* ✉ *5347 Shelburne Rd., Shelburne* ☎ *802/985–9060* 🌐 *www.heartofthevillage.com* 🛏 *9 rooms* 🍴 *Free Breakfast.*

★ **The Inn at Shelburne Farms**

$ | **B&B/INN** | It's hard not to feel like an aristocrat at this exquisite turn-of-the-20th-century Tudor-style inn, perched at the edge of Lake Champlain—even Teddy Roosevelt stayed here. **Pros:** stately lakefront setting in a historic mansion; endless activities; proposal-worthy restaurant. **Cons:** lowest-priced rooms have shared baths; closed in winter; no air-conditioning. [$] *Rooms from: $170* ✉ *1611 Harbor Rd., Shelburne* ☎ *802/985–8498* 🌐 *www.shelburnefarms.org* 🕒 *Closed mid-Oct.–mid-May* 🛏 *28 rooms* 🍴 *No Meals.*

★ **Mt. Philo Inn**

$$$ | **B&B/INN** | Practically on the slopes of Mt. Philo State Park in Charlotte, the 1896 inn offers gorgeous views of Lake Champlain from its outdoor porches and an ideal blend of historical and contemporary boutique decor. **Pros:** walking trail goes directly to Mt. Philo State Park; lots of local stonework incorporated; complimentary breakfast basket includes all the fixings. **Cons:** not walking distance to any sights; rooms too big for just one guest; you cook breakfast yourself. [$] *Rooms from: $320* ✉ *27 Inn Rd., Charlotte* ☎ *802/425–3335* 🌐 *www.mtphiloinn.com* 🛏 *4 suites* 🍴 *No Meals.*

Shopping

The Flying Pig Bookstore

BOOKS | It should come as no surprise that this bookstore is notable for its whimsy and carefully curated children's section: one of the owners is a stand-up comedian, and the other is a picture-book author. ✉ *5247*

At the Shelburne Museum, the restored 220-foot Ticonderoga steamboat is the last existing walking beam side-wheel passenger steamer.

Shelburne Rd., Shelburne ☎ *802/985–3999* ⊕ *www.flyingpigbooks.com.*

The Shelburne Country Store

GENERAL STORE | As you enter this store, you'll feel as though you've stepped back in time. Walk past the potbelly stove and take in the aroma emanating from the fudge neatly piled behind huge antique glass cases, alongside a vast selection of penny candies and chocolates. There are creemees, of course, but here the specialties are candles, weather vanes, glassware, and local foods. ☒ *29 Falls Rd., off U.S. 7, Shelburne* ☎ *802/985–3657, 800/660–3657* ⊕ *www.shelburne-countrystore.com.*

Lake Champlain Islands

Lake Champlain stretches more than 100 miles south from the Canadian border and forms the northern part of the boundary between New York and Vermont. Within it is an elongated archipelago comprising several islands—Isle La Motte, North Hero, Grand Isle, and South Hero—and the Alburgh Peninsula. Enjoying a temperate climate, the islands hold several apple orchards and are a center of water recreation in summer and ice fishing in winter. A scenic drive through the islands on U.S. 2 begins at Interstate 89 and travels north to Alburgh Center; Route 78 takes you back to the mainland.

ESSENTIALS

VISITOR INFORMATION Lake Champlain Islands Chamber of Commerce. ☒ *North Hero* ☎ *802/372–8400, 800/262–5226* ⊕ *www.champlainislands.com.* **Lake Champlain Regional Chamber of Commerce.** ☒ *Burlington* ☎ *802/863–3489, 877/686–5253* ⊕ *www.vermont.org.*

◉ Sights

Alburgh Dunes State Park

STATE/PROVINCIAL PARK | This park has one of the longest sandy beaches on Lake Champlain and some fine examples of rare flora and fauna along the hiking trails. The wetlands are also an important area for wildlife refuge, providing a safe habitat for breeding, feeding, and nesting for surrounding animals like deer and wild turkey. ✉ *151 Coon Point Rd., off U.S. 2, Alburgh* ☎ *802/796–4170* 🌐 *www.vtstateparks.com/alburgh.html* 🎟 *$5.*

★ Allenholm Farm

FARM/RANCH | The pick-your-own apples at this farm are amazingly tasty—if you're here at harvest time, don't miss out. The farm also has a petting area with donkeys, miniature horses, sheep, goats, and other animals. At the store, you can buy cheeses, dried fruit, homemade pies, and maple creemees. ✉ *111 South St., South Hero* ☎ *802/372–5566* 🌐 *www.allenholm.com* 🎟 *Free.*

Grand Isle State Park

STATE/PROVINCIAL PARK | You'll find hiking trails, boat rentals, and shore fishing at Grand Isle. ✉ *36 E. Shore S, off U.S. 2, Grand Isle* ☎ *802/372–4300* 🌐 *www.vtstateparks.com/grandisle.html* 🎟 *$5.*

Hyde Log Cabin

HISTORIC HOME | Built in 1783, this log cabin on South Hero is often cited as the country's oldest surviving specimen. It's now home to the Grand Isle Historical Society. ✉ *228 U.S. 2, Grand Isle* ☎ *802/828–3051* 🎟 *$3* ⏰ *Closed weekdays mid-Oct.–May.*

Missisquoi National Wildlife Refuge

WILDLIFE REFUGE | On the mainland east of the Alburgh Peninsula, the refuge consists of 6,729 acres of federally protected wetlands, meadows, and woods. It's a beautiful area for bird-watching, canoeing, and walking nature trails. ✉ *29 Tabor Rd., 36 miles north of Burlington, Swanton* ☎ *802/868–4781* 🌐 *www.fws.gov/refuge/missisquoi.*

North Hero State Park

STATE/PROVINCIAL PARK | The 399-acre North Hero has a swimming beach and nature trails. It's open to rowboats, kayaks, and canoes. ✉ *3803 Lakeview Dr., North Hero* ☎ *802/372–8727* 🌐 *www.vtstateparks.com/northhero.html* 🎟 *$5.*

Snow Farm Vineyard and Winery

WINERY | Vermont's first vineyard was started here in 1996; today, the winery specializes in nontraditional botanical hybrid grapes designed to take advantage of the island's microclimate, similar to that of Burgundy, France. Take a self-guided tour and sip some samples in the tasting room—dessert wines are the strong suit. On Thursday evening, late May–September, you can picnic and enjoy the free concerts on the lawn. ✉ *190 W. Shore Rd., South Hero* ☎ *802/372–9463* 🌐 *www.snowfarm.com* 🎟 *Free* ⏰ *Closed late Dec.–Apr.*

Sand Bar State Park

STATE/PROVINCIAL PARK | One of Vermont's best swimming beaches is at Sand Bar State Park, along with a snack bar, a changing room, and boat rentals. ✉ *1215 U.S. 2, South Hero* ☎ *802/893–2825* 🌐 *vtstateparks.com/sandbar.html* 🎟 *$5.*

St. Anne's Shrine

HISTORIC SIGHT | This spot marks the site where, in 1665, French soldiers and Jesuits put ashore and built a fort, creating Vermont's first European settlement. Vermont's first Roman Catholic Mass was celebrated here on July 26, 1666. ✉ *92 St. Anne's Rd., Isle La Motte* ☎ *802/928–3362* 🌐 *www.saintannesshrine.org* 🎟 *Free.*

🍴 Restaurants

Blue Paddle Bistro

$$ | **AMERICAN** | This cozy, white clapboard house with an indicative blue awning has been a community staple for 17 years. Co-owner Mandy Hotchkiss and chef-owner Phoebe Bright share a decades-spanning friendship; today, their ongoing collaboration manifests in the bistro's seasonal menu and hand-written, daily changing nightly specials inspired by farm-sourced ingredients. **Known for:** Sunday brunch; crab cakes with mango chutney; plenty of Vermont-grown vegetables. [$] *Average main: $24* ✉ *316*

U.S. Rte. 2, South Hero ☎ *802/372–4814* ⊕ *www.bluepaddlebistro.com.*

Kraemer & Kin

$ | AMERICAN | This family-owned micro-brewery started in a Grand Isle garage in 2020. Now, it occupies the basement of the clubhouse at Alburg Golf Links, an 18-hole course with stunning views of Lake Champlain. **Known for:** creative small-batch beers brewed on site; local takes on classic clubhouse bites; golf course on the lake. $ *Average main: $12* ✉ *230 Rt.129, Alburgh* ☎ *802/796–3586* ⊕ *kraemerandkin.com* ⊗ *Closed Mon.–Wed.*

🛏 Hotels

Ruthcliffe Lodge & Restaurant

$ | HOTEL | If you're looking for an inexpensive summer destination—to take in the scenery, canoe the lake, or go biking—this will do quite nicely as the lodge is on the rarely visited Isle La Motte. **Pros:** inexpensive rates; high-quality restaurant; laid-back vibe. **Cons:** two-night minimum stays on weekends and holiday periods; quite remote; simple, bland design. $ *Rooms from: $142* ✉ *1002 Quarry Rd., Isle La Motte* ☎ *802/928–3200* ⊕ *www.ruthcliffe.com* ⊗ *Closed mid-Oct.–mid-May* ⇥ *7 rooms* ❑ *Free Breakfast.*

🏃 Activities

Apple Island Resort

BOATING | The resort's marina rents pontoon boats, rowboats, canoes, kayaks, and pedal boats. ✉ *71 U.S. 2, South Hero* ☎ *802/372–3922* ⊕ *www.appleislandresort.com.*

Hero's Welcome

BOATING | This general store rents bikes, canoes, kayaks, and paddleboards; come winter, they switch to ice skates, cross-country skis, and snowshoes. ✉ *3537 U.S. 2, North Hero* ☎ *802/372–4161* ⊕ *www.heroswelcome.com.*

Montgomery and Jay

51 miles northeast of Burlington.

Montgomery is a small village near the Jay Peak ski resort and the Canadian border. Amid the surrounding countryside are seven covered bridges.

GETTING HERE AND AROUND
Montgomery lies at the junction of Routes 58, 118, and 242. From Burlington, take Interstate 89 north to Routes 105 and 118 east. Route 242 connects Montgomery and, to the northeast, the Jay Peak Resort.

👁 Sights

Lake Memphremagog

BODY OF WATER | Vermont's second-largest body of water, Lake Memphremagog extends 33 miles north from Newport into Canada. Prouty Beach in Newport has tennis courts, boat rentals, and a 9-hole disc-golf course. Watch the sunset from the deck of the East Side Restaurant, which serves excellent burgers and prime rib. ✉ *242 Prouty Beach Rd., Newport* ☎ *802/334–6345* ⊕ *www.newportrecreation.org.*

☕ Coffee and Quick Bites

Miso Hungry

$ | JAPANESE | At the base of mammoth Jay Peak sits a wood-shingled food truck cooking arguably the best ramen in the state. Owners Momoko and Jordan Antonucci met as rafting guides in Japan, and spent three winters in Hokkaido gravitating towards the steaming bowls of noodles made at après-ski ramen trucks parked mountainside. **Known for:** spicy miso ramen; seasonal onigiri; authentic Japanese cooking made with Vermont-sourced ingredients. $ *Average main: $13* ✉ *830 Jay Peak Rd., Jay* ☎ *518/605–4474* ⊕ *www.misohungryramen.com.*

Did You Know?

Long and skinny Lake Champlain is sometimes called the sixth Great Lake. Several small and scenic islands, like Grand Isle, are popular seasonal getaways in warm weather.

🛏 Hotels

⭐ The INN

$ | **B&B/INN** | This smart chalet-style lodge comes with tons of character. **Pros:** Trout River views from back rooms; within walking distance of shops and supplies; smart, individually designed rooms. **Cons:** noise from bar can seep into nearby rooms; two-night minimum stay; outside food and alcohol not allowed. $ *Rooms from: $169 ✉ 241 Main St., Montgomery ☎ 802/326–4391 ⊕ www.theinn.us ⇄ 11 rooms ⦿ Free Breakfast.*

Jay Peak Resort

$$ | **HOTEL** | **FAMILY** | Accommodations at Jay Peak include standard hotel rooms, suites, condominiums, town houses, and cottage and clubhouse suites. **Pros:** slopes never far away; 60,000-square-foot indoor water park; kids 14 and under stay and eat free and complimentary childcare is provided. **Cons:** can get noisy; not very intimate; service can be lackluster. $ *Rooms from: $239 ✉ 830 Jay Peak Rd., Montgomery ☎ 802/988–2611 ⊕ www.jaypeakresort.com ⇄ 515 units ⦿ Free Breakfast.*

Phineas Swann Bed & Breakfast Inn

$ | **B&B/INN** | The top-hatted bulldog on the sign of this 1880 farmhouse isn't just a mascot: it reflects the hotel's welcoming attitude to pet owners. **Pros:** walking distance from shops and supplies; lots of dogs; each room has different design. **Cons:** decor is a tad old-fashioned; dog theme (and actual dogs) not for everyone; no outside alcohol allowed. $ *Rooms from: $199 ✉ 195 Main St., Montgomery ☎ 802/326–4306 ⊕ www.phineasswann.com ⇄ 9 rooms ⦿ Free Breakfast.*

🏃 Activities

ICE-SKATING

Ice Haus Arena

HOCKEY | **FAMILY** | The sprawling arena contains a professional-size hockey rink and seating for 400 spectators. You can practice your stick handling, and the rink is open to the public for skating several times a week. There are tournaments throughout the year. ✉ *830 Jay Peak Rd., Jay ☎ 802/988–2727 ⊕ www.jaypeakresort.com ⦿ $6.*

SKIING

Hazen's Notch Association

SKIING & SNOWBOARDING | Delightfully remote at any time of the year, this center has 40 miles of marked and groomed trails and rents equipment and snowshoes. ✉ *1423 Hazen's Notch Rd., Montgomery ☎ 802/326–4799 ⊕ www.hazensnotch.org.*

Jay Peak

SKIING & SNOWBOARDING | Sticking up out of the flat farmland, Jay Peak averages 349 inches of snow per year—more than any other Vermont ski area—and it's renowned for its glade skiing and powder. There are two interconnected mountains, the highest reaching nearly 4,000 feet. The smaller mountain has straight-fall-line, expert terrain that eases mid-mountain into an intermediate pitch. Beginners should stay near the bottom on trails off the Metro quad lift. There are also five terrain parks, snowshoeing, telemark skiing, and a state-of-the art ice arena for hockey, figure skating, and curling. The Pump House, an indoor water park with pools and slides, is open year-round. **Facilities:** 78 trails; 385 acres; 2,153-foot vertical drop; 9 lifts. ✉ *830 Jay Peak Rd., Jay ☎ 802/988–2611 ⊕ www.jaypeakresort.com ⦿ Lift ticket: $99.*

Lake Willoughby

30 miles southeast of Montgomery (summer route; 50 miles by winter route), 28 miles northeast of Greensboro.

The jewel of the Northeast Kingdom is clear, deep, and chilly Lake Willoughby, edged by sheer cliffs and surrounded by state forest. The only town on its shores is tiny Westmore, which has a beach and a few shops that cater to campers and seasonal residents.

◎ Sights

Bread and Puppet Museum
OTHER MUSEUM | FAMILY | This ramshackle barn houses a surrealistic collection of props used by the world-renowned Bread and Puppet Theater. The troupe has been performing social and political commentary with the towering (they're supported by people on stilts) and eerily expressive puppets for more than 50 years. In July and August, there are performances on Saturday night and Sunday afternoon, with museum tours before Sunday shows. ⊠ *753 Heights Rd., 1 mile east of Rte. 16, Glover* ☎ *802/525–3031* ⊕ *www. breadandpuppet.org* 🖃 *Donations accepted* ۞ *Closed Nov.–May.*

Lake Willoughby
BODY OF WATER | The cliffs of Mt. Pisgah and Mt. Hor drop to the edge of Lake Willoughby on opposite shores, giving this beautiful, deep, glacially carved lake a striking resemblance to a Norwegian fjord. The trails to the top of Mt. Pisgah reward hikers with glorious views. Take note: the beach on the southern end is Vermont's most famous nude beach. ⊠ *Westmore.*

Greensboro

27 miles southwest of Lake Willoughby.

Tucked along the southern shore of Caspian Lake, Greensboro has been a summer resort for literati, academics, and old-money types for more than a century. Yet it exudes an unpretentious, genteel character—most of the people running about on errands seem to know each other. The town beach is right off the main street.

◎ Sights

★ Hill Farmstead Brewery
BREWERY | It is difficult to quantify owner and master brewer Shaun Hill's contribution to the international explosion of craft beer. Hill Farmstead has won Best Brewery in the World six times in the past decade, and it's a key player in Vermont tourism, where beer contributes as much to the state economy as skiing and hiking. Since opening in 2010, Hill's eighth generation family farmstead off a rural mountain pass, miles from cell service, has drawn millions of local and international travelers pilgrimaging for a coveted pint and a growler to-go. A beautiful bar is surrounded by acres of woods and lawnspace, and a small lake sits at the bottom of a sloping field—a nice spot for pondering over a pint. ⊠ *403 Hill Rd., Greensboro* ☎ *802/533–7450* ⊕ *hillfarm-stead.com.*

⊜ Shopping

The Willey's Store
GENERAL STORE | This is a classic general store of the "if-we-don't-have-it-you-don't-need-it" kind. It's also the spot where locals in the know can snag hard-to-find Vermont gems like Jasper Hill Farm cheeses and bottles of Hill Farmstead beer. ⊠ *7 Breezy Ave., Greensboro* ☎ *802/533–2621.*

Chapter 5

NEW HAMPSHIRE

Updated by
Andrew Collins

⊙ Sights	🍴 Restaurants	🛏 Hotels	🛍 Shopping	🍸 Nightlife
★★★★★	★★★☆☆	★★★★☆	★★★★☆	★★★☆☆

WELCOME TO NEW HAMPSHIRE

TOP REASONS TO GO

★ **The White Mountains:** Offering spectacular hiking and skiing, these dramatic peaks and notches are unforgettable.

★ **Lake Winnipesaukee:** Beaches, arcades, boat cruises, and classic summer camps fuel a whole season of family fun.

★ **Fall Foliage:** Head to the Kancamagus Highway or drive through the Monadnock mountain towns for absolutely stunning scenery.

★ **Portsmouth:** An hour's drive from Boston, this small, upbeat American city abounds with colorful Colonial architecture, trendy dining, and easy access to New Hampshire's only stretch of the Atlantic coastline.

★ **Pristine Towns:** Peterborough, Walpole, Tamworth, Center Sandwich, Bethlehem, and Jackson are among the most charming small villages in New England.

1 Portsmouth. Colonial homes meet hip dining.

2 Rye. Sweeping beaches and lavish oceanfront homes.

3 Exeter. Café culture and a famous prep school.

4 Durham. Home of the University of NH.

5 Wolfeboro. The U.S.'s oldest summer resort.

6 Laconia and Weirs Beach. Lake Winnipesaukee's hub of family fun.

7 Meredith. A bustling marina and mills converted to hotels.

8 Plymouth. A lively college town and gateway to the White Mountains.

9 Holderness. Base camp for Squam and Little Squam lakes.

10 Center Sandwich. Lake Winnipesaukee's quiet, scenic side.

11 Tamworth. Tranquility and Mt. Chocorua views.

12 North Conway. Outlet shops and family-friendly amusements.

13 Jackson. A storybook White Mountains town.

14 Mt. Washington. Highest peak in the northeastern United States.

15 Bartlett. A scenic ski and hiking hub.

16 Bretton Woods. Cog railway and a grand resort.

17 Bethlehem. An artsy alpine hamlet.

18 Littleton. A scenic river town with a lively Main Street.

19 Franconia. One of the White Mountains' favorite recreation hubs.

20 Lincoln and North Woodstock. Ski resorts and kitschy family spots.

21 Waterville Valley. A four-season resort and recreation village.

22 New London. Charming gateway to Lake Sunapee.

23 Newbury and Lake Sunapee. Skiing, boating, and the nation's oldest crafts fair.

24 Hanover. Home to Dartmouth College.

25 Cornish. Covered bridges and the Saint-Gaudens estate.

26 Walpole. A pretty village green and Connecticut River views.

27 Keene. A classic Main Street and views of Mt. Monadnock.

28 Peterborough. The inspiration for Thornton Wilder's *Our Town.*

29 Milford. A bustling river town near myriad appealing attractions.

30 Manchester. The Granite State's largest city.

31 Concord. The small but lively state capital.

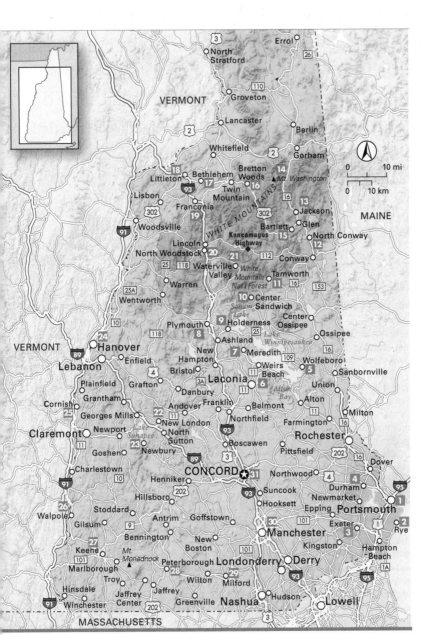

New Hampshire's precipitous terrain, clear air, and sparkling lakes attract trailblazers, artists, and countless tourists. A varied geography and endless outdoor activities are part of the draw, but visitors also appreciate this place of beauty, history, and hospitality. Whether you're seeking adventure or just want to laze on the porch swing of a century-old inn, you'll find ample ways to engage with this rugged, diverse state that stretches from the sea to the Northeast's highest mountain peaks.

Ralph Waldo Emerson, Henry David Thoreau, Nathaniel Hawthorne, and Louisa May Alcott all visited and wrote about the state, sparking a fervent literary tradition. It also has a strong political history: this was the first colony to declare independence from Great Britain, the first to adopt a state constitution, and the first to require its constitution be referred to the people for approval. Politically, it remains a fiercely independent swing state that holds some of the earliest election primaries in the country and that's known for both its libertarian and progressive tendencies.

The state's varied terrain makes it popular with everyone from hard-core climbers and skiers to young families looking for easy access to nature. You can hike, ski, snowboard, snowshoe, and fish, as well as explore on snowmobiles, sailboats, kayaks, and mountain bikes. New Hampshirites have no objection to others enjoying the beauty here as long as they leave a few dollars behind: it's the only state in the union with neither sales nor income taxes, so tourism brings in much-needed revenue (and tourists can enjoy tax-free shopping).

With a few communities consistently rated among the most livable in the nation, New Hampshire has grown a bit faster than most other northeastern states over the past two decades. The state is gradually developing two distinct personalities: one characterized by rapid urbanization in the southeast and the other by quiet village life in the west and north. Although newcomers have brought change, the free-spirited sensibility of the Granite State remains intact, as does its natural splendor.

MAJOR REGIONS

The **Seacoast,** New Hampshire's 18-mile stretch of coastline, packs in plenty of gorgeous scenery and lively diversions. The northern portion of the shoreline, from the charmingly historic regional hub, **Portsmouth**, south through the affluent town of **Rye**, is especially pristine and free from the honky-tonk excess of the southern section (around Hampton Beach and Seabrook). From Rye, you can branch inland to the prep-school town of **Exeter**, and then cut north through **Durham** (home to the University of New Hampshire). From here it's a short drive to the Lakes Region.

Throughout central New Hampshire, you'll encounter lakes and more lakes in the aptly named **Lakes Region.** The largest, Lake Winnipesaukee, has 180 miles of coastline and attracts all sorts of water-sports enthusiasts to the towns of **Wolfeboro**, **Laconia** (with its bustling **Weirs Beach** section), and **Meredith**. You'll find smaller and more secluded lakes with enchanting bed-and-breakfasts in **Holderness**, which adjoins famously scenic Squam Lake. **Plymouth**, **Center Sandwich**, and **Tamworth** are great bases to explore the surrounding lakes and as well as the southern reaches of the White Mountains.

Skiing, snowshoeing, and snowboarding in the winter; hiking, biking, and riding scenic railways in the summer: the Whites, as locals call **The White Mountains,** have plenty of natural wonders. **Mt. Washington**, the tallest mountain in the Northeast, can be conquered by trail, train, or car; other towns with strong railroad ties include up-and-coming **Littleton** and touristy **North Conway**. **Lincoln** and **North Woodstock** and **Waterville Valley** are lively resort areas, and **Bethlehem, Jackson**, and **Franconia** are stunning alpine jewels. **Bretton Woods** and **Bartlett** are great skiing and hiking towns.

Quiet villages proliferate in the **Lake Sunapee** region; the lake itself is a wonderful place to swim, fish, or enjoy a cruise. **Hanover**, home to Dartmouth College (founded 1769), retains that true New England college-town feel, with ivy-draped buildings and cobblestone walkways. The charming town of **New London** is one of the area's main hubs, while **Newbury**, on the edge of Mt. Sunapee State Park, is a popular base for outdoor recreation. **Cornish**, once the haunt of J. D. Salinger, is where you'll find Cornish-Windsor Bridge, the country's second-longest covered bridge.

New and old coexist in **the Monadnocks and Merrimack Valley,** the state's southwestern and south-central regions, respectively. Here high-tech firms have helped reshape the cities of **Manchester** and **Concord** while small towns in the hills surrounding Mt. Monadnock, southern New Hampshire's largest peak, like **Keene** and **Peterborough**, celebrate tradition and history. **Walpole** has one of the state's loveliest town greens.

Planning

Getting Here and Around

Although New Hampshire is a small state, roads curve around lakes and mountains, making distances sometimes much longer than they appear on a map. You can get a taste of the coast, lake, and mountain areas in three to five days; eight days will give you time to make a more complete loop.

AIR

Manchester-Boston Regional Airport, the state's largest, has nonstop service from more than a dozen U.S. cities. The drive from Boston's Logan Airport to most places in New Hampshire takes one to three hours; the same is true for Bradley International Airport, outside Hartford, Connecticut.

CAR

In this generally rural state with limited public transportation, a car is definitely the easiest and most practical way to get around. Interstate 93 stretches from Boston to Littleton and on into neighboring Vermont. Interstate 89 will get you from Concord to Hanover en route to Burlington, Vermont. And Interstate 95 (a toll road) passes through New Hampshire's short coastal region on the way from Boston to Maine. Throughout the state, quiet and winding backcountry lanes can take a little longer but reward travelers with gorgeous scenery.

The speed limit on interstate and limited-access highways is usually 65 to 70 mph. On state and U.S. routes, speed limits vary considerably, from 25 mph to 55 mph, so watch signs carefully. The website of the **New Hampshire Department of Transportation** (⊕ www.nhtmc.com) has up-to-the-minute information about traffic and road conditions.

TRAIN

Amtrak's *Downeaster* passenger rain operates between Boston and Portland, Maine, with New Hampshire stops in Exeter, Durham, and Dover.

Hotels

In the mid-19th century, wealthy Bostonians retreated to imposing New Hampshire country homes in the summer. Grand hotels were built across the state, especially in the White Mountains, which at that time competed with Saratoga Springs, Newport, and Bar Harbor to draw the nation's elite vacationers. A handful of these hotel-resorts survive, and many of those country houses have since been converted into romantic inns. You'll also find quite a few well-kept motor lodges and cottage compounds, particularly in the White Mountains and Lakes regions. In ski areas, expect the usual ski condos and lodges, but most slopes are also within a short drive of a country inn or two. In the Merrimack River valley, as well as along major highways, chain hotels and motels predominate. The state is rife with campgrounds, especially in the White Mountains.

Hotel reviews have been shortened. For full information, visit Fodors.com.

Restaurants

With a dining scene that's still dominated by old-fashioned hotels, lively pubs, laid-back seafood shacks, and unfussy diners, delis, and pizza parlors, New Hampshire is still generally a bit more traditional than its neighboring states, but the times are definitely changing. You'll find a growing array of contemporary, locavore-driven bistros, international restaurants, third-wave coffee roasters, mixology-minded cocktail bars, and artisanal craft breweries around the state—especially in Portsmouth and Manchester, but also in an increasing number of smaller communities, such as Bethlehem, Exeter, Jackson, Keene, New London, and Walpole. In quite a few smaller hamlets, the best restaurant in town is often inside the historic inn. Reservations are seldom required, and dress is casual.

Restaurant reviews have been shortened. For full information, visit Fodors. com.

What It Costs in U.S. Dollars			
$	$$	$$$	$$$$
RESTAURANTS			
under $18	$18–$24	$25–$35	over $35
HOTELS			
under $150	$150–$225	$226–$300	over $300

Outdoor Activities

Skiing: Ski areas abound in New Hampshire, among them Bretton Woods, Mt. Sunapee, Waterville Valley, and Cannon Mountain. For cross-country skiing, nothing beats Gunstock Mountain Resort, with 32 miles of trails, also open for snowshoeing. Or visit Franconia Village, which has 40 miles of cross-country trails.

Biking: Many ski resorts in the White Mountains offer mountain biking, providing chairlift rides to the mountaintop and trails for all skill levels at the bottom. Some of the state's most scenic road biking is along the Kancamagus Highway and around Lake Sunapee.

Hiking: New Hampshire is a fantastic state for trekking, whether you're up for an arduous hike in the White Mountains or along the Appalachian Trail, or you'd rather something a bit less taxing, maybe around the shore of Lake Sunapee or Lake Winnipesaukee, or in one of the dozens of beautiful state parks, such as Crawford Notch, Franconia Notch, and Mt. Monadnock.

Shopping

One of five U.S. states without a sales tax, New Hampshire is famously popular with bargain hunters. From outlet shopping centers to state-run liquor stores to bustling downtowns packed with independent boutiques, you'll find great deals in every corner of the state.

Visitor Information

CONTACTS Lakes Region Tourism Association. ⊠ *Tilton* ☎ *603/286–8008* ⊕ *www.lakesregion.org.* **Lake Sunapee Region Chamber of Commerce.** ⊠ *New London* ☎ *603/526–6575* ⊕ *www.lakesunapeeregionchamber.com.* **Ski New Hampshire.** ☎ *603/745–9396* ⊕ *www.skinh.com.* **Visit New Hampshire.** ⊠ *Concord* ☎ *603/271–2665* ⊕ *www.visitnh.gov.* **White Mountains Visitors Center.** ⊠ *North Woodstock* ☎ *603/745–8720* ⊕ *www.visitwhitemountains.com.* **Chamber Collaborative of Greater Portsmouth.** ⊠ *Portsmouth* ☎ *603/610–5510* ⊕ *www.goportsmouthnh.com.*

When to Go

Summer and fall are the most popular and expensive times to visit New Hampshire. Fans of boating, swimming, and hiking flock to the state's many lakes as well as the short section of coastline starting around Memorial Day and continuing through mid-September. After that, for the next few weeks, the state is a magnet for fans of fall foliage. Winter is popular for skiers and other winter-sports enthusiasts, especially in the White Mountains, but outside of ski areas, many businesses and attractions close or have shorter hours from late fall until May or June. Spring's unpredictable weather—along with April's mud and late May's black flies—tends to deter visitors. Still, the season has its joys, not the least of which is the appearance, mid-May–early June, of the state flower, the purple lilac, soon followed by the blooming of colorful rhododendrons and fields of lupine.

Portsmouth

47 miles east of Concord, 50 miles south of Portland, Maine, 56 miles north of Boston.

A small but lively Colonial port across the river from Kittery, Maine, upscale Portsmouth buzzes with hip restaurants, swank cocktails bars, contemporary art galleries and boutiques, and acclaimed cultural venues that host nationally recognized speakers and performers—the action is focused largely around downtown's Market Square. Settled in 1623 as Strawbery Banke, Portsmouth grew into a prosperous port before the Revolutionary War, during which it harbored many Tory sympathizers. These days, this city of 22,000 has many grand residences from the 18th to the early 20th centuries, many of them preserved within or near the engaging Strawbery Banke Museum. For a scenic drive or bike ride, follow Rte. 1B east from downtown across the Piscataqua River, following it around leafy New Castle Island—where you'll pass Fort Constitution and the grand, historic Wentworth by the Sea Hotel.

GETTING HERE AND AROUND

Both Interstate 95 and U.S. 1 connect Portsmouth with the rest of coastal New England, while U.S. 4 and Route 101 are the easiest ways to get here from inland New Hampshire. Downtown Portsmouth is walkable, though you'll need a car for attractions farther afield.

BOAT TOURS

Gundalow Company

BOAT TOURS | FAMILY | Sail the Piscataqua River in a flat-bottom gundalow (a type of barge) built at Strawbery Banke. Help the crew set sail, steer the vessel, and trawl for plankton while learning about the region's history from an onboard educator. Passengers are welcome to bring food and beverages. Afternoon and evening sails are offered. ⊠ *60 Marcy St., Portsmouth* ☎ *603/433–9505* ⊕ *www.gundalow.org* ✉ *From $18* ۞ *Closed mid-Oct.–late May.*

Portsmouth Harbor Cruises

BOAT TOURS | Tours of Portsmouth Harbor and the Isles of Shoals, inland-river foliage trips, and sunset and wine cruises are all in this company's repertoire. ⊠ *64 Ceres St., Portsmouth* ☎ *603/436–8084, 800/776–0915* ⊕ *www.portsmouthharbor. com* ✉ *From $21* ۞ *Closed Nov.–early May.*

WALKING TOURS

★ Discover Portsmouth

WALKING TOURS | FAMILY | The Portsmouth Historical Society operates this combination visitor center–museum, where you can pick up maps, get the scoop on what's happening while you're in town, and view cultural and historical exhibits. Here you can also learn about self-guided historical tours and sign up for guided ones. ⊠ *10 Middle St., Portsmouth* ☎ *603/436–8433* ⊕ *www.portsmouthhistory.org* ✉ *Tours from $20* ۞ *No tours Nov.–Apr.*

★ Portsmouth Black Heritage Trail

WALKING TOURS | FAMILY | Important local sites in African American history can be seen on the 75-minute guided Sankofa Tour. Included are the African Burying Ground and historic homes of local slave traders and abolitionists. Tours, which begin at the Old Meeting House, are conducted on Saturday afternoon throughout the summer. ⊠ *222 Court St., Portsmouth* ☎ *603/570–8469* ⊕ *www. blackheritagetrailnh.org* ✉ *$20* ۞ *No tours Nov.–Apr.*

Portsmouth Eats

WALKING TOURS | On White Table, Best of Portsmouth, and Sweet and Savory walking tours—mostly on weekends—you get to taste the culinary delights of four or five establishments in New Hampshire's coastal city. ☎ *603/571–3287* ⊕ *www. portsmouth-eats.com* ✉ *From $45.*

VISITOR INFORMATION

Chamber Collaborative of Greater Portsmouth

✉ *Portsmouth* ☎ *603/610–5510* ⊕ *www. portsmouthchamber.org.*

⊙ Sights

Albacore Park

MILITARY SIGHT | Built in Portsmouth in 1953, the USS *Albacore* is the centerpiece of Albacore Park. You can board this prototype submarine, which served as a floating laboratory to test an innovative hull design, dive brakes, and sonar systems for the Navy. The visitor center exhibits *Albacore* artifacts, and the nearby Memorial Garden is dedicated to those who have lost their lives in submarine service. ✉ *600 Market St., Portsmouth* ☎ *603/436–3680* ⊕ *www. ussalbacore.org* 🎟 *$9* ⊙ *Closed Tues.*

Great Bay Estuarine National Research Reserve

NATURE PRESERVE | **FAMILY** | Just inland from Portsmouth is one of southeastern New Hampshire's most precious assets. In this 10,235 acres of open and tidal waters, you can spot blue herons, ospreys, and snowy egrets, particularly during the spring and fall migrations. The Great Bay Discovery Center has indoor and outdoor exhibits, a library and bookshop, and a 1,700-foot boardwalk, as well as other trails, which wind through mudflats and upland forest. ✉ *89 Depot Rd., Greenland* ☎ *603/778–0015* ⊕ *www. greatbay.org* 🎟 *Free* ⊙ *Discovery Center closed Sun. and Mon. and Nov.–Apr.*

Isles of Shoals

ISLAND | **FAMILY** | Four of the nine small, rocky Isles of Shoals belong to New Hampshire (the other five belong to Maine), many of them still known by the earthy names—Hog and Smuttynose, to cite but two—17th-century fishermen bestowed on them. A history of piracy, murder, and ghosts suffuses the archipelago, long populated by an independent lot who, according to one writer, hadn't the sense to winter on the mainland. Celia Thaxter, a native islander, romanticized these islands with her poetry in *Among the Isles of Shoals* (1873). In the late 19th century, Appledore Island became an offshore retreat for Thaxter's coterie of writers, musicians, and artists. Star Island contains a small museum, the Rutledge Marine Lab, with interactive family exhibits. From May to early October you can take a narrated history cruise of the Isles of Shoals and walking tours of Star Island with Isles of Shoals Steamship Company. ✉ *Barker Wharf, 315 Market St., Portsmouth* ☎ *800/441–4620, 603/431–5500* ⊕ *www.islesofshoals. com* 🚢 *Cruises from $41* ⊙ *No cruises mid-Oct.–Apr.*

John Paul Jones House

HISTORIC HOME | **FAMILY** | Revolutionary War hero John Paul Jones lived at this boardinghouse while he supervised construction of the USS *America* for the Continental Navy. The 1758 hip-roof building displays furniture, costumes, glass, guns, portraits, and documents from the late 18th century. The collection's specialty is textiles, among them some extraordinary early-19th-century embroidery samplers. ✉ *43 Middle St., Portsmouth* ☎ *603/436–8420* ⊕ *www. portsmouthhistory.org* 🎟 *$10* ⊙ *Closed mid-Oct.–late May.*

★ Moffatt-Ladd House and Garden

HISTORIC HOME | The period interior of this striking 1763 mansion tells the story of Portsmouth's merchant class through portraits, letters, and furnishings. The Colonial Revival garden includes a horse chestnut tree planted by General William Whipple when he returned home after signing the Declaration of Independence in 1776. ✉ *154 Market St., Portsmouth* ☎ *603/436–8221* ⊕ *www.moffattladd. org* 🎟 *$10; garden only $2* ⊙ *Closed mid-Oct.–May.*

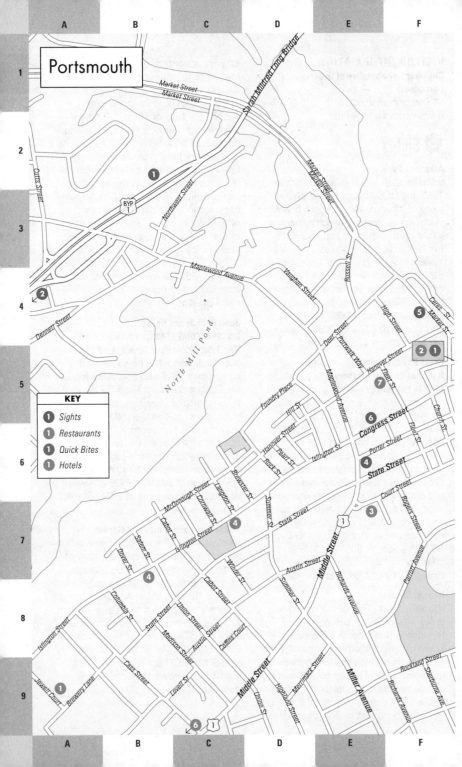

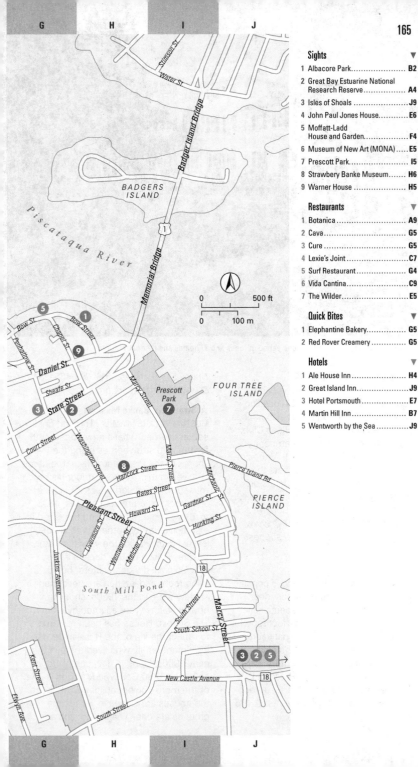

Strawbery Banke Museum includes period gardens and 37 homes and other structures.

Museum of New Art (MONA)

ART MUSEUM | Set in the same handsomely restored 1905 YMCA building in downtown Portsmouth that also houses acclaimed Jimmy's Jazz & Blues Club, this 6,800-square-foot contemporary art museum opened in 2021. A non-collecting institution, MONA hosts three exhibits each year, with the focus on emerging artists and often large-scale, site-specific works. ⊠ *135 Congress St., Portsmouth* ☎ *603/450–1011* ⊕ *www. monaportsmouth.org* 🖃 *$10 suggested donation* 🕘 *Closed Mon.*

Prescott Park

CITY PARK | **FAMILY** | Picnicking is popular at this 3½-acre waterfront park near Strawbery Banke, whose spectacular garden with fountains is perfect for whiling away an afternoon. The park contains Point of Graves, Portsmouth's oldest burial ground, and two 17th-century warehouses. The summerlong Prescott Park Arts Festival features concerts, outdoor movies, and food-related events. ⊠ *105 Marcy St., Portsmouth* ☎ *603/436–2848* ⊕ *www.prescottpark.org.*

★ Strawbery Banke Museum

MUSEUM VILLAGE | **FAMILY** | The first English settlers named what's now Portsmouth for the wild strawberries along the shores of the Piscataqua River. The name survives in this 10-acre outdoor history museum, which comprises 37 homes and other structures dating from 1695 to 1954, some restored and furnished to a particular period, others with historical exhibits. Half of the interior of the Shapley-Drisco House depicts its use as a Colonial dry-goods store, but its living room and kitchen are decorated as they were in the 1950s, showing how buildings were adapted over time. The Shapiro House has been restored to reflect the life of the Russian-Jewish immigrant family who lived there in the early 1900s. Done in decadent Victorian style, the 1860 Goodwin Mansion is one of the more opulent buildings. Although the houses are closed in winter, the grounds are open year-round, and an outdoor skating rink operates December–early March. ✉ *14 Hancock St., Portsmouth* ☎ *603/433–1100* ⊕ *www.strawberybanke.org* 🎫 *$19.50* 🕙 *Homes closed Nov.–Apr. except for guided tours on Nov. weekends.*

Warner House

HISTORIC HOME | The highlight of this circa-1716 gem is the curious folk-art murals lining the hall staircase, which may be the oldest-known murals in the United States still gracing their original structure. The house, a notable example of brick Georgian architecture, contains original art, furnishings, and extraordinary examples of area craftsmanship. The west-wall lightning rod is believed to have been installed in 1762 under the supervision of Benjamin Franklin. ✉ *150 Daniel St., Portsmouth* ☎ *603/436–5909* ⊕ *www.warnerhouse.org* 🎫 *$10* 🕙 *Closed mid-Oct.–late May and Mon.–Wed.*

🍴 Restaurants

★ Botanica

$$$ | **MODERN FRENCH** | This swanky spot in a gorgeous old brick brewery building in Portsmouth's up-and-coming West End is a magnet for fans of artisan gin, which figures in about a dozen intriguing cocktails, but the exquisite French-accented cuisine appeals to all. Highlights from the seasonal menu include classic steak frites with brandy jus, and grilled monkfish in a squash bisque with corn and lobster. **Known for:** imaginative gin-centric cocktails; attractive side patio; chocolate soufflé. 💲 *Average main: $30* ✉ *110 Brewery La., Portsmouth* ☎ *603/373–0979* ⊕ *www.botanicanh.com* 🕙 *Closed Sun.–Mon. No lunch.*

★ Cava

$$$ | **TAPAS** | Having a meal at this sophisticated little wine and tapas bar down a tiny alley near the downtown riverfront can feel like going to a special dinner party. It has a small exhibition kitchen and bar, and just a handful of tables and chairs, where

guests can enjoy a selection of stellar bocadillos, tapas, and pintxos—from piquillo peppers with goat cheese and artichokes to char-grilled baby octopus—plus a few larger plates, such as paella. **Known for:** a superb wine list; authentic Spanish tapas; churros with hot chocolate. 💲 *Average main: $26* ✉ *10 Commercial Alley, Portsmouth* ☎ *603/319–1575* ⊕ *www.cavatapasandwinebar.com* 🕙 *Closed Mon. and Tues. No lunch.*

★ Cure

$$$ | **MODERN AMERICAN** | As its name hints, this buzzy neighborhood bistro in a lively dining room with redbrick walls, beam ceilings, and hardwood floors specializes in cured, brined, and slow-cooked meats, which you can sample through beautifully presented charcuterie boards, smoked ribs, and slow-roasted Moroccan lamb shank. But take heart if you're less disposed toward red meat—you'll find plenty of creative seafood and veggie dishes on the menu, including gooey lobster mac and cheese. **Known for:** locally sourced ingredients; well-chosen wine list; lively but romantic dining room. 💲 *Average main: $29* ✉ *189 State St., Portsmouth* ☎ *603/427–8258* ⊕ *www.curerestaurantportsmouth.com* 🕙 *No lunch.*

Lexie's Joint

$ | **BURGER** | **FAMILY** | What began as a humble downtown burger joint has blossomed into a regional mini empire, thanks to the high-quality ingredients, upbeat service, and groovy "peace, love, and burgers"–themed decor. The burgers are reasonably priced and topped with all sorts of goodies, but there are also hot dogs and a few sandwiches, plus plenty of addictive sides. **Known for:** milk shakes with Shain's of Maine homemade ice cream; fried pickles with chipotle aioli; the farmhouse burger, with cheddar, bacon, avocado, and fried egg. 💲 *Average main: $9* ✉ *212 Islington St., Portsmouth* ☎ *603/815–4181* ⊕ *www.peaceloveburgers.com.*

Surf Restaurant

$$$ | SEAFOOD | Whether you eat inside the conversation-filled, high-ceilinged dining room or out on the breezy deck, you'll be treated to expansive views of Old Harbour and the Piscataqua River—an apt setting for consistently fresh and tasty seafood. The menu branches into several directions, including lobster rolls, shrimp-pork ramen, sushi, and Tuscan-style shrimp with marinara sauce, but manages everything well, and there's a well-curated wine and cocktail selection to complement your choice. **Known for:** raw-bar specialties; water views; creative sushi rolls. $ *Average main: $29* ✉ *99 Bow St., Portsmouth* ☎ *603/334–9855* ⊕ *www.surfseafood.com* ⊙ *Closed Mon. and Tues. No lunch Wed. and Thurs.*

Vida Cantina

$$ | MODERN MEXICAN | In a state sorely lacking in notable Latin restaurants, this airy contemporary space south of downtown stands out for the ambitious modern Mexican cuisine of chef-owner and James Beard award–nominated chef David Vargas. Several kinds of street-food-style tacos are offered, including barbacoa and pork belly, along with a tangy goat cheese version of queso fundido and sous vide short rib with pistachio salsa macha. **Known for:** adobo shrimp mole; interesting sides, like blue cornbread and shishito peppers; boozy weekend brunches. $ *Average main: $21* ✉ *2456 Lafayette Rd., Portsmouth* ☎ *603/501–0648* ⊕ *www. vidacantinanh.com.*

The Wilder

$$$ | MODERN AMERICAN | Have a seat at the bar or at one of the banquette seats along the wall at this convivial, upscale gastropub with offbeat artwork and a diverse crowd. The kitchen serves up well-executed takes on comfort classics like Nashville-style hot chicken sandwiches with maple-cayenne sauce; poutine smothered in roasted-bone gravy and glazed pork belly; and braised beef short rib with mushroom-onion jam and crispy

shallots. **Known for:** late-night dining; lively and friendly bar scene; fun weekend brunch. $ *Average main: $25* ✉ *174 Fleet St., Portsmouth* ☎ *603/319–6878* ⊕ *www.wilderportsmouth.com* ⊙ *No lunch weekdays.*

☕ Coffee and Quick Bites

★ Elephantine Bakery

$ | BAKERY | Master bakers Sherif and Nadine Farag run this cozy, conversation-filled bakery and cafe that's known for its meticulously crafted Middle Eastern and French pastries, sandwiches, and breakfast dishes. Start the day with poached eggs *cilbir* (over garlic labneh with aleppo butter, parsley gremolata, and toasted sourdough), and make every effort to save room for a slice of cardamom-rosewater cake or a brown-butter brownie. **Known for:** perfectly poured espresso drinks; Egyptian bread pudding with coconut milk; outdoor seating on a redbrick sidewalk. $ *Average main: $14* ✉ *10 Commercial Alley, Portsmouth* ☎ *603/319–6189* ⊕ *www.elephantinebakery.com* ⊙ *No dinner.*

★ Red Rover Creamery

$ | ICE CREAM | FAMILY | This tiny parlor in historic downtown produces ice cream in big, bold flavors—think black currant tea–caramel, brown sugar–nectarine, and classic cookies-and-cream. They also bake dense and chewy cookies in interesting flavors, which you can enjoy on their own or in an ice-cream sandwich. **Known for:** fresh-baked cookies; decadent ice-cream sandwiches; steps from Strawbery Banke Museum. $ *Average main: $6* ✉ *150 State St., Portsmouth* ☎ *603/427–8172* ⊕ *www.redrovercreamery.com* ⊙ *Closed Mon. and Tues.*

🛏 Hotels

Ale House Inn

$$ | B&B/INN | Each of the stylish rooms in this urbane inn occupying a converted Victorian redbrick brewery on the historic riverfront has plenty of handy amenities,

such as wine glasses with corkscrews, iPod docks, and plush robes, and the modern bathrooms have handsome Italian tilework. **Pros:** welcome beers from local breweries upon arrival; free parking; bicycles for local jaunts. **Cons:** no breakfast; several steps to enter hotel; rooms are a bit compact. $ *Rooms from: $195* ⊠ *121 Bow St., Portsmouth* ☎ *603/431–7760* ⊕ *www.larkhotels.com* ⤵ *10 rooms* ⦿ *No Meals.*

Great Island Inn

$$$ | **B&B/INN** | From downtown Portsmouth, it's a picturesque 2-mile drive or bike ride along the Piscataqua River to this urbane inn set inside an 1820s home that's been given a nautical-chic redesign, all of its six apartment-style studios equipped with well-stocked kitchens, washers and dryers, and light-filled living spaces. **Pros:** smart, contemporary decor; free parking if you book through the inn's website; pretty setting on historic New Castle Island. **Cons:** housekeeping services aren't offered; not directly on the water; a little far to walk to dining and shopping. $ *Rooms from: $280* ⊠ *3 Walbach St., New Castle* ☎ *603/436–2778* ⊕ *www.greatislandinn.com* ⤵ *6 rooms* ⦿ *No Meals.*

Hotel Portsmouth

$$ | **HOTEL** | This downtown Victorian mansion built in 1881 by a sea captain is now a 32-room boutique hotel with elegantly updated furnishings, plush bed linens, and such modern conveniences as iPad docks, fast Wi-Fi, and flat-screen TVs. **Pros:** close to Market Square; free parking; lounge serving wine, beer, and small bites. **Cons:** thin walls result in occasional noise; some rooms have bland views; two-night minimum during busy times. $ *Rooms from: $220* ⊠ *40 Court St., Portsmouth* ☎ *603/433–1200* ⊕ *www.larkhotels.com* ⤵ *32 rooms* ⦿ *Free Breakfast.*

Martin Hill Inn

$$ | **B&B/INN** | The quiet rooms in this yellow 1815 house surrounded by flower-filled gardens are furnished with antiques and

decorated with fine period antiques; a generous full breakfast is served each morning, featuring lemon-ricotta pancakes or other delectable treats. **Pros:** refrigerators in rooms; excellent breakfast; off-street parking. **Cons:** a little outside the downtown core on busy street; breakfast is served at a communal table; no children under 12. $ *Rooms from: $220* ⊠ *404 Islington St., Portsmouth* ☎ *603/436–2287* ⊕ *www.martinhillinn.com* ⤵ *7 rooms* ⦿ *Free Breakfast.*

★ Wentworth by the Sea

$$$$ | **RESORT** | Nearly demolished in the 1980s, one of coastal New England's most elegant Victorian grand resorts— where the likes of Harry Truman and Gloria Swanson once vacationed—has been meticulously restored and now ranks among the cushiest golf, boating, and spa getaways in New Hampshire. **Pros:** amenities include an expansive full-service spa, heated indoor pool, and an outstanding golf course; marina with charters for harbor cruises and deep-sea fishing; excellent food in main restaurant and casual waterfront bistro. **Cons:** 10- to 15-minute drive from downtown Portsmouth; steep rates in summer and fall; large property lacks intimacy. $ *Rooms from: $365* ⊠ *588 Wentworth Rd., New Castle* ☎ *603/422–7322, 866/384–0709* ⊕ *www.marriott.com* ⤵ *161 rooms* ⦿ *No Meals.*

▼ Nightlife

BARS AND BREWPUBS

★ Earth Eagle Brewings

BREWPUBS | This bustling gastropub produces unusual, boldly flavorful ales in the Belgian style, some using distinctive botanicals—lemongrass, ginger root— rather than hops. The food is terrific, there's an airy outdoor beer garden, and musicians perform many evenings. ⊠ *175 High St., Portsmouth* ☎ *603/502–2244* ⊕ *www.eartheaglebrewings.com.*

Four of the nine rocky Isles of Shoals belong to New Hampshire; the other five belong to Maine.

Portsmouth Book & Bar

BARS | Combine an old-school indie bookstore with a funky café–cocktail bar, set it inside a restored 1817 customhouse, and you've got this endearing hangout that's popular with everyone from college students to artists to tourists. Live music, comedy, and readings are offered, too. ✉ *40 Pleasant St., Portsmouth* ☎ *603/427–9197* ⊕ *www.bookandbar. com.*

MUSIC CLUBS

⭐ Jimmy's Jazz & Blue Club

LIVE MUSIC | Downtown's early 1900s YMCA building has been converted into this gorgeous, high-ceilinged music venue with brick walls, color artwork, and a snug mezzanine. An impressive lineup of jazz and blues bands perform here, and full dinner service from a Southern-accented menu is available before each show. ✉ *135 Congress St., Portsmouth* ☎ *888/603–5299* ⊕ *www.jimmysoncongress.com.*

🎭 Performing Arts

⭐ Music Hall

CONCERTS | Beloved for its acoustics, the 895-seat hall built in 1878 presents top-drawer music concerts, from pop to classical, along with dance and theater. The more intimate Music Hall Lounge, around the corner, presents performances by noted musicians, authors, and comedians and serves light food and drinks. ✉ *28 Chestnut St., Portsmouth* ☎ *603/436–2400* ⊕ *www.themusichall. org.*

Seacoast Repertory Theatre

THEATER | Here you'll find a year-round schedule of musicals, classic dramas, and works by up-and-coming playwrights, as well as everything from a youth theater to drag cabaret nights. ✉ *125 Bow St., Portsmouth* ☎ *603/433–4472* ⊕ *www. seacoastrep.org.*

🛍 Shopping

The historic city center, especially around Market Square, abounds with gift and clothing boutiques, book and gourmet food shops, and crafts stores and art galleries.

Byrne & Carlson

CHOCOLATE | Watch elegant cream truffles and luscious chocolates being made in the European tradition at this small artisanal shop. ✉ 121 State St., Portsmouth ☎ 207/439–0096 ⊕ www.byrneandcarlson.com.

New Hampshire Art Association

ART GALLERIES | Since 1940, this venerable local arts organization has served as an incubator of local painters, sculptors, and other talented creatives. Works by the association's more than 300 juried members appear on the walls of this lively downtown gallery. NHAA also organizes other shows throughout the state—check the website for the latest schedule. ✉ 136 State St., Portsmouth ☎ 603/431–4230 ⊕ www.nhartassociation.org.

Off Piste

SOUVENIRS | Look to this quirky emporium for offbeat gifts and household goods— everything from painted buoy birdhouses to irreverent books, games, and mugs. ✉ 37 Congress St., Portsmouth ☎ 603/319–6910.

Portsmouth Farmers' Market

MARKET | FAMILY | One of the best and longest-running farmers' markets in the state showcases seasonal produce along with regional treats such as maple syrup and artisanal cheeses. There's live music, too. It's held Saturday morning, May–early November. ✉ City Hall parking lot, 1 Junkens Ave., Portsmouth ☎ 888/600–0128 ⊕ www.seacoasteatlocal.org.

Rye

8 miles south of Portsmouth.

In 1623 the English established a settlement at Odiorne Point in what is now the minimally developed and picturesque town of Rye, making it the birthplace of New Hampshire. Top draws include a lovely state park, beaches, and the views from Route 1A, which is prettiest if you follow it south, passing the group of late-19th- and early-20th-century mansions known as Millionaires' Row. Strict town laws prohibit commercial development in Rye, creating a dramatic contrast with its frenetic neighbor, Hampton Beach.

GETTING HERE AND AROUND
Interstate 95 and U.S. 1, just west of town, provide easy access, but Rye shows its best face from coastal Route 1A.

👁 Sights

★ Fuller Gardens

GARDEN | Arthur Shurtleff, a noted landscape architect from Boston, designed this late-1920s estate garden in the Colonial Revival style. In a gracious seaside residential neighborhood a couple of miles south of Jenness Beach, this peaceful little botanical gem encompasses 1,700 rosebushes, hosta and Japanese gardens, and a tropical conservatory. ✉ 10 Willow Ave., North Hampton ☎ 603/964–5414 ⊕ www.fullergardens.org 🖾 $9 🕙 Closed mid-Oct.–early May.

★ Odiorne Point State Park

STATE/PROVINCIAL PARK | FAMILY | These 135 acres of protected seaside land are where David Thompson established New Hampshire's first permanent English settlement. Several signed nature trails provide vistas of the nearby Isles of Shoals and interpret the park's military history. The rocky shore's tidal pools shelter crabs, periwinkles, and sea anemones. The park's **Seacoast Science Center** hosts exhibits on the area's natural history. Its tidal-pool touch tank and 1,000-gallon Gulf of Maine deepwater aquarium are popular with kids. ✉ *570 Ocean Blvd., Rye* ☎ *603/436–8043* ⊕ *www.seacoastsciencecenter.org* 🎫 *Park $4, Science Center $10* 🕙 *Closed Tues.*

🏖 Beaches

Jenness State Beach

BEACH | FAMILY | Good for swimming and sunbathing, this long, sandy beach is a favorite among locals who enjoy its light crowds and nice waves for bodysurfing. Wide and shallow, Jenness Beach is a great place for kids to run and build sand castles. **Amenities:** lifeguards; parking (fee); showers; toilets. **Best for:** surfing; swimming; walking. ✉ *2280 Ocean Blvd., Rye* ☎ *603/227–8722* ⊕ *www.nhstateparks.org* 🎫 *Parking $2/hr Apr.–Sept., $1/hr Oct.*

★ Wallis Sands State Beach

BEACH | FAMILY | This family-friendly swimmers' beach has bright white sand, a picnic area, a store, and beautiful views of the Isles of Shoals. **Amenities:** food and drink; lifeguards; parking (fee); showers; toilets. **Best for:** swimming; walking. ✉ *1050 Ocean Blvd.; Rye* ☎ *603/436–9404* ⊕ *www.nhstateparks.org* 🎫 *$15 per car (late May–mid-Sept.).*

🍴 Restaurants

The Carriage House

$$$ | SEAFOOD | Across from Jenness Beach, this elegant cottage serves innovative dishes with an emphasis on local seafood, from raw bar specialties like scallop crudo and littleneck clams on the half shell to roasted cod and tarragon lobster salad. A first-rate hanger steak and lamb stew with eggplant and fry bread round out the menu. **Known for:** classic daily blue-plate specials; breezy, refreshing cocktails; cozy upstairs tavern with ocean views. 💲 *Average main: $31* ✉ *2263 Ocean Blvd., Rye* ☎ *603/964–8251* ⊕ *www.carriagehouserye.com* 🕙 *Closed Sun. and Mon. No lunch.*

🛏 Hotels

★ Rye Motor Inn

$$$$ | MOTEL | This chicly remade mid-century motel, comprising 12 spacious apartment-style suites with kitchens and retro-cool decor, enjoys direct beach access along a mostly undeveloped and gorgeous stretch of Atlantic coastline between Odiorne Point and Wallis Sands Beach. **Pros:** all units have fully equipped kitchens; directly across the road from the beach; adults (21 and over) only. **Cons:** adults (21 and over) only; rooms themselves don't actually overlook the ocean; two-night minimum stay on weekends. 💲 *Rooms from: $349* ✉ *741 Ocean Blvd., Rye* ☎ *603/436–2778* ⊕ *www.ryemotorinn.com* 🍽 *12 rooms* 🍴 *No Meals.*

🍸 Nightlife

★ Throwback Brewery

BREWPUBS | FAMILY | After a day of fun at the beach, head a few miles inland to this working farm on 12 acres and its sustainable brewery that crafts first-rate ales using as much local ingredients as possible—some of the hops are grown on-site. On sunny days, sample Throwback's beers in the tented beer garden, and any time of year, you can sip and dine on farm-to-table pub fare, from cheese plates to Korean beef bowls. You can also buy seasonal produce at the farmstand. ✉ *7 Hobbs Rd., North Hampton* ☎ *603/379–2317* ⊕ *www.throwbackbrewery.com.*

🏃 Activities

Granite State Whale Watch

WILDLIFE-WATCHING | FAMILY | This respected outfitter conducts naturalist-led whale-watching tours aboard the 100-passenger *Granite State*, along with excursions around the Isles of Shoals and to Star Island. ✉ *Rye Harbor*

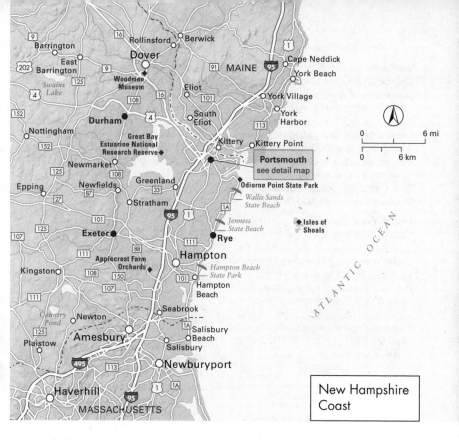

New Hampshire
Coast

State Marina, 1870 Ocean Blvd., Rye
☎ 603/964–5545, 800/964–5545 ⊕ www.
granitestatewhalewatch.com ⊠ $46
⊘ Closed mid-Oct.–mid-May.

Exeter

11 miles west of Rye.

During the Revolutionary War, Exeter served as the state capital, and it was here amid intense patriotic fervor that the first state constitution and the first Colonial Declaration of Independence from Great Britain were put to paper. These days this dapper river town shares more in appearance and personality with Boston's blue-blooded satellite communities than the rest of New Hampshire. Cheerful cafés, coffeehouses, and boutiques with artisanal wares fill the bustling town center.

GETTING HERE AND AROUND
Amtrak's *Downeaster* stops here between Boston and Portland, Maine. By car, Route 101 provides access from the east and west.

ESSENTIALS
VISITOR INFORMATION Exeter Area Chamber of Commerce. ⊠ *Exeter* ☎ *603/772–2411* ⊕ *www.exeterarea.org.*

◉ Sights

American Independence Museum
HISTORY MUSEUM | Guided tours of this museum that celebrates the nation's birth focus on the family who lived here during the Revolutionary War. Among 3,000 artifacts, see drafts of the U.S. Constitution and the first Purple Heart, as

well as letters and documents written by George Washington and the household furnishings of John Taylor Gilman, one of New Hampshire's early governors. In July, the museum hosts the two-week American Independence Festival, and occasional architectural tours are offered, too. ✉ *Ladd-Gilman House, 1 Governor's La., Exeter* ☎ *603/772–2622* 🌐 *www.independencemuseum.org* 🎟 *$8* 🕒 *Closed Sun.–Tues. and Dec.–Apr.*

Phillips Exeter Academy
COLLEGE | The grounds of this elite 1,100-student prep school, open to the public, resemble an Ivy League university campus. The school's library is one of the masterworks of modernist architect Louis I. Kahn. The Lamont Gallery, in the Frederick R. Mayer Art Center, mounts free contemporary art exhibitions. ✉ *20 Main St., Exeter* ☎ *603/772–4311* 🌐 *www.exeter.edu.*

🍴 Restaurants

★ Il Cornicello
$$$ | **ITALIAN** | At this intimate, romantic downtown restaurant overlooking the Exeter River, artfully prepared dishes like gemelli with chestnut mushrooms and smoked ham in a leek-taleggio-mustard sauce, and classic shrimp linguine with a garlicky scampi sauce take center stage. There's also a long and impressively curated list of Italian wines. **Known for:** lovely views of the downtown riverfront; seasonally inspired antipasti; fresh, hand-cut pasta. [$] *Average main: $27* ✉ *11 Water St., Exeter* ☎ *603/580–4604* 🌐 *www.ilcornicello.com* 🕒 *Closed Sun.–Tues. No lunch.*

★ Otis
$$$$ | **MODERN AMERICAN** | This romantic, urbane restaurant set inside the early-19th-century Inn by the Bandstand offers exceptional five-course tasting menus featuring farm-to-table fare that changes often to reflect what's in season. Typical offering include sea scallops with orange and fennel, and lamb with Brussels sprouts, shallots, and a sherry sauce, and everything is always plated beautifully. **Known for:** market-fresh, seasonal ingredients; views of charming village center; sticky toffee pudding with a bourbon caramel sauce. [$] *Average main: $70* ✉ *Inn by the Bandstand, 4 Front St., Exeter* ☎ *603/580–1705* 🌐 *www.otisrestaurant.com* 🕒 *Closed Sun.–Wed. No lunch.*

☕ Coffee and Quick Bites

Laney & Lu
$ | **CAFÉ** | **FAMILY** | This snug counter service café is a handy option for organic coffees, blended tea elixirs, and creative smoothies and bowls—the blueberry-basil with banana, avocado, spinach, and almond milk is a standout. Or tuck into a salad of locally sourced fruit, veggies, and greens, or try one of the hearty but healthy salads made on locally baked sourdough. **Known for:** artisan toasts with different toppings; fresh smoothies; a great kids' menu. [$] *Average main: $13* ✉ *26 Water St., Exeter* ☎ *603/580–4952* 🌐 *www.laneyandlu.com* 🕒 *No dinner.*

🛏 Hotels

★ Inn by the Bandstand
$$$$ | **B&B/INN** | This gorgeously appointed luxury B&B in the heart of downtown Exeter exudes character and comfort, with individually themed rooms furnished with fine antiques, Oriental rugs, and cushy bedding. **Pros:** steps from downtown shopping and dining; exceptional dining in Otis and Ambrose restaurants; fabulous breakfasts. **Cons:** minimum stay on busy weekends; in a busy part of downtown; steep rates. [$] *Rooms from: $329* ✉ *6 Front St., Exeter* ☎ *603/772–6352* 🌐 *www.innbythebandstand.com* 🛏 *8 rooms* 🍽 *Free Breakfast.*

📧 Shopping

Applecrest Farm Orchards

FOOD | FAMILY | At this 250-acre farm, pick apples and berries or buy freshly baked fruit pies and cookies and outstanding homemade ice cream. A café serves ice cream. Fall brings cider pressing, hayrides, pumpkins, and music on weekends. Author John Irving's experiences working here as a teen inspired *The Cider House Rules.* ✉ *133 Exeter Rd., Hampton Falls* ☎ *603/926–3721* ⊕ *www. applecrest.com.*

★ Exeter Fine Crafts

CRAFTS | This acclaimed nonprofit cooperative formed in 1966 features creations by more than 300 of Northern New England's top pottery, painting, jewelry, textile, glassware, and other artisans. ✉ *61 Water St., Exeter* ☎ *603/778–8282* ⊕ *www.exeterfinecrafts.com.*

Durham

12 miles north of Exeter, 11 miles west of Portsmouth.

A lively college town settled in 1635, Durham became a maritime hub in the 19th century thanks to its easy access to Great Bay via the Oyster River. With the University of New Hampshire anchoring its town center, it's a good hub for exploring two other nearby riverfront communities with thriving historic downtowns, Dover and Newmarket.

GETTING HERE AND AROUND

You can reach Durham on Route 108 from the north or south and on U.S. 4 from Portsmouth or Concord. The *Downeaster* Amtrak train stops here.

👁 Sights

★ Bedrock Gardens

GARDEN | FAMILY | It's easy to lose yourself for a couple of hours, or longer if you pack a picnic lunch, as you wander along the peaceful trails and through the astoundingly gorgeous flower beds of this 30-acre former farm that's now a thriving public garden dotted with hundreds of sculptures and art installations. Features range from formal parterre and spiral gardens to more whimsical and impressionistic plantings. ✉ *19 High Rd., Lee* ☎ *603/659–2993* ⊕ *www. bedrockgardens.org* 🖻 *$15* ⊙ *Closed mid-Oct.–mid-May.*

Children's Museum of New Hampshire

CHILDREN'S MUSEUM | FAMILY | The state's best and largest museum for kiddos is set inside a LEED-certified 1920s armory with big windows overlooking downtown Dover's Cocheco River. In this bright and colorful space, well-designed interactive exhibits on submarines, river ecosystems, dinosaurs, and music are geared to kids up to around age 12, and storytelling sessions are offered regularly. ✉ *6 Washington St., Dover* ☎ *603/742–2002* ⊕ *www.childrens-museum.org* 🖻 *$12.50* ⊙ *Closed Mon.*

★ Woodman Museum

HISTORY MUSEUM | FAMILY | This campus of four impressive, historic museums consists of the 1675 Damm Garrison House, the 1813 Hale House (home to abolitionist Senator John P. Hale from 1840 to 1873), the 1818 Woodman House, and the 1825 Keefe House, which contains the excellent Thom Hindle Gallery. Exhibits focus on Early American cooking utensils, clothing, furniture, and Native American artifacts, as well as natural history and New Hampshire's involvement in the Civil War. ✉ *182 Central Ave., Dover* ☎ *603/742–1038* ⊕ *www.*

woodmanmuseum.org 🎫 *$15* 🕒 *Closed Mon. and Tues. and Dec.–Mar.*

🍴 Restaurants

Hop + Grind

$ | **BURGER** | Students and faculty from UNH, whose campus is just a few blocks away, congregate over mammoth burgers with flavorful, original sides (kimchi, fries topped with cilantro-pickled peppers or black-garlic-truffle aioli) and other creative takes on gastropub fare. This is a hot spot for craft-beer aficionados, who appreciate the long list of options, including a rotating cache of rare and seasonal selections. **Known for:** impressive local beer selection; fun and lively student crowd; malted milk shakes with unusual flavors. [$] *Average main: $11* ✉ *Madbury Commons, 17 Madbury Rd., Durham* ☎ *603/397–5564* 🌐 *www.hopandgrind.com.*

Savannah Kitchen

$$ | **SOUTHERN** | Located inside a restored mill building on the Lamprey River in the historic village of Newmarket, this festive tavern and bar with boldly colored walls and timber-beam ceilings specializes in flavorful—if decadent—regional Southern dishes like classic shrimp and grits, braised pork shoulder with Creole spices and red gravy, and grilled New Orleans–style oysters. It's also a fun spot for cocktails and conversation. **Known for:** $1 oysters on the half shell at happy hour; colorful drinks served in tiki-style tumblers; warm blueberry-peach bread pudding. [$] *Average main: $19* ✉ *55 Main St., Newmarket* ☎ *603/292–5158* 🌐 *www.savannahkitchennewmarket.com* 🕒 *No lunch.*

★ **Stages at One Washington**

$$$$ | **MODERN AMERICAN** | Offering stunning, reservation-only prix-fixe dinners featuring 8 to 10 small courses, this intimate open-kitchen space occupies the third floor of a converted redbrick mill building in Dover. The daily menu is based on what the talented culinary team here has sourced from farms and fishing boats—perhaps cured monkfish with green pea dashi and ramps, or lobster mushrooms with coffee, razor clams, and hazelnuts. **Known for:** artfully presented food; lavish multicourse dinners; optional wine pairings. [$] *Average main: $150* ✉ *1 Washington St., Dover* ☎ *603/842–4077* 🌐 *www.stages-dining.com* 🕒 *Closed Sun.–Tues. No lunch.*

🛏 Hotels

Three Chimneys Inn

$$ | **B&B/INN** | Since 1649, this stately yellow house has graced a hill overlooking the Oyster River; it now offers attractive rooms filled with period antiques and reproductions in the main house and a 1795 barn. **Pros:** charming, historic ambience; free parking and continental breakfast; reasonable rates. **Cons:** a long walk (or short drive) into town; restaurant is uneven in quality; books up on fall and spring weekends. [$] *Rooms from: $179* ✉ *17 Newmarket Rd., Durham* ☎ *603/868–7800, 888/399–9777* 🌐 *www.threechimneysinn.com* 🔑 *23 rooms* 🍴 *Free Breakfast.*

🍸 Nightlife

Garrison City Beerworks

BREWPUBS | In a stylish light-filled storefront space in downtown Dover with a large redbrick side patio, sip some of the state's most inventive craft beers, from saisons to stouts. Globally inspired street tacos (Korean beef, Nashville chicken) are offered too. ✉ *455 Central Ave., Dover* ☎ *603/343–4231* 🌐 *www.garrisoncity-beerworks.com.*

★ **Stone Church**

LIVE MUSIC | This cool music club and pub in beautifully restored 1835 former Methodist church on a hilly bluff in

New Hampshire Lakes Region

historic Newmarket presents first-rate rock, reggae, folk, jazz, and blues. ✉ *5 Granite St., Newmarket* ☎ *603/659–7700* ⊕ *www.stonechurchrocks.com.*

👜 Shopping

★ Emery Farm

FOOD | FAMILY | In the same family since 1655, Emery Farm sells berries and produce in summer, pumpkins in fall, and Christmas trees in winter. The farm shop carries breads, pies, and local crafts, and a café serves sandwiches, ice cream, cider doughnuts, and other light fare. Enjoy pumpkin-patch hayrides in autumn and visit the petting barn May–October. ✉ *147 Piscataqua Rd., Durham* ☎ *603/742–8495* ⊕ *www.emeryfarm.com.*

Wolfeboro ·

40 miles northwest of Durham, 40 miles northeast of Concord.

Quietly upscale and decidedly preppy Wolfeboro has been a vacation getaway since Royal Governor John Wentworth built a home on the shore of Lake Winnipesaukee in 1768—hence its reputation as the country's oldest summer resort. Its waterfront downtown bursts with tony boutiques and eateries, while smaller Lake Wentworth—a few miles east— offers a quieter vibe. The century-old, white clapboard buildings of Brewster Academy prep school bracket the town's southern end.

With 240 miles of shoreline, Lake Winnipesaukee has something for everyone.

GETTING HERE AND AROUND
Route 28 connects Wolfeboro with the rest of Lake Winnipesaukee. Be prepared for lots of traffic in the summer.

ESSENTIALS
VISITOR INFORMATION Wolfeboro Area Chamber of Commerce. ⊠ *Wolfeboro* ☎ *603/569–2200* ⊕ *www.wolfeboro-chamber.com.*

 Sights

Alton Bay
TOWN | FAMILY | Two mountain ridges frame picturesque Alton Bay, which is the name of both a narrow 4-mile inlet and village at the southern tip of Lake Winnipesaukee, near Wolfeboro. Cruise boats dock here, and small float planes buzz just over the bay, sometimes flying in formation. There's a boardwalk, mini golf, a public beach, and a Victorian-style bandstand, and a few basic but fun short-order eateries near the waterfront, such as Pop's Clam Shell and Stillwells Ice Cream. ⊠ *Rte. 11 at Rte. 28A, Alton Bay.*

★ New Hampshire Boat Museum
OTHER MUSEUM | FAMILY | Set in a 1950s quonset hut–style former dance hall near Lake Wentworth, this small but fascinating museum and boat-building center celebrates New Hampshire's maritime legacy with displays of vintage wooden boats, models, antique engines, racing photography, trophies, and vintage marina signs. You can also attend workshops on boat building and restoration, take sailing lessons, and go on 45-minute narrated rides on Lake Winnipesaukee in the *Millie B.*, reproduction 1928 triple-cockpit Hacker-Craft. ⊠ *399 Center St., Wolfeboro* ☎ *603/569–4554* ⊕ *www.nhbm.org* ⊠ *$9, boat tours $40* ⊙ *Closed mid-Oct.–late May.*

Wright Museum
HISTORY MUSEUM | Uniforms, vehicles, and other artifacts at this museum illustrate the contributions of those on the home front to the U.S. World War II effort. ⊠ *77 Center St., Wolfeboro* ☎ *603/569–1212* ⊕ *www.wrightmuseum.org* ⊠ *$14* ⊙ *Closed Nov.–Apr.*

Beaches

Wentworth State Park

BEACH | FAMILY | Away from the hustle and bustle of Wolfeboro on pretty little Lake Wentworth, this simple park features a quiet beach with good fishing, picnic tables and grills, and ball fields. **Amenities:** parking (no fee); showers; toilets. **Best for:** swimming; walking. ✉ *297 Governor Wentworth Hwy., Wolfeboro* ☎ *603/569–3699* 🌐 *www.nhstateparks.org* 🎟 *$4.*

Restaurants

East of Suez

$$ | ASIAN | In a countrified lodge on the south side of town, this friendly restaurant serves creative Asian cuisine, with an emphasis on Philippine fare, such as *lumpia* (pork-and-shrimp spring rolls with a sweet-and-sour fruit sauce) and *pancit canton* (panfried egg noodles with sautéed shrimp and pork and Asian vegetables with a sweet oyster sauce). You can also sample Thai red curries, Japanese tempura, and Korean-style flank steak. **Known for:** BYOB policy; banana tempura with coconut ice cream; plenty of vegan options. [$] *Average main: $24* ✉ *775 S. Main St., Wolfeboro* ☎ *603/569–1648* 🌐 *www.eastofsuez.com* 🕓 *Closed Mon. and early Sept.–late May. No lunch.*

★ Pavilion

$$$ | MODERN AMERICAN | Guests of the Pickering House hotel had become so enamored of the inn's occasional dinners and other food events that the owners opened this full-time restaurant in the Victorian house next door. Showcasing creative American fare sourced locally and seasonally as much as possible, the kitchen serves an oft-changing menu that might feature pan-roasted duck breast with garlic-roasted radicchio and roasted figs, and mussels in a green curry–coconut broth with lime and cilantro. **Known for:** elegant early-19th-century building; exceptional wine list; creative seasonal fruit desserts and house-made ice creams. [$] *Average main: $33* ✉ *126 S. Main St., Wolfeboro* ☎ *603/393–0851* 🌐 *www.pavilionwolfeboro.com* 🕓 *Closed Mon. and Tues. No lunch.*

Hotels

Lake Wentworth Inn

$ | MOTEL | This attractively renovated vintage motor lodge, just a five-minute walk from Lake Wentworth and Albee Beach, has been brightened up with an inviting midcentury cottage look and such family-friendly features as a game room and guest library. **Pros:** pool, game room, and library; short walk to beach; clean and very affordable. **Cons:** no breakfast; not directly on the water; a short drive from downtown. [$] *Rooms from: $149* ✉ *427 Center St., Wolfeboro* ☎ *603/569–1700* 🌐 *www.lakewentworthinn.com* 🛏 *43 rooms* 🍴 *No Meals.*

★ Pickering House

$$$$ | B&B/INN | Following an extensive renovation by amiable innkeepers Peter and Patty Cook, this striking yellow 1813 Federal mansion ranks among New Hampshire's most luxurious small inns. **Pros:** ultracushy rooms; the adjacent restaurant, Pavilion, is superb; in-town location. **Cons:** on busy street; among the highest rates in the state; not suitable for children. [$] *Rooms from: $610* ✉ *116 S. Main St., Wolfeboro* ☎ *603/569–6948* 🌐 *www.pickeringhousewolfeboro.com* 🛏 *10 rooms* 🍴 *Free Breakfast.*

Nightlife

Lone Wolfe Brewing

BREWPUBS | Sample raspberry sours and the heady Dippah Double IPA in the cheerful taproom of this downtown brewhouse that also serves tasty pub fare and presents live music many weekends inside or in the outdoor beer garden. ✉ *36 Mill St., Wolfeboro* ☎ *603/515–1099* 🌐 *www.thelonewolfe.com.*

🛍️ Shopping

Black's Paper Store

SOUVENIRS | Browse regionally made soaps, chocolates, maple products, pottery, candles, lotions, potions, yarns, toys, and gifts at this vast old-fashioned emporium that dates back to the 1860s. ✉ *8 S. Main St., Wolfeboro* ☎ *603/569–4444* ⊕ *www.blacksgiftsnh.com.*

The Country Bookseller

BOOKS | **FAMILY** | You'll find an excellent regional-history section and plenty of children's titles at this independent bookstore, where you can do a little reading in the small café. ✉ *23A N. Main St., Wolfeboro* ☎ *603/569–6030* ⊕ *www. thecountrybookseller.com.*

Yum Yum Shop

FOOD | Picking up freshly baked breads, pastries, cookies, ice cream, and other sweets here has been a tradition since 1948. ✉ *16 N. Main St., Wolfeboro* ☎ *603/569–1919* ⊕ *www.yumyumshop. com.*

🏃 Activities

HIKING
Abenaki Tower

HIKING & WALKING | **FAMILY** | A quarter-mile hike to this 100-foot post-and-beam tower north of town, followed by a climb to the top, rewards you with views of Lake Winnipesaukee and the Ossipee mountain range. It's particularly photogenic at sunset. ✉ *Rte. 109, Tuftonboro.*

Blue Job Mountain

HIKING & WALKING | A wildflower-strewn 3.3-mile loop trail reaches the summit of Blue Job Mountain, 25 miles south of Wolfeboro, where a 1913 fire tower provides a panoramic view of the Atlantic Ocean, White Mountains, and even Boston on a clear day. ✉ *First Crown Point Rd., Strafford.*

★ Mt. Major

HIKING & WALKING | About 5 miles north of Alton Bay, a rugged 3-mile trail up a series of granite cliffs leads to this dramatic summit. At the top you'll find a four-sided stone shelter built in 1925, but the real reward is the spectacular view of Lake Winnipesaukee. ✉ *Rte. 11, Alton Bay.*

Laconia and Weirs Beach

25 miles west of Wolfeboro, 27 miles north of Concord.

The arrival of the railroad in 1848 turned the sleepy hamlet of Laconia into the Lakes Region's chief manufacturing hub—downtown's 1823 Belknap Mill still stands as a monument to this legacy. At the north end of town, Weirs Beach is a hub of summertime arcade activity, with souvenir shops, fireworks, the Bank of NH outdoor concert pavilion, and legions of kids. Cruise boats also depart from here, and the refurbished Winnipesaukee Pier has family-oriented restaurants and other amusements. In June, bikers from around the world arrive for Laconia Motorcycle Week.

GETTING HERE AND AROUND
Laconia offers easy access from Interstate 93 in Tilton, where you'll find a clutch of outlet shops, and to both Winnisquam and Winnipesaukee lakes, via U.S. 3 or Route 11.

👁️ Sights

★ Canterbury Shaker Village

MUSEUM VILLAGE | **FAMILY** | Established in 1792, this community 15 miles south of Laconia flourished in the 1800s and practiced equality of the sexes and races, common ownership, celibacy, and pacifism. The last member of the religious community passed away in 1992. Shakers invented such household items as the clothespin and the flat broom and were known for the simplicity and integrity of their designs. Engaging

View simple yet functional furniture, architecture, and crafts at Canterbury Shaker Village.

guided tours—you can also explore on your own—pass through some of the 694-acre property's nearly 30 restored buildings, many of them with original furnishings. Crafts demonstrations take place daily. An excellent shop sells handcrafted wares. ⊠ *288 Shaker Rd., Canterbury* ☎ *603/783–9511* ⊕ *www. shakers.org* ⊠ *Grounds free, guided tours $25* ⊙ *Closed Dec.–Apr.*

Funspot

AMUSEMENT PARK/CARNIVAL | FAMILY | The mothership of Lake Winnipesaukee's family-oriented amusement parks, Funspot's more than 600 video games make it the world's largest arcade—there's even an arcade museum. You can also work your way through an indoor minigolf course and 20 lanes of bowling. Rates vary depending on the activity. ⊠ *579 Endicott St. N, Weirs Beach* ☎ *603/366–4377* ⊕ *www.funspotnh.com.*

★ MS Mount Washington

MARINA/PIER | FAMILY | The 230-foot MS *Mount Washington* offers 2½-hour scenic cruises of Lake Winnipesaukee, departing Weirs Beach with stops at Wolfeboro, Alton Bay, Center Harbor, and Meredith depending on the day. Sunset cruises include live music and a buffet dinner. The same company operates the *Sophie C.* ($42), which has been the area's floating post office for more than a century. The boat departs from Weirs Beach with mail and passengers, passing through parts of the lake not accessible to larger ships. The *Winnipesaukee Spirit* ($30) offers summer cocktail cruises on Meredith Bay. ⊠ *211 Lakeside Ave., Weirs Beach* ☎ *603/366–5531* ⊕ *www. cruisenh.com* ⊠ *From $42* ⊙ *Closed mid-Oct.–mid-May.*

Winnipesaukee Scenic Railroad

TRAIN/TRAIN STATION | FAMILY | You can board this scenic railroad's restored cars at Weirs Beach or Meredith for one- or two-hour rides along the shoreline. Special excursions include fall foliage and the Santa train. ⊠ *211 Lakeside Ave., Weirs Beach* ☎ *603/745–2135* ⊕ *www.hoborr. com* ⊠ *From $22.*

🏖 Beaches

Ellacoya State Park

BEACH | FAMILY | Families enjoy this secluded 600-foot sandy beach and park on the southwestern shore of Lake Winnipesaukee. Ellacoya, with views of the Sandwich and Ossipee mountains, has a shallow beach that's safe for small children, sheltered picnic tables, and a small campground. **Amenities:** parking (fee); toilets. **Best for:** solitude; swimming. ✉ *266 Scenic Rd., Gilford* ☎ *603/293–7821* ⊕ *www.nhstateparks. org* 💲 *$5 mid-May–late Sept.*

🍴 Restaurants

Local Eatery

$$$ | MODERN AMERICAN | Proof that impressive dining in the Lakes Region isn't always near the water, this elegant restaurant is set beneath the soaring ceiling of downtown Laconia's historic train depot. Favoring local ingredients, the kitchen turns out inventive renditions of classic American dishes, like scallops and grits with a sweet corn butter sauce, and coffee-rubbed pork tenderloin. **Known for:** artisan butter boards with roasted garlic and focaccia; inviting patio; apple tart tatin with caramel sauce. 💲 *Average main: $30* ✉ *21 Veterans Sq., Laconia* ☎ *603/527–8007* ⊕ *www.laconialocaleatery.com* 🕐 *Closed Sun. and Mon. No lunch.*

🛏 Hotels

★ Lake House at Ferry Point

$$ | B&B/INN | This gracious red Victorian farmhouse, built as a summer getaway for the Pillsbury family of baking fame, has a peaceful setting on Lake Winnisquam. **Pros:** hearty full breakfast included; free use of kayaks; private dock and a small beach. **Cons:** not within walking distance of dining or shopping; may be a little quiet for some families; two-night minimum many weekends. 💲 *Rooms from: $215* ✉ *100 Lower Bay Rd., Sanbornton* ☎ *603/637–1758* ⊕ *www.new-hampshire-inn.com* 🛏 *9 rooms* 🍴 *Free Breakfast.*

Lake Opechee Inn & Spa

$$$ | HOTEL | Slightly removed from, but within a short drive of, the crowds of Weirs Beach, this boutique spa hotel set in a converted mill is a great place to chill out, enjoy a shiatsu massage or cranberry facial, and savor dinner and cocktails on a patio overlooking the lake. **Pros:** views of Lake Opechee; appealing spa and restaurant; many rooms have balconies, gas fireplaces, and jetted tubs. **Cons:** indoor pool is small; in a busy part of Laconia; 10-minute drive to Winnipesaukee. 💲 *Rooms from: $244* ✉ *62 Doris Day Ct., Laconia* ☎ *603/524–0111* ⊕ *www.opecheeinn.com* 🛏 *34 rooms* 🍴 *Free Breakfast.*

🏃 Activities

SKIING

Gunstock Mountain Resort

SKIING & SNOWBOARDING | FAMILY | This ski resort with a 2,267-foot summit and ample snowmaking capacity offers plenty of beginner terrain along with snow-tubing and a 22-acre terrain park. Nearly half of the trails offer night skiing, and you'll find 14 miles of cross-country and snowshoeing runs. In summer the Adventure Park offers a fantastic zipline system—the longest run at 3,981 feet—an aerial obstacle course, a 4,100-foot mountainside roller coaster (also open in winter), and scenic chairlift rides that access great hiking (the Ridge Trail is especially scenic). There's also mountain biking, a wetlands boardwalk, e-bike tours, kayak rentals, and a stocked fishing pond. **Facilities:** 49 trails; 227 acres; 1,340-foot vertical drop; 7 lifts. ✉ *719 Cherry Valley Rd., Gilford* ☎ *603/293–4341* ⊕ *www. gunstock.com* 💲 *Lift ticket: $100.*

What's your vessel of choice for exploring New Hampshire's Lakes Region: kayak, canoe, powerboat, or sailboat?

Meredith

11 miles north of Laconia.

For many years a workaday mill town with relatively little touristic appeal, Meredith has become a popular summer getaway thanks largely to the transformation of several historic buildings into Mill Falls, now a cluster of hotels, restaurants, and shops overlooking Lake Winnipesaukee. Take a stroll down Main Street, which is dotted with boutiques and antiques stores, and along the lakefront, where you'll find a bustling marina, sculpture walk, and some lively dockside restaurants.

GETTING HERE AND AROUND

You can reach Meredith from Interstate 93 via Route 104, or from points south on U.S. 3 (beware the heavy weekend traffic). In town, it's easy to get around on foot.

ESSENTIALS

VISITOR INFORMATION Meredith Area Chamber of Commerce. ⊠ *Meredith* ☎ *603/279–6121* ⊕ *www.meredithareachamber.com.*

Sights

Hermit Woods Winery

WINERY | Stop by this contemporary downtown winery to sample the light and fruity wines and hard ciders, made with local blueberries, apples, cranberries, and honeys as well as imported grapes. Tours, which include a barrel tasting, are available, and you can order cheese, charcuterie, and other treats from the deli to enjoy while sipping outside on the deck. On weekend evenings, there's live piano in the Loft lounge. ⊠ *72 Main St., Meredith* ☎ *603/253–7968* ⊕ *www.hermitwoods.com.*

Meredith Sculpture Walk

PUBLIC ART | **FAMILY** | Throughout town, especially in parks beside the lake and at the gardens at Mill Falls Marketplace, you'll see colorful contemporary artworks. They're part of the Annual Meredith Sculpture walk, a year-round juried event featuring 33 distinctive pieces by renowned sculptors. Each June, a new collection of sculptures is installed. For a detailed look, take a free guided tour, offered at 10 am daily, mid-July and early September. ✉ *Meredith* 🌐 *www.meredithsculpturewalk.org.*

🍴 Restaurants

Canoe

$$ | MODERN AMERICAN | Just up the road in Center Harbor, this boathouse-inspired bistro sits high above Lake Winnipesaukee and has seating in both a quieter dining room and a convivial bar with an open kitchen. It's known for seafood, including wood-fired, bacon-wrapped scallops and a creamy, entrée-size haddock chowder topped with herbs and crushed Ritz Crackers. **Known for:** fun people-watching at the bar; great wine and beer selection; salted-caramel brownie sundaes. [$] *Average main: $25* ✉ *232 Whittier Hwy., Center Harbor* ☎ *603/253–4762* 🌐 *www.canoecenterharbor.com* 🕑 *Closed Wed. No lunch weekdays.*

Lakehouse Grille

$$$ | AMERICAN | With big windows overlooking the lake and timber posts and ceiling beams, this popular restaurant inside the Church Landing at Mill Falls hotel captures the rustic ambience of an old-fashioned camp dining room. Feast on classic American favorites with interesting twists, such as eggs Benedict topped with Maine lobster in the morning, and char-grilled steaks, chops, and seafood in the evening. **Known for:** blueberry pie with lemon ice cream; water views; Sunday jazz brunch. [$] *Average main: $32* ✉ *Church Landing, 281 Daniel Webster Hwy., Meredith* ☎ *603/279–5221* 🌐 *www.thecman.com.*

🛏 Hotels

Mill Falls at the Lake

$$$ | HOTEL | Choose from four lodgings at this rambling resort: relaxing Church Landing and Bay Point are both on the shore of Lake Winnipesaukee; convivial Mill Falls—with a pool—and Chase House are across the street, next to a 19th-century mill that houses shops and restaurants. **Pros:** activity center with boat rentals and lake cruises; many dining options; spa with heated indoor-outdoor pool. **Cons:** rooms with water views are expensive; some properties aren't directly on the lake; somewhat impersonal, corporate feel. [$] *Rooms from: $239* ✉ *312 Daniel Webster Hwy., Meredith* ☎ *603/279–7006, 844/745–2931* 🌐 *www.millfalls.com* 🔑 *188 rooms* 🍽 *No Meals.*

🍸 Nightlife

Twin Barns Brewing

BEER GARDENS | Serving a roster of well-crafted ales along with tasty comfort food (flatbread pizzas, burgers), this beer-centric compound occupies a handsome 1850s restored barn with a large tented beer garden. ✉ *194 Daniel Webster Hwy., Meredith* ☎ *603/279–0876* 🌐 *www.twinbarnsbrewing.com.*

🎟 Performing Arts

Interlakes Summer Theatre

THEATER | During its 10-week season of summer stock, this striking 420-seat theater presents classic Broadway musicals like *42nd Street, Evita,* and *West Side Story.* ✉ *1 Laker La., Meredith* ☎ *603/707–6035* 🌐 *www.interlakestheatre.com.*

★ **Winnipesaukee Playhouse**

THEATER | Since this critically lauded theater opened in a rustic yet state-of-the-art red-barn-style venue in 2013, it's become one of the top performing arts centers in the region, presenting well-known Broadway shows and original dramas and comedies year-round. ✉ *33 Footlight Circle, Meredith* ☎ *603/279–0333* ⊕ *www.winnipesaukeeplayhouse.org.*

Shopping

Annalee Dolls

TOYS | FAMILY | Everyone from young kids to ardent collectors makes the pilgrimage to the showroom of this internationally renowned shop that's been hand-crafting whimsical dolls since 1934. Annalee's expressive mice are a top draw, but holiday figurines are also highly popular. ✉ *339 Daniel Webster Hwy., Meredith* ☎ *800/433–6557* ⊕ *www.annalee.com.*

★ League of New Hampshire Craftsmen

CRAFTS | This eclectic gallery offers wares by more than 250 artisans working in everything from stained glass and ceramics to wrought iron and mixed media. Prices are surprisingly reasonable for many items, and there are additional branches in Center Sandwich, Concord, Hookset, Littleton, Nashua, and North Conway. ✉ *279 Daniel Webster Hwy., Meredith* ☎ *603/279–7920* ⊕ *www.meredith.nhcrafts.org.*

🏃 Activities

BOATING

Home to a popular marina, Meredith is also near the quaint village of Center Harbor, another boating hub in the middle of three bays at the north end of Lake Winnipesaukee.

★ EKAL

WATER SPORTS | At the lakefront activity center at Mill Falls, you can rent standup paddleboards, kayaks, canoes, aqua cycles, and bicycles, and book excursions on a restored 1931 Chris Craft runabout. ✉ *285 Daniel Webster Hwy. (U.S. 3), Meredith* ☎ *603/677–8646* ⊕ *www.ekalactivitycenter.com.*

GOLF

Waukewan Golf Club

GOLF | This beautiful, well-groomed course with undulating fairways and several challenging blind shots has been a local favorite since the late '50s. ✉ *166 Waukewan Rd., Center Harbor* ☎ *603/279–6661* ⊕ *www.waukewangolfclub.com* 💲 *$34* ⛳ *18 holes, 5828 yards, par 72.*

Plymouth

16 miles northwest of Meredith, 22 miles south of North Woodstock.

Home to Plymouth State University, whose small but attractive campus clings to a steep hill looming over an attractive, bustling downtown, Plymouth acts as a bridge between White Mountains and the Lakes Region; it's especially convenient for visiting 4,000-acre Newfound Lake, one of the state's deepest and purest bodies of water, as well as Squam Lake. It's also close to some great hiking to the west, including 3,121-foot Mt. Cardigan, in nearby Alexandria, and Big and Little Sugarloaf peaks, the trailhead for which is reached along West Shore Road, near the entrance to Wellington State Park.

GETTING HERE AND AROUND
Plymouth is just off Interstate 93.

👁 Sights

Polar Caves Park

CAVE | FAMILY | From the attractive log cabin–style main lodge, an easy trail leads to nine granite caves that formed some 50,000 years ago, during the last ice age. This family-friendly attraction begun in 1922 also contains a small petting zoo with a herd of adorable fallow deer. ✉ *705 Rte. 25, Rumney* ☎ *603/536–1888* ⊕ *www.polarcaves.com* 💲 *$27* 🕐 *Closed mid-Oct.–mid-May.*

★ Wellington State Park

STATE/PROVINCIAL PARK | **FAMILY** | At this picturesque 220-acre park on the west shore of glorious Newfound Lake, about 12 miles from Plymouth, you'll find the largest freshwater beach in the state park system. Enjoy the picnic and fishing areas, numerous hiking trails, and boat launch. ✉ *614 W. Shore Rd., Bristol* ☎ *603/744–2197* 🌐 *www.nhstateparks.org* 🎟 *$5 mid-May–mid-Sept.*

🍴 Restaurants

★ Benton's Sugar Shack

$ | **AMERICAN** | **FAMILY** | A legit contender in New Hampshire's fierce battle for the best pancake house, this rustic timber-frame roadhouse is run by a family who've been producing maple syrup for five generations. Open only on weekends, Benton's serves stacks of pancakes in several flavors, including strawberry shortcake, Mounds Bar, and Grandma's apple cinnamon. **Known for:** sides of maple kielbasa and baked beans; "design your own" pancakes with custom fillings; raspberry-stuffed French toast. [$] *Average main: $9* ✉ *2010 Rte. 175, Thornton* ☎ *603/726–3867* 🌐 *www.bentonssugarshack.com* 🕒 *Closed Mon.–Wed. No dinner.*

Covered Bridge Farm Table

$$ | **MODERN AMERICAN** | With tall windows as well as a large deck overlooking the historic Blair Covered Bridge and the Pemigewasset River, this rustic restaurant serves an eclectic mix of Asian, Mediterranean, and American dishes and is a favorite place to refuel after hiking in the White Mountains or boating on Squam Lake. Good bets include wild-caught salmon with a ginger-scallion vinaigrette and butter chicken with garam masala, ginger, and jasmine rice. **Known for:** apple-cider-donut ice cream sandwiches; diverse, international menu; expansive riverfront deck. [$] *Average main: $23* ✉ *57 Blair Rd., Campton* ☎ *603/238–9115* 🌐 *www.farmtablenh.com* 🕒 *Closed Sun. and Tues.*

★ Little Red Schoolhouse

$$ | **AMERICAN** | **FAMILY** | Lobster-roll aficionados flock to this funky converted schoolhouse with screened-in and outdoor seating high on a bluff above the Pemigewasset River. Start with a cup of lobster bisque or clam chowder before digging into a traditional (lightly dressed, with mayo) or hot-buttered lobster roll—both come on a warm, buttered brioche roll, best enjoyed with a side of garlic fries. **Known for:** pretty river and forest views; good craft beer selection; homemade ice-cream sandwiches. [$] *Average main: $22* ✉ *1994 Daniel Webster Hwy., Campton* ☎ *603/726–6142* 🌐 *www.littleredschoolhousenh.com* 🕒 *Closed mid-Oct.–mid-May.*

Six Burner Bistro

$$$ | **MODERN AMERICAN** | In this charming red Victorian house on Plymouth's bustling Main Street, with some seats on the front veranda and others set in a warren of cozy rooms with art on the walls, this casually elegant spot offers tasty American and international fare. Consider Szechuan-style salmon ramen, and blackened grilled chicken with honeydew-melon salsa and tzatziki sauce. **Known for:** sourcing from local farms; well-selected wine and beer list; creative salad options with myriad protein add-ons. [$] *Average main: $28* ✉ *13 S. Main St., Plymouth* ☎ *603/536–9099* 🌐 *www.sixburnerbistro.com* 🕒 *Closed Sun.–Tues.*

🛏 Hotels

Common Man Inn & Spa

$$ | **HOTEL** | This contemporary hotel with country lodge–inspired furnishings, just off I–93 a little north of downtown, contains warmly appointed rooms in a variety of configurations; some have whirlpool tubs and fireplaces, and a few have cozy sleeping lofts. **Pros:** pets are welcome; relaxing spa; convenient to White Mountains and Lakes Region. **Cons:** often booked up with weddings; small pool; 15-minute walk from

downtown. $ *Rooms from: $159* ✉ *231 Main St., Plymouth* ☎ *603/536–2200, 866/843–2626* ⊕ *www.thecmaninnplymouth.com* ⇆ *38 rooms* ⦿ *Free Breakfast.*

🎭 Performing Arts

★ Flying Monkey

CONCERTS | Set in downtown Plymouth's brightly restored 1920s movie house, this cinema and performing arts center presents dinner theater and other live comedy and music shows, plus retro movies. A balcony bar serves wine and beer. ✉ *39 Main St., Plymouth* ☎ *603/536–2551* ⊕ *www.flyingmonkeynh.com.*

Holderness

7 miles southeast of Plymouth, 8 miles northwest of Meredith.

This peaceful village straddles two of the state's most scenic lakes, Squam and Little Squam, both of which have been spared from excessive development but do offer some memorable inns that are perfect for a tranquil getaway. *On Golden Pond,* starring Katharine Hepburn and Henry Fonda, was filmed on Squam, whose beauty attracts nature lovers.

GETTING HERE AND AROUND
Holderness is easy to reach from Interstate 93 and U.S. 3.

⊙ Sights

★ Squam Lakes Natural Science Center

NATURE PRESERVE | **FAMILY** | This 230-acre property includes a ¾-mile nature trail that passes by trailside live-animal exhibits of black bears, bobcats, otters, fishers, mountain lions, red foxes, and raptors. A pontoon boat cruise offers the best way to tour the waterfront—naturalists talk about native fauna, from bald eagles to loons; dinner and sunset options are available. Kids' programs teach about insects and wilderness

survival skills. The center also operates nearby 1-acre Kirkwood Gardens and maintains three short hiking trails, all of which you can access for free. ✉ *23 Science Center Rd., Holderness* ☎ *603/968–7194* ⊕ *www.nhnature.org* ✆ *Trail $22, lake cruise $27* ⊙ *Live-animal exhibits closed Nov.–Apr.*

🍴 Restaurants

Walter's Basin

$$$ | **AMERICAN** | A former bowling alley in the heart of Holderness makes an unlikely but charming setting for meals overlooking Little Squam Lake—local boaters dock right beneath the dining room. Among the specialties on the seafood-intensive menu are shellfish paella, and sea scallops with a creamy bacon-corn-poblano succotash, while sandwiches and salads are among the lighter options. **Known for:** dockside setting; live music some summer evenings; fried whole-belly clams. $ *Average main: $26* ✉ *859 U.S. 3, Holderness* ☎ *603/968–4412* ⊕ *www.waltersbasin.com.*

🛏 Hotels

Cottage Place on Squam

$$ | **MOTEL** | This sweet, old-fashioned compound of cottages and suites on Little Squam Lake is a terrific find—and value—for families, as nearly all units have partial or full kitchens, and many can comfortably sleep up to five guests (there's also a six-bedroom lodge that groups can rent entirely). **Pros:** reasonably priced; lots of on-site activities, from kayaking to shuffleboard; well-curated shop has fun one-of-a-kind gifts. **Cons:** the retro ambience isn't at all fancy; family popularity might be a turnoff if seeking peace and quiet; no restaurant. $ *Rooms from: $159* ✉ *1132 U.S. 3, Holderness* ☎ *603/968–7116* ⊕ *www.cottageplaceonsquam.com* ⇆ *15 rooms* ⦿ *No Meals.*

★ Inn on Golden Pond
$$$$ | **B&B/INN** | The hospitable innkeepers at this comfortable and informal B&B a short distance from Squam Lake make every possible effort to accommodate their guests—many of whom are repeat clients—from providing them with hiking trail maps to using rhubarb grown on property to make the jam served during the delicious country breakfasts. **Pros:** 50-acre property with woodland and lake views; comfortable indoor and outdoor common spaces; generous full breakfast. **Cons:** not directly on the lake; a bit pricey; can't accommodate pets. [$] *Rooms from: $315* ✉ *1080 U.S. 3, Holderness* ☎ *603/968–7269* 🌐 *www.innongoldenpond.com* 🛏 *8 rooms* 🍴 *Free Breakfast.*

Manor on Golden Pond
$$$ | **B&B/INN** | A name like this is a lot to live up to, but the Manor generally succeeds: it's one of the region's most atmospheric inns, situated on a slight rise overlooking Squam Lake, with 15 acres of lawns, towering pines, and hardwood trees; a grand restaurant serving lavish modern European fare; and a small but well-outfitted spa. **Pros:** fireplaces and Jacuzzis in many rooms; gracious common spaces; afternoon high tea is served in the library. **Cons:** the top-tier suites are quite expensive; furnishings could stand a little refreshing; not suitable for younger kids. [$] *Rooms from: $245* ✉ *31 Manor Rd., off Shepard Hill Rd., Holderness* ☎ *603/968–3348, 800/545–2141* 🌐 *www.manorongoldenpond.com* 🛏 *24 suites* 🍴 *Free Breakfast.*

Activities

★ Squam Lakes Association
BOATING | **FAMILY** | You can rent kayaks and canoes, reserve campsites, enroll kids in education programs, and learn about local wildlife watching, fishing, and hiking opportunities at this nonprofit organization that's been focused on lake conservation since it formed in 1904. ✉ *534 U.S. 3, Holderness* ☎ *603/968–7336* 🌐 *www.squamlakes.org.*

West Rattlesnake Mountain
HIKING & WALKING | The nearly 500-foot elevation gain of this moderately strenuous but fairly short 2.3-mile loop trail to the top of West Rattlesnake Mountain will get your heart pounding, but the panoramic views over Squam Lake are a satisfying reward. ✉ *Rte. 113, Holderness.*

Center Sandwich

12 miles northeast of Holderness.

With Squam Lake to the west, Lake Winnipesaukee to the south, and the Sandwich Mountains to the north, Center Sandwich offers one of the prettiest settings in the Lakes Region. So appealing are the town and its views that John Greenleaf Whittier used the Bearcamp River as the inspiration for his poem "Sunset on the Bearcamp." The town attracts artisans—crafts shops abound among its clutch of charming 18th- and 19th-century buildings.

GETTING HERE AND AROUND

You reach this rural town from Holderness via Route 113 and Meredith—by way of Center Harbor and Moultonborough—by Routes 25 and 109.

Sights

★ Castle in the Clouds
CASTLE/PALACE | Resembling a fairy-tale castle, this grand 1914 mountaintop estate is anchored by an elaborate mansion with 16 rooms, 8 bathrooms, and doors made of lead. Owner Thomas Gustave Plant spent $7 million—the bulk of his fortune—on this project and died penniless in 1941. Tours include the mansion and the Castle Springs water facility on this high Ossipee Mountain Range property overlooking Lake Winnipesaukee. Hiking (and cross-country skiing in winter) and pony and horse rides are

also offered, along with lakeview terrace jazz dinners many summer evenings at the Carriage House restaurant, which is also open for lunch when mansion tours are offered. ⌧ *455 Old Mountain Rd., Moultonborough* ☎ *603/476–5900* ⊕ *www.castleintheclouds.org* ⌁ *$20* ⊘ *Closed late Oct.–late May.*

Loon Center

WILDLIFE REFUGE | FAMILY | Recognizable for its eerie calls and striking black-and-white coloring, the loon resides on many New Hampshire lakes but is threatened by the gradual loss of its habitat. Two trails wind from the modern visitor center through this 200-acre lakeside wildlife sanctuary, which has made great progress in helping to restore the state's loon population, which currently stands at around 550; vantage points on the Loon Nest Trail overlook the spot resident loons sometimes occupy in late spring and summer. ⌧ *183 Lee's Mills Rd., Moultonborough* ☎ *603/476–5666* ⊕ *www.loon.org* ⌁ *Free* ⊘ *Closed Sun.–Wed. in late-Oct.–Apr.*

🍴 Restaurants

Corner House Inn

$$ | AMERICAN | In a converted barn adorned with paintings by local artists, this rustic tavern in an 1840s building in charming Center Sandwich village dishes up classic American fare. Salads made with local greens and a maple vinaigrette are a house specialty, but don't overlook the mac and cheese with house-made sauce and steak tips–and–lobster surf and turf. **Known for:** inviting art-filled dining room; tender steaks and prime rib; good list of reasonably priced wines. Ⓢ *Average main: $23* ⌧ *22 Main St., Center Sandwich* ☎ *603/476–3060* ⊕ *www.nhcornerhouse.com* ⊘ *Closed Sun.–Tues. No lunch.*

☕ Coffee and Quick Bites

Sandwich Creamery

$ | CAFÉ | FAMILY | This artisan dairy is located inside a converted general store that now carries gifts and foods from a few other local vendors, which you pick out from shelves and refrigerator cases and pay for yourself with cash or Venmo (the shop is unstaffed). The creamery sells delicious farmstead-made cheddar cheese as well as ice cream and ice cream sandwiches in about two-dozen flavors, including cinnamon, blueberry, and ginger. **Known for:** PB&J ice cream sandwiches; artisan cheddar cheeses; fresh-baked breads and other foods from local purveyors. Ⓢ *Average main: $4* ⌧ *22 Main St., Center Sandwich* ☎ *603/284–6675* ⊕ *www.facebook.com/thesandwichcreamery* ⊘ *Closed Mon. and Tues.*

🛍 Shopping

Old Country Store and Museum

GENERAL STORE | A quirky spot to pick up maple syrup, aged cheeses, jams, molasses, penny candy, and other treats, this rambling shop dates to 1781 and also contains antique farm and forging equipment and other artifacts. ⌧ *1011 Whittier Hwy., Moultonborough* ☎ *603/476–5750* ⊕ *www.nhcountrystore.com.*

🏃 Activities

BOATING
Wild Meadow Canoes & Kayaks

BOATING | Canoes and kayaks at this shop at the north tip of Lake Winnipesaukee, near the Center Harbor town line. ⌧ *6 Whittier Hwy., Moultonborough* ☎ *603/253–7536* ⊕ *www.wildmeadowcanoes.com.*

HIKING
Red Hill

HIKING & WALKING | FAMILY | This 2,030-foot mountain really does turn red in autumn. At the top of the moderately steep 1.7-mile Fire Tower Trail, you can climb a fire tower for 360-degree views of Lake Winnipesaukee and Squam Lake, as well as the White Mountains beyond. To make a loop, return via the Cabin Trail. At the parking area, a small snack bar (open mostly on weekends) dispenses organic coffee, ice cream, and other treats. ⊠ *Red Hill Rd., 2 miles west of Rte. 25, Moultonborough.*

Tamworth

13 miles east of Center Sandwich.

President Grover Cleveland summered in what remains a place of almost unreal quaintness: Tamworth is equally photogenic in verdant summer, during the fall foliage season, or under a blanket of winter snow. Cleveland's son, Francis, returned and founded the acclaimed Barnstormers Theatre in 1931. One of America's first summer theaters, it continues to this day. Tamworth has a clutch of villages within its borders, and six historic churches. In the hamlet of Chocorua, the view through the birches of Chocorua Lake has been so often photographed that you may experience déjà vu. Rising above the lake is Mt. Chocorua (3,490 feet), which has many good hiking trails.

GETTING HERE AND AROUND

Tamworth's main village, at the junction of Routes 113 and 113A, is tiny and can be strolled.

⊙ Sights

Remick Country Doctor Museum and Farm

FARM/RANCH | FAMILY | For 99 years (1894–1993) Dr. Edwin Crafts Remick and his father provided medical services to the Tamworth area and operated a family farm. These two houses now comprise a farm museum, with the second floor of the house kept as it was when Remick passed away, providing a glimpse into the life of a country doctor. The still-working farm features special activities, such as maple-syrup making, and has hiking trails and picnicking areas. ⊠ *58 Cleveland Hill Rd., Tamworth* ☎ *603/323–7591* ⊕ *www.remickmuseum.org* ⊠ *Pay as you wish* ⊙ *Museum closed Sat.–Tues. in Nov.–Apr.*

★ Tamworth Distilling & Mercantile

DISTILLERY | Using a 250-gallon copper still constructed in Kentucky, this artisanal distillery set in a stately barn just a short stroll from famed Barnstormers Theatre produces exceptional craft spirits, including Chocorua Straight Rye, Von Humboldt's Turmeric Cordial, Tamworth Garden Spruce Gin, and several flavorful cordials. If you're lucky, your stop will include a chance to sample Eau de Musc, a limited-release whiskey infused with an oil extracted from the castor glands of beavers. ⊠ *15 Cleveland Hill Rd., Tamworth* ☎ *603/323–7196* ⊕ *www.tamworthdistilling.com* ⊙ *Closed Mon.–Tues.*

🎟 Performing Arts

★ Barnstormers Theatre

THEATER | Founded in 1931, this highly respected theater company presents dramas and comedies June–August. ⊠ *104 Main St., Tamworth* ☎ *603/323–8500* ⊕ *www.barnstormerstheatre.org.*

🏃 Activities

White Lake State Park

HIKING & WALKING | The 72-acre stand of native pitch pine here is a National Natural Landmark. The park has a picnic area and a sandy beach, trails you can hike, trout you can fish for, and canoes you can rent. ⊠ *94 State Park Rd., Tamworth* ☎ *603/323–7350* ⊕ *www.nhstateparks.org* ⊠ *$5 late May–mid-Oct.*

North Conway

20 miles north of Tamworth, 42 miles east North Woodstock, 62 miles northwest of Portland, Maine.

Before the arrival of the popular Settlers Green outlet stores, this town drew visitors for its inspiring scenery, ski resorts, and access to White Mountain National Forest. Today, however, the feeling of natural splendor is gone. Shopping is the big sport, and businesses line Route 16 for several miles. You'll get a close look at them as traffic often slows to a crawl. It's a bit of a food desert, too, with plenty of options but few of them notable.

GETTING HERE AND AROUND
Route 16 bisects town but can be clogged with traffic. Take the scenic West Side Road from Conway to Intervale, or even on to Bartlett if you're headed farther north, to circumvent the traffic and take in splendid views.

ESSENTIALS
VISITOR INFORMATION Mt. Washington Valley Chamber of Commerce. ⊠ *North Conway* ☎ *877/948–6867* ⊕ *www.visitmwv. com.*

Sights

Conway Scenic Railroad
TRAIN/TRAIN STATION | FAMILY | Departing from historic North Conway Station, the railroad operates various trips aboard vintage trains. The Notch Train to Crawford Depot or to Fabyan Station travels through rugged territory yielding wonderful views, which are best enjoyed from the premium-class Upper Dome cars. The shorter Conway Valley Train offers glimpses of Mt. Washington during a 55-minute round-trip journey to Conway or a 1¾-hour excursion to Bartlett. The 1874 station displays lanterns, old tickets and timetables, and other artifacts. Reserve early during foliage season. Some rides include box lunches or full dinners. ⊠ *38*

Norcross Cir., North Conway ☎ *603/356–5251* ⊕ *www.conwayscenic.com* ⊠ *From $21* ⊙ *Closed Dec.–Mar.*

Echo Lake State Park
STATE/PROVINCIAL PARK | FAMILY | You don't have to be a rock climber to enjoy the views from the 700-foot White Horse and Cathedral ledges, which you can reach via a 1.7-mile road. From the top, you'll see the entire valley, including Echo Lake, which offers fishing, swimming, boating, and, on quiet days, an excellent opportunity to shout for echoes. ⊠ *68 Echo Lake Rd., Conway* ☎ *603/356–2672* ⊕ *www. nhstateparks.org* ⊠ *$4 early May–Oct.*

🍴 Restaurants

Muddy Moose
$ | AMERICAN | FAMILY | This playfully themed lodge-style restaurant buzzes with the sound of happy kids, but everyone seems to enjoy the rustic trappings, which include a huge stone fireplace, moose-antler chandeliers, and mounted animals. The comfort food here is reliably good, from barbecue rack of ribs to peppercorn-mushroom burgers, and there's a good selection of local beers. **Known for:** half-pound burgers with plenty of toppings; extensive kids offerings; Paradise four-layer chocolate cake. $ *Average main: $17* ⊠ *2344 White Mountain Hwy., North Conway* ☎ *603/356–7696* ⊕ *www. muddymoose.com.*

Table + Tonic Farm Cafe
$ | MODERN AMERICAN | The green-thumb-savvy proprietors of the popular and adjacent Local Grocer natural foods market operate this hip farm-to-table café. In this sleek, solar-powered establishment you can feast on fresh baked goods, organic-egg dishes, leafy salads, healthy sandwiches, and smoothies and espresso drinks. **Known for:** healthy breakfast and lunch fare; good selection of local beers and craft cocktails; attractive side patio overlooking a leafy garden. $ *Average main: $11* ⊠ *3358 White Mountain Hwy.,*

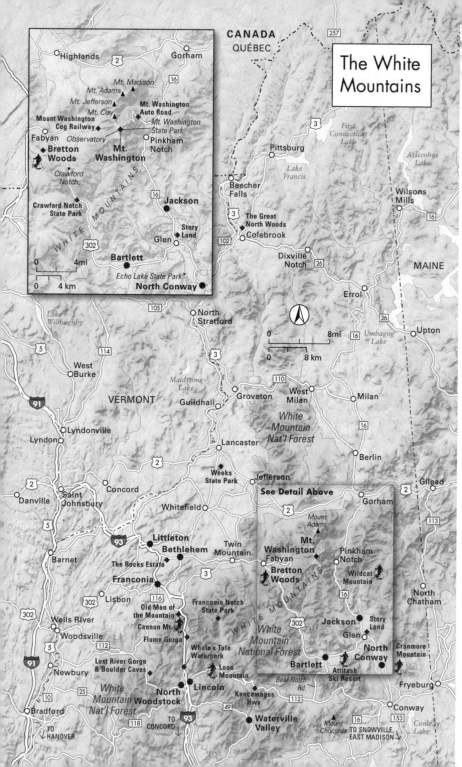

The White Mountains

Detail (inset map)

CANADA
QUÉBEC

Highlands
Gorham
Mt. Madison
Mt. Adams
Mt. Jefferson
Mt. Clay
Mt. Washington Auto Road
Mount Washington Cog Railway
Mt. Washington State Park
Fabyan
Observatory
Pinkham Notch
Bretton Woods
Mt. Washington
Crawford Notch
Jackson
Crawford Notch State Park
Story Land
Glen
Bartlett
Echo Lake State Park
North Conway

WHITE MOUNTAINS

0   4mi
0   4 km

Main map

First Connecticut Lake
Aziscohos Lake
Pittsburg
Lake Francis
Wilsons Mills
Beecher Falls
MAINE
The Great North Woods
Colebrook
Dixville Notch
Errol
Upton
Umbagog Lake
North Stratford
0   8mi
0   8 km
Lake Willoughby
West Burke
VERMONT
Maidstone Lake
Groveton
West Milan
Milan
White Mountain Nat'l Forest
Lyndon
Lyndonville
Guildhall
Lancaster
Berlin
Weeks State Park
Jefferson
See Detail Above
Gorham
Gilead
Concord
Whitefield
Mount Adams
Saint Johnsbury
Danville
Mt. Washington
Fabyan
Pinkham Notch
Littleton
Bethlehem
Twin Mountain
Bretton Woods
Wildcat Mountain
The Rocks Estate
Franconia
North Chatham
Old Man of the Mountain
Franconia Notch State Park
WHITE MOUNTAINS
Jackson
Story Land
Lisbon
Cannon Mt.
White Mountain National Forest
Glen
Cranmore Mountain
Wells River
Flume Gorge
North Conway
Woodsville
Whale's Tale Waterpark
Bartlett
Lost River Gorge & Boulder Caves
Loon Mountain
Bear Notch Rd.
Attitash Ski Resort
Fryeburg
Newbury
North Woodstock
Lincoln
Conway
White Mountain Nat'l Forest
Kancamagus Hwy.
Bradford
TO HANOVER
TO CONCORD
Waterville Valley
Mount Chocorua
TO SNOWVILLE, EAST MADISON
Conway Lake

North Conway ☎ *603/356–6068* 🌐 *www.tableandtonic.com* 🕒 *Closed Tues. and Wed. No dinner.*

Hotels

The Buttonwood Inn
$$$ | **B&B/INN** | A tranquil oasis in a busy resort area, the Buttonwood sits on Mt. Surprise, 2 miles northeast of North Conway village—close enough to access area dining and shopping, but far away from noise and crowds of downtown. **Pros:** delicious breakfasts; year-round outdoor hot tub and fire pit; 6 acres of peaceful grounds. **Cons:** too secluded for some; swimming pool is seasonal; some rooms have private baths down the hall. [$] *Rooms from: $238* ✉ *64 Mt. Surprise Rd., North Conway* ☎ *603/356–2625* 🌐 *www.buttonwoodinn.com* 🛏 *10 rooms* 🍴 *Free Breakfast.*

Cranmore Inn
$$ | **B&B/INN** | **FAMILY** | Just a block from the restaurants, shops, and attractions along Route 16 in North Conway, this rambling structure built in 1863 offers a nice range of upscale accommodations with modern furnishings, from two-bedroom apartments with kitchens and balconies to cozier standard rooms. **Pros:** very friendly and kind innkeepers; short walk from local dining and attractions; a wide range of room sizes and configurations. **Cons:** no elevator; in a town that can get very crowded in high season; some noise from street traffic. [$] *Rooms from: $174* ✉ *80 Kearsarge Rd., North Conway* ☎ *603/356–5502* 🌐 *www.cranmoreinn.com* 🛏 *20 rooms* 🍴 *Free Breakfast.*

Huttopia White Mountains
$ | **RESORT** | **FAMILY** | Convenience to the Kancamagus Highway and the Lakes Region are among the draws of this 50-acre glamping (cabins and canvas tents) compound on a pristine mountain lake and offering a wealth of amenities, including a food truck, pool, beach, yoga classes, and recreational activities. Kayak and paddleboard rentals are available. Some units overlook the lake. **Pros:** plenty to keep kids and families entertained; high-quality bedding and cooking equipment; good range of accommodation types and styles. **Cons:** at some sites you can hear cars from the road; lively, family-oriented vibe may not suit everyone; units can be hard to heat on cool spring and fall nights. [$] *Rooms from: $112* ✉ *Pine Knoll Rd., Albany* ☎ *844/488–8674, 603/447–3131* 🌐 *www.canada-usa.huttopia.com* 🕒 *Closed mid-Oct.–mid-May* 🛏 *97 units* 🍴 *No Meals.*

Inn at Crystal Lake
$$ | **B&B/INN** | In the quaint village of Eaton Center, about 10 miles south of North Conway, this stately 1884 Greek Revival inn contains finely appointed rooms with dramatic themes, each filled with a mix of curious and whimsical art and collectibles from the innkeepers' travels. **Pros:** short walk to the lake; convivial pub with good food; good base for White Mountains, Lakes Region, and Maine's Stone Mountain Arts Center. **Cons:** secluded area; few dining options nearby; may feel a bit old-fashioned for some. [$] *Rooms from: $169* ✉ *2356 Eaton Rd., Eaton Center* ☎ *603/447–2120* 🌐 *www.innatcrystallake.com* 🛏 *11 rooms* 🍴 *Free Breakfast.*

Purity Spring Resort
$$ | **RESORT** | **FAMILY** | Set on the pine-shaded shore of a rippling outdoor lake and adjacent to the slopes of King Pine Ski Area, this inviting boutique resort is a year-round destination for family-friendly recreation. Amenities are extensive and include lawn games, an indoor pool, free use of kayaks and canoes, and a restaurant with traditional but reliably good food. Accommodations come in a variety of shapes and sizes, and many have kitchens. This is a great option for a family getaway or reunion. **Pros:** wide range of accommodations (some that are perfect for large families); scenic

lakefront setting; lots of recreational activities. **Cons:** lots of very active families; resort fee; remote location with few dining options nearby. $ *Rooms from: $159* ⊠ *1256 Eaton Rd. Madison* ☎ *603/367–8896, 800/373–3754* ⊕ *www. purityspring.com* ⟲ *67 units* ⟨⊙⟩ *No Meals.*

★ Snowvillage Inn

$$ | B&B/INN | The finest room in this pastoral inn's main gambrel-roof house (built in 1916) has 12 windows that look out over the Presidential Range, and many guest rooms—some in a carriage house and a new outbuilding—have fireplaces. **Pros:** spectacular views; use of snowshoes and 10 acres of trails; delicious full breakfasts. **Cons:** off the beaten path; no TVs in rooms; not many dining options nearby. $ *Rooms from: $179* ⊠ *136 Stewart Rd., Eaton Center* ☎ *603/447–2818* ⊕ *www.snowvillageinn. com* ⟲ *17 rooms* ⟨⊙⟩ *Free Breakfast.*

ⓨ Nightlife

Delaney's Hole in the Wall

PUBS | This legendary après-ski tavern has a real fondness for ski history, displaying early photos of local ski areas, old signs and placards, and odd bits of lift equipment. Enjoy watching games on TV in the sports-bar area and noshing on comforting pub fare. ⊠ *2966 White Mountain Hwy., North Conway* ☎ *603/356–7776* ⊕ *www.delaneys.com.*

★ Tuckerman Brewing Co.

BEER GARDENS | Offering live music on weekends, seating inside as well as—during the warmer months—in a huge tented beer garden, light snacks, and some of the freshest and tastiest beer in the state, this venerable craft brewery on the edge of downtown Conway is a fun place to relax after a hike or mingle with friends. ⊠ *66 Hobbs St., Conway* ☎ *603/447–5400* ⊕ *www.tuckerman-brewing.com.*

🛍 Shopping

More than 120 factory outlets—including L.L. Bean, J. Crew, New Balance, Columbia, Talbots, Polo, Nike, Banana Republic, and American Eagle—line Route 16.

Handcrafters Barn

CRAFTS | The work of 150 area artists and artisans are sold in this attractive red-clapboard building. ⊠ *2473 White Mountain Hwy., North Conway* ☎ *603/356–8996* ⊕ *www.handcrafters-barn.com.*

🏃 Activities

SKIING

Cranmore Mountain Resort

SKIING & SNOWBOARDING | FAMILY | This fun-to-ski area has been a favorite with families since it opened in 1938. Most runs are naturally formed intermediates that weave in and out of glades. Beginners have several slopes and routes from the summit; experts must be content with a few short, steep pitches. Snowboarders can explore five different terrain parks. A mountain coaster, a tubing park, a giant swing, and a zipline provide additional entertainment, and there's night skiing on Saturdays and holidays. **Facilities:** 56 trails; 170 acres; 1,200-foot vertical drop; 8 lifts. ⊠ *1 Skimobile Rd., North Conway* ☎ *800/786–6754* ⊕ *www.cranmore.com* ⟐ *Lift ticket: $94.*

Mt. Washington Valley Ski Touring and Snowshoe Foundation

SKIING & SNOWBOARDING | Nearly 30 miles of groomed cross-country trails weave through the North Conway countryside, maintained by this foundation. Membership to the Mt. Washington Valley Ski Touring Club, available by the day or year, is required. Equipment rentals are available. ⊠ *279 Rte. 16/U.S. 302, Intervale* ☎ *603/356–9920* ⊕ *www.mwvskitouring. org.*

Jackson

9 miles north of North Conway.

Just off Route 16 via a red covered bridge, photogenic Jackson retains its storybook New England character. Art and antiques shopping, tennis, golf, fishing, and hiking to waterfalls are among the draws, as well as a high concentration of upscale country inns. When the snow falls, Jackson becomes the state's cross-country skiing capital, and there are also four downhill ski areas nearby—hotels and inns provide ski shuttles.

ESSENTIALS

Jackson is on Route 16, just north of the junction with U.S. 302.

VISITOR INFORMATION Jackson Area Chamber of Commerce. ☎ *603/383–9356* 🌐 *www.jacksonnh.com.*

Sights

Story Land

AMUSEMENT PARK/CARNIVAL | FAMILY | This theme park with life-size storybook and nursery-rhyme characters is geared to kids (ages 2–12). The two-dozen rides include a flumer, a river raft, and the Roar-O-Saurus and Polar Coaster roller coasters. Play areas and magic shows provide additional entertainment. There's also the Living Shores Aquarium, which offers 32,000-square-feet of mostly interactive, touch-friendly pools and exhibits. ✉ *850 Rte. 16, Glen* ☎ *603/383–4186* 🌐 *www.storylandnh.com* 🎟 *$55, aquarium $25.*

Restaurants

★ Thompson House Eatery

$$$ | MODERN AMERICAN | The domain of celebrated chef-owner Jeff Fournier, who's cooked at some of Boston's most acclaimed restaurants, this exceptional eatery is set inside a chicly restored farmhouse in the village of Jackson. Ethereal highlights from the oft-changing menu include seared Maine bluefin tuna with a leek-fennel emulsion and brown sugar–and–chili-roasted delicata squash, and a superb cheese board with raspberry-hibiscus jam, nuts, and local honey. **Known for:** elegant and historic farmhouse setting; on-site shop with gourmet goods to go; seasonally flavored house-made ice creams. [$] *Average main: $34* ✉ *193 Main St., Jackson* ☎ *603/383–9341* 🌐 *www.thethompsonhouseeatery.com* 🕐 *Closed Mon. and Tues. No lunch.*

Hotels

Inn at Ellis River

$$ | B&B/INN | Most of the rooms—which are all outfitted with armchairs and ottomans and floral-print duvet covers and featherbeds—in this unabashedly romantic 1893 inn on the Ellis River have fireplaces, and some also have balconies with Adirondack chairs and whirlpool tubs. **Pros:** pretty riverside location; abundantly charming; multicourse breakfasts and afternoon refreshments included. **Cons:** some rooms up steep stairs; not suitable for kids under 12; the least expensive rooms are quite compact. [$] *Rooms from: $179* ✉ *17 Harriman Rd., Jackson* ☎ *603/383–9339, 800/233–8309* 🌐 *www.innatellisriver.com* 🛏 *21 rooms* 🍴 *Free Breakfast.*

Inn at Jackson

$ | B&B/INN | This homey yet distinctive B&B—designed in 1902 by famed architect Stanford White for the Baldwin family of piano fame—is reasonably priced, charmingly furnished, and in the heart of the village. **Pros:** great value considering its many charms; peaceful setting; wonderful breakfasts. **Cons:** top-floor rooms lack fireplaces; rooms could use some updating; a bit frilly for some tastes. [$] *Rooms from: $149* ✉ *Thorn Hill Rd. and Main St., Jackson* ☎ *603/383–4321, 800/289–8600* 🌐 *www.innatjackson.com* 🛏 *14 rooms* 🍴 *Free Breakfast.*

★ The Inn at Thorn Hill & Spa

$$$ | B&B/INN | With a large reception room and sweeping staircase, a deck overlooking the rolling hills around the village, and a common area with a wet bar and a cozy fireplace, this lovely inn—modeled after an 1891 Victorian designed by Stanford White—is breathtaking throughout. **Pros:** superb restaurant; soothing full spa; exceptional full breakfasts. **Cons:** rigid peak-season cancellation policy; not suitable for kids; carriage house and cottages are less sumptuous. $ *Rooms from: $259* ✉ *42 Thorn Hill Rd., Jackson* ☎ *603/383–4242* ⊕ *www.innatthornhill. com* ⮩ *22 rooms* ⦿ *No Meals.*

Wentworth

$$ | B&B/INN | FAMILY | Thoughtful renovations have given new life and elegance to the guest rooms at this baronial 1869 Victorian, whose amenities include a full spa, a first-rate restaurant, and access to a terrific golf course and cross-country ski trails. **Pros:** discounts at neighboring Wentworth Golf Club; interesting architecture; very good farm-to-table restaurant. **Cons:** some rooms up steep stairs; two-night minimum many weekends; at a somewhat busy intersection. $ *Rooms from: $189* ✉ *1 Carter Notch Rd., Jackson* ☎ *603/383–9700, 800/637–0013* ⊕ *www.thewentworth.com* ⮩ *61 rooms* ⦿ *Free Breakfast.*

🏃 Activities

CROSS-COUNTRY SKIING

★ Jackson Ski Touring Foundation

SKIING & SNOWBOARDING | FAMILY | This acclaimed cross-country ski operation has an attentive staff and 90 miles of groomed trails for skiing, skate skiing, and snowshoeing. The varied terrain offers something for all abilities—lessons and rentals are offered, too. Trails wind through covered bridges and into the picturesque village of Jackson, where you can warm up in cozy trailside restaurants. ✉ *153 Main St., Jackson* ☎ *603/383–9355* ⊕ *www.jacksonxc.org.*

ICE-SKATING

Nestlenook Farm

ICE SKATING | FAMILY | This picturesque farm maintains an outdoor ice-skating rink with rentals, music, and a bonfire as well as offering snowshoeing and sleigh rides. ✉ *66 Dinsmore Rd., Jackson* ☎ *603/383–7101* ⊕ *www.nestlenook-farmsleighrides.com.*

Mt. Washington

12 miles north of Jackson, 39 miles east of Bretton Woods.

At 6,288 feet, Mt. Washington is the tallest peak in the northeastern United States. The world's highest winds, 231 mph, were recorded here in 1934. You can take a guided van tour, a drive, or a hike to the summit. A number of trails circle the mountain and access the other peaks in the Presidential Range, but all of them are fairly strenuous and best attempted only if you're somewhat experienced and quite fit. It gets cold up here: even in the summer, you'll want a jacket.

GETTING HERE AND AROUND

Mt. Washington Auto Road climbs west from Route 16, about 2 miles north of Wildcat Mountain ski resort and 8 miles south of Gorham.

👁 Sights

★ Mt. Washington Auto Road

MOUNTAIN | FAMILY | The drive to the top of this imposing summit is truly memorable. Your route: the narrow, curving Mt. Washington Auto Road, which climbs 4,600 feet in about 7 miles. Drivers can download an app with a narrated tour and receive a bumper sticker that reads, "This car climbed Mt. Washington." The narration is fascinating, and the views are breathtaking. Once at the top, check out **Extreme Mount Washington,** an interactive museum dedicated to science and weather. If you're nervous about heights or the condition of your car, book a guided van tour or a ride up the cog railway in Bretton Woods. ✉ *1 Mt. Washington Auto Rd., Gorham* ☎ *603/466–3988* 🌐 *www.mt-washington.com* 🎟 *Car and driver $39–$45; guided bus tour from $45–$51* ⏲ *Closed late Oct.–early May.*

🍴 Restaurants

Big Day Brewing

$ | **AMERICAN** | You certainly don't have to be a beer lover to appreciate this airy, modern brewpub that serves exceptionally good pub fare like fries topped with house-made curry aioli, roasted–sweet potato tacos, and farm-raised-beef burgers with bacon and barbecue sauce—the kind of sustenance that warms the soul after a day of White Mountains hiking. But Big Day does produce some of the region's best brews, including European-style classics like a golden Munich Dunkel and a citrusy Hefeweizen. **Known for:** churros house-made strawberry compote; spacious, pet-friendly beer garden; distinctive, well-crafted beers. [$] *Average main: $15* ✉ *20 Glen Rd., Gorham* ☎ *603/915–9006* 🌐 *www.bigdaybrewing.com* ⏲ *Closed Mon.–Tues. No lunch Wed.–Thurs.*

Nonna's Kitchen

$$ | **ITALIAN** | **FAMILY** | Set in a vintage barber shop in downtown Gorham—8 miles north of the Mt. Washington Auto Road—this homey restaurant is a tribute to the owners' Italian grandmothers. Indeed, the menu reads like a roll call of favorites from the best restaurants in Boston's or New Haven's Little Italy neighborhoods—classic antipasto, feathery gnocchi with pesto, eggplant parmigiana, veal piccata, and linguine with clams and red sauce. **Known for:** friendly service; cod puttanesca; fresh handmade pastas, cooked to order. [$] *Average main: $20* ✉ *19 Exchange St., Gorham* ☎ *603/915–9203* 🌐 *www.nonnasgorham.com* ⏲ *Closed Mon. and Tues. No lunch.*

🛏 Hotels

★ **Glen House Hotel**

$$$ | **HOTEL** | The latest of four Glen House hotels that have stood on this site at the base of the Mt. Washington Auto Road since 1852, this upscale three-story retreat opened in 2018 in a Shaker-inspired building whose soaring windows, a yellow clapboard exterior, and simple lines hark back to its predecessors. **Pros:** easy access to Mt. Washington activities; beautifully designed; excellent on-site restaurant. **Cons:** remote area; may be a bit shiny and new for some tastes; limited dining options in the area. [$] *Rooms from: $284* ✉ *979 Rte. 16, Gorham* ☎ *603/466–3420* 🌐 *www.theglenhouse.com* 🛏 *68 rooms* 🍽 *Free Breakfast.*

🏃 Activities

All trails to Mt. Washington's peak are demanding and require a considerable investment of time and effort. Perhaps the most famous is the **Tuckerman Ravine Trail,** the path used by extreme skiers who risk life and limb to fly down the face of the steep ravine. The hike to the top can easily take six–nine hours round-trip. However you get to the top, because the weather here is so erratic, it's critical to check weather conditions, to be prepared, and to keep in mind that Mt. Washington's summit is much colder than the base.

CROSS-COUNTRY SKIING

★ **Great Glen Trails Outdoor Center**

SKIING & SNOWBOARDING | **FAMILY** | Featuring a dramatic 28-mile network of both mild and wild cross-country ski and mountain-biking trails at the foot of Mt. Washington, Great Glen provides access to more than 1,100 acres of backcountry. You can also book to the summit via SnowCoach, a nine-passenger van refitted with triangular snowmobile-like treads. You have the option of skiing or snowshoeing down or just enjoying the magnificent winter view. There's

The highest peak in New England, Mt. Washington rewards those who drive or hike to the top with spectacular views.

also a huge ski and sports shop, a food court, and a climbing wall. In summer you can also rent kayaks and book excellent paddling, rafting, and float trips along the Androscoggin River. ⊠ *1 Mt. Washington Auto Rd., at Rte. 16, Gorham* ☎ *603/466–3988* ⊕ *www.greatglentrails. com* ⌨ *SnowCoach tours $65.*

HIKING
Pinkham Notch
HIKING & WALKING | On Mt. Washington's eastern slopes, scenic Pinkham Notch encompasses several ravines, including famous Tuckerman. The Appalachian Mountain Club operates a visitor center that provides trail information. Guided hikes leave from here, and outdoor skills workshops are offered. On-site are an outdoors shop, a lodge with basic overnight accommodations, and a dining hall. Not all the trails ascend Mt. Washington or are necessarily strenuous. Good bets for shorter, moderate hikes include Glen Ellis Falls and Crystal Cascade, which

both lead to scenic waterfalls. ⊠ *AMC Pinkham Notch Visitor Center, 361 Rte. 16, Gorham* ☎ *603/466–2727* ⊕ *www. outdoors.org.*

SKIING
Wildcat Mountain
SKIING & SNOWBOARDING | Glade skiers love Wildcat's 80 acres of tree skiing. Runs include some stunning double–black diamond trails; experts can really zip down the Lynx. Beginners, as long as they can hold a wedge, should check out the 2½-mile-long Polecat, which offers excellent views of the Presidential Range. The trails are classic New England—narrow and winding—and the vistas are stunning. For an adrenaline rush, there's a terrain park. In summer you can dart to the top on the four-passenger gondola, hike the many trails, and fish in the crystal clear streams. **Facilities:** 48 trails; 225 acres; 2,112-foot vertical drop; 5 lifts. ⊠ *Rte. 16, Gorham* ☎ *603/466–3326* ⊕ *www.skiwildcat.com* ⌨ *$115.*

Bartlett

19 miles south of Mt. Washington, 9 miles northwest of North Conway.

With Bear Mountain to its south, Mt. Parker to its north, Mt. Cardigan to its west, and the Saco River to its east, Bartlett—incorporated in 1790—has an unforgettable setting. Lovely Bear Notch Road (closed in winter) has the only midpoint access to the Kancamagus Highway. There isn't much town to speak of: the dining options listed here are actually nearby in Glen. It's best known for the Attitash Ski Resort.

GETTING HERE AND AROUND

U.S. 302 passes through Bartlett from Bretton Woods and west from Glen.

🍴 Restaurants

White Mountain Cider Co.

$$$ | **MODERN AMERICAN** | Set in a historic cider mill near the Saco River, this rustic yet elegant bistro and adjacent gourmet market and deli presses fresh cider in the fall—it's served with traditional homemade cider doughnuts. But it's also a terrific farm-to-table restaurant, featuring a seasonal menu of eclectic, contemporary dishes. **Known for:** flavorful sandwiches and soups in the adjacent market; creative cocktails; friendly, knowledgeable service. [$] *Average main: $32* ✉ *207 U.S. 302, Glen* ☎ *603/383–9061* 🌐 *www.ciderconh.com* 🕒 *Closed Tues. No lunch in restaurant.*

🛏 Hotels

★ **Alpine Garden Camping Village**

$$ | **RESORT** | This relatively cozy glamping compound nestled in a serene wooded property in the heart of the White Mountains consists of charming cabins, a couple of campers, and a pair of luxurious, beautifully designed tree houses. There's reliable Wi-Fi, and each of the individually decorated units have climate-control, record players, and minibars stocked with wine and cider. **Pros:** peaceful, wooded setting; on-site winery and tasting room; heated pool. **Cons:** there's a small charge for linens; no pets; not a great fit for kids. [$] *Rooms from: $165* ✉ *125 U.S. 302, Bartlett* ☎ *603/374–5154* 🌐 *www.alpinegardenglamping.com* 🕒 *Closed mid-Apr.–Nov.* 🛏 *11 units* 🍴 *No Meals.*

★ **Bernerhof Inn**

$$ | **B&B/INN** | Skiers, hikers, and adventurers who favor a luxurious, intimate lodging over a bustling condo resort adore this grand Victorian inn operated with eco-friendly practices and furnished with a mix of fine antiques and period reproductions. **Pros:** excellent on-site cooking school; exudes old-world charm; small but wonderfully relaxing spa. **Cons:** guests under 21 not permitted; some rooms receive a little road noise. [$] *Rooms from: $189* ✉ *342 U.S. 302, Glen* ☎ *603/383–4200* 🌐 *www.bernerhof-inn.com* 🛏 *12 rooms* 🍴 *Free Breakfast.*

Golden Apple Inn

$ | **MOTEL** | **FAMILY** | This small, attractively updated, and economical motel is an easy drive from the Mt. Washington Auto Road, skiing at Attitash Mountain Resort, and the inviting villages of Jackson and North Conway. **Pros:** well-tended gardens and grounds with a pool, playground, and barbecue grill; superb value; excellent base for skiing and hiking. **Cons:** on a somewhat busy road; no breakfast or restaurant; simple decor. [$] *Rooms from: $109* ✉ *322 U.S. 302, Glen* ☎ *603/383–9680* 🌐 *www.goldenappleinn.com* 🛏 *17 rooms* 🍴 *No Meals.*

Grand Summit Hotel at Attitash

$$ | **RESORT** | **FAMILY** | All of the pleasantly furnished rooms at this ski-in, ski-out condo-style resort at the base of Bear Peak have kitchenettes, and many have private balconies with splendid views. **Pros:** appealing slope-side setting; ski-package deals; kitchenettes in rooms. **Cons:** generally bland decor; could use some sprucing up; restaurants are a bit

meh. [$] *Rooms from: $159* ✉ *104 Grand Summit Rd., Bartlett* ☎ *603/374–6700* 🌐 *www.grandsummitattitash.com* 🛏 *143 rooms* 🍴 *No Meals.*

Nightlife

Red Parka Pub

PUBS | This homey pub decorated with license plates and ski memorabilia has been an institution, especially during winter ski season, since the early 1970s, providing a fun and festive venue for après-ski or-hike socializing. Beer is served in Mason jars, the kitchen serves up juicy steaks and comfort fare, and there's live music many evenings. ✉ *3 Station St., Glen* ☎ *603/383–4344* 🌐 *www.redparkapub.com.*

Activities

SKIING

Attitash Ski Resort

SKIING & SNOWBOARDING | **FAMILY** | With one of New Hampshire's higher vertical drops, Attitash Mountain has dozens of trails to explore, and there are more on the adjacent Attitash Bear Peak. You'll find traditional New England ski runs and challenging terrain alongside wide-open cruisers that suit all skill levels. There are acres of glades, plus a progressive freestyle terrain park. The Attitash Adventure Center offers rentals, lessons, and children's programs. **Facilities:** 68 trails; 311 acres; 1,750-foot vertical drop; 9 lifts. ✉ *775 U.S. 302, Bartlett* ☎ *800/223–7669* 🌐 *www.attitash.com* 🎟 *Lift ticket: $115.*

Bretton Woods

21 miles northwest of Bartlett.

In the early 1900s private railcars brought the elite from New York and Philadelphia to the Mount Washington Hotel, the jewel of the White Mountains. A visit to this property, which was the site of the 1944 United Nations conference that created the International Monetary Fund and the International Bank for Reconstruction and Development (and the birth of many conspiracy theories), is not to be missed. This rural area—there's no real town per se—is also known for the cog railway to the summit of Mt. Washington, Bretton Woods ski resort, and unparalleled hiking at Crawford Notch State Park.

GETTING HERE AND AROUND

Bretton Woods is in the heart of the White Mountains on U.S. 302. A free shuttle makes it easy to get around the resort's many venues.

Sights

★ **Crawford Notch State Park**

STATE/PROVINCIAL PARK | **FAMILY** | Scenic U.S. 302 winds southeast of Bretton Woods through the steep, wooded mountains on either side of spectacular Crawford Notch. At this 5,775-acre state park, you can picnic and hike to Arethusa Falls, the longest drop in New England, or to the Silver and Flume cascades—they're among more than a dozen outstanding trails. Roadside photo ops abound, and amenities include an Adirondack-style visitor center, gift shop, snack bar, and fishing pond. ✉ *1464 U.S. 302, Hart's Location* ☎ *603/374–2272* 🌐 *www.nhstateparks.org.*

★ **Mount Washington Cog Railway**

TRAIN/TRAIN STATION | **FAMILY** | In 1858, Sylvester Marsh petitioned the state legislature for permission to build a steam railway up Mt. Washington. One politico retorted that Marsh would have better luck building a railroad to the moon, but 11 years later the Mount Washington Cog Railway chugged its way up to the summit along a 3-mile track on the mountain's west side. Today it's a beloved attraction—a thrill in either direction. A small museum has exhibits about the cog rail, and a casual restaurant offers great views of the trains beginning their ascent. The full trip on these eco-friendly, biodiesel trains takes three hours including an hour at the summit. In winter, the railway runs shorter and less-expensive trips to the Waumbek Station (elevation 3,900 feet), which still offers impressive vistas of the snow-covered countryside. ✉ *3168 Base Station Rd., Bretton Woods* ☎ *603/278–5404, 800/922–8825* ⊕ *www. thecog.com* ✉ *Summit from $72, Waumbek Station from $41.*

🛏 Hotels

★ The Notchland Inn
$$$ | B&B/INN | Built in 1862 by Sam Bemis, America's grandfather of landscape photography, the gracious granite manor house exudes mountain charm and is popular with Crawford Notch hikers who favor luxury. **Pros:** set amid soaring mountains; marvelous house and common rooms; outstanding breakfasts and dinners. **Cons:** very isolated; fills up well in advance on summer and fall weekends; not ideal for young kids. Ⓢ *Rooms from: $295* ✉ *2 Morey Rd., Hart's Location* ☎ *603/374–6131, 800/866–6131* ⊕ *www.notchland.com* 🛏 *15 rooms* ⦿ *Free Breakfast.*

★ Omni Mount Washington Hotel
$$$$ | RESORT | FAMILY | The two most memorable sights in the White Mountains might just be Mt. Washington and this dramatic 1902 resort with a 900-foot veranda, glimmering public rooms, astonishing views of the Presidential Range, and dozens of recreational activities like tubing, sleigh rides, horseback riding, and fly-fishing. **Pros:** incomparable setting and ambience; loads of amenities and dining options; free shuttle to skiing and activities. **Cons:** lots of kids running around the property; a drive from nearest decent-size town; rates soar on summer–fall weekends. Ⓢ *Rooms from: $386* ✉ *310 Mt. Washington Hotel Rd., Bretton Woods* ☎ *603/278–1000, 888/444–6664* ⊕ *www.mountwashingtonresort.com* 🛏 *269 rooms* ⦿ *No Meals.*

🏃 Activities

SKIING
★ Bretton Woods
SKIING & SNOWBOARDING | FAMILY | New Hampshire's largest ski area is also one of the country's best family ski resorts. The views of Mt. Washington alone are worth the visit, and the scenery is especially beautiful from the two-story restaurant at the dramatically contemporary Rosewood Lodge, which sits at 3,000 feet in elevation and is reached via the all-glass eight-passenger Skyway Gondola. The resort has something for everyone, from extensive kids' programs and lessons to some seriously steep pitches near the top of the 1,500-foot vertical. And the 35 glades will keep experts busy, while snowboarders enjoy the three terrain parks. The Nordic trail system has 62 miles of cross-country ski tracks. Both night skiing and snowboarding are available on weekends and holidays. There's also the year-round Canopy Tour, with nine ziplines, two sky bridges, and three rappelling stations. **Facilities:** 63 trails; 464 acres, 1,500-foot vertical drop; 10 lifts. ✉ *99 Ski Area Rd., Bretton Woods* ☎ *603/278–3320* ⊕ *www. brettonwoods.com* ✉ *Lift ticket: $104.*

HIKING
Sugarloaf Trail
HIKING & WALKING | A relatively easy hike offering impressive views of Mt. Washington and the Presidential Range, this 3.4-mile round-trip hike starts near a tributary of the Ammonoosuc River, a 10-minute drive west of Bretton Woods. The trail runs alongside the river for a short way before ascending the somewhat steep eastern slope of Sugarloaf Mountain (the total elevation gain is about 1,050 feet). At the top of the ridge, you can cut across to both the North and South Sugarloaf summits; if you're short on time, choose the southern summit, which offers the most impressive panoramas. ✉ *Zealand Rd. Twin Mountain* ✛ *1 miles south of US 302.*

Bethlehem

14 miles west of Bretton Woods.

In the days before antihistamines, hay-fever sufferers came by the trainload to this enchanting village whose crisp air has a blissfully low pollen count. Today this progressive, artsy hamlet with fewer than 1,000 residents is notable for its art deco Colonial Theatre (which presents indie films and concerts), distinctive galleries and cafés, and stately Victorian and Colonial homes, many of which line the village's immensely picturesque Main Street, a highly enjoyable locale for a stroll.

GETTING HERE AND AROUND

U.S. 302 and Route 142 intersect in the heart of this small village center that's easy to explore on foot.

Sights

The Rocks Estate

NATURE PRESERVE | FAMILY | The estate of John Jacob Glessner (1843–1936), one of the founders of International Harvester, now serves as a 1,400-acre conservation and education center. The property is named for the many surface boulders on the estate when Glessner bought it—some were used to erect the rambling rock walls that flanks the estate's striking shingle-style restored buildings. The Rocks presents natural-history programs and has self-guided tours and hiking trails with excellent views of the Presidential Range. Come winter, cross-country ski trails and a select-your-own-Christmas-tree farm open up. In early spring, you can watch how maple syrup is made. Note that the property's trails have been closed during an extensive restoration project but are expected to reopen in summer 2023. ✉ *4 Christmas La., Bethlehem* ☎ *603/444–6228* 🌐 *www.forestsociety.org/the-rocks.*

Restaurants

★ Cold Mountain Cafe

$$ | ECLECTIC | Adjacent to the Marketplace at WREN, this homey art-filled storefront eatery and wine bar is one of the area's social focal points, with a welcoming staff and a thoughtful, international menu. Pork tacos, Indian lamb stew, and heirloom tomato caprese salads are a few of the best dishes, but save room for the flourless chocolate torte with strawberry-balsamic coulis. **Known for:** friendly, upbeat crowd and staff; bounteous salads; intriguing cocktail list. [$] *Average main: $22* ✉ *2015 Main St., Bethlehem* ☎ *603/869–2500* 🌐 *www.coldmountaincafe.com* 🕒 *Closed Sun.*

Coffee and Quick Bites

Maia Papaya

$ | CAFÉ | Pause during your stroll through inviting Bethlehem for breakfast, lunch, smoothies, lattes, or homemade chai tea at this quirky organic café that specializes in vegetarian fare and made-from-scratch baked goods (try not to pass up one of the justly renowned scones). On cool mornings, warm up with a hearty breakfast burrito; terrific lunchtime options include the artichoke melt panini or the bountiful green salad. **Known for:** plenty of gluten-free and vegetarian options; fruit-filled oat bars; organic oatmeal with local maple syrup. [$] *Average main: $9* ✉ *2161 Main St., Bethlehem* ☎ *603/869–9900* 🌐 *www.themaiapapaya.com* 🕒 *Closed Tues. No dinner.*

★ Super Secret Ice Cream

$ | ICE CREAM | FAMILY | It may have the word "secret" in its name, but this artisan ice-cream shop with a walk-up window and deck as well as a spacious indoor seating area has a devoted following—let's just say the cat's out of the bag. This is some of the richest and delicious ice cream in the state, and there's always a great lineup of unusual flavors, such as Thai tea, roasted cherry chip, honeycomb, and strawberry buttermilk. **Known for:** unusual flavors; the milk and many ingredients are sourced locally; sunny patio seating. $ *Average main: $6* ✉ *2213 Main St., Bethlehem* ☎ 🌐 *www.supersecreticecream.com* 🕓 *Closed Mon.–Tues.*

Hotels

★ **Adair Country Inn and Restaurant**

$$$ | B&B/INN | An air of yesteryear refinement suffuses Adair, a three-story Georgian Revival home that attorney Frank Hogan built as a wedding present for his daughter in 1927—her hats adorn the place, as do books and old photos from the era. **Pros:** a superb, romantic restaurant; rates include a memorable breakfast and afternoon tea; cross-country skiing and hiking trails. **Cons:** not within walking distance of town; sometimes books up with weddings; closed for a month each fall and spring. $ *Rooms from: $279* ✉ *80 Guider La., Bethlehem* ☎ *603/444–2600, 888/444–2600* 🌐 *www.adairinn.com* 🕓 *Closed mid-Nov. and Apr.* 🛏 *11 rooms* 🍴 *Free Breakfast.*

Nightlife

★ **Rek-Lis Brewing Company**

BEER GARDENS | After a day of hiking or skiing, grab a seat inside this cozy tavern or out on one of the expansive decks and savor the outstanding house-made beers along with guest taps from other notable breweries. There's great pub food, too, and a popular Sunday brunch. ✉ *2085 Main St., Bethlehem* ☎ *603/991–2357* 🌐 *www.reklisbrewing.com.*

Shopping

★ **Marketplace at WREN**

ART GALLERIES | WREN (the Women's Rural Entrepreneurial Network) has been a vital force in little Bethlehem's steady growth into a center of more than 100 artists, craftspersons, and other business owners. At WREN's headquarters, there's an outstanding gallery that presents monthly juried exhibits and a retail gift boutique, Local Works, featuring crafts, foods, books, and one-of-a-kind gifts. ✉ *2011 Main St., Bethlehem* ☎ *603/869–9736* 🌐 *www.wrenworks.org.*

Littleton

5 miles west of Bethlehem.

One of northern New Hampshire's largest towns (this isn't saying much, mind you) sits on a granite shelf along the Ammonoosuc River, whose swift current and drop of 235 feet enabled the community to flourish as a mill center in its early days. The railroad came through later, and Littleton grew into the region's commercial hub. Long merely a place to stock up than a real destination, it's reinvented itself in recent decades, and lively Main Street now abounds with intriguing shops and eateries set inside tidy 19th- and early-20th-century buildings you might expect to see in an old Jimmy Stewart movie.

GETTING HERE AND AROUND

Littleton sits just off Interstate 93, and its downtown is easily explored on foot.

ESSENTIALS

VISITOR INFORMATION Littleton Area Chamber of Commerce. ✉ *Littleton* ☎ *603/444–6561* 🌐 *www.littletonareachamber.com.*

Restaurants

★ **Schilling Beer Taproom**

$ | PIZZA | With a storybook setting in a converted 18th-century mill on the Ammonoosuc River, this craft brewpub offers tasty wood-fired pizzas, bratwurst sandwiches, house-baked soft pretzels, and other fare that pairs well with its distinctive European ales. The pie topped with prosciutto, pears, chèvre, mozzarella, and beer-caramelized onions is a favorite, best enjoyed with a farm-house-style saison. **Known for:** seating overlooking the river; beer tastings; great pizzas. $ *Average main: $14* ✉ *18 Mill St., Littleton* ☎ *603/444–4800* ⊕ *www.schillingbeer.com.*

Taste the Thai & Sushi House

$$ | **THAI** | This friendly, laid-back Asian restaurant excels with just about everything it offers, from creative sushi rolls and sashimi (try the salmon topped with house-made truffle sauce) to well-seasoned (or fiery hot, on request) curries to boba teas. House specialties include the sweet-and-tangy shrimp pineapple curry, ginger stir-fried salmon, and basil crispy duck. **Known for:** quite possibly the most authentic Thai food in New Hampshire; Thai tea shaved ice; colorful cocktails. $ *Average main: $19* ✉ *406 Union St., Littleton* ☎ *603/575–5488* ⊕ *www.tastethethaiandsushihouse.com* ⊗ *Closed Wed.*

★ Tim-Bir Alley

$$$$ | **MODERN AMERICAN** | In this terrific contemporary downtown restaurant, you can sample some of the tastiest farm-to-table fare in the White Mountains. The menu changes frequently and uses regional American ingredients in creative ways—try country pâté with venison and pistachio, followed by crispy maple-glazed duck breast with smashed carrots and bok choy. **Known for:** stylish yet unpretentious; local artisan cheese plates; beautifully plated desserts. $ *Average main: $36* ✉ *7 Main St., Littleton* ☎ *603/444–6142* ⊕ *www.timbiralleyrestaurant.com* ▭ *No credit cards* ⊗ *Closed Mon. and Tues. No lunch.*

☕ Coffee and Quick Bites

★ Crumb Bum

$ | **CAFÉ** | Stop by this cute cake shop to stock up on creative, and utterly delectable, baked goods, such as grapefruit-rosemary-cardamom short bread cookies, maple cinnamon rolls, and macarons in a variety of flavors, and egg-bacon-cheese breakfast sandwiches constructed on ethereal duck-fat biscuits. Fine coffees are available, too. **Known for:** great baked goods; duck-fat angel biscuit breakfast sandwich; vegan options. $ *Average main: $5* ✉ *97 Main St., Littleton* ☎ *603/575–1773* ⊕ *www.crumbbumbakery.com* ⊗ *Closed Tues.–Wed.*

The Inkwell

$ | **CAFÉ** | Drop by this hip café with two downtown Littleton locations, both of them with ample indoor and outdoor seating, for a light bite, to relax with a book, or sip one of the well-crafted fair-trade coffee or organic loose-leaf tea drinks. Several kinds of toast with tasty toppings (ricotta and lemon honey; cheddar, ham, and egg) are available at breakfast, along with myriad scones, cookies, and gluten-free pastries. **Known for:** creative panini sandwiches for lunch; lots of outdoor seating; iced and hot coffees with local maple syrup. $ *Average main: $8* ✉ *24 Beacon St,, Littleton* ☎ *603/575–5335* ⊕ *www.inkwellnh.com* ⊗ *Closed Sun. No dinner.*

 ## Hotels

Mountain View Grand Resort & Spa

$$ | **RESORT** | **FAMILY** | Casual elegance and stunning views of the White Mountains define this stately yellow wedding cake of a hotel that dates to 1865 and sprawls over 1,700 acres that include a working farm and a well-maintained golf course. **Pros:** full-service spa; dozens of activities; babysitting service and summer camp. **Cons:** breakfast not included in rates; not too many dining options nearby; sometimes fills up with corporate meetings and retreats. $ *Rooms from: $219* ✉ *101 Mountain View Rd., Whitefield* ☎ *855/837–2100* ⊕ *www.mountainviewgrand.com* ⇆ *144 rooms* ⊠ *No Meals.*

Thayers Inn

$ | **HOTEL** | This former grande dame with a distinguished roster of past guests— including Ulysses S. Grant, Henry Ford, and PT Barnum—offers quirky and fun budget accommodations and a great location in one of the liveliest little downtowns in the White Mountains. **Pros:** some rooms have kitchenettes; fascinating building filled with memorabilia and exhibits; on lively and festive Main Street. **Cons:** no elevator; functional decor; tiny bathrooms. Ⓢ *Rooms from: $129* ✉ *111 Main St., Littleton* ☎ *603/444–6469* ⊕ *www.thayersinn.com* ⇲ *34 rooms* ❙⊘❙ *Free Breakfast.*

Shopping

Chutters

CANDY | **FAMILY** | Boasting the world's longest candy counter, at 112 feet, this kid- and adult-approved century-plus-old candy shop with satellite locations in Lincoln, Loon Mountain Resort, and Bretton Woods carries just about every variety of sweet treat you could imagine. ✉ *43 Main St, Littleton* ☎ *603/444–5787* ⊕ *www.chutters.com.*

★ Just L Modern Antiques

ANTIQUES & COLLECTIBLES | Fans of mid-century furnishings, from low-slung modern sofas and sleek Danish coffee tables to both fashionable and kitschy housewares, vintage paintings, and kitchen items flock to this enormous two-floor emporium set along Littleton's increasingly hip Main Street. ✉ *35 Main St., Littleton* ☎ *603/259–3125* ⊕ *www. facebook.com/midmodliving.*

Little Village Toy and Book Stop

TOYS | **FAMILY** | Maps, history books, unusual children's toys and many adult fiction and nonfiction titles fill this cheerful shop, the lower level of which contains a branch of the venerable League of New Hampshire Craftsmen's gallery. ✉ *81B Main St., Littleton* ☎ *603/444–4869* ⊕ *www.littlevillagetoy.com.*

Pentimento

SOUVENIRS | This eclectic shop, packed into a Victorian house a few steps from the historic Opera House, is a great place to find unusual jewelry, candles, fashion eyewear, and handmade cards. ✉ *34 Union St., Littleton* ☎ *603/444–7797* ⊕ *www.facebook.com/pentimentonh.*

Franconia

7 miles south of Littleton.

Travelers have long passed through spectacular Franconia Notch, and in the late 18th century this town just to the north existed just to serve them. It and the region's jagged rock formations and heavy coat of evergreens stirred the imaginations of Washington Irving, Henry Wadsworth Longfellow, and Nathaniel Hawthorne, who penned a short story about the iconic—though now crumbled—cliff known as the Old Man of the Mountain. Tiny downtown consists of a handful of businesses and the remains of the interesting old 1840s Besaw Iron Furnace. Drive west 4 miles to visit Sugar Hill, a village of about 500 people that's famous for its spectacular sunsets and views of Franconia Ridge, best seen from Sunset Hill, where a row of grand hotels and mansions once stood.

GETTING HERE AND AROUND
Franconia is right off Interstate 93.

ESSENTIALS
VISITOR INFORMATION Franconia Notch Chamber of Commerce. ✉ *Franconia* ☎ *603/823–2000* ⊕ *www.franconianotch. org.*

◉ Sights

★ Franconia Notch State Park

STATE/PROVINCIAL PARK | **FAMILY** | Traversed by the Appalachian Trail and a stretch of Interstate 93 that narrows for 8 miles to become Franconia Notch Parkway, this stunning 6,692-acre state park feels as awesome as a national park and offers dozens of diversions, including myriad hiking trails, summer swimming at **Echo Lake Beach,** and winter downhill skiing at **Cannon Mountain,** whose 4,080-foot summit observation deck you can explore on the **Aerial Tramway,** an 80-passenger cable car. One of the top park draws, the dramatic, narrow 800-foot-long **Flume Gorge** is reached from a modern visitor center via a picturesque 2-mile loop hike along wooden boardwalks and stairways. The park was long famous as the site of the **Old Man of the Mountain,** an iconic profile high on a granite cliff that crumbled unexpectedly in 2003. Overlooking Profile Lake, at the small Old Man of the Mountain Park, you can walk the short but pretty paved trail to view the mountain face through steel rods that seem literally to put the beloved visage back on the mountain. You can see related photographs and memorabilia in a small museum, and also visit the **New England Ski Museum** (which has a second location in North Conway) to learn how skiing was popularized as a sport in New England, through artifacts, clothing, and equipment, as well as Bode Miller's five Olympic medals. ✉ *260 Tramway Dr., Franconia* ☎ *603/823–8800* 🌐 *www.nhstateparks.org* 🎟 *Aerial Tramway $28, Echo Lake parking $4, Flume Gorge $18, museums free.*

The Frost Place

HISTORIC HOME | Robert Frost's year-round home from 1915 to 1920, this modest homestead on a peaceful unpaved road is surrounded by well-tended gardens and offers stunning mountain views. The place is imbued with the spirit of his work—two rooms contain memorabilia and signed editions of his books. Poetry readings are scheduled some summer evenings. Out back, you can follow short trails marked with lines from his poetry. The grounds are always open and beautiful for a stroll. ✉ *158 Ridge Rd., Franconia* ☎ *603/823–5510* 🌐 *www.frostplace.org* 🎟 *$5* 🕒 *Closed mid-Oct.–Apr.*

🍴 Restaurants

★ Polly's Pancake Parlor

$ | **AMERICAN** | **FAMILY** | In the Dexter family for generations, Polly's has been serving up pancakes and waffles (from its own original recipe, with several batter options available, including cornmeal and gingerbread) since the 1930s—the current space dates to 2015 but retains the original country charm. Try the smoked bacon and ham, eggs Benedict, sandwiches on homemade bread, delicious baked beans, and such tempting desserts as raspberry pie. **Known for:** gift shop with maple products; gingerbread pancakes with blueberries and walnuts; pretty hilltop setting. [$] *Average main: $14* ✉ *672 Rte. 117, Franconia* ☎ *603/823–5575* 🌐 *www.pollyspancakeparlor.com* 🕒 *Closed Wed. No dinner.*

🛏 Hotels

Franconia Inn

$ | **RESORT** | **FAMILY** | At this 107-acre family-friendly resort anchored by an affordable three-story inn with unfussy country furnishings, you can play tennis on four clay courts, soak in the outdoor heated pool or hot tub, hop on a mountain bike, or soar in a glider, and cross-country ski on 40 miles of groomed trails. **Pros:** tons of family-oriented activities; outdoor heated pool; peaceful setting with mountain views. **Cons:** a bit remote; historic hotel with some quirks; popularity with families can make it a little noisy. [$] *Rooms from: $135* ✉ *1172 Easton Rd., Franconia* ☎ *603/823–5542, 800/473–5299* 🌐 *www.franconiainn.com* 🕒 *Closed Apr.–mid-May* 🛏 *34 rooms* 🍽 *No Meals.*

Sunset Hill House

$$ | **HOTEL** | It's all about the view at this striking Victorian inn set high on a ridge in tiny Sugar Hill, its 70 acres holding lovely gardens, a seasonal outdoor pool, and a great little golf course. **Pros:** mesmerizing views; excellent 9-hole golf course; unusually good restaurant with outdoor dining. **Cons:** slightly remote setting; not a great option for kids; some bathrooms are shower-only. $ *Rooms from: $160* ⊠ *231 Sunset Hill Rd., Sugar Hill* ☎ *603/823–7244* ⊕ *www.thesunsethillhouse.com* ⇆ *28 rooms* ⦿ *Free Breakfast.*

★ Sugar Hill Inn

$$$ | B&B/INN | Although this upscale inn surrounded by neatly manicured gardens dates to 1789, it has a decidedly current vibe, from its sumptuous rooms with such modern perks as whirlpool tubs, gas fireplaces, and Bose sound systems, to the superb prix-fixe restaurant serving sublime contemporary American fare. **Pros:** many rooms have private decks; dining packages available; gorgeous countryside setting. **Cons:** somewhat remote; books up well ahead on weekends; not a good fit for kids. $ *Rooms from: $239* ⊠ *116 Sugar Hill Rd. (Rte. 117), Sugar Hill* ☎ *603/823–4100* ⊕ *www.sugarhillinn.com* ⇆ *15 rooms* ⦿ *Free Breakfast.*

🛍 Shopping

★ Harman's Cheese & Country Store

GENERAL STORE | It's worth a slight but pretty detour over the hill from Franconia to visit this rambling old village store and dairy that turns out legendarily rich, sharp aged cheddar, which is also available smoked and in port-and-cognac spreads. The venerable red-clapboard shop carries plenty of other foodie-pleasing products. ⊠ *1400 Rte. 117, Sugar Hill* ☎ *603/823–8000* ⊕ *www.harmanscheese.com.*

🤸 Activities

SKIING

Cannon Mountain

SKIING & SNOWBOARDING | FAMILY | Serviced by the first aerial tramway in North America, which was built in 1938, this classic New England ski resort inside Franconia Notch State Park offers terrain

that runs the gamut from steep pitches off the peak to gentle blue cruisers. Beginners may want to head over to the separate Tuckerbrook family area, which offers 13 trails and four lifts. Adventurous types will want to try out the Mittersill area, which has 86 acres of lift-accessed "side country" trails and glades where the snow is au naturel. **Facilities:** 97 trails; 285 acres; 2,180-foot vertical drop; 10 lifts. ⊠ *260 Tramway Dr., Franconia* ☎ *603/823–8800* ⊕ *www.cannonmt.com* 🎫 *Lift ticket: $99.*

Lincoln and North Woodstock

17 miles south of Franconia, 42 miles west of North Conway, 64 miles north of Concord.

These neighboring towns at the White Mountains' southwestern corner are the western gateway to the famed Kancamagus Highway. They form a lively resort base camp, especially for metro Boston families who get here via the easy two-hour drive straight up Interstate 93. Although the town itself isn't much of an attraction, myriad festivals and activities keep Lincoln swarming with visitors year-round.

Tiny North Woodstock maintains a more inviting village feel and is close to some easy, scenic, family-friendly hikes, such as Georgiana Falls and the slightly more ambitious Indian Head Trail.

GETTING HERE AND AROUND

Accessed from Interstate 93, Lincoln and North Woodstock are connected by Route 112—it's a short 1-mile drive between the two.

ESSENTIALS

VISITOR INFORMATION Western White Mountains Chamber of Commerce. ⊠ *North Woodstock* ☎ *603/745–6621* ⊕ *www.westernwhitemtns.com.*

TOURS
Pemi Valley Moose Tours
WILDLIFE-WATCHING | FAMILY | If you're eager to see a mighty moose, embark on a moose-watching bus tour into the northernmost White Mountains. The 3- to 3½-hour trips depart at 8:30 pm May to late September for the best wildlife-sighting opportunities. ⊠ *136 Main St., Lincoln* ☎ *603/745–2744* ⊕ *www.moosetoursnh. com* ⊠ *$45.*

Sights

Hobo Railroad
TRAIN/TRAIN STATION | FAMILY | Restored vintage train cars take you on 80-minute excursions along the scenic banks of the Pemigewassett River. A Santa Express runs late November–mid-December. ⊠ *64 Railroad St., Lincoln* ☎ *603/745–2135* ⊕ *www.hoborr.com* ⊠ *$20* ⊘ *Closed mid-Dec.–Apr.*

★ Kancamagus Highway
SCENIC DRIVE | FAMILY | In 1937, two old local roads were connected from Lincoln to Conway to create this remarkable 34.5-mile national designated scenic byway through a breathtaking swath of the White Mountains. This section of Route 112 known as the Kancamagus—often called simply "the Kanc"—contains no businesses or billboards and is punctuated by overlooks, picnic areas, and memorable hiking trailheads. These include **Lincoln Woods,** an easy 6-mile round-trip trek along a railroad bed that departs from the Lincoln Woods Visitor Center, crosses a dramatic suspension bridge over the Pemigewasset River, and ends at a swimming hole formed by dramatic Franconia Falls. There's also **Sabbaday Falls,** a short ½-mile stroll to a multilevel cascade that plunges through two potholes and a flume. For a slightly harder but less crowded trek, take the 3.5-mile **Boulder Loop Trail,** which rises precipitously some 1,000 feet from the banks of the Swift River to a granite-crowned summit with mountain

views. The road's highest point, at 2,855 feet, crosses the flank of Mt. Kancamagus, near Lincoln—a great place to view the fiery displays of foliage each autumn. On-site in lots and overlooks costs $5. ☎ *603/536–6100* ⊕ *www.fs.usda.gov/ whitemountain.*

★ Lost River Gorge & Boulder Caves
NATURE SIGHT | FAMILY | Parents can enjoy the looks of wonder on their kids' faces as they negotiate wooden boardwalks and stairs leading through a granite gorge formed by the roaring waters of the Lost River. One of the 10 caves they can explore is called the Lemon Squeezer (and it's a tight fit). Visitors can also pan for gems and search for fossils and walk through a fascinating giant man-made birdhouse, venture across a suspension bridge, and climb up into a big tree house. The park offers lantern tours on weekend evenings. ⊠ *1712 Lost River Rd., North Woodstock* ☎ *603/745–8720* ⊕ *www.lostrivergorge.com* ⊠ *$22* ⊘ *Closed mid-Oct.–Apr.*

Seven Birches Winery
WINERY | With a tasting room at Lincoln's RiverWalk resort and steps away in a bright and modern wine bar with a big patio, this respected winery offers its classic European-varietal dry wines and sweeter fruit wines by the glass or flight, along with a selection of snacks. ⊠ *22 S. Mountain Dr., Lincoln* ☎ *603/745–7550* ⊕ *www.sevenbirches.com.*

Whale's Tale Waterpark
WATER PARK | FAMILY | You can float on an inner tube along a gentle river, plunge down one of five waterslides, hang five on the Akua surf simulator, or bodysurf in the large wave pool at Whale's Tale. There's plenty here for toddlers and small children, too. ⊠ *481 Daniel Webster Hwy. (U.S. 3), Lincoln* ☎ *603/745–8810* ⊕ *www. whalestalewaterpark.net* ⊠ *From $44* ⊘ *Closed early Oct.–Apr.*

Continued on page 218

HIKING THE APPALACHIAN TRAIL

Tucked inside the nation's most densely populated corridor, a simple footpath in the wilderness stretches more than 2,200 miles, from Georgia to Maine. The Appalachian Trail passes through some of New England's most spectacular regions, and daytrippers can experience the area's beauty on a multitude of accessible, rewarding hikes.

Running along the spine of the Appalachian Mountains, the trail was fully blazed in 1937 and designed to connect anyone and everyone with nature. Within a day's drive of two-thirds of the U.S. population, it draws an estimated three million people every year. Through-hikers complete the whole trail in one daunting six-month season, but all ages and abilities can find renewal and perspective here in just a few hours. One-third of the AT passes through New England, and it's safe to say that the farther north you go, the harder the trail gets. New Hampshire and Maine challenge experienced hikers with windy, cold, and isolated peaks.

Top, hiking in New Hampshire's White Mountains. Above, autumn view of Profile Lake, Pemigewasset, NH.

ON THE TRAIL

New England's prime hiking season is in late summer and early fall, when the blaze of foliage viewed from a high peak is unparalleled. Popular trails see high crowds; if you seek solitude, try hiking at sunrise, a peaceful time that's good for wildlife viewing. You'll have to curb your enthusiasm in spring and early summer to avoid mud season in late April and black flies in May and June.

With the right gear, attitude, and preparation, winter can also offer fine opportunities for hiking, snowshoeing, and cross-country skiing.

FOLLOW THE TRAIL

Most hiking trails are marked with blazes, blocks of colored paint on a tree or rock. The AT, and only the AT, is marked by vertical, rectangular 2-by-6-inch white blazes. Two blazes mark route changes; turn in the direction of the top blaze. At higher elevations, you might also see cairns, small piles of rocks carefully placed by trail rangers to show the way when a blaze might be obscured by snow or fog.

Scenic U.S. 302—and the AT—pass through Crawford Notch, a spectacular valley in New Hampshire's White Mountains.

Hikers gather outside Lakes of the Clouds Hut, near the peak of Mount Washington.

TRIP TIPS

WHAT TO WEAR: For clothes, layer with a breathable fabric like polypropylene, starting with a shirt, a fleece, and a wind- or water-resistant shell. Bring gloves, a hat, and a change of socks.

WHAT TO BRING: Carry plenty of water and lightweight high-energy food. Don't forget sunscreen and insect repellent. Bring a map and compass. Just in case: a basic first-aid kit, a flashlight or headlamp, whistle, multi-tool, and matches.

PLAN AHEAD: In your car, leave a change of clothing, especially dry socks and shoes, as well as extra water and food.

PLAY IT SAFE: Tell someone your hiking plan and take a hiking partner. Carry a rescue card with emergency contact information and allergy details.

BE PREPARED: Plan your route and check the weather forecast in advance.

REMEMBER YOUR BEGINNINGS: Look back at the trail especially at the trailhead and at tricky junctions. If you've got a digital camera, photograph trail maps posted at the trailhead or natural landmarks to help you find your way.

WHERE TO STAY

Day hikers looking to extend the adventure can also make the experience as hard or as soft as they choose. Through-hikers combine camping with overnight stays in primitive shelters, mountain huts, comfortable lodges, and resorts just off the trail.

Rustic cabins and lean-tos provide basic shelter in Maine's Baxter State Park. In Maine and New Hampshire, the Appalachian Mountain Club runs four-season lodges as well as a network of mountain huts for backcountry hikers. A hiker code of camaraderie and conviviality prevails in these huts. Experience a night and you might just find yourself dreaming of a through-hike.

FOR MORE INFORMATION

Appalachian Trail Conservancy
(⊕ www.appalachiantrail.org)

Appalachian National Scenic Trail
(⊕ www.nps.gov/appa)

Appalachian Mountain Club
(⊕ www.outdoors.org)

ANIMALS ALONG THE TRAIL

❶ Black bear

Black bears are the most common—and smallest—bear in North America. Clever and adaptable, these adroit mammals will eat whatever they can (though they are primarily vegetarian, favoring berries, grasses, roots, blossoms, and nuts). Not naturally aggressive, black bears usually make themselves scarce when they hear hikers. The largest New England populations are in New Hampshire and Maine.

❷ Moose

Spotting a moose in the wild is unforgettable: their massive size and serene gaze are truly humbling. Treasure the moment, then slowly back away. At more than six feet tall, weighing 750 to 1,200 pounds, a moose is not to be trifled with, particularly during rutting and calving seasons (fall and spring, respectively). Dusk and dawn are the best times to spot the iconic animal; you're most likely to see one in Maine, especially in and around ponds.

⚠ Black flies

Especially fierce in May and June, these pesky flies can upset the tranquility of a hike in the woods as they swarm your face and bite your neck. To ward them off, cover any exposed skin and wear light colors. You'll get some relief on a mountain peak; cold weather and high winds also keep them at bay.

❸ Bald eagles

Countless bird species can be seen and heard along the AT, but what could be more exciting than to catch a glimpse of our national bird as it bounces back from near extinction? Now it's not uncommon to see the majestic bald eagle with its tremendous wing span, white head feathers, and curved yellow beak. The white head and tail distinguish the bald from the golden eagle, a bit less rare but just as thrilling to see. Most of New England's bald eagles are in Maine, but they are now present—albeit in small numbers—in all six states.

WILDFLOWERS ALONG THE TRAIL

❹ Mountain laurel

The clusters of pink and white blooms of the mountain laurel look like bursts of fireworks. Up close, each one has the delicate detail of a lady's parasol. Blooms vary in color, from pure white to darker pink, and have different amounts of red markings. Connecticut's state flower, mountain laurel flourishes in rocky woods, blooming in May and June. Look for the shrub in southern New England; it's rare along the Appalachian trail in Vermont and Maine.

❺ Mountain avens

A member of the rose family, these showy yellow flowers abound in New Hampshire's White Mountains. You can't miss the large buttercup-like blooms on long green stems when they are in bloom from June through August. So common here, yet extremely rare: the only other place in the whole world where you can find mountain avens is on an island off the coast of Nova Scotia.

❻ Painted trillium

You might smell a trillium before you see it; these flowers have an unpleasant odor that may attract the flies that pollinate it. To identify this impressive flower, look for sets of three: three large pointed blue-green leaves, three sepals (small leaves beneath the petals), and three white petals with a brilliant magenta center. It can take four or five years for a trillium to produce one flower, which blooms in May and June in wet woodlands.

❼ Pink lady slippers

These delicate orchids can grow from 6 to 15 inches high and favor specific wet wooded areas in dappled sunlight. The slender stalk rises from a pair of green leaves, then bends a graceful neck to suspend the paper-thin pale pink closed flower. The slow-growing plant needs help from fungus and bees to survive and can live to be 20 years old. New Hampshire's state wildflower, the pink lady slipper blooms in June throughout New England.

● = Somewhat Common ● = Rare

CHOOSE YOUR DAY HIKE

MAINE

GULF HAGAS, Greenville

Difficult, 8-plus miles round-trip, 6–7 hours

This National Natural Landmark in the North Maine Woods is a spectacular sight for the adventurous day hiker. It involves a long drive on logging roads east from Greenville (see Inland Maine section) to a remote spot and a slippery, sometimes treacherous 8-mile hike around the rim of what's been dubbed Maine's Grand Canyon. Swimming in one of the sparkling pools under a 30-foot-high waterfall and admiring the views of cliffs, cascades, gorges, and chasms in this slate canyon, otherwise unthinkable in New England, will take your breath away.

TABLE ROCK, Bethel

Medium, 2.7 miles round-trip, 2 hours

Maine's Mahoosuc Range is thought to be one of the most difficult stretches of the entire AT, but north of Bethel at Grafton Notch State Park, day hikes range from easy walks in to cascading waterfalls to strenuous climbs up Old Speck's craggy peak. The Table Rock trail offers interesting sights—great views of the notch from the immense slab of granite that gives this trail its name, as well as one of the state's largest system of slab caves—narrow with tall openings unlike underground caves.

NEW HAMPSHIRE

ZEALAND TRAIL, Bretton Woods

Easy, 5.6 miles round-trip, 3.5–4 hours

New Hampshire's Presidential range gets so much attention and traffic that sometimes the equally spectacular Pemigewasset Wilderness, just to its west, gets overlooked. Follow U.S. 302 to the trailhead on Zealand Rd. near Bretton Woods. For an easy day hike to one of the Appalachian Mountain Club's excellent overnight huts, take the mostly flat Zealand Trail over bridges and past a beaver swamp to Zealand Pond. The last tenth of a mile is a steep ascent to the mountain retreat, where you might spot an AT through-hiker taking a well-deserved rest. (Most north-bound through-hikers reach this section around July or August.) In winter, you can get here by a lovely cross-country ski trip.

TRAIL NAMES

For through-hikers, doing the AT can be a life-altering experience. One of the trail's most respected traditions is taking an alter ego: a trail name. Lightning Bolt: fast hiker. Pine Knot: tough as one. Bluebearee: because a bear got all her food on her very first night on the trail.

VERMONT

HARMON HILL, Bennington

Medium to difficult, 3.3 miles round-trip, 3–4 hours

This rugged hike in the Green Mountains goes south along the AT where it coincides with the Long Trail, Vermont's century-old "footpath in the wilderness." From the trailhead on Route 9 just east of Bennington, the first half mile or so is strenuous, with some rock and log staircases and hairpins. The payback is the sweeping view from the top; you'll see Mount Anthony, Bennington and its iconic war monument, and the rolling green hills of the Taconics to the west.

STRATTON MOUNTAIN, Stratton

Difficult, 6.6 miles round-trip, 5–6 hours

A steep and steady climb from the trailhead on Stratton Arlington Rd. (west of the village of Stratton) up the 3,936-foot-high Stratton Mountain follows the AT and Long Trail through mixed forests. It's said that this peak is where Benton MacKaye conceived of the idea for the Appalachian Trail in 1921. An observation tower at the summit gives you a great 360-degree view of the Green Mountains. From July to October, you can park at Stratton resort and ride the gondola up (or down) and follow the .75-mile Fire Tower Trail to the southern true peak.

MASSACHUSETTS

MOUNT GREYLOCK, North Adams

Easy to difficult, 2 miles round-trip, less than 1 hour

There are many ways to experience Massachusetts's highest peak. From North Adams, follow Route 2 to the Notch Rd. trailheads. For a warm-up, try the Rounds Rock trail (Easy, 0.7 mi) for some spectacular views. Or drive up the 8-mile-long summit road and hike down the Robinson's Point trail (Difficult, 0.8 miles) for the best view of the Hopper, a glacial cirque that's home to an old-growth red spruce forest. At the summit, the impressive **Bascom Lodge**, built in the 1930s by the Civilian Conservation Corps, provides delicious meals and overnight stays (⊕ www.bascomlodge.net).

CONNECTICUT

LION'S HEAD, Salisbury

Medium, 4.6 miles round-trip, 3.5–4 hours

The AT's 52 miles in Connecticut take hikers up some modest mountains, including Lion's Head in Salisbury. From the trailhead on Route 41, follow the white blazes of the AT for two easy miles, then take the blue-blazed Lion's Head Trail for a short, steep push over open ledges to the 1,738-foot summit with its commanding views of pastoral southern New England. Try this in summer when the mountain laurels—Connecticut's state flower—are in bloom.

EXPERIENCE MOUNT WASHINGTON

Looking at Mt. Washington from Mt. Bond in the Pemigewasset Wilderness Area, New Hampshire.

Mount Washington is the Northeast's peak of superlatives: worst weather in the world, highest spot in the northeast, windiest place on Earth. It snows in the summer, there are avalanches in winter, and it's foggy 60 percent of the time. Strong 35-mile-per-hour winds are the average, and extreme winds of 100 miles per hour with higher gusts blow year-round. Here, you can literally get blown away.

Explorers, scientists, artists, and botanists have been coming to the mountain for hundreds of years, drawn by its unique geologic features, unusual plants, and exceptional climate.

WHY SO WINDY? The 6,288-foot-high treeless peak is the highest point for miles around, so nothing dampens the force of the wind. Also, the sharp vertical rise causes wind to accelerate. Dramatic changes in air pressure also cause strong, high winds. Add to that the fact that three major storm tracks converge here, and you've got a mountain that has claimed more than 150 lives in the past 175 years.

GOING UP THE MOUNTAIN

An ascent up Mount Washington is for experienced hikers who are prepared for severe, unpredictable weather. Even in summer, cold, wet, foggy, windy conditions prevail. The most popular route to the top is on the eastern face up the Tuckerman Ravine Trail. But countless trails offer plenty of moderate day hikes, like the Alpine Garden Trail, as an alternative to a summit attempt. Start at the Pinkham Notch Visitor Center on Route 16 to review your options.

BACKPACKING ON THE MOUNTAIN

Lakes of the Clouds Hut perches 5,050 feet up the southern shoulder, providing bunkrooms and meals in summer; reservations are required. On the eastern face, the **Hermit Lake Shelter Area** has shelters and tent platforms; to camp here you'll need a first-come, first-served permit from the Visitors Center. Both are operated by the **AMC** (☎ 603/466-2727; ⊕ www.outdoors.org).

NON-HIKING ALTERNATIVES

In the summer, the **Auto Road** (☎ 603/466-3988 ⊕ *www.mt-washington.com*) and the **Cog Railway** (☎ 800/922-8825 ⊕ *www.thecog.com*) present alternate ways up the mountain; both give you a real sense of the mountain's grandeur. In winter, a **Snow-Coach** (☎ 603/466–3988 ⊕ *www.mt-washington.com*) hauls visitors 4.5 miles up the Auto Road with an option to cross-country ski, telemark, snowshoe, or ride the coach back down.

🍴 Restaurants

Woodstock Inn Brewery
$$ | AMERICAN | This big and festive brewpub inside a late-1800s train station is decorated with old maps, historic photographs, and other fun curiosities. The kitchen turns out reliably good pub fare—pizza, burgers, steaks, seafood—and filling breakfasts, and the brewery produces nearly 20 different varieties of exceptionally good beers. **Known for:** game room and kids' menu; brewery tours; inviting indoor and outdoor seating. [$] *Average main: $21* ✉ *135 Main St., North Woodstock* ☎ *603/745-3951* 🌐 *www.woodstockinnnh.com.*

☕ Coffee and Quick Bites

The Moon Bakery & Cafe
$ | CAFÉ | A must for delicious sustenance and potent lattes before hitting the slopes or hiking along the Kancamagus Highway, this homey café offers ample indoor seating in exposed-brick-wall nooks or outside on the sidewalk. Popular items include ham and cheddar sandwiches with maple mustard, avocado-egg breakfast sandwiches, and matcha green tea smoothies. **Known for:** fresh smoothies; hefty sandwiches on house-baked bread; trail mix cookies. [$] *Average main: $11* ✉ *28 S. Mountain Dr., Lincoln* ☎ *603/745-5013* 🌐 *www.facebook.com/themoonlincoln* 🕒 *Closed Tues. No dinner.*

🛏 Hotels

Indian Head Resort
$ | RESORT | FAMILY | This early-20th-century resort, identified by its 100-foot-tall observation tower and its lovely setting overlooking Shadow Lake, offers inexpensive and spacious rooms, making it a good choice for families on a budget. **Pros:** near kid-friendly attractions; fun, old-school personality; a free ski shuttle to Cannon or Loon Mountain. **Cons:** some rooms overlook parking lot; on busy road 5 miles north of Woodstock; shows wear in places. [$] *Rooms from: $139* ✉ *664 Daniel Webster Hwy. (U.S. 3)* ☎ *603/745-8000, 800/343-8000* 🌐 *www.indianheadresort.com* 🛏 *148 rooms* 🍽 *Free Breakfast.*

★ **Lumen Nature Retreat**
$ | RESORT | With easy access to the many recreational activities of Waterville and Woodstock, this 20-acre glamping hideaway offers downright plush accommodations in stylish safari tents and A-frame cabins, all with premium linens, cooking utensils, and battery chargers. **Pros:** units are well-stocked for cooking and campfires; all units have patios and smokeless firepits; spotless accommodations with plush bedding. **Cons:** no camp store or reception area; two-night minimum stay on weekends; some noise from Interstate 93. [$] *Rooms from: $109* ✉ *11 Sugar Plum La., North Woodstock* ☎ *603/764-7244* 🌐 *www.stayatlumen.com* 🕒 *Closed Nov.–Apr.* 🛏 *15 units.*

Mountain Club on Loon
$$ | RESORT | FAMILY | With a diverse range of accommodations, including large family suites, and many units with full kitchens, this functional if pretty standard condo-style lodge provides convenient ski-in, ski-out accommodations on Loon Mountain. **Pros:** within walking distance of the lifts; full-service spa; easy proximity to great hiking. **Cons:** very busy on winter weekends; decor is a bit perfunctory; not within walking distance of town. [$] *Rooms from: $171* ✉ *90 Loon Mountain Rd., Lincoln* ☎ *603/745-2244, 800/229-7829* 🌐 *www.mtnclub.com* 🛏 *235 rooms* 🍽 *No Meals.*

🛍 Shopping

Fadden's General Store
GENERAL STORE | The Fadden family, who have been making maple syrup for several generations, operates this inviting general store, sugarhouse, and maple

museum that dates to 1896. Come in to buy syrup, souvenirs, and gourmet treats, or for a self-guided tour of the operations. ⊠ *109 Main St., North Woodstock* ☎ *603/745–8371* ⊕ *www.nhmaplesyrup. com.*

Activities

HIKING
Mt. Moosilauke
HIKING & WALKING | One of the most rewarding, though heavily trafficked, summits in the White Mountains, 4,802-foot Mt. Moosilauke soars high to the west of the Pemigewasset Valley and can be approached via a few routes, including the Appalachian Trail and from Route 112 near Lost River Gorge. The most enjoyable trek is via the 7-mile South Peak Loop. It begins near Route 118 at the 1930s Moosilauke Ravine Lodge, which is operated by Dartmouth College and offers basic overnight accommodations. However you ascend to the treeless peak, you'll enjoy sweeping views of the Presidential Range, Lake Winnipesaukee, and even the Adirondacks. ⊠ *Ravine Rd., North Woodstock.*

SKIING
Loon Mountain
SKIING & SNOWBOARDING | **FAMILY** | Wide, straight, and consistent intermediate ski trails prevail at this modern resort on the Pemigewasset River. The most advanced runs are grouped on the North Peak, with beginner trails set apart. There's snow tubing on the lower slopes, and eight terrain parks suitable for all ability levels. A base lodge offers dining and lounges. You'll also find 13 miles of cross-country trails, an outdoor ice-skating rink, snowshoeing and snowshoeing tours. During the summer months, popular resort activities include disc golf, ziplining, mountain-biking, e-bikes, a rock-climbing wall, and exploring glacially carved caves. **Facilities:** 61 trails; 370 acres; 2,100-foot vertical drop; 11 lifts. ⊠ *90 Loon*

Mountain Rd., Lincoln ☎ *603/745–8111* ⊕ *www.loonmtn.com* ⛷ *Lift ticket: $116.*

Waterville Valley

25 miles southeast of North Lincoln.

Although visitors have been exploring this dramatic alpine landscape since 1835, and the first ski trails were installed on 3,997-foot Mt. Tecumseh in the 1930s, Watervalley Valley didn't become a major destination until a group of developers led by Olympic skier Tom Corcoran built a full-service ski area here in 1966. That led to a planned resort with several hotels and condominiums, a town square with shops and restaurants, a golf course, and other amenities. Today it's a terrific family-friendly winter-sports destination, but there's also plenty to do in warmer months, including great hiking and mountain-biking. Rates at the resort hotels come with passes that include cross-country ski and bike rentals, access to the well-equipped White Mountain Athletic Club, and other perks—it's a remarkable value.

GETTING HERE AND AROUND
You get here from Interstate 93 in Campton, via Route 49, which runs alongside the Mad River and dead-ends at the Town Square. Free shuttle buses whisk guests from hotels to the ski area. In summer, you can also get here by way of unpaved Tripoli Road, a bumpy but beautiful route through White Mountain National Forest that accesses some amazing campgrounds and hikes, such as Mt. Osceola and Mt. Tecumseh. It leads out to Interstate 93 in Woodstock.

Restaurants

Coyote Grill
$$ | **AMERICAN** | **FAMILY** | On the second floor of the White Mountain Athletic Club, Waterville Valley's best restaurant is a rambling space with big windows

offering up grand views of the White Mountains. The food is hearty and well-prepared, just what you need after a day of hiking or skiing. **Known for:** mountain views; lighter fare served downstairs by the pool; Oreo-crusted white-chocolate cheesecake. [$] *Average main: $22* ✉ *98 Valley Rd., Waterville Valley* ☎ *603/236–4919* 🌐 *www.wildcoyotegrill.com* 🕒 *Closed Mon. and Tues. No lunch.*

Hotels

Golden Eagle Lodge

$$ | **HOTEL** | **FAMILY** | Waterville Valley's premier condominium resort, its steep roof punctuated by dozens of gabled dormers, recalls the grand hotels of an earlier era. **Pros:** steps from Town Square; units all have kitchens and lots of elbow room; sweeping mountain views. **Cons:** decor is a little dated; no a/c in many units; lots of kids and families create a sometimes hectic pace. [$] *Rooms from: $179* ✉ *28 Packard's Rd., Waterville Valley* ☎ *603/236–4600* 🌐 *www.goldeneaglelodge.com* 🛏 *139 condos* 🍴 *No Meals.*

Valley Inn

$ | **HOTEL** | **FAMILY** | One of the region's better values, the Valley Inn offers few frills, but when you factor in the free activities pass and the quiet but convenient location, it's an excellent option. **Pros:** very reasonable rates; largest units have kitchens and can sleep six; peaceful setting. **Cons:** a few minutes' walk to Town Square; cookie-cutter decor; very basic breakfast. [$] *Rooms from: $119* ✉ *17 Tecumseh Rd., Waterville Valley* ☎ *603/236–8425, 800/343–0969* 🌐 *www.valleyinn.com* 🛏 *48 rooms* 🍴 *Free Breakfast.*

Activities

HIKING

★ Welch-Dickey Trail

HIKING & WALKING | This at times steep but gorgeous 4½-mile loop hike ascends a wooded hillside before climbing above the sheer granite faces of 2,605-foot Welch and 2,734-foot Dickey mountains. There are higher climbs in the White Mountains, but this trail offers incredible views in every direction. Parking costs $5. ✉ *Orris Rd., Waterville Valley.*

SKIING

Waterville Valley Resort

SKIING & SNOWBOARDING | **FAMILY** | This family-friendly ski area has hosted many World Cup races, so advanced skiers can look forward to a challenge. About two-thirds of the 50 trails are intermediate: straight down the fall line, wide, and agreeably long. About 20 acres of tree-skiing and six terrain parks add heart-pounding stimulus, and full snowmaking coverage ensures good skiing even when nature doesn't cooperate. The resort also offers 46 miles of groomed cross-country trails. **Facilities:** 50 trails; 220 acres; 2,020-foot vertical drop; 11 lifts. ✉ *1 Ski Area Rd., Waterville Valley* ☎ *603/236–8311, 800/468–2553* 🌐 *www.waterville.com* 🎟 *Lift ticket: $112.*

New London

60 miles southwest of Waterville Valley, 33 miles west of Laconia, 40 miles northwest of Concord.

The progressive and quaint town of New London is anchored by the campus of Colby-Sawyer College (1837) and makes a good base for exploring Lake Sunapee. You'll find an engaging array of eateries and boutiques in town.

GETTING HERE AND AROUND

New London is just off Interstate 89.

Sights

★ Mt. Kearsarge

MOUNTAIN | There are two main ways to access this dramatic 2,937-foot granite peak east of Lake Sunapee. Approach it through **Winslow State Park,** which is closer to New London, by driving to the picnic area and hiking a 1.8-mile loop

Lake Sunapee

trail to the top. Or, more popularly, drive the 3½-mile scenic auto route through **Rollins State Park,** which snakes up the mountain's southern slope and leads to a ½-mile summit trail. However you get there, the views from the top are astounding. The park road at Rollins State Park closes at 5 pm nightly and from mid-November to late May, but from Winslow State Park you can hike Mt. Kearsarge any time of day or night, year-round. Rollins State Park is accessed from the cute Colonial village of Warner, which is worth a quick stroll. ⊠ *Rollins State Park, 1066 Kearsarge Mountain Rd., Warner* ✛ *20.3 miles south of New London via I-89* ☎ *603/456–3808* ⊕ *www. nhstateparks.org* ⊠ *$4.*

Mt. Kearsarge Indian Museum
INDIGENOUS SIGHT | Learn about not only the Native tribes of New England but also indigenous culture throughout the rest of the United States at this terrific museum set on a 12½-acre tract of meadows and forest on the road to Rollins State Park and Mt. Kearsarge. Exhibits are organized by region and feature ancient dugout birch canoes, headdresses and jewelry, basketry, textiles, pottery, musical instruments, and wood carvings, and docents are happy to provide free guided tours. Outside, you can stroll through Medicine Woods to discover the many kinds of plants used by Native communities for food, healing, and tools, and around a small arboretum with local flora. ⊠ *18 Highlawn Rd., Warner* ✛ *16.4 miles south of New London via I-89 South* ☎ *603/456–2600* ⊕ *www.indianmuseum.org* ⊠ *$11* ⊘ *Closed Dec.–Apr. and weekdays in Nov.*

Restaurants

★ Oak & Grain

$$$$ | **MODERN AMERICAN** | The refined yet relaxed restaurant in the historic Inn at Pleasant Lake makes a splendid destination for a special occasion dinner, or simply to savor a delicious brunch in the window-lined dining room or out on the patio—both areas have views of the lake in the near distance. The kitchen here turns out artfully plated contemporary fare, such as grilled octopus with Spanish chorizo and a smoked-paprika vinaigrette, and sea scallops with a ginger-citrus chimichurri. **Known for:** pretty lake views; knowledgeable, friendly service; locally sourced meats and seafood. [$] *Average main: $37* ✉ *Inn at Pleasant Lake., 853 Pleasant St., New London* ☎ *603/873–4833* 🌐 *innatpleasantlake.com* ⏲ *Closed Mon. and Tues. No lunch.*

Peter Christian's Tavern

$$ | **MODERN AMERICAN** | Exposed beams, wooden tables, a smattering of antiques, and half shutters on the windows make the amiable Peter Christian's a cool summer oasis and a warm winter haven. From shepherd's pie to seafood and grits with lobster butter, the flavorful comfort fare relies heavily on seasonal ingredients. **Known for:** outstanding seafood chowder; well-curated craft-beer and wine selection; dog-friendly patio. [$] *Average main: $22* ✉ *195 N. Main St., New London* ☎ *603/526–2964* 🌐 *www.peterchristiansnh.com.*

Coffee and Quick Bites

Blue Loon Bakery

$ | **BAKERY** | Have a seat in this cheerful bakery's sunny seating nooks or out on the back patio, while you savor an egg-cheddar croissant, house-made granola, a Brie-fig-apple baguette, or one of the delectable pastries or cakes. Favorite treats include maple-pumpkin pie, seasonal fruit tarts, raspberry scones, and praline sticky buns. **Known for:** savory artisan breads; fresh-baked pies; picnic supplies for nearby hiking and beach adventures. [$] *Average main: $9* ✉ *12 Lovering La., New London* ☎ *603/526–2892* 🌐 *www.blueloonbakery.com* ⏲ *Closed Mon. and Tues. No dinner.*

Hotels

★ Follansbee Inn

$$ | **B&B/INN** | **FAMILY** | Built in 1840, this rambling country inn on the shore of Kezar Lake is the kind of place that almost instantly turns strangers into fast friends. **Pros:** relaxed lakefront setting with 3-mile walking trail; free use of canoes, kayaks, sailboats, rowboats, and bicycles; excellent breakfast. **Cons:** not all rooms have lake views; Wi-Fi can be spotty in places; no restaurants within walking distance. [$] *Rooms from: $165* ✉ *2 Keyser St., North Sutton* ✥ *5½ miles south of New London via Rte. 114 South* ☎ *603/927–4221* 🌐 *www.follansbeeinn.com* 🛏 *17 rooms* 🍴 *Free Breakfast.*

★ Inn at Pleasant Lake

$$$ | **B&B/INN** | Overlooking the shore of Pleasant Lake, and offering views of majestic Mt. Kearsarge in the distance, and just a short drive from downtown New London, this beautifully appointed 1790s inn has spacious, bright rooms filled with fine country antiques and high-end bedding. **Pros:** adjacent to lakefront and a small beach; tennis courts; rates includes an outstanding full breakfast and afternoon tea. **Cons:** not within walking distance of town; not a good fit for kids; minimum stay at busy times. [$] *Rooms from: $229* ✉ *853 Pleasant St., New London* ☎ *603/526–6271, 800/626–4907* 🌐 *innatpleasantlake.com* 🛏 *10 rooms* 🍴 *Free Breakfast.*

Nightlife

Flying Goose Brew Pub

BREWPUBS | Offering a regular menu of about a dozen handcrafted beers, including a much lauded black IPA and a heady barley wine as well as a few seasonal varieties—made with hops grown on-site—this pub, and solar-powered brewery is a hit with beer connoisseurs. The kitchen serves juicy ribs, paper-thin onion rings, excellent burgers, and other tasty victuals. ⊠ *40 Andover Rd., New London* ☎ *603/526–6899* ⊕ *www.flying-goose.com.*

🎭 Performing Arts

New London Barn Playhouse
THEATER | FAMILY | Broadway-style musicals and children's plays are presented here every summer in New Hampshire's oldest continuously operating theater. ⊠ *84 Main St., New London* ☎ *603/526–6710* ⊕ *www.nlbarn.org.*

Newbury and Lake Sunapee

8 miles southwest of New London.

In the west-central part of the state, the towns around prestigious Dartmouth College and rippling Lake Sunapee vary from sleepy, old-fashioned outposts that haven't changed much in decades to bustling, sophisticated towns filled with cafés, art galleries, and boutiques. Newbury lies at the southern edge of 6-square-mile Lake Sunapee, one of the highest—and cleanest—lakes in the state, and a wonderful destination for boating, swimming, and fishing. Mt. Sunapee State Park has a picturesque beach on the lake as well as a mountain section that rises to an elevation of nearly 3,000 feet and offers some of the best skiing in southern New Hampshire. The popular League of New Hampshire Craftsmen's Fair, the oldest crafts fair in the nation, is held here in early August.

GETTING HERE AND AROUND
From Interstate 89, Route 103A leads here via the eastern shore of Lake Sunapee.

For a great drive, follow the Lake Sunapee Scenic and Cultural Byway, which runs about 25 miles from Georges Mills (a bit west of New London) down into Warner, tracing much of the Lake Sunapee shoreline.

👁 Sights

★ John Hay Estate at the Fells
GARDEN | The former home of the statesman who served as private secretary to Abraham Lincoln and U.S. Secretary of State to Presidents William McKinley and Theodore Roosevelt, built the 22-room Fells on Lake Sunapee as a summer home in 1890. House tours offer a glimpse of late Victorian life on a New Hampshire estate. The grounds, a gardener's delight, include a 100-foot-long perennial garden and a rock garden with a brook flowing through it. Miles of hiking trails can also be accessed from its 83½ acres. ⊠ *456 Rte. 103A, Newbury* ☎ *603/763–4789* ⊕ *www.thefells. org* 🎫 *$10 when house open, $8 when house closed* 🕙 *House closed Mon. and Tues. and mid-Oct.–late May.*

★ Sunapee Harbor
TOWN | On the west side of Lake Sunapee, this old-fashioned summer resort community has a large marina, a few restaurants and shops on the water, a tidy village green with a gazebo, and a small museum. ⊠ *Main St. at Lake Ave., Sunapee.*

🏖 Beaches

Mt. Sunapee State Park Beach
BEACH | FAMILY | A great family spot, this beach adjoining a 4,085-acre mountain park has picnic areas, fishing, and a bathhouse, plus access to great hiking trails. You can also rent canoes and kayaks, and there's a campground. **Amenities:**

lifeguards; parking (fee); showers; toilets. **Best for:** swimming; walking. ✉ *86 Beach Access Rd., Sunapee* ☎ *603/763–5561* 🌐 *www.nhstateparks.org* 🎫 *$5 mid-May–mid-Oct.*

🍴 Restaurants

Suna

$$ | **MODERN AMERICAN** | On a wooded country road just up the hill from Lake Sunapee, this lively little bar and bistro is great for a romantic meal or a relaxed bite after a day on the water or the mountain. The eclectic menu features a mix of classic American and Continental dishes with creative touches. **Known for:** excellent craft cocktails; lively après-ski scene; sublime desserts. [$] *Average main: $22* ✉ *6 Brook Rd., Sunapee* ☎ *603/843–8998* 🌐 *www.sunarestaurant-nh.com* 🕒 *Closed Mon. No lunch.*

Wildwood Smokehouse

$$ | **BARBECUE** | The hulking metal smoker outside this Old West–inspired tavern with high pressed-tin ceilings, chandeliers, and red Victorian wallpaper hints at the delicious barbecue served inside. Plates heaped with ribs, beef brisket, pulled chicken, and smoked bratwurst reveal the considerable skill of Wildwood's pit master, and plenty of tasty sides are offered, too, from mac and cheese to dirty rice. **Known for:** pecan pie; "hog wings" (pork shanks in barbecue sauce); popular early evening happy hour. [$] *Average main: $19* ✉ *45 Main St., Sunapee* ☎ *603/763–1178* 🌐 *www.wildwoodsmokehousesunapee.com* 🕒 *Closed Sun. and Mon. No lunch.*

☕ Coffee and Quick Bites

Sanctuary Dairy Farm Ice Cream

$ | **ICE CREAM** | **FAMILY** | Enjoy a scoop or two of rich homemade ice cream at this 10th-generation dairy farm a couple of miles from Lake Sunapee. Interesting flavors like hazelnut, lemon cookie, and maple pecan keep regulars coming back for more, but the barnyard with adorable goats, bunnies, and other critters is almost as big a draw. **Known for:** unusual ice-cream flavors; seating in picturesque pasture; cute barnyard animals to feed. [$] *Average main: $5* ✉ *209 Rte. 103, Sunapee* ☎ *603/863–8940* 🌐 *www.icecreamkidbeck.com* 🕒 *shop closed mid-Oct.–late May.*

🛏 Hotels

Sunapee Harbor Cottages

$$$ | **HOTEL** | **FAMILY** | This cozy compound of six charming, eco-friendly cottages—each sleeping five–eight people and with small but well-equipped kitchens—is a stone's throw from Sunapee Harbor and an easy drive from winter skiing at nearby Mt. Sunapee. **Pros:** ideal for families or friends traveling together; free beach passes; pet-friendly. **Cons:** no maid service; limited clothes storage; cottage porches overlook one another. [$] *Rooms from: $265* ✉ *4 Lake Ave., Sunapee Harbor* ☎ *603/763–5052* 🌐 *www.sunapeeharborcottages.com* 🔑 *6 cottages* 🍽 *No Meals.*

🛍 Shopping

Wild Goose Country Store

SOUVENIRS | On the harbor in Sunapee, this old-fashioned general store carries teddy bears, penny candy, pottery, and other engaging odds and ends. ✉ *77 Main St., Sunapee* ☎ *603/763–5516.*

🏃 Activities

BOAT TOURS

Sunapee Cruises

ENTERTAINMENT CRUISE | This company operates narrated afternoon and dinner cruises of Lake Sunapee from June to mid-October. Ninety-minute afternoon cruises on the *M/V Mt. Sunapee* focus on Lake Sunapee's history and the mountain scenery. A buffet dinner is included on the two-hour sunset cruises aboard the *M/V Kearsarge*, a vintage-style steamship.

✉ *Town Dock, 81 Main St., Sunapee Harbor* ☎ *603/938–6465* ⊕ *www.sunapee-cruises.com* ⊠ *From $24.*

HIKING
Monadnock-Sunapee Greenway Trail
HIKING & WALKING | This 50-mile trail starts in Newbury at Mt. Sunapee and snakes through verdant forests and the handsome village greens of Washington and Nelson and over jagged granite peaks south to Mt. Monadnock. One of the most enjoyable ways to access this trail is to hike the 2.3-mile (one-way) Andrew Brook Trail up to the granite ledges above Lake Solitude, where you'll cross with it. ✉ *Andrew Brook Trailhead, Mountain Rd., Newbury* ⊕ *www.msgtc.org.*

SKIING
Mt. Sunapee
SKIING & SNOWBOARDING | **FAMILY** | This family-friendly resort is one of New England's best-kept secrets. The owners have spent millions upgrading their snow machines and grooming equipment and turning this into a four-season resort. Mt. Sunapee offers 67 trails and slopes for all abilities. There are four terrain parks and nine glade trails. In summer, the adventure park features a canopy zipline tour, an aerial challenge course, an 18-hole disc-golf course, miniature golf, and numerous hiking trails. **Facilities:** 67 trails; 233 acres; 1,510-foot vertical drop; 9 lifts. ✉ *1398 Rte. 103, Newbury* ☎ *603/763–3500* ⊕ *www.mountsunapee.com* ⊠ *Lift ticket: $114.*

Hanover

30 miles northwest of New London, 60 miles southwest of Littleton, 20 miles east of Woodstock, Vermont.

Eleazar Wheelock founded Hanover's Dartmouth College in 1769 to educate the Abenaki "and other youth." When he arrived, the town consisted of about 20 families. Over time the college and the town grew symbiotically, with Dartmouth eventually becoming the northernmost Ivy League school. Hanover is still synonymous with Dartmouth, but it's also a respected medical and cultural center. Mostly independent shops fill the town's commercial district, which blends almost imperceptibly with Dartmouth's campus. Hanover and West Lebanon, with Woodstock, Quechee, Norwich, and White River Junction across the Connecticut River in Vermont, form an appealing two-state vacation destination.

GETTING HERE AND AROUND
Lebanon Municipal Airport is served by Cape Air from Boston and White Plains, New York. By car, there's easy access from Interstates 91 and 89.

ESSENTIALS
AIRPORT Lebanon Municipal Airport. ✉ *5 Airpark Rd., West Lebanon* ☎ *603/298–8878* ⊕ *www.flyleb.com.*

VISITOR INFORMATION Upper Valley Business Alliance. ✉ *Lebanon* ☎ *603/448–1203* ⊕ *www.uppervalleybusinessalliance.com.*

◉ Sights

Dartmouth College
COLLEGE | The poet Robert Frost spent part of a brooding freshman semester at this Ivy League school before giving up college altogether, but the school counts politician Nelson Rockefeller, actor Mindy Kaling, TV producer Shonda Rhimes, and author Theodor ("Dr.") Seuss Geisel among its many illustrious grads. The buildings clustered around the picturesque green, which is lovely for strolling, include the **Baker Memorial Library,** which houses such literary treasures as 17th-century editions of William Shakespeare's works. The library is also well-known for Mexican artist José Clemente Orozco's 3,000-square-foot murals that depict the story of civilization in the Americas. Free campus tours are available. ✉ *N. Main and Wentworth Sts., Hanover* ☎ *603/646–1110* ⊕ *www.dartmouth.edu.*

Enfield Shaker Museum

MUSEUM VILLAGE | In 1782, two Shaker brothers from Mt. Lebanon, New York, arrived on the still-beautiful shores of Lake Mascoma. Eventually, they formed Enfield, the ninth of 18 Shaker communities in the United States, and relocated to the lake's southern shore, where they erected more than 200 buildings. The Enfield Shaker Museum preserves the legacy of these Shakers, who numbered 330 members at the village's peak. By 1923, interest in the society had waned, and the last 10 members joined the Canterbury community, south of Laconia. A self-guided walking tour takes you through 13 of the remaining buildings, among them an 1849 stone mill. Demonstrations of Shaker crafts techniques also take place, and overnight accommodations are available in the community's stately six-story Great Stone Dwelling. ✉ *447 Rte. 4A, Enfield* ✢ *12 miles southeast of Hanover* ☎ *603/632–4346* 🌐 *www.shakermuseum.org* 🎟 *$14* 🕒 *Closed Mon.–Wed., Nov.–mid-May, and weekdays mid-May–June.*

★ **Hood Museum of Art**

ART MUSEUM | Dartmouth's excellent art museum owns Picasso's *Guitar on a Table,* silver by Paul Revere, a set of Assyrian reliefs from the 9th century BC, along with other noteworthy examples of African, Peruvian, Oceanic, Asian, European, and American art. The range of contemporary works—including pieces by John Sloan, William Glackens, Mark Rothko, Fernand Léger, and Joan Miró—is particularly notable. Rivaling the collection is the museum's architecture: a series of austere, copper-roof, redbrick buildings arranged around a courtyard. The museum galleries received an ambitious renovation and expansion in 2019 that added five new galleries and a striking new entrance designed by the husband-and-wife architectural team of Tod Williams and Billie Tsien (known for the Barnes Foundation in Philadelphia and New York's downtown Whitney Museum). ✉ *Wheelock St., Hanover* ☎ *603/646–2808* 🌐 *hoodmuseum.dartmouth.edu* 🕒 *Closed Sun.–Tues.*

Hopkins Center for the Arts

ARTS CENTER | If the towering arcade at the entrance to the center appears familiar, it's probably because it resembles the project that architect Wallace K. Harrison completed just after designing it: New York City's Metropolitan Opera House at Lincoln Center. The complex includes a 900-seat theater for concerts and film screenings, a 480-seat theater for plays, and a black-box theater for new plays. This is the home of the Dartmouth Symphony Orchestra and several other performance groups. ✉ *2 E. Wheelock St., Hanover* ☎ *603/646–2422* 🌐 *hop.dartmouth.edu.*

🍴 Restaurants

★ **Ariana's**

$$$ | **MODERN AMERICAN** | With its stone fireplace, cathedral ceiling, and rustic-elegant barnlike interior, this inviting restaurant in the venerable Lyme Inn turns out farm-fresh modern American fare with international influences. Try the blackened scallops with an orange-chili-butter sauce or sliced-duck salad with shaved fennel and a ginger dressing, before moving on to herb-crusted swordfish with a saffron-sherry butter sauce. **Known for:** five-course prix-fixe chef dinners; a well-curated wine list; peaceful setting in a historic hamlet. [$] *Average main: $29* ✉ *1 Market St., Lyme* ✢ *10.8 miles north of Hanover via Rte. 10* ☎ *603/353-4405* 🌐 *www.arianasrestaurant.com* 🕒 *Closed Sun.–Tues.*

Base Camp

$$ | **NEPALESE** | This inviting restaurant in the lower level of a downtown retail-dining complex serves authentic, prepared-to-order Nepalese cuisine. Start with an order of momos (steamed dumplings) bursting with buffalo, paneer-and-spinach, wild boar, or several other

A Lovely Drive Through the Upper Valley ⊙

From Hanover, make the beautiful 60-mile drive up Route 10 to Littleton for a stunningly scenic tour of the upper Connecticut River and lower Ammonoosuc river valleys. You'll have views of Vermont's Green Mountains from many points. The road passes through groves of evergreens, over leafy ridges, and through delightful hamlets abundant with fine Georgian- and Federal-style mansions. Grab gourmet picnic provisions at the historic general stores in Lyme or Bath, view several covered bridges on nearby side roads, and, stop by pastoral family farms, like Hatchland Farm's Dairy Delites, for ice cream and Collins Farm for its corn maze. There are numerous spots for a picnic, including little-visited Bedell Bridge State Park in Haverhill, which overlooks the Connecticut River.

fillings, and then try one of the easily shared *tarkari* (tomato-based) curries or chilies, offered with an extensive variety of meats and vegetables, from goat and duck to sweet potato and mushroom. **Known for:** everything can be prepared from mild to very spicy; plenty of meatless options; helpful, friendly staff. $ *Average main: $22* ⊠ *3 Lebanon St., Hanover* ☎ *603/643–2007* ⊕ *www. basecampcafenh.com.*

Latham House Tavern

$$ | AMERICAN | This convivial, easygoing gastropub in historic Lyme's rambling Dowd's Country Inn—which also has pleasant guest accommodations—features an impressive list of New England craft beers as well as an enticing selection of reasonably priced comfort fare. Favorites include the half-pound house burger topped with bacon and a beer–smoked gouda fondue, and the confit-pork poutine with a chipotle-cider barbecue sauce. **Known for:** elevated pub fare; interesting list of beers on tap; warmly lighted dining room with beam ceiling. $ *Average main: $20* ⊠ *9 Main St., Lyme* ✛ *10.7 miles north of Hanover via Rte. 10* ☎ *603/795–9995* ⊕ *www. lathamhousetavern.com* ⊙ *Closed Tues.*

Murphy's On the Green

$$ | AMERICAN | Students, visiting alums, and locals regularly descend on this wildly popular pub, which has walls lined with shelves of old books. The varied menu features burgers and salads as well as meat loaf, lobster mac and cheese, and vegetarian dishes like crispy-tofu pad Thai and house-smoked tofu street tacos. **Known for:** sourcing ingredients from local farms; good people-watching; extensive beer list. $ *Average main: $20* ⊠ *5 Main St., Hanover* ☎ *603/643–7777* ⊕ *www. murphysonthegreen.com* ⊙ *No lunch Mon.–Wed.*

☕ Coffee and Quick Bites

Lou's Restaurant

$ | AMERICAN | FAMILY | A Hanover tradition since 1947, this diner-cum-café-cum-bakery serves possibly the best breakfast in the valley, with favorites that include blueberry-cranberry buttermilk pancakes, and corned beef brisket hash with free-range poached eggs. Or just grab a seat at the old-fashioned soda fountain for a juicy burger and an ice-cream sundae. **Known for:** colorful mix of locals and Dartmouth folks; fresh-baked pastries and brownies; breakfast served all day. $ *Average main: $15* ⊠ *30 S. Main St.,*

The Cornish–Windsor Bridge is the second-longest covered bridge in the United States.

Hanover ☎ *603/643–3321* 🌐 *www.lousrestaurant.com* 🕓 *No dinner.*

Hotels

Hanover Inn

$$$ | **HOTEL** | A sprawling Georgian-style brick structure rising six white-trimmed stories above the gracious Dartmouth Green contains this chichi boutique hotel and is also home to the acclaimed farm-to-table restaurant, Pine. **Pros:** overlooks campus green in center of town; excellent restaurant and bar; well-equipped fitness center. **Cons:** in a busy area; pricey during busy times; books up way in advance many weekends. [$] *Rooms from: $265* ✉ *2 E. Wheelock St., Hanover* ☎ *603/643–4300* 🌐 *www.hanoverinn.com* 🛏 *108 rooms* 🍴 *No Meals.*

★ **Lyme Inn**

$$$ | **B&B/INN** | With an enchanted setting on the elliptical village common in Colonial Lyme, this four-story inn that began life as a stagecoach stop in the early 1800s offers an elegant, tranquil respite from the crowds of Hanover and offers meals in an esteemed restaurant. **Pros:** quiet setting; rates include a tasty but light breakfast; good base for exploring Hanover as well as Norwich and Woodstock, Vermont. **Cons:** can book up well in advance at busy times; a 15-minute drive to Hanover; minimum-night stays during some periods. [$] *Rooms from: $239* ✉ *1 Market St., Lyme* ✣ *10.8 miles north of Hanover via Rte. 10* ☎ *603/795-4824* 🌐 *www.thelymeinn.com* 🛏 *14 rooms* 🍴 *Free Breakfast.*

Six South St Hotel

$$$ | **HOTEL** | With its bold black and red color scheme and angular light fixtures and furnishings, this redbrick boutique hotel just off Hanover's bustling Main Street is a perfect roost for visiting Dartmouth and its museums. **Pros:** hip contemporary design; great little bistro and bar; downtown location steps from campus. **Cons:** expensive parking; breakfast buffet costs extra; busy in-town setting. [$] *Rooms from: $239* ✉ *6 South*

St., Hanover ☎ *603/643–0600* 🌐 *www.sixsouth.com* 🛏 *63 rooms* 🍴 *No Meals.*

Activities

Ledyard Canoe Club

BOATING | On the banks of the Connecticut River, this outfitter rents canoes, kayaks, and standup paddleboards by the hour, as well as rustic cabins. ✉ *9 Boathouse Rd., Hanover* ☎ *603/643–6709* 🌐 *www.ledyardcanoeclub.org.*

Cornish

22 miles south of Hanover.

Today Cornish is best known for its covered bridges and for having been the home of the late reclusive author J. D. Salinger, but at the turn of the 20th century the village was acclaimed as the home of the country's then-most-popular novelist, Winston Churchill (no relation to the British prime minister). His novel *Richard Carvel* sold more than a million copies. Churchill was such a celebrity that he hosted President Theodore Roosevelt in 1902. At that time Cornish was an artistic enclave: painter Maxfield Parrish lived and worked here, and sculptor Augustus Saint-Gaudens set up his studio here, where he created the heroic bronzes for which he is known.

GETTING HERE AND AROUND

About 5 miles west of town off Route 12A, the Cornish–Windsor Bridge crosses the Connecticut River, leading to Interstate 91 in Vermont.

Sights

Cornish-Windsor Bridge

BRIDGE | This 460-foot bridge, 1½ miles south of the Saint-Gaudens National Historic Site, connects New Hampshire to Vermont across the Connecticut River. Erected in 1866, it is the longest covered wooden bridge in the United States. The notice on the bridge reads, "Walk your horses or pay two dollar fine." ✉ *Bridge St., Cornish.*

★ **Saint-Gaudens National Historic Site**

HISTORIC HOME | On a bluff in rural Cornish with views of Vermont's stately Mt. Ascutney, this pastoral property celebrates the life and artistry of Augustus Saint-Gaudens, a leading 19th-century sculptor with renowned works on Boston Common, Manhattan's Central Park, and Chicago's Lincoln Park. In summer you can tour his house (with original furnishings), studio, and galleries, and year-round it's a pleasure to explore the 150 gorgeous acres of lawns, gardens, and woodlands dotted with casts of his works and laced with 2½ miles of hiking trails. Concerts are held Sunday from late June through August. ✉ *139 Saint-Gaudens Rd., Cornish* ☎ *603/675–2175* 🌐 *www.nps.gov/saga* 🎟 *$10* 🕒 *Buildings closed Nov.–late May.*

Hotels

Common Man Inn

$ | **HOTEL** | New Hampshire's distinctive Common Man hotel and restaurant group runs this quirky boutique hotel fashioned out of a striking 19th-century redbrick mill on downtown Claremont's Sugar River; the on-site restaurant serves hearty pub fare and has great water views. **Pros:** distinctive, historic architecture; deck and hot tub overlooking river; good location for exploring both sides of Connecticut River. **Cons:** 12 miles from Cornish; in a quiet town with few attractions; not many good dining options in area. [$] *Rooms from: $129* ✉ *21 Water St., Claremont* ☎ *603/542–6171* 🌐 *www.thecmaninnclaremont.com* 🛏 *30 rooms* 🍴 *Free Breakfast.*

Walpole

33 miles south of Cornish.

Walpole possesses one of the state's prettiest town greens. Bordered by Elm and Washington streets, it's surrounded by homes dating to the 1790s, when the townsfolk constructed a canal around the Great Falls of the Connecticut River, bringing commerce and wealth to the area. This upscale little town now has 4,000 inhabitants. Walpole is also home to Florentine Films, documentarian Ken Burns's production company.

■ TIP→ Charlestown, which boasts one of the state's largest historic districts, with about 60 homes—all handsome examples of Federal, Greek Revival, and Gothic Revival architecture (and 10 built before 1800), is just down the road from Walpole.

GETTING HERE AND AROUND

Walpole is a short jaunt up Route 12 from Keene, and is just across the Connecticut River from Bellows Falls, Vermont.

👁 Sights

Fort at No. 4

MILITARY SIGHT | FAMILY | In 1747, this timber fort overlooking the Connecticut River, 15 miles north of Walpole, served as an outpost on the periphery of Colonial civilization. That year fewer than 50 militiamen at the fort withstood an attack by 400 French soldiers, ensuring that northern New England remained under British rule. Today, costumed interpreters at this living-history museum cook dinner over an open hearth and demonstrate weaving, gardening, and candle making. The museum also holds reenactments of militia musters and the battles of the French and Indian War. ✉ *267 Springfield Rd. (Rte. 11), Charlestown* ✥ *13.3 miles north of Walpole via Hwy 12* ☎ *603/826–5700* 🌐 *www.fortat4.org* 🎟 *$10* 🕒 *Closed Mon. and Tues. and Nov.–Apr.*

🍴 Restaurants

★ Hungry Diner

$ | MODERN AMERICAN | FAMILY | A departure from the old-school greasy-spoon diners that proliferate in New England, this contemporary space with a white-tile and light-wood interior and a big, inviting outdoor seating area serves delicious, eclectic comfort fare that relies heavily on seasonal, local ingredients, including pasture-raised meats. Think Korean barbecue tacos with house-made kimchi and pickled carrots, or the buttermilk-fried chicken sandwich with a tangy secret sauce and dill pickles. **Known for:** superb craft beer, wine, and cocktail program; mac and cheese with bacon; milk shakes and soft-serve ice cream. [$] *Average main: $17* ✉ *9 Edwards La., Walpole* ☎ *603/756–3444* 🌐 *www.hungrydinerwalpole.com* 🕒 *Closed Tues.*

The Restaurant at Burdick's

$$$ | MODERN AMERICAN | Famous artisanal chocolatier and Walpole resident Larry Burdick, who sells his hand-filled, hand-cut chocolates to top restaurants around the country, founded this acclaimed restaurant next door to his shop in Walpole's charming little downtown. With the easygoing sophistication of a Parisian café and incredibly rich desserts, the restaurant features a French-inspired international menu that utilizes fresh, often local, ingredients and changes daily. **Known for:** noteworthy wine list; adjacent gourmet grocery with delicious picnic supplies; decadent desserts featuring house-made chocolates and pastries. [$] *Average main: $27* ✉ *47 Main St., Walpole* ☎ *603/756–9058* 🌐 *www.47mainwalpole.com* 🕒 *Closed Sun. and Mon.*

☕ Coffee and Quick Bites

★ Walpole Creamery

$ | CAFÉ | FAMILY | Arguably the state's best purveyor of artisanal, small-batch ice cream, this unassuming parlor in Walpole always features a long list of both regular and seasonal flavors, such as Fijan ginger, fresh peach, wild blueberry, and mint dark-chocolate-chip. Thick, rich, and using only all-natural ingredients, this luscious ice cream is also sold in many of the region's restaurants, farmstands, and groceries. **Known for:** using many local, seasonal ingredients; sandwiches and light lunch fare in the parlor; brownie sundaes. [$] *Average main: $5* ✉ *532 Main St., Walpole* ☎ *603/445–5700* 🌐 *www.walpolecreamery.com.*

Keene

17 miles southeast of Walpole, 20 miles northeast of Brattleboro, Vermont.

Keene, the largest city in southwestern New Hampshire (population 23,000), has one of the prettiest and widest main streets in the state, with several engaging boutiques and cafés—you can spend a fun few hours strolling along it. Home to Keene State College, the city feels both youthful and lively, with its funky crafts stores and eclectic entertainment, like the Monadnock International Film Festival, held in late September.

GETTING HERE AND AROUND

Routes 9 and 101 pass through Keene, connecting it with Brattleboro, Vermont and Peterborough.

ESSENTIALS

VISITOR INFORMATION Greater Keene and Peterborough Chamber of Commerce. ✉ *Keene* ☎ *603/352–1303* 🌐 *www.keenechamber.com.*

👁 Sights

Madame Sherri Forest

NATURE SIGHT | FAMILY | The focal point of this rugged 513-acre tract of deciduous forest in West Chesterfield are the stone chimney, grand staircase, and foundation of a chateau-style summer house owned by Parisian-born socialite and theatrical costume designer Madame Antoinette Sherri (the house burned down in 1963, and she died shortly after). A short woodland path from the parking area accesses the ruins, which are still fascinating despite a partial collapse of the staircase following heavy rains in 2021. Two fairly easy but hilly trails offer longer hikes through the surrounding forest, including the 3-mile round-trip trek up Wantastiquet Mountain, which offers clear views up and down the Connecticut River and across to Vermont. Trails also lead into the adjacent Wantastiquet State Forest, and there's more great hiking nearby in Pisgah State Park. ✉ *Gulf and Egypt Rds., West Chesterfield* ✣ *23.1 miles south of Walpole via I-91 N* ☎ *603/224–9945* 🌐 *www.forestsociety.org.*

Stonewall Farm

FARM/RANCH | FAMILY | At this picturesque nonprofit early-1800s farm and educational center, you can stop by to pick up produce and goods raised on-site (including delicious Frisky Cow Gelato) and procured from other artisanal producers in the area. Leave time to explore the grounds, dairy and small-animal barns, gardens, and chicken coops—a wide range of education tours are offered, plus seasonal hay and sleigh rides. There's also a maple sugaring house and small farm tool museum, and the property is traversed by hiking trails and accesses the 20-mile Cheshire Rail Trail, which stretches from Walpole through Keene and down to the Massachusetts border. ✉ *242 Chesterfield Rd., Keene* ☎ *603/357–7278* 🌐 *www.stonewallfarm.org.*

🍴 Restaurants

★ Luca's Mediterranean Café

$$ | MEDITERRANEAN | A deceptively simple storefront bistro with sidewalk tables overlooking Keene's graceful town square, Luca's dazzles with epicurean creations influenced by Italy, France, Greece, Spain, and North Africa. There's always an extensive selection of small plates, such as almond-crusted fried mozzarella and roasted Brussels sprouts with bacon and pomegranate-infused honey, plus handmade pastas and complexly flavored grills and stews. **Known for:** fresh, creative pastas; affable but knowledgeable service; great wine list. $ *Average main: $22* ⊠ *10 Central Sq., Keene* ☎ *603/358–3335* ⊕ *www.lucascafe.com* ⊗ *Closed Sun.*

Machina Kitchen & Art Bar

$$ | ECLECTIC | This farm-to-table restaurant in downtown Keene is a vital force in the community, offering not only stellar, sustainably sourced food and craft cocktails but also an art gallery with rotating exhibits and occasional live music performances. The menu changes often but always features a mix of classics and unexpected adventures like the salt cod croquettes with preserved-lemon remoulade, fried frog legs with mango-habanero salsa, or Korean-spiced-brisket bulgogi bowls with fresh pears and sesame. **Known for:** interesting cocktails and mocktails; friendly, creative-spirited crowd; occasional prix-fixe dinners with cocktail pairings. $ *Average main: $20* ⊠ *9 Court St., Keene* ☎ *603/903–0011* ⊕ *www.machinaarts.org* ⊗ *Closed Sun. No lunch weekdays.*

🛏 Hotels

★ Chesterfield Inn

$$ | B&B/INN | Fine antiques and Colonial-style fabrics adorn the spacious guest quarters in this opulent yet unpretentious country inn nestled on a 10-acre farmstead a couple of miles from the Connecticut River. **Pros:** beautifully tended gardens; kids and pets are welcome; excellent full breakfast included. **Cons:** restaurant closed on Sunday; two-night minimum at busy times; 20-minute drive from Keene. $ *Rooms from: $194* ⊠ *20 Cross Rd., off Rte. 9, West Chesterfield* ⊹ *14 miles west of Keene via Rte. 9* ☎ *603/256–3211* ⊕ *www.chesterfieldinn.com* ⇥ *15 rooms* ⦿ *Free Breakfast.*

Fairfield Inn and Suites Keene Downtown

$$ | HOTEL | It's unusual to find a midrange chain property set in a historic building on a picturesque downtown Main Street, but this well-kept hotel—inside the restored early 1900s Goodnow department store—is a rarity with its reasonably priced rooms, exposed-brick walls, 12-foot ceilings, and modern furnishings. **Pros:** the bilevel loft suites have two bathrooms; good fitness room; steps from great dining and shopping. **Cons:** bustling downtown center can be a little noisy; complimentary breakfast is pretty basic; historic building with quirky layout. $ *Rooms from: $175* ⊠ *30 Main St., Keene* ☎ *603/357–7070* ⊕ *www.fairfieldinnkeene.com* ⇥ *40 rooms* ⦿ *Free Breakfast.*

The Inn at East Hill Farm

$$$ | RESORT | FAMILY | For those with kids who like animals, East Hill Farm is heaven: a family resort with daylong children's programs on a 160-acre farm overlooking Mt. Monadnock that include milking cows; collecting eggs; feeding the sheep, donkeys, cows, rabbits, horses, chickens, goats, and ducks; horseback and pony rides; hiking and hay rides in summer; and sledding and sleigh rides in winter. **Pros:** family-friendly; farm fun and activities galore; beautiful setting. **Cons:** very remote location; noisy dining room; not an ideal choice for adults seeking a romantic retreat. $ *Rooms from: $334* ⊠ *460 Monadnock St., Troy* ⊹ *11 miles southeast of Keene* ☎ *603/242–6495, 800/242–6495* ⊕ *www.east-hill-farm.com* ⇥ *65 rooms* ⦿ *All-Inclusive.*

Riverside Hotel

$$ | HOTEL | With a boat dock and dazzling views of the Connecticut River, this simple but nicely kept three-story hotel is perfect for price-conscious travelers exploring the southwestern Monadnocks as well as nearby Brattleboro, Vermont. **Pros:** stunning river views; just a hop across river from Brattleboro; reasonable rates. **Cons:** decor is pleasant but not especially distinctive; noise travels between rooms; pretty basic breakfast. $ Rooms from: $170 ⊠ 20 Riverside Dr., West Chesterfield ☎ 603/256–4200 ⊕ www.riversidehotelnh.com ⇥ 34 rooms ❖❖ Free Breakfast.

▼ Nightlife

Branch and Blade Brewing
BEER GARDENS | Don't be put off by the location inside a small industrial park— this convivial taproom offers seating at picnic tables with wooden-keg tables, a big outdoor seating area where you can nosh on tasty pub fare, and, most importantly, great beer, including a tart Gose and potent triple IPA. ⊠ 17 Bradco St., Keene ☎ 603/354–3478 ⊕ www. babbrewing.com.

🎭 Performing Arts

Colonial Theatre
CONCERTS | This beautifully renovated 1924 vaudeville theater presents comedy, music, and dance performances as well as occasional indie film screenings. ⊠ 95 Main St., Keene ☎ 603/352–2033 ⊕ www.thecolonial.org.

🛍 Shopping

Hannah Grimes Marketplace
CRAFTS | The pottery, kitchenware, soaps, greeting cards, toys, and specialty foods of more than 250 artisans are on display in this colorful downtown gallery. ⊠ 42 Main St., Keene ☎ 603/352–6862 ⊕ www.hannahgrimesmarketplace.com.

Peterborough

20 miles east of Keene.

Thornton Wilder's play *Our Town* was based on Peterborough, which was the first in the region to be incorporated (1760) and remains a commercial and cultural hub, drawing big crowds for its theater

and concerts in summer. Downtown's charming Depot Square district abounds with distinctive boutiques, galleries, and restaurants. At Putnam Park on Grove Street, stand on the bridge and watch the roiling waters of the Nubanusit River.

GETTING HERE AND AROUND
Walkable downtown Peterborough is easily reached via Route 101 and U.S. 202.

ESSENTIALS
VISITOR INFORMATION Monadnock Travel Council. ⊠ Peterborough ⊕ www.monadnocktravel.com.

◉ Sights

Cathedral of the Pines
NATURE SIGHT | This 236-acre outdoor memorial pays tribute to Americans who have sacrificed their lives in service to their country. There's an inspiring view of Mt. Monadnock and Mt. Kearsarge from the Altar of the Nation, which is composed of rock from every U.S. state and territory. All faiths are welcome, and you can hear organ music some afternoons. The Memorial Bell Tower, built in 1967 with a carillon of bells from around the world, is built of native stone. Norman Rockwell designed the bronze tablets over the four arches. Flower gardens, an indoor chapel, and a museum of military memorabilia share the hilltop, and several trails lace the property, leading to tranquil peaceful areas. ⊠ 10 Hale Hill Rd., Rindge ☎ 603/899–3300 ⊕ www. cathedralofthepines.org.

Mariposa Museum
ART MUSEUM | FAMILY | You can play instruments or try on costumes from around the world and indulge your cultural curiosity at this nonprofit museum dedicated to hands-on exploration of international folk art. The three-floor museum is housed inside a historic Baptist church, across from the Universalist church in the heart of town. The museum hosts workshops and presentations on dance and arts and crafts. ⊠ 26 Main St., Peterborough

Charming Peterborough was the inspiration for the fictional Grover's Corners in Thornton Wilder's play, Our Town.

☎ *603/924–4555* 🌐 *www.mariposamuseum.org* 🎟 *$8* 🕒 *Closed Mon. and Tues.*

Monadnock State Park

STATE/PROVINCIAL PARK | Said to be America's most-climbed mountain—more than 400 people sometimes crowd its bald peak—Monadnock rises to 3,165 feet, and on clear days you can see the Boston skyline. When the parking lots are full, rangers close the park, so it's prudent to make a reservation online or get a very early morning start, especially during fall foliage. Five trailheads branch out into more than two dozen trails of varying difficulty (though all rigorous) that wend their way to the top. Allow three–five hours for any round-trip hike. The visitor center has free maps as well as exhibits documenting the mountain's history. In winter, you can cross-country ski along roughly 12 miles of groomed trails on the lower elevations. Pets are not permitted in the park. ✉ *116 Poole Rd., off Rte. 124* ✣ *7½ miles west of Peterborough* ☎ *603/532–8862* 🌐 *www.nhstateparks.org* 🎟 *$15 parking.*

🍴 Restaurants

Coopershill Public House

$$ | **IRISH** | Choose a sidewalk table overlooking bustling Depot Square or a table inside the conversation-filled dining room at this lively gastropub adjacent to Peterborough's popular independent cinema and steps from Mariposa Museum. The specialty here is rare whiskies, and there's also a nice selection of wines, craft beers, and other drinks, but don't overlook the consistently excellent Irish-influenced pub fare, including Guinness stew, mushroom-and-kale flatbread, bangers and mash, and terrific burgers. **Known for:** superb whiskey selection; ingredients sourced from New England farms; pecan bread pudding. [$] *Average main: $18* ✉ *6 School St., Peterborough* ☎ *603/371–9036* 🌐 *www.coopershillpublichouse.com.*

Pearl Restaurant & Oyster Bar

$$ | **ASIAN FUSION** | Despite its prosaic setting in a shopping center a little south of Peterborough's historic downtown, this sleek, contemporary Asian bistro and oyster bar is quite welcoming once inside. Several types of fresh oysters are always available, along with such diverse offerings as ahi tuna poke, Hanoi-style pork spring rolls, Korean barbecue pork, and coconut-veggie rice bowls. **Known for:** creative fusion fare; superb wine list; oysters on the half shell. $ *Average main: $22* ⊠ *1 Jaffrey Rd., Peterborough* ☎ *603/924–5225* ⊕ *www.pearl-peterborough.com* ☯ *Closed Sun. No lunch.*

🛏 Hotels

Benjamin Prescott Inn
$ | **B&B/INN** | Thanks to the dairy farm surrounding this 1853 Colonial house—with its stenciling and wide pine floors—you'll feel as though you're miles out in the country rather than just 10 minutes from Peterborough and even closer to the cute downtown of Jaffrey. **Pros:** reasonably priced; relaxing, scenic grounds; delicious breakfast included. **Cons:** minimum-night stays at busy times; not within walking distance of town; not suitable for young children. $ *Rooms from: $135* ⊠ *433 Turnpike Rd., Jaffrey Center* ✛ *8 miles southeast of Peterborough* ☎ *603/532–6637* ⊕ *www.benjaminprescottinn.com* ⇆ *10 rooms* ⭘ *Free Breakfast.*

Birchwood Inn
$ | **B&B/INN** | Overlooking the village green of tiny, quiet Temple, this affordable and friendly B&B built in 1775 once hosted Henry David Thoreau. **Pros:** friendly, old-fashioned tavern; quite affordable; good base for exploring Peterborough and Milford areas. **Cons:** secluded small town; quirky place with just three rooms; not suited for kids. $ *Rooms from: $139* ⊠ *340 Rte. 45, Temple* ✛ *7.3 miles east of Peterborough via Rte. 101* ☎ *603/878–3285* ⊕ *www.thebirchwoodinn.com* ⇆ *3 rooms* ⭘ *Free Breakfast.*

Jack Daniels Inn
$ | **MOTEL** | **FAMILY** | This clean, bright, and handsomely decorated 17-room motor inn just a half-mile north of downtown Peterborough is a terrific find with large, affordable rooms furnished with attractive reproduction antiques. **Pros:** great value; one of the only lodgings in Peterborough; continental breakfast included. **Cons:** unfancy motel-style rooms; some street noise; a 10-minute walk from downtown. $ *Rooms from: $134* ⊠ *80 Concord St. (U.S. 202), Peterborough* ☎ *603/924–7548* ⊕ *www.jackdanielsinn.com* ⇆ *17 rooms* ⭘ *Free Breakfast.*

🍸 Nightlife

Post & Beam Brewing
BREWPUBS | Serving boldly flavored saisons, grisettes, and other fine, mostly old-world-style ales and lagers as well as soft pretzels with hummus, chili, and other tasty edibles, this terrific brewery in downtown Peterborough has a beautiful setting inside the stately 1837 G.A.R. (Grand Army of the Republic) meeting hall. ⊠ *40 Grove St., Peterborough* ☎ *603/784–5361* ⊕ *www.postandbeambrewery.com.*

🎭 Performing Arts

Monadnock Music
CONCERTS | From early summer through late autumn, Monadnock Music sponsors a series of solo recitals, chamber music concerts, and orchestra and opera performances by renowned musicians. Events take place throughout the area, and some of the offerings are free. ⊠ *Peterborough* ☎ *603/852–4345* ⊕ *www.monadnockmusic.org.*

Peterborough Folk Music Society
CONCERTS | The Music Society presents folk concerts by artists such as John Gorka, Red Molly, and Cheryl Wheeler at the Peterborough Players Theatre and Bass Hall at Monadnock Center.

⊠ *Peterborough* ☎ *603/827–2905*
⊕ *www.pfmsconcerts.org.*

★ **Peterborough Players**

THEATER | FAMILY | This first-rate summer (mid-June–mid-September) theater troupe has been performing since 1933, these days presenting seven main-stage productions in a converted 18th-century barn throughout the summer. The Players also present children's shows in July and August. ⊠ *55 Hadley Rd., Peterborough* ☎ *603/924–7585* ⊕ *www.peterborough-players.org* ⊘ *Closed mid-Sept.–late June.*

⊖ Shopping

★ **Harrisville Designs**

FABRICS | Hand-spun and hand-dyed yarn, as well as looms, felt, knitting yarn, and instruction books, are sold at this famous shop that occupies a striking redbrick, water-powered mill in the heart of a Monadnock village that's been famous for textiles since 1794. The shop also conducts classes in knitting, spinning, and weaving.

■**TIP**➜ **Across the street, the inviting Harrisville General Store—open since 1838—serves tasty salads and sandwiches using locally sourced ingredients.** ⊠ *4 Mills Alley, Harrisville* ✛ *10 miles northwest of Peterborough* ☎ *800/338–9415* ⊕ *www. harrisville.com.*

Milford

18 miles east of Peterborough.

A once thriving mill town in the Souhegan River Valley, between the eastern peaks of the Monadnocks and the state's busy Nashua–Manchester corridor, Milford has a lively downtown centered around a leafy oval green and a growing crop of notable restaurants and bars. The town is a good base for exploring several interesting area attractions, from the neatly preserved Colonial historic district

of neighboring Amherst to the twisting back country roads that lead to offbeat shops, eateries, and scenic hikes in Brookline, Mason, and Wilton. Although Milford lacks hotels, nearby Nashua has about a dozen chain properties in every price range.

GETTING HERE AND AROUND

Routes 101 and 114 cross in Milford, providing easy access to Manchester to the northeast and Peterborough to the west.

⊙ Sights

Andres Institute of Art

ART MUSEUM | More than 80 contemporary sculptures, reached by 11 hiking trails, dot this 140-acre former ski hill. Established in 1996 by local engineer Paul Andres and sculptor John Weidman, it's the largest outdoor sculpture park in New England. Exploring this tranquil site, you'll discover these abstract works set amid leafy woodlands and occasional garden clearings. Some trails are open to mountain bikers in summer and snowmobilers in winter. ⊠ *98 Rte. 13, Brookline* ✛ *8 miles south of Milford* ☎ *603/673–8441* ⊕ *www.andresinstitute. org.*

LaBelle Winery

WINERY | Set on a leafy hilltop midway between Milford and Manchester, this contemporary winery with high ceilings and tall windows contains a tasting room, a bistro serving excellent lunch and dinner fare, an art gallery with rotating exhibits, and a spacious dog-friendly terrace. ⊠ *345 Rte. 101, Milford* ☎ *603/672–9898* ⊕ *www.labellewinery.com.*

★ **Pickity Place**

HISTORIC HOME | The winding 10-mile drive through Russell-Abbott State Forest is part of the fun of visiting this enchanted—and secluded—1786 red clapboard cottage on which artist Elizabeth Orton Jones based her illustrations in *Little Red Riding Hood* in the 1940s. Surrounded by fragrant, organic herb and flower gardens (you can buy seeds and plants in the nursery in back), the house today contains a sweet gift shop that sells dried herbal blends and other gourmet products, a small museum with Little Red Riding Hood memorabilia, and a wonderful little restaurant that serves five-course lunches featuring herbs and produce grown on-site. ✉ *248 Nutting Hill Rd., Mason* ✣ *9.4 miles southwest of Milford via Mason Rd.* ☎ *603/878–1151* 🌐 *www.pickityplace.com.*

🍴 Restaurants

★ Greenleaf

$$$ | MODERN AMERICAN | Set in an arresting redbrick Victorian bank building with soaring windows and a private dining room inside an old vault, Greenleaf is worth the trip for absolutely sublime modern American fare. Consider cast-iron New York strip steak with sweet potato and black garlic, or poached lobster tossed with angel hair pasta with tomatoes and mustard greens. James Beard–nominated chef Chris Viaud also runs the acclaimed Haitian Creole restaurant, Ansanm, around the corner. **Known for:** superb cocktail program; food sourced from local purveyors; inventive, delicious desserts. [$] *Average main: $33* ✉ *54 Nashua St., Milford* ☎ 🌐 *www.greenleafmilford.com* ⏲ *Closed Sun. and Mon. No lunch.*

Parker's Maple Barn

$ | AMERICAN | FAMILY | At this rustic establishment begun in the late 1960s on a country lane in Mason, the word "maple" appears no fewer than 15 times on the menu, accenting everything from the maple-infused coffee to maple-glazed ribs to maple milk shakes. Naturally, pancakes—available with wild blueberries, chocolate chips, or pumpkin seasoning—are the big draw, but don't overlook the savory fare, including corned-beef-hash omelets and waffle breakfast sandwiches. **Known for:** Belgian waffles with maple ice cream; maple chicken sausage; maple milk shakes and root beer floats. [$] *Average main: $11* ✉ *1316 Brookline Rd., Mason* ✣ *10.3 miles southwest of Milford via Rte. 13* ☎ *603/878–2308* 🌐 *www.parkersmaplebarn.com* ⏲ *Closed Tues. and Wed. No dinner.*

🛍 Shopping

★ Frye's Measure Mill

CRAFTS | Since 1858, this picturesque sawmill on a tranquil a pond has been a destination in rural Wilton. Since the 1960s, it's produced and sold classic Shaker-style maple-wood boxes, but the shop here also sells all sorts of beautiful folk art pieces, from hand-blown glass to finely forged ironware. Tours of the mill and its old print shop are also available. ✉ *12 Frye Mill Rd., Wilton* ✣ *7.6 miles west of Milford via Rte. 101A/Elm St.* ☎ *603/654–6581* 🌐 *www.fryesmill.com.*

Manchester

17 miles northeast of Milford, 45 miles west of Portsmouth, 53 miles north of Boston.

With 117,000 residents, New Hampshire's largest city grew up around the Amoskeag Falls on the Merrimack River, which drove small textile mills through the 1700s. By 1828 Boston investors had bought the rights to the Merrimack's water power and built the Amoskeag Mills, which became a testament to New England's manufacturing capabilities. In 1906 the mills employed 17,000 people and churned out more than 4 million yards of cloth weekly. When this vast enterprise closed in 1936, the town was devastated. Today Manchester is the state's most prominent business center, but many of the old mill buildings have been converted into condos, restaurants, museums, and office space, and the downtown dining, nightlife, and arts scenes have flourished in recent years.

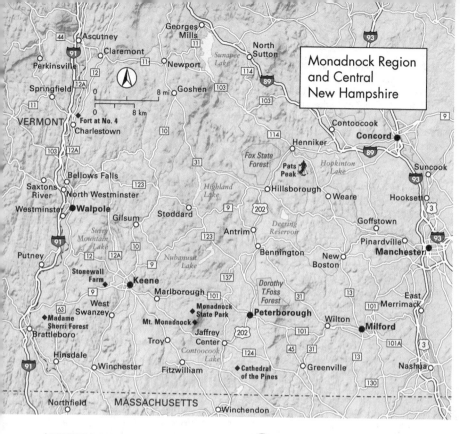

Map: Monadnock Region and Central New Hampshire

GETTING HERE AND AROUND

The state's largest airport, Manchester-Boston Regional Airport, is a modern, cost-effective, and hassle-free alternative to Boston's Logan Airport, with nonstop service from about a dozen cities. Public transit is limited here—a car is the best way for visitors to get around.

ESSENTIALS

AIRPORT Manchester-Boston Regional Airport. ✉ *1 Airport Rd., Manchester* ☎ *603/624–6539* ⊕ *www.flymanchester. com.*

VISITOR INFORMATION Greater Manchester Chamber of Commerce. ✉ *Manchester* ☎ *603/792–4100* ⊕ *www.manchester-chamber.org.*

◉ Sights

★ Currier Museum of Art

ART MUSEUM | The Currier maintains an astounding permanent collection of works by European and American masters, among them Claude Monet, Edward Hopper, Winslow Homer, John Marin, Andrew Wyeth, and Childe Hassam, and it presents changing exhibits of contemporary art. The museum also arranges guided tours of the nearby Zimmerman House. Completed in 1950, it's New England's only Frank Lloyd Wright–designed residence open to the public. Wright called this sparse, utterly functional living space "Usonian," a term he used to describe several dozen similar homes based on his vision of distinctly American architecture. ✉ *150 Ash St., Manchester* ☎ *603/669–6144* ⊕ *www.currier.org* 🎟 *$15; $35 for Zimmerman House.*

Millyard Museum

OTHER ATTRACTION | **FAMILY** | In one of the most architecturally striking Amoskeag Mills buildings, state-of-the-art exhibits depict the region's history from when Native Americans lived here and fished the Merrimack River to when the machines of Amoskeag Mills wove cloth. The museum also offers lectures and walking tours, and has a child-oriented Discovery Gallery. There's a very good book and gift shop, too. ✉ *200 Bedford St., Manchester* ☎ *603/622–7531* 🌐 *www.manchesterhistoric.org* 🎟 *$10* 🕒 *Closed Sun. and Mon.*

SEE Science Center

SCIENCE MUSEUM | **FAMILY** | The world's largest permanent LEGO installation at minifigure scale, depicting Amoskeag Millyard and Manchester as they looked a century ago, is the star attraction at this hands-on science lab and children's museum. The mind-blowing exhibit, covering 2,000 square feet, is made up of about 3 million LEGO bricks. It conveys the massive size and importance of the mills, which ran a mile on each side of the Merrimack. The museum also contains touch-friendly interactive exhibits and offers daily science demonstrations. ✉ *Amoskeag Millyard, 200 Bedford St., Manchester* ☎ *603/669–0400* 🌐 *www.see-sciencecenter.org* 🎟 *$10.*

🍴 Restaurants

Cotton

$$ | **MODERN AMERICAN** | Mod lighting and furnishings lend this restaurant inside an old Amoskeag Mills building a swanky atmosphere, although on warm days you may want to have a seat on the patio, set in an arbor. The farm-to-table-inspired comfort food changes regularly but has featured pan-seared crab cakes, grilled Atlantic salmon with sweet corn and gnocchi, and Delmonico steak with a choice of sauces. **Known for:** well-prepared comfort food; creative mixed drinks; handsome converted-warehouse setting. [$] *Average main: $23* ✉ *75 Arms St., Manchester* ☎ *603/622–5488* 🌐 *www.cottonfood.com* 🕒 *Closed Sun. and Mon. No lunch.*

Red Arrow Diner

$ | **AMERICAN** | One of New England's most celebrated diners, this bustling downtown greasy spoon has been catering to students, artists, and most famously U.S. Presidential candidates since 1922. This colorful restaurant, open around the clock, is a friendly place with fresh daily specials as well as such classics as kielbasa-and-cheese omelets and triple-bun Dinahmoe burgers. **Known for:** filling breakfasts; colorful people-watching; house-brewed root beer and cream soda. [$] *Average main: $11* ✉ *61 Lowell St., Manchester* ☎ *603/626–1118* 🌐 *www.redarrowdiner.com.*

☕ Coffee and Quick Bites

Restoration Cafe

$ | **CAFÉ** | Set on the ground floor of a vintage redbrick apartment building on the east side of downtown, this hip café and gathering spot excels both with drinks—everything from nitro cold brews to creative smoothies—and healthy, well-crafted food. At breakfast, consider the egg-cheddar-chive brioche sandwich, while tandoori bowls and rare-seared tuna sandwiches, along with craft cocktails and beers, are popular in the afternoon and for brunch. **Known for:** healthy smoothies; sleek industrial vibe; cheerful outdoor patio. [$] *Average main: $10* ✉ *235 Hanover St., Manchester* ☎ *603/518–7260* 🌐 *www.restorationcafenh.com* 🕒 *Closed Mon. No dinner.*

🛏 Hotels

★ **Ash Street Inn**

$$ | **B&B/INN** | Each of the five rooms in this striking sage-green 1885 B&B near the Currier Museum of Art and a few blocks from Elm Street dining is painted a different color, and all have soft bathrobes, flat-screen satellite TVs, and beds topped with Egyptian cotton linens. **Pros:** stylishly decorated rooms; excellent full breakfast included; free off-street parking. **Cons:** pricey for Manchester; not a great choice for children; urban setting isn't for those seeking quiet. $ *Rooms from: $219* ✉ *118 Ash St., Manchester* ☎ *603/668–9908* ⊕ *www.ashstreetinn.com* ⇆ *5 rooms* ⦿ *Free Breakfast.*

★ Bedford Village Inn

$$$ | **RESORT** | A few miles southwest of Manchester, this upscale complex consisting of an 1810 Federal inn and a bigger, contemporary boutique hotel is all about luxury and pampering, with Italian marble bathrooms, whirlpool tubs, sumptuous linens, four-poster beds, and Molton Brown bath products in the rooms. **Pros:** ultraposh accommodations and amenities; gorgeous gardens and grounds; outstanding food and beverage. **Cons:** in a suburb outside Manchester; breakfast not included in rates; often booked with weddings on weekends. $ *Rooms from: $278* ✉ *2 Olde Bedford Way, Bedford* ☎ *603/472–2001, 800/852–1166* ⊕ *www.bedfordvillageinn.com* ⇆ *64 rooms* ⦿ *No Meals.*

🍸 Nightlife

Crown Tavern

BARS | Set in a stunningly restored downtown theater with a huge adjacent outdoor patio, the Crown is a splendid venue for dining, but it's the natty bar—with noteworthy craft-cocktail list, exposed-brick walls, and tile floor—that's especially alluring. If you are hungry, try the thick-cut truffle fries or Nashville hot chicken sandwich. ✉ *99 Hanover St., Manchester* ☎ *603/218–3132* ⊕ *www.thecrownonhanover.com.*

815

BARS | A scene-y crowd mixes and mingles at this dimly lighted Prohibition Era–inspired, speakeasy-style cocktail bar with plush arm chairs and sofas and

Oriental rugs, and an impressive list of both innovative and classic cocktails, plus unusual local and international beers. ✉ *825 Elm St., Manchester* ☎ *603/782–8086* ⊕ *www.815nh.com.*

🎭 Performing Arts

The Palace Theatre

CONCERTS | This 1914 former vaudeville house presents musicals and plays, comedy, and concerts throughout the year. ✉ *80 Hanover St., Manchester* ☎ *603/668–5588* ⊕ *www.palacetheatre.org.*

🛍 Shopping

★ Dancing Lion Chocolate

CHOCOLATE | This acclaimed confectioner produces edible works of art in the form of strikingly designed chocolate bars like the WhiteSand with juniper, cardamom, and white chocolate, and the earthy Silk Flowers bar colored and flavored with peppercorns, chrysanthemums, and marigolds. Other specialties include bonbons and Mayan drinking chocolate, which you can sip in the adjacent café. ✉ *917 Elm St., Manchester* ☎ *603/625–4043* ⊕ *www.dancinglion.us.*

Concord

20 miles north of Manchester, 47 miles west of Portsmouth.

New Hampshire's capital (population 42,000) is a small and somewhat quiet city that tends to state business and little else. With that said, downtown has seen a steady influx of new restaurants and bars. Stop in town to get a glimpse of New Hampshire's State House, which is crowned by a gleaming, eagle-topped gold dome.

GETTING HERE AND AROUND

Interstate 93 bisects Concord north–south and is intersected by Interstate 89 and U.S. 202, which becomes Interstate 393 near the city line. Main Street near the State House is walkable, but a car is the best way to explore farther afield.

ESSENTIALS

VISITOR INFORMATION Greater Concord Chamber of Commerce. ✉ *Concord* ☎ *603/224–2508* 🌐 *www.concordnhchamber.com.*

Sights

McAuliffe-Shepard Discovery Center
SCIENCE MUSEUM | FAMILY | New England's only air-and-space center offers a full day of activities focused mostly on the heavens. See yourself in infrared light, learn about lunar spacecraft, examine a replica of the Mercury-Redstone rocket, or experience what it's like to travel in space—you can even try your hand at being a television weather announcer. There's also a café. ✉ *2 Institute Dr., Concord* ☎ *603/271–7827* 🌐 *www.starhop.com* 🎫 *$12* 🕒 *Closed Mon.–Thurs. in Sept.–May.*

New Hampshire Historical Society
HISTORY MUSEUM | Steps from the state capitol, this museum is a great place to learn about the Concord coach, a popular mode of transportation before railroads. The Discovering New Hampshire exhibit delves into a number of facets of the state's heritage, from politics to commerce. Rotating shows might include locally made quilts or historical portraits of residents. ✉ *30 Park St., Concord* ☎ *603/228–6688* 🌐 *www.nhhistory.org* 🎫 *$7* 🕒 *Closed Sun.–Wed.*

★ State House
GOVERNMENT BUILDING | The gilded-dome state house, built in 1819, is the nation's oldest capitol building in which the legislature still uses the original chambers. From January through June, you can watch the two branches in action. The Senate has 24 members, and the House house has 400—a ratio of 1 representative per 3,500 residents (a world record). The visitor center coordinates guided and self-guided tours, bookable online or on-site, and displays history exhibits and paraphernalia from presidential primaries. ✉ *Visitor center, 107 N. Main St., Concord* ☎ *603/271–2154* 🌐 *www.gencourt.state.nh.us* 🎫 *Free* 🕒 *No tours on weekends.*

Restaurants

Barley House
$$ | AMERICAN | A lively, old-fashioned tavern with Irish overtones, the Barley House is steps from the state capitol and typically buzzes with a mix of politicos, businesspeople, and tourists. The melting pot of a menu includes chorizo-topped pizzas, burgers smothered with a peppercorn-whiskey sauce, chicken potpies, beer-braised bratwurst, and Mediterranean chicken salad—all reliably prepared. **Known for:** live Irish music some nights; great beer selection; hefty, delicious burgers. [$] *Average main: $20* ✉ *132 N. Main St., Concord* ☎ *603/228–6363* 🌐 *www.thebarleyhouse.com* 🕒 *Closed Wed.*

★ Revival
$$$ | MODERN AMERICAN | In this handsome, high-ceilinged redbrick building on a downtown side street, foodies and revelers congregate for some of the most creative and accomplished regional American cuisine in the Merrimack Valley. Highlights, in addition to an impressive selection of whiskies and cognacs, might include an artful platter of charcuterie and New England artisanal cheeses, hearty beef and veal Bolognese with mushroom tagliatelle, and seared salmon with pancetta and olive tapenade, but the menu changes regularly. **Known for:**

ingredients sourced from local farms; see-and-be-seen vibe; decadent desserts. $ *Average main: $26* ⊠ *11 Depot St., Concord* ☎ *603/715–5723* ⊕ *www. revivalkitchennh.com* ⊘ *Closed Sun. and Mon. No lunch.*

 Hotels

The Centennial

$$ | HOTEL | Concord's most distinctive and romantic hotel occupies an imposing brick-and-stone building constructed in 1892 for widows of Civil War veterans, but the interior has been given a head-to-toe makeover: boutique furnishings and contemporary art immediately set the tone in the lobby; pillow-top beds sport luxurious linens and down pillows; and bathrooms have stone floors, granite countertops, and stand-alone showers. **Pros:** elegant redesign of historic structure; attractive residential setting; great bar and restaurant. **Cons:** not within walking distance of downtown dining; rooms facing road can get a little road noise; breakfast costs extra. $ *Rooms from: $179* ⊠ *96 Pleasant St., Concord* ☎ *603/227–9000* ⊕ *www.thecentennialhotel.com* ⇌ *32 rooms* ⦿ *No Meals.*

★ Hotel Concord

$$$ | HOTEL | This sleek, stunning contemporary boutique hotel lies within a short stroll of the city's top arts venues and eateries; the airy and light-filled rooms, many with balconies, have hardwood floors, distinctive artwork, big windows, and are outfitted with Amazon Echo devices, huge HD TVs, and spacious marble baths. **Pros:** inexpensive parking; hip, cosmopolitan design; lots to see and do within walking distance. **Cons:** on a busy street; some may find the in-room high-tech gadgets a little challenging; books up when statehouse is in session. $ *Rooms from: $239* ⊠ *11 S. Main St., Concord* ☎ *603/504–3500* ⊕ *www.hotelconcordnh.com* ⇌ *38 rooms* ⦿ *Free Breakfast.*

Performing Arts

★ Capitol Center for the Arts

ARTS CENTERS | The Egyptian-motif artwork, part of the original 1927 decor, has been restored in this historic 1,304-seat venue that now hosts touring Broadway shows, dance companies, and musical acts. A few blocks away (at 16 S. Main Street), the organization also operates **Bank of NH Stage**, a restored historic movie house that presents music, comedy, and other notable shows. ⊠ *44 S. Main St., Concord* ☎ *603/225–1111* ⊕ *www. ccanh.com.*

Chapter 6

INLAND MAINE

Updated by
Mary Ruoff

● Sights 🍴 Restaurants 🛏 Hotels 🛍 Shopping 🍸 Nightlife
★★★★☆ ★★★☆☆ ★★★☆☆ ★★☆☆☆ ★★☆☆☆

WELCOME TO INLAND MAINE

TOP REASONS TO GO

★ **Baxter State Park:** Mt. Katahdin, the state's highest peak, stands sentry over Baxter's forestland in its "natural wild state."

★ **Moosehead Lake:** Surrounded by mountains, Maine's largest lake—dotted with islands and chiseled with inlets and coves—retains the rugged beauty that so captivated author Henry David Thoreau in the mid-1800s.

★ **Water Sports:** It's easy to get out on the water on scheduled cruises on large inland lakes; guided or self-guided boating, canoeing, and kayaking trips; and white-water rafting excursions on several rivers.

★ **Winter Pastimes:** Downhill skiing, snowmobiling, snowshoeing, cross-country skiing, fat-tire biking, and ice fishing are all popular winter sports. You can even go dogsledding!

★ **Foliage Drives:** Maine's best fall foliage is inland, where hardwoods outnumber spruce, fir, and pine trees in many areas.

Though Maine is well known for its miles of craggy coastline, the inland part of the state is surprisingly vast and far less populated. Not one hour's drive from the bays and ocean, huge swaths of forestland are punctuated by lakes (sometimes called ponds, despite their size). Summer camps, ski areas, and small villages populate the mountainous western part of the state, which stretches north along the New Hampshire border to Québec. In the remote North Woods, wilderness areas beckon outdoors lovers. You can take a drive (go slow!) down a "moose alley" in both regions.

1 **Sebago Lake Area.** Less than 20 miles northwest of Portland, the Sebago Lake area bustles with activity in summer.

2 **Bridgton.** Bridgton is a classic New England town with many nearby lakes to explore.

3 **Bethel.** In the valley of the Androscoggin River, Bethel is home to Sunday River, one of Maine's major ski resorts.

4 **Rangeley.** Rangeley, along its namesake lake, anchors a lake-dotted region with long stretches of pine, beech, spruce, and sky.

5 **Kingfield.** Just north of Kingfield is Sugarloaf ski resort, Maine's other big ski resort, which has plenty to offer year-round.

6 **Greenville.** The woodsy town, on Moosehead Lake, Maine's largest, is a great base for day trips.

7 **Millinocket.** The gateway to the premier wilderness destinations of Baxter State Park and the Allagash Wilderness Waterway.

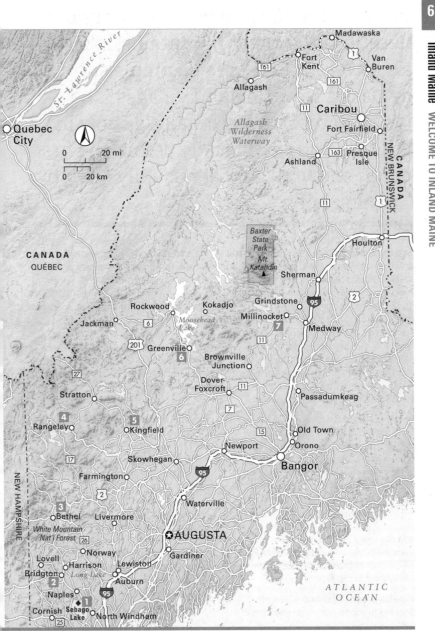

St. Lawrence River

Quebec City

CANADA
QUÉBEC

NEW HAMPSHIRE

0   20 mi
0   20 km

Madawaska

Fort Kent

Van Buren

161

1

Allagash

161

11

Caribou

Allagash Wilderness Waterway

Fort Fairfield

163

Presque Isle

Ashland

11

1

CANADA
NEW BRUNSWICK

Baxter State Park
Mt. Katahdin ▲

Houlton

Sherman

2

Rockwood

Kokadjo

Grindstone

95

6

Jackman

Moosehead Lake

Millinocket

7

Medway

201

Greenville

6

Brownville Junction

11

27

Dover-Foxcroft

11

Passadumkeag

Stratton

7

4

5

15

Old Town

Rangeley

Kingfield

Orono

17

Newport

Bangor

Skowhegan

95

Farmington

2

Waterville

3

Bethel

Livermore

White Mountain Nat'l Forest

26

AUGUSTA

Norway

Gardiner

Lovell

Harrison

Lewiston

Bridgton

Long Lake

2

Auburn

Naples

95

1

Cornish

Sebago Lake

North Windham

25

ATLANTIC OCEAN

Unlike the state's higher-profile coastline, inland Maine is a four-season destination. Natural beauty is abundant here, in the form of mountains, lakes, and rivers, and there's an ample supply of classic New England villages. The large ski resorts start making snow in late autumn, so typically before the first major snowfall, and are usually open by Thanksgiving.

Sebago and Long lakes, north of Portland and the gateway to the Western Lakes and Mountains region, hum with boaters and watercraft in the summer. Bridgton and Bethel ooze quintessential New England charm and draw skiers come winter. Rangeley, a mountain town in western Maine, has been a haven for anglers since the 19th century, but these days this lake-strewn area is also known for hiking and winter sports and activities, from snowmobiling to alpine skiing.

In the North Woods, remote forestland lines most of Moosehead Lake, New England's largest lake within a single state. Greenville, at its southern end, is the hub in this neck of the woods. Visitors come to enjoy the lake, explore nearby wilderness locales, snowmobile, ice fish, and downhill and cross-country ski. Mt. Katahdin, Maine's highest peak and the terminus of the Appalachian Trail, rises in 210,000-acre Baxter State Park, an outdoor enthusiast's mecca outside Millinocket in the North Woods.

Wealthy urban "rusticators" began flocking to inland Maine on vacation in the mid-1800s. Their legacy, and that of the locals who catered to them, lives on at sporting camps still found—albeit in smaller numbers—on remote lakes and rivers, in displays at small but impressive regional museums, and through Maine's unique system of licensed outdoor guides. Known as Registered Maine Guides, these well-qualified practitioners lead such excursions as kayaking, white-water rafting, hiking, fishing, hunting, canoeing, or moose spotting.

MAJOR REGIONS

The sparsely populated **Western Lakes and Mountains** region stretches north and west, bordered by New Hampshire and Québec. Each season offers different outdoor highlights: you can choose from snow sports, hiking, mountain biking, leaf peeping, fishing, swimming, and paddling. The **Sebago Lake Area** bustles with activity in summer. **Bridgton** is a classic New England town, as is **Bethel**, in the valley of the Androscoggin River. Sunday River, a major ski resort nearby, also offers summer activities. The more remote **Rangeley** Lakes region contains long stretches of pine, beech, spruce, and sky, and classic inns. Just north of **Kingfield** is Sugarloaf ski resort, Maine's other big ski resort, which has plenty to offer year-round.

Much of the **North Woods** is best experienced by canoeing or kayaking, fishing, hiking, snowshoeing, cross-country skiing, or snowmobiling. The woodsy town of **Greenville**, on Moosehead Lake, is a great base for day trips, including excursions into Maine's 100 Mile Wilderness. **Millinocket** is the gateway to Baxter State Park, Allagash Wilderness Waterway, and Katahdin Woods and Waters National Monument, all premier wilderness destinations open for public recreation.

Planning

Visitors to inland Maine often spend their entire vacation in the region. That's certainly true of those who come to ski at a resort, fish at a remote sporting camp, or just relax at a lakeside cabin. Resort towns offer scenic cruises, intriguing small museums, and nearby hiking but are also hubs for exploring farther afield. Visitors may head out early for white-water rafting, to recreate in a renowned wilderness area, or day trip among the lake towns closer to Portland. The farther inland you go, the farther between destinations. Lodgings and rentals often have minimum stays during peak times.

Getting Here and Around

AIR
Two primary airports serve Maine: Portland International Jetport (PWM) and Bangor International (BGR). Portland is closer to the Western Lakes and Mountains area; Bangor is more convenient to the North Woods. Offering charter as well as scenic flights, regional flying services pick visitors up at major airports and transport them to remote locales.

CAR
Because Maine is large and rural, a car is essential. U.S. 2 is the major east–west thoroughfare in Western Maine, winding from Bangor to New Hampshire. Interstate 95 is a departure point for many visitors to inland Maine, especially the North Woods. The highway heads inland at Brunswick and becomes a toll road (the Maine Turnpike) from the New Hampshire border to Augusta. Because of the hilly terrain and abundant lakes and rivers, inland Maine can get curvy. Traffic rarely gets heavy, though highways often pass right through instead of around the larger towns, which can slow your trip a bit.

In Maine's North Woods, private logging roads are often open to the public (sometimes by permit and fee). When driving these roads, always give lumber-company trucks the right-of-way; loggers must drive in the middle of the road and often can't move over or slow down for cars. Be sure to have a full tank of gas before heading onto private roads in the region.

Activities

People visit inland Maine year-round, coming to hike, bike, camp, fish, canoe, kayak, white-water raft, downhill and cross-country ski, snowshoe, and snowmobile.

BIKING
Bicycle Coalition of Maine
BIKING | The coalition provides information about biking in the state. ☎ *207/623–4511* ⊕ *www.bikemaine.org.*

FISHING
Maine Department of Inland Fisheries and Wildlife
FISHING | You can buy hunting and fishing licenses online through this state agency, which has a wealth of information about where and how to enjoy these outdoor activities in Maine. ☎ *207/287–8000* ⊕ *www.maine.gov/ifw.*

GUIDE SERVICES

Maine Professional Guides Association

The association can help you find a state-licensed guide to lead a fishing, hunting, hiking, kayaking, canoeing, white-water rafting, snowshoeing, birding, or wildlife-watching trip. ⊕ *www.maineguides.org.*

HIKING

Maine Appalachian Trail Club

HIKING & WALKING | The club publishes seven Appalachian Trail maps ($8 per map for nonmembers, $6.40 for members), all of which are bound together in its Maine trail guide ($34.95 for nonmembers, $27.96 for members). Maps are also available (free and for purchase) via a free app (*see the website for details*). The organization's interactive online map has information on everything from side trails to communities along the AT in Maine. ⊕ *www.matc.org.*

Maine Trail Finder

HIKING & WALKING | The website has trail descriptions, photos, user comments, directions, and interactive maps for trails to hike, walk, mountain bike, paddle, snowshoe, and cross-county ski. ⊕ *www.mainetrailfinder.com.*

SKIING

Ski Maine Association

SURFING | For alpine and cross-country skiing information. ☎ *207/773–7669* ⊕ *www.skimaine.com.*

SNOWMOBILING

Maine Snowmobile Association

SNOW SPORTS | The website has contacts and links for about 10,000 miles of local and regional trails and an excellent state-wide map of the approximately 4,000-mile Interconnected Trail System (ITS). ☎ *207/622–6983* ⊕ *www.mainesnowmobileassociation.com.*

WHITE-WATER RAFTING

Raft Maine Association

WHITE-WATER RAFTING | An association of four white-water rafting outfitters, the website has information on the companies and Maine's three major white-water rafting rivers—the Kennebec, the Dead, and the West Branch of the Penobscot, which together make Maine New England's premier destination for white-water rafting. The Kennebec and Dead rivers converge at The Forks in Western Maine, while the West Branch of the Penobscot flows near Millinocket in the North Woods.

■ **TIP** → **Family-friendly rafting trips are available.** ⊕ *www.raftmaine.com.*

Hotels

Well-run inns, bed-and-breakfasts, and motels can be found throughout inland Maine, including some more sophisticated lodgings. During high season, or seasons, you may be required to stay two nights minimum. At places near ski resorts, you'll find peak-season rates in winter as well as at the height of summer and the fall foliage peak. Both hotel rooms and condo units are among the options at the two largest ski resorts, Sunday River and Sugarloaf. Greenville has the largest selection of lodgings in the North Woods region, with elaborate and homey accommodations alike. Lakeside sporting camps are popular around Rangeley and the North Woods; many have cozy cabins heated with wood stoves and provide three hearty meals a day (lunch is packed to go), perhaps featuring fish you caught. Conservation organizations also operate wilderness retreats.

Hotel reviews have been shortened. For full reviews visit Fodors.com.

Maine Campground Owners Association

The association's helpful membership directory is available by mail and on its website, which also has an interactive map. Many campgrounds have RV spaces and cabin rentals. ☎ *207/782–5874* ⊕ *www.campmaine.com.*

Maine Sporting Camp Association

Representing 45 camps, the association's goal is to "preserve the sporting camp's uniqueness" in Maine. Visit the website to search for camps by activity, meal plan, season of operation, and even the fish in local waters. ☎ 207/888–3931 ⊕ www.mainesportingcamps.com.

Maine State Parks Campground Reservations Service

You can get information about and make reservations for 12 state park campgrounds through this service. Note: reservations for Baxter State Park, which is administered separately, are not handled by the service. ☎ 207/624–9950, 800/332–1501 in Maine ⊕ www.campwithme.com.

What It Costs in U.S. Dollars			
$	$$	$$$	$$$$
RESTAURANTS			
under $18	$18–$24	$25–$35	over $35
HOTELS			
under $200	$200–$299	$300–$399	over $399

Restaurants

Fear not, lobster lovers: this succulent, emblematic Maine food is on the menu at many inland restaurants, from fancier establishments to roadside places. Dishes containing lobster are more common than boiled lobster dinners; look for daily specials. Shrimp, scallops, and other seafood are also menu mainstays, and you may find bison burgers or steaks from a nearby farm. Organic growers and natural foods producers are found throughout the state and often sell their products to nearby restaurants. Pumpkins, blackberries, apples, and strawberries make their way into homemade desserts, as do Maine's famed blueberries. Many lakeside resorts and sporting camps have

a reputation for good food—some of the latter will even cook the fish you catch.

Restaurant reviews have been shortened. For full reviews visit Fodors.com.

Visitor Information

The more than 2 million acres overseen by the Maine Bureau of Parks and Lands encompass 33 state parks, 15 historic sites, three scenic waterways, and about 300 miles of multiuse trails (popular with ATV riders and snowmobilers). Its free public lands—approximately 600,000 acres—are wilderness areas managed for recreation, wildlife preservation, and timbering. Some are in remote areas accessible only by logging roads; others are relatively close to town centers; and some have trails, outhouses, and primitive campsites.

CONTACTS Maine Office of Tourism. ☎ 888/624–6345 ⊕ www.visitmaine. com. **Maine Tourism Association.** ⊕ www. mainetourism.com. **Maine Bureau of Parks and Lands.** ☎ 207/287–3821 ⊕ www. parksandlands.com.

When to Go

As a rule, inland Maine's most popular hiking trails and lakeside beaches get busier when the weather gets warmer, but if splendid isolation is what you crave, you can still find it. In summertime, lodging rates rise with the temperature and traffic picks up—though rarely jams, outside of a few spots. Inland Maine gets hotter than the coast in July and August; lakes and higher elevations are naturally cooler. Of course the weather also makes it a beautiful time of year to visit. September is a good bet: temperatures are more moderate, and the crowds thinner. Western Maine is the state's premier destination for leaf peepers—hardwoods are more abundant inland. Peak foliage season runs late September–mid-October.

Maine's largest ski resorts typically start making snow for the trails before the first large snowfall and are open by Thanksgiving. As the weather has warmed in recent years, winters here have started later and ended sooner. In northerly and mountain destinations, snowmobiling and cross-country skiing are unlikely to be in full swing before mid-January. Early spring snowmelt ushers in mud season, which leads to black fly season mid-May–mid-June. The flies are especially pesky in the woods but less bothersome in town. Spring is prime time for canoeing and fishing.

Sebago Lake Area

20 miles northwest of Portland.

Seasonal and year-round dwellings, from simple camps to sprawling showplaces, line the shores of sprawling Sebago Lake and fingerlike Long Lake. Both are popular with water-sports enthusiasts, as is Brandy Pond and other bodies of water in the area. Several rivers flow into Sebago Lake—Maine's second largest—linking nearby lakes and ponds to form a 43-mile waterway. Naples, on the causeway separating Long Lake from Brandy Pond, pulses with activity in the summer, when the area swells with seasonal residents and weekend visitors. Open-air cafés overflow with patrons, boats buzz along the water, and families parade along the sidewalk edging Long Lake. On clear days the view includes snowcapped Mt. Washington. The nonextant Cumberland and Oxford Canal was part of a water route from Long Lake to Portland in the mid-1800s. At Sebago Lake State Park, the one remaining canal lock operates on the Songo River, which connects Brandy Pond and Sebago Lake.

GETTING HERE AND AROUND

Sebago Lake, gateway to Maine's Western Lakes and Mountains, is less than 20 miles from Portland on U.S. 302.

VACATION RENTALS

CONTACTS Krainin Real Estate. ⊠ *1539 Roosevelt Tr., Raymond* ☎ *207/655–5189 for vacation rentals* ⊕ *www.krainin.com.*

VISITOR INFORMATION

CONTACTS Sebago Lakes Region Chamber of Commerce. ⊠ *909 Roosevelt Tr., Suite A, Windham* ☎ *207/892–8265* ⊕ *www. sebagolakeschamber.com.*

◉ Sights

Sabbathday Lake Shaker Village

MUSEUM VILLAGE | FAMILY | Established in the late 18th century, this is the last active Shaker community in the world. The farmstead's many structures include the 1794 Meetinghouse; the 1839 Ministry's Shop, where the elders and eldresses lived until the early 1900s; and the 1821 Sister's Shop, where household goods and candies were made. Visitors can take self-guided exterior building tours; check out free exhibits in the 1850 Boys' Shop, about Shaker childhood, and the 1816 Granary, on the community's history and evolution; and walk the gardens and grounds. The Shaker Store sells community-produced foods and goods as well as handicrafts by area artisans and has an antique shop whose offerings may include "fancy goods" made here years ago for sale to tourists. Check the website for events, including workshops. ⊠ *707 Shaker Rd., New Gloucester* ☎ *207/926–4597* ⊕ *www.maineshakers.com* ⊠ *Free* ⊘ *Closed mid-Oct.–late May and Sun. late May–mid-Oct.*

Sebago Lake State Park

STATE | PROVINCIAL PARK | This 1,400-acre expanse on the north shore of Sebago Lake is a great spot for swimming, boating, and fishing for both salmon and togue (lake trout). Its 250-site campground is the largest at any Maine state park. Bicycling along the park's roads is a popular pastime in warm weather, as is hiking. Come winter, the park offers 5½ miles of groomed cross-country trails and 6 miles of ungroomed trails, also used for snowshoeing. On the park's edge, Songo Lock State Historic Site, an operational lock along the twisting, narrow Songo River and a remnant of a 19th-century canal system, is a pleasant—and free—picnic area. You can also fish off the handicapped-accessible pier and launch a kayak or canoe. ✉ *11 Park Access Rd., Casco* ☎ *207/693–6231* 🌐 *www.maine.gov/sebagolake* 🎟 *Nonresident $8, Maine resident $6.*

Hotels

Lakeview Inn

$ | **B&B/INN** | Built in 1906 as a hotel annex, the four-story inn has 16 rooms and suites—all on the upper floors—and a wide, inviting front porch that overlooks gardens and offers an angled view of Long Lake beyond Naples' main thoroughfare. **Pros:** cornhole outside, pool table inside; convenience center has kitchenette (no stove top) with courtesy coffee and tea; several deluxe larger rooms and family-friendly suites. **Cons:** third-floor rooms but no elevator; stairs a bit steep; "comfy" rooms are smallish. [$] *Rooms from: $189* ✉ *15 Lake House Rd., Naples* ☎ *207/693–9099* 🌐 *www.lakeviewinnmaine.com* 🛏 *16 rooms* 🍴 *Free Breakfast.*

Activities

Sebago and Long lakes are popular areas for sailing, fishing, and motorboating. As U.S. 302 cuts through the center of Naples, you'll find rental craft for fishing or cruising at the causeway.

TOURS

Songo River Queen II

BOAT TOURS | **FAMILY** | Departing from the Naples causeway, the *Songo River Queen II*, a 93-foot stern-wheeler, takes passengers on scheduled cruises on Long Lake and also offers private charters. The narration is awash in local history and fun facts about noteworthy dwellings along the shore, including a former home of horror writer and Mainer Stephen King. There's a bar and snack bar on board. Check the website for themed evening cruises with live music, offered most weekends. ✉ *841 Roosevelt Tr., Naples* ☎ *207/693–6861* 🌐 *www.songoriverqueen.net* 🎟 *From $35.*

WATER SPORTS

Dingley's Wharf

WATER SPORTS | **FAMILY** | Smack in the middle of the Naples causeway on Long Lake, Dingley's offers lots of choices for getting out on the water. Wakeboarding, waterskiing, wake surfing, knee boarding, and tube riding excursions with a certified instructor include lessons. If you have your own boat, you can rent equipment for these activities. Dingley's rental options include Jet Skis, aqua trikes, kayaks, canoes, and standup paddleboards. Need to make a bigger splash? Rent a pontoon boat or Boston Whaler. ✉ *851 Roosevelt Tr., Naples* ✣ *On Naples causeway* ☎ *207/693–5253* 🌐 *www.dingleyswharf.com.*

Bridgton

8 miles north of Naples, 30 miles south of Bethel.

Downtown Bridgton is a great place to spend the day, with restaurants, a movie theater, museums, a nice mix of shops and galleries, and a handful of parks. Steps from the action, a covered pedestrian bridge leads to 66-acre Pondicherry Park, a nature preserve with wooded trails and two streams. Highland Beach is off the north end of Main Street, across from an inviting small park. On hot summer days, kids dive off the dock as mountains lounge on the horizon. Come winter, skiers head to Pleasant

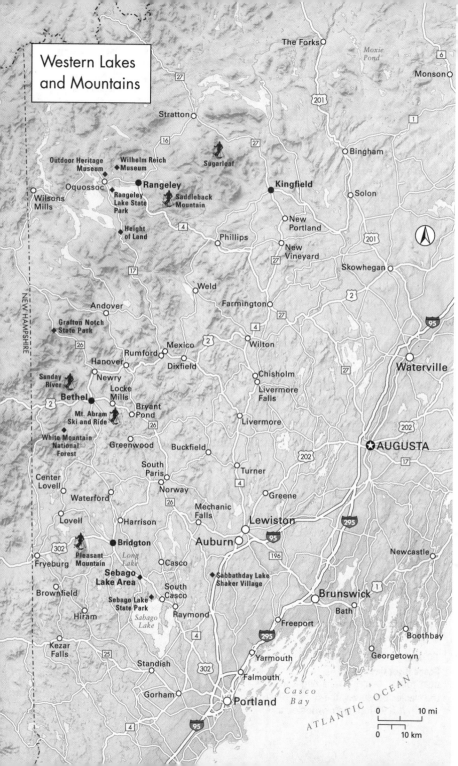

Western Lakes and Mountains

The Forks

Moxie Pond

Monson

27

201

6

1

Stratton

Bingham

16

27

Sugarloaf

Kingfield

Solon

Outdoor Heritage Museum

Wilhelm Reich Museum

Oquossoc

Rangeley

Saddleback Mountain

New Portland

Wilsons Mills

Rangeley Lake State Park

201

Height of Land

4

Phillips

New Vineyard

Skowhegan

27

Weld

Farmington

2

Waterville

Andover

27

95

Grafton Notch State Park

Rumford

Mexico

Wilton

4

26

Hanover

Dixfield

Chisholm

Sunday River

Newry

Livermore Falls

Bethel

Locke Mills

2

Bryant Pond

Livermore

202

Mt. Abram Ski and Ride

26

AUGUSTA

White Mountain National Forest

Greenwood

Buckfield

17

Center Lovell

South Paris

Turner

4

Waterford

Norway

Greene

Lovell

26

Mechanic Falls

Lewiston

Newcastle

Harrison

Pleasant Mountain

Bridgton

Long Lake

Casco

Auburn

95

196

302

Fryeburg

Sebago Lake Area

South Casco

Sabbathday Lake Shaker Village

295

Brunswick

Brownfield

Sebago Lake State Park

Raymond

Bath

1

Hiram

Sabago Lake

4

Freeport

Boothbay

Kezar Falls

25

Yarmouth

Georgetown

Standish

Falmouth

Casco Bay

302

Gorham

Portland

ATLANTIC OCEAN

95

4

NEW HAMPSHIRE

0   10 mi

0   10 km

Mountain (formerly Shawnee Peak) and cross-country ski at Bridgton's ridgetop golf course. The town is the hub for a region strewn with lakes and large ponds popular for boating, fishing, and swimming; the surrounding countryside is a good choice for leaf peepers and hikers. Harrison is a few miles north at the end of Long Lake. Beyond here, Waterford's villages evoke Old New England. In fall, head west to Fryeburg, home to Fryeburg Fair (🌐 www.fryeburgfair.org), Maine's largest agricultural fair. North of the New Hampshire border town, Center Lovell draws boaters to Kezar Lake (author and Mainer Stephen King summers here) and hikers to Mount Sabattus.

GETTING HERE AND AROUND

From Portland, U.S. 302 runs northwest to Bridgton along the east side of Sebago Lake and the west side of Long Lake, then continues west 15 miles to Fryeburg, where Route 5 continues north to Center Lovell. Route 117 skirts the west side of Long Lake en route to Harrison, north of Bridgton. Both Route 37 (in North Bridgton) and Route 35 (in Harrison) depart Route 117 for Waterford.

VISITOR INFORMATION

CONTACTS Greater Bridgton Lakes Region Chamber of Commerce. ✉ *257 Main St., Suite 1, Bridgton* ☎ *207/647–3472* 🌐 *www.gblrcc.org.*

Sights

★ Rufus Porter Museum of Art and Ingenuity

ART MUSEUM | FAMILY | Local youth Rufus Porter became a leading folk artist in the early 1800s, painting landscape and harbor murals on the walls of New England homes, like this museum's barn red Cape Cod–style Nathan Church House, which bears unsigned murals by Porter (or one of his apprentices). In 2016, the late-18th-century structure was moved to the museum's downtown setting, where an eye-catching circa-1830s former residence on Main Street has exhibits about Porter, who was also an "ahead of his time" inventor, writer, and founder of *Scientific American* magazine. Early issues are on display, as are models of some of his inventions and his miniature portraits. A video about this ingenious man is shown. Both buildings have changing exhibits, and the museum's excellent gift shop has books about Porter. ✉ *121 Main St., Bridgton* ☎ *207/647–2828* 🌐 *www.rufusportermuseum.org* 🎟 *$8* 🕓 *Closed mid-Oct.–mid-June and Sun.–Tues. mid-June–mid-Oct.*

Beaches

With many lakes in the Bridgton area, it's not surprising the town has three public beaches. Two have playgrounds and a dock: the crown jewel, Highland Beach, at the end of Highland Lake at the edge of downtown on Highland Road, and Woods Pond Beach off Route 117. Salmon Point Beach, part of the town-owned campground of the same name, has fewer amenities but is on one of the area's premier bodies of water, Long Lake.

Restaurants

Standard Gastropub

$ | AMERICAN | FAMILY | Like the facade, a cooler wall—stocked with hundreds of beers from around Maine and the world, sold to diners and to go—attests to Gastropub's gas station past (it even served gas initially). Craft brews, many hard to find, accompany snazzy, farm-to-table takes on American classic and foreign-inspired comfort foods. **Known for:** smash burgers (local grass-fed beef) with house sauce and twice-fried fries; chili mayo–smothered smoked street corn and street corn dip and chips (at least one is always on the menu); Sunday brunch. [$] *Average main: $15* ✉ *233 Main St., Bridgton* ☎ *207/647–4100* 🌐 *www.standardgastropub.com* 🕓 *Closed Tues.*

Hotels

★ Bear Mountain Inn + Barn

$$ | **B&B/INN** | Aside Bear Pond in South Waterford, this 1800s 25-acre homestead inn features country chic decor with plaid accents and handsome baths (some with tub and shower); most accommodations—nine guest rooms and family-friendly suites, plus the snuggly cottage and post-and-beam apartment—have lake views and a fireplace (or wood stove). **Pros:** small beach and docks for swimming, boating, and fishing on Bear Pond, and courtesy canoes, kayaks, standup paddleboards, and row boats to use on the lake-like body of water; hot tub, hammocks, picnic areas, and 1-mile riverside trail; woodsy yet luxurious suite-like Mountain Ash has a fireplace, two-person Jacuzzi tub (plus walk-in shower), wet bar, armchairs, king bed, built-in daybed, and private deck. **Cons:** no shops and restaurants in immediate vicinity; some third-floor rooms but no elevator; typically fully booked on weekends for weddings spring through fall. [$] *Rooms from: $225* ✉ *364 Waterford Rd., Waterford* ☎ *866/450–4253, 207/583–4404* 🌐 *www.bearmtninn.com* 🕓 *Closed mid-Nov.–late Dec. and Apr.* 🛏 *9 rooms, 1 cabin, 1 apartment* 🍴 *Free Breakfast.*

★ Noble House Inn

$$ | **B&B/INN** | Just beyond downtown, state Senator Winburn Staples (1855–1939) built this stately 1903 home above Highland Lake on large grounds that include a pine grove; guests enjoy luxury comforts and a relaxing atmosphere where they can kick back on the wraparound porch, in an Adirondack chair by one of the fire pits, or in the living room or den (both have fireplaces)—perhaps with a drink from the intimate guests-only bar. **Pros:** distinctive suites have king or queen beds and queen sleeper sofas, one has an electric fireplace, and two guest rooms can be joined as a family suite; courtesy canoes and kayaks for Highland Lake; enjoy a massage (fee, by appointment) in your room or the inn's massage suite. **Cons:** limited lake views; during the warm season, some weekends are fully booked for weddings; third-floor suite but no elevator. [$] *Rooms from: $225* ✉ *81 Highland Rd., Bridgton* ☎ *207/647–3733* 🌐 *www.noblehouseinn.com* 🛏 *8 rooms* 🍴 *Free Breakfast.*

Activities

SKIING

Pleasant Mountain

SKIING & SNOWBOARDING | **FAMILY** | Just a few miles from Bridgton, Pleasant Mountain (formerly Shawnee Peak) appeals to families and those who enjoy nighttime skiing—nearly half the trails are lighted except most Sundays. The ski area got its original name back in 2022 after its sale to Boyne Resorts, owner of Maine's largest ski resorts, Sugarloaf and Sunday River. Opened in the 1930s and Maine's first ski area to add a lift, Pleasant Mountain's three terrain parks and glade areas offer alternatives to downhill runs. A great room looks up at the slopes in the main base lodge, which has a cafeteria and a pub restaurant with an expansive deck; the smaller East Lodge anchors some of the more challenging terrain and has an eatery. Summer visitors can hike and pick blueberries. For a rustic stay, the ski area offers a slope-side mountaintop yurt (sleeps four) and cabin (sleeps six) year-round via Airbnb; guests hike up or, in winter, can opt for the chairlift. **Facilities:** 42 trails; 239 acres; 1,300-foot vertical drop; 6 lifts. ✉ *119 Mountain Rd., off U.S. 302, Bridgton* ☎ *207/647–8444* 🌐 *www.pleasantmountain.com* 🎟 *Lift ticket: $89.*

🛍 Shopping

Whether you are a browser or a shopper, downtown Bridgton beckons. Main Street often looks and feels like a Norman Rockwell painting, and it's here that you'll find mostly year-round shops selling books, antiques, gifts, art, handcrafts, chocolates, souvenirs, T-shirts, and clothing, anchored by a branch of Renys (⊕ www.renys.com), the state's friendly, spic-and-span outlet department store chain, aka "A Maine Adventure."

Firefly Boutique

WOMEN'S CLOTHING | Picture windows line the walls of this welcoming corner boutique that sells unique women's attire from the "USA and beyond" including cashmere and cashmere-feel print shawls, leggings in fun prints, and lively dresses for evenings out as well as running about. In business since 2009, Firefly is also known for jewelry: more than 30 of its jewelry and clothing lines are American-made. Several of the former are by Maine artisans. ⊠ *103 Main St., Bridgton* ☎ *207/647–3672* ⊕ *www. fireflyshopmaine.com.*

Gallery 302

ART GALLERIES | Creative shop windows showcase an individual artist on a rotating biweekly basis, inviting passersby into Bridgton Art Guild's wide-open tin-ceilinged gallery in a former hardware store. Eclectic and fun—definitely not stuffy—the gallery opened in 2003 and represents more than 40 local and regional artists working in various media. Artists' displays have their bio and photograph. Don't miss the back-corner gift shop with cards, small prints, and the like. Along with hosting wine and cheese receptions and community events, the guild holds classes and workshops— many for a day or half day, so consider signing up. ⊠ *112 Main St., Bridgton* ☎ *207/647–2787* ⊕ *www.gallery302. com.*

Bethel

27 miles north of Bridgton, 66 miles south of Rangeley.

Bethel is pure New England: a town with white clapboard houses, a large green, white-steeple churches, and a mountain vista at the end of every street. Gould Academy, a college prep school founded in 1836, anchors the east side of downtown. On Main Street, the world class Maine Mineral & Gem Museum honors the region's storied mining history—and has a moon rock collection that rocks. In winter, Bethel is ski country. Sunday River, one of Maine's big ski resorts, is only a few miles north in Newry, while family-friendly Mt. Abram is east of town. On the third weekend in July, Bethel Area Summerfest includes a parade, fireworks, and live music. Whatever the season, folks hit Bethel Village Trails on the edge of the village, and the 978-acre Bethel Community Forest a few miles from the town center. Under the tutelage of nonprofit Inland Woods + Trails (⊕ www. woodsandtrails.org), the locales welcome hikers, mountain bikers, fat-tire cyclists, snowshoers, and cross-country skiers.

GETTING HERE AND AROUND

From the south, both Routes 35 and 5 lead to Bethel, overlapping several miles south of town. Route 5 from Bethel to Fryeburg is especially pretty come fall, with long stretches of overhanging trees and glimpses of Kezar Lake as the road passes through tiny Center Lovell. If you're coming to Bethel from the west on U.S. 2, you'll pass White Mountain National Forest.

VACATION RENTALS

CONTACTS Four Seasons Realty & Rentals. ⊠ *303 Mayville Rd., Bethel* ☎ *207/824– 3776* ⊕ *www.fourseasonsrealtymaine. com.*

VISITOR INFORMATION

CONTACTS Bethel Area Chamber of Commerce. ⊠ *8 Station Pl., off Cross St., Bethel* ☏ *207/824–2282, 800/442–5826* ⊕ *www.bethelmaine.com.*

Sights

Artist's Bridge

SCENIC DRIVE | FAMILY | The most painted and photographed of Maine's nine covered bridges can be found on a detour from Newry. Head south on U.S. 2 and then northwest on Sunday River Road (stay to the right at "Y" intersections). Trails flow alongside Sunday River from the pedestrian-only bridge, which is a popular swimming spot. ⊠ *Sunday River Rd., 4 miles northwest of U.S. 2, Newry.*

Grafton Notch State Park

STATE/PROVINCIAL PARK | FAMILY | Grafton Notch Scenic Byway along Route 26 runs through Grafton Notch, a favorite destination for viewing fall foliage that stretches along the Bear River Valley 14 miles north of Bethel. It's an easy walk from roadside parking areas to the distinctive Screw Auger Falls, which drops through a gorge, creating pools; Mother Walker Falls; and Moose Cave. Trailhead parking and the nicely shaded Spruce Meadow picnic area are also right along the road. Table Rock Loop Trail (2.4 miles roundtrip) rewards hikers with views of the mountainous terrain. More challenging is the 7.6-mile round-trip trek along the Appalachian Trail to the viewing platform atop 4,180-foot Old Speck Mountain, one of the state's highest peaks. The Appalachian Trail also traverses the 31,764-acre Mahoosuc Public Land—its two tracts sandwich the park—whose trails offer stunning, if strenuous, backcountry hiking (there are backcountry campsites). In winter, a popular snowmobile trail follows the river through the park. ⊠ *1941 Bear River Rd., Newry* ☏ *207/824–2912 mid-May–mid-Oct. only, 207/624–6080* ⊕ *www.maine.gov/graftonnotch* ⊠ *Nonresidents $4, Maine residents $3.*

★ Maine Mineral & Gem Museum

SCIENCE MUSEUM | FAMILY | Moon rocks, Maine mineralogy, and western Maine's mineral and gem mining legacy converge at this interactive 15,000-square-foot museum—unexpected in a town of Bethel's size. Opened in 2019 and founded by philanthropists, the handsome structure (two Main Street buildings were joined) is surrounded by garden beds with large rocks, some resembling modern sculpture and all placarded with interesting facts about their origins, etc. Inside, 19 exhibits are spread about four galleries on two floors. Kids love the simulated mining blast, part of an exhibit on gem discoveries and mica and feldspar mining in the Bethel area. When the "Space Rocks" gallery darkens, a 3D film beams about, making it look as if a meteorite shower has blown up the walls, revealing Bethel. The windowless space displays more moon meteorites than the world's other natural history museums combined. This museum's collection includes the biggest chunk of Mars on earth, weighing 32 pounds; 6,000 meteorites from the moon, Mars, and the asteroid belt; and nearly 38,000 mineral specimens, some 15,000 of them Maine-mined. A replica of a shuttered Maine mineral store, once a tourist hot spot, showcases prized specimens. In the "Hall of Gems" (and the gift shop!), Maine's famed pink and "watermelon" tourmaline and other gems bedazzle. ⊠ *99 Main St., Bethel* ☏ *207/824–3036* ⊕ *www.minemineralmuseum.org* ⊠ *$15* ⊗ *Closed Tues.*

Museums of the Bethel Historical Society

HISTORY MUSEUM | Across from the Village Common, the society's campus comprises two buildings: the 1821 O'Neil Robinson House and the 1813 Dr. Moses Mason House, both on the National Register of Historic Places. The O'Neil Robinson House has well-done exhibits about the region's history and a Maine Ski and Snowmobile Museum display. One parlor room serves as a gift shop with a nice book selection. The Moses Mason House has nine period rooms, and the front hall and stairway are decorated with Rufus Porter School folk art murals. The barn gallery has changing exhibits. In town when the museum is closed? Touch base as it does open by appointment.

■ **TIP→ Head out back to check out the Sunday River snow roller, pulled by a team of horses back in the day, and a giant Mt. Zircon Moon Tide Spring "Ginger Champagne" soda bottle lunch stand, a 1920s promotion for a defunct western Maine spring and soda water company.** ✉ *10 Broad St., Bethel* ☎ *207/824–2908* 🌐 *www.bethelhistorical.org* 🎫 *By donation* 🕒 *O'Neil Robinson closed mid Oct.–late May, Sun. and Mon. July and Aug., and Sat.–Mon. June and Sept.; Moses Mason closed Sept.–June and Sun.–Wed. July and Aug.*

White Mountain National Forest
FOREST | FAMILY | This forest straddles New Hampshire and Maine, with the highest peaks on the New Hampshire side. The Maine section, though smaller, has magnificent rugged terrain. Hikers can enjoy everything from hour-long nature loops to a day hike up Speckled Mountain. The mountain is part of the 14,000-acre Caribou-Speckled Mountain Wilderness Area, one of several in the forest, but the only one entirely contained within Maine. The most popular Maine access to the national forest is via Route 113, which runs south from its terminus at U.S. 2 in Gilead, 10 miles from downtown Bethel. Most of the highway is the Pequawket Trail Maine Scenic Byway, and the section through the forest is spectacular come fall. This stretch is closed in winter but is used by snowmobilers and cross-country skiers. Two of the forest's campgrounds are in Maine; backcountry camping is allowed. ✉ *Rte. 113, off U.S. 2, Gilead* ☎ *603/466–2713* 🌐 *www.fs.usda.gov/whitemountain* 🎫 *From $5 per car.*

🍴 Restaurants

Cho Sun
$$$ | KOREAN | Offering sushi and more, dishes here are deeply rooted in Korea and Maine: the chef's Korean mother owns the restaurant, which she founded in 2002, and spices for the kimchi are grown at the family's local homestead. On summer nights, dining on the wide front porch—lit by torches and candles and right above the sidewalk on Main Street in downtown Bethel—is delightful, but the lively storm-blue dining rooms are also inviting, and perfect for a post-ski meal. **Known for:** dolsot bibimbop (a dish of steamed rice and veggies) served in a hot stone pot with tofu, beef, chicken, shrimp, or calamari to mix in at your table; seasonal satellite restaurant, Cho Sun Sushi and Noodle Bar (has a full bar) at Sunday River ski resort; Sunday karaoke night in the cabin-like bar at the back of the main restaurant. [$] *Average main: $25* ✉ *141 Main St., Bethel* ☎ *207/824–7370* 🌐 *www.chosun207.com* 🕒 *No lunch. Closed Mon. and Tues.*

☕ Coffee and Quick Bites

Good Food Store
$ | AMERICAN | FAMILY | A cheery red door welcomes customers to this hip, cozy grocery, opened in 1994 and selling specialty, organic, and Maine-produced foods and goods, from sodas to local poultry. Friendly staff will help you select from the specials-friendly takeout menu and the great to-go beer and wine selection, or suggest grocery items for a picnic or dinner at your lodging. **Known for:** pumpkin whoopie pies; "heat and eat" meals; outdoor Smokin' Good BBQ. [$] *Average main: $8* ✉ *212 Mayville Rd., Bethel* ☎ *207/824–3754* 🌐 *www.goodfoodbethel.com* 🕒 *Smokin' Good BBQ closed mid-Apr.–mid-May and mid-Oct.–mid-Nov.*

One of the Rangeley Lakes, Mooselookmeguntic is said to mean "portage to the moose feeding place" in the Abenaki language.

Hotels

Holidae House Bed & Breakfast

$ | **B&B/INN** | Welcoming hospitality keeps guests returning year after year to this charming, affordable, light blue downtown B&B, where innkeepers are at the ready with day-trip tips (or to kindly help guests as needed), and eight guest rooms occupy two floors of the antiques-filled home, which was originally built for a lumber executive in 1906. **Pros:** military and first responder discounts and walk-in rates; fresh-baked treats in afternoon; blow-up mattresses available. **Cons:** nice porch and a brick patio out front but otherwise no yard; no mountain views; no king beds. [$] *Rooms from: $160* ✉ *85 Main St., Bethel* ☎ *207/824–3400* 🌐 *www.holidaehouse.com* 🛏 *8 rooms* 🍴 *Free Breakfast.*

Activities

CANOEING AND KAYAKING

Bethel Outdoor Adventure and Campground

CANOEING & ROWING | **FAMILY** | On the Androscoggin River, this outfitter rents canoes, kayaks, tubes, and standup paddleboards, with and without shuttle service, and has a campground. There's also an open-air facility where you can sluice for precious and semiprecious gems and minerals (the Bethel region has a long history of mining for them). All Bethel Outdoor Adventure activities get customers a free trek on the Burma Bridge, which leads to a walking trail on the company's private, wild river island. This outfitter also sells state fishing licenses. ✉ *121 Mayville Rd., Bethel* ☎ *207/824–4224* 🌐 *www.betheloutdoor-adventure.com.*

Inland Maine BETHEL

Whoopie Pies

When a bill aiming to make the whoopie pie Maine's official dessert was debated in state legislature, some lawmakers countered that the blueberry pie (made with Maine wild blueberries, of course) should have the honor. The blueberry pie won out, but what might have erupted into civil war instead ended civilly, with whoopie pies designated the official state "treat." Spend a few days anywhere in Maine and you'll soon know what a sweet, and popular, treat they are.

The name is misleading: it's a "pie" only in the sense of a having a filling between two "crusts"—namely, a thick layer of sugary frosting sandwiched between two saucers of rich cake, usually chocolate. It may have acquired its distinctive moniker from the jubilant "yelp" farmers emitted after discovering it in their lunchboxes. The whoopie pie is said to have Pennsylvania Dutch roots, but many Mainers insist that it originated here. Typically, the filling is made with butter or shortening; some recipes add Marshmallow Fluff. Many bakers have indulged the temptation to experiment with flavors and ingredients, particularly in the filling but also in the cake, offering pumpkin, raspberry, oatmeal cream, red velvet, peanut butter, and more.

DOGSLEDDING

Mahoosuc Guide Service

ADVENTURE TOURS | This acclaimed guide company leads day and multiday dog-sledding trips in the Umbagog National Wildlife Refuge on the Maine–New Hampshire border. The outfitter also offers overnight dogsledding, fly fishing, and canoe excursions inside and outside Maine. One of the multiday canoe trips is an immersion in the ways of the Penobscot Nation, a Maine Native American tribe. Mahoosuc has lodging that's good for groups. ✉ *1513 Bear River Rd., Newry* ☎ *207/824–2073* ⊕ *www.mahoosuc. com* 🎫 *Dogsledding trips from $450 per person.*

SKIING

Carter's Cross-Country Ski Center

SKIING & SNOWBOARDING | FAMILY | Mountain views await at this acclaimed cross-country ski center, which offers 34 miles of trails for all levels of skiers. Skis, snowshoes, and sleds to pull children are all available for rent, as are fat-tire bikes. Both bike and ski lessons are offered.

Carter's also rents three rustic ski-in cabins (available off-season except for April–mid-May) and has a ski shop. ✉ *786 Intervale Rd., Bethel* ☎ *207/824–3880 Bethel location* ⊕ *www.cartersxcski.com* 🎫 *$22.*

Mt. Abram Ski & Ride

SKIING & SNOWBOARDING | FAMILY | Family-friendly and affordable, Mt. Abram is open Thursday–Sunday during ski season. It allows off-trail "boundary-to-boundary" skiing, has two terrain parks, and welcomes uphill snowshoers and skiers ($5 day pass). Westside, the popular lift-served beginner area, has its own base lodge. The main lodge is home to Loose Boots Lounge, which occasionally features live music. Mountain biking is big here during the warm months: Mt. Abram offers rentals and lessons and trails are lift-served. **Facilities:** 44 trails; 650 acres; 1,150-foot vertical drop; 5 lifts. ✉ *308 Howe Hill Rd., off Rte. 26, Greenwood* ☎ *207/875–5000* ⊕ *www. mtabram.com* 🎫 *Lift ticket: $35.*

★ **Sunday River**

SKIING & SNOWBOARDING | FAMILY | Once-sleepy Sunday River has evolved into a sprawling resort that attracts skiers from around the world. Stretching for 3 miles, it encompasses eight trail-connected peaks and six terrain parks. Off-trail "boundary-to-boundary" skiing is allowed, and there's night skiing (well, "twilight" as it's from 3–6:30) on select Fridays and Saturdays and some holidays. Fireworks light the skies at the main South Ridge base lodge, one of three at the resort, for some holidays and special events. Sunday River has several lodging choices, including condos and two slope-side hotels: the family-friendly Grand Summit, at one of the mountain bases, and the more upscale Jordan Grand, near a summit at the resort's western end. (It's really up there, several miles by vehicle from the base areas, but during ski season a shuttle serves the resort, or you can ski over for lunch.)

■ TIP→ **At both slope-side hotels, the outdoor heated pool and hot tub are open year-round.**

From the less costly Snow Cap Inn, it's a short walk to the slopes. Come summer, the resort offers archery, kayaking, and standup paddleboarding lessons and guided kayak tours, and at the main South Ridge Base Lodge, chairlift rides to North Peak. Many visitors opt to hike down, or hit a trail up top, before riding down. Perhaps take in a chairlift ride after a game of golf: Sunday River Golf Club is acclaimed for its wide-open mountain and valley views and challenging elevation changes.

■ TIP→ **Don't golf? Grab a drink or a bite at the clubhouse and hit those views—there's a building-length deck and a soaring Palladian window framed by polished wood walls.**

Facilities: 139 trails; 884 acres; 2,340-foot vertical drop; 19 lifts. ✉ *15 S. Ridge Rd.* ☎ *207/824–3000, 207/824–5200 for* snow conditions, *800/543–2754 for reservations* ⊕ *www.sundayriver.com* ✉ *Lift ticket: $122.*

Rangeley

66 miles north of Bethel.

With 100-plus lakes and ponds linked by rivers and streams, the vastly forested Rangeley region has a rough, wilderness feel and has long attracted winter-sports enthusiasts, hikers, and anglers—it's been hailed for centuries as a "fly-fishing mecca." The four-season resort town of Rangeley stretches along the north side of its namesake lake. Right behind Main Street, Lakeside Park ("Town Park" to locals) has a large swimming area, a playground, picnic shelters, and a boat launch. Come winter, Saddleback Mountain ski resort lures downhill skiers, many of them families. Other winter activities in these parts include cross-country skiing, snowshoeing, fat-tire biking, snowmobiling, and pond skating. In late January, the Rangeley Snowmobile Snodeo offers thrilling snowmobile acrobatics, fireworks, a parade, and a cook-off for which area restaurants enter their chilies and chowders. Seven miles west on Route 4, tucked at the east end of Rangeley Lake near Mooselookmeguntic Lake, tiny Oquossoc is another hub for outdoor activities and dining. At the main crossroads, the Outdoor Heritage Museum beckons visitors; nearby Bald Mountain is a family-friendly day hike. South of the hamlet on Route 17 is the western gateway to the region, Height of Land—a must-see overlook with distant views stretching to mountains on the New Hampshire border.

GETTING HERE AND AROUND

To reach Rangeley on a scenic drive through Western Maine, take Route 17 north from U.S. 2 in Mexico past Height of Land to Route 4 in Oquossoc, then head east into town. Much of the drive is the Rangeley Lakes National Scenic Byway. From Rangeley, Route 16 continues east to Sugarloaf ski resort and Kingfield.

VACATION RENTALS

CONTACTS Morton & Furbish Vacation Rentals. ⊠ *2478 Main St., Rangeley* ☎ *888/218–4882* ⊕ *www.rangeleyrentals. com.*

VISITOR INFORMATION

CONTACTS Rangeley Lakes Chamber of Commerce. ⊠ *6 Park Rd., Rangeley* ☎ *207/864–5571* ⊕ *www.rangeleymaine. com.*

Sights

★ Height of Land

SCENIC DRIVE | FAMILY | Height of Land is the highlight of Rangeley Lakes National Scenic Byway, with unforgettable views of mountains and lakes. One of Maine's best overlooks, it hugs Route 17 atop Spruce Mountain several miles south of Rangeley's Oquossoc village. On a clear day, you can look west to mountains on the New Hampshire border. There's off-road parking, interpretive panels, stone seating, and a short path to the Appalachian Trail. Rangeley Lake unfolds at a nearby overlook on the opposite side of the road. ⊠ *Rte. 17, Rangeley.*

★ Moose Alley

OTHER ATTRACTION | FAMILY | Bowling is just one reason families, couples, locals, and visitors head here for a night out, or indoor fun on a rainy—or sunny!—day. There's arcade games, billiards, foosball, cornhole, shuffleboard, darts, air hockey, and dancing and live music (check the website for details), plus ten bowling lanes. Moose Alley's Spirit Bar Grill & Cafe serves breakfast, lunch, and dinner. Folks also stop here for ice cream or baked goods, espresso or bubble tea, settling in upfront at the soda fountain-style and curvy lounge seating. Images of fish, moose, loons, and Rangeley Lake are smattered on the dance

floor and antler chandeliers provide a mellow glow, but the woodsy decor is modern, stylish, and hip, not overdone. The cool curved bar in the center is faced to resemble river stones, as are pillars inside and out. There's table seating, couches, and around the firepit, roomy armchairs (put your feet on the surround but not your food, as the sign reminds!). Order at the counter: your meal or snack is delivered to your table, bar seat, lane, or game spot. The pub fare is delish (try the chipotle sweet potato fries), and food is served until close. ⊠ *2809 Main St., Rangeley* ☎ *207/864–9955* ⊕ *www. moosealley.me* ⊗ *Closed Wed.*

★ Outdoor Heritage Museum

HISTORY MUSEUM | FAMILY | Spruce railings and siding on the museum's facade replicate a local taxidermy shop from about 1900. Inside, there's an authentic log sporting camp from the same period, when grand hotels and full-service sporting lodges drew well-to-do rusticators to Rangeley for long stays. One of the big draws is the exhibit on local flytier Carrie Stevens, whose famed streamer flies increased the region's fly-fishing fame in the 1920s. The many diverse exhibits include displays on U.S. presidents Dwight D. Eisenhower and Herbert Hoover fishing in Rangeley; vintage watercraft; Native American birch-bark canoes and artifacts; art of the region; and gleaming fish mounts of world-record-size brook trout. With free exhibits out front, this is a popular stop even when closed—don't miss the 12,000-year-old Native American meat cache. ⊠ *8 Rumford Rd., Oquossoc* ☎ *207/864–3091* ⊕ *www.outdoorheritagemuseum.org* ⊠ *$8* ⊗ *Closed Nov.–Apr., closed Mon. May–Oct. and also Tues. May, June, Sept., and Oct.*

Rangeley Lake State Park

STATE/PROVINCIAL PARK | FAMILY | On the south shore of Rangeley Lake, this 869-acre park has superb lakeside scenery, swimming, picnic tables, a playground, a boat ramp, a few short trails, and a campground. In the off-season, visitors can park outside the gate and walk-in. ✉ *1 State Park Rd., Rangeley* ✣ *Turn on S. Shore Rd. from Rte. 17 or Rte. 4* ☎ *207/864–3858 May–mid-Oct. only, 207/624–6080 regional state parks office (off-season contact)* 🌐 *www.maine.gov/rangeleylake* 🎟 *Nonresident $6, Maine resident $4* 🕓 *Closed Oct.–Apr.*

Wilhelm Reich Museum

SCIENCE MUSEUM | **FAMILY** | The museum showcases the life and work of Austrian physician, scientist, and writer Wilhelm Reich (1897–1957), who believed that all living matter and the atmosphere contain a force called orgone energy. The hilltop Orgone Energy Observatory exhibits biographical materials, inventions, and equipment used in his experiments, whose results were disputed by the Food and Drug Administration and other government agencies. Stone faces the exterior of the boxy 1949 structure, which is listed on the National Register of Historic Places. A mid-century gem inside and out, Reich's second-floor study, library, and laboratory look as they did in his day, with original sleek modern furniture. The observatory deck has magnificent countryside views. In July and August, the museum presents engaging nature programs; trails lace the largely forested 175-acre property, known as Orgonon, which has a waterside vacation rental cottage. Reich's tomb sits next to one of his inventions, a cloud accumulator. ✉ *19 Orgonon Cir., off Rte. 4, Rangeley* ☎ *207/864–3443* 🌐 *wilhelmreichmuseum.org* 🎟 *Museum $10, grounds free* 🕓 *Museum closed Oct.–June, Sun.–Tues. in July and Aug. and Sun.–Fri. in Sept. Private tours May–Oct. by appt.*

🍴 Restaurants

Loon Lodge

$$$ | **AMERICAN** | Built as a summer home, this rustically elegant 1909 log lodge alongside Rangeley Lake on Rangeley village's outskirts has been a restaurant and inn for much of its life; lovely lake views float beyond midcentury picture windows in dining spaces that were part of a porch. Locally sourced seasonal fine dining thrives with updated classics such as Moroccan-spiced rack of lamb with English mint and Indian curry spices, ginger-crusted tuna with Asian slaw, and desserts like skillet du jour. **Known for:** six original guestrooms with gleaming wood walls on the second floor, two modern ones on the lower level, and four in a separate building; the restaurant menu is available at Pickford Pub, where folks grab a drink while waiting for a table in the dining rooms, often heading down to the lakefront lawn or the dock below that; specials are big on less pricey comfort foods, as is the winter menu. [$] *Average main: $35* ✉ *16 Pickford Rd., Rangeley* ☎ *207/864–5666* 🌐 *www.loonlodgeme.com* 🕓 *No lunch. Closed late Oct.–late Nov. and Mon. late Nov.–late Oct., also Tues. early April–mid-May (inn open year-round).*

☕ Coffee and Quick Bites

Pine Tree Frosty

$ | **FAST FOOD** | **FAMILY** | A summertime visit to Rangeley isn't complete without a stop at this cash-only snack bar—in business since 1964—for ice cream and simple meals like burgers and fries. Both hard and soft ice cream are served, as are sundaes, milk shakes, flurries, and banana splits. **Known for:** Maine-made Gifford's hard ice cream; lobster rolls; waterside Adirondack chairs and picnic tables. [$] *Average main: $7* ✉ *2459 Main St., Rangeley* 🌐 *facebook.com/pinetreefrosty* 💳 *No credit cards* 🕓 *Closed early Sept.–late May.*

Hotels

The Rangeley Inn

$ | HOTEL | FAMILY | Painted eggshell blue, this historic downtown hotel was built around 1900 for wealthy urbanites on vacation—from the wide covered front porch, you step into a grand lobby with polished pine wainscoting, statement oversized cushioned red chairs, and a brick fireplace. **Pros:** warms the dinner-only tavern in winter, and the elegant original dining room is a breakfast-only restaurant; on Hayley Pond, paddle a courtesy canoe or kayak or take a guided kayak photography trip (fee); nice variety of suites (largest sleeps six). **Cons:** no elevator; not on Rangeley Lake; a couple minutes walk from lodge to main inn. [$] *Rooms from: $195* ✉ *2443 Main St., Rangeley* ☎ *207/864–3341* 🌐 *www.therangeleyinn.com* 🕓 *Closed mid-Nov.–early Dec. and mid-April–mid-May* 🛏 *42 rooms* 🍴 *No Meals.*

Activities

Rangeley and Mooselookmeguntic lakes are good for canoeing, kayaking, sailing, fishing, and motorboating. For paddlers, options abound whether you're a novice or an expert. Lake fishing for landlocked salmon and the region's famed brook trout is at its best in May, June, and September. The area's rivers and streams are especially popular with fly-fishers, who enjoy the sport May–October. Ice fishing shacks dot Rangeley Lake come winter.

Saddleback Mountain ski resort and Rangeley Lakes Trails Center offer mountain biking; trails are groomed in winter for fat-tire biking as well as cross-country skiing and snowshoeing.

GOLF

Mingo Springs Golf Course

GOLF | FAMILY | This popular course is known for its mountain and water views. The course is short but challenging, with very angled drives. The front nine holes are the hilliest; the back nine holes the longest. You can also take in the views and spot wildlife on the Mingo Springs Trail & Bird Walk, an easy 3-mile loop trail through the woods along the course. ✉ *43 Country Club Rd., Rangeley* ☎ *207/864–5021* 🌐 *www.mingosprings.com* 🎟 *$23 for 9 holes, $34 for 18 holes* 🏌 *18 holes, 6024 yards, par 71.*

HIKING

Hiking options in the Rangeley Lakes region include 39 miles of trails and access roads on Rangeley Lakes Heritage Trust's 16,250 acres of conserved lands, which also welcome many other types of outdoor recreation. Trail maps and information are available at the organization's website (🌐 www.rlht.org) and its downtown Rangeley office (✉ 2424 Main Street).

MULTISPORT OUTFITTERS

Ecopelagicon Rangeley Adventure Co.

KAYAKING | FAMILY | Off Main Street on Hayley Pond, this outfitter and retailer has an easy, affordable way to get you on the water: rent a kayak, canoe, standup paddleboard, or paddle boat by the hour ($10–$18) and head out back to the pond. Or rent one (paddle boats excepted) for a half-, full-, or multiday trip and paddle where you please; shuttle service is offered to locales on the Northern Forest Canoe Trail and the Appalachian Trail. Come winter you can rent snowshoes ($15 adults, $10 kids). In business since 1993, this welcoming "nature store" sells outdoor recreation gear galore, books and guides, and a slew of gifts, many Maine-themed. Shoppers linger at the back window to gaze at Saddleback Mountain and ducks and loons on the pond. ✉ *7 Pond St., Rangeley* ☎ *207/864–2771* 🌐 *www.rangeleyadventureco.com.*

★ River's Edge Sports

BOATING | FAMILY | Hugging Route 4 in Oquossoc and resembling a sporting lodge, this is a convenient stop for gear galore and great way to get out on the water. Rent a kayak, canoe, or standup paddleboard for the day or week. If you'd like you can put in at the dock out back on Rangeley Lake, near the outflow into Rangeley River. This outfitter will also deliver, and pick up, your rental craft (fee). River's Edge sells Maine fishing licenses, and owner Gerry White, a Registered Maine Guide, leads fishing trips on Rangeley and Mooselookmeguntic lakes. Other guided trips are offered, too. Along with camping, fishing, hunting, and hiking gear, the 8,000-some-item store stocks souvenirs, apparel—from jackets to Rangeley and Oqussoc hoodies and tees—and gifts, many Maine-made. Don't miss the bins of colorful flies for fishing and the mounted wildlife: the "indoor zoo" has salmon, bobcats, bears, moose, and more. River's Edge's website has detailed information to help you enjoy the great outdoors in Rangeley. Gerry and his wife, Sally, happily share tips in person, too. ⊠ *38 Carry Rd. (Rte. 4), Rangeley* ☏ *207/864–5582* ⊕ *www. riversedgesports.com* ⊠ *Rentals from $30.*

SEAPLANES

★ Acadian Seaplanes

AIR EXCURSIONS | In addition to 15-, 30- and 75-minute scenic flights high above the mountains by seaplane, this operator offers enticing "fly-in" excursions: travel by seaplane to wilderness locales to dine at a sporting camp or go white-water rafting on the remote Rapid River. The 1¼-hour "Mountain Explorer" scenic flight splash lands on a remote pond. Yes, seaplane passengers spot moose from the air. Acadian also provides charter service, including between the Rangeley area and Boston, New York, Portland, Bangor, and other places in Maine. ⊠ *2640 Main St., Rangeley* ☏ *207/864– 5307* ⊕ *www.acadianseaplanes.com* ⊠ *From $99.*

SKIING

Rangeley Lakes Trails Center

LOCAL SPORTS | FAMILY | A largely wooded, 34-mile trail network stretches along lower Saddleback Mountain and leads to Saddleback Lake. In winter, trails are groomed (double- and single-track) for cross-country skiing, back country skiing, snowshoeing, and fat-tire biking. A yurt lodge has ski, snowshoe, and fat-tire rentals and a snack bar known for tasty soups. Call ahead for ski, snowshoe, and fat-tire tours and cross-country lessons. In warmer weather, the trails are popular with mountain bikers, hikers, and runners. ⊠ *524 Saddleback Mountain Rd., Dallas* ☏ *207/864–4309 winter only* ⊕ *www.rangeleylakestrailscenter.org* ⊠ *From $12.*

Saddleback Mountain

SKIING & SNOWBOARDING | FAMILY | Maine's third largest ski area has a high-speed quad lift, and the beginner ski area is one of New England's best, partly because it is below the base lodge. At the other end of the spectrum, it's black diamonds only all the way down at Kennebago Steeps!, touted as the East's largest steep-skiing area. Saddleback also has extensive glade areas, two terrain parks, and lots of natural snow. A fieldstone fireplace keeps things warm in the post-and-beam base lodge, which has a cafe and an upper-level pub (open most of the year) where diners savor mountain views with a hand-tossed pizza or smash burger. Or grab a bite between runs in the mid-mountain lodge (to open in early 2023). On-mountain lodging choices include ski-in, ski-out homes and trailside condos. Come summer the resort offers hiking and mountain biking, including rentals (lift-served mountain biking is to start in 2023), and guided kayak, canoe, standup paddleboard, and birding trips. **Facilities:** 68 trails; 600 acres; 2,000-foot vertical drop; 6 lifts. ⊠ *976 Saddleback Mountain Rd., Dallas* ☏ *207/864–5671, 866/918–2225* ⊕ *www.saddlebackmaine. com.*

SNOWMOBILING

More than 100 miles of maintained trails link lakes and towns to wilderness camps in the Rangeley area.

Rangeley Snowmobile Rentals

SNOW SPORTS | Rangeley is one of Maine's top snowmobiling destinations, but you don't need to bring a sled: you can rent one here (one seat or two) for two hours, half a day, or a full day. ☒ *11 Swains Rd., Rangeley* ☎ *207/491–6625* ⊕ *www. rangeleysnowmobiles.com.*

Kingfield

38 miles east of Rangeley.

Dotted with white clapboard churches, and in the shadows of Mt. Abraham ("Mt. Abram" to locals) and Sugarloaf Mountain, home to the eponymous ski resort, Kingfield is "real" New England. The pretty Carrabassett River slices the village and flows over a dam downtown, creating a great swimming spot below the Route 16 bridge. Small pullouts mark swimming holes along Route 27 as it flows north along the rock-strewn river through Carrabassett Valley (also the name of the neighboring town) to the resort. On the other side of the water-way, the 6.6.-mile Narrow Gauge Path-way rail-trail wends through the narrow, steep-walled valley. The path was first cleared in the late 1800s for a narrow-er-than-standard railway that transported timber and tourists. Today it's part of an extensive and growing mountain biking network and one of many activities along the 47-mile State Route 27 Maine Scenic Byway from Kingfield to the remote Canadian border crossing at Coburn Gorge. Fantastic backcountry recreation awaits in the northern half of the drive around Eustis and Stratton. Near these small recreation hubs, the state's 36,000-acre Bigelow Preserve takes in the entire Bigelow Range and borders 20,000-acre Flagstaff Lake.

GETTING HERE AND AROUND

From Rangeley it's 37 miles to Kingfield, traveling south on Route 4 to Phillips, and from there, north on Route 142. Or head over from Rangeley on Route 16 via Strat-ton, where the road joins State Route 27 Maine Scenic Byway and continues south to Kingfield. This route is just 5 miles longer, and you can link the two for a scenic loop or fall foliage drive.

VISITOR INFORMATION

CONTACTS Franklin County Chamber of Commerce. ☒ *615 Wilton Rd., Farmington* ☎ *207/778–4215* ⊕ *www.franklincounty-maine.org.*

⊙ Sights

Stanley Museum

HISTORY MUSEUM | Original Stanley Steamer cars built by twin brothers Francis and Freelan Stanley—Kingfield's most famous natives—are the main draw at this museum inside a 1903 Geor-gian-style former school. Also well worth the stop here are exhibits about the glass-negative photography business the identical twins sold to Eastman Kodak, and the well-composed photographs, taken by their sister, Chansonetta Stanley Emmons, of everyday country life at the turn of the 20th century. ☒ *40 School St., Kingfield* ☎ *207/265–2729* ⊕ *www. stanleymuseum.org* ⊠ *$8* ⊗ *Closed Jan.–Feb., Sat.–Mon. Mar.–May and Nov. and Dec., and Mon. June–Oct.*

☕ Coffee and Quick Bites

Orange Cat Cafe

$ | AMERICAN | FAMILY | Just past down-town en route to Sugarloaf, this café serves breakfast items (bagels with a choice of spreads, burrito and sandwich with or without meat), flavor-filled lunch fare (wraps, sandwiches, salads), and scrumptious baked goods; local and organic ingredients are kitchen staples, even the salsa is made right here, and the coffee is great. In a landmark

Federal-style former residence known as the "Brick Castle," it's presently drive-through only, but there's colorful seating on the large front lawn. **Known for:** turmeric-flavored coconut Golden Milk; Vegetarian's Revenge wrap with hummus; huge chocolate chip cookies. $ *Average main: $10* ⊠ *329 Main St., Kingfield* ☎ *207/265–2860* ⊕ *www. orangecatcafe.com.*

 ## Activities

BIKING

Carrabassett Valley and environs has emerged as a prime mountain biking destination, with Carrabassett Valley Trails offering a network of 80-plus miles of trails for all abilities. Signed, well-maintained trails link with the 6.6-mile Narrow Gauge Pathway (nonmotorized) aside the Carrabassett River. Several trailheads with kiosks are in the valley along or near Route 27. Come winter, some trails are groomed for cross-country skiing and fat-tire biking. Maps, trail conditions and closures, and suggested loops are available at the Carrabassett Region of the New England Mountain Bike Association website (www.carrabassettnemba. org). Area businesses distribute its large printed maps, and you can rent mountain bikes in-season and get maps and trail advice at a couple of valley spots. Freeman Ridge Bike Park south of Kingfield town center has single-track trails with berms, jumps, etc. (⊕ www.freemanridgebike.com; $12 day pass). North of Carrabassett Valley in the Eustis-Stratton area, mountain biking trails offer a rugged wilderness ride.

Allspeed Cyclery

BIKING | FAMILY | Portland-based Allspeed Cyclery rents mountain bikes from late May through early October at its satellite operation at Sugarloaf's Outdoor Center, where there is a trailhead. Adult rentals are $109 per day, and there are less expensive options for kids; the rate drops if you rent for multiple days. The locale is also a bike repair shop and sells items from tires and tubes to helmets and apparel, but not bikes. ⊠ *3001 Outdoor Center Rd., Carrabassett Valley* ⊹ *Off Route 27* ☎ *207/779–3951* ⊕ *www. allspeed.com.*

Carrabassett Valley Bike

BIKING | A local mountain biking enthusiast runs this rental, repair, and sales outfit from late spring through early fall at Happy Tunes! Ski Service Center, where he works come winter. Rentals are $50 for a full day and $35 half day. ⊠ *1106 Valley Crossing, Carrabassett Valley* ⊹ *Just off Rte. 27 next to Tufulio's Restaurant* ☎ *207/235–6019* ⊕ *www.facebook.com/ CarrabassettValleyBike.*

SKIING
Sugarloaf

SKIING & SNOWBOARDING | FAMILY | An eye-catching setting, abundant natural snow, and the only above-the-tree-line lift-service skiing in the East have made Sugarloaf one of Maine's best-known ski resorts. Glade areas, six terrain parks—including a border-cross track—amp up the skiing options, as do ski bike rentals and ungroomed Sidecountry on Burnt Mountain and Brackett Basin. Snowshoers and uphill skiers (fee, regardless of what's on your feet) can attack this terrain as well as "the Loaf." Cat Skiing is offered on Burnt Mountain: hop a snowcat ride to the top and ski down (fee; slots fill fast). Along with hundreds of slope-side condos and rental homes with ski-in, ski-out access, the resort has two slope-side hotels: Sugarloaf Mountain Hotel is in the ski village, as are shops and restaurants; smaller, more affordable Sugarloaf Inn is a bit down the mountain. Just off Route 27 below the mountain, the Outdoor Center has an NHL-size ice rink; is the gateway to a 56-mile network of groomed trails for cross-country skiing, snowshoeing, and fat-tire biking; and rents equipment for all these activities.

■ **TIP→** After skiing or other winter fun, unwind on-mountain at the **Sports & Fitness**

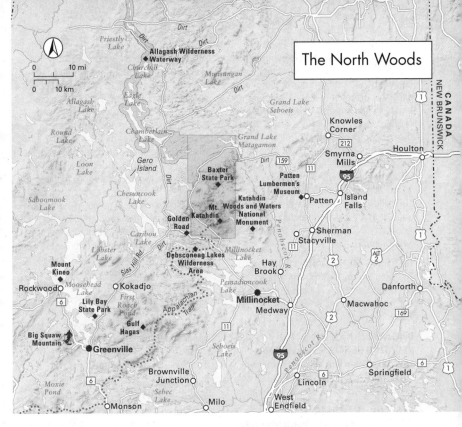

The North Woods

Center (fee), which includes a pool, sauna, hot tubs, steam rooms, and by-appointment massages (fee).

Once at Sugarloaf, you'll find a car unnecessary—a shuttle connects all operations during the season. In summer you can mountain bike, hike, or zipline; take a scenic lift ride or rent a Onewheel, kayak, or standup paddleboard; or play golf, either disc golf or a round on what many consider Maine's best golf course. Designed by Robert Trent Jones Jr., it's known for challenging elevation changes.

Facilities: 162 trails (includes glades); 1,240 acres; 2,820-foot vertical drop; 14 lifts. ⊠ *5092 Sugarloaf Access Rd., Carrabassett Valley* ☎ *207/237–2000, 800/843–5623 for reservations* ⊕ *www. sugarloaf.com* 🎫 *Lift ticket: $129.*

Greenville

155 miles northeast of Portland, 70 miles northwest of Bangor.

Greenville, tucked at the southern end of island-dotted, mostly forest-lined Moosehead Lake, has the best selection of shops, restaurants, and inns in the North Woods region. In the mid-1800s, Henry David Thoreau departed from here on two of his three famous trips into Maine's wilderness, led by Penobscot guides Chief Joseph Attean and Joseph Polis. The region encompassing the lake—at 75,000 acres, Maine's largest and the largest entirely within New England—is an outdoors lover's paradise. In summer, boating, fishing, kayaking, canoeing, and hiking are popular on Moosehead Lake. Come winter, folks head to the Greenville area for ice fishing, snowmobiling, snowshoeing, and cross-country and downhill skiing—you can enjoy both at Big Squaw Mountain ski area northeast of town. Restaurants and lodgings are also clustered 20 miles north of Greenville in Rockwood, where the Moose River flows through the village and—across from Mt. Kineo's majestic cliff face—into the lake. There's also a gaggle in hip hiking hub Monson, 14 miles south of Greenville. Maine's 100 Mile Wilderness, home to the most difficult and most northerly stretch of the Appalachian Trail, stretches from here to Mt. Katahdin.

GETTING HERE AND AROUND

To reach Greenville from Interstate 95, get off at Exit 157 in Newport and head north, successively, on Routes 7, 23, and 15.

VACATION RENTALS

VACATION RENTALS Vacasa (Moosehead Lake Cabin Rentals). ⊠ *Greenville* ☎ *207/695–4300, 855/861–5757* ⊕ *www. vacasa.com/usa/Moosehead-Lake.*

VISITOR INFORMATION

CONTACTS Destination Moosehead Lake. ⊠ *480 Moosehead Lake Rd., Greenville* ☎ *207/695–2702* ⊕ *www.destination-moosehead lake.com.*

◉ Sights

The busy Moosehead Historical Society has several museums in Greenville. Two are in a former church in the small downtown and several more are about a mile east of there at the society's campus in the town's Greenville Junction section.

★ Moosehead Cultural Heritage Center and Moosehead Lake Aviation Museum

HISTORY MUSEUM | FAMILY | At East Cove in downtown Greenville, a former church houses two of five Moosehead Historical Society museums. The center exhibits Native American artifacts and items from the Moosehead Lake region dating from 9,000 BC. Displays about Native

American residents spotlight Henry Perley, a guide and author who gained fame as a performer in Wild West shows and movies. Changing exhibits explore local history and culture. The adjoining aviation museum reveals the impact of aviation—from early bush pilots to Greenville's annual International Seaplane Fly-In the weekend after Labor Day—in this remote region. One room focuses on the Air Force B-52 crash here in 1963 that killed seven of nine crew members (you can get information on hiking to the debris-littered crash site, now a memorial). Outside, sculptures honor Henry David Thoreau and his Penobscot guides, Chief Joseph Attean and Joseph Polis, who departed with him from Greenville for Maine's wilds. ⊠ *6 Lakeview St., Greenville* ☎ *207/695–2909 Moosehead Historical Society office* ⊕ *www.moose-headhistory.org* ☞ *$3 (includes both museums)* ۞ *Closed mid-Oct.–late June and Sun.–Wed. late June–mid-Oct.*

Gulf Hagas

NATURE SIGHT | Called the "Grand Canyon of the East" and part of the Appalachian Trail Corridor, this National Natural Landmark has chasms, cliffs, four major waterfalls, pools, exotic flora, and intriguing rock formations. The West Branch of the Pleasant River flows through the 3-mile, slate-walled gorge east of Greenville in a remote, privately owned commercial forest, KI Jo-Mary, which allows access via gravel logging roads (always yield to trucks). A fee (cash or check only) is charged from late spring to late fall at forest checkpoints, where you can get trail maps and hiking information.

From either parking area you can hike to one of the showcase falls and mostly avoid the difficult rim trail. A good choice for families with young children: start at Head of Gulf parking area for a 3½-mile round-trip hike to Stair Falls on the gorge's western end. From the Gulf Hagas parking area, it's a 3-mile round-trip hike to spectacular Screw Auger Falls on the gulf's eastern end. Gulf hikers who start from this parking area must ford the Pleasant River—usually easily done in summer, but dangerous in high water—and pass through the Hermitage, a stand of old pines and hemlock. A loop route that follows the rim and the less difficult Pleasant River Tote Trail is an 8- to 9-mile trek; there are shorter loops as well. Slippery rocks and rugged terrain make for challenging progress along the rim trail. ✉ Greenville ✛ From Greenville, travel 11 miles east via Pleasant St., which becomes Katahdin Iron Works Rd., to Hedgehog checkpoint. Follow signs to parking areas: Head of Gulf, 2½ miles; Gulf Hagas, 6½ miles ⊕ www.north-mainewoods.org.

Lily Bay State Park

STATE/PROVINCIAL PARK | FAMILY | Nine miles northeast of Greenville on Moose-head Lake, this 925-acre park has good lakefront swimming, a 2-mile walking trail with water views, two boat-launch-ing ramps, a playground, and two campgrounds with a total of 90 sites. In winter, the entrance road is plowed to access the groomed cross-country ski trails and the lake for ice fishing and snowmobiling. ✉ 13 Myrle's Way, Green-ville ✛ Turn onto State Park Rd. from Lily Bay Rd. ☎ 207/695–2700 ⊕ www.maine.gov/lilybay ✉ Nonresident $6, Maine resident $4.

★ Moosehead Historical Society Museums

HISTORY MUSEUM | FAMILY | Anchoring the society's campus in Greenville Junction is the Eveleth-Crafts-Sheridan Histori-cal House, a large 1890s home that's changed little since the last resident of a prominent Greenville family lived here. Each year there's a new changing exhibit within the period rooms. The original kitchen, state of the art back in the day, is a highlight of the guided tours; cooks will also savor the museum's collection of old utensils and kitchen items in a basement gallery. You can even check out the attic. In the home's carriage

house the Moosehead Lumbermen's Museum has exhibits about the region's logging history. A highlight here is a 30-foot bateau used on log drives until the 1960s. Upstairs next to the society's office, a display about hotels on Mt. Kineo, where wealthy Americans flocked to vacation in the rusticator era, is a visitor favorite. In the barn, the Moose-head Outdoor Heritage Museum's covers subjects like Maine Warden Service flight rescues and wildlife—there are bobcat, moose, and caribou mounts. Outside is a sunken garden. ✉ 444 Pritham Ave., Greenville Junction ☎ 207/695–2909 ⊕ www.mooseheadhistory.org ✉ $7.50 (includes guided tours of all three museums) ⊘ Closed mid-Oct.–late June and Sat.–Tues. late June–mid-Oct. (Lumbermen's Museum open year-round Tues.-Fri., $3 off-season).

Mount Kineo

MOUNTAIN | FAMILY | Accessible primar-ily by steamship, Kineo House was a thriving upscale summer resort that sits below its namesake's 700-foot cliff on an islandlike, 1,200-acre peninsula jutting into Moosehead Lake. The last of three successive hotels with this name was built in 1884 and became America's largest inland waterfront hotel. It was torn down in 1938, but Kineo remains an outstanding day trip. Trails to the summit of the spectacular landmark, now part of Mount Kineo State Park, lead to a fire tower that rewards with a 360-degree sweep of Maine's largest lake and rugged mountains. Hikers scramble on the challenging Indian Trail, but it also has amazing views. All hikes begin on the Carriage Trail, a flat, shore-hugging remnant of the halcyon hotel days. You can play a round on the 9-hole Mount Kineo Golf Course, one of New Eng-land's oldest. There is no road access, but you can take a 15-minute boat trip to Mount Kineo from Rockwood on the golf course's seasonal shuttle (fee). Historic summer "cottages" line the greens near the small clubhouse, which has a snack bar and welcomes hikers. ✉ *Kineo Dock, Village Rd., Rockwood* ☎ *207/534–9012 for golf course and shuttle, 207/941–4014 for park regional office* 🌐 *www.maine.gov/mountkineo* 🎟 *Nonresident $4, Maine resident $3.*

Coffee and Quick Bites

Harris Drug Store and Dairy Bar

$ | AMERICAN | FAMILY | Inside this tidy, well-stocked downtown drug store you can twist on a red stool at the well-kept 1960s-era soda fountain while enjoying a sundae or scoop of ice cream. Hot and cold drinks are also served. **Known for:** soda fountain milk shakes served in traditional glasses; owned by the Harris family since 1896 (not the original locale); soft and hard serve at the seasonal Dairy Bar next door. [$] *Average main: $5* ✉ *10 Pritham Ave., Greenville* ☎ *207/695–2921* 🌐 *facebook.com/harrisdrugstore* 🕒 *Dairy Bar closed mid-Sept.–mid-May.*

Hotels

★ Appalachian Mountain Club Maine Wilderness Lodges

$$$ | RESORT | FAMILY | In Maine's 100-Mile Wilderness, the Appalachian Mountain Club's 100,000-plus acres includes three historic sporting-camp retreats, each with a woodsy main lodge with a fireplace, sitting area with games and books, and long tables where meals (included in rates) are served family-style. **Pros:** courtesy canoes (some on outlying ponds), kayaks, and standup paddleboards (no boards at Little Lyford); Little Lyford and Gorman Chairback are near Gulf Hagas; Medawisla has some self-service cabins (otherwise lodge rates include meals). **Cons:** winter access only by cross-country skiing, snowshoeing, hiking, or snowmobile transport (fee) at Little Lyford and Gorman Chairback, but gear is transported for you; no waterfront cabins at Little Lyford; no courtesy bikes. [$] *Rooms from: $300* ✉ *North Woods outside Greenville, Greenville* ☎ *603/466–2727 reservations* 🌐 *www.outdoors.org/lodging/mainelodges* 🕒 *Gorman Chairback and Medawisla closed early March–late June and mid-Oct.–mid-Jan.; Little Lyford closed early March–mid-May and mid-Oct.–mid-Jan.* 🛏 *Gorman Chairback: 12 cabins, 1 bunkhouse (sleeps 10); Little Lyford: 10 cabins, 1 bunkhouse (sleeps 14); Medawisla, 9 cabins, 2 bunkhouses (each sleeps 16)* 🍴 *All-Inclusive.*

★ Blair Hill Inn & Restaurant

$$$$ | B&B/INN | Beautiful gardens, high stone walls, and a hilltop location with marvelous views over Moosehead Lake distinguish this 1891 country estate, one of New England's top inns, with spacious elegant rooms and baths (many have oversize tubs and showers) and a fine dining restaurant. **Pros:** free concierge plans outdoor excursions; two two-room suites nice for families; amenities range from snacks, hiking guides, and beach towels to a fitness center, hillside hot tub, and flat or bubbly artesian well water. **Cons:** when open, the dinner-only restaurant uses most of the inside common space; not on Moosehead Lake; no elevator to three third-floor guestrooms. [$] *Rooms from: $529* ✉ *351 Lily Bay Rd., Greenville* ☎ *207/695–0224* 🌐 *www.blairhill.com* 🕒 *Closed Nov.–mid-Dec. and Apr.–mid-May* 🛏 *10 rooms* 🍴 *Free Breakfast.*

Activities

BOATING

Capt. Rogers Pontoon Rental

BOATING | Operated by a captain with decades of experience on local waters, the business rents swim ladder-equipped pontoon boats (8–13 passengers) for full-day excursions and overnight trips on 40-mile-long Moosehead Lake. The Rockwood business is on the Moose River just a mile from where it enters the lake across from Mount Kineo, Moosehead's famed landmark. Boat rentals start at $275 per day. You can also rent a tube (with rope for towing) for $35 per day. ✉ *9 Maynard Rd., Rockwood* ✛ *At Moose River Bridge* ☎ *207/233–3820* ⊕ *www. captrogerspontoonrental.com.*

MULTISPORT OUTFITTERS

Northwoods Outfitters

WATER SPORTS | You can rent canoes, kayaks, standup paddleboards, camping and fishing equipment, UTVs and ATVs, comfort and mountain bikes, snowmobiles, snowshoes, cross-country skis, and winter clothing here. Northwoods also guides a host of outdoor trips (some multiday), including open-water and ice fishing, waterfall hikes, photography, snowmobiling, and moose-watching (by land or water); operates a shuttle to remote areas; and offers recreation packages with area lodging establishments. At the base in downtown Greenville, you can pick up sporting goods, souvenirs, and clothing; get trail advice; and kick back in the Hard Drive Café. ✉ *5 Lily Bay Rd., Greenville* ☎ *207/695–3288, 866/223–1380* ⊕ *www.maineoutfitter. com.*

SKIING

Big Squaw Mountain

SKIING & SNOWBOARDING | **FAMILY** | A local nonprofit was formed in 2013 to reopen the lower portion of Big Moose Mountain (the resort uses Moose Mountain's old name) after it closed for a few years, and the ski area now operates Friday through Sunday, on holidays, and during school vacation weeks. The summit chairlift, unused since 2004, and the shuttered hotel loom trailside like something out of a Stephen King novel (he is a Mainer, remember), but the mostly intermediate trails on the lower mountain are plenty high enough to wow skiers with views up and down Moosehead Lake, Maine's largest. On a clear day, Mt. Katahdin, the state's highest peak, accents the mountainous horizon. The terrain, cheap prices, a surface lift for beginners, and the spacious, retro-fun chalet lodge draw families. The resort also has free trails

for cross-country skiing, snowshoeing, and fat-tire biking. **Facilities:** 28 trails; 58 acres; 660-foot vertical drop; 2 lifts. ✉ *447 Ski Resort Rd., Greenville Junction* ☎ *207/695–2400* ⊕ *www.skibigsquaw. com* ⛷ Lift ticket: $40.

TOURS

Currier's Flying Service

AIR EXCURSIONS | You can take sightseeing flights, either a tour or a custom trip, in vintage seaplanes over the Moosehead Lake region from ice-out until mid-October. ✉ *447 Pritham Ave., Greenville Junction* ☎ *207/695–2778* ⊕ *www.curri-ersflyingservice.com* ⛷ From $70.

Katahdin Cruises & Moosehead Marine Museum

BOAT TOURS | The Moosehead Marine Museum runs 2-, 3- and 5-hour afternoon trips on Moosehead Lake aboard the *Katahdin*, a 115-foot 1914 steamship converted to diesel. Cruisers learn about the rich logging and tourism history of Maine's largest lake and environs on the narrated excursions. (The longer one skirts Mt. Kineo's cliffs.) Also called the *Kate,* this ship carried resort guests to Mt. Kineo until 1938; the logging industry then used it until 1975. The boat and the free shoreside museum have displays about the steamships that transported people and cargo on Moosehead Lake for a century starting in the 1830s. ✉ *12 Lily Bay Rd., Greenville* ☎ *207/695–2716* ⊕ *www.katahdincruises.com* ⛷ From $40.

Millinocket

67 miles north of Bangor, 88 miles northwest of Greenville.

Millinocket, a former paper-mill town with a population of about 4,000, is the gateway to "forever wild" Baxter State Park and a jumping-off point for Maine's North Woods. The town is the place to stock up on supplies, fill your gas tank, grab a meal, and nab a motel room (and hit the shower!) before heading into or upon returning from the wilderness. On the east side of Baxter, President Obama created the Katahdin Woods and Waters National Monument in 2016. Numerous rafting and canoeing outfitters and guides are based in the region. Katahdin Woods & Waters Scenic Byway, much of which flows along Route 11, links the region's conserved lands and scattered towns.

GETTING HERE AND AROUND

From Interstate 95, take Route 157 (Exit 244) west to Millinocket. From here follow signs to Baxter State Park (Millinocket Lake Road becomes Baxter Park State Road), 18 miles from town.

VISITOR INFORMATION

CONTACTS Katahdin Chamber of Commerce. ✉ *1029 Central St., Millinocket* ☎ *207/723–4443* ⊕ *www.katahdinmaine. com.*

⊙ Sights

Allagash Wilderness Waterway

BODY OF WATER | A spectacular 92-mile corridor of lakes, ponds, streams, and rivers, the waterway park cuts through vast commercial forests, beginning near the northwestern corner of Baxter State Park and running north to the town of Allagash, 10 miles from the Canadian border. From May to mid-October, the Allagash is prime canoeing and camping country. The Maine Bureau of Parks and Lands has campsites along the waterway, most not accessible by vehicle. The complete 92-mile course, part of the 740-mile Northern Forest Canoe Trail, which runs from New York to Maine, requires 7–10 days to canoe. Novices may want to hire a guide, as there are many areas with strong rapids. A good outfitter can help plan your route and provide equipment and transportation. ✉ *Millinocket* ☎ *207/941–4014 for regional parks bureau office* ⊕ *www.maine.gov/ allagash.*

★ **Baxter State Park**
STATE/PROVINCIAL PARK | FAMILY | A gift from Governor Percival Baxter, this is the jewel in the crown of northern Maine: a 210,000-acre wilderness area that surrounds Mt. Katahdin, Maine's highest mountain and the terminus of the Appalachian Trail. Every year, the 5,267-foot Katahdin draws thousands of hikers to make the daylong summit, rewarding them with stunning views of forests, mountains, and lakes. There are three parking-lot trailheads for Katahdin. *If you're not an expert hiker, skip the hair-raising Knife Edge Trail.*

■ TIP→ **Reserve a day-use parking space at the trailheads June 1–October 15.**

The crowds climbing Katahdin can be formidable on clear summer days and fall weekends, so if it's solitude you crave, head for one of the many other park mountains accessible from the extensive trail network, including 11 peaks exceeding an elevation of 3,000 feet. The Brothers and Doubletop Mountain are challenging daylong hikes; the Owl takes about six hours; and South Turner can be climbed in a morning—its summit has a great view across the valley. A trek around Daicey Pond, or from the pond to Big and Little Niagara Falls, are good options for families with young kids. Another option if you only have a couple of hours is renting a canoe at Daicey or Togue Pond (bring cash for this honor system); many of the park's ponds, including some of the most remote ones, have rental canoes. Roads are unpaved, narrow, winding, and not plowed in winter; there are no pay phones, gas stations, or stores; and cell phone service is unreliable. Dogs are not allowed. Camping is primitive and reservations are required; there are 10 campgrounds plus backcountry sites.

■ TIP→ **The park has a visitor center at its southern entrance, but you can get information and make parking and camping reservations at park headquarters in Millinocket**

There are amazing views from the top of the 5,267-foot-tall Mt. Katahdin.

(64 Balsam Drive). ✉ *Baxter State Park Rd.* ✛ *Togue Pond Gate (southern entrance) is 18 miles northwest of Millinocket; follow signs from Rte. 157. Matagamon Gate (northern entrance) is 27 miles west of Patten; follow signs from Rte. 159.* ☎ *207/723–5140* ⊕ *www.baxter-stateparkauthority.com* 🎟 *$16 per vehicle; Maine residents free* ⊘ *Mt. Katahdin trails are closed and park access is limited in Nov. and Apr.–mid-May.*

Debsconeag Lakes Wilderness Area
NATURE PRESERVE | Bordering the south side of the Golden Road below Baxter State Park, the Nature Conservancy's 46,271-acre Debsconeag Lakes Wilderness Area is renowned for its rare ice cave, old forests, abundant pristine ponds, and views of Mt. Katahdin—they are mesmerizing along a challenging 5-mile circuit hike that includes the Rainbow Loop Trail. The access road for the Ice Cave Trail (2 miles round-trip) and Hurd Pond is 17 miles northwest of Millinocket, just west of the Golden Road's Abol Bridge. The kiosk at this

entrance has information about the preserve, including a large map. Nearby the Appalachian Trail exits the conservancy land, crossing the bridge en route to Baxter. Hugging the curving, scenic West Branch of the Penobscot River and revealing Katahdin, the first few miles of the 5-mile dirt access road deserve a drive even if you aren't stopping to recreate. Before hiking, paddling, fishing, or camping in the remote preserve (no fees or reservations required), visit the conservancy's website for directions, maps, and other information. ✉ *Golden Rd., Millinocket* ⊕ *www.nature.org/maine.*

Golden Road
SCENIC DRIVE | Near Baxter State Park, a roughly 20-mile no-fee stretch of this private east–west logging road—named for the huge sum a paper company paid to build it, according to one story—offers access to Maine's wilderness without venturing too far in. Though paved, it's rutty and bumpy; yield (keep right!) to logging trucks. From Millinocket follow signs for Baxter State Park from

Route 157; eight miles from the railroad overpass at the edge of town there's a crossover from Millinocket Lake Road to the Golden Road. This is where the drive begins. North Woods Trading Post is here, across from Ambajejus Lake on the Millinocket Lake Road side of the crossover. Stop not just for gas, coffee, a bite, or to shop but to pick up the free handout highlighting stops along the drive, with mileage—you'll need it, since ponds for moose spotting aren't signed and hiking spots that are can be easy to miss. At the end of the drive, drive or walk across Ripogenus Dam, just off the Golden Road between Ripogenus lake and gorge. Below the dam is the best spot (marked on the handout) for watching white-water rafters.

■ TIP→ Take photos of Baxter's Mt. Katahdin from the footbridge alongside Abol Bridge: this view is famous. ⊠ *Golden Rd., Millinocket.*

Katahdin Woods and Waters National Monument

NATIONAL PARK | Two rivers flow and streams and ponds abound at this 87,500-acre North Woods preserve, created east of Baxter State Park in 2016 and home to moose, bald eagles, salmon, and bobcats. There's no visitor center, but you can get information from late May to mid-October at the staffed welcome center in Patten at the Patten Lumbermen's Museum (61 Shin Pond Road). Access and park roads are gravel; sanitary facilities are limited; and there is no water, food, fuel, or reliable cell service. In the monument's southern portion, 17-mile Katahdin Loop Road has scenic views of Baxter's Mt. Katahdin and trailheads to short hikes and Barnard Mountain, a 4-mile round-trip that links with the International Appalachian Trail. There are mountain biking options as bike-designated routes link with the loop road (biking is allowed on park roads). In the northern section, visitors hike, mountain bike, cross-country ski (some

groomed trails), and snowshoe along and near the waterfall-dotted East Branch of the Penobscot River. Folks paddle and fish on the river and other monument waters. ⊠ *Patten* ✛ *Southern entrance: From Rte. 11 in Stacyville, head west on gravel Swift Brook Rd. (use caution when turning; it's about 12 miles to Katahdin Loop Dr.). Northern entrance: from Pattern turn on Rte. 159 (becomes Grand Lake Rd.); it's about 30 miles to entrance (take 2nd left after crossing the East Branch of the Penobscot River).* ☎ *207/456–6001* ⊕ *www.nps.gov/kaww.*

Patten Lumbermen's Museum

HISTORY MUSEUM | FAMILY | Two reproduction 1800s logging camps are among the 10 buildings filled with exhibits depicting the history of logging in Maine. They include sawmill and towboat models, dioramas of logging scenes, horse-drawn sleds, and a steam-powered log hauler. Exhibits also highlight local artists and history as well as logging-related topics. The museum is a welcome center for nearby Katahdin Woods and Waters National Monument. ⊠ *61 Shin Pond Rd., Patten* ☎ *207/528–2650* ⊕ *www.lumbermensmuseum.org* 🖭 *$12* ⊘ *Closed mid-Oct.–mid-May; Mon.–Thurs. late May–June; and Mon. (except holidays) July–early Oct.*

Penobscot River Trails

TRAIL | FAMILY | A New York philanthropist was so taken with the Mt. Katahdin region he spurred creation of 16 miles of free public recreation trails along the East Branch of the Penobscot River, conveniently off Route 11. Opened in 2019, the "crusher dust" paths are akin to the famed carriage trails at coastal Maine's Acadia National Park. The trails are used for mountain biking and walking and, after the snow flies, groomed for cross-country skiing. Folks also snowshoe and fat-tire bike here in winter. You can chill after a workout or eat your lunch in the woodsy chic visitor center. Come winter, wood stoves heat up two warming huts—one offers an outstanding view of Mt. Katahdin—along the trails. Courtesy (donation requested) bikes, snowshoes, and cross-country skis are available, as are strollers. Paddlers head to the hand-carry boat launch. ✉ *2540 Grindstone Rd., Stacyville* 🌐 *www.penobscotrivertrails.org.*

🍴 Restaurants

River Drivers Restaurant

$$ | **AMERICAN** | **FAMILY** | At the deservedly popular restaurant at the New England Outdoor Center resort—serving lunch and dinner, and breakfast too in winter and summer—wood for the trim, wainscoting, bar, and floors was milled from old logs salvaged from local waters, and diners enjoy views of Mt. Katahdin from beyond rows of windows or the patio. Many dishes feature local ingredients; for dinner, entrees join offerings like sandwiches, tacos, and fish and chips. **Known for:** dining as Katahdin anchors the sunset across Millinocket Lake; crab cake appetizer with remoulade sauce; sister restaurant Knife Edge Brewing has a wood-fired pizzeria. [$] *Average main: $21* ✉ *30 Twin Pines Rd., Millinocket* ✥ *7 miles from the railroad overpass at the edge of Millinocket, en route to Baxter State Park, turn right on Black Cat Road, drive approximately 1 mile, NEOC entrance on left* ☎ *207/723–8475* 🌐 *www.neoc.com.*

☕ Coffee and Quick Bites

North Woods Trading Post

$ | **AMERICAN** | **FAMILY** | Yummy, freshly prepared to-go fare includes pizza, breakfast and regular sandwiches, and house-made baked goods at this cabin-style "last stop" for gear, supplies, and gas before Baxter State Park. Quality Maine-made gifts and souvenirs, Baxter and Mt. Katahdin art and attire, and Maine- and park-theme books are tastefully arrayed; gear basics, packaged wine and beer, and grocery essentials are also sold. **Known for:** provides area information, as do placards at rest area next door; co-owned by a former Baxter ranger; across from Ambajejus Lake at a crossover to the Golden Road. [$] *Average main: $12* ✉ *1605 Baxter State Park Rd., Millinocket* ☎ *207/723–4326* 🌐 *www.northwoodstradingpostme.com* 🕒 *Closed late Oct.–early May.*

🛏 Hotels

Libby Camps

$$$$ | **RESORT** | **FAMILY** | Run by a fifth-generation Libby family member, this sporting camp on Millinocket Lake draws fishing and hunting enthusiasts as well as folks who want to unplug and relax in nature; well-kept log cabins have handmade quilts, wood stoves, gas lamps, modern baths, and coolers with lake-cut ice. **Pros:** courtesy kayaks, canoes, and motorboats and pistols for shooting skeet and sporting clays (lessons and ammunition, fee); fishing, hunting, and paddling guides, fly-casting equipment and lessons, and seaplane trips to remote ponds with stashed canoes and Baxter State Park (fees); dreamy hiking trail from camp edges Millinocket Lake en route to a wooden dam. **Cons:** 20 miles on private gravel roads into camp; 4x4 vehicle recommended if driving to fishing and hiking locales beyond camp; Wi-Fi only in the lodge (though for most guests that's a pro). [$] *Rooms from: $600* ✉ *Millinocket* ✥ *Off Oxbow Rd. (private logging road, fee) on Millinocket Lake (Maine has two) north of Baxter State Park* ☎ *207/435–8274* 🌐 *www.libbycamps.com* 🕒 *Closed late Nov.–mid-Jan. and mid-Mar.–mid-May* 🛏 *9 cabins* 🍴 *All-Inclusive.*

★ **New England Outdoor Center**

$$$ | **RESORT** | **FAMILY** | Just 8 miles from Baxter State Park, Mt. Katahdin rises across Millinocket Lake from this 1,400-acre four-season great outdoors resort, with older renovated log cabins—and a

few newer ones— scattered beneath tall pines on a grassy nub of land jutting into Millinocket Lake. **Pros:** kayaks and canoes to use on the lake; resort trails for cross-country skiing, snowshoeing, mountain and fat-tire biking, and hiking link with nearby trails; two restaurants: River Drivers, with a wonderful Katahdin view, and more casual Knife Edge Brewing. **Cons:** no or limited water views from newer cabins near the cove; no lodge with common space for relaxing; only six smaller cabins (sleep four–six). $ *Rooms from: $300* ✉ *30 Twin Pines Rd., Millinocket* ✛ *7 miles from the railroad overpass at the edge of Millinocket, en route to Baxter State Park, turn right on Black Cat Road, drive approximately 1 mile, NEOC entrance on left* ☎ *800/766–7238, 207/723–5438* ⊕ *www.neoc.com.*

🏃 Activities

MULTISPORT OUTFITTERS
Katahdin Outfitters
BOATING | This company provides trip planning, gear, and shuttles for overnight canoe and kayak expeditions on the Allagash River, the West Branch of the Penobscot River, and the St. John River. ✉ *360 Bates St., Millinocket* ☎ *207/723–5700* ⊕ *www.katahdinoutfitters.com* 🖃 *Call for prices.*

★ New England Outdoor Center *(NEOC)*
ADVENTURE TOURS | FAMILY | A major player in North Woods tourism and conveniently located between Millinocket and Baxter State Park, NEOC offers a full slate of guided excursions: fishing, hiking, canoeing, and kayaking; white-water rafting on the West Branch of the Penobscot River; photography, moose- and wildlife-spotting; and snowmobiling and ice fishing. It also rents canoes, kayaks, standup paddleboards, snowmobiles (attire, too), fat-tire bikes, cross-country skis, and snowshoes and offers cross-country skiing and paddling lessons. The onsite Knife Edge

Brewing (open daily for lunch and dinner and breakfast too in winter and summer), has wood-fired pizzas, salads, and sandwiches, along with house and other craft brews. Nonguests can use showers (fee) after hiking or camping at Baxter. ✉ *30 Twin Pines Rd., Millinocket* ✛ *6.3 miles from railroad overpass at the edge of Millinocket en route to Baxter State Park, turn right on Katahdin View Drive (across from Duck Cove Road) and drive about a mile.* ☎ *207/723–5438, 800/766–7238* ⊕ *www.neoc.com.*

SEAPLANES
Katahdin Air Service
AIR EXCURSIONS | In addition to operating ½- and 1-hour scenic flights over the Katahdin area, this seaplane operator offers fly-in excursions to backcountry locales to picnic at a pond beach, dine at a sporting camp, or moose-watch and bask in nature. Or take a one-way trip to a remote spot to begin a hiking or canoe trip. Katahdin Air also provides charter service, including to and from Maine airports and the region's small towns and remote locales and sporting camps. ✉ *1888 Golden Rd., Millinocket* ☎ *207/723–8378* ⊕ *www.katahdinair.com* 🖃 *From $135.*

WHITE-WATER RAFTING
North Country Rivers
WHITE-WATER RAFTING | North Country Rivers's base for white-water rafting trips on the West Branch of the Penobscot River is at Big Moose Inn, Cabins & Campground, on Millinocket Lake south of Baxter State Park. The businesses team up on lodging packages. (In Western Maine, the outfitter runs white-water rafting trips on the Dead and Kennebec rivers in The Forks and has a resort south of there in Bingham.) ✉ *102A Baxter State Park Rd., Millinocket* ☎ *800/348–8871* ⊕ *www. northcountryrivers.com.*

Chapter 7

THE MAINE COAST

Updated by
Alexandra Hall, Annie Quigley,
Christine Burns Rudalevige,
Mary Ruoff, Mimi Steadman

👁 **Sights**
★★★★☆

🍴 **Restaurants**
★★★★☆

🛏 **Hotels**
★★★★★

🛍 **Shopping**
★★★☆☆

🍸 **Nightlife**
★★★☆☆

WELCOME TO THE MAINE COAST

TOP REASONS TO GO

★ **Lobster and Wild Maine Blueberries:** It's not a Maine vacation unless you don a bib and dig into a steamed lobster with drawn butter, and finish with a wild blueberry pie for dessert.

★ **Boating:** Maine's coastline was made for boaters, so make sure you get out on the water.

★ **Hiking the Bold Coast:** Miles of unspoiled coastal and forest paths Down East make for a hiker's (and a birdwatcher's) dream.

★ **Cadillac Mountain:** Drive a winding 3½ miles to the 1,530-foot summit in Acadia National Park for the sunrise.

★ **Dining in Portland:** With more than 250 restaurants and counting, Forest City is a foodie haven with one of the highest per capita restaurant densities in the United States.

1 **Kittery.**

2 **The Yorks and Cape Neddick.**

3 **Ogunquit.**

4 **Wells.**

5 **Kennebunk, Kennebunkport, and Cape Porpoise.**

6 **Biddeford.**

7 **Scarborough, Prout's Neck, and Cape Elizabeth.**

8 **Portland.**

9 **Casco Bay Islands.**

10 **Freeport.**

11 **Brunswick.**

12 **Bath.**

13 **Wiscasset.**

14 **Boothbay.**

15 **Damariscotta.**

16 **Monhegan Island.**

17 **Rockland.**

18 **Rockport.**

19 **Camden.**

20 **Belfast.**

21 **Bucksport.**

22 **Blue Hill.**

23 **Deer Isle.**

24 **Bar Harbor.**

25 **Bass Harbor.**

26 **Schoodic Peninsula.**

27 **Lubec.**

28 **Campobello Island, Canada.**

29 **Eastport.**

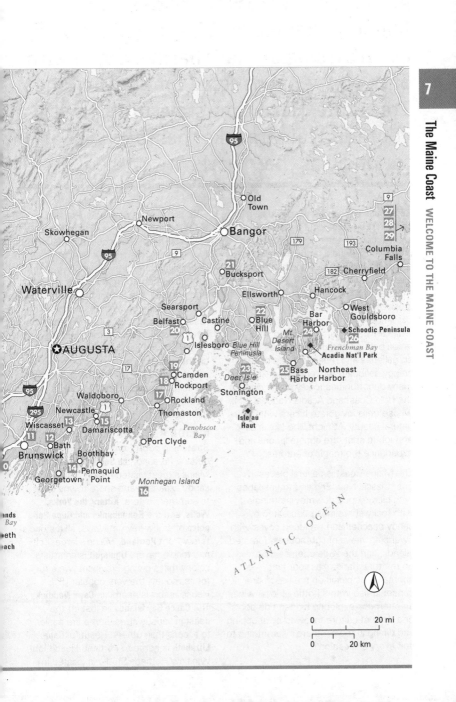

As you drive across the border into Maine, a sign reads, "The way life should be." It's a slogan that's hard to argue with once you've spent some time in the Pine Tree State. Here, time stays in step with you, and Mainers take their play just as seriously as their work.

Romantics thrill at the wind and salt spray in their faces on a historic windjammer. Birders fill their notebooks to the brim with new field notes. Families love the unspoiled beaches and sheltered inlets dotting the shoreline—not to mention the numerous homemade-ice-cream stands. Foodies revel in greater Portland's booming restaurant scene, while artists and art lovers find inspiration both on and off the canvas amid art galleries and museums or along the craggy seaboard. Adventure-seekers find many opportunities to kayak and cycle at the Bold Coast and Acadia National Park, whose trails invigorate hikers with their natural beauty. At night, the sky is dark enough to spot rare constellations and experience the magic of auroras.

The Maine Coast is several places in one. Classic New England townscapes with picturesque downtowns mingle with rocky shorelines punctuated by sandy beaches and secluded coves with sweeping views of lighthouses, forested islands, and the wide-open sea. So, no matter what strikes your fancy—a spontaneous picnic on the beach or a sunset cruise with a bottle of local wine, an afternoon exploring hidden tide pools or a dose of culture followed by shopping and dining in town—there's something to suit every disposition.

Counting all its nooks, crannies, and crags, Maine's coast would stretch thousands of miles if you could pull it straight, which means there's always some new, undiscovered territory awaiting you. Stretching north from Kittery to just outside Portland, the Southern Coast is the most popular area, with many top-notch restaurants, museums, and wineries. Don't let that stop you from heading farther Down East (Maine-speak for "way up the coast"), where you'll be rewarded with the majestic mountains and rugged coastline of Acadia National Park, as well as the unspoiled, dramatic scenery of the Bold Coast.

MAJOR REGIONS

Stretching north from Kittery to just outside Portland, **the Southern Coast** is Maine's most visited region; miles of sandy expanses and shore towns cater to summer visitors. **Kittery, the Yorks, Wells,** and the **Kennebunks and Cape Porpoise** offer low-key getaways, all a stone's throw from **Portland**, Maine's largest city and foodie haven. **Ogunquit** is an artists' colony that's giving Provincetown a run for its money; the very popular Cliff House resort is nearby in **Cape Neddick**. The **Casco Bay Islands** lie just off the coast in various sizes, some are easier to access than others. Beautiful **Cape Elizabeth** is home to Portland Head Light; Winslow Homer's Studio is located in nearby **Scarborough,** which is also home to the tiny hamlet of **Prout's Neck**.

North of Portland, **the Mid-Coast Region** has a craggy coastline that winds its way around pastoral peninsulas. Its villages boast maritime museums, innovative restaurants, antique shops, and beautiful architecture. **Freeport** is home to the headquarters of L.L. Bean and a lovely harbor. **Brunswick**, while a bigger, more commercial city, has rows of historic brick and clapboard homes and is home to Bowdoin College. **Bath** is known for its maritime heritage. On the **Wiscasset** waterfront, you can choose from a variety of seafood shacks competing for the best lobster rolls. **Damariscotta**, too, is worth a stop for its good seafood restaurants, and you'd be hard-pressed to find better-tasting oysters than those from the Damariscotta River. **Boothbay** is one of the Mid-Coast's quaintest towns, and it's where you'll find the Coastal Maine Botanical Gardens. It's also one of three towns from which you can take a ferry to **Monhegan Island**, which seems to be inhabited exclusively by painters at their easels, intent on capturing the windswept cliffs and weathered homes with colorful gardens. **Pemaquid Point** sits at the tip of the Pemaquid Peninsula, while the sleepy town of **Port Clyde** and neighboring **Tenants Harbor** sit on the St. George Peninsula.

Penobscot Bay covers an estimated 1,070 square miles and is home to more than 1,800 islands. Its dramatic natural scenery highlights its picture-perfect coastal towns, which include **Belfast, Rockport,** and **Camden**. **Rockland** gets lots of attention thanks to a trio of attractions: the renowned Farnsworth Art Museum, the popular summer Lobster Festival, and the lively North Atlantic Blues Festival. **Bucksport** has the stunning Penobscot Narrows Bridge and the Fort Knox historic site.

The large **Blue Hill Peninsula** juts south into Penobscot Bay. Painters,

photographers, sculptors, and other artists are drawn to the peninsula; you can find more than 20 galleries on **Deer Isle** and at least half as many on the mainland. Not far from the mainland are the islands of Little Deer Isle and Deer Isle. **Blue Hill** and Castine are the area's primary business hubs. Isle Au Haut is only accessible by mail boat, but worth the effort.

Millions come to enjoy Acadia National Park and the region around it. **Ellsworth** is the gateway town for Mount Desert Island. **Bar Harbor** is fun to explore, with its many gift shops and restaurants, while **Bass Harbor** offers quieter retreats.

The "real Maine," as some call the region known as **Down East,** unfurls in thousands of acres of wild blueberry barrens, congestion-free coastlines, vast wilderness preserves, and a tangible sense of rugged endurance. The landscape of **Schoodic Peninsula's** craggy coastline, towering evergreens, and views over Frenchman Bay are breathtaking year-round. Towns on the peninsula include Grindstone Neck, Winter Harbor, and Gouldsboro; the peninsula's southern tip is home to the Schoodic section of Acadia National Park. **Lubec** is a frequent destination for outdoor enthusiasts; a popular excursion is New Brunswick's **Campobello Island**, which has the Roosevelt Campobello International Park. **Eastport** is connected to the mainland by a granite causeway; it was once one of the nation's busiest seaports.

Planning

You could easily spend a lifetime's worth of vacations along the Maine Coast and never truly see it all. But if you are determined to travel the coast end-to-end, allot at least two weeks at a comfortable pace. Count on longer transit time getting from place to place in summer, as traffic along U.S. 1 can be agonizing in high season, especially in the areas around Wiscasset and Acadia National Park.

Getting Here and Around

AIR

Maine has two international airports, Portland International Jetport and Bangor International Airport, near the coast. Manchester–Boston Regional Airport in New Hampshire is about 45 minutes away from the southern end of the Maine coastline. Boston's Logan Airport is the only major international airport in the region; it's about 90 minutes south of the Maine's border with New Hampshire.

BUS

The seasonal Shoreline Explorer trolleys link southern Maine's beach towns from the Yorks to the Kennebunks, allowing travel in this region without a car.

Concord Coach Lines has express service between Portland and Boston's Logan Airport and South Station. Concord operates out of the Portland Transportation Center (✉ *100 Thompson's Point Road*).

CONTACTS Shoreline Explorer. ⊕ *www. shorelineexplorer.com/*.

CAR

Once you're here, the best way to experience the craggy Maine Coast, with its scenic and winding country roads, is in a car. There are miles and miles of roads far from the larger towns that have no bus service, and you won't want to miss the chance to discover your own favorite ocean vista while on a scenic drive. From the New Hampshire border through Portland to Brunswick, you can greatly cut down on travel time by following the dull but efficient interstates, I–95 and I–295; note that from York to Augusta, I–95 is a toll road.

TRAIN

Amtrak offers regional service from Boston to Portland via its *Downeaster* line, which originates at Boston's North Station and makes six stops in Maine: Wells, Saco, Old Orchard Beach (seasonal), Portland, Freeport, and Brunswick.

When to Go

Maine's dramatic coastline and pure natural beauty welcome visitors year-round, but note that many smaller museums and attractions are open only in high season (Memorial Day–mid-October), as are many waterside attractions and eateries.

Summer begins in earnest on July 4, and you'll find that many smaller inns, bed-and-breakfasts, and hotels from Kittery on up to Bar Harbor are booked a month or two in advance for dates through August. That's also the case come fall, when the fiery foliage draws leaf peepers. After Halloween, hotel rates drop significantly until ski season begins around Thanksgiving. B&Bs that stay open year-round but are not near ski slopes will often rent rooms at far lower prices than in summer.

In spring, the fourth Sunday in March is designated as Maine Maple Sunday, and farms throughout the state open their doors to visitors not only to watch sap turn into golden syrup but to sample the sweet results.

Activities

No visit to the Maine Coast is complete without some outdoor activity—on two wheels, two feet, holding two paddles, or pulling a bag full of clubs.

If your adventures find you swimming in the ocean or floating close to its surface on a kayak, be on the lookout for sharks. Their populations have rebounded in recent years following conservation and regulatory efforts. In the summer of 2020, off Bailey

Driving in Coastal Maine

	Miles	Time
Boston–Portland	112	2 hours
Kittery–Portland	50	50 minutes
Portland–Freeport	18	20 minutes
Portland–Camden	80	2 hours
Portland–Bar Harbor	175	3 hours 20 minutes

Island, a swimming woman was killed by a great white shark in Maine's first recorded shark fatality; authorities surmised her wet suit caused her to appear to be a seal, a favored prey of sharks.

BIKING

Both the Bicycle Coalition of Maine and Explore Maine by Bike are excellent resources for trail maps and other riding information.

CONTACTS Bicycle Coalition of Maine. ✉ *34 Diamond St., Portland* ☎ *207/623–4511* ⊕ *www.bikemaine.org.*

HIKING

Exploring the Maine Coast on foot is a quick way to acclimate yourself to the relaxed pace of life here—and sometimes the only way to access some of the best coastal spots. Many privately owned lands are accessible to hikers, especially Down East. Inquire at a local establishment about hikes that may not appear on a map.

KAYAKING

Nothing gets you literally off the beaten path like plying the saltwaters in a graceful sea kayak.

CONTACTS Maine Association of Sea Kayak Guides and Instructors. ☎ ⊕ *maskgi.org.* **Maine Island Trail Association.** ✉ *100 Kensington St., 2nd fl., Portland* ☎ *207/761–8225* ⊕ *www.mita.org.*

Hotels

Beachfront and roadside motels, historic-home B&Bs and inns, as well as a handful of newer boutique hotels, make up the majority of lodging along the Maine Coast. There are a few larger luxury resorts, such as the Samoset Resort in Rockport or the Bar Harbor Inn in Bar Harbor, but most accommodations are simple, comfortable, and relatively inexpensive. You will find some chain hotels in larger cities and towns, including major tourist destinations like Portland, Freeport, and Bar Harbor. Many properties close during the off-season (mid-October–mid-May); those that stay open year-round often drop their rates dramatically after high season. (It is often possible to negotiate a nightly rate with smaller establishments during low season.) There is a 9% state hospitality tax on all room rates.

Hotel reviews have been shortened. For full reviews visit Fodors.com.

What It Costs in U.S. Dollars

	$	$$	$$$	$$$$
RESTAURANTS				
	under $18	$18–$24	$25–$35	over $35
HOTELS				
	under $200	$200–$299	$300–$399	over $399

Restaurants

Many breakfast spots along the coast open as early as 6 am to serve the working crowd, and as early as 4 am for fishermen. Lunch generally runs 11–2:30; dinner is usually served 5–9. Only in larger cities will you find full dinners offered much later than 9, although in larger towns you can usually find a bar or bistro with a limited menu available late into the evening.

Many restaurants in Maine are closed Monday. Resort areas make an exception to this in high season, but these eateries often shut down altogether in the off-season.

Unless otherwise noted in reviews, restaurants are open daily for lunch and dinner.

Credit cards are generally accepted at restaurants throughout Maine, even in more modest establishments, but it's still a good idea to have cash on hand wherever you go, just in case.

The one signature meal on the Maine Coast is, of course, the lobster dinner. It typically includes a whole steamed lobster with drawn butter for dipping, a clam or seafood chowder, corn on the cob, coleslaw, and a bib. Lobster prices vary from day to day, but generally a full lobster dinner should cost around $25–$30, or about $18–$20 without all the extras.

Restaurant reviews have been shortened. For full reviews visit Fodors.com.

Visitor Information

CONTACTS DownEast and Acadia Regional Tourism. ⊠ *7 Ames Way, Machias* ☎ *207/255–0983, 888/665–3278* ⊕ *www. downeastacadia.com.* **Maine Lobster Marketing Collaborative.** ⊠ *2 Union St., Suite 204, Portland* ☎ *207/541–9310* ⊕ *www. lobsterfrommaine.com.* **Southern Midcoast Maine Chamber.** ⊠ *Brunswick* ☎ *207/725–8797* ⊕ *www.midcoastmaine.com.* **State of Maine Visitor Information Center.** ⊠ *Hallowell* ☎ *800/767–8709* ⊕ *www. mainetourism.com.*

Kittery

60 miles north of Boston, 4 miles north of Portsmouth, New Hampshire.

Known as the "Gateway to Maine," Kittery has become primarily a major shopping destination thanks to its massive complex of factory outlets. Flanking both sides of U.S. 1 are more than 120 stores, which attract serious shoppers year-round. But Kittery has more to offer than just retail therapy: head east on Route 103 to the area around Kittery Point to experience the great outdoors.

Here you'll find hiking and biking trails, as well as fantastic views of Portsmouth, New Hampshire, Whaleback Light, and, in the distance, Isles of Shoals. The isles and the light, along with two others, can be seen from two forts near this winding stretch of Route 103: Fort McClary State Historic Site (closed to vehicles off-season) and Fort Foster, a town park (with vehicle access to parking lots in the off-season, except in the case of ice or snow).

The Kittery Visitor Information Center is an excellent place to get information for mapping out your tour of Maine (and for a quick photo op with Smokey the Bear). Sometimes local organizations are on hand selling delicious homemade goodies for the road.

GETTING HERE AND AROUND
Three bridges—on U.S. 1, U.S. 1 Bypass, and Interstate 95—cross the Piscataqua River from Portsmouth, New Hampshire, to Kittery. Interstate 95 has three Kittery exits. Route 103 is a scenic coastal drive through Kittery Point to York.

VISITOR INFORMATION
CONTACTS Kittery Visitor Information Center. ⊠ *U.S. 1 and I-95, at Maine mile marker 3.5 on I-95 northbound, Kittery* ☎ *207/439–1319* ⊕ *www.mainetourism. com.*

🍽 Restaurants

Chauncey Creek Lobster Pier
$$ | SEAFOOD | FAMILY | From the road you can barely see the red roof hovering below the trees, but chances are you can see the line of cars parked at this popular outdoor restaurant that has been serving up fresh lobster for more

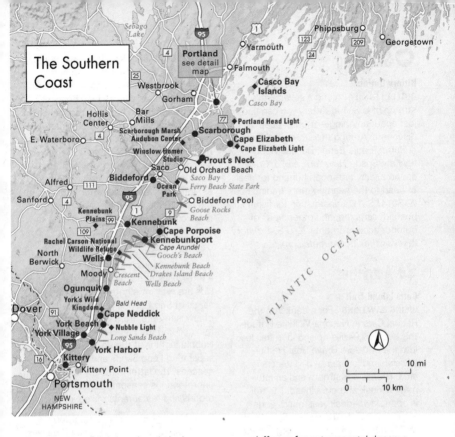

The Southern Coast

than 70 years. Brightly colored picnic tables fill the deck, and enclosed eating areas sit atop the high banks of the tidal river, beside a working pier, which delivers fresh seafood straight to your plate. **Known for:** classic lobster dinners; BYOB; ocean-to-plate. $ *Average main: $25 ⊠ 16 Chauncey Creek Rd., Kittery* ☏ *207/439–1030* ⊕ *www.chaunceycreek. com* ⊗ *Closed Mon. post-Labor Day– Columbus Day. Closed post-Columbus Day–Mother's Day.*

☕ Coffee and Quick Bites

Bob's Clam Hut

$$ | **SEAFOOD** | **FAMILY** | With fresh (never frozen) shellfish and a cheery, old-school vibe, Bob's also serves up scrumptious, homemade sauces to smother over golden fried clams, alongside some of the creamiest New England clam chowders

around. **Known for:** retro-coastal decor; a classic stop since 1956; tangy Moxie barbecue sauce. $ *Average main: $16 ⊠ 315 U.S. 1, Kittery* ☏ *207/439–4233* ⊕ *www. bobsclamhut.com.*

★ Lil's

$ | **CAFÉ** | This Kittery Foreside café is named for the woman who worked the register at nearby Bob's Clam Hut for two decades, but you'll find no shellfish here—just excellent pastries and breads, made on-site daily. Don't miss the top-notch old-fashioned crullers, and duck into the vault in back—filled with vintage records—while you're at it. **Known for:** chill spot to refuel between explorations; lots of parking; a variety of excellent house-made crullers. $ *Average main: $6 ⊠ 7 Wallingford Sq., Unit 106, Kittery* ☏ *207/703–2800* ⊕ *lilscafe.com* ⊗ *No dinner.*

🛍 Shopping

Kittery Outlets

OUTLET | FAMILY | Along a several-mile stretch of U.S. 1 in Kittery you can find just about anything—often at deep discounts. Among the stores are Crate & Barrel, Eddie Bauer, Banana Republic, Kate Spade New York, and J. Crew; spend a rainy afternoon hunting for deals, or head to the nearby Kittery Trading Post (⊠ 301 U.S. 1), a destination for fishing, boating, camping, and other types of outdoor accoutrements. ⊠ *U.S. 1, Kittery* ⊕ *www.thekitteryoutlets.com.*

🏃 Activities

Cutts Island Trail

HIKING & WALKING | For a peek into the Rachel Carson National Wildlife Refuge, this scenic 1.8-mile upland loop trail leads into the 800-acre Brave Boat Harbor Division and is a prime bird-watching area. There's a restroom and an information kiosk at the trailhead. The trail is open dawn–dusk year-round; dogs are not allowed. ⊠ *Seapoint Rd., Kittery* ☎ *207/646–9226* ⊕ *www.fws.gov/refuge/ rachel-carson/visit-us.*

The Yorks and Cape Neddick

8 miles north of Kittery via I–95, U.S. 1, and U.S. 1A.

Spending an afternoon in York Village is like going back in time—and you really only need a couple of hours here to roam the historic streets of this pint-size but worthwhile town. One of the first permanent settlements in Maine, the village museums detail its rich history. York is also home to the flagship store of Stonewall Kitchen, one of Maine's signature gourmet-food purveyors; the store has a café, too. There's also a cluster of vibrant contemporary-art galleries.

A short distance from the village proper, York Harbor opens to the water and offers many places to linger and explore. The harbor itself is busy with boats of all kinds, while the sandy harbor beach is good for swimming. Much quieter and more formal than York Beach to the north, this area has a somewhat exclusive air. Perched along the cliffs on the north side of the harbor are huge "cottages" built by wealthy summer residents in the late 1800s, when the area became a premier seaside resort destination with several grand hotels.

York Beach is a real family destination, devoid of all things staid and stuffy, and a throwback to nostalgic summers past: kids are welcome here. Just beyond the sands of Short Sands Beach are a host of amusements, from bowling to indoor minigolf and the Fun-O-Rama arcade. Nubble Light is at the tip of the peninsula separating Long Sands and Short Sands beaches. The latter is mostly lined with unpretentious seasonal homes, with motels and restaurants mixed in.

Cape Neddick is 1 mile north of York Beach via U.S. 1A. It's still one of the less developed of York's areas, and there's no distinct village hub, though it's become something of an elevated destination, with acclaimed restaurants and trendy lodgings popping up. Cape Neddick Harbor is at its southern end, beyond York Beach village.

GETTING HERE AND AROUND

York is Exit 7 off I–95; follow signs to U.S. 1, the modern commercial strip. From here, U.S. 1A will take you to the village center and on to York Harbor and York Beach before looping back up to U.S. 1 in Cape Neddick. After passing through York Village to York Harbor (originally called Lower Town), U.S. 1A winds around and heads north to York Beach's village center, a 4-mile trip.

It's a scenic 6 miles to York Beach via the loop road, U.S. 1A, from its southern intersection with U.S. 1. Although 2 miles longer, it's generally faster to continue north on U.S. 1A to Cape Neddick and then U.S. 1A south to the village center, home to Short Sands Beach. Here U.S. 1A is known as Ocean Avenue as it heads north from York Harbor along Long Sands Beach en route to York Beach village and Short Sands Beach.

You can get from beach to beach on a series of residential streets that wind around Nubble Point between these beaches. Also, from late June through Labor Day, the bright-red vehicles of the York Trolley Company link Short Sands Beach in York Beach village with nearby Long Sands Beach, running along U.S. 1A, making a number of stops. Maps can be picked up throughout York; fares are $2 one-way, $4 round-trip, cash only (payable to driver upon boarding). You can also connect with a shuttle service to Ogunquit.

TRANSPORTATION York Trolley Co.. ⊠ *York* ☎ *207/363–9600* ⊕ *www.yorktrolley.com.*

VISITOR INFORMATION
CONTACTS Greater York Region Chamber of Commerce. ⊠ *1 Stonewall La., off U.S. 1, York* ☎ *207/363–4422* ⊕ *www.gateway-tomaine.org.*

◉ Sights

Cliff Walk and Fisherman's Walk
TRAIL | Two walking trails begin near Harbor Beach. Starting in a small nearby park, the Cliff Walk ascends its granite namesake and passes the summer "cottages" at the harbor entrance. There are some steps, but, as signs caution, tread carefully because of erosion. Fisherman's Walk, on the other hand, is an easy stroll. Starting across Stage Neck Road from the beach, it passes waterfront businesses, historic homes, and rocky harbor beaches on the way to York's beloved Wiggly Bridge. This pedestrian suspension bridge alongside Route 103 (there is minimal parking here) leads to Steedman Woods, a public preserve with a shaded loop trail

along the York River estuary's ambling waters. You can also enter the preserve near the George Marshall Store in York Village. ⊠ *Stage Neck Rd., off U.S. 1A, York.*

Old York Historical Society
HISTORY MUSEUM | FAMILY | Nine historic 18th- and 19th-century buildings, clustered on York Street and along Lindsay Road and the York River, highlight York's rich history, which dates from the early colonial period. Start your visit at the museum's visitor center in the Remick Barn at the corner of U.S. 1A and Lindsay Road. The Old Gaol (established 1656) was once the King's Prison for the Province of Maine; step inside for a look inside its dungeons, cells, and jailer's quarters. The 1731 Elizabeth Perkins House reflects the Victorian style of its last occupants, the prominent Perkins family. ⊠ *Old York Museum Center, 3 Lindsay Rd., York Village* ☎ *207/363–1756* ⊕ *www.oldyork.org* ☞ *$10* ⊗ *Closed Nov.–Memorial Day.*

★ Nubble Light
LIGHTHOUSE | On a small island just off the tip of Cape Neddick, Nubble Light is one of the most photographed lighthouses on the globe. Direct access is prohibited, but the small Sohier Park right across from the light has parking, historical placards, benches, and a seasonal information center that shares the 1879 light's history. ⊠ *11 Sohier Park Rd., York* ☎ *207/363–3569 May 1–mid-Oct.* ⊕ *www.nubblelight.org.*

Sayward-Wheeler House
HISTORIC HOME | FAMILY | Built in 1718, this waterfront home was remodeled in the 1760s by Jonathan Sayward, a local merchant who had prospered in the West Indies trade. By 1860, his descendants had opened the house to the public to share the story of their Colonial ancestors. Accessible only by guided tour (first and third Saturday, June through mid-October, 11–4 with the last tour at 3), the house reveals the decor of a prosperous New England family and the stories of

the free and enslaved people who lived here at the outset of the Revolutionary War. The parlor—considered one of the country's best-preserved Colonial interiors, with a tall clock and mahogany Chippendale-style chairs—looks pretty much as it did when Sayward lived here. ✉ *9 Barrell La. Ext., York Harbor* ☎ *207/384–2454* 🌐 *www.historicnewengland.org/property/sayward-wheeler-house* 🎟 *$10* 🕓 *Closed mid-Oct.–June.*

Beaches

Long Sands Beach

BEACH | FAMILY | In the peak of summer, each day sees thousands of visitors along this swath of white sand, which stretches for more than a mile. They come to sunbathe, surf (in designated areas), play volleyball, and explore tide pools. You can rent umbrellas and rafts here, but you'll have to walk to nearby restaurants for a bite to eat. Dogs are allowed (however, between late May and late September, only before 8 am and after 6:30 pm). **Amenities:** lifeguards (seasonal); parking (fee); toilets. **Best for:** surfing; swimming; walking. ✉ *189 Long Beach Ave., Rte. 1A, York Beach.*

Restaurants

Dockside Restaurant

$$ | SEAFOOD | On an islandlike peninsula overlooking York Harbor, this restaurant has plenty of seafood on the menu. Floor-to-ceiling windows in the stepped modern dining space transport diners to the water beyond—every seat has a water view. **Known for:** "drunken" lobster (lobster and seared scallops in an Irish-whiskey cream); decadent seafood chowder and lobster bisque; lively, dockside vibe with spectacular views. [$] *Average main: $25* ✉ *22 Harris Island Rd., off Rte. 103, York Harbor* ☎ *207/363–2722* 🌐 *www.dockside-restaurant.com* 🕓 *Closed Tues. in summer and late Oct.–mid-May.*

The Goldenrod

$$ | AMERICAN | FAMILY | People line the windows to watch Goldenrod Kisses being made the same way they have since 1896—and thousands of pounds are made every year at this York Beach classic. Aside from the famous taffy (there's penny candy, too), this eatery is family-oriented, very reasonably priced, and a great place to get homemade ice cream from the old-fashioned soda fountain. **Known for:** laid-back, kid-friendly atmosphere; breakfast served all day; classic American fare, like burgers, hot dogs, and baked dinners. [$] *Average main: $10* ✉ *2 Railroad Ave., York Beach* ☎ *207/363–2621* 🌐 *www.thegoldenrod.com* 🕓 *Closed mid-Oct.–mid-May.*

Coffee and Quick Bites

Flo's Steamed Hot Dogs

$ | AMERICAN | Yes, it seems crazy to highlight a hot-dog stand, but this is no ordinary place—who would guess that a hot dog could make it into *Saveur* and *Gourmet* magazines? There is something grand about this shabby, red-shingle shack, where the classic dog has mayo and a special sauce—consisting of, among other things, onions and molasses (you can buy a bottle to take home, and you'll want to). **Known for:** family-owned and-operated; in business since 1959; lines out the door (but efficient service means waits aren't that long). [$] *Average main: $3* ✉ *1359 U.S. 1, Cape Neddick* ☎ *No phone* 🌐 *www.floshotdogs.com* 💳 *No credit cards* 🕓 *Closed Wed. No dinner.*

Hotels

★ Cliff House

$$$ | HOTEL | FAMILY | At this luxurious hotel overlooking the Atlantic Ocean, you can watch the white crests smash the craggy bluffs below while nestled in a hooded flannel robe on your balcony. **Pros:** the views; rooms have private terraces;

plenty of activities to keep everyone busy. **Cons:** no in-room coffee setups (only one communal coffee station per floor to help reduce waste); meals not included; central location means a drive to the nearest town centers. [$] *Rooms from: $600* ✉ *591 Shore Rd., Cape Neddick* ☎ *207/361–1000* 🌐 *www.cliffhouse-maine.com* 🛏 *226 rooms* 🍴 *No Meals.*

★ Stage Neck Inn

$$ | RESORT | FAMILY | A family-run operation that is now in the competent hands of the second generation, this resort hotel takes full advantage of its gorgeous harborside location, with Adirondack chairs, chaise longues, and a fire pit on the surrounding lawns; water views from most guest rooms; and floor-to-ceiling windows in the common spaces. **Pros:** elaborate breakfast buffet with scrumptious baked goods; poolside service and snack bar in season; rooms have balconies or deck areas and most have water views. **Cons:** spa is on the small side; some rooms have only partial water views; rooms with two beds have doubles rather than queens. [$] *Rooms from: $300* ✉ *8 Stage Neck Rd., off U.S. 1A, York Harbor* ☎ *800/340–1130, 207/363–3850* 🌐 *www.stageneck.com* 🕓 *Closed 1st 2 wks in Jan.* 🛏 *60 rooms* 🍴 *Free Breakfast.*

York Harbor Inn

$ | B&B/INN | A mid-17th-century fishing cabin with dark timbers and a fieldstone fireplace forms the heart of this historic inn, which now includes several neighboring buildings. **Pros:** many rooms have harbor views; close to beaches, scenic walking trails; kid-friendly. **Cons:** rooms vary greatly in style, size, and appeal; no ocean views at the Chapman Cottage; only Harbor Crest Inn is pet-friendly. [$] *Rooms from: $199* ✉ *480 York St., York Harbor* ☎ *207/363–5119* 🌐 *www.yorkharborinn.com* 🛏 *65 rooms* 🍴 *Free Breakfast.*

Shopping

Stonewall Kitchen

FOOD | FAMILY | You've probably seen Stonewall Kitchen's jars of chutneys, jams, jellies, salsas, and sauces in specialty stores back home. This complex houses the expansive flagship store, which has a viewing area of the bottling process. Sample all the mustards, salsas, and dressings you can stand, or have lunch at the café, then meander through the stunning gardens to the Stonewall Home Company Store, offering candles, hand lotions, and essentials for the garden and home. ✉ *2 Stonewall La., off U.S. 1, York* ☎ *207/351–2712* 🌐 *www.stonewallkitchen.com.*

Activities

Shearwater Charters

FISHING | Shearwater offers light-tackle and fly-fishing charters in the York River and along the shoreline from Kittery to Ogunquit. Bait-fishing trips are also available. Departures are from Town Dock #2 in York Harbor; just note that trips are capped at three people. ✉ *Town Dock #2, 20 Harris Island Rd., York* ☎ *207/363–5324* 🌐 *www.mainestripers.net.*

Ogunquit

7 miles north of the Yorks via U.S. 1.

A resort village since the late 19th century, Ogunquit made a name for itself as an artists' colony. Today it has become a mini Provincetown, with a population that swells in summer, boutique shops and galleries, and many inns and small clubs that cater to an LGBTQ+ clientele.

Nightlife in Ogunquit revolves around the precincts of Ogunquit Square and Perkins Cove, where people stroll, often enjoying an after-dinner ice-cream cone or espresso. For a scenic drive, take Shore Road from downtown to the 175-foot Bald

Ogunquit's Perkins Cove is a pleasant place to admire the boats (and wonder at the origin of their names).

Head Cliff; you'll be treated to views up and down the coast. On a stormy day the surf can be quite wild here.

GETTING HERE AND AROUND

Parking in the village and at the beach is costly and limited, so leave your car at the hotel or in a public parking space and hop the trolley. It costs $5 per trip and runs Memorial Day weekend–Columbus Day, with weekend-only service during the last few weeks, after Labor Day. From Perkins Cove, the trolley runs through town along Shore Road and then down to Ogunquit Beach; it also stops along U.S. 1.

TRANSPORTATION Shoreline Explorer.
☎ *800/965–5762* ⊕ *www.shorelineexplorer.com.*

VISITOR INFORMATION

CONTACTS Ogunquit Chamber of Commerce. ✉ *36 Main St., Ogunquit* ☎ *207/646–1279* ⊕ *www.ogunquit.org.*

👁 Sights

Marginal Way

PROMENADE | FAMILY | This mile-plus-long, paved footpath hugs the shore of a rocky promontory just beyond Ogunquit's downtown. Thirty-nine benches along the easygoing path allow you to appreciate the open sea vistas. Expect heavy foot traffic, even in the off-season—which is the only time of the year that dogs are allowed. ✉ *Perkins Cove Rd., Ogunquit* ⊕ *www.marginalwayfund.org.*

★ Ogunquit Museum of American Art

ART MUSEUM | FAMILY | Ogunquit has long been an important site for artists, and this stellar museum—the only one in Maine focused solely on American art—continues that legacy. The collection includes 3,000 early modern and contemporary paintings, sculptures, drawings, and more, including works with ties to Ogunquit's once-famous artist colony. The main gallery offers sweeping views of Perkins Cove. Leave time to stroll around the 3-acre seaside sculpture park in good weather. ✉ *543 Shore Rd., Ogunquit* ☎ *207/646–4909* 🌐 *ogunquitmuseum.org* 🎫 *$12* ⏲ *Closed Nov. 1–Apr. 30.*

Perkins Cove

OTHER ATTRACTION | FAMILY | This neck of land off Shore Road in the lower part of Ogunquit village has a jumble of sea-weathered fish houses and buildings that were part of an art school. These have largely been transformed by the tide of tourism into shops and restaurants, including the classic Barnacle Billy's seafood spot. When you've had your fill of browsing, stroll out along the mile-long Marginal Way. ✉ *Perkins Cove Rd., off Shore Rd., Ogunquit.*

Beaches

Ogunquit Beach

BEACH | FAMILY | Perfect for just about every beach fan—sunbathers to beachcombers and bodysurfers—this 3-mile-long, sandy beach is located between the Atlantic Ocean and the Ogunquit River. Beach chairs and umbrellas are available for rent seasonally. Dogs are welcome from September through March. **Amenities**: food and drink; lifeguards; parking (fee); toilets. **Best For:** sunset; swimming; walking. ✉ *Ogunquit* ✣ *End of Ocean Ave.* 🌐 *www.ogunquit.org/our-beaches* 🎫 *Parking $35 a day (mid-Apr.–Oct.).*

Restaurants

Barnacle Billy's

$$$ | SEAFOOD | Overlooking Perkins Cove, Barnacle Billy's has been serving up fresh, local seafood since 1961. Place your order at the counter before settling into a table on the deck to await delivery of your clam chowder, fried clams, broiled scallops, or lobster roll. **Known for:** lobster rolls and chowder; takeout counter and ice cream; deck seating overlooking Perkins Cove. [$] *Average main: $38* ✉ *50–70 Perkins Cove Rd., Ogunquit* ☎ *207/646–5575* 🌐 *www.barnbilly.com* ⏲ *Closed late Oct.–late Apr.*

The Lobster Shack

$$ | SEAFOOD | A fixture since 1947 in Ogunquit's bustling Perkins Cove, this cozy, weathered-shingle lobster pound is just across from the oft-photographed footbridge. Choose from a ¼- to a whopping 1-pound lobster roll, or try the delicious roll with hand-picked Maine crab meat. **Known for:** Maine beers on tap; lobsters rolls; chowder. [$] *Average main: $26* ✉ *110 Perkins Cove Rd., Ogunquit* ☎ *207/646–2941* 🌐 *www.lobster-shack.com.*

★ **Northern Union**

$$ | CONTEMPORARY | From the moment you walk into Northern Union you know you're going to be in very good hands. A genuine, welcoming staff and laid-back yet elegant design scheme put you in the mood for a slow, very memorable dinner of seasonally inspired small plates like braised pork belly or duck confit and rotating entrées like seared scallops and lobster fettuccine—all available with spot-on wine pairings that you won't find anywhere else in the area. **Known for:** almost everything is made in-house; dishes that can easily be shared; a terrific selection of cured meats and cheese boards with a local, seasonal bent. [$] *Average main: $27* ✉ *261 Shore Rd., Ogunquit* ☎ *207/216–9639* 🌐 *www.northern-union.me* ⏲ *No lunch.*

Performing Arts

Ogunquit Playhouse

THEATER | FAMILY | Over its nearly century-long history, this classic summer theater has brought some the country's best talent to its stage. The stately green-and-white building feels like a relic from an old-time summer resort, and with an average of five productions each season, the Playhouse offers a good reason to take a break from the beach and spend an evening indoors. ✉ *10 Main St., Ogunquit* ☎ *207/646–5511* 🌐 *www.ogunquitplayhouse.org* 🎫 *Show tickets: from $47* ⏲ *Closed Nov.–May.*

Wells

6 miles north of Ogunquit via U.S. 1.

Lacking any kind of discernible village center, Wells could be easily overlooked as nothing more than a commercial stretch of U.S. 1 between Ogunquit and the Kennebunks. But look more closely: this is a place where people come to enjoy some of the best beaches on the coast. Until 1980 the town of Wells incorporated Ogunquit, and today this family-oriented beach community has 7 miles of densely populated shoreline, along with nature preserves, where you can explore salt marshes and tidal pools.

GETTING HERE AND AROUND

Amtrak's *Downeaster* train stops at Wells Transportation Center, but from there, this town is best explored by car. U.S. 1 is the main thoroughfare, with antiques stores, shops, and diners lining both sides. Venture down the roads that branch off U.S. 1 to the east (and the coast), like Mile Road, which has spots to eat and drink and leads to Wells Beach. Just north, where U.S. 1 intersects with Route 9, is the Rachel Carson National Wildlife Refuge.

VISITOR INFORMATION

CONTACTS Wells Chamber of Commerce. ⊠ *136 Post Rd., Wells* ✛ *At intersection of Post Rd. (U.S. 1) and Kimballs La.* ☎ *207/646–2451* ⊕ *www.wellschamber. org.*

Sights

Rachel Carson National Wildlife Refuge
WILDLIFE REFUGE | FAMILY | At the headquarters of the Rachel Carson National Wildlife Refuge, which has 11 divisions from Kittery to Cape Elizabeth, is the Carson Trail, a 1-mile loop. The trail traverses a salt marsh and a white-pine forest where migrating birds and waterfowl of many varieties are regularly spotted, and it borders Branch Brook and the Merriland River. ⊠ *321 Port Rd., Wells*

☎ *207/646–9226* ⊕ *www.fws.gov/refuge/ rachel_carson.*

🏖 Beaches

Crescent Beach
BEACH | FAMILY | Lined with summer homes, this sandy strand is busy in the summer, but the beach and the water are surprisingly clean, considering all the traffic. The swimming's good, and beachgoers can also explore tidal pools and look for seals on the sea rocks nearby. **Amenities:** lifeguards; parking (fee); toilets. **Best for:** swimming. ⊠ *Webhannet Dr., south of Mile Rd., Wells.*

Wells Beach
BEACH | FAMILY | The northern end of a 2-mile stretch of golden sand, Wells Beach is popular with families and surfers, who line up in the swells and suit up on the boardwalk near the arcade and snack shop. The beach's northern tip is a bit quieter, with a long rock jetty perfect for strolling. **Amenities:** food and drink; lifeguards; parking (fee); toilets. **Best for:** surfing; walking. ⊠ *Atlantic Ave., north of Mile Rd., Wells.*

🍴 Restaurants

★ Batson River Fish Camp
$$ | AMERICAN | This outpost of the popular Batson River brewing and distilling company channels the feel of a trendy lakeside camp (think vintage thermoses and prize catches mounted on the walls) all year round. The menu includes standout cocktails, well-done bar fare, and beers brewed on-site, just behind Fish Camp. **Known for:** limited-edition brews; throwback camp decor; fun spot for a well-made cocktail after a day at the beach. Ⓢ *Average main: $20* ⊠ *73 Mile Rd., Wells* ☎ *207/360–7255* ⊕ *batsonriver.com/wells-maine* ⊘ *Closed Wed. No lunch.*

Billy's Chowder House

$$ | SEAFOOD | FAMILY | Locals and vacationers head to this roadside seafood restaurant and bar in the midst of a salt marsh en route to Wells Beach. The menu features classic seafood dishes like lobster rolls and chowders, but there are plenty of nonseafood choices, too. **Known for:** views of the Rachel Carson National Wildlife Refuge; generous lobster rolls; one of the oldest waterfront restaurants in Wells. Ⓢ *Average main: $24 ✉ 216 Mile Rd., Wells ☏ 207/646–7558 ⊕ www. billyschowderhouse.com ☉ Closed mid-Dec.–mid-Jan.*

★ Bitter End

$$ | SEAFOOD | Pete and Kate Morency, the duo originally behind the ever-popular Pier 77 and the Ramp Bar and Grill in Kennebunkport, are also the masterminds behind this seafood spot, where Mediterranean and American classics are given brilliant, contemporary twists. The fabulous decor consists of an unlikely marriage of old-school American sports memorabilia and something that might be described as shabby ballroom chic—crystal chandeliers hang above old leather boxing gloves, and shiny trophies (including a 1961 Miss Universe cup) and black-and-white photos of sports icons line the bar. **Known for:** cuisine fusion and a rotating menu; outdoor seating area with firepit; superbly curated bevy of liquors. Ⓢ *Average main: $24 ✉ 2118 Post Rd., Wells ☏ 207/360–0904 ⊕ www. bitterend.me ☉ Closed Tues.*

Maine Diner

$$ | AMERICAN | One look at the 1953 exterior, and you'll start craving diner food, but be prepared to get a little more than you bargained for: after all, how many greasy spoons make an award-winning lobster pie? There's plenty of fried seafood in addition to the usual diner fare, and breakfast is served all day. **Known for:** classic diner fare; wild Maine blueberry pie; sources a lot of produce from its very own vegetable garden.

Ⓢ *Average main: $15 ✉ 2265 Post Rd., Wells ☏ 207/646–4441 ⊕ www.mainediner.com ☉ No dinner. Closed Wed. and at least 2 wks in Jan.*

☕ Coffee and Quick Bites

Congdon's Doughnuts

$ | AMERICAN | FAMILY | These superior doughnuts have been made by members of the same family since 1945 and at the same location since 1955. Congdon's has about 40 different varieties, some seasonal, though the plain variety really gives you an idea of just how good these doughnuts are: it's the biggest seller, along with the honey dipped and black raspberry jelly. **Known for:** perfect spot to start a rainy day; Congdon's After Dark features food trucks and live music nightly in summer; outrageously good, classic doughnuts. Ⓢ *Average main: $3 ✉ 1090 Post Rd., Wells ☏ 207/646–4219 ⊕ www. congdons.com ☉ No dinner. Closed Wed. in season and Mon.–Wed. off-season; check website for details.*

🛏 Hotels

Haven by the Sea

$$ | B&B/INN | Once the summer mission of St. Martha's Church in Kennebunkport, this exquisite inn, just a block from the beach, has retained many details from its former life, including cathedral ceilings and stained-glass windows. **Pros:** rotating breakfasts that cater to dietary restrictions without compromising taste; nightly happy hour with complimentary appetizers and sherry, port, and brandy; beach towels and beach chairs available. **Cons:** not an in-town location; distant ocean views; $50 cancellation fee no matter how far in advance. Ⓢ *Rooms from: $260 ✉ 59 Church St., Wells ☏ 207/646–4194 ⊕ www.havenbythesea. com ⇥ 9 rooms ⃝ Free Breakfast.*

Kennebunk, Kennebunkport, and Cape Porpoise

6 miles north of Wells via Rte. 9.

The town centers of Kennebunk and Kennebunkport are separated by 5 miles and two rivers, but, what are probably best described as the Hamptons of the Pine Tree State are united by a common history and laid-back seaside vibe. Kennebunkport has been a resort area since the 19th century, and its most recent residents have made it even more famous: the dynastic Bush family is often in residence on its immense estate, which sits dramatically out on Walker's Point on Cape Arundel. Newer homes have sprung up alongside the old, and a great way to take them all in is with a slow drive out Ocean Avenue along the cape.

Sometimes bypassed on the way to its sister town, Kennebunk has its own appeal. Once a major shipbuilding center, Kennebunk today retains the feel of a classic New England small town, with an inviting shopping district, steepled churches, and fine examples of 18th- and 19th-century brick and clapboard homes. There are also plenty of natural spaces for walking, swimming, birding, and biking, and the area's major beaches are along its shores.

Just north of Kennebunkport is the fishing village of Cape Porpoise, with a working lobster pier, spectacular views of the harbor and lighthouse, and excellent restaurants.

GETTING HERE AND AROUND
Kennebunk's main downtown sits along U.S. 1, extending west from the Mousam River. The Lower Village is along routes 9 and 35, 4 miles down Route 35 from downtown, and the way between is lined on both sides by mansions, making it a spectacular drive.

To reach the beaches of Kennebunk, continue straight (the road becomes Beach Avenue) at the intersection with Route 9. If you turn left instead, Route 9 will take you across the Kennebunk River, into Kennebunkport's touristy downtown, called Dock Square (or sometimes just "the Port"). Here you'll find the most activity (and crowds) in the Kennebunks, thanks to restaurants, shops, galleries, and boats that offer cruises.

The Intown Trolley runs narrated jaunts in season, passing Kennebunk's beaches and Lower Village as well as neighboring Kennebunkport's scenery and sights. The main stop is at 21 Ocean Avenue in Kennebunkport, around the corner from Dock Square.

TRANSPORTATION Intown Trolley. ⊠ *Kennebunkport* ☎ *207/967–3686* ⊕ *www. intowntrolley.com.*

WALKING TOURS
To take a little walking tour of Kennebunk's most notable structures, begin at the Federal-style Brick Store Museum at 117 Main Street. Head south on Main Street (turn left out of the museum) to see several extraordinary 18th- and early-19th-century homes, including the **Lexington Elms** at No. 99 (1799), the **Horace Porter House** at No. 92 (1848), and the **Benjamin Brown House** at No. 85 (1788).

When you've had your fill of historic homes, head back up toward the museum, pass the 1773 **First Parish Unitarian Church** (its Asher Benjamin–style steeple contains an original Paul Revere bell), and turn right onto **Summer Street.** This street is an architectural showcase, revealing an array of styles from Colonial to Federal. Walking past these grand beauties will give you a real sense of the economic prowess and glamour of the long-gone shipbuilding industry.

At noon on Thursday and Saturday from June through October (or by appointment off-season), the museum offers a guided architectural walking tour of Summer

Street. You can also purchase a $4.95 map that marks historic buildings or a $15.95 guidebook, *Windows on the Past.*

For a dramatic walk along Kennebunk-port's rocky coastline and beneath the views of Ocean Avenue's grand mansions, head out on the **Parson's Way Shore Walk,** a paved 4.8-mile round-trip. Begin at Dock Square and follow Ocean Avenue along the river, passing the Colony Hotel and St. Ann's Church, all the way to Walker's Point. Simply turn back from here.

VISITOR INFORMATION

CONTACTS Kennebunk-Kennebunkport Chamber of Commerce. ☒ *16 Water St., Kennebunk* ☎ *207/967–0857* ⊕ *www. gokennebunks.com.*

◉ Sights

Brick Store Museum

HISTORY MUSEUM | FAMILY | The cornerstone of this block-long preservation of early-19th-century commercial and residential buildings is William Lord's Brick Store. Built as a dry-goods store in 1825 in the Federal style, the building has an openwork balustrade across the roofline, granite lintels over the windows, and paired chimneys. Exhibits chronicle the Kennebunk area's history, art, and culture for kids and adults alike. In addition, museum staffers lead walking tours of Kennebunk's National Historic District (at noon on Thursday and Saturday from June through October) and of the town's beaches (at 11 on Saturday from July through September). ☒ *117 Main St., Kennebunk* ☎ *207/985–4802* ⊕ *www. brickstoremuseum.org* ☞ *$5* ⊙ *Closed Mon.*

★ Dock Square

PLAZA/SQUARE | Restaurants, art galleries, clothing boutiques, and other shops—both trendy and touristy—line this bustling square and nearby streets and alleys. Walk onto the drawbridge to admire the tidal Kennebunk River; cross to the other side and you are in the Lower Village of neighboring Kennebunk. ☒ *Dock Sq., Kennebunkport.*

Seashore Trolley Museum

OTHER MUSEUM | FAMILY | This fun, visitor-favorite museum is an homage to transport from years past. Get an up-close look at trolleys from major metropolitan areas worldwide—from Boston to Budapest, New York to Nagasaki, and San Francisco to Sydney—beautifully restored and displayed (and, sometimes, operational). Best of all, you can take a nearly 4-mile ride on the tracks of the former Atlantic Shore Line Railway, with a stop along the way at the museum restoration shop, where trolleys are transformed from junk into gems. The outdoor museum is self-guided. ☒ *195 Log Cabin Rd., Kennebunkport* ☎ *207/967–2800* ⊕ *www.trolleymuseum.org* ☞ *$13* ⊙ *Closed weekdays in May and Mon. and Tues. June 1–Oct. 31. Closed Nov.– Apr. except 1st 2 weekends in Dec.*

◉ Beaches

Kennebunk Beach

BEACH | FAMILY | Kennebunk Beach has three distinct stretches, one after another, along Beach Avenue, which is lined with cottages and old Victorians. The southernmost **Mother's Beach** is popular with families. Rock outcroppings lessen the waves, and a playground and tidal pools keep kids busy. This is followed by the stony **Middle Beach.** The most northerly, and the closest to downtown Kennebunkport, is **Gooch's Beach,** the main swimming beach. **Amenities:** lifeguards; parking (fee); toilets. **Best for:** walking; swimming. ☒ *Beach Ave., south of Rte. 9, Kennebunk.*

★ Goose Rocks Beach

BEACH | FAMILY | Three-mile-long Goose Rocks, a 10-minute drive north of Kennebunkport, has a good long stretch of smooth sand and plenty of shallow pools for exploring. It's a favorite of families with small children. Pick up a $25 daily

292

parking permit at one of two kiosks along the beach: one outside of Goose Rocks Beach General Store at 3 Dyke Road and the other at the Proctor Avenue beach path. Dogs are allowed (on a leash), but only before 9 and after 5 during the summer season. There is one porta potty behind the General Store, but otherwise no facilities are available at the beach. **Amenities:** parking (fee). **Best for:** walking; swimming. ⊠ *Dyke Rd., off Rte. 9, Kennebunkport* ⊕ *www.kennebunkportme. gov.*

 Restaurants

★ The Clam Shack

$$ | SEAFOOD | FAMILY | For more than a half century, this shack has been known for speedy service and great takeout fare, like its traditional boiled lobster dinners and lobster rolls on freshly baked buns. Eat at one of several wooden picnic tables that overlook the Kennebunk River. **Known for:** clam chowder; lobster rolls and fried clams; ships lobster nationally. Ⓢ *Average main: $17* ⊠ *2 Western Ave., Kennebunk* ☎ *207/967–3321* ⊕ *www. theclamshack.net.*

★ Earth at Hidden Pond

$$$ | FUSION | Each and every meal feels like a special occasion at his splurge-worthy place, which offers thoughtful attention to flavor and texture and uses the freshest locally sourced ingredients. The seasonally inspired menu is always in flux, but you can be sure that even hard-core foodies will be delighted with this culinary experience. **Known for:** wood-fire surf-and-turf dishes; ingredients culled from its own garden; private dining sheds and cabanas for special occasions and groups. Ⓢ *Average main: $38* ⊠ *354 Goose Rocks Rd., Kennebunkport* ☎ *207/967–6550* ⊕ *hiddenpondmaine. com/earth.*

★ Old Vines Wine Bar

$$ | MODERN AMERICAN | Housed in a historic barn, this wine bar and its front patio get busy in summer, and for good reason: artisan cocktails and flavorful small plates are expertly made, and, as the name suggests, the wine list is stellar. Except for a six-week break in midwinter, it's open year-round and cozy on cold nights, too. **Known for:** regular entertainment by Maine musicians; wine list featuring small vineyards and unique varietals; lively Yard Bar open outdoors in summer. Ⓢ *Average main: $24* ⊠ *173 Port Rd., Kennebunk* ☎ *207/967–2310* ⊕ *oldvineswinebar.com* ◷ *No lunch. Closed for 6 wks in Feb. and Mar.*

★ Pier 77 Restaurant

$$ | AMERICAN | Here, phenomenal views share center stage with a sophisticated menu that emphasizes seafood. The ground-level restaurant's large windows overlook Cape Porpoise harbor, ensuring that every seat has a view of the water; tucked around the corner, the tiny but funky and fun Ramp Bar & Grill pays homage to a really good burger, fried seafood, and other pub-style classics; and, up a flight of stairs, Ramp Up offers crow's-nest harbor views and a place to wait for your table when lines to get in are long. **Known for:** live music in summer; great spot for cocktails on the water while watching boats and sea life pass by; a packed house almost every meal in the summer (reservations highly recommended). Ⓢ *Average main: $25* ⊠ *77 Pier Rd., Cape Porpoise* ☎ *207/967–8500* ⊕ *www.pier77restaurant.com.*

★ The Tides Beach Club Restaurant

$$$ | SEAFOOD | Maritime accents and a crisp color palette help to make this unfussy, beachside restaurant a good place to relax and enjoy a prebeach bite or a post-beach sit-down meal. The menu features lighter seafood fare and salads alongside heartier options, such as lobster rangoons, crispy fried-chicken

Maine's rocky coastline stretches for about 3,400 miles, including Kennebunkport.

sandwiches, and burgers. **Known for:** no dress code—think beach-hair-don't-care chic; delicious craft cocktails; exceptional service that isn't cloying. [$] *Average main: $35* ✉ *930 Kings Hwy., Kennebunkport* ☎ *207/967–3757* 🌐 *tidesbeachclubmaine.com/food.*

Coffee and Quick Bites

Dock Square Coffee House

$ | **AMERICAN** | European-style coffee drinks, tea, pastries, smoothies, and other seasonal snacks are on the menu at this small café built over a tidal river in the midst of Dock Square. The coffee is sourced from Portland-based and nationally recognized Coffee By Design, one of the state's best. **Known for:** locally sourced coffee, pastries and breakfast sandwiches; quiet place to sit amid the bustle of Dock Square; central location. [$] *Average main: $5* ✉ *18 Dock Sq., Kennebunkport* ☎ *207/967–4422* 🌐 *www.docksquarecoffeehouse.biz* 🕒 *Closed Jan.–Mar.*

Hotels

★ **Hidden Pond**

$$$$ | **RESORT** | Tucked away on 60 wooded acres near Goose Rocks Beach, this resort enclave has hiking trails, two pools, a sumptuous spa, a phenomenal restaurant, a working farm and a variety of lodging options—from luxurious one-bedroom bungalows and two-bedroom cottages to rustic-chic lodges with interconnected suites and studios. **Pros:** use of beach facilities at nearby Tides Beach Club and free beach shuttle and beach-cruiser bikes; lots of on-site activities for adults and children; guests can cut fresh flowers and harvest vegetables from the property's many gardens. **Cons:** steep prices; away from the center of town; no dogs allowed. [$] *Rooms from: $1050* ✉ *354 Goose Rocks Rd., Kennebunkport* ☎ *207/967–9050* 🌐 *hiddenpondmaine.com* 🕒 *Closed Nov.–Apr.* 🛏 *46 units* 🍴 *No Meals.*

★ Kennebunkport Captains Collection

$$ | **B&B/INN** | The four historic inns and houses in this Lark Hotels collection were painstakingly restored in 2020 and 2021, and each was given its own sumptuous, traditional-meets-modern twists. **Pros:** complimentary bikes; easy walk into town; fireplaces in the guest rooms. **Cons:** the nontraditional resort layout may not be everyone's ideal; no pool; no elevators (as these are historic homes). $ *Rooms from: $349* ✉ *6 Pleasant St., Kennebunkport* ☎ *207/967–3141* ⊕ *www.larkhotels.com/hotels/kennebunkport-captains-collection* ⇆ *45 rooms* ⏲ *Free Breakfast.*

The Nonantum Resort

$$$ | **RESORT** | **FAMILY** | Hands down the most family-friendly resort in the Kennebunks, this place is a dream for parents who want to have a quality family vacation without stress. **Pros:** comfortable beds from local Portland Mattress Makers; seasonal, Maine-centric childrens' activities; friendly, service-oriented staff. **Cons:** wedding events add to bustle; heavy visitor traffic; no indoor pool. $ *Rooms from: $449* ✉ *95 Ocean Ave., Kennebunkport* ☎ *207/967–4050* ⊕ *nonantumresort.com* ⏲ *Closed mid-Dec.–late Apr.* ⇆ *109 rooms* ⏲ *Free Breakfast.*

★ Sandy Pines Campground

$ | **RESORT** | The "glamping" (glamorous camping) tents, camp cottages, and A-frame hideaway huts on wheels at Sandy Pines Campground deliver every bit as much comfort and luxury as a fine hotel (with a few caveats, including communal bathing areas), but give you a chance to get up close and personal with nature. **Pros:** the glamping areas of Sandy Pines are quiet zones; nightly bonfires under the stars without roughing it; all lodgings equipped with outdoor sitting area, picnic table, and fire ring. **Cons:** expect all that comes with being in nature; glamping options are not pet-friendly; three-night minimum stay (seasonal). $ *Rooms from:*

$109 ✉ *277 Mills Rd., Kennebunkport* ☎ *207/967–2483* ⊕ *sandypinescamping.com* ⏲ *Closed mid-Oct.–mid-May* ⇆ *60 units* ⏲ *No Meals.*

The Wanderer Cottages

$$ | **MOTEL** | This cluster of tidy, well-appointed cottages opened in summer 2022 in a quiet area that's still a stone's throw from beaches and Dock Square. **Pros:** serene, nicely landscaped setting; heated saltwater pool; private, spacious-feeling cottages, some with sitting areas. **Cons:** no food or bar on-site; no kids allowed; 1.5 miles from Dock Square and 1.2 miles from Parson's Beach. $ *Rooms from: $349* ✉ *195 Sea Rd., Kennebunk* ☎ *207/849–7400* ⊕ *wanderercottages.com* ⇆ *17 cottages* ⏲ *Free Breakfast.*

🛍 Shopping

★ Daytrip Society

SOUVENIRS | **FAMILY** | The impossibly hip and well-selected array of goods at this modern-design shop makes it an excellent place for both window-shopping and finding gifts for just about anyone on your list (including yourself). A refreshing departure from the rest of the somewhat stodgy gift shops in the village, this boutique is chock-full of eye candy, most of which is also functional. There are many locally sourced and contemporary products, from hats and jewelry to novelty books, home decor, and outdoor adventure essentials. Check out Daytrip Jr., its equally hip children's store around the corner. ✉ *4 Dock Sq., Kennebunkport* ☎ *207/967–4440* ⊕ *www.daytripsociety.com.*

★ Farm + Table

HOUSEWARES | This delightful shop is housed in a bright-red Maine barn filled with household items both useful and pleasing to the eye. Browse the collection of ceramics, linens, kitchen essentials, and more by small-batch makers, and pick up a few artisan treats, too. ✉ *8 Langsford Rd., Cape Porpoise* ☎ *207/604–8029* ⊕ *www.farmtablekennebunkport.com.*

Port Canvas

HANDBAGS | Since 1968, Port Canvas has been hand-crafting sporty, customizable canvas totes and duffels perfect for lugging your souvenirs home. Other products range from raincoats to keychains. Each stitcher puts their initials inside the bag ensuring authenticity and quality. ✉ *39 Limerick Rd., Kennebunkport* ☎ *207/985–9767* 🌐 *www.portcanvas.com* 🕓 *Closed Fri.–Sun.*

Activities

Rugosa Lobster Tours

BOATING | **FAMILY** | Lobster-trap hauling trips aboard the *Rugosa* in the scenic waters off the Kennebunks run daily, from Memorial Day through Columbus Day. ✉ *Nonantum Resort, 95 Ocean Ave., Kennebunkport* ☎ *207/468–4095* 🌐 *www.rugosalobstertours.com* 🎟 *$49 per person for a group tour.*

★ The Pineapple Ketch

SAILING | **FAMILY** | One terrific way to get out on the water and see some marine life is aboard a classic 38-foot, Downeaster ketch steered by a knowledgeable captain and crew. Tours last 90 minutes, and soft drinks are provided. You'll have to bring your own snacks, as well as wine, beer, or cocktails, which are especially good to have on hand during the sunset cruises. ✉ *95 Ocean Ave., Kennebunkport* ☎ *207/888–3445* 🌐 *pineappleketch.com* 🎟 *From $55 per person* 🕓 *Closed mid-Oct.–late May.*

Biddeford

11 miles north of Kennebunkport, 18 miles south of Portland.

Biddeford is waking from a deep sleep, having devolved into something of a ghost town for a good deal of the past half century. Chefs and small-business owners who have relocated from Portland are giving Biddeford's beautiful old-mill-town architecture a new lease on life. Developers have taken note as well, revamping many historic buildings, including the imposing 233,000-square-foot Lincoln Mill. Today, Biddeford is filled with art galleries and quirky boutiques, a distillery, an art school, and top-notch restaurants.

GETTING HERE AND AROUND

From I–95, get off at Exit 32 and follow Alfred Street to Biddeford's downtown. U.S. 1 also runs right through town. Amtrak's *Downeaster* train stops at Saco; the train station is just steps from Biddeford's mill buildings, breweries, and restaurants.

VISITOR INFORMATION

CONTACTS Biddeford-Saco Chamber of Commerce. ✉ *28 Water St., Biddeford* ☎ *207/282–1567* 🌐 *www.biddefordsacochamber.org.*

Restaurants

★ Elda

$$$$ | **MODERN AMERICAN** | Award-winning chef Bowman Brown is behind this restaurant, situated in an old mill building—transformed with exquisite, Scandinavian-style decor—and offering just two tasting-menu seatings (at 5 and 8:30) a night. This is one of Maine's most highly regarded and splurge-worthy dining experiences, featuring meticulously prepared, seasonally inspired dishes, but if your budget is tight, note that the first-floor Jackrabbit Cafe serves small plates and pastries for a fraction of the tasting-menu price. **Known for:** unhurried, indulgent dining (meals often last three hours); focus on locally sourced ingredients; impeccable, modern-meets-original design, with an old vault serving as bar. [$] *Average main: $160* ✉ *14 Main St., 2nd fl., Biddeford* ☎ *207/602–0359* 🌐 *www.eldamaine.com* 🕓 *No lunch. Closed Sun.–Tues. and for 2-wk break in spring.*

★ **Goldthwaite's Pool Lobster**

$$ | SEAFOOD | FAMILY | This classic spot has been a go-to in the seaside hamlet of Biddeford Pool for over 100 years. Now part general store, part takeout spot, it's a one-stop-shop for sunscreen, wine and beer, and locally made pies; the kitchen offers a bevy of Maine classics (including lobster dinners and fresh lobster rolls), sometimes with a twist (like haddock tacos with ginger-cucumber salsa or a blueberry cream cheese tart for dessert). **Known for:** award-winning clam chowder; decadent desserts made in-house; reasonable prices with million-dollar views. ⓢ *Average main: $22 ⊠ 3 Lester B. Orcutt Blvd., Biddeford ☎ 207/284–5000 ⊕ poollobster.com ⊗ General store closed mid-Sept.–mid-May; restaurant closed Labor Day–early June.*

★ **Palace Diner**

$$ | AMERICAN | Everything about this diner, set in an old-fashioned train car just off Main Street, is retro except the food. Hop on a stool at the counter (that's all there is), enjoy the Motown tunes, and tuck into one of the deluxe sandwiches for breakfast or lunch. **Known for:** diner food that's anything but standard; delicious fried-chicken sandwich with cabbage slaw and French fries; fantastic collaboration with local chefs from regional restaurants. ⓢ *Average main: $12 ⊠ 18 Franklin St., Biddeford ☎ 207/284–0015 ⊕ www.palacedinerme.com ▭ No credit cards ⊗ No dinner.*

🛏 Hotels

★ **The Lincoln Hotel**

$$ | HOTEL | A far cry from Maine's coastal bed-and-breakfasts and quaint inns, this hotel in the massive, revitalized Lincoln Mill has a distinctly urban feel. **Pros:** cool base for exploring Biddeford's many watering holes; gas fireplaces in every room; soaring ceilings and huge windows with city views. **Cons:** not close to beaches or outdoor activities; no room service (only grab-and-go food in the lobby); trendy vibe might not appeal to some. ⓢ *Rooms from: $299 ⊠ 17 Lincoln St., Biddeford ☎ 207/815–3977 ⊕ www.lincolnhotelmaine.com ⇥ 33 rooms ⦿ No Meals.*

Scarborough, Prout's Neck, and Cape Elizabeth

Scarborough and Prout's Neck: 10 miles northeast of Biddeford. Cape Elizabeth: 10 miles southeast of Scarborough, 8 miles southeast of Portland.

Among the noteworthy attractions in the affluent Portland bedroom community of Cape Elizabeth are the famed Portland Head Light and the Cape Elizabeth Light, the subject of a well-known Edward Hopper painting.

Speaking of famous artists, Winslow Homer painted many of his famous oceanscapes from a tiny studio on the rocky peninsula known as Prout's Neck, a now-exclusive gated community 7 miles south of Cape Elizabeth. The studio is open to tours only through the Portland Museum of Art. The only other way to access Prouts Neck is by parking outside the gates and walking along a popular cliff trail.

GETTING HERE AND AROUND

The somewhat rural landscapes of Scarborough, the hamlet of Prout's Neck, and Cape Elizabeth are best explored by car. From Route 1 North, Routes 207 and 77 travel along the coast; most of the state parks, preserves, and vistas are along this route. From Portland, take the Casco Bay Bridge and continue onto Route 77 South.

◉ Sights

Cape Elizabeth Light

LIGHTHOUSE | FAMILY | This was the site of twin lighthouses erected in 1828—and locals still call it Two Lights—but one of the lighthouses was dismantled in 1924 and converted into a private residence.

Old Orchard Beach

Located between Kennebunkport and Portland, Old Orchard Beach was a classic, upscale, place-to-be-seen resort area in the late 19th century, when the railroad brought wealthy families looking for entertainment and the benefits of fresh sea air. During the 1940s and '50s, the pier had a dance hall where stars of the time performed. Although the luster has dulled and Old Orchard is now a little tacky (though pleasantly so) these days, it remains a good place for seaside entertainments.

The center of the action is a 7-mile strip of sand beach that's accompanied by Palace Playland, New England's only boardwalk amusement park (think Coney Island or Seaside Heights). Fire claimed the end of the pier—at one time it jutted out nearly 1,800 feet into the sea—but rides, miniature golf, midway games, and souvenir stands still line both sides. Despite the peak-season crowds and fried-food odors, the atmosphere is captivating; the town even sponsors a fireworks display every Thursday night in the summer. Places to stay range from cheap motels to cottage colonies to full-service seasonal hotels. You won't find free parking, but there are ample lots. Amtrak has a seasonal stop here, too.

For even more family fun, Saco's Funtown Splashtown USA is just 10 minutes from the Old Orchard Beach Pier. Kids of all ages can cool off and play for hours amid the thrill adventures, kiddie rides, waterslides, and play pools.

The other half still operates, and you can get a great photo of it from the end of Two Lights Road (note that it's not quite visible from the nearby Two Lights State Park). The lighthouse itself is closed to the public, but you can explore the tidal pools at its base, looking for small, edible snails known as periwinkles, or just "wrinkles," as they're sometimes referred to in Maine. Picnic tables are also available. ⊠ At end of Two Lights Rd., across from The Lobster Shack at Two Lights (225 Two Lights Rd.), Cape Elizabeth.

★ Portland Head Light
LIGHTHOUSE | FAMILY | Familiar to many from photographs and the Edward Hopper painting Portland Head-Light (1927), this lighthouse was commissioned by George Washington in 1790. The towering, white-stone structure stands over the keeper's quarters, a white home with a blazing red roof, today the Museum at Portland Head Light. The lighthouse is in 90-acre Fort Williams Park, a sprawling green space with walking paths, picnic facilities, a beach and—you guessed it—a cool old fort. ⊠ 1000 Shore Rd., Cape Elizabeth ☎ 207/799–2661 ⊕ www.portlandheadlight.com ⊠ Museum $2 ⊙ Museum closed mid-Oct.–late May.

★ Winslow Homer Studio
HISTORIC HOME | FAMILY | The great American landscape painter created many of his best-known works in this seaside home between 1883 until his death in 1910. It's easy to see how this rocky, jagged peninsula might have been inspiring. The only way to get a look is on a tour with the Portland Museum of Art, which leads 2½-hour strolls through the historic property. ⊠ 5 Winslow Homer Rd., Scarborough ☎ 207/775–6148 ⊕ www.portlandmuseum.org ⊠ $65 ⊙ Closed Nov.–Apr.

🍴 Restaurants

⭐ Bite Into Maine

$$ | SEAFOOD | FAMILY | Hands down Maine's best lobster roll is found at this food truck that overlooks the idyllic Portland Head Light in Cape Elizabeth. Traditional rolls smothered in ungodly amounts of drawn butter are delicious, but you've also got the option to get out of the lobster comfort zone with rolls featuring flavors like wasabi, curry, and chipotle. **Known for:** quick and informal spot for a bite; unbeatable view over the ocean; always fresh lobster. $ *Average main: $24 ⊠ 1000 Shore Rd., Cape Elizabeth ☎ 207/289–6142 ⊕ www.biteinto-maine.com ⊗ Closed mid-Nov.–mid-Apr.*

⭐ The Lobster Shack at Two Lights

$$ | SEAFOOD | FAMILY | A classic spot since the 1920s, you can't beat the location—right on the water, below the lighthouse pair that gives Two Lights State Park its name—and the food's not bad either. Enjoy fresh lobster whole or piled into a hot-dog bun with a dollop of mayo, or opt for the delicious chowder, fried clams, or fish-and-chips. **Known for:** picnic tables with unparalleled views; family-friendly environment; mini-homemade blueberry pies. $ *Average main: $25 ⊠ 225 Two Lights Rd., Cape Elizabeth ☎ 207/799–1677 ⊕ www.lobstershacktwolights.com ⊗ Closed late Oct.–late Mar.*

⭐ Shade Eatery at Higgins Beach Inn

$$ | SEAFOOD | FAMILY | This charming neighborhood restaurant and bar just steps from the beach serves up generous, deeply satisfying dishes filled with locally sourced ingredients. Seafood plays a big role in the menu, with lobster rolls brimming with fresh meat; fish tacos stuffed with cilantro, lime crema, and coleslaw; a seafood chowder; and a lobster tostada. **Known for:** family-friendly environment; three-season-porch dining; casual and perfect for a postbeach bite. $ *Average main: $24 ⊠ Higgins Beach Inn, 36 Ocean Ave., Scarborough ☎ 207/883–1479 ⊕ www.higginsbeach-inn.com/dining ⊗ Breakfast daily and dinner Wed.–Sun. mid-May–mid-Oct. Lunch daily Memorial Day–Labor Day.*

🛏 Hotels

⭐ Higgins Beach Inn

$$ | B&B/INN | FAMILY | Decidedly "new Maine," this lovingly renovated 1892 inn with a laid-back, summer-casual kind of nonchalance is just steps from the surfer's paradise that is Higgins Beach. **Pros:** very family-friendly; exceptionally efficient and warm service; small touches (beach towels, sparkling-water dispenser) that make a difference. **Cons:** no pets allowed; a short walk to the beach; limited common areas. $ *Rooms from: $269 ⊠ 34 Ocean Ave., Scarborough ☎ 207/883–6684 ⊕ www.higginsbeach-inn.com ⊗ Closed Oct.–Apr. ⇌ 23 rooms ❅ Free Breakfast.*

⭐ Inn by the Sea

$$$$ | B&B/INN | With a location on stunning Crescent Beach, some of the state's most gracious service, and a top-notch restaurant that delights at every meal, you might never want to leave the aptly named Inn by the Sea. **Pros:** amenities like a spa and an outdoor pool with water views; hands down the most dog-friendly accommodations in Maine; direct access to Crescent Beach with chic beach chairs, towels, and umbrellas on hand. **Cons:** a little removed from Portland's food scene; not for the budget-minded; minimum stays in the high season. $ *Rooms from: $719 ⊠ 40 Bowery Beach Rd., Cape Elizabeth ☎ 207/799–3134 ⊕ www.innbythesea.com ⇌ 62 rooms ❅ No Meals.*

Portland

28 miles from Kennebunk via I–95 and I–295; 122 miles from Boston via I-95.

Maine's largest city may be considered small by national standards—its population is just 66,000—but its character, spirit, and appeal make it feel much larger. It's well worth at least a day or two of exploration, even if all you do is spend the entire time eating and drinking at the many phenomenal restaurants, bakeries and specialty dessert shops, craft cocktail bars, and microbreweries scattered across the city.

Portland's burgeoning Arts District centers on a revitalized Congress Street, which runs the length of the peninsular city from alongside the Western Promenade in the southwest to the Eastern Promenade on Munjoy Hill in the northeast. Washington Street, home to some of the city's newest and most exciting restaurants, runs through the East End and Munjoy Hill. Congress Street is peppered with interesting shops, eclectic restaurants, and excellent museums.

Just beyond the Arts District is the West End, an area of extensive architectural wealth. Predominantly residential, it's filled with stunning examples of the city's emphasis on preserving this past. Water tours of the harbor and excursions to the Casco Bay islands depart from the piers of Commercial Street.

GETTING HERE AND AROUND

If you're flying, the Portland International Jetport is about a 20-minute drive from Old Port. It offers direct flights to many domestic destinations; airlines include American, United, Delta, Elite Airways, Frontier, JetBlue, Southwest, and Sun Country.

If you're driving, take Interstate 95 to Interstate 295 to get to the Portland Peninsula and downtown. Commercial Street runs along the harbor, Fore Street

is one block up in the heart of the Old Port, and the Arts District stretches along diagonal Congress Street. Munjoy Hill is on the eastern end of the peninsula and the West End on the opposite side.

Alternatively, there is Amtrak (via the Downeaster train) and bus (Concord Coach Lines) service from Boston.

Portland is wonderfully walkable, but there are taxis and ride-shares available. To get to many islands in Casco Bay, hop aboard a waterfront ferry or taxi.

TOURS

Casco Bay Lines

BOATING | FAMILY | Casco Bay Lines operates ferry service to the seven bay islands with year-round populations. Summer offerings include music cruises, lighthouse excursions, and a trip to Bailey Island with a stopover for lunch. Round-trip fees range from $7.70 to $11.55, depending on which island you're visiting.

Peaks Island is the only island to allow cars to be transported by ferry, and those car reservations are often tough to get during the busy summer months. On most islands, bikes and/or golf carts are available for rent close to the ferry terminal. You can bring along your own bike on the ferry for $6.50 per adult and $3.25 per child. ✉ *Maine State Pier, 56 Commercial St., The Old Port and the Waterfront* ☎ *207/774–7871* ⊕ *www. cascobaylines.com.*

Lucky Catch Cruises

BOATING | FAMILY | Set sail in a real lobster boat: This company gives you the genuine experience, which includes hauling traps and the chance to purchase the catch. ✉ *Long Wharf, 170 Commercial St., The Old Port and the Waterfront* ☎ *207/761–0941* ⊕ *www.luckycatch.com* ▥ *From $25* ☉ *Closed Nov.–Apr.*

Maine Foodie Tours

SPECIAL-INTEREST TOURS | Learn about Portland's culinary history and sample such local delights as lobster tacos,

Portland's busy harbor is full of working boats, pleasure craft, and ferries headed to the Casco Bay Islands.

organic cheese, and the famous Maine whoopie pie. The culinary walking tours include stops at fishmongers, bakeries, and cheese shops that provide products to Portland's famed restaurants. From summer into early fall, you can also take a chocolate tour, a bike-and-brewery tour, or a trolley tour with a stop at a micro-brewery. Tours begin at various locales in the Old Port. ✉ *320 Fore St., Portland* ☎ *207/233–7485* ⊕ *www.mainefoodi-etours.com* ✉ *From $29.*

Odyssey Whale Watch

BOATING | FAMILY | From mid-May to mid-October, Odyssey Whale Watch leads whale-watching and deep-sea-fishing excursions. ✉ *Long Wharf, 170 Commercial St., The Old Port and the Waterfront* ☎ *207/775–0727* ⊕ *www. odysseywhalewatch.com* ✉ *From $29* ⊘ *Closed Nov.–Apr.*

★ Portland Schooner Co.

BOATING | FAMILY | May through Octo-ber this company and its efficient crew offers daily two-hour windjammer cruises aboard the beautiful vintage schooners, *The Bagheera, Timberwind,* and *Wendameen.* The sunsets alone are worth the sail, but breezes on a hot summer day and views of the islands put the experience over the top. You can also arrange private charters. ✉ *Maine State Pier, 56 Commercial St., The Old Port and the Waterfront* ☎ *207/766–2500* ⊕ *www.portlandschooner.com* ✉ *Prices vary according to time of sails* ⊘ *Closed Nov.–Apr.*

Portland Discovery Land and Sea Tours

BUS TOURS | FAMILY | These informative trolley tours detail the city's historical and architectural highlights, Memorial Day–October. It's one of the best ways to tour the harbor and Casco Bay, including an up-close look at several lighthouses. Options include combining a city tour with a bay or lighthouse cruise. ✉ *Long Wharf, 170 Commercial St., Portland* ☎ *207/774–0808* ⊕ *www.portland-discovery.com* ✉ *From $23* ☞ *Closed Nov.–Apr.*

305

The Maine Coast PORTLAND

7

Portland Fire Engine Co. Tours
SPECIAL-INTEREST TOURS | FAMILY | See Portland on a vintage Fire Engine on these narrated, 50-minute tours that highlight the city's lighthouses, civil war forts, and historical buildings, and architecture. Tours leave from the waterfront and circle through the city, passing everything from the Maine State Pier and East End Beach to Longfellow Square, Portland Museum of Art, and Monument Square. ⊠ 180 Commercial St., Old Port, Portland ☎ 207/252–6358 ⊕ portlandfiretours.com ⊠ From $30 ⊘ Closed Nov.–May.

VISITOR INFORMATION
CONTACTS Downtown Portland. ⊠ 549 Congress St., Portland ☎ 207/772–6828 ⊕ www.portlandmaine.com. **Greater Portland Convention and Visitors Bureau.** ⊠ 14 Ocean Gateway Pier, Portland ☎ 207/772–4994 ⊕ www.visitportland. com.

The Old Port and the Waterfront

A major international port and a working harbor since the early 17th century, Portland's Old Port and the Waterfront bridge the gap between the city's historic commercial activities and those of today. It is home to fishing boats docked alongside whale-watching charters, luxury yachts, cruise ships, and oil tankers from around the globe. Commercial Street parallels the water and is lined with brick buildings and warehouses that were built following the Great Fire of 1866. In the 19th century, candle makers and sail stitchers plied their trades here; today specialty shops, art galleries, and restaurants have taken up residence.

Cannabis in Vacationland ◉

Though Maine voters approved legalizing the recreational use and sales of marijuana in November 2016, various delays prevented retail shops from opening until October 2020. Since then a deluge of outlets has opened in the Greater Portland area, and although availability has expanded statewide, Portland is by far the place to find the most retail options.

◉ Sights

Harbor Fish Market
STORE/MALL | A Portland favorite since 1968, this freshest-of-the-fresh seafood market ships lobsters and other Maine delectables almost anywhere in the country. A bright-red facade on a working wharf opens into a bustling space with bubbling lobster tanks and fish, clams, and other shellfish on ice; employees are as skilled with a fillet knife as sushi chefs. There is also a small retail store. ⊠ 9 Custom House Wharf, The Old Port and the Waterfront ☎ 207/775–0251 ⊕ www.harborfish.com ⊠ Free.

🍽 Restaurants

Flatbread
$$ | PIZZA | FAMILY | Families, students, and bohemian types gather at this popular New England chain flatbread-pizza place where two massive wood-fire ovens are the heart of the soaring, warehouselike space. Waits can be long on weekends and in summer, but you can call a half-hour ahead to put your name on the list, or grab a drink from the bar and wait outside with a view of the harbor. **Known for:** unfussy, kid-friendly atmosphere;

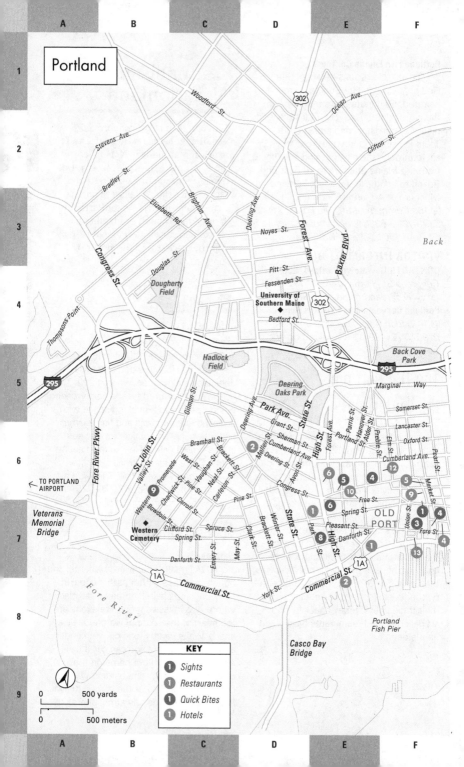

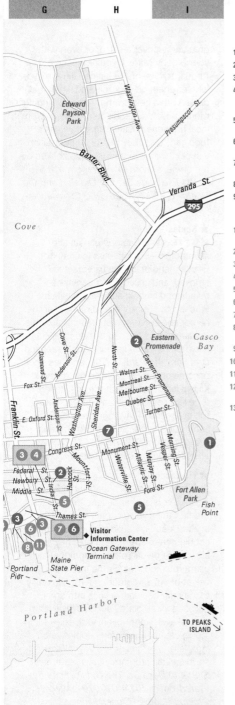

outdoor dining on a deck that overlooks the working waterfront; dogs allowed on outside deck. $ *Average main: $18* ✉ *72 Commercial St., The Old Port and the Waterfront* ☎ *207/772–8777* 🌐 *www.flatbreadcompany.com.*

★ Fore Street

$$$ | MODERN AMERICAN | One of Maine's most legendary chefs, Sam Hayward, opened this much-lauded restaurant in a renovated warehouse on the edge of the Old Port in 1996; today every copper-top table in the main dining room has a view of the enormous brick oven and soapstone hearth that anchor the open kitchen. The menu changes daily to reflect the freshest ingredients from Maine's farms and waters, as well as the tremendous creativity of the staff. **Known for:** turnspit roasted meats; handmade charcuterie; last-minute planners take heart: a third of the tables are reserved for walk-ins. $ *Average main: $30* ✉ *288 Fore St., The Old Port and the Waterfront* ☎ *207/775–2717* 🌐 *www.forestreet.biz* 🕒 *No lunch.*

Gilbert's Chowder House

$$ | SEAFOOD | FAMILY | This is the real deal, as quintessential as old-school Maine dining can be. Clam rakes and nautical charts hang from the walls of this unpretentious waterfront diner, and the flavors come from the depths of the North Atlantic, prepared and presented simply: fried scallops, haddock, clams and extraordinary clam cakes, and fish, clam, and seafood chowders (corn, too). **Known for:** family-friendly environment; classic lobster rolls, served on toasted hot-dog buns bursting with claw and tail meat; an ice-cream parlor to round out your meal; chalkboard daily specials. $ *Average main: $19* ✉ *92 Commercial St., The Old Port and the Waterfront* ☎ *207/871–5636* 🌐 *www.gilbertschowderhouse.com.*

Highroller Lobster Co.

$$ | SEAFOOD | FAMILY | Opened in early 2018, this high-energy spot serves lobster numerous ways—in a roll, on a stick, on a burger, over a salad, or even with your Bloody Mary. If you're feeling adventurous, try one of the sauces (lime mayo, lobster ghee) on your roll, and wash it all down with a beer from the ever-changing menu, which depends on availability from local breweries. **Known for:** origins as a food cart; the lobby pop (a lobster tail on a stick); Highroller whoopie pies baked by the owner's mom. $ *Average main: $15* ✉ *104 Exchange St., The Old Port and the Waterfront* ☎ *207/536–1623* 🌐 *highroller-lobster.com.*

★ Scales

$$$$ | SEAFOOD | Seafood purists and adventurers alike find bliss in chef Fred Elliot's menu of superb pan-roasted, smoked, and grilled fish; fresh-as-can-be seafood crudos; and fried shellfish. Perched on Maine Wharf directly over the harbor, the contemporary-but-comfortable restaurant was opened by two local culinary heroes, restaurateur Dana Street and chef Sam Hayward, in 2016, and has since become one of Portland's most beloved. **Known for:** beautiful waterfront location; excellent pan-roasted and grilled seafood; fun bar scene. $ *Average main: $39* ✉ *68 Commercial St., The Old Port and the Waterfront* ☎ *207/8050444* 🌐 *www.scalesrestaurant.com* 🕒 *Closed Mon.*

★ Via Vecchia

$$$ | MODERN ITALIAN | Sparkling and gigantic crystal chandeliers aren't exactly the first thing you'd expect to greet you in a brick-and-ivy building tucked into a cobblestoned street, yet here they are—along with myriad other unapologetically glamorous touches. Settle into a green velvet booth and order up a meticulously made craft cocktail, or tuck into small Italian-inspired plates such as juicy lamb belly skewers or bucatini with spicy 'nduja cream. **Known for:** people-watching; Italian small plates; an excellent craft cocktail program. $ *Average main: $29* ✉ *10 Dana St., The Old Port and the Waterfront* ☎ *207/407–7070* 🌐 *www.vvoldport.com* 🕒 *Closed Mon.*

Coffee and Quick Bites

Bard Coffee

$ | **CAFÉ** | The beans sourcing this shop's delicious brew are bought from a handful of small growers—you can read their bios on the website—and roasted in-house. Enjoy your brew hot, cold, or iced with a locally made baked good. **Known for:** close relationships with sources; passionate, knowledgeable baristas; bulk coffee and tea. [$] *Average main: $5* ✉ *185 Middle St., The Old Port and the Waterfront* ☎ *207/899–4788* 🌐 *www.bardcoffee.com.*

★ **Gelato Fiasco**

$ | **CAFÉ** | **FAMILY** | Proper Italian gelato and *sorbetto* here come in traditional flavors as well as more offbeat varieties like torched marshmallow s'more, mascarpone pistachio caramel, and mint brownie cookie. There are new flavors every day, along with espresso and other hot drinks. **Known for:** you can try every single flavor before deciding on what you'll get; long lines out the door in the summer; multigenerational bonding spot. [$] *Average main: $5* ✉ *425 Fore St., The Old Port and the Waterfront* ☎ *207/699–4314* 🌐 *www.gelatofiasco.com.*

The Holy Donut

$ | **CAFÉ** | **FAMILY** | Don't pass up a chance to try these sweet and savory, all-natural, Maine potato-based doughnuts glazed in flavors such as dark chocolate–sea salt, maple, pomegranate, triple berry, and chai, or stuffed with delicious fillings like bacon and cheddar, or ricotta. There are always new inventions, too, such as salted chocolate caramel and key lime pie. **Known for:** long lines, but worth the wait; shop closes for the day once all the doughnuts are sold; vegan and gluten-free options are available. [$] *Average main: $5* ✉ *177 Commercial St., The Old Port and the Waterfront* ☎ *207/331–5655* 🌐 *www.theholydonut.com.*

★ **Standard Baking Co.**

$ | **BAKERY** | **FAMILY** | You'd be hard-pressed to find a more pitch-perfect bakery in the Pine Tree State, but you'll have to pop by early (or put in an order in advance) to get your mitts on these delectable baked goods. The perfectly airy croissants, crusty baguettes, beguiling tarts, dainty Madeleines, and creative breads incorporate locally sourced grains and are nothing short of revelations. **Known for:** good selection of locally roasted coffees; amazing galettes and brioches; creative scones. [$] *Average main: $3* ✉ *75 Commercial St., The Old Port and the Waterfront* ☎ *207/772–5519* 🌐 *www.standardbakingco.com.*

Hotels

Hilton Garden Inn Portland Downtown Waterfront

$$$ | **HOTEL** | This bright, clean, and modern hotel is a perfect base for exploring on foot the adjacent Old Port and nearby East End, and it's only a walk across the street to catch a ferry to the Casco Bay islands. **Pros:** heated saltwater lap pool; central location for exploring; some rooms with harbor view. **Cons:** no pets; no self-parking; some rooms face neighboring businesses. [$] *Rooms from: $379* ✉ *65 Commercial St., The Old Port and the Waterfront* ☎ *207/780–0780* 🌐 *www.hilton.com/en/hilton-garden-inn* 🛏 *120 rooms* 🍴 *No Meals.*

The Portland Regency Hotel and Spa

$$ | **HOTEL** | Not part of a chain despite the "Regency" name, this brick building in the center of the Old Port served as Portland's armory in the late 19th century. **Pros:** easy walk to sites; pet-friendly ($75 nonrefundable cleaning fee); full-service spa with lounges, saunas, steam rooms, hot tub, and an array of luxurious treatments. **Cons:** no pool; busy downtown location; not all rooms have noteworthy views. [$] *Rooms from: $300* ✉ *20 Milk St., The Old Port and the Waterfront* ☎ *207/774–4200, 800/727–3436* 🌐 *www.*

theregency.com 🔊 *95 rooms* |O| *No Meals.*

★ The Press Hotel

$$$ | **HOTEL** | **FAMILY** | In a former newspaper building, this boutique hotel is part of Marriott's Autograph Collection; the hotel feels both broadly cosmopolitan and distinctly Maine. **Pros:** Frette bed linens and Maine-made Cuddledown comforters and bed throws; sparkling-clean rooms with a modern-design feel; art gallery and excellent public spaces with tasteful furnishings. **Cons:** right next to the fire department; valet parking can be expensive; some rooms have underwhelming views. $ *Rooms from: $375* ✉ *119 Exchange St., The Old Port and the Waterfront* ☎ *877/890–5641* ⊕ *www.thepresshotel.com* 🔊 *110 rooms* |O| *No Meals.*

Y Nightlife

Gritty McDuff's Portland Brew Pub

BREWPUBS | Maine's original brewpub serves fine ales, British pub fare, and seafood dishes. There are between six and eight rotating ales on tap, and there's always a seasonal offering. ✉ *396 Fore St., The Old Port and the Waterfront* ☎ *207/772–2739* ⊕ *www.grittys.com.*

★ Portland Hunt and Alpine Club

BARS | Scandinavian-inspired dishes and serious craft cocktails drive this hip locale that also offers excellent charcuterie and seafood boards. If it's free, grab a seat in the intimate alpine-style hut, off to the side of the main room. And don't miss the excellent happy hour, weekdays 1–6. ✉ *75 Market St., The Old Port and the Waterfront* ☎ *207/747–4754* ⊕ *www.huntandalpineclub.com.*

🛍 Shopping

Abacus Gallery

ANTIQUES & COLLECTIBLES | This appealing crafts gallery has gift items in glass, wood, and textiles, as well as fine modern jewelry. ✉ *44 Exchange St., The Old Port and the Waterfront* ☎ *207/772–4880* ⊕ *www.abacusgallery.com.*

Lisa Marie's Made in Maine

SOUVENIRS | Here you'll find an excellent selection of locally sourced items from soaps and candles to dish towels, pottery, and jewelry, all made in the great state of Maine. ✉ *35 Exchange St., The Old Port and the Waterfront* ☎ *207/828–1515* ⊕ *www.lisamariesmadeinmaine.com.*

★ Sea Bags

OTHER SPECIALTY STORE | The brand's flagship location displays totes in every shape and size made from recycled sailcloth and decorated with bright, graphic patterns. Check out the display that shows you exactly how a sail is used to create all the different bags and accessories. The factory store, located just a few blocks away on the Custom House Wharf, is where the bags are actually sewn; you can find some factory sales as well. ✉ *123 Commercial St., The Old Port and the Waterfront* ☎ *207/835–0096* ⊕ *www.seabags.com.*

★ Sherman's Maine Coast Book Shops

BOOKS | Open since 1886, Sherman's is Maine's oldest bookstore chain. The Portland store has an impressive stock of well-selected books interspersed with excellent gift choices, such as stationery, candles, and holiday decor, as well as a fun array of toys. It's a good place to spend a cold or rainy day perusing the selection. ✉ *49 Exchange St., The Old Port and the Waterfront* ☎ *207/773–4100* ⊕ *www.shermans.com.*

🏃 Activities

Casco Bay Lines

BOATING | **FAMILY** | Casco Bay Lines operates ferry service to the seven bay islands with year-round populations. Summer offerings include music cruises, lighthouse excursions, and a trip to Bailey Island with a stopover for lunch. Round-trip fees range from $7.70 to $11.55, depending on which island you're visiting.

Peaks Island is the only island to allow cars to be transported by ferry, and those car reservations are often tough to get during the busy summer months. On most islands, bikes and/or golf carts are available for rent close to the ferry terminal. You can bring along your own bike on the ferry for $6.50 per adult and $3.25 per child. ✉ *Maine State Pier, 56 Commercial St., The Old Port and the Waterfront* ☎ *207/774–7871* ⊕ *www. cascobaylines.com.*

Lucky Catch Cruises

BOATING | FAMILY | Set sail in a real lobster boat: This company gives you the genuine experience, which includes hauling traps and the chance to purchase the catch. ✉ *Long Wharf, 170 Commercial St., The Old Port and the Waterfront* ☎ *207/761–0941* ⊕ *www.luckycatch.com* ➥ *From $25* ⊙ *Closed Nov.–Apr.*

Odyssey Whale Watch

BOATING | FAMILY | From mid-May to mid-October, Odyssey Whale Watch leads whale-watching and deep-sea-fishing excursions. ✉ *Long Wharf, 170 Commercial St., The Old Port and the Waterfront* ☎ *207/775–0727* ⊕ *www. odysseywhalewatch.com* ➥ *From $29* ⊙ *Closed Nov.–Apr.*

★ Portland Schooner Co.

BOATING | FAMILY | May through October this company and its efficient crew offers daily two-hour windjammer cruises aboard the beautiful vintage schooners, *The Bagheera, Timberwind,* and *Wendameen.* The sunsets alone are worth the sail, but breezes on a hot summer day and views of the islands put the experience over the top. You can also arrange private charters. ✉ *Maine State Pier, 56 Commercial St., The Old Port and the Waterfront* ☎ *207/766–2500* ⊕ *www.portlandschooner.com* ➥ *Prices vary according to time of sails* ⊙ *Closed Nov.–Apr.*

East End, Munjoy Hill, and Washington Ave.

These three sections of town are often referred to independently, but they also overlap in large parts; Washington Avenue runs through both areas, and Munjoy Hill is part of the East End. The latter includes the Eastern Promenade, East End Beach, and the Portland Observatory. Meanwhile, Washington Avenue has become one of the most concentrated areas of fantastic food in all Maine. From authentic Thai fixings and ultrafresh oysters to creative barbecue and locally made kombucha, it's all here.

◉ Sights

East End Beach

BEACH | FAMILY | Portland's only public beach, it's set at the bottom of the hill of the Eastern Promenade. Its panoramic views of Casco Bay make it a popular summer spot, as do amenities like convenient parking, picnic tables, and a boat launch. **Amenities:** food and drink; parking (fee); toilets; water sports. **Best for:** sunrise; sunsets; swimming; walking. ✉ *Cutter St., East End.*

Eastern Promenade

PROMENADE | FAMILY | Between the city's two promenades, this one, often overlooked by tourists, has by far the best view. Gracious Victorian homes, many now converted to condos and apartments, border one side of the street. On the other is 68 acres of hillside parkland that includes Ft. Allen Park and, at the base of the hill, the Eastern Prom Trail and tiny East End Beach and boat launch. On a sunny day the Eastern Prom is a lovely spot for picnicking, snacking (there are always a few top-notch food trucks), and people-watching. ✉ *Washington Ave. to Fore St., East End.*

Maine Narrow Gauge Railroad Museum

TRAIN/TRAIN STATION | FAMILY | Whether you're crazy about old trains or just want to see the sights from a different perspective, the railroad museum has an extensive collection of locomotives and rail coaches, and offers scenic tours on narrow-gauge railcars. The 3-mile jaunts run on the hour, at 10, 11, noon, 1, 2, and 3 every day in the operating season. Rides take you along Casco Bay, at the foot of the Eastern Promenade. The operating season caps off with a fall harvest ride (complete with cider), and during the Christmas season there are special Polar Express rides, based on the popular children's book. ✉ *58 Fore St., East End* ☎ *207/828–0814* ⊕ *www.mainenarrow-gauge.org* ☞ *Museum $5, train rides $12* ⊙ *Closed Nov.–Apr.*

Portland Observatory

OBSERVATORY | FAMILY | This octagonal observatory on Munjoy Hill was built in 1807 by Captain Lemuel Moody, a retired sea captain, as a maritime signal tower. Moody used a telescope to identify incoming ships, and flags to signal to merchants where to unload their cargo. Held in place by 122 tons of ballast, it's the last remaining historic maritime signal station in the country. The guided tour leads all the way to the dome, where you can step out on the deck and take in views of Portland, the islands, and inland toward the White Mountains. ✉ *138 Congress St., East End* ☎ *207/774–5561* ⊕ *www.portlandlandmarks.org* ☞ *$10* ⊙ *Closed mid-Oct.–late May.*

 Restaurants

★ Duckfat

$$ | MODERN AMERICAN | FAMILY | Even in midafternoon, this small, casual, and cool panini-and-more shop in the Old Port is packed. The focus here is everyday farm-to-table fare: the signature Belgian fries are made with Maine potatoes cooked,

yes, in duck fat and served in paper cones, and standards include meat loaf and the BGT (bacon, goat cheese, tomato). **Known for:** decadent poutine with duck-fat gravy; hopping atmosphere—waits for a table can be long; thick milk shakes prepared with local gelato by Gelato Fiasco. Ⓢ *Average main: $12* ✉ *43 Middle St., East End* ☎ *207/774–8080* ⊕ *www.duckfat.com* ⊙ *Closed Wed.*

★ East Ender

$$$ | AMERICAN | FAMILY | The emphasis at this cozy neighborhood restaurant is on the superb food rather than the atmosphere, which isn't surprising, given that the owners formerly served their tasty, no-fuss fare from a truck. Lunch and dinner feature locally sourced, sustainable ingredients in dishes that reflect the seasons. **Known for:** mouthwatering house-smoked bacon; crispy, thrice-cooked fries; brunch cocktails that incorporate ingredients from local distilleries and house-made cordials. Ⓢ *Average main: $24* ✉ *47 Middle St., East End* ☎ *207/879–7669* ⊕ *www.eastenderport-land.com* ⊙ *Closed Sun. and Mon.*

★ Eventide Oyster Co.

$$ | SEAFOOD | Not only does Eventide have fresh, tasty oysters from all over Maine and New England, artfully prepared with novel accoutrements like kimchi, ginger ices, and cucumber-champagne mignonette, it also serves delicious crudos and ceviches with unique ingredients like blood orange and chili miso. The menu constantly changes, depending on what's in season. **Known for:** brown-butter lobster rolls; a decent selection of alternatives for nonseafood lovers; teaming up with other local restaurants for special cook-offs and menus. Ⓢ *Average main: $15* ✉ *86 Middle St., East End* ☎ *207/774–8538* ⊕ *www.eventideoysterco.com.*

☕ Coffee and Quick Bites

★ Coffee By Design

$ | CAFÉ | Housed in a former bakery building, this small and local coffeehouse company pours specialty coffee employing unusually high standards for environmental and economic sustainability. Flavor-wise, the sturdy coffee is brewed from beans they roast themselves, which have become a staple in many locals' home kitchens. **Known for:** among Portland's original artisanal coffee roasters; community commitment; three locations citywide. $ *Average main: $6* ✉ *67 India St., East End* ☎ *207/780–6767* ⊕ *www.coffeebydesign.com.*

The Arts District

This district starts at the top of Exchange Street, near the upper end of the Old Port, and extends west past the Portland Museum of Art. Congress Street is the district's central artery. Much of Portland's economic heart is here, including several large banking and law firms. It's also where Maine College of Art and the Portland Public Library make their homes. Art galleries, specialty stores, and a score of restaurants line Congress Street. Parking is tricky; two-hour meters dot the sidewalks, but there are several nearby parking garages.

◉ Sights

★ Maine Historical Society and Longfellow House

HISTORIC HOME | The boyhood home of the famous American poet was the first brick house in Portland and the oldest building on the peninsula. It's particularly interesting, because most of the furnishings, including the young Longfellow's writing desk, are original. Wallpaper, window coverings, and a vibrant painted carpet are period reproductions. Built in 1785, the large dwelling (a third floor was added in 1815) sits back from the street and has a small portico over its entrance and four chimneys surmounting the roof. It's part of the Maine Historical Society, which includes an adjacent research library and a museum with exhibits about Maine life. After your guided tour, stay for a picnic in the Longfellow Garden; it's open to the public during museum hours. ✉ *489 Congress St., Arts District* ☎ *207/774–1822* ⊕ *www.mainehistory.org* ✉ *House and museum $15, gardens free* ⊙ *Closed Nov.–Apr.*

★ Portland Museum of Art

ART MUSEUM | Maine's largest public art institution's collection includes fine seascapes and landscapes by Winslow Homer, John Marin, Andrew Wyeth, Edward Hopper, Marsden Hartley, and other American painters. Homer's *Weatherbeaten*, a quintessential Maine Coast image, is here, and the museum owns and displays, on a rotating basis, 16 more of his paintings, plus more than 400 of his illustrations (and it offers tours of the Winslow Homer Studio in nearby Prouts Neck). The museum has works by Monet and Picasso, as well as Degas, Renoir, and Chagall. I.M. Pei's colleague Henry Cobb designed the strikingly modern Charles Shipman Payson building. ✉ *7 Congress Sq., Arts District* ☎ *207/775–6148* ⊕ *www.portlandmuseum.org* ✉ *$18 (free Fri. 4–8 pm)* ⊙ *Closed Mon. and Tues.*

Victoria Mansion

HISTORIC HOME | Built between 1858 and 1860, this Italianate mansion is widely regarded as the most sumptuously ornamented dwelling of its period remaining in the country. Architect Henry Austin designed the house for hotelier Ruggles Morse and his wife, Olive. The interior design—everything from the plasterwork to the furniture (much of it original)—is the only surviving commission of New York designer Gustave Herter. Behind the elegant brownstone exterior of this National Historic Landmark are colorful frescoed walls and ceilings, ornate marble mantelpieces, gilded gas chandeliers, a magnificent 6-foot-by-25-foot stained-glass ceiling window, and a freestanding mahogany staircase. A guided tour runs about 45 minutes and covers all the architectural highlights. Victorian era–themed gifts and art are sold in the museum shop, and the museum often has special theme events. ✉ *109 Danforth St., Arts District* ☎ *207/772–4841* ⊕ *www.victoriamansion.org* 🎫 *$18* ☉ *Closed Nov.–Apr.*

⊕ Restaurants

★ Leeward

$$$ | **ITALIAN** | With nods from critics far and wide, one of the state's most celebrated restaurants is also one of its newest. This high-ceilinged, Italian-centric restaurant comes from husband and wife team Jake and Raquel Stevens who turn out exquisite handmade pasta like the spaghettini Nero laced with squid, serrano chile, pork brood, white wine, and bread crumbs—a revelation of flavors both strong and soothing. **Known for:** thoughtfully chosen wine list; delicious handmade pastas; happening bar scene on weekend nights. $ *Average main: $25* ✉ *85 Free St., Arts District* ☎ *207/8088623* ⊕ *www.leewardmaine. com* ☉ *Closed Sun. and Mon. No lunch.*

⊖ Coffee and Quick Bites

Speckled Ax Wood Roasted Coffee

$ | **CAFÉ** | The Speckled Ax serves up a seriously delicious coffee, whether cold brewed or piping hot with frothy milk. The secret to the richness of the beans is the painstaking roasting process, using a vintage Italian Petroncini roaster fired with local hardwood—ask to take a peek at that contraption while you wait for your drink. **Known for:** pastries and other baked goods; local gathering space; a hip vibe. $ *Average main: $4* ✉ *567 Congress St., Arts District* ☎ *207/660–3333* ⊕ *www. speckledax.com.*

🛏 Hotels

The Westin Portland Harborview

$$ | **HOTEL** | This imposing structure was New England's largest hotel, the Eastland, when built in 1927 and is a well-known part of the Portland skyline. **Pros:** the views from the rooftop bar and lounge; pet friendly; on-site laundry. **Cons:** rooms with city views cost more; not all rooms have harbor views; often bustling with event attendees. $ *Rooms from: $254* ✉ *157 High St., Arts District* ☎ *207/775–5411* ⊕ *www.marriott.com* ☞ *289 rooms* ❙❙ *No Meals.*

🛍 Shopping

Renys Department Store

DEPARTMENT STORE | With its emphasis on high-value merchandise—from Timberland shoes and Carhartt jackets to locally made products like Maine Chefs Wild Blueberry Jam, Raye's Mustard, and bamboo cutting boards made into a map of Maine—this third-generation family-run Maine-centric department has been serving Mainers since 1949. There are 17 stores around the state, but this location is an excellent place to pick up clever souvenirs, a sweater for chilly nights, gifts for folks back home, or just a home accessory to reinforce your love of the Pine Tree State. ✉ *540 Congress St., Arts District* ☎ *207/553–9061* ⊕ *www.renys.com.*

The West End

A leisurely walk through Portland's West End, beginning at the top of the Arts District, offers a real treat to historic architecture buffs. Elaborate building began in the mid-1800s, encouraged by both a robust economy and Portland's devastating fire of 1866, which leveled nearly one-third of the city. The neighborhood, on the National Register of Historic Places, reveals an extraordinary display of architectural splendor, from High

Victorian Gothic to lush Italianate, Queen Anne, and Colonial Revival.

Sights

Western Promenade

PROMENADE | FAMILY | Developed beginning in 1836 and landscaped by the Olmsted Brothers, this 18-acre park is one Portland's oldest preserved spaces. It offers wonderful sunset views in spots, as well as a network of wooded trails, places to sit and people-watch, and paths that pass by the neighborhood's historic homes.

A good place to start is at the head of the Western Promenade, which has benches and a nice view. From the Old Port, take Danforth Street all the way up to Vaughn Street; take a right on Vaughn and then an immediate left onto Western Promenade. Pass by the Western Cemetery, Portland's second official burial ground, laid out in 1829—inside is the ancestral plot of poet Henry Wadsworth Longfellow—and look for street parking. ✉ *Danforth St. to Bramhall St., West End.*

Restaurants

BaoBao Dumpling House

$$ | ASIAN | FAMILY | In a historic town house with traditional Asian decor (a 30-foot copper dragon watches over diners) in Portland's quaint West End, this dumpling house serves deeply satisfying Asian-inspired comfort food in an intimate setting. Start with the house-made Asian slaw, then move to dumplings filled with tried-and-trues such as pork and cabbage or something less traditional, like beef bulgogi or shrimp and bacon. **Known for:** dishes integrating local, seasonal ingredients; tap takeovers by local brewmasters; dishes other than the namesake dumplings. [$] *Average main: $12* ✉ *133 Spring St., at Park St., West End* ☎ *207/772–8400* 🌐 *www.baobaodumplinghouse.com* 🕒 *Closed Mon. and Tues.*

Becky's Diner

$$ | DINER | FAMILY | You won't find a more local or unfussy place—or one more abuzz with conversation at 4 am—than this waterfront institution way down on the end of Commercial Street. The food is cheap, generous in proportion, and has that satisfying, old-time-diner quality. **Known for:** classic Maine diner food featuring many seafood dishes; very lively atmosphere commingling locals and visitors; parking is easy—a rarity in Portland. [$] *Average main: $14* ✉ *390 Commercial St., West End* ☎ *207/773–7070* 🌐 *www.beckysdiner.com.*

★ **Slab Sicilian Street Food**

$$ | PIZZA | FAMILY | Let the fact that this incredibly popular outfit doesn't even bother to call its signature foodstuff "pizza" (but instead, "Sicilian street food") be your first hint that the pie here is a different animal altogether. And while there are perfectly good sandwiches on offer, almost everyone's here for the pillowy, chewy, old world–style pizza, by turns smothered in mushrooms or meats, freshly chopped herbs, or graced with a dollop of blue cheese dip. **Known for:** excellent thick- and thin-crust pizzas; dough and pizza fixings to make at home; good sandwiches. [$] *Average main: $14* ✉ *25 Preble St., West End* ☎ *207/245–3088* 🌐 *www.slabportland.com* 🕒 *Closed Tues. and Wed.*

Hotels

Canopy by Hilton Portland Waterfront

$$$$ | HOTEL | FAMILY | One of the newest additions to Portland's hotel landscape, there's a soft contemporary feel throughout the property—abstract carpets, plenty of warm lighting, textured headboards, compact tables, and multimedia artwork give guest rooms a nice mix of sleekness and coziness. **Pros:** pet-friendly room available; two good on-site restaurants; well-equipped fitness center. **Cons:** a short walk from Old Port; no self-parking available; valet parking is $38. [$] *Rooms*

from: $460 ✉ 9 Center St., West End
☎ 207/791–5000 ⊕ www.hilton.com
↝ 135 rooms ♚ No Meals.

★ The Francis

$$$ | HOTEL | In the beautifully restored
Mellen E. Bolster House, this charming
boutique hotel has a mid-century-modern
vibe that seamlessly compliments the
building's immaculately preserved histori-
cal design elements. **Pros:** bars in rooms;
smart spa on second floor; guest rooms
feature custom-built furniture. **Cons:** only
15 rooms; some rooms not accessible
by elevator; no bathtubs. $ Rooms from:
$300 ✉ 747 Congress St., West End
☎ 207/772–7485 ⊕ www.thefrancis-
maine.com ↝ 15 rooms ♚ No Meals.

🍸 Nightlife

Luna Rooftop Bar

COCKTAIL LOUNGES | Sophisticated and
blessed with stunning views of the
city and waterfront, Luna has plenty to
recommend as a spot to grab drinks
before or after an evening stroll around
the city. Perched atop the Canopy by
Hilton Portland Waterfront, its talented
bar staff pour creative cocktails and the
kitchen turns out enough filling small
plates to snack on or make a dinner out
of. (The eclectic menu spotlights petite
lobster rolls; tuna tataki; Korean BBQ
beef sliders; and desserts like ricotta
lavender fritters.) ✉ Canopy Portland
Waterfront, 285 Commercial St., West
End ☎ 207/791–0011 ⊕ lunarooftopbar-
maine.com.

Casco Bay Islands

The islands of Casco Bay are also known
as the Calendar Islands, because an early
explorer mistakenly thought there was
one for each day of the year (in reality
there are only 140 or so). These islands
range from ledges visible only at low tide
to populous Peaks Island, a suburb of
Portland. Some are uninhabited; others

support year-round communities, as well
as stores and restaurants. Ft. Gorges
commands Hog Island Ledge, and Eagle
Island is the site of Arctic explorer Admi-
ral Robert Peary's home.

The brightly painted ferries of Casco
Bay Lines are the islands' lifeline. There
is service to the most populated ones,
including: Bailey Island, Chebeague
Island, Cliff Island, Great Diamond / Little
Diamond, Long Island, and Peaks Island.

There is little in the way of overnight lodg-
ing on the islands—the population swells
during the warmer months due to summer
residents—and there are few restaurants
or organized attractions other than the
natural beauty of the islands themselves.
Meandering about by bike or on foot is a
good way to explore on a day trip.

GETTING HERE AND AROUND

Casco Bay Lines provides year-round ferry
service from Portland to the following
islands in Casco Bay: Little Diamond and
Great Diamond; Chebeague; Bailey; Cliff;
Peaks; and Long Islands. Boats leave from
the terminal in Old Port, and schedules
vary according to season—ferries leave
more often in summer, less so in fall and
spring, and only several times per day
in the winter. Islands also have different
schedules; Peaks Island, the closest to
Portland and the most populated, has the
most frequent ferries. On-island transpor-
tation should be planned for. Peaks Island
is the only one allowing cars to be trans-
ported by ferry, and if your aim is to do
that, plan in advance, as ferries fill up fast
in the summer. On most of the islands,
you can rent a bike or a golf cart as soon
as you get off the ferry terminal. You can
also bring your own bike on the ferry to all
islands; rates are $6.50 per adult bike and
$3.25 per child's bike. Pets can tag along,
too, for an additional $4.10 round-trip.

Specialty cruises are offered (also with
differing schedules and prices according
to season) passing by various islands,
depending on the theme. There's a

Moonlight Run, Sunset Run, Sunrise Run, and the popular Mailboat Run, which lets passengers join as the working ferry delivers real mail to Little Diamond, Great Diamond, Long, Cliff, and Chebeague Islands.

CONTACTS Casco Bay Lines. ✉ *56 Commercial St., Portland* ☎ *207/774–7871* ⊕ *www.cascobaylines.com.*

Sights

Chebeague Island

ISLAND | FAMILY | About 5 miles long and 1½ miles wide, Chebeague (pronounced shah-big) has a year-round population of about 390, which more than quadruples in the summer season. Originally used as a fishing ground by Abenaki Indigenous people, the island later became a place known for stone slooping—those workers who carried ballast and granite for 19th-century ships, to be used in grand buildings. The island has a number of impressive Greek Revival homes built by them. There are a couple of small beaches, but most visitors come to spend time at The Chebeague Island Inn, where there's golf and tennis to play, and a very good restaurant open for lunch, dinner, or just drinks. ✉ *Great Chebeague Island* ☎ *207/846–3148* ⊕ *www.townofchebeagueisland.org.*

Cliff Island

ISLAND | FAMILY | Little wonder that the farthest island from Portland served by ferry service is also the most secluded and natural. Roads are unpaved, and most of the woods and beaches here are conservation land. Food isn't always easy to find here; there is but one store, and hours can be limited, so bring a lunch if you're looking to picnic. If a beach is on your agenda, head toward Stone Beach for great views of the nearby islands. ✉ *Cliff Island.*

Great Diamond Island and Little Diamond

ISLAND | FAMILY | Though most of Great Diamond is closed to the public, the Inn at Diamond Cove welcomes visitors and offers plenty to do. Housed in what was once Fort McKinley, a United States Army coastal defense fort built in the late 1800s and retired in the 1940s, it's a combination resort, with several eateries as well as private residences. Guests can play tennis and indoor basketball, lounge at the pool, or use the complimentary bikes. Visitors often take the ferry just for the day, or for dinner at the property's fine dining establishment, Diamond's Edge. The area is car-free, so if you're not staying at the Inn, be prepared to explore on foot or bring your own bike. Meanwhile, Little Diamond can be accessed on foot at low tide via Lamson Cove, and is filled with private residences, many of which can be rented during the summer months. ✉ *Great Diamond Island.*

Long Island

ISLAND | FAMILY | Three miles long and one-mile wide, Long Island lives up to its name in shape, and is home to 200 year-round residents (many of whom work in the fishing industry) and 1,000 summer dwellers. There are a few lovely beaches here, including South Beach, Andrews Beach, and Fowler Beach. A few country stores and a bakery can supply you with vittles for a picnic. Bike rentals are not available, so bring your own over on the ferry or rent a golf cart close to the ferry landing when you arrive. ✉ *Long Island* ⊕ *townoflongisland.us/wp/.*

Peaks Island

ISLAND | FAMILY | Nearest to Portland (only a 15-minute ferry ride away), this is the most developed of the Calendar Islands, but it still allows you to experience the relaxed pace of island life. Explore an art gallery or an old fort, and meander along the alternately rocky and sandy shore on foot, or rent a kayak, bike, or golf cart once off the ferry. A number of spots are open for both lunch and dinner.

The Fifth Maine Museum, a small museum with Civil War artifacts, open only in summer, is maintained in the building of the 5th Maine Regiment. (☒ $8; ☎ 207/766–3330, ⊕ www. fifthmainemuseum.org). When the Civil War broke out in 1861, Maine was asked to raise a single regiment to fight, but the state came up with several (the number eventually totaled 40), and sent the 5th Maine Regiment into the war's first battle, at Bull Run. The museum also offers guidebooks for a two-hour self-guided tour of the World War II Peaks Island Reservation. ☒ Peaks Island ⊕ peaksisland.info.

Freeport

6 miles northeast of Yarmouth.

Boston may be called Beantown, but Freeport could easily lay claim to the moniker: L.L. Bean put the town on visitors' radar. The company's flagship store and impressive campus dominate Main Street, and a plethora of outlets and specialty stores edge both the main drag and nearby streets. But those who visit Freeport only to shop are missing out.

Lovely old clapboard houses line the town's shady backstreets, and, a few miles away, South Freeport's pretty harbor sits on the Harraseeket River. In addition, the area's nature preserves have miles of walking trails.

GETTING HERE AND AROUND
Interstate 295 has three Freeport exits and passes by on the edge of the downtown area. U.S. 1 is Main Street here. Note that parking in Freeport is free. The Amtrak Downeaster stops in the heart of town, and the Metro Breez bus travels between Portland and Freeport several times every day except Sunday.

CONTACTS Metro Breez Buses. ☒ Portland ☎ 207/774–0351 ⊕ gpmetro.org.

VISITOR INFORMATION
CONTACTS Visit Freeport. ☒ 115 Main St., Freeport ☎ 207/865–1212 ⊕ www. visitfreeport.com.

◉ Sights

Freeport Historical Society
HISTORY MUSEUM | FAMILY | Pick up a village walking map and delve into Freeport's rich past through the exhibits at the Freeport Historical Society, located in Harrington House, a hybrid Federal- and Greek Revival-style home built in the 1830s. It's a good idea to call ahead to make sure it's open. The historical society also offers walking tours a few times a month in the summer. ☒ 45 Main St., Freeport ☎ 207/865–3170 ⊕ www. freeporthistoricalsociety.org ◐ Closed Sat.–Mon.

★ L.L. Bean
STORE/MALL | FAMILY | Founded in 1912 after its namesake invented the iconic hunting boot, L.L. Bean began as a mail-order merchandiser with a creaky old retail store. Today, the giant flagship store attracts more than 3 million visitors annually. Open 365 days a year, 24 hours a day, it is the anchor in the heart of Freeport's outlet-shopping district. You can still find the original hunting boots, along with cotton and wool sweaters; outerwear of all kinds; casual clothing, boots, and shoes for men, women, and kids; and camping equipment. Nearby are the company's home furnishings store and its bike, boat, and ski store. Don't miss the chance to snap a photo with the 16½-foot-tall statue of its signature rubber boot outside the main entrance, or visit its discount outlet, across the street in the Freeport Village Station mall. ☒ 95 Main St., Freeport ☎ 877/755–2326 ⊕ www.llbean.com.

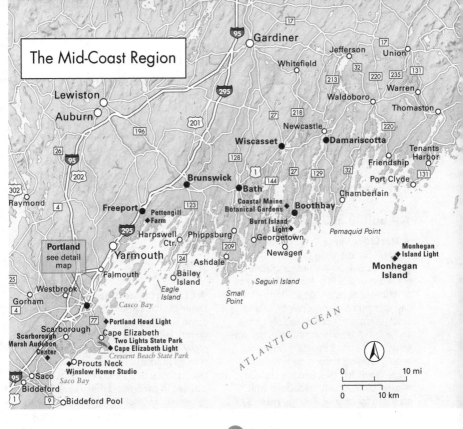

The Mid-Coast Region

Pettengill Farm

FARM/RANCH | **FAMILY** | The grounds of the Freeport Historical Society's saltwater Pettengill Farm—140 beautifully tended acres along an estuary of the Harraseeket River—are open to the public. It's about a 15-minute walk from the parking area down a farm road to the circa-1800 saltbox farmhouse, which is open by appointment. Little has changed since it was built, and it has rare etchings (called sgraffiti) of ships and sea monsters on three bedroom walls. ⊠ *31 Pettengill Rd., Freeport* ☎ *207/865–3170* ⊕ *www. freeporthistoricalsociety.org* ✉ *Free (donations appreciated).*

🍴 Restaurants

Harraseeket Lunch and Lobster Co.

$$ | **SEAFOOD** | **FAMILY** | Take a break from Main Street's bustle and drive 3 scenic miles to South Freeport, where this popular, bare-bones, counter-service place sits beside the town landing and serves up seafood baskets and lobster dinners. Save room for strawberry shortcake,. blueberry crisp, bread pudding, whoopie pies, or another of the homemade desserts. **Known for:** great seafood; harbor views; picnic table dining inside or out. $ *Average main: $18* ⊠ *36 S. Main St., South Freeport* ☎ *207/865–3535, 207/865–4888* ⊕ *www.harraseeketlunchandlobster.com* ➡ *No credit cards* 🕑 *Closed mid-Oct.–May.*

Maine Beer Company

$$ | PIZZA | FAMILY | Of the half dozen breweries in Freeport, the Maine Beer Company is a standout. Its beer is well crafted, as are its salads, charcuterie, and wood-fired pizzas, and you can dine indoors or out. **Known for:** delicious IPAs; beautiful bilevel space; community-spirited owners. $ *Average main: $20* ⊠ *525 U.S. 1, Freeport* ☎ *207/221–5711* ⊕ *www.mainebeercompany.com.*

☕ Coffee and Quick Bites

★ Met Coffee House

$ | CAFÉ | Sit at a table to enjoy a bagel, croissant, Belgian waffles, or quiche at breakfast or a cold or toasted sandwich or flatbread at lunch. At any time of the day, sink into a comfy chair or sofa to indulge in a great cup of regular coffee, an "artistic" latte (try the Heath Bar version), or one of 15 specialty hot chocolates, including almond joy and peppermint. **Known for:** 16 smoothie choices; relaxed atmosphere; decorated with art that's for sale. $ *Average main: $13* ⊠ *48 Main St., Freeport* ☎ *207/869–5809* ⊕ *www.metropolitancoffeehouse.com.*

🛏 Hotels

★ Harraseeket Inn

$ | HOTEL | FAMILY | The welcome is warm at this inn, where gas fireplaces glow in the lobby, and guest rooms—about half of them in a historic wing—have serene color schemes and reproduction Federal-style furnishings. **Pros:** generous breakfast buffet; amenities include an indoor pool and a gym; easy walk to shopping district. **Cons:** rooms in newer wings lack historic charm; not all rooms have a garden view; fireplaces only in select rooms. $ *Rooms from: $179* ⊠ *162 Main St., Freeport* ☎ *207/865–9377, 800/342–6423* ⊕ *www.harraseeketinn.com* 🛏 *84 rooms* ⑩ *Free Breakfast.*

🎭 Performing Arts

L.L. Bean Summer Concert Series

CONCERTS | FAMILY | Throughout the summer, L.L. Bean hosts free activities, including concerts, at the L.L. Bean Discovery Park, part of the company's large campus. It's set back from Main Street, along a side street that runs between the company's flagship and home furnishings stores. Additional offerings include family movie nights and wellness classes. ⊠ *18 Morse St., Freeport* ☎ *877/755–2326* ⊕ *www.llbean.com* 🎫 *Free* ☞ *Bring chairs.*

🏃 Activities

★ L.L. Bean Outdoor Discovery Programs

GROUP EXERCISE | FAMILY | It shouldn't come as a surprise that one of the world's largest outdoor outfitters also provides instructional adventures to go with its products. L.L. Bean's year-round Outdoor Discovery Programs include courses in canoeing, biking, kayaking, fly-fishing, snowshoeing, cross-country skiing, and other outdoor sports. Some last for only a few hours, while others are multiday experiences. Special offerings include women's-only adventures and team-building programs. ⊠ *11 Desert Rd., Freeport* ☎ *888/552–3261* ⊕ *www.llbean.com.*

🛍 Shopping

You really do need a strategy to shop smartly in Freeport, where Maine retailers and major brands—including Levi's, Dooney & Bourke, J.Crew, Under Armour, Vineyard Vines, and Ralph Loren—are all represented. Visit Freeport's guide (complete with coupons) to area offerings lists hundreds of stores on Main Street, Bow Street, and elsewhere. It's available at the visitor information center and other places in town.

Brunswick

10 miles north of Freeport.

Lovely brick or clapboard buildings are the highlight of Brunswick's Federal Street Historic District, which includes Federal Street, Park Row, and the stately campus of Bowdoin College. From the intersection of Pleasant and Maine streets, in the center of town, you can walk in any direction and discover an array of restaurants, bookstores, boutiques, and jewelers. Bowdoin's campus is home to several museums, and the college's performing-arts events are open to the public.

GETTING HERE AND AROUND

From I–295, take the Coastal Connector to U.S. 1 in Brunswick. The Concord Coach Lines bus that runs along the coast stops at the Brunswick Visitor Center, which is next to the train tracks and has a self-service ticket kiosk for Amtrak's *Downeaster* train. Brunswick Link buses can shuttle you around town and to Brunswick Landing and Cook's Corner every day (between 6:45 am and 6:30 pm) except Sunday.

CONTACTS Brunswick Link. ☎ *207/721–9600* 🌐 *brunswicklink.org.*

VISITOR INFORMATION

CONTACTS Brunswick Visitor Center. ✉ *16 Station Ave., Brunswick* ☎ *207/721–0999* 🌐 *brunswickdowntown.org.*

Sights

★ Bowdoin College Museum of Art

ART MUSEUM | FAMILY | This small museum housed in a stately building on Bowdoin's main quad features one of the oldest permanent collections of art in the United States. The more than 20,000 objects include paintings, sculpture, decorative arts, and works on paper. They range from Ancient, European, Asian, and Indigenous works to modern and contemporary art. The museum often mounts well-curated, rotating exhibitions and has programs for getting children excited about art. ✉ *245 Maine St., Brunswick* ☎ *207/725–3275* 🌐 *www.bowdoin.edu/art-museum* 🎟 *Free* 🕒 *Closed Mon.*

Restaurants

★ 555 North

$$$ | AMERICAN | Set within the gracious Federal hotel, 555 North is the rebirth of chef-owner Steve Corry's popular Portland restaurant, which closed in 2019 after an 18-year run. Diners will find the same exceptionally creative, seasonal approach to food as well as a sophisticated but relaxed atmosphere. **Known for:** imaginative menu; prominent, accomplished chef; attentive and polished service. [$] *Average main: $30* ✉ *The Federal, 10 Water St., Brunswick* ☎ *207/481–4535* 🌐 *555-north.com* 🕒 *Closed Tues. and Wed.*

Coffee and Quick Bites

Little Dog Coffee Shop

$ | MODERN AMERICAN | FAMILY | The coffee is freshly roasted and richly flavorful, the baked goods are straight from the oven, and the atmosphere is chill. Have a muffin or croissant, select from several toasties with imaginative fillings, or try the delicious avocado toast on homemade wheat bread. **Known for:** exhibits of local art; excellent light bites; grab-and-go burritos. [$] *Average main: $10* ✉ *87 Maine St., Freeport* ☎ *207/721–9500* 🌐 *www.littledogcoffeeshop.com.*

Hotels

★ The Federal

$$ | HOTEL | With a large modern wing attached to a historic Federal house, this refined hotel offers an airy, contemporary atmosphere blended with period-appropriate warmth. **Pros:** excellent on-site restaurant; personalized welcome; sophisticated decor. **Cons:** 20-minute walk to

Bowdoin College campus; a bit tricky to find; no elevator to third floor in Federal House. [$] *Rooms from: $287* ✉ *10 Water St., Brunswick* ☎ *207/481–4066* 🌐 *www.thefederalmaine.com* 🛏 *30 rooms* 🍴 *No Meals.*

Bath

18 miles northeast of Harpswell Neck.

Bath's tradition of shipbuilding dates from 1607 with the construction of the pinnace *Virginia*, the first oceangoing ship built by Europeans in the Americas. (A full-size replica of the small sailing vessel was launched in June 2022.) It was a very lucrative industry, as evidenced by the historic district's architecture, including the 1820 Federal-style home at 360 Front Street; the 1810 Greek Revival, white-clapboard mansion at 969 Washington Street; and the raspberry-color Victorian gem at 1009 Washington Street. All three operate as inns.

In 1890, the venerable Bath Iron Works (BIW as it's known locally) completed its first passenger ship. During World War II, the company was capable of launching a new ship every 17 days. Today, BIW is one of the state's largest employers, with about 6,800 workers building destroyers for the U.S. Navy. (It's a good idea to avoid U.S. 1 on weekdays 3:15–4:30 pm, when a major shift change takes place.)

The must-see Maine Maritime Museum highlights shipbuilding history in Bath and elsewhere along the Maine Coast. It also offers tours to the perimeter of BIW's grounds (due to security concerns, it's a restricted property). Also, be sure to look up at City Hall, on Front Street: the bell in its tower was cast by Paul Revere in 1805.

Dangling to seaward of Woolwich, just east of Bath, Georgetown Island is connected to the mainland via a series of bridges. The island's exceptional beauty makes it well worth a detour. Along miles of corrugated shoreline, you'll find a few charming seafood eateries, old-fashioned lodging, and the natural jewel that is Reid State Park.

GETTING HERE AND AROUND

U.S. 1 passes through downtown and across the Kennebec River at Bath. Downtown is on the north side of the highway along the river. The Maine Maritime Museum is on the south side of the highway. Concord Coach Lines bus service that runs along the coast stops in Bath.

VISITOR INFORMATION

CONTACTS Bath Regional Information Center. ✉ *15 Commercial St., Bath* ☎ *207/443–1513* 🌐 *visitbath.com.*

👁 Sights

★ Maine Maritime Museum

HISTORY MUSEUM | FAMILY | No trip to Bath is complete without visiting the cluster of preserved 19th- and early 20th-century buildings that were once part of the historic Percy & Small Shipyard. Plan to spend at least half a day exploring them and the adjacent modern museum. Indeed, there's so much to see that admission tickets are good for two days.

During hour-long shipyard tours, you'll learn how massive wooden ships were built, and you might see shipwrights and blacksmiths at work. One of the vintage buildings houses a fascinating, 6,000-square-foot lobstering exhibit. In the main building ship models, paintings, photographs, and artifacts showcase maritime history. The grounds also contain a gift shop and bookstore; a seasonal café; and a huge, modern sculpture representing the 450-foot-long, six-masted schooner *Wyoming*, built right here and one of the longest wooden vessels ever launched.

From late May through late October, daily nature and lighthouse cruises, ranging from 30 minutes to three hours, are offered aboard the motor vessel *Merrymeeting,* which travels along the scenic

Kennebec River. The museum also has guided tours of Bath Iron Works (June–mid-October). ✉ *243 Washington St., Bath* ☎ *207/443–1316* 🌐 *www.mainemaritimemuseum.org* 🎟 *$18, good for 2 days within 7-day period.*

★ Popham Beach State Park

BEACH | FAMILY | At the tip of the Phippsburg Peninsula, Popham Beach State Park faces the open Atlantic between the mouths of the Kennebec and Morse rivers. At low tide, you can walk several miles of tidal flats and also out to small Fox Island, where you can explore tide pools or fish off the ledges (pay attention to the incoming tide unless you want to swim back). Shifting sand and beach and sea dynamics have led to dramatic erosion here, and, in recent years, the sea has taken a big bite out of the beach. There are picnic tables, plus a bathhouse, showers, and toilets. About a mile from the beach, the road ends at the Civil War–era Fort Popham State Historic Site, an unfinished semicircular granite fort overlooking the sea. The site of the Popham Colony, an early 1600s English settlement, is also nearby. Enjoy beach views and some fresh seafood at nearby Spinney's Restaurant. ✉ *10 Perkins Farm La., off Rte. 209, Bath* ☎ *207/389–1335* 🌐 *www.maine.gov/pophambeach* 🎟 *$8.*

★ Reid State Park

BEACH | FAMILY | On Georgetown Island, this park's jewel is a gorgeous, unspoiled, mile-long beach framed by sand dunes; there's a second, ½-mile beach as well. Climb to the top of rocky Griffith Head to take in sea views that stretch to lighthouses on Seguin Island, Hendricks Head, and The Cuckolds. If you're swimming, be aware of the possibility of an undertow. Walking along the beach or following one of the hiking trails are popular pastimes as well. During a storm, this is a great place to observe the ferocity of the waves crashing onto the shore. In summer, parking lots fill by 11 am on weekends and holidays. ✉ *375 Seguinland Rd., Georgetown* ☎ *207/371–2303* 🎟 *$8* 🕓 *Closed sunset to 9 am.*

🍴 Restaurants

★ Bath Brewing Company

$$ | MODERN AMERICAN | You'll feel right at home in this intimate modern pub, offering casual dining on two floors plus an upper outdoor deck. The beer ranges from IPAs to stouts and sours. **Known for:** surprising pub food; welcoming modern pub in the heart of downtown; tasty craft beers. [$] *Average main: $20* ✉ *141 Front St., Bath* ☎ *207/389–6039* 🌐 *www.bathbrewing.com* 🕓 *Closed Mon. and Tues.*

★ Five Islands Lobster Company

$$ | SEAFOOD | Drive to the end of Route 127 and relax in the breezes off Sheepscot Bay in the tiny fishing village of Five Islands, not too far from Reid State Park. This award-winning lobster shack overlooks at least islands from its perch atop the working wharf, and you can watch lobstermen unload their traps onto the dock while you feast on fresh lobster rolls or a full lobster dinner and sample Maine-made ice cream. **Known for:** BYOB; authentic Maine setting with gorgeous scenery; excellent lobster rolls. [$] *Average main: $24* ✉ *1447 5 Islands Rd., Georgetown* ☎ *207/371–2990* 🌐 *www.fiveislandslobster.com* 🕓 *Closed Wed. in summer; closed weekdays spring and fall; closed early May–early Oct.*

☕ Coffee and Quick Bites

Café Crème

$ | BAKERY | FAMILY | Located in the heart of downtown, this café with its own on-site bakery draws visitors and locals alike for delicious coffee paired with made-that-day goods served with a smile. The cinnamon roll with maple bacon is a savory Maine take on a classic

Continued on page 331

MAINE'S LIGHTHOUSES
GUARDIANS OF THE COAST

Perched high on rocky ledges, on the tips of wayward islands, and sometimes seemingly on the ocean itself are the more than five dozen lighthouses standing watch along Maine's craggy and ship-busting coastline.

Marshall Point Light

LIGHTING THE WAY: A BIT OF HISTORY

Portland Head Light

Most lighthouses were built in the first half of the 19th century to protect vessels from running aground at night or when the shoreline was shrouded in fog. Along with the mournful siren of the foghorn and maritime lore, these practical structures have come to symbolize Maine throughout the world.

SHIPWRECKS AND SAFETY

These alluring sentinels of the eastern seaboard today have more form than function, but that certainly was not always the case. Safety was a strong motivating factor in the erection of the lighthouses. Commerce also played a critical role. For example, in 1791 Portland Head Light was completed, partially as a response to local merchants' concerns about the rocky entrance to Portland Harbor and the varying depths of the shipping channel. In 1789, the federal government created the U.S. Lighthouse Establishment (later the U.S. Lighthouse Service) to manage them. In 1939 the U.S. Coast Guard took on the job.

Maine's lighthouses were built in much-needed locations, but the points and islands upon which they sat were prone to storm damage. Along with poor construction, this meant that over the years many lighthouses had to be rebuilt or replaced.

LIGHTHOUSES TODAY

In modern times, many of the structures still serve a purpose. Technological advances, such as GPS and radar, are mainly used to navigate through the choppy waters, but a lighthouse or its foghorns are helpful secondary aids, and sometimes the only ones used by recreational boaters. The numerous channel-marking buoys still in existence also are testament to the old tried-and-true methods.

Of the 66 lighthouses along this far northeastern state, 57 are still working, alerting ships (and even small aircraft) of the shoreline's rocky edge. Government agencies, historic preservation organizations, and mostly private individuals own the decommissioned lights.

KEEPERS OF THE LIGHT

Some keepers also used bells and sirens, like this Fog Signal Station on Manana Island in 1898.

Pemaquid Point's fourth-order Fresnel lens

LIFE OF A LIGHTKEEPER

One thing that has changed with the modern era is the disappearance of the lighthouse keeper. In the early 20th century, lighthouses began the conversion from oil-based lighting to electricity. A few decades later, the U.S. Coast Guard switched to automation, phasing out the need for an on-site keeper.

While the keepers of tradition were no longer needed, the traditions of these stalwart, 24/7 employees live on through museum exhibits and retellings of Maine's maritime history, legends, and lore. The tales of a lighthouse keeper's life are the stuff romance novels are made of: adventure, rugged but lonely men, and a beautiful setting along an unpredictable coastline.

The lighthouse keepers of yesterday probably didn't see their own lives so romantically. Their daily narrative was one of hard work and, in some cases, exceptional solitude. A keeper's primary job was to ensure that the lamp was illuminated all day, every day. This meant that oil (whale or coal oil and later kerosene) had to be carried about and wicks trimmed on a regular basis. When fog shrouded the coast, they sounded the solemn horn to pierce through the damp darkness that hid their light. Their quarters were generally small and often attached to the light tower itself. The remote locations of the lights added to the isolation a keeper felt, especially before the advent of radio and telephone, let alone the Internet. Though some brought families with them, the keepers tended to be men who lived alone.

THE LIGHTS 101

Over the years, Fresnel (fray-NELL) lenses were developed in different shapes and sizes so that ship captains could distinguish one lighthouse from another. Invented by Frenchman Augustin Fresnel in the early 19th century, the lens design allows for a greater transmission of light perfectly suited for lighthouse use. Knowing which lighthouse they were near helped captains know which danger was present, such as a submerged ledge or shallow channel. Some lights, such as those at Seguin Island Light, are fixed and don't flash. Other lights are colored red.

DID YOU KNOW?

A lighthouse's personality shines through its flash pattern. For example, Bass Harbor Light (pictured) is on for three seconds, off for one second. Some lights, such as Seguin Island Light, are fixed and don't flash.

LIGHTHOUSE FINDER

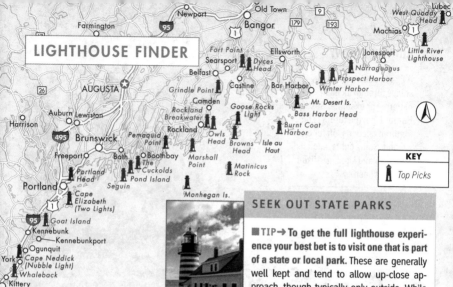

Map labels: Farmington, Newport, Old Town, Bangor, West Quoddy Head, Lubec, Machias, Fort Point, Ellsworth, Jonesport, Little River Lighthouse, AUGUSTA, Searsport, Dyces Head, Narraguagus, Prospect Harbor, Belfast, Castine, Bar Harbor, Winter Harbor, Grindle Point, Camden, Goose Rocks Light, Mt. Desert Is., Bass Harbor Head, Rockland Breakwater, Burnt Coat Harbor, Auburn Lewiston, Harrison, Brunswick, Pemaquid Point, Rockland, Owls Head, Browns Head, Isle au Haut, Freeport, Bath, Boothbay, The Cuckolds, Marshall Point, Matinicus Rock, Portland Head, Pond Island, Seguin, Monhegan Is., Portland, Cape Elizabeth (Two Lights), Goat Island, Kennebunk, Kennebunkport, Ogunquit, Cape Neddick (Nubble Light), York, Whaleback, Kittery, Portsmouth

KEY

🛨 Top Picks

West Quoddy Head

VISITING MAINE'S LIGHTHOUSES

As you travel along the Maine Coast, you won't see lighthouses by watching your odometer—there were no rules about the spacing of lighthouses. The decision as to where to place a lighthouse was a balance between a region's geography and its commercial prosperity and maritime traffic.

Lighthouses dot the shore from as far south as York to the country's eastern-most tip at Lubec. Accessibility varies according to location and other factors. A handful are so remote as to be out-right impossible to reach (except perhaps by kayaking and rock climbing). Some don't allow visitors according to Coast Guard policies, though you can enjoy them through the zoom lens of a camera. Others you can walk right up to and, occasionally, even climb to the top. Lighthouse enthusiasts and preservation groups restore and maintain many of them. All told, approximately 30 lighthouses allow some sort of public access.

SEEK OUT STATE PARKS

■ **TIP→** To get the full lighthouse experience your best bet is to visit one that is part of a state or local park. These are generally well kept and tend to allow up-close approach, though typically only outside. While you're at the parks you can picnic or stroll on the trails. Wildlife is often abundant in and near the water; you might spot sea birds and even whales in certain locations (try West Quoddy Head, Portland Head, or Two Lights).

MUSEUMS, TOURS, AND MORE

Most keeper's quarters are closed to the public, but some of the homes have been converted to museums, full of intriguing exhibits on lighthouses, the famous Fresnel lenses used in them, and artifacts of Maine maritime life in general. Talk to the librarians at the **Maine Maritime Museum** in Bath (⊕ www.mainemaritimemuseum. org) or sign up for one of the museum's daily lighthouse cruises to pass by up to ten on the Lighthouse Lovers Cruise. In Rockland, the **Maine Lighthouse Museum** (⊕ www.mainelighthousemuseum.org) has the country's largest display of Fresnel lenses. The museum also displays keepers' memorabilia, foghorns, brassware, and more. Maine Open Lighthouse Day is the second Saturday after Labor Day; you can tour and even climb about two dozen lights usually closed to the public.

For more information, check out the lighthouse page at Maine's official tourism site: ⊕ visitmaine.com.

SLEEPING LIGHT: STAYING OVERNIGHT

Goose Rocks, where you can play lighthouse keeper for a week.

Want to stay overnight in a lighthouse? There are several options to do so.

■ TIP→ Book lighthouse lodgings as far in advance as possible, up to one year ahead.

Our top pick is **Pemaquid Point Light** (*L. Dewey Chase Rentals* ☎ *207/677–2100* ⊕ *newharborrentals.com)* because it has one of the most dramatic settings on the Maine coast. Two miles south of **New Harbor**, the second floor of the lighthouse keeper's house is rented out on a weekly basis early May through mid-November to support upkeep of the grounds. When you aren't enjoying the interior, head outdoors: the covered front porch has a rocking-chair view of the ocean. The one-bedroom, one-bath rental sleeps up to a family of four.

Situated smack dab in the middle of a major maritime thoroughfare between two Penobscot Bay islands, **Goose Rocks Light** (☎ *203/400–9565* ⊕ *www.beaconpreservation.org)* offers lodging for the adventuresome—the 51-foot "spark plug" lighthouse is completely surrounded bywater. Getting there requires a ferry ride from Rockland to nearby **North Haven**, a 5- to 10-minute ride by motorboat, and then a climb up an iron-rung ladder from the pitching boat—all based on high tide and winds, of course. There's room for up to six people. It's a bit more cushy experience than it was for the original keepers: there's a flat-screen TV with DVD player and a selection of music and videos for entertainment. In addition, a hammock hangs on the small deck that encircles the operational light; it's a great place from which to watch the majestic windjammers and the fishing fleet pass by.

Little River Lighthouse (☎ *877/276–4682* ⊕ *www.littleriverlight.org)*, along the far northeastern reaches of the coast in **Cutler**, has three rooms available for rent from mid-June to September. You're responsible for food and beverages, linens, towels, and other personal items (don't forget the bug spray), but kitchen and other basics are provided. The lighthouse volunteers with Friends of Little River Lighthouse will provide a boat ride to the island upon which the lighthouse sits.

TOP LIGHTHOUSES TO VISIT

BASS HARBOR HEAD LIGHT

Familiar to many as the subject of countless photographs is Bass Harbor Head Light, at the southern end of **Mount Desert Island.** It is within Acadia National Park and 17 miles from the town of Bar Harbor. The station grounds are open year-round.

CAPE ELIZABETH LIGHT

Two Lights State Park is so-named because it's next to two lighthouses. Both of these **Cape Elizabeth** structures were built in 1828. The western light was closed in 1924 and eventually converted into a private residence; the eastern light, Cape Elizabeth Light, still projects its automated cylinder of light. The grounds surrounding the building and the lighthouse itself are closed to the public, but the structure is easily viewed and photographed from nearby at the end of Two Lights Road.

Cape Neddick

CAPE NEDDICK LIGHT

More commonly known as Nubble Light for the smallish offshore expanse of rock it rests upon, Cape Neddick Light sits a few hundred feet off a rock point in **York Beach.** With such a precarious location, its grounds are inaccessible to visitors, but close enough to be exceptionally photogenic, especially during the Christmas season.

MONHEGAN ISLAND LIGHT

Only the adventuresome and the artistic see this light, because **Monhegan Island** is accessible by an approximately one-hour ferry ride. To reach the lighthouse, you have an additional half-mile walk uphill from the ferry dock. The former keeper's quarters is home to the Monhegan Museum, which has exhibits about the island. The tower itself is closed to the public.

Portland Head

PORTLAND HEAD LIGHT

One of Maine's most photographed lighthouses (and its oldest), the famous Portland Head Light was completed in January 1791. At the edge of Fort Williams Park, in **Cape Elizabeth**, the towering white stone lighthouse stands 101 feet above the sea. The Coast Guard operates it and it is not open for tours. However the adjacent keeper's dwelling is now a museum.

WEST QUODDY HEAD LIGHT

Originally built in 1808 by mandate of President Thomas Jefferson, West Quoddy Head Light sits in **Lubec** on the easternmost tip of land in the mainland United States. The 49-foot-high lighthouse with distinctive red and white stripes, is part of Quoddy Head State Park.

West Quoddy Head

sweet treat. **Known for:** sweet and savory stuffed croissants; creative coffee drinks; friendly staff. $ *Average main: $7* ⊠ *56 Front St., at Centre St., Bath* ☎ *207/443–6454* ⊕ *www.cafecremebath.com.*

Hotels

Sebasco Harbor Resort
$$$$ | RESORT | FAMILY | This nearly century-old resort on 450 water-side acres at the western side of the Phippsburg Peninsula is a good choice for both couples and families. **Pros:** very good on-site restaurant; children's activities and an array of lawn games; golf course, tennis courts, and heated saltwater pool. **Cons:** no sandy beach; heavy traffic and large number of rooms can diminish quality and service; golf fee not included in stay. $ *Rooms from: $420* ⊠ *29 Kenyon Rd., off Sebasco Rd., Phippsburg* ☎ *866/389–2072, 207/389-1161* ⊕ *www.sebasco. com* ☉ *Closed late Oct.–mid-May* ⇆ *89 rooms* ⦿ *No Meals.*

Wiscasset

10 miles north of Bath.

Settled in 1663, Wiscasset sits on the bank of the Sheepscot River. It bills itself as "Maine's Prettiest Village," and it's easy to see why: it has graceful churches, old cemeteries, and elegant sea captains' homes (many converted into antiques shops and galleries).

This is where everyone wants to stop for a lobster roll. Red's Eats gets all the publicity—and the resulting long, long lines—for its positively overflowing rolls. At Sprague's, just across the street, the quality is just as high, and although they don't stuff the rolls with quite as much lobster, you do pay a few dollars less.

GETTING HERE AND AROUND
U.S. 1 becomes Wiscasset's Main Street. Traffic often slows to a crawl in summer, as everyone traveling along the coast here must funnel onto a two-lane bridge across the Sheepscot River. The speed limit is reduced in town, and there are several stop lights, both of which further slow things down. There's no parking on Main Street in front of the shops, but there are several free nearby lots to either side of the main drag. The Concord Coach Lines bus that goes along the coast stops in Wiscasset.

🍴 Restaurants

★ Red's Eats
$$$ | SEAFOOD | FAMILY | The customers lined up beside this little red shack at the bottom of Wiscasset's Main Street, just before the bridge across the Sheepscot River, have come from far and wide for one of the Maine Coast's best lobster rolls—namely, a perfectly buttered and griddled split-top roll that's absolutely, positively stuffed with fresh, sweet meat and served with melted butter and mayo on the side. Devotees swear that the wait (up to two hours!) is worth it, and it helps that staffers hand out ice water, popsicles, umbrellas to protect from rain or hot sun, and even dog biscuits for the pups. **Known for:** more than a whole lobster goes into each roll; the unholy "Puff Dog," a hot dog loaded with bacon and cheese and deep-fried; long lines in summer, especially on weekends. $ *Average main: $25* ⊠ *41 Water St., Wiscasset* ⊹ *Corner of U.S. 1* ☎ *207/882–6128* ⊕ *www.redseatsmaine.com* ▭ *No credit cards* ☉ *Closed late-Oct.–mid-Apr.*

★ Water Street Kitchen and Bar
$$$ | MEDITERRANEAN | Step into this welcoming, airy space, and settle at a table with a view of the Sheepscot River to enjoy local seafood, meats, and produce. Many of the pastas, paellas, and risottos have a Mediterranean flavor; other dishes showcase the chef's creative approach to modern American cuisine. **Known for:** eclectic menu; raw bar; pleasant atmosphere. $ *Average main: $25* ⊠ *15 Water*

St., Wiscasset ☎ *207/687–8076* 🌐 *www.waterstreetkitchen.com.*

☕ Coffee and Quick Bites

Treats

$ | **AMERICAN** | What started as a candy shop over 30 years ago has grown into a Wiscasset staple featuring baked goods, coffee, wine, craft beer, cheese, and more. All of the "treats"—scones, cookies, croissants, muffins, cakes, sweet buns, babka, coffee cake—are baked right here every day. **Known for:** scones made from owner's nana's recipe; a morning gathering spot for locals; locally sourced ingredients. [$] *Average main: $5* ✉ *80 Main St., Wiscasset* ☎ *207/882–6192* 🌐 *www.treatsofmaine.com* 🕓 *Closed Mon.*

Boothbay

11 miles south of Wiscasset.

The shoreline of the Boothbay Peninsula is a craggy stretch of inlets where pleasure craft of all sizes and types bob alongside lobster boats and sightseeing vessels. Boothbay Harbor is something of a smaller version of Bar Harbor: touristy, but friendly and fun, with pretty, winding streets and lots to explore. Commercial Street, Wharf Street, Townsend Avenue, and the By-Way are lined with shops and ice-cream parlors.

Be sure to take in the coast and islands from the water aboard one of many sightseeing cruises. One of the biggest draws here is the stunning Coastal Maine Botanical Gardens, a short drive north in the town of Boothbay. Its more than 300 acres encompass spectacular plantings and natural landscapes, walking trails, and a delightful children's garden.

GETTING HERE AND AROUND

Soon after crossing the Sheepscot River bridge just east of Wiscasset, turn right onto Route 27 and follow it to Boothbay and all the way into the heart of Boothbay Harbor, just 2 miles farther south. For some incredible scenery, take Route 96 off Route 27 out to Ocean Point in East Boothbay.

Note that, in season, a daily boat to Monhegan Island leaves from a dock on Boothbay Harbor's Commercial Street.

VISITOR INFORMATION

CONTACTS Boothbay Harbor Region Chamber of Commerce. ✉ *192 Townsend Ave., Boothbay* ☎ *207/633–2353* 🌐 *www.boothbayharbor.com.*

👁 Sights

★ Coastal Maine Botanical Gardens

GARDEN | **FAMILY** | Reserve your admission tickets in advance online (required), and set aside a couple of hours to explore New England's largest botanical garden, where, depending on the time of year, you can stroll amid the lupines, rhododendrons, or roses. Regardless of the season, you'll encounter the site's biggest (literally and figuratively) draws: the five gigantic and utterly irresistible trolls constructed by Danish artist Thomas Danbo using scrap wood and other found materials that are placed in wooded areas throughout the 323-acre grounds.

The children's garden is a wonderland of stone sculptures, rope bridges, small teahouse-like structures with grass roofs, and even a hedge maze. Children and adults alike adore the separate woodland fairy area. The Garden of the Five Senses lets you experience flora through much more than just sight. Inside the main building are a café, grab-and-go market, shop, and resource library. During the holiday season, the gardens mount a dazzling, nighttime Gardens Aglow show, with 650,000 LED bulbs lighting up the darkness.

Comfortable walking shoes are a must, but, if you'd prefer not to walk everywhere, there's free shuttle service to several key locales. In addition, free, hour-long, docent-led tours of the central gardens leave from the visitor center at 11 each day from May through October. There's also a one-hour golf cart tour ($10; free on Wednesday). ✉ *132 Botanical Gardens Dr., off Rte. 27, Boothbay* ☎ *207/633–8000* 🌐 *www.mainegardens.org* 🎫 *$22* 🕓 *Closed late Oct.–May 1, except for holiday season Gardens Aglow extravaganza* ✍ *Reservations required.*

🍴 Restaurants

★ The Deck Bar & Grill

$$ | AMERICAN | Located at Linekin Bay Resort, this casual, mostly outdoor restaurant offers a serene waterside setting coupled with fresh lobster rolls, haddock BLTs, mussels, crab cakes, crudo yellowfin tuna, fish tacos, and clams linguine. There are plenty of meat, gluten-free, and vegan options, too. **Known for:** stunning view down Linekin Bay; a wonderful escape from the bustle; live music on weekends. [$] *Average main: $20* ✉ *Linekin Bay Resort, 92 Wall Point Rd., Boothbay Harbor* ☎ *207/633–2494* 🌐 *www.linekinbayresort.com/dining* 🕓 *Closed mid-Oct.–mid May.*

★ Shannon's Unshelled

$ | SEAFOOD | FAMILY | The namesake of this shack first got the idea to set up shop when her father posed the simple question: "Where can you buy a quick lobster roll in Boothbay Harbor?" Unable to answer, Shannon's Unshelled was born, and the shack is now beloved for its grilled, buttered buns stuffed with whole lobsters and served with a side of garlicky, sea-salted, drawn butter. **Known for:** fried seafood features gluten-free batter; seaweed salads; trap-to-table lobster. [$] *Average main: $16* ✉ *23 Granary Way, Boothbay Harbor* ☎ *207/350–7313* 🌐 *www.shannonsunshelled.biz* 🕓 *Closed Sun. and Wed.*

☕ Coffee and Quick Bites

★ Downeast Ice Cream Factory

$ | ICE CREAM | FAMILY | Stop in at this cute little house next to the boardwalk and order an ice-cream cone to enjoy at a nearby picnic table or as you stroll along the waterfront. You'll probably want to make it a two-scooper, so you can try at least two of the many flavors, all made right here in Boothbay Harbor. **Known for:** more than 50 flavors; super-premium ice cream; vegan sorbets. [$] *Average main: $6* ✉ *1 By-Way, Boothbay Harbor* ☎ *207/315–6670* 🌐 *www.downeasticecreamfactory.com* 🕓 *Closed Nov.–mid-May.*

🛏 Hotels

Spruce Point Inn

$$$ | RESORT | FAMILY | Since 1892, this refined seaside resort has welcomed guests, including members of the Kennedy family, to its own sea-lapped point at the eastern side of the outer harbor. **Pros:** two on-site restaurants; private boat tour of harbor; lots of included amenities and activities. **Cons:** a few private residences close to premises; no elevators; some of the more-historic buildings have quirks. [$] *Rooms from: $300* ✉ *88 Grandview Ave., Boothbay Harbor* ☎ *207/633–4152, 800/553–0289* 🌐 *www.sprucepointinn.com* 🕓 *Closed mid-Oct.–mid-May* 🛏 *63 rooms* 🍽 *No Meals.*

★ Topside Inn

$$$$ | B&B/INN | Dating from 1865 and once the home of a wealthy sea captain, this grand, hilltop inn has an immense lawn dotted with Adirondack chairs, a wraparound porch, and a fireside lounge with a stylish bar. **Pros:** knockout harbor views; exceptional breakfasts; walking distance to downtown. **Cons:** two-person maximum per room; books up quickly in summer; steep, short walk back up the hill from town. [$] *Rooms from: $550* ✉ *60 McKown St., Boothbay Harbor* ☎ *207/633–5404* 🌐 *www.topsideinn.*

com ⏲ *Closed late Oct.–early May* 🛏 *22 rooms* 🍴 *Free Breakfast.*

Damariscotta

18 miles northeast of Boothbay Harbor.

Near the head of the Damariscotta River, and flanked by the Boothbay and Pemaquid peninsulas, this vibrant little town has a bevy of shops, many tucked into 150-year-old brick buildings in the three-block-long National Historic District. This is also the place to slurp your fill of freshly plucked oysters.

Indigenous peoples summered on these shores millennia ago, leaving behind huge, still-visible, oyster-shell middens. By the late 1800s, the shellfish had disappeared. A century later, aquaculture programs spawned new enterprises, and today some of the country's most prized oysters come from the clear, clean Damariscotta River. Some say this is the Napa Valley of oyster growing.

Damariscotta is also the commercial hub of an eponymous region made up of several communities along the rocky coast. The closest is Newcastle, just a stroll across the bridge. It was settled in the early 1600s and later had shipyards and mills. The oldest Catholic church in New England, St. Patrick's, is here, and it still rings its original Paul Revere bell. South of Damariscotta on the Pemaquid Peninsula are the towns of Bristol, South Bristol, Round Pond, New Harbor, and Pemaquid Point.

Thousands descend on Damariscotta every October over Indigenous Peoples Day/Columbus Day Weekend for the zany Pumpkinfest, whose events include pumpkin-boat races on the harbor—yes, people actually race around in giant, tubby, tippy, paddle- and outboard-powered pumpkins.

GETTING HERE AND AROUND

From Boothbay Harbor follow Route 27 north to U.S. 1. Turn off U.S. 1 onto business U.S. 1, which runs through the village of Damariscotta.

At the northern end of downtown, Routes 129 and 130 lead south from business U.S. 1. In a few miles, 129 turns off to South Bristol and Christmas Cove. Route 130 continues down to Bristol, New Harbor, and Pemaquid. From there, you can take Route 32 north up through New Harbor, Round Pond, and Bremen, returning to U.S. 1 in Waldoboro.

The Concord Coach Lines bus that travels the coast stops in Damariscotta daily.

VISITOR INFORMATION

CONTACTS Damariscotta Region Chamber of Commerce. ✉ *67–A Main St., Damariscotta* ☎ *207/563–8340* 🌐 *www.damariscottaregion.com.*

🍴 Restaurants

King Eider's Pub and Restaurant

$$$$ | **AMERICAN** | **FAMILY** | At this restaurant in an adorable building just off Main Street, the acclaimed crab cakes and the oysters fresh from the Damariscotta River are good bets, but so are the steak-and-ale pie, seafood stew, and fish-and-chips (made with fresh haddock that's sautéed rather than fried). With exposed-brick walls and low, wood-beamed ceilings hung with pottery beer mugs, the downstairs is a snug place to enjoy a Maine craft ale. **Known for:** live music in the pub; cozy atmosphere; extensive whiskey collection. [$] *Average main: $36* ✉ *2 Elm St., Damariscotta* ✣ *Just off Main St.* ☎ *207/563–6008* 🌐 *www.kingeiderspub.com.*

Newcastle Publick House

$$ | **AMERICAN** | **FAMILY** | In a large, historic, handsomely renovated brick building, Newcastle Publick House serves delicious comfort food in a pleasant dining room and welcoming bar. Specialties include

Maine is the largest lobster-producing state in the United States.

fresh oysters prepared several ways, a selection of burgers, and one of the best French onion soups around. **Known for:** stacked burgers; cozy, old-school atmosphere; desserts and breads made by nearby Oysterhead Pizza Co.. [$] *Average main: $20* ✉ *52 Main St., Newcastle* ☎ *207/563–3434* 🌐 *www.newcastlepublickhouse.com* 🕓 *Closed Mon.*

Coffee and Quick Bites

Barn Door Baking Company Cafe

$ | **BAKERY** | **FAMILY** | Connected to Sherman's Maine Coast Book Shop through an arched doorway, this little café turns out excellent coffee and hot and cold coffee drinks, plus fresh-from-the-oven sweet and savory baked items. It's hard to choose among the scones, slices of cake and pie, sinful cookies, cupcakes, and old-fashioned dessert bars. **Known for:** daily selection of irresistible baked goodies; good place to chill and catch up on email; friendly service. [$] *Average main: $5* ✉ *162 Main St., Damariscotta* ☎ *207/563–3662* 🌐 *www.barndoorbakingcompany.com.*

S. Fernald's Country Store

$ | **SANDWICHES** | **FAMILY** | Settle into the couch or sit at a table for breakfast and try the Eggs Bigelow (two eggs in a hole, bacon, cheddar, and locally baked sourdough) or grab a sandwich, wrap, or sub for lunch. The biggest challenge is deciding among the many breads and filling choices on the extensive menu. **Known for:** a local favorite; penny candy, toys, and other nostalgic items; great for picnic provisions. [$] *Average main: $10* ✉ *50 Main St., Damariscotta* ☎ *207/563–8484* 🌐 *www.sfernalds.com* 🕓 *Closed Sun. and Mon.*

Hotels

★ **Newcastle Inn**

$$ | **B&B/INN** | **FAMILY** | A riverside location, tasteful decor, and lots of common areas (inside and out) make this an especially relaxing country inn. **Pros:** guests can order beer or wine; suites have sitting areas; water views from many rooms. **Cons:** flights of stairs to rooms on upper floors; not all rooms have water views;

some rooms lack ample sitting areas. [$] *Rooms from: $250* ✉ *60 River Rd., Newcastle* ☎ *207/563–5685* 🌐 *www.newcastleinn.com* 🛏 *13 rooms* 🍴 *Free Breakfast.*

Monhegan Island

East of Pemaquid Peninsula, about 10 miles offshore.

If you like the idea of a slow-paced vacation on a remote island, Monhegan is for you. What's more, if you're also an artist or an art aficionado, you might never want to leave: there's a reason this has been a haven for artists for over a century.

To get here you'll need to take a ferry. A tiny hamlet greets you at the harbor. There are no paved roads. It doesn't take long to grasp that Monhegan is the place where simple and artful living is the order of the day.

The island was known to Basque, Portuguese, and Breton fishermen well before Columbus discovered America. English fishermen spent summers catching cod here in the 1600s. About a century ago, Monhegan was discovered by some of America's finest painters—Rockwell Kent, Robert Henri, A.J. Hammond, and Edward Hopper among them—who sailed out to paint its open meadows, savage cliffs, wild ocean views, and fishermen's shacks.

In summer, the tiny village and its dirt lanes buzz with day trippers who've come to hike the island's trails, visit a few shops and artists' studios, lunch in a handful of eateries, and enjoy the unspoiled remoteness. The island has 17 miles of trails, and serenity awaits at the lighthouse atop the hill overlooking the harbor and at the high cliffs of White Head, Black Head, and Burnt Head. From these rugged headlands, you can gaze across the ocean, where the next landfall is Spain.

GETTING HERE AND AROUND

Excursion vessels transport passengers between three mainland harbors and Monhegan. The boat trip is almost as exhilarating as exploring the island itself. Be on the lookout for seals, porpoises, and perhaps even small whales. Note that visitors are not allowed to bring cars to the island, so be prepared to wander on foot.

The Port Clyde boat landing is home to Monhegan Boat Line's *Elizabeth Ann* and the *Laura B.* There are three round-trips daily mid-June through mid October, one trip daily in late fall and early spring, and three trips weekly in the winter. In season, Hardy Boat offers daily trips between New Harbor and Monhegan, while Balmy Days Cruises makes crossings from Boothbay Harbor. All three companies also offer a variety of regional sightseeing cruises.

CONTACTS Balmy Days Cruises. ✉ *42 Commercial St., Pier 8, Boothbay Harbor* ☎ *207/633–2284* 🌐 *www.balmydayscruises.com.* **Hardy Boat Cruises.** ✉ *129 State Rte. 32, New Harbor* ☎ *207/677–2026* 🌐 *hardyboat.com.* **Monhegan Boat Line.** ✉ *880 Port Clyde Rd., Port Clyde* ☎ *207/372–8848* 🌐 *www.monheganboat.com.*

Sights

★ Monhegan Brewing Company

BREWERY | There's something to be said for enjoying a cold beer after a long hike. You can slake your thirst at a seasonal tap "room" (seating is actually outdoors beneath umbrellas and tents) of this tiny brewery owned by a local lobstering family. Options could include Crow's Nest IPA, Balmy Days Citra Kölsch, or Mad Cow Milk Stout. There might also be icy cold root beer, and you can get lunch to go at the on-site Bait Bag food trailer. ✉ *1 Boody La., Monhegan* ☎ *297/596–0011* 🌐 *monheganbrewing.com* 🕒 *Closed mid-Oct.–late May.*

Monhegan Island Light
LIGHTHOUSE | **FAMILY** | Getting a close-up look at this squat stone lighthouse, which was automated in 1959, requires a ½-mile, slightly steep uphill walk from the island's ferry dock. The tower is open sporadically throughout the summer for short tours. In the former keeper's quarters, the small Monhegan Museum of Art & History provides a peek into island life past and present. It also exhibits works by artists with a connection to this special place. ✉ *Lighthouse Hill Rd., ½ mile east of dock, Monhegan* ☎ *207/596–7003* 🌐 *monheganmuseum.org* 🎟 *$10 (museum)* 🕒 *Closed Oct.–late June.*

🍴 Restaurants

★ **Fish House Market**
$$ | **SEAFOOD** | Although everything served at this seafood shack and market beside Fish Beach is delicious and simply prepared, the crab roll—a large, split-top roll buttered and griddled and stuffed with fresh, sweet, mayo-tossed crabmeat—may just be the best on the Maine coast. Order at the window, carry your tray to a picnic table inches from the water, and lap up the view of lobster boats in the harbor. **Known for:** BYOB; outstanding fish chowder; lovely waterside location. [$] *Average main: $18* ✉ *98 Fish Beach La., Monhegan* ☎ *207/594–8368* 🌐 *www.facebook.com/fishhousemonhegan* 🕒 *Closed late Sept.–late May.*

☕ Coffee and Quick Bites

The Barnacle
$ | **AMERICAN** | On the wharf a few steps from the boat landing, The Barnacle serves espresso and a selection of coffees from Monhegan Coffee Roasters along with baked goods such as scones and brownies, and ice cream. For lunch, choose from prepared sandwiches, chowders, and salads, which you can eat at a picnic table or take with you. **Known for:** a place to wait for the ferry; eat outdoors or grab-and-go; locally roasted coffee. [$] *Average main: $15* ✉ *Monhegan Boat Landing, wharf, Monhegan* ☎ *207/596–0371* 🌐 *www.islandinnmonhegan.com/the-barnacle* 🕒 *Closed mid-Oct.–late May.*

Rockland

25 miles north of Damariscotta via U.S. 1.

This town is considered the gateway to Penobscot Bay and is the first stop on U.S. 1 offering a glimpse of the often-sparkling and island-dotted blue bay. Though previously considered by visitors to be a place to pass through on the way to places like Camden, Rockland now gets lots of attention on its own. This is thanks to a great selection of small but excellent restaurants; a terrific Main Street lineup of shops and galleries; the renowned Farnsworth Art Museum and the Center for Maine Contemporary Art; and several popular summer festivals. Despite all of these developments, Rockland continues to be a fishing port and the commercial hub of this coastal area.

The best place to view Rockland's windjammers as they sail in and out of the harbor is the mile-long granite breakwater that protects Rockland Harbor. To get there, from U.S. 1, head east on Waldo Avenue and then right on Samoset Road; follow this short road to its end.

GETTING HERE AND AROUND

U.S. 1 runs along Main Street here. It is one way (headed north) as it goes through downtown. U.S. 1A curves through the residential neighborhood just west of the business district, offering a southbound route as well as a faster route if you are just passing through in either direction.

The Concord Coach Lines bus that runs along the coast stops in Rockland.

Ferries to the islands of Vinalhaven, North Haven, and Matinicus leave from the ferry terminal at the northern end of Main Street.

VISITOR INFORMATION

CONTACTS Penobscot Bay Area Chamber of Commerce. ✉ *Rockland* ☎ *207/596–0376, 800/562–2529* ⊕ *www.camdenrockland. com.*

WHEN TO GO

Late summer is an ideal time to visit Rockland—if you don't mind the crowds. The Maine Lobster Festival highlights the calendar in August. September is a beautiful month, with bright, clear skies and cooling breezes. In addition, it may be easier than it is at the height of summer to book a reservation at the many popular restaurants.

March is a dreary month. The skies are often gray, and it isn't too late in the season for snow. Some restaurants and shops that close in winter may not yet be open. But if you enjoy solitude, this is a great time for walking the shore, watching the waves, and searching for intriguing finds brought ashore by winter storms.

FESTIVALS AND EVENTS

Maine Lobster Festival

FESTIVALS | FAMILY | Rockland's annual Maine Lobster Festival, held in early August, is the region's largest annual event. About 10 tons of lobsters are steamed in a huge lobster cooker—you have to see it to believe it. The festival, held in Harbor Park, includes a parade, live entertainment, food booths, and, of course, the crowning of the Maine Sea Goddess. ✉ *Harbor Park, Main St., south of U.S. 1, Rockland* ☎ *800/576–7512* ⊕ *www.mainelobsterfestival.com.*

North Atlantic Blues Festival

FESTIVALS | FAMILY | About a dozen well-known musicians gather for the North Atlantic Blues Festival, a two-day affair held the first or second full weekend after July 4. The show officially takes place at the public landing on Rockland Harbor Park, but it also includes a "club crawl" through downtown Rockland on Saturday night. Admission to the festival is $45 at the gate, $75 for a weekend pass. ✉ *Public Landing, 275 Main St., Rockland* ☎ *207/596–6055* ⊕ *www. northatlanticbluesfestival.com.*

◉ Sights

★ Center for Maine Contemporary Art

ART MUSEUM | The impressive Center for Maine Contemporary Art sprang from a 50-year legacy that originated in makeshift exhibitions in barns and a potato-barrel storage loft before settling into a small, antique fire house in Rockport. Since 2016, this striking, light-filled building designed by Toshiko Mori has allowed the museum to showcase modern works by accomplished artists with a Maine connection in a space that befits the quality of the art. Expect envelope-pushing, changing exhibitions and public programs. Visitors are invited to drop into the museum's ArtLab to gain greater insight into current exhibitions by trying their own hand at making art inspired by the works on display. ArtLab is open weekends in summer; daily the rest of the year. ✉ *21 Winter St., Rockland* ☎ *207/701–5005* ⊕ *cmcanow.org* ⚲ *$8.*

★ Farnsworth Art Museum

ART MUSEUM | FAMILY | One of the most highly regarded small museums in the country, the Farnsworth's collection is largely devoted to works by three generations of the famous Wyeth family, who have spent summers on the Maine Coast for a century. N.C. Wyeth was an accomplished illustrator whose works were featured in many turn-of-the-20th-century adventure books; his son Andrew was one of the country's best-known and-loved painters; and Andrew's son Jamie is an accomplished painter in his own right. Galleries in the main building always display some of Andrew Wyeth's works, such as *The Patriot, Witchcraft,* and *Turkey Pond.* Across the street, the Wyeth Center, in a former church, exhibits art by Andrew's father and son. The museum's collection also includes works by such lauded, Maine-connected artists as Fitz Henry Lane, George Bellows, Winslow Homer, Edward Hopper, Louise Nevelson, and Rockwell Kent. Changing exhibits are shown in the Jamien Morehouse Wing.

Just across the garden from the museum, the Farnsworth Homestead, the handsome, circa-1850 Greek Revival home of the museum's original benefactor, retains its original lavish Victorian furnishings and is open late June–mid-October.

In Cushing, a village on the St. George River about 10 miles south of Thomaston (a half-hour drive from Rockland), the museum operates the Olson House. The large, weathered-shingle structure was the home of Christina Olson and her brother, Alvarez, who were good friends of Andrew Wyeth. He depicted them and their home in numerous works, including his famous painting *Christina's World*. It is open spring through fall. ✉ *16 Museum St., Rockland* ☎ *207/596–6457* 🌐 *www.farnsworthmuseum.org* 🎟 *$15* 🕒 *Closed Tues. Nov.–Dec.; closed Mon. and Tues. Jan.–May; Wyeth Center closed Jan.–May.*

Maine Lighthouse Museum

HISTORY MUSEUM | FAMILY | The lighthouse museum has more than 25 Fresnel lighthouse lenses, as well as what's said to be the nation's largest collection of lighthouse and life-saving artifacts, and Coast Guard memorabilia. Permanent exhibits spotlight topics like lighthouse heroines—women who manned the lights when the keepers couldn't—and lightships. ✉ *1 Park Dr., Rockland* ☎ *207/594–3301* 🌐 *www.mainelighthousemuseum.org* 🎟 *$10.*

🍴 Restaurants

Claws

$$$ | SEAFOOD | FAMILY | Set right beside the road at the northern end of town, this lobster shack gets consistently enthusiastic reviews—many say the overstuffed lobster roll is one of the best. The large menu includes all the usual suspects plus a great selection of "snacky things" and entrées, and even a taco bar—butter-poached lobster tacos, anyone? **Known for:** wild Maine blueberry shortcake; lobster rolls stuffed with a pound of meat; award-winning lobster bisque. [$] *Average main: $25* ✉ *743 Main St., Rockland* ☎ *207/596–5600* 🌐 *www.clawsrocklandmaine.com.*

★ In Good Company

$$$ | MODERN AMERICAN | As the name suggests, this is an excellent spot to slow down and catch up with good friends over a bottle of wine while savoring small, internationally flavored plates or a full meal. The creative blend of textures and flavors that comes out of the kitchen is exceptional. **Known for:** outside dining in summer; excellent wine pairings; pared-down aesthetic with a focus on the food. [$] *Average main: $30* ✉ *415 Maine St., Rockland* ☎ *207/593–9110* 🌐 *www.ingoodcompanymaine.com.*

★ Primo

$$$$ | MEDITERRANEAN | Chef Melissa Kelly has twice won the James Beard Best Chef: Northeast, and she and her world-class restaurant have been written up in such magazines as *Gourmet, Bon Appétit,* and *O.* Named for the chef-owner's Italian grandfather, Primo serves masterfully prepared pasta, fresh seafood, and local meats. **Known for:** house-made pasta; fresh Maine ingredients with Mediterranean influences; consistently excellent; $1 oysters every Sunday. [$] *Average main: $38* ✉ *2 N. Main St., Rockland* ☎ *207/596–0770* 🌐 *www.primorestaurant.com* 🕒 *Closed Tues.*

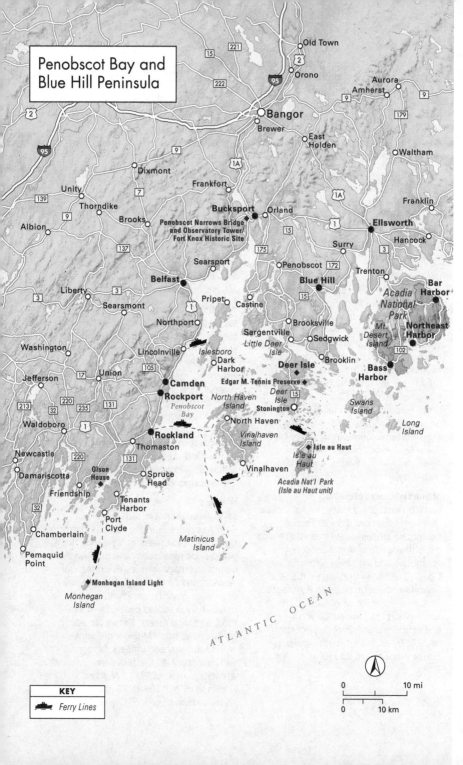

Penobscot Bay and Blue Hill Peninsula

Old Town
Orono
Aurora
Amherst
Waltham
Bangor
Brewer
East Holden
Franklin
Dixmont
Frankfort
Bucksport
Orland
Ellsworth
Hancock
Penobscot Narrows Bridge and Observatory Tower/ Fort Knox Historic Site
Surry
Unity
Thorndike
Brooks
Searsport
Penobscot
Trenton
Albion
Belfast
Blue Hill
Bar Harbor
Liberty
Pripet
Castine
Acadia National Park
Northeast Harbor
Searsmont
Northport
Brooksville
Sargentville
Sedgwick
Mt. Desert Island
Washington
Lincolnville
Islesboro
Little Deer Isle
Brooklin
Bass Harbor
Dark Harbor
Deer Isle
Jefferson
Union
Camden
Edgar M. Tennis Preserve
Deer Isle
Swans Island
Rockport
North Haven Island
Long Island
Penobscot Bay
Stonington
Waldoboro
Rockland
North Haven
Thomaston
Vinalhaven Island
Isle au Haut
Newcastle
Spruce Head
Vinalhaven
Isle au Haut
Damariscotta
Olson House
Acadia Nat'l Park (Isle au Haut unit)
Friendship
Tenants Harbor
Chamberlain
Port Clyde
Matinicus Island
Pemaquid Point
Monhegan Island Light
Monhegan Island

ATLANTIC OCEAN

KEY

Ferry Lines

0 — 10 mi
0 — 10 km

Windjammer Excursions

Nothing defines the Penobscot Bay area better than its fleet of historic windjammers, and a sailing trip on one of these beauties, whether for just a few hours or a few days, is an unforgettable experience. Originally designed to carry cargo and built along the East Coast in the 19th and early 20th centuries, the wooden-hulled vessels once plied coastal waters in such trades as lumbering, granite, fishing, and oystering. Members of today's windjammer fleet range from as small as 46 feet, accommodating six passengers (plus a couple of crew members), to more than 130 feet, carrying 30 passengers.

In the past few years, nearly all of the windjammers have been passed on to new, young captain-owners who bring fresh energy as well as solid qualifications to their stewardship of these beloved tall ships.

On a windjammer excursion, passengers are welcome to participate in on-board tasks, be it helping to hoist a sail or taking a turn at the wheel. Exceptional meals help keep them fueled for the effort.

During the Camden Windjammer Festival (⊕ www.facebook.com/WindjammerFestival), held Labor Day weekend, crowds gather to watch the region's fleet sail into the harbor, and most boats are open for tours. The schooner-crew talent show later in the weekend is a bit more irreverent than the majestic arrival ceremony.

A windjammer cruise gives you a chance to soak up Maine's dramatic coast from the water. Overnight cruises can run anywhere from two to eight days; day trips—usually just a couple of hours long—feature a tour of the harbor and some lighthouse and wildlife sightseeing. Prices depend on trip length; overnight cruises include all meals. Trips leave from Camden, Rockland, and Rockport. You can find information on the fleets by visiting the individual vessels' websites or by contacting the Penobscot Bay Regional Chamber of Commerce (⊕ camdenrockland.com), the Maine Windjammer Association (⊕ www.mainewindjammercruises.com), or Maine Windjammer Cruises (⊕ www.sailmainecoast.com).

Rockland Café

$ | **DINER** | **FAMILY** | Famous for the size of its breakfasts—don't pass up the lobster or fish-cake Benedict—Rockland Café has been a local favorite for decades. The large menu includes plenty of lunch and dinner choices from the excellent clam, fish, and seafood chowder to fried haddock, clams, shrimp, and scallops or lobster, clam, shrimp, and scallop rolls. **Known for:** lots of traditional seafood dishes; classic liver and onions; lively place where locals come to catch up. $ *Average main: $12* ⊠ *441 Main St., Rockland* ☎ *207/596–7556* ⊕ *www.rocklandcafe.com.*

☕ Coffee and Quick Bites

★ **Atlantic Baking Company**

$ | **AMERICAN** | **FAMILY** | Classic European and American breads such as batards, baguettes, ciabatta, focaccia, sourdough boules, and rolls come out of French ovens every morning at this popular little spot. The cases are also filled with just-baked croissants, scones, muffins, cookies, and more. **Known for:** French macarons; apricot pistachio oat cookies; classic sourdough. $ *Average main: $5* ⊠ *351 Main St., Rockland* ☎ *207/596–0505* ⊕ *atlanticbakingco.com* ⊗ *Closed Sun.*

Hotels

Berry Manor Inn

$$$ | **B&B/INN** | Originally the residence of Rockland merchant Charles H. Berry, this 1898 shingle-style B&B sits in Rockland's National Historic District. **Pros:** guest pantry stocked with drinks, sweets, and treats—there's always pie; 10-minute walk to downtown and the harbor; some rooms can be combined to create two-room suites. **Cons:** view limited to gardens; somewhat fussy decor consistent with Victorian-era property; not pet-friendly. [$] *Rooms from: $350* ✉ *81 Talbot Ave., Rockland* ☎ *207/596–7696, 800/774–5692* 🌐 *www.berrymanorinn.com* 🛏 *18 rooms* 🍴 *Free Breakfast.*

★ 250 Main Hotel

$$$$ | **HOTEL** | Finely crafted by local shipwrights, this jazzy little boutique hotel is filled with stylish and colorful mid-century-modern design. **Pros:** heated bathroom floors; complimentary afternoon wine-and-cheese hour; walk to shops and restaurants. **Cons:** no pool; some noise from the street and from the harbor in the morning; parking (free) is across the street and down the hill. [$] *Rooms from: $450* ✉ *250 Main St., Rockland* ☎ *207/594–5994* 🌐 *250mainhotel.com* 🛏 *26 rooms* 🍴 *Free Breakfast.*

Activities

Schooner Heritage

SAILING | **FAMILY** | Designed and built specifically for passengers, the 95-foot *Heritage* carries up to 30 guests. Both captains are musicians and enjoy playing their guitars for guests in the evening. Trips range from three to six nights in length, and children aged 10 and up are welcome. ✉ *North End Shipyard, 11 Front St., Rockland* ☎ *207/594–8007, 800/648–4544* 🌐 *www.schoonerheritage.com* 🎫 *From $780* 🕓 *Closed Oct.–early June.*

Schooner J. & E. Riggin

SAILING | **FAMILY** | The schooner *J. & E. Riggin*, originally an oyster dredger, offers multiday sailing cruises that thoroughly immerse passengers in traditional life under sail. Measuring 120 feet overall, the *Riggin* carries up to 24 overnight guests plus six crew. The experience is highlighted by three daily meals, plus snacks, all prepared using locally sourced seafood, vegetables, and other ingredients. ✉ *Windjammer Wharf, 3 Captain Spear Dr., Rockland* ☎ *207/594–1875, 800/869–0604* 🌐 *www.mainewindjammer.com* 🎫 *From $615* 🕓 *Closed early Oct.–late May.*

★ Schooner Ladona

SAILING | Unlike her windjammer sisters, which were built to work hard, the schooner *Ladona* began her career as a private racing yacht, though she was later called into duty during World War II. Built in 1922 (rebuilt in 1971), and restored from bow to stern before joining the windjammer fleet a few years ago, this graceful schooner takes guests on cruises of three to seven nights. The on-board experience recalls *Ladona*'s past as a private yacht, with greater comfort and luxury, as well as more elegant dining, than the other members of the windjammer fleet. All trips include breakfast, lunch, and dinner, as well as a selection of fine wines and beers every evening. One trip features daily wine tastings led by an experienced wine professional. ✉ *40 Tillson Ave., Rockland* ☎ *800/999–7352, 207/594–4723* 🌐 *www.schoonerladona.com* 🎫 *From $1108* 🕓 *Closed mid-Oct.–early June.*

Rockport

4 miles north of Rockland via U.S. 1.

Heading north on U.S. 1 from Rockland, you enter Rockport before you reach the tourist mecca of Camden. Hugging the harbor, Rockport Village is a short drive off U.S. 1. It's home to a handful of very good small restaurants.

Originally called Goose River, Rockport was part of Camden until 1891. The cutting and burning of limestone was once a major industry in this area. The stone was cut in nearby quarries and then burned in hot kilns; the resulting lime powder was used to create mortar. Some of the kilns can still be seen down on the harbor.

If you drive from Rockport to Camden on Union Street, you'll pass under the Camden-Rockport Arch at the town line. It has appeared in a number of movies, including *Peyton Place* and *In the Bedroom*.

GETTING HERE AND AROUND

Rockport is off U.S. 1 between Rockland and Camden. Turn on Pascal Avenue to get to the village center.

The Concord Coach Lines bus that runs along the coast makes a stop near Rockport village on Route 1 just over the town line in Camden.

Restaurants

★ 18 Central Oyster Bar and Grill

$$$ | SEAFOOD | 18 Central Oyster Bar and Grill produces excellent, creative dishes in a cozy spot high above Rockport's working harbor. Seasonally inspired, locally harvested seafood plus dishes with a hint of Southern comfort make up the backbone of the menu—think fried green tomatoes with local peekytoe crab, chili oil, and microgreens, or crispy fried chicken accompanied by collards and heirloom grits. **Known for:** evenly paced, well-balanced dinners transition gracefully from one course to the next; lively atmosphere encouraged by botanically infused cocktails; packed as soon as the door opens for dinner. $ *Average main: $30* ⊠ *18 Central St., Rockport* ☎ *207/466–9055* ⊕ *www.18central.com* ⊗ *Closed Tues.–Thurs.* ☞ *Reservations strongly advised; credit card required to secure reservations for more than 4; max party size 8 people.*

Nina June

$$$ | MEDITERRANEAN | FAMILY | This lovely trattoria is known for its cheery harbor-view setting and frequently changing menus where locally sourced ingredients shine. Highly regarded chef-owner Sara Jenkins's fresh but authentic takes on Mediterranean-spanning dishes use seafood harvested along Maine's rocky coast, including local oysters, and everything from the pasta to the pickled veggies is made in-house; the presentation of each dish makes for sheer eye candy. **Known for:** weekly five-course prix-fixe menu plus a small à la carte café menu; craft cocktails; harbor views, especially from outdoor deck; cooking classes with Sara Jenkins and guest chefs. $ *Average main: $26* ⊠ *24 Central St., Rockport* ☎ *207/236–8880* ⊕ *www. ninajunerestaurant.com* ⊗ *Closed Sun.– Tues. No lunch.*

Hotels

Samoset Resort

$$$$ | RESORT | FAMILY | Located on the Rockland-Rockport town line along the edge of Penobscot Bay and the eastern side of Rockland harbor, this 230-acre resort offers luxurious rooms, suites, and cottages, all with a private balcony or patio and an ocean or garden view. **Pros:** sweeping ocean views; choice of restaurants on-site; a beautiful resort that seems to meet every need. **Cons:** not for those who prefer quiet, intimate lodging; not within easy walking distance of downtown Rockland or Camden; no beach. $ *Rooms from: $400* ⊠ *220 Warrenton St., off Rte. 1, Rockport* ☎ *207/594–2511* ⊕ *www.samosetresort. com* ⊗ *Closed weeknights Dec.–Apr.* ⇆ *178 rooms* ⦿ *Free Breakfast* ☞ *Daily $40 resort fee; 2 dogs under 30 lbs. permitted ($75 per night per dog).*

🏃 Activities

Schooner Heron

SAILING | FAMILY | Docked in the Rockport Marine Park, the lovely 65-foot, Alden-designed schooner takes passengers sailing on Penobscot Bay three times a day, weather permitting. She was built and is operated by a very experienced, qualified, and licensed couple who sail their schooner to the Caribbean every winter. In Maine from June through early October, they offer an Educational Eco Sail, a happy-hour sunset sail, and private morning charters. While underway, they share their knowledge of local maritime history, sea life, and lobstering. ✉ *Rockport Marine Park, Rockport* ☎ *207/236–8605* ⊕ *www.sailheron.com* ⊗ *Closed late Oct.–June.*

Camden

8 miles north of Rockland.

Known as the Jewel of the Maine Coast, Camden is one of the region's most popular spots. The town's compact size makes it perfect for exploring on foot: shops, restaurants, and galleries line Main Street, as well as the side streets and alleys around the harbor. But be sure to include Camden's residential area on your tour. It is quite charming and filled with lovely period houses from the time when Federal, Greek Revival, and Victorian architectural styles were the rage among the wealthy; many of them are now B&Bs. The Chamber of Commerce, on the Public Landing, can provide you with a walking map.

Rising on the north side of town are the Camden Hills. Drive or hike to the summit of Mt. Battie, in Camden Hills State Park, to enjoy panoramic views of the town, harbor, and island-dotted bay. This perch is where Pulitzer-winning poet Edna St. Vincent Millay penned

"Renascence," describing the view in the lines: All I could see from where I stood / Was three long mountains and a wood; / I turned and looked another way, / And saw three islands in a bay."

Camden's not only famous for its geography, but also for its fleet of windjammers—originals from the age of sailing as well as replicas—with their romantic histories and great billowing sails. If possible, sign up for a cruise, whether for a couple of hours or as much as a week.

GETTING HERE AND AROUND

U.S. 1 runs right through the middle of Camden. If you're driving from farther south on U.S. 1 and would like to bypass Thomaston and Rockland on your way to Camden, turn left off onto Route 90 in Warren and rejoin Route 1 at the other end of Route 90 in Rockport.

U.S. 1 has lots of names as it runs through Maine. Within Camden's town limits, it begins at the southern end of town as Elm Street, changes to Main Street in the downtown area, and then becomes High Street.

The Concord Coach Lines bus that drives the coastal route stops on Route 1 in Camden, just south of town.

VISITOR INFORMATION

CONTACTS Penobscot Bay Regional Chamber of Commerce. ✉ *Visitor Center, 2 Public Landing, Camden* ☎ *207/236–4404, 800/562–2529* ⊕ *www.camdenrockland. com.*

WHEN TO GO

From June to September, the town is crowded with visitors, but that doesn't detract from its charm. Just make reservations for lodging and restaurants well in advance and be prepared for busy traffic on the town's Main Street. This is also the best time to book a windjammer excursion.

FESTIVALS AND EVENTS

Camden Shakespeare Festival

THEATER | **FAMILY** | Every year, a professional troupe of actors presents a midsummer festival of Shakespeare plays beside the harbor. Held in Camden's beautiful amphitheater, the performances strive to engage audiences of all ages, including children. The festival is presented in association with the Camden Public Library. ✉ *Box 1206, Camden* ☎ *207/464–0008* 🌐 *camdenshakespeare.org* 🎫 *$28* 🕒 *Closed Aug.–June.*

★ **Camden Windjammer Festival**

FESTIVALS | **FAMILY** | One of the biggest and most colorful events of the year is the Camden Windjammer Festival, which takes place over Labor Day weekend. The harbor is packed with historic vessels, there are lots of good eats, and visitors can tour the magnificent ships. ✉ *Camden* ☎ *207/236–3438* 🌐 *www.facebook.com/WindjammerFestival/.*

🍴 Restaurants

★ **Natalie's Restaurant**

$$$$ | **MODERN AMERICAN** | Located in the stylish and elegant Camden Harbour Inn, this fine-dining restaurant serves imaginative, beautifully plated creations starring local seafood, meats, and other seasonal ingredients like vegetables and herbs from the property's garden. Probably the most sophisticated dining spot in Camden, Natalie's is the creation of Dutch owners Raymond Brunyanszki and Oscar Verest, who have brought in talented chefs to create splurge-worthy dishes that are served by a polished waitstaff. **Known for:** phenomenal service with true attention to detail; signature five-course lobster tasting menu; grand views of the Camden Hills, harbor, and bay. [$] *Average main: $38* ✉ *Camden Harbour Inn, 83 Bay View St., Camden* ☎ *866/658–1542, 207/236–7008* 🌐 *www.nataliesrestaurant.com* 🕒 *Closed Sun. Nov.–May. No lunch.*

The Waterfront

$$ | **AMERICAN** | Come to this long-standing local favorite for a ringside seat on Camden Harbor; the best view, when the weather cooperates, is from the deck. The menu features fresh local seafood, but there are also beef and chicken entrées and salads. **Known for:** great salad choices; harborside dining, including outdoor deck; solid menu that never disappoints. [$] *Average main: $20* ✉ *48 Bay View St., Camden* ☎ *207/236–3747* 🌐 *www.waterfrontcamden.com* 🕒 *Closed Tues.* ☞ *No groups larger than 8 people.*

☕ Coffee and Quick Bites

Harbor Dogs

$ | **SEAFOOD** | **FAMILY** | A summertime fixture for five decades, the Harbor Dogs shack on the town landing is the perfect place to grab lunch to enjoy at a nearby bench beside the harbor or before or after a cruise. Hot dog toppings include southwestern, Asian, and Chicago, and there are also lobster and crab rolls, fish tacos, haddock Reubens, and fried-seafood platters. **Known for:** lengthy hot-dog menu; watching the sightseeing boats and sailboats coming and going; delicious takeout to enjoy on a harborfront bench. [$] *Average main: $15* ✉ *1 Public Landing, Camden* ☎ *207/230–9638* 🌐 *www.harbordogs.com* 🕒 *Closed Wed. and Thurs. and mid-Oct.–mid-May. No dinner.*

★ **Owl and Turtle Bookshop and Café**

$ | **CAFE** | **FAMILY** | This pint-size but well-stocked independent bookstore with a tiny café has been serving Camden for more than 50 years. The full menu of coffee drinks is based on locally roasted beans and includes a selection of homemade baked goods. **Known for:** locally roasted coffee beans; homemade baked goods; independent bookstore. [$] *Average main: $5* ✉ *33 Bay View St., Camden* ☎ *207/230–7335* 🌐 *www.owlandturtle.com* 🕒 *Closed Sun. and Mon.*

Zoot Coffee

$ | **CAFÉ** | Locals and visitors alike are drawn to this community gathering spot by the irresistible aroma of freshly roasted coffee; it's a great spot to visit with friends or open your tablet to do some work. There's a wide selection of hot and cold coffee drinks, chai variations, and hot chocolate, as well as Italian ices and to-go choices that include porridge, yogurt, toast, soup, quiche, grilled cheese, pie, and even beans on toast! **Known for:** well-prepared coffee drinks; relaxed atmosphere; simple breakfast and lunch choices. $ *Average main: $5* ✉ *5 Elm St., Camden* ☎ *207/236–9858* ⊕ *www.facebook.com/ZootCoffee* ☾ *No dinner.*

🛏 Hotels

Hartstone Inn & Hideaway

$$$ | **B&B/INN** | Inside this circa-1835 mansard-roofed Victorian home at the southern edge of Camden's downtown area is a plush, sophisticated retreat and a culinary destination. **Pros:** pet-friendly; extravagant breakfasts; some private entrances. **Cons:** not on water; no wheelchair access; not all rooms have fireplaces. $ *Rooms from: $300* ✉ *41 Elm St., Camden* ☎ *207/236–4259* ⊕ *www.hartstoneinn.com* ☾ *Restaurant closed Mon. and Tues.* ⇌ *22 rooms* ⧦ *Free Breakfast.*

Lord Camden Inn

$$ | **HOTEL** | **FAMILY** | If you want to be in the midst of the shops and not far from the harbor, this handsome Main Street brick building with bright blue-and-white awnings is the perfect choice. **Pros:** buffet breakfast with hot entrées; all rooms have mini-refrigerators and microwaves; most rooms have balconies. **Cons:** Main Street noise can drift up into front rooms; no on-site restaurant; $15/night parking unless room is booked directly with hotel. $ *Rooms from: $299* ✉ *24 Main St., Camden* ☎ *207/236–4325,* *800/336–4325* ⊕ *www.lordcamdeninn.com* ⇌ *36 rooms* ⧦ *Free Breakfast.*

★ The Norumbega

$$$$ | **B&B/INN** | With a commanding position overlooking the bay just north of downtown Camden, this impressive, turreted "castle" exudes Old World grandeur. **Pros:** eye-popping architecture; beautiful views of both the ocean and the sloping, waterside lawn; elegant rooms and suites. **Cons:** stairs to climb; a short drive from the center of town; no pets. $ *Rooms from: $450* ✉ *63 High St., Camden* ☎ *207/236–4646* ⊕ *www.norumbegainn.com* ⇌ *11 rooms* ⧦ *Free Breakfast.*

🏃 Activities

★ Mary Day

SAILING | **FAMILY** | Sailing for more than 50 years, the *Mary Day* was the first schooner in Maine built specifically for vacation excursions. Accommodating up to 28 guests and seven crew, she is continually maintained and upgraded. Cruise lengths range from one night to six nights. ✉ *Camden Harbor, Atlantic Ave., Camden* ☎ *800/992–2218* ⊕ *www.schoonermaryday.com* ⊠ *From $450* ☾ *Closed Nov.–mid-June.*

Olad

SAILING | Captain Aaron Lincoln skippers two-hour sailing trips aboard the 57-foot *Olad* and the smaller *Owl*. Out on Penobscot Bay, passengers spot lighthouses, coastal mansions, seals, and the occasional red-footed puffin cousins known as guillemots. Either boat can also be chartered for longer trips. ✉ *Camden Harbor, 1 Bay View Landing, Camden* ☎ *207/236–2323* ⊕ *www.maineschooners.com* ⊠ *$55* ☾ *Closed Oct.–June 1* ⇌ *BYOB and snacks.*

🛍 Shopping

⭐ Swans Island Company

CRAFTS | For luxurious handcrafted blankets, throws, pillows, wraps, and scarves, look no further. All products are made in Maine using natural, heirloom-quality yarns. The expert craftsmanship explains the hefty price tag. ✉ *2 Bayview St., Camden* ☎ *207/706–7926* ⊕ *swansislandcompany.com.*

⭐ Hearth and Harrow

HOUSEWARES | Featuring tea towels, napkins, the softest T-shirts, and other textiles hand-printed in Rockport with delightful animals and other nature themes, this inviting shop also stocks home goods, glassware, cards, cooking and gardening books, and plants. ✉ *20 Main St., Camden* ☎ *207/252–9675* ⊕ *www.hearthandharrow.com.*

Belfast

13 miles north of Lincolnville via U.S. 1.

Along with several other Maine communities, Belfast is a strong contender for being named the state's prettiest town. Old-fashioned street lamps set the streets aglow at night and there are handsome ship captain's mansions and a tantalizing selection of shops, galleries, and restaurants all along Main and adjacent streets as well as a lively arts scene. Take the time to stroll down one side of Main Street all the way to the harbor, and then back up the other side. Within a few blocks, you can enjoy not only fresh local seafood, but also a taste of Thai, Lao, Japanese, Italian, and Jamaican cuisines. It's a delightful place to spend a day or two.

■ **TIP→ As you walk around town, you will see a number of cream-color signs labeled THE MUSEUM IN THE STREETS. Be sure to read them. The signs present all sorts of interesting facts and factoids about the history of Belfast.**

GETTING HERE AND AROUND

As it traces the coast, U.S. 1 runs through Belfast, though the center of town is a short drive off the highway. If you're traveling Interstate 95, take U.S. 3 East in Augusta to get here. The highways meet in Belfast, heading north. Concord Coach Lines' coastal bus stops in Belfast.

VISITOR INFORMATION

The information center has a large array of magazines, guidebooks, maps, and brochures that cover the entire Mid-Coast. It also can provide you with a free walking-tour brochure that describes the various handsome, historic buildings.

CONTACTS Belfast Area Chamber of Commerce. ✉ *Belfast* ☎ *207/338–5900* ⊕ *www.belfastmaine.org.*

👁 Sights

Belfast is infused with a decidedly artistic atmosphere, thanks in part to its having been a magnet for artists, artisans, and back-to-the-landers in the late 20th century. Today, the streets are lined with eclectic and sophisticated boutiques as well as a surprising array of restaurants. And, there's still evidence of the wealth of the mid-1800s, as High Street and the residential area above it are lined with the Greek Revival and Federal-style mansions of business tycoons, shipbuilders, and ship captains. Indeed, the town has one of the best showcases of Greek Revival homes in the state. Don't miss the privately owned "White House," an especially imposing mansion that stands where High and Church streets merge, several blocks south of downtown. Built in 1840, it's named for James P. White, its original owner; while it also used to be painted white, it's actually more cream-colored these days.

Islesboro

If you would like to visit a Penobscot Bay island but don't have much time, Islesboro (⊕ *townofislesboro. com*) is a pleasant choice, as it's only a 20-minute ferry ride from Lincolnville Beach on the mainland. But do plan accordingly as the ferry terminal on Islesboro is miles from the heart of the island, so you'll need wheels—a car or a bike—to explore the 14-mile-long island that includes the tiny village of Dark Harbor. ■TIP→ If you plan on simply walking, you won't have time before boarding the return ferry to see much other than a country road and the museum at the lighthouse (the ferry landing is right beside it)—if the museum is open.

Round-trip ferry passage for a driver and one passenger plus car is $42. When you add a reservation for your car—optional but strongly recommended in-season to ensure space on the ferry for your car—the total comes to $82.

The drive along Islesboro's main road from one end of the island to the other is lovely, though, and a number of nature preserves offer hiking trails that wend through woodlands to bold shores. Most visitor-oriented businesses are open seasonally (Memorial Day to Labor Day) including the Dark Harbor Shop, which sells sandwiches and ice cream. You can also buy picnic supplies at two stores: the Island Market, on the main road a short distance from the road to the ferry terminal; and Durkee's General Store (⊠ *867 Main Rd.*), 5 miles farther north. There are no full-service restaurants on the island. Next to the ferry terminal is the Grindle Point Lighthouse; the Sailor's Memorial Museum is in the keeper's house (open on summer weekends).

The Islesboro Ferry (⊕ *www.maine. gov/mdot/ferry/islesboro*), operated by the Maine State Ferry Service, makes nine daily round trips from Lincolnville April through October and seven daily trips November through March. Try to head out on one of the early ferries so you have enough time to drive around and get back without missing the last ferry. There are *no* public lodging accommodations on the island.

🍽 Restaurants

Darby's Restaurant and Pub
$$ | AMERICAN | FAMILY | With pressed-tin ceilings, this charming, old-fashioned restaurant and bar—it's been such since 1865—is a perennial local favorite with a welcoming community feel to it. Pad Thai, chicken chili salad with cashews, a Buddha bowl, and a few Mexican-flavored items are signature dishes, but the menu also serves hearty, scratch-made soups, sandwiches on homemade bread, and classic fish-and-chips. **Known for:** excellent happy hour; gluten-free menu

choices; homemade breads. $ *Average main: $18* ⊠ *155 High St., Belfast* ☎ *207/338–2339* ⊕ *www.darbys-restaurant.com* ⊗ *Closed Sun.*

★ Young's Lobster Pound
$$$ | SEAFOOD | FAMILY | Right on the water's edge, across the harbor from downtown Belfast, this corrugated-steel building looks more like a fish cannery than a restaurant, but it's one of the best places for an authentic Maine lobster dinner, known here as the "shore dinner." Lobster rolls, surf-and-turf dinners, steamed clams, steak tips, and hot dogs

are popular, too. As this is a real-deal lobster pound, with absolutely no frills, lobstermen tie up at the dock to unload their catch. **Known for:** "shore dinner": clam chowder or lobster stew, steamed clams or mussels, a 1½-pound boiled lobster, corn on the cob, and chips; family-friendly environment; BYOB. [$] *Average main: $30* ✉ *2 Fairview St., off U.S. 1, Belfast* ☎ *207/338–1160* 🌐 *www.youngslobsters.com* 🕒 *Takeout only Jan.–Mar.*

Coffee and Quick Bites

Must Be Nice Lobster

$$ | SEAFOOD | Not only does Sadie Samuels captain her own lobster boat, the *Must Be Nice*, but she also transforms her haul into lobster rolls that she sells—along with crab rolls, fries, hot dogs, and burgers—from a lunch wagon parked at the bottom of Main Street, just up from the harbor. There are outdoor tables plus indoor seating alongside a small shop of items Samuels crafts herself. **Known for:** made by a local lobsterwoman; award-winning lobster rolls; mini lobster rolls at half the price of the full-size rolls. [$] *Average main: $18* ✉ *2 Cross St., Belfast* ☎ *207/218–1431* 🌐 *www.mustbenicelobster.com* 🕒 *Closed Mon.*

★ **The Scone Goddess**

$ | BAKERY | FAMILY | In a petite gray Cape (look for the mini red-and-white-striped lighthouse beside it), the Scone Goddess makes what are almost certainly the best scones you've ever tasted. Tender and a little crumbly—they bear no resemblance to those stone-hard lumps so often passed off as scones—flavors, which change daily, include ginger lemon, wild Maine blueberry lemon, raspberry cream, and bacon cheddar. **Known for:** unusual flavors; lattes and other beverages; easy-to-mix-and-bake mixes. [$] *Average main: $4* ✉ *1390 Atlantic Hwy., Northport* ✣ *3 miles from downtown Belfast* ☎ *207/323–0249* 🌐 *www.thesconegoddess.com* 🕒 *Closed Sun. and Mon.*

Bucksport

9 miles north of Searsport via U.S. 1.

Bucksport experienced a bumpy time following the closing a few years ago of a large paper mill that was a major employer. Happily, it is now experiencing a renaissance with new restaurants and shops popping up along Main Street. Just across from town, the stunning and graceful Penobscot Narrows Bridge and Observatory (the world's tallest public bridge observatory) stands taller than the Statue of Liberty. Take the time to ascend via elevator to the bridge-top observatory for sweeping views of land and sea. Fort Knox, Maine's largest historic fort, also overlooks the town from across the Penobscot River. Stroll the paved, garden-bordered riverfront walkway that edges Bucksport's downtown to take in magnificent vistas of both the imposing fort and the bridge.

GETTING HERE AND AROUND

Driving north on Route 1, pass over the spectacular Penobscot Narrows Bridge onto small Verona Island. Then cross a second bridge to Bucksport. Turn left to head down Main Street.

Sights

Fort Knox Historic Site

HISTORIC SIGHT | FAMILY | Next to the Penobscot Narrows Bridge is Fort Knox, Maine's largest historic fort. It was built of granite on the west bank of the Penobscot River between 1844 and 1869 when, despite a treaty with Britain settling boundary disputes, invasion was still a concern—after all, the British controlled this region during both the Revolutionary War and the War of 1812. The fort never saw any real action, but it was used for troop training and as a garrison during the Civil War and the Spanish-American War. Ghost hunters have reported a range of paranormal activities here. Visitors are welcome to explore the many rooms and passageways. Guided tours are given between 11 and 3 when volunteers are available. ✉ *740 Ft. Knox Rd., Prospect* ☎ *207/469–6553* 🌐 *www.fortknoxmaine.com* 🎫 *Fort $7; fort and observatory $9* 🕓 *Fort closed Nov.–Apr.*

★ Penobscot Narrows Bridge and Observatory Tower
VIEWPOINT | FAMILY | An "engineering marvel" is how experts describe this beautiful, cable-stayed, 2,120-foot-long Penobscot Narrows Bridge, which is taller than the Statue of Liberty. As one approaches, the bridge appears in the distance like the towers of a fairy-tale castle. The observatory, perched near the top of a 437-foot-tall tower and accessed by an elevator, is the tallest public bridge observatory in the world. Don't miss it—the panoramic views, which take in the hilly countryside and the Penobscot River as it widens into Penobscot Bay, are breathtaking. ✉ *711 Ft. Knox Rd., off U.S. 1, Prospect* ☎ *207/469–6553* 🌐 *www.maine.gov/mdot/pnbo* 🎫 *Fort and observatory $9* 🕓 *Closed Nov.–May.*

🍴 Restaurants

★ Friar's Brewhouse Taproom
$ | AMERICAN | FAMILY | You probably wouldn't expect to find an eatery run by Franciscan friars in this little town, but you'll be glad you did. Dressed in long brown habits, your hosts happily serve excellent European-style beers brewed in their nearby mountainside friary, which pair well with sandwiches on freshly baked baguettes, or hearty entrées that blend Maine and French Canadian flavors like family-recipe meat loaf, from-scratch soups, pâté, and fresh local fish dishes. **Known for:** fresh-baked breads; thoughtfully prepared dishes; warm and welcoming friars. [$] *Average main: $15* ✉ *84A Main St., Bucksport* ☎ *207/702–9156* 🌐 *www.facebook.com/friarbrew.hotmail/* 🕓 *Closed Sun. and Mon.*

Blue Hill

20 miles east of Castine; 20.6 miles south of Bucksport

Nestled snugly between Blue Hill Mountain and Blue Hill Bay, the village of Blue Hill sits right beside Blue Hill Harbor. About 30 miles from Acadia National Park, the village is a good laid-back base for exploring the Mount Desert Island area, though summertime traffic can significantly increase out-and-back travel times.

Originally known for its granite quarries, copper mines, and shipbuilding, today Blue Hill has galleries, boutiques, and a modest but varied dining scene that offers everything from good coffee at Bucklyn's to fine dining at Arborvine. Tucked near the harbor, a charming little park explodes with sound on Monday nights in summer, when a renowned steel-drum band gives free concerts.

GETTING HERE AND AROUND

From Castine, take Route 166 to 166A. Turn right onto Route 199 North, and follow it to Route 175 South. Turn left onto Route 177 East, which takes you right into town.

From Bucksport, take Route 15 south into town.

☕ Coffee and Quick Bites

★ Bucklyn Coffee
$ | CAFÉ | This tiny, friendly shop serves big, flavorful coffee and interesting sweet and savory pastries. **Known for:** great place for a morning or early afternoon pick-me-up; Maine-roasted beans; coffee served anyway you like it. [$] *Average main: $9* ✉ *103 Main St., Blue Hill* ☎ *917/971–3246* 🌐 *bucklyncoffee.square.site* 🕓 *Closed Sun.*

★ The Co-Op Cafe

$ | AMERICAN | FAMILY | Housed in the Blue Hill Co-Op Community Market, this is a prime place for soups, sandwiches, and pastries. The bread selection alone is worth a stop. **Known for:** eat in or takeout; gluten-free and vegan options; great salad and hot-entrée bars. [$] *Average main: $11* ✉ *70 South St., Blue Hill* ☎ *207/374–2165* 🌐 *www.bluehill.coop/the-coop-cafe.*

Hotels

Blue Hill Inn

$$$ | B&B/INN | At this Federal-style inn, which was built as a home in 1835 and expanded into a lodging in the 1850s, wide-plank, pumpkin-pine floors perfectly complement the mix of antiques that fill the parlor, library, and guest rooms, several of which have working fireplaces, clawfoot tubs, and flower-garden views. **Pros:** plenty of charm; modern suites with kitchens in separate building; excellent service. **Cons:** narrow stairs; thin walls; only some rooms available in winter. [$] *Rooms from: $315* ✉ *40 Union St., Blue Hill* ☎ *207/374–2844* 🌐 *www.bluehillinn.com* 🛏 *13 rooms* 🍴 *Free Breakfast.*

Under Canvas

$$$$ | RESORT | FAMILY | Amid 100 acres on Union River Bay, this glamping property has luxury tents with king-size beds, bathrooms, organic toiletries, wood stoves, and other creature comforts. **Pros:** breathtaking coast and Cadillac Mountain views; good base for Acadia National Park visits; lots of on-site amenities and activities. **Cons:** it still feels like camping; pricey rates and food and activities cost extra; some might find 10 pm quiet time restricting. [$] *Rooms from: $620* ✉ *702 Surry Rd., Surry* ☎ *888/496–1148* 🌐 *www.undercanvas.com/camps/acadia* 🕒 *Closed mid-Oct.–mid-May* 🛏 *63 tents* 🍴 *No Meals.*

Shopping

★ Blue Hill Wine Shop

WINE/SPIRITS | In a restored barn and Cape-style house, one of Blue Hill's earliest residences, this shop carries more than 3,000 carefully selected wines, as well as cheeses, breads, groceries, local and imported beer, cider, cooking ingredients, and coffees and teas. ✉ *138 Main St., Blue Hill* ☎ *207/374–2161* 🌐 *www.bluehillwineshop.com* 🕒 *Closed Sun.*

★ Handworks Gallery

CRAFTS | Set in what was once a department store, this gallery sells fine art; contemporary fabric, metal, wood, glass, and ceramic decorative items and housewares; and jewelry and accessories. Everything is handcrafted by a diverse group of established and emerging Maine artists. ✉ *48 Main St., Blue Hill* ☎ *207/374–5613* 🌐 *handworksgallery.org* 🕒 *Closed Sun.* ☞ *Limited hrs Jan.–Apr.*

Deer Isle

16 miles south of Blue Hill.

Reachable by a bridge, the thick woods of Deer Isle and Little Deer Isle give way to tidal coves at almost every turn. Stacks of lobster traps populate the backyards of shingled houses, and dirt roads lead to secluded summer cottages.

The village of Deer Isle is nestled between Northwest Harbor and Mill Pond. While it's only got one of each, it's got a great coffee shop, a lovely inn with a beer garden, an art gallery, and a quirky shop with all Maine-made books, toys, and crafts.

GETTING HERE AND AROUND

From Sedgwick, Route 15 crosses a 1930s suspension bridge onto Little Deer Isle and continues on to the larger Deer Isle.

From Blue Hill, follow Route 175 south to Route 172 through Sedgwick and then follow the directions above.

VISITOR INFORMATION

CONTACTS Deer Isle–Stonington Chamber of Commerce. ✉ *114 Little Deer Isle Rd., Deer Isle* ☎ *207/348–6124* 🌐 *www.deer-isle.com.* **Isle au Haut Boat Services.** ✉ *37 Seabreeze Ave., Stonington* ☎ *207/367–5193* 🌐 *isleauhaut.com.*

Sights

Edgar M. Tennis Preserve

NATURE PRESERVE | While enjoying miles of woodland and shore trails at the Edgar M. Tennis Preserve, you can look for hawks, eagles, and ospreys, and wander among old apple trees, fields of wildflowers, and ocean-polished rocks. ✉ *Tennis Rd., off Sunshine Rd., Deer Isle* ☎ *207/348–2455* 🌐 *www.islandheritagetrust.org* 🎟 *Free.*

Stonington

TOWN | A charming seaside town with only 1,000 year-round residents, Stonington sits at the southern end of Route 15, which has helped retain its unspoiled small-town flavor. This picturesque working waterfront, where boats arrive overflowing with the day's catch, is Maine's largest lobster port. It's also a tranquil tourist destination with boutiques and galleries lining Main Street that cater mostly to out-of-towners.

Stonington includes the villages of Burnt Cove, Oceanville, Green Head, and Clam City. It also serves as the gateway to Isle au Haut, which is home to a remote section of Acadia National Park. ✉ *Stonington.*

Restaurants

★ Aragosta at Goose Cove

$$$$ | CONTEMPORARY | Executive chef and proprietor Devin Finigan has created magic in this location with endless views of East Penobscot Bay and food that speaks to the prowess of this region's fishermen and farmers. Whether you're experiencing the chef's tasting menu—think scallops with sorrel and whey; Wagyu with ramps and new potato; and rhubarb with lemon and shortbread—Sunday a-la-carte brunch (seasonal), or a summer happy hour, you're in for a high-quality treat. **Known for:** seasonal tasting menu; delicious hand-crafted cocktails; locally sourced ingredients that dictate the menu. [$] *Average main: $150* ✉ *300 Goose Cove Rd., Deer Isle* ☎ *207/348–6900* 🌐 *aragostamaine.com* 🕒 *Closed Nov. and Dec. No lunch Mon.–Sat.*

★ 44 North Coffee

$ | BAKERY | This place offers amazing (and equitably sourced) coffee and invites you to take a minute to have a conversation while you wait for your slow-pour brew to flow through a colorful, custom-built wooden drip bar. Grab a pastry supplied by a variety of local bakers—if there are any left when you arrive. **Known for:** no Wi-Fi; pastries from Brooksville's Tinder Hearth Bakery; great coffee. [$] *Average main: $15* ✉ *7 Main St., Deer Isle* ☎ *207/348–5208* 🌐 *44northcoffee.com* 🕒 *Closed Sun.*

Hotels

★ Aragosta

$$$$ | RESORT | Nestled among spruces, moss-covered rocks, and the Barred Island Nature Preserve, Aragosta is one of Maine's most tranquil oceanfront complexes. **Pros:** excellent on-site restaurant; postcard-perfect location; cottages are dog-friendly. **Cons:** a car is a must; Wi-Fi is only available in the restaurant; suites are not dog-friendly. [$] *Rooms from: $500* ✉ *300 Goose Cove Rd., Deer Isle* ☎ *207/348–6900* 🌐 *aragostamaine.com* 🕒 *Closed mid-Oct.–mid-May* 🛏 *9 cottages, 3 suites* 🍴 *Free Breakfast.*

🏃 Activities

★ Isle au Haut Boat Services

BOATING | FAMILY | To get to and from Isle au Haut, the mail boat operated by this company is your best bet, with four trips a day Monday through Saturday and two trips on Sunday in summer. Parking is available at the Stonington ferry terminal and at several lots in town that are within walking distance. This company also offers regular puffin and lighthouse tours and private charters to Camden and Mt. Desert Island. ✉ *27 Seabreeze Ave., Stonington* ☎ *207/367–5193* ⊕ *www. isleauhaut.com* ✆ *Mail boat: $20 each way. Tours: $80.*

Ellsworth Area

140 miles northeast of Portland, 28 miles south of Bangor.

Ellsworth is the main gateway to Acadia National Park making it a good spot for refueling—literally and figuratively. With two supermarkets, several good restaurants, and a range of shops, the city has nearly everything you need. Big box stores are along Route 3 and there's a nice downtown area on Main Street with unique shops set in attractive brick buildings. From here you continue through to Trenton, where there are souvenir shops, roadside eateries, and less expensive lodgings before crossing onto Mount Desert Island. ■**TIP→ Folks stay in Ellsworth and Trenton for the less expensive lodging.**

GETTING HERE AND AROUND

Ellsworth is the eye of the storm through which all vehicles traveling to Mount Desert Island must pass. As such, the few short miles of U.S. 1 that pass through the city can be gnarled with traffic in summer.

VISITOR INFORMATION

CONTACTS Ellsworth Area Chamber of Commerce. ✉ *151 High St., Ellsworth* ☎ *207/667–5584* ⊕ *www.ellsworthchamber.org.*

🍴 Restaurants

Airline Brewing Company

$ | BURGER | With red cushioned seating and wood walls around the bar, this cozy-as-can-be brew pub (the brewery itself is inland) right on Main Street has a decor and menu that reflects its British ownership. Several of the dozen or so beers served are hand-pulled, and food options include steak and ale pie and bangers and mash. **Known for:** being a community gathering place; warm beer cheese appetizers; "signature toasties" (yes, British for toasted sandwiches). Ⓢ *Average main: $13* ✉ *173 Main St., Ellsworth* ☎ *207/412–0045* ⊕ *www. abcmaine.beer/.*

Fogtown Brewing Company

$ | PIZZA | FAMILY | Though tucked back on an Ellsworth residential street, folks find this hip brewpub—yes, the brewery is right here—with a large, inviting beer garden, housed on the lower level of an old brick warehouse. The simple menu includes hotdogs and bratwurst, and pizza cooked in the outdoor oven. **Known for:** live music; seasonal pizza toppings; community gathering spot. Ⓢ *Average main: $15* ✉ *25 Pine St., Ellsworth* ☎ *207/370–0845* ⊕ *www.fogtownbrewing.com* ⊙ *No lunch Closed Mon. from late May–mid-Oct. and Mon.–Wed. from mid-Oct.–late May.*

🛍 Shopping

John Edwards Market

FOOD | With a selection of organic and natural foods, and soup, sandwiches, salads, baked goods, and coffee to go, John Edwards Market is a pleasant option whether you're packing a picnic or stocking the kitchenette at your rental.

Downstairs, a wine cellar and an art gallery showcase work by area artists. Wine tastings are on the first Friday of the month 5–7 pm. ⊠ *158 Main St., Ellsworth* ☎ *207/667–9377* ⊕ *www.johnedwards-market.com.*

Bar Harbor

20 miles from Ellsworth via Route 3.

A resort town since the 19th century, Bar Harbor is the artistic, culinary, and social center of Mount Desert Island, providing visitors to nearby Acadia National Park with lodging, shops, and restaurants. Around the turn of the last century, the town was a premier summer haven for the very rich because of its cool breezes and stunning interplay of mountains and sea. Many of their lavish mansions in and near town burned down in the Great Fire of 1947. The business district—centered around Main, Mount Desert, Cottage, and West streets—was spared. You can stroll past mansions that survived the fire on the shore path and West Street, a national historic district.

Bar Harbor has a few excellent museums and numerous greens and parks. Some were the sites of grand hotels like Agamont Park overlooking the harbor, and the Village Green, a gathering spot with a piano (that anyone can play) under the gazebo. Spring through fall, scenic cruises and whale-watching trips come and go from the town pier, boats cluster in the harbor, and visitors linger on the many sidewalk benches. At low tide, folks walk to Bar Island.

GETTING HERE AND AROUND

Route 3 leads to Bar Harbor. Acadia National Park's Hulls Cove Visitor Center is off the highway three miles before downtown, near the oceanside hamlet of Hulls Cove. The Cadillac Mountain entrance for Acadia's Park Loop Road (two-way section) is on Route 233 just west of downtown. Continuing on Route 233 to its terminus at Route 198, turn left for Northeast Harbor or right to reach Route 102, which loops the western side of Mount Desert Island. A few miles from downtown Bar Harbor on Route 3 is an entrance for Acadia's Sieur de Monts section and the loop road (one-way section). A more scenic and only slightly longer route to Northeast Harbor is via Route 3. Tiny Otter Creek is about midway along the drive, which has hilly forested sections and ocean views in Seal Harbor and Northeast Harbor.

VISITOR INFORMATION

CONTACTS Bar Harbor Chamber of Commerce. ⊠ *2 Cottage St., Bar Harbor* ☎ *207/288–5103* ⊕ *www.visitbarharbor.com.*

◉ Sights

★ Abbe Museum

HISTORY MUSEUM | FAMILY | This important museum dedicated to Maine's Indigenous tribes—collectively known as the Wabanaki—is the state's only Smithsonian-affiliated facility and one of the few places in Maine to experience Native culture as interpreted by Native peoples themselves. Spanning 12,000 years, the "core" exhibit, People of the First Light, features items such as birch bark canoes, basketry, and bone tools as well as photos and interactive displays. Changing exhibits often showcase contemporary Native American art. A birchbark canoe made at the Abbe anchors the free Orientation Gallery beside the gift shop at the entrance. Check the website for events, from basket weaving and boatbuilding demonstrations to author talks and family-friendly pop-up rainy days activities.

Opened in 1928, the Abbe's Acadia National Park location at Sieur de Monts is its original home. Longtime exhibits in the small eight-sided building include artifacts from early digs on Mount Desert Island and dioramas of Native American

Long ramps on Maine's many docks make it easier to access boats at either high or low tide.

life here before European settlement. ⊠ *26 Mount Desert St., Bar Harbor* ☎ *207/288–3519* ⊕ *www.abbemuseum. org* 🎟 *$10* ⏱ *Closed Nov.–early May; Fri. and Sat. mid-May–Oct.*

★ La Rochelle Mansion and Museum

HISTORY MUSEUM | Stepping into the large foyer of this 1903 brick chateau, your view flows through glass doors on the opposite side, then across the piazza and flat lawn to a serene coastal expanse. A business partner of J.P. Morgan, George Bowdoin, and his wife, Julia, built this 13,000-square-foot, 41-room mansion near downtown Bar Harbor as their seasonal residence. Unlike many of the area's summer "cottages" of the nation's elite, it was spared from the Great Fire of 1947. In 2020, La Rochelle became Bar Harbor Historical Society's museum and the town's only Gilded Age mansion open to the public. While the Bowdoins' story weaves through displays, each room has themed exhibits on local history: in the foyer, baskets the Wabanaki made to sell to tourists; the dining room, grand hotels

of yesteryear; the master bedroom, old maps (one shows where the fire raged); a guest room, the town's famous visitors; and so on. Under the elegant wishbone staircase, a "flower room" with a curved wall spotlights the famous landscape artist who created the long-gone sunken garden. In the servants' quarters on the third floor, their story is shared—don't miss the hallway callbox. ⊠ *127 West St., Bar Harbor* ☎ *207/288–0000* ⊕ *www. barharborhistorical.org* 🎟 *$15* ⏱ *Closed Nov.–late May.*

🍴 Restaurants

Atlantic Brewing Co. Midtown

$ | **AMERICAN** | **FAMILY** | Glass walls let you see this busy craft brewery spot in action even before you enter, but look up or head up—there's rooftop seating with great Bar Harbor views. After ordering a flight or glass of beer, choose from a food menu offering soups, sandwiches, salads, and lobster and crab rolls. ⊠ **Known for:** jumbo pretzel with cheese and mustard made with an English Brown

Ale; Old Soaker natural blueberry soda and root beer for the kids; also selling beer to go. $ *Average main: $16* ✉ *52 Cottage St., Bar Harbor* ☎ *207/288–2326* ⊕ *www.atlanticbrewing.com.*

Jeannie's Great Maine Breakfast

$ | AMERICAN | FAMILY | After enjoying the sunrise atop Acadia National Park's Cadillac Mountain, snuggle into a wooden booth or grab a table at this homey, yellow-walled eatery that opens at 6 am to catch the crowds who flock to the spectacle. Signature items include homemade oatmeal bread, stuffed French toast, and the Great Maine Breakfast, with three eggs, meat, pancakes, and vegetarian baked beans—the tradition here is to eat leftovers from Saturday night's bean supper on Sunday morning. **Known for:** gluten-free and vegan options; strawberry rhubarb fruit spread; serving breakfast through lunch (closes 1 pm). $ *Average main: $13* ✉ *15 Cottage St., Bar Harbor* ☎ *207/288–4166* ⊕ *www.jeanniesbreakfast.com* ⊗ *Closed mid-Oct.–early May and Tues. early May–mid-Oct. No dinner.*

★ Side Street Cafe

$ | AMERICAN | FAMILY | On a side street near the Village Green, this place (and its sister arm, The Annex) hops on busy summer evenings as folks line up for its comfort food like fish tacos and burgers. Outdoor and indoor dining spaces, one anchored by a horseshoe bar, flow together and exposed brick, and a cork wall and ceiling, add warmth to the welcoming, modern, family-friendly vibe; friendly dogs are allowed outside. **Known for:** handcrafted cocktails and live music nightly in The Annex; "signature" mac-and-cheese including lobster and meatball as well as "create-your-own"; margaritas. $ *Average main: $14* ✉ *49 Rodick St., Bar Harbor* ☎ *207/801–2591* ⊕ *www.sidestreetbarharbor.com* ⊗ *Main restaurant: closed late Oct.–early Apr.; The Annex: no lunch, closed mid-Oct.–late May.*

☕ Coffee and Quick Bites

★ Burning Tree

$ | AMERICAN | An early standout in Maine's farm-to-table movement, this acclaimed establishment not far from Bar Harbor in tiny Otter Creek sells to-go foods—prepared (including breakfast pastries) and ready-to-cook, all made on-site and largely featuring ingredients from the owners' extensive gardens. The retail side has a small gardenside outdoor eating area and also sells small-scale wines (natural, organic, and biodynamic) as well as ciders. **Known for:** crab cakes with jalapenos; inventive seasonal items like pickled plums; nice selection of vegetarian offerings. $ *Average main: $10* ✉ *69 Otter Creek Dr., Otter Creek* ✛ *5 miles from Bar Harbor, 7 miles from Northeast Harbor* ☎ *207/288–9331* ⊕ *www.theburningtreerestaurant.com* ⊗ *Closed late Oct.–late May; closed Tues. late May–late Oct.*

Downeast Deli & Boxed Lunch Co.

$ | AMERICAN | Don't be fooled by this tiny takeout-only joint's no-frills storefront: many praise its lobster rolls as the best around. On summer mornings, the line often stretches around the corner by 10 am as folks come to get lobster rolls as well as wraps, sandwiches, salads, and slices of blueberry pie for outings to Acadia National Park and elsewhere around Mount Desert Island. **Known for:** taking orders the night before; several lobster roll options, including just plain "naked"; selling a few breakfast items, too. $ *Average main: $13* ✉ *65 Main St., Bar Harbor* ☎ *207/288–1001* ⊕ *www. downeastdeli.com* ⊗ *Closed late Oct.– early May.*

Mount Desert Island Ice Cream

$ | ICE CREAM | Madagascar Vanilla Bean has specks from beans scraped from vanilla pods—just one example of the prep work that goes into creating these heralded artisanal ice creams (and a few sorbets), made at a nearby production facility with as many local ingredients as possible. The shop's double doors open like a huge window, welcoming passers-by right in; grab a seat or head across the street to the Village Green to savor every bite. **Known for:** unique rotating flavors like Bay of Figs; locations in Portland, Maine; Washington, D.C.; and Japan; ice cream on menus at area restaurants. *$ Average main: $5 ✉ 7 Firefly La., Bar Harbor ☎ 207/801–4007 🌐 www.mdiic.com ⏲ Closed late Oct.–early Apr.*

Hotels

Bar Harbor Grand Hotel

$$$ | **HOTEL** | **FAMILY** | Taking one of the well-appointed, modern rooms in this 2011 replica of Bar Harbor's famed Rodick House hotel puts you a stone's throw from the town's lively restaurants, cafés, and gift shops, and though it's a short walk to the waterfront, you can relax here with a dip in the hotel's heated pool or Jacuzzi. **Pros:** "extended stay" suites with kitchenettes; standard rooms have a king or two queens; courtesy full breakfast includes local pastries. **Cons:** summer street noise in front-facing rooms; no restaurant or bar on-site; not on or in sight of the ocean. *$ Rooms from: $389 ✉ 269 Main St., Bar Harbor ☎ 207/288–5226, 888/766–2599 🌐 www.barharborgrand.com ⏲ Closed mid-Nov.–early Apr. 🛏 72 rooms 🍴 Free Breakfast.*

★ Salt Cottages

$$$$ | **MOTEL** | **FAMILY** | Renovated into a chic family-friendly resort in 2022, these 1940s-era roadside cottages surround a green that sweeps uphill across Route 3 from Hulls Cove beach just 3 miles from Bar Harbor—Acadia is even closer. **Pros:** stylish lodge where you can relax by the fireplace and go to Picnic, a takeout restaurant serving breakfast, lunch, and dinner; kids 12 and under stay free in cabins with adults; resort amenities include heated pool, hot tubs, bocce, lawn games, "game shed," and courtesy s'mores for the firepit. **Cons:** cabins aren't stocked with utensils or dishes; no courtesy coffee in the lodge (but provided for cottage coffeemakers); limited or no water views from inside most cabins. *$ Rooms from: $480 ✉ 20 Rte. 3, Hulls Cove ☎ 207/288–9918 🌐 www.saltcottagesbarharbor.com ⏲ Closed Nov.–mid-May 🛏 31 cottages 🍴 No Meals.*

★ Terramor Outdoor Resort

$$$$ | **RESORT** | **FAMILY** | Luckily for visitors to Acadia National Park, Kampgrounds of America transformed one of its traditional campgrounds into its first glampground in 2020; anchoring 64 tents (all with floors, beds, private fire rings, and hotel-like amenities) on well-shaded, well-spaced sites is an impressive lodge with a high sloped wood ceiling and restaurant (eat in or get items to go), bar, fireplaces, chic chairs and couches, and decks. **Pros:** activities galore, including yoga, stargazing, concerts, and lobster bakes; big fancy grill sites (fee; all you need is provided including food); covered sitting area by swank pool and hot tub. **Cons:** no "en tent" baths in four tents remaining from KOA campground (but baths are private and the price is right); not on the water; road noise at some sites. *$ Rooms from: $400 ✉ 1453 Rte. 102, Bar Harbor ☎ 207/288–7500 🌐 terramoroutdoorresort.com ⏲ Closed mid-Oct.–mid-May 🛏 64 units 🍴 Free Breakfast.*

★ West Street Hotel

$$$$ | **RESORT** | With only 85 mostly water-view rooms and suites, attention to detail comes naturally here, and the panoramic views from the fabulous adults-only infinity pool on the rooftop deck are hands down the best in town. **Pros:** each floor is equipped with guest pantries filled with snacks and goodies; one of Maine's most tastefully decorated boutique hotels; many rooms and suites have balconies. **Cons:** $35 daily resort fee; chilly Maine weather can limit use of resort amenities; near but not on the water. *$ Rooms from: $700 ✉ 50 West*

St., Bar Harbor ☎ *207/288–0825* ⊕ *www. opalcollection.com/west-street* ⊙ *Closed from late Oct.–early May* ⊐ *85 rooms* ⦿ *No Meals.*

 ## Activities

BIKING
Bar Harbor Bicycle Shop
BIKING | FAMILY | Rent bikes for a half day, full day, or week at the Bar Harbor Bicycle Shop. The selection includes hybrid and Class 1 e-bikes as well as tag-alongs, child trailers, and car racks. ⊠ *141 Cottage St., Bar Harbor* ☎ *207/288–3886* ⊕ *www.barharborbike.com.*

BOATING
Coastal Kayaking Tours
GUIDED TOURS | FAMILY | This outfitter has been leading trips in the scenic waters off Mount Desert Island since 1982. Trips are limited to no more than 12 people. The season is mid-May–mid-October. ⊠ *48 Cottage St., Bar Harbor* ☎ *207/288–9605* ⊕ *www.acadiafun.com.*

★ **Downeast Windjammer Cruises**
BOAT TOURS | FAMILY | Cruises among the islands of Frenchman Bay are offered on the 151-foot four-masted schooner *Margaret Todd* and 58½-foot two-masted *Bailey Louise Todd,* both with distinctive red sails, as well as 72-foot, two-masted Schooner *Joshua,* with traditional white sails. Trips run morning, afternoon, and at sunset for 1½ to 2 hours, except in the fall when sunset cruises are a bit shorter than usual. Whatever the season, these evening excursions feature live folk music. The tour operator often offers longer specialty cruises and does fishing and sailing charters. ⊠ *Bar Harbor Inn pier, 7 Newport Dr., Bar Harbor* ☎ *207/288–4585* ⊕ *www.downeastwindjammer.com* ⧉ *From $44 per person* ⊙ *Closed mid-Oct.–mid-May.*

WHALE-WATCHING
Bar Harbor Whale Watch Co.
BOAT TOURS | FAMILY | This company has six boats, one of them a 130-foot jet-propelled double-hulled catamaran with spacious decks. There are lighthouse and puffin-watching, lobstering and seal-watching, whale-watching, nature, and sunset cruises. The Somes Sound trip takes in four lighthouses; one to Acadia National Park's Baker Island is led by a park ranger. ⊠ *1 West St., Bar Harbor* ☎ *207/288–2386, 888/942–5374* ⊕ *www. barharborwhales.com* ⧉ *From $43.*

⊖ Shopping

Cadillac Mountain Sports
SPORTING GOODS | One of the best sporting-goods stores in the state, Cadillac Mountain Sports has developed a following of locals and visitors alike. Here you'll find top-quality climbing, hiking, boating, paddling, and camping equipment, and in winter you can rent cross-country skis, ice skates, and snowshoes. ⊠ *26 Cottage St., Bar Harbor* ☎ *207/288–4532* ⊕ *www. cadillacsports.com.*

Island Artisans
ART GALLERIES | Works by more than 100 Maine artisans are sold here, including basketry, pottery, fiber work, embossed paper, wood bowls and objects, and jewelry. ⊠ *99 Main St., Bar Harbor* ☎ *207/288–4214* ⊕ *www.islandartisans. com* ⊙ *Closed Jan.–Apr.*

Northeast Harbor

12 miles south of Bar Harbor via Rtes. 3 and 198.

A summer community for some of the nation's wealthiest families, Northeast Harbor on the eastern side of the entrance to Somes Sound has one of the best harbors on the Maine coast. Filled with yachts and powerboats, you can catch a cruise or hop the year-round ferry to the Cranberry Isles.

The small downtown—two blocks from the harbor on Sea Street—is nicely clustered with shops, galleries, and eateries. The village's extensive trail network (maintained by a village improvement association) provides access to Acadia National Park's Lower Hadlock Pond (you can hike around the pond or connect with other trails). Most of the Land & Garden Preserve, which stretches from Northeast Harbor to Seal Harbor, was formerly part of John D. Rockefeller Jr.'s summer estate; the preserve encompasses the world-renowned Asticou Azalea Garden, Thuya Garden, and the Abby Aldrich Rockefeller Garden.

GETTING HERE AND AROUND

After crossing onto Mount Desert Island, it's 11 miles via Route 198 to Northeast Harbor. Be sure to slowly cruise Sargeant Drive during your stay—about 4 miles long and well-shaded with a few small pullovers, this narrow scenic drive edges the fjord-like deep sound between its terminuses in the village center and at Route 198.

From Northeast Harbor, Route 3 travels eastward to Seal Harbor, affording lovely ocean views. Here, Acadia National Park's Stanley Brook Road (closed off-season; about 2 miles long) connects to Park Loop Road where it becomes two-way near Jordan Pond. Continuing to Bar Harbor from Seal Harbor, Route 3 passes through Otter Creek and by lovely forested Acadia slopes. The 11½-mile route to Bar Harbor from Northeast Harbor via Route 198/Route 3 and Route 233 is only a few minutes faster and a half-mile shorter than the Route 3 way. Both routes pass through sections of Acadia.

VISITOR INFORMATION

CONTACTS Town of Mount Desert Chamber of Commerce. ✉ *41 Harbor Dr., Northeast Harbor* ☎ *207/276–5040* ⊕ *mtdesertchamber.org.*

◉ Sights

Land & Garden Preserve manages and cares for 1,400 acres in Northeast Harbor and Seal Harbor that encompasses the Abby Aldrich Rockefeller Garden, Asticou Azalea Garden, Little Long Pond Natural Lands, and Thuya Garden.

Parking areas at the Preserve's gardens are small and fill quickly at peak times; you may have to return later in the day. Thuya Garden also has a parking area below the garden on Route 3, from which you can ascend to the garden on a trail with granite stairs. In lieu of a day hike, consider walking up to Thuya and Asticou Azalea gardens from the village at the end of Route 198. It's about 2 miles from there to Asticou at the corner of Route 198/Route 3. Take the sidewalk all the way or hit the preserve's Asticou Stream Trail for the last leg. It's a 15-minute walk along Route 3 between Asticou and Thuya. You can also hike between them on a route that includes a side road and a bit of the sidewalk near Asticou (see the preserve map online or at parking area kiosks).

Abby Aldrich Rockefeller Garden

GARDEN | The Abby Aldrich Rockefeller Garden is the creation of its namesake and famed landscape designer Beatrix Farrand. An ever-present Narnia vibe begins on the drive up through the woods to the hilltop locale: leaf blowers keep the large mossy granite rocks free of leaves and needles, to magical effect. Even before entering on the Spirit Path, lined with Korean funerary statues, the garden's earthy pink high wall is entrancing as it resembles walls in Beijing's Forbidden City. The English-style main border garden has many colorful annuals; one side is more shaded so bed heights vary, adding whimsy to the symmetrical space. In smaller garden spaces nearby, you can rest on a bench, step through a pagoda, look out on Little Long Pond, and contemplate more Eastern sculptures, from seated Buddhas to guardian animals. An easy forest trail leads to the large terrace—with commanding extended ocean views—that fronted The Eyrie, the Rockefellers' massive summer "cottage," until it was torn down in 1962. ⊠ *Lawn & Garden Preserve, Seal Harbor* ⊕ *www.gardenpreserve.org/abby-aldrich-rockefeller-garden* ☒ *$15* ⊙ *Closed early Sept.–early July* ⚠ *Reservations only.*

Asticou Azalea Garden

GARDEN | With many varieties of rhododendrons and azaleas, the Japanese-style garden is spectacular from late May to mid-June as the pink, white, and blue flowers not only bloom but reflect in a stream-fed pond. Whatever the season there's plenty to admire, especially in fall when the many native plants brighten the landscape. You can contemplate on a bench along the winding paths as intended, perhaps by the white sand garden—raked to evoke moving water. Created with azaleas from famed landscape designer Beatrix Farrand's Bar Harbor garden, Asticou was designed by Charles Savage, a self-educated garden designer who managed his family's nearby Asticou Inn. ⊠ *Land & Garden Preserve, 3 Sound Dr., on corner of Rte. 3 and Rte. 198, Northeast Harbor* ☎ *207/276–3699* ⊕ *www.gardenpreserve.org/asticou-azalea-garden* ☒ *$5 suggested donation* ⊙ *Closed Nov.–early May.*

Little Long Pond Natural Lands

NATURE PRESERVE | The Land & Garden preserve expanded greatly in 2015 when David Rockefeller, son of Acadia National Park founder John D. Rockefeller Jr., donated about 1,000 acres of largely forested land in Seal Harbor to the conversation group. The property includes 17 acres of meadows; 12 acres of marsh; a bog and streams; carriage roads and trails, some connecting with Acadia's trails; stone staircases on the Richard Trail, steep in sections, similar to those in Acadia; and a pond you can hike around and swim in (at designated areas). Upon David Rockefeller's death in 2017, the preserve was gifted the old estate's formal garden, the Abby Aldrich Rockefeller Garden.

Two of several preserve parking areas on Route 3 are for Little Long Pond Natural Lands. The one beside the pond across from Bracy Cove is small, so consider using the parking area west of here, where a 0.4-mile trail leads to the cove and pond. ⊠ *Lawn & Garden Preserve, Rte. 3 Seal Harbor* ⊕ *www.gardenpreserve.org/little-long-pond.*

Thuya Garden

GARDEN | Hidden atop a hill above Route 3, this garden is part of what was once the summer home of Boston landscape designer and engineer Joseph Henry Curtis. Today the site is a peaceful and elegant spot to take in formal perennial gardens. Designed by Charles Savage and named for the property's majestic white cedars, Thuja occidentalis, the garden is filled with colorful blooms throughout summer. Walk the immaculately groomed grass paths or enjoy the view from a well-placed bench. You'll find delphiniums, daylilies, dahlias, heliotrope, snapdragons, and other types of vegetation. You can take a look at the sitting room in the Curtis home, which has a large collection of books compiled by Savage. Check the website for docent-led tours of the "lodge" as it's known. ⊠ *Land & Garden Preserve, 15 Thuya Dr., Northeast Harbor* ☎ *207/276–5130* ⊕ *www. gardenpreserve.org* ☒ *$5 suggested donation* ⊙ *Closed mid-Oct.–mid-June.*

🍴 Restaurants

★ Abel's Lobster

$$$ | **SEAFOOD** | **FAMILY** | Located on a nub jutting into Somes Sound a few miles from Northeast Harbor, this place hums on summer nights as adults grab a drink from the outside bar, kids and dogs romp, and folks angle to watch lobsters cook in an open-air kitchen before eating at tables about the sloping lawn; the window-lined mid-century wood-walled dining room has views from every table. There are separate menus for each dining space though there is some overlap including the wood-fired boiled lobster, a lobster roll, fried clams, and the 9-ounce house burger. **Known for:** outside bar-type table curves above the shore; largely locally sourced menu; house-made cornbread. $ *Average main: $33* ⊠ *13 Abels Lane, Mount Desert, Somesville* ☎ *207/276–8221* ⊕ *www.abelslobster-mdi.com* ⊗ *Closed mid-Oct.-mid-May and Sun. and Mon. from mid-May–mid-Oct.*

Asticou Inn
$$$ | **AMERICAN** | **FAMILY** | Overlooking the water out back and practically hugging Route 3 out the front, this 1883 four-story gray-shingled restaurant and inn can't be missed nor is the opportunity to dine here and savor the spectacular view of picturesque Northeast Harbor, especially from the large deck fronting the classic old New England dining room. The menu offers a handful of entrées, including filet mignon, and lighter fare like fish tacos. **Known for:** popovers with strawberry jam; award-winning seafood chowder; lodging choices outside the main inn include funky six-sided 1960s cottages nicknamed "spaceships". $ *Average main: $33* ⊠ *15 Peabody Rd., Northeast Harbor* ☎ *207/276–3344* ⊕ *www.asticou.com* ⊗ *Closed Tues. and early Oct.–mid May.*

Bass Harbor

9 miles south of Somesville via Rtes. 102 and 102A.

Tucked below Southwest Harbor at the bottom of Mount Desert Island, this small lobstering village doesn't bustle with seasonal tourists like larger island villages, but it does have a few restaurants. It's also the departure point for the ferry to Frenchboro and Swans Island.

Two miles south of Bass Harbor and part of Acadia National Park, Bass Harbor Head Light is the most popular attraction on the island's "quiet side" and one of the most photographed lighthouses in Maine. Acadia's Ship Harbor and Wonderland trails, both easy and under 1½ miles, are also nearby.

GETTING HERE AND AROUND
Bass Harbor is 2.7 miles from Southwest Harbor via Route 102 and Route 102A (Seawall Road), but many visitors travel between them on the 7-mile-long scenic route that loops below Route 102 on a coastal swath bordered by the ocean and both harbors: Southwest on the north and Bass on the west. The road provides access to several popular Acadia National Park attractions.

ESSENTIALS
CONTACTS Southwest Harbor & Tremont Chamber of Commerce. ⊠ *329 Main St., Southwest Harbor* ☎ *207/244–9264* ⊕ *www.acadiachamber.com.*

⊙ Sights

Burnt Coat Harbor Lighthouse and Swans Island
LIGHTHOUSE | **FAMILY** | Swans Island is a picturesque 6-mile ferry ride from Bass Harbor at the bottom of Mount Desert Island. There are numerous outdoor activities, like hiking, swimming, fishing, and biking, but the 35-foot-tall white Burnt Coat Harbor Lighthouse on the south shore is not to be missed. Both the light and the keeper's house, which has history exhibits, an art gallery, bathrooms, and a small gift shop, are open from late June to early September. An apartment upstairs can be rented on a weekly basis from June through October. Aside from vacation rentals, there's only one lodging, the five-room Harbor Watch Inn (⊕ *www. harborwatchinnswansisland.com*). The Island Market & Supply (⊕ *www.tims-swans-island.com*) is a great place to get picnic supplies or other general store

needs. ✉ *Swans Island, Bass Harbor* 🌐 *www.burntcoatharborlight.com.*

🍴 Restaurants

Thurston's Lobster Pound

$$ | SEAFOOD | FAMILY | Right on Bass Harbor, Thurston's is easy to spot because of the bright yellow awnings covering much of its outdoor-only seating. You can order everything from a grilled-cheese crab sandwich, haddock chowder, or hamburger to a boiled lobster served with clams or mussels. **Known for:** selling fresh cooked or uncooked lobsters to go—it's also a lobster wholesaler; lobster fresh off the boat sold in three size ranges; good place to watch sunsets. [$] *Average main: $20* ✉ *9 Thurston Rd., Bernard* ☎ *207/244–7600* 🌐 *www.thurstonforlobster.com* 🕒 *Closed mid-Oct.–late spring; closed Sun. and Mon. late spring–mid-Oct.*

Schoodic Peninsula

25 miles east of Ellsworth via U.S. 1 and Rte. 186.

Acadia National Park's only mainland section sits at the bottom of Schoodic Peninsula, extending to its very tip. As at the park over on Mount Desert Island, visitors to the Schoodic District hike, bike, camp, and savor spectacular views. Crowds are smaller, though they are increasing, and it's here that you'll find Winter Harbor and Gouldsboro.

On the peninsula's western side, Winter Harbor's small but sweet downtown is en route to Grindstone Neck. Granite steps lead to rocky shorefront on tucked-away street ends in the wealthy summer community, which gives an inkling of Bar Harbor before a 1947 fire destroyed many mansions there. Surrounding Winter Harbor, Gouldsboro is also a proud lobstering and fishing community, sprinkled with coastal villages. Guarded by its namesake light, Prospect Harbor stretches along Route 186. Tiny Wonsqueak and Birch harbors flash after you exit Acadia. On the peninsula's most easterly shore, Corea is tucked away from it all on a small roundish harbor, the open ocean beyond.

GETTING HERE AND AROUND

Route 186 loops Schoodic Peninsula, intersecting with the U.S. Route 1 twice.

A seasonal passenger ferry travels Frenchman Bay between Bar Harbor and Winter Harbor, where visitors can connect with the seasonal free Island Explorer bus service to Acadia National Park's Schoodic District and nearby villages . Route 195 runs down the middle of the peninsula from U.S. 1 to Prospect Harbor and continues east to Corea, where it ends.

VISITOR INFORMATION

CONTACTS Schoodic Chamber of Commerce. ✉ *Winter Harbor* 🌐 *schoodicchamber.com.*

👁 Sights

For more information on the Schoodic District area of Acadia National Park, see the Acadia National Park chapter.

🍴 Restaurants

Lunch on the Wharf

$$ | SEAFOOD | FAMILY | A fisherman's wife owns this popular establishment, which buys lobster right off the boat and has covered tables spread about a deck atop a wharf. As stunning as the setting is, folks also come for the excellent food, including boiled lobster with sides; there are plenty of non-seafood choices, too, including pulled pork. **Known for:** BYOB; lobster rolls; whoopie pies. [$] *Average main: $18* ✉ *13 Gibbs La., Corea, Gouldsboro* ☎ *207/276–5262* 🌐 *www.corealunch.com.*

Did You Know?

A far cry from the bloated berries at most grocery stores, Maine's small, flavor-packed wild blueberries are a must in-season, late July–early September. Try a handful fresh, in pancakes, or a pie.

Wild for Blueberries

Native only to northern New England, Atlantic Canada, and Quebec, wild blueberries have long been a favorite food and a key ingredient in cultural and economic life Down East. Maine's crop averages 85 million pounds annually, accounting for virtually all U.S. production and one-fourth of North America's. Washington County yields about 75% of Maine's crop, which is why the state's largest wild blueberry processors are here: Jasper Wyman & Son in Milbridge and the predecessor of what is now Cherryfield Foods in Cherryfield were founded shortly after the Civil War, during which Maine blueberries were shipped to Union soldiers.

Wild blueberries, which bear fruit every other year, thrive in the region's cold climate and sandy, acidic soil. Undulating blueberry barrens stretch for miles in Deblois and Cherryfield (the "Blueberry Capital of the World") and are scattered throughout Washington County. Look for tufts among low-lying plants along roadways. In spring, the fields shimmer as the small-leaf plants turn myriad shades of mauve, honey orange, and lemon yellow. White flowers appear in June. Fall transforms the barrens into a sea of otherworldly red.

Amid Cherryfield's barrens, a plaque on a boulder lauds the late J. Burleigh Crane for helping advance an industry that's not as wild as it used to be. Fields are irrigated, honeybees have been brought in to supplement native pollinators, and rocks and boulders are removed to literally "level" the field. In the past, barrens were typically burned to rid plants of disease and insects, reducing the need for pesticides to improve yield. Native Americans, who are still active in the industry, taught European settlers the practice, now used mostly by organic growers.

Most of the barrens in and around Cherryfield are owned by large blueberry processors. At least 90% of Maine's crop is harvested with machinery. That requires moving boulders, so the rest continues to be harvested by hand with blueberry rakes, which resemble large forks and pull the berries off their stems. Years ago, year-round residents did this work; today, it's mostly seasonal migrant workers.

Blueberries get their dark color from anthocyanins, which act as an antioxidant. Wild blueberries have more of these antiaging, anticancer compounds than their cultivated cousins; they're also smaller and more flavorful, and therefore mainly used in packaged foods, many of the frozen variety. Just 1% of the state's crop (some 500,000 pints) is consumed fresh, most of it in Maine. Look for fresh berries (usually starting in late July and lasting until early September) at roadside stands, farmers' markets, and supermarkets.

Find farm stores, stands, and markets statewide selling blueberries and blueberry jams and syrups at ⊕ *www. realmaine.com*, a Maine Department of Agriculture, Conservation and Forestry site that promotes Maine foods. Wild blueberries are the state's official berry and pies made with them are its official dessert.

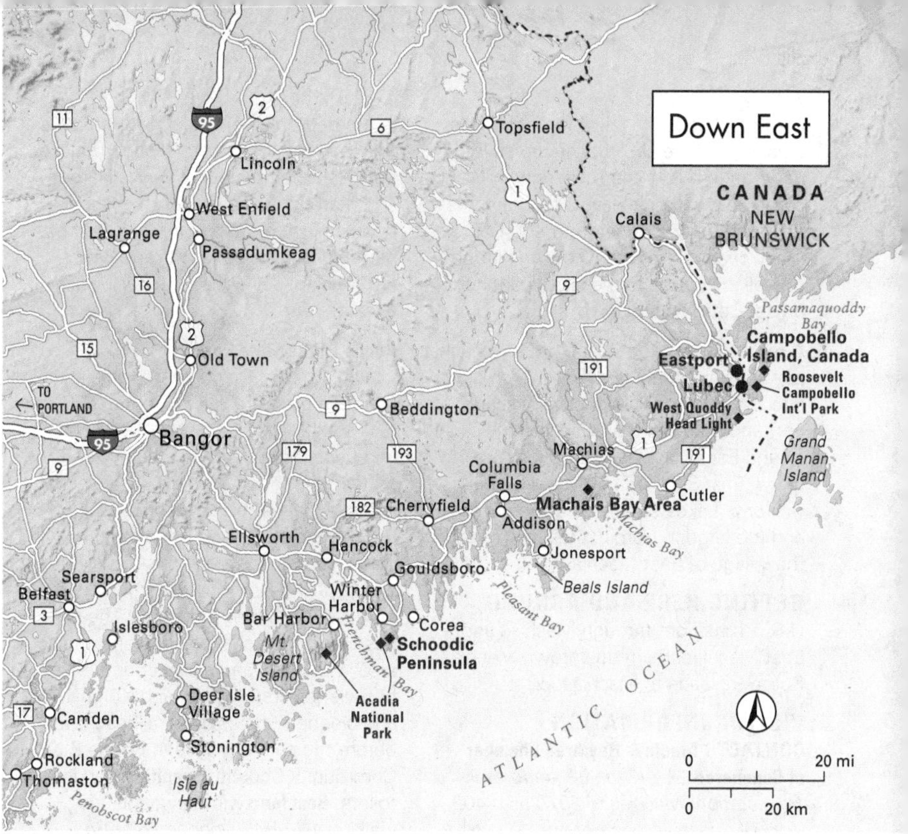

Hotels

★ **Acadia Oceanside Meadows Inn**

$ | B&B/INN | FAMILY | A must for nature lovers, this lodging sits on a 200-acre preserve dotted with woods, streams, salt marshes, and ponds, with spacious guest rooms in two historic buildings overlooking a private white sand beach (rare for these parts); it's also home to Oceanside Meadows Innstitute for the Arts and Sciences, which holds lectures, musical performances, art exhibits, and other events in the restored barn. **Pros:** separate guest kitchen and picnic area with a grill; sea captain's home has three two-room suites that are ideal for families; laminated pamphlets with daily itineraries for exploring Schoodic Peninsula and beyond are available for guest use and purchase. **Cons:** beach is across the road; some dated baths; some third floor rooms. [$] *Rooms from: $199* ✉ *202 Corea Rd., Prospect Harbor* ☎ *207/963–5557* 🌐 *gomaine.com* 🕒 *Closed mid-Oct.–late May* 🛏 *15 rooms* 🍴 *Free Breakfast.*

Machias Bay Area

20 miles northeast of Jonesport.

The Machias area—Machiasport, East Machias, and Machias (Washington County's seat)—was the site of the Revolutionary War's first naval battle. Despite being outnumbered and out-armed, a small group of Machias men under the leadership of Jeremiah O'Brien captured the armed British schooner *Margaretta.* That battle, fought on June 12, 1775, is known as the "Lexington of the Sea." "Machias" is a Native American word meaning "bad little falls," for those falls crashing beside U.S. 1 as it curves into downtown below the University of Maine campus. If you only have a few minutes to watch the water churn through the rocky channel from the viewing platform or walking bridge at the small park here, do so. Better yet, picnic.

A few miles on, the village of East Machias flanks its namesake river, which flows into the Machias River above Machiasport and Machias Bay. Also linking Machias and East Machias is the multi-use Down East Sunrise Trail (🌐 *www.sunrisetrail.org*). Lakes streak the countryside, and the largest, Gardiner Lake, is outside the village of East Machias.

GETTING HERE AND AROUND

U.S. 1 runs right through Machias and East Machias. From downtown Machias, Route 92 leads to Machiasport.

VISITOR INFORMATION

CONTACTS Machias Bay Area Chamber of Commerce. ✉ *2 Kilton La., in former train station, Machias* ☎ *207/255–4402* 🌐 *www.machiaschamber.org.*

Beaches

★ Jasper Beach

BEACH | FAMILY | Sea-polished stones fascinate with glistening tones—many reddish but also heather, bluish, and creamy white—at this mesmerizing rock beach; removing stones from the beach is illegal. Banked in unusual geologic fashion, you must walk up and over a rock dune to get to the beach. When you do, you know you have arrived at a special place. Stones graduate from gravel at the shore to palm-size further back. Reddish volcanic rhyolite stones were mistaken for jasper, hence the name. Stretching a half mile across the end the rectangular-ish Howard Cove, bedrock at both ends deems this a pocket beach, but it's not your typical small one. A saltmarsh and fresh and saltwater lagoons intrigue visitors, and there are sea caves in the bedrock (be careful if you tread that way—the rocks are slippery). Tucked between the hamlets of Bucks Harbor and Starboard, Jasper Beach has long been a place of respite for folks in these parts. **Amenities:** parking (free). **Best for:** walking; solitude. ✉ *Jasper Beach, Machiasport.*

Roque Bluffs State Park

BEACH | FAMILY | Down East's rock- and fir-bound shores give way to the 274-acre park's half-mile crescent-shaped sand and pebble beach: one with any sand is a rarity in the region, and expansive ocean views enhance this one's beauty. Just beyond the beach you'll find a freshwater pond that's ideal for swimming and kayaking—rent flatwater kayaks here—and stocked for fishing. The park has changing areas (no showers), picnic area with grills, and a playground. Miles of trails traverse woods, apple orchards, and blueberry fields. The trailhead is just before the park entrance at Roque Bluffs Community Church. **Amenities:** parking; toilets. **Best for:** swimming; solitude, walking. ✉ *145 Schoppee Point Rd., Roque Bluffs, Machias* ✣ *Follow signs from U.S. 1 in Jonesboro or Machias* ☎ *207/255–3475* 🌐 *www.maine.gov/dacf/park* 🎟 *$4 Maine residents, $6 nonresidents.*

Restaurants

Helen's Restaurant

$$ | AMERICAN | FAMILY | In business for many years, the look here is updated and fresh, as the family-run establishment was rebuilt after a fire in 2014; it serves lunch and dinner, with entrées as well as burgers, sandwiches, salads, and the like. While the menu is big on seafood, don't expect only fried: try choices like charbroiled salmon topped with a maple glaze made with mustard, maple syrup, and blueberry jam, all Maine-made. **Known for:** fish-and-chips; lunch or dinner on the riverside deck come summer; Maine wild blueberry pie. [$] *Average main: $20*

✉ *111 Main St., Machias* ☎ *207/255–8423*
🌐 *www.helensrestaurantmachias.com*
🕑 *Closed Sun. and Mon.*

Lubec Area

*28 miles northeast of Machias via U.S. 1
and Rte. 189.*

Lubec is one of the first places in the
United States to see the sunrise and
a popular destination for outdoors
enthusiasts. The Bold Coast of high cliffs
between here and the quaint fishing
hamlet Cutler offers some of the best
coastal hiking in the Eastern United
States, with sweeping views and rocky
beaches. But there are trails throughout
the area, not just on the high Bold Coast,
and many aren't especially difficult. Along
with government parks and lands, many
conservation groups have preserves in
and near Lubec. Birding is renowned as
many migratory seabirds head this way;
mudflats, marshes, and headlands offer
diverse habitats for observing birds.

Lubec is a good base for visiting New
Brunswick's Campobello Island across
the bridge from downtown—the only
one to the island, so don't forget your
passport! The village itself is perched at
the end of a neck, so you can often see
water in three directions. While there are
some rundown buildings in and around
the small downtown, there's also a small
cluster of restaurants, inns, shops, and
lively murals that reveal the spirit of this
remote, peaceful, and beautiful place.

GETTING HERE AND AROUND
From U.S. 1 in Whiting, Route 189 runs
11 miles to Lubec. To travel here on a
slightly longer scenic route through the
seaside hamlet of Cutler, take Route 191
from U.S. 1 in East Machias to Route 189
in West Lubec. From Lubec to Eastport,
it's 3 miles by boat but 38 miles by
the circuitous northerly land route. In
summer, a water taxi links the towns, as
does a seasonal ferry.

◉ Sights

**West Quoddy Head Light/Quoddy
Head State Park**
STATE/PROVINCIAL PARK | FAMILY | Candy
cane–stripe West Quoddy Head Light
marks the easternmost point of land in
the United States. One of Maine's most
famous lighthouses, it guards Lubec
Channel as it flows into much wider
Atlantic waters that also demarcate
Canada and the United States. Author-
ized by President Thomas Jefferson, the
first light here was built in 1808. West
Quoddy, just inside the park entrance,
was constructed in 1858. You can't climb
the tower, but the former lightkeeper's
house is a seasonal museum; there are
displays about the lighthouse and its former keepers, works by local artists, and a
gift shop. Plan for more than a lighthouse
visit at this enticing 541-acre Bold Coast
park. Whales are often sighted offshore,
the birding is world-famous, and there's a
seaside picnic area. Visitors beachcomb,
walk, or hike several miles of trails; a
2-mile trail along the cliffs yields magnificent views of Canada's cliff-clad Grand
Manan Island, while the 1-mile roundtrip
Bog Trail reveals arctic and subarctic
plants rarely found south of Canada.
Leading to a lookout with views of Lubec
across the channel, the western leg of
the 1-mile Coast Guard Trail is wheelchair
accessible. In the off-season, visitors can
park outside the gate and walk in. ✉ *973
S. Lubec Rd., Lubec* ☎ *207/733–0911*
🌐 *www.maine.gov/dacf/parks* 💲 *$4*
🕑 *Closed mid-Oct.–mid-May.*

🍴 Restaurants

Water Street Tavern & Inn
$$$ | SEAFOOD | FAMILY | Perched on the
water in a shingled building downtown,
this popular restaurant serves some of
the sweetest scallops you'll ever eat;
moqueca (a Brazilian seafood stew); and
filet mignon for those so inclined. It's
also a great place to grab a glass of wine

or a beer at the bar or a cup of coffee while gazing out at the water. **Known for:** laid-back, friendly atmosphere; specialty house-baked cake changes daily; also three guest rooms and a cozy suite. [$] *Average main: $25* ✉ *12 Water St., Lubec* ☎ *207/733–0122* 🌐 *www.watersttavernandinn.com* 🕓 *No lunch; closed late Oct.–late Apr.*

Hotels

★ **Peacock House**

$ | **B&B/INN** | Five generations of the Peacock family lived in this 1860 sea captain's home in the middle of the village before it was converted to an inn in 1989; with a large foyer, living room with fireplace, and cozy library, the white-clapboard house has plenty of places where you can relax—there's even a sunroom that opens to a deck and gardens. **Pros:** guests welcome to play the instruments in the living room; four suites, including two on the first floor with sitting rooms and a primo open-plan one upstairs; innkeepers direct guests to area's tucked-away spots. **Cons:** not on the water; no self-check-in; one bedroom has slanted ceiling. [$] *Rooms from: $175* ✉ *27 Summer St., Lubec* ☎ *207/733–2403, 888/305–0036* 🌐 *www.peacockhouse.com* 🛏 *7 rooms* 🍴 *Free Breakfast.*

Campobello Island, Canada

Across the international bridge from downtown Lubec.

A popular excursion from Lubec, New Brunswick's Campobello Island has two small fishing villages, Welshpool and Wilson's Beach, but Roosevelt International Park, the former summer home of Franklin and Eleanor Roosevelt, is the big draw. If you have the time, you can take a whale-watching excursion, explore the large provincial park, or check out two lighthouses: Mulholland Point across from Lubec and East Quoddy just off the opposite end of the island. There are a few places to stay or grab a bite scattered around the lowkey island.

GETTING HERE AND AROUND

The only land route is the bridge from Lubec, but in summer a car ferry shuttles passengers from Campobello Island to Deer Island, where you can continue to the Canadian mainland on the free government ferry.

After coming across the bridge from Lubec, Route 774 runs from one end of the island to the other, taking you through the two villages and to Roosevelt Campobello International Park.

VISITOR INFORMATION

Campobello Island is part of New Brunswick, Canada, so U.S. Citizens will need their passports to get here.

CONTACTS Visit Campobello Island. ✉ *Campobello* 🌐 *www.visitcampobello.com.*

Sights

East Quoddy Lighthouse (*Head Harbour Lighthouse*)

LIGHTHOUSE | **FAMILY** | Get an update on the tides before heading here if you want to walk out to the lighthouse (also known as Head Harbour Lighthouse) as you can only do so at low tide, via the ladders there—be careful on the wet rocks. On a tiny island off the eastern end of Campobello, this distinctive lighthouse is marked with a large red cross and is accessible only at and around low tide, but it's worth a look no matter the sea level. You may spot whales in the island-dotted waters off the small park on the rock-clad headland across from the light. Seasonal tours of the light may be offered. ✉ *East end of Rte. 774, Campobello.*

★ **Roosevelt Campobello International Park**

HISTORIC HOME | FAMILY | President Franklin D. Roosevelt and his family spent summers at this estate, which is now an international park with neatly manicured lawns that stretch out to the beach. Guided tours of the 34-room Roosevelt Cottage run every 15 minutes. Presented to Eleanor and Franklin as a wedding gift, the wicker-filled structure looks essentially as it did when the family was in residence. A visitor center has displays about the Roosevelts and Canadian-American relations. In the neighboring Wells-Shober Cottage, Eleanor's Tea is held at 11 am (10 am EST) and 3 pm (2 pm EST) daily. A joint project of the American and Canadian governments, this park is crisscrossed with interesting hiking trails. Groomed dirt roads attract bikers. Eagle Hill Bog has a wooden walkway and signs identifying rare plants. ⊠ *459 Rte. 774, Welshpool* ☎ *506/752–2922, 877/851–6663* ⊕ *www.fdr.net* ☜ *Free* ⊙ *Roosevelt Cottage closed late Oct.– late May* ☞ *Islands are on Atlantic Time, which is an hour later than Eastern Standard Time.*

Eastport

38 miles northeast of Lubec via Rte. 189, U.S. 1, and Rte. 190.

Occupying Moose Island on Cobscook and Passamaquoddy bays, a causeway links Eastport to the mainland. "Island City" has wonderful island views, and downtown looks across Friar Roads (part of Passamaquoddy Bay) to Canada's Campobello Island. The water is so deep that whales are often spotted off the large municipal pier (a.k.a. the Breakwater), where you can eye fishing boats and freighters. Among the highest in the world, tides fluctuate as much as 28 feet—thus the ladders and steep gangways for accessing boats. Old Sow, the Western Hemisphere's largest whirlpool, is offshore.

Smuggling with British-controlled Canada thrived here in the early 1800s and sardine-canning at the century's end. Fishing, aquaculture, and a marine terminal are part of today's economy, as is tourism. Art galleries and interesting shops fill storefronts in the largely brick downtown; folks amble on a waterfront walkway with an amphitheater and sculptures. One with a granite-carved fish is on the Maine Sculpture Trail; there's also a tall, jolly fisherman and Nerida, a sweet bronze-cast mermaid. Known for artsy flair with a quirky twist, Eastport drops a sardine on New Year's Eve, plus a maple leaf for the Canadians. In September, buccaneers from Eastport and Lubec battle during the pirate festival.

GETTING HERE AND AROUND

From U.S. 1, Route 190 leads to Eastport, the only road to the city. Before the causeway over, it passes through Sipayik (Pleasant Point) Passamaquoddy reservation. Continue on Washington Street to the water. In the summer, you can take a water taxi from here to Lubec—a few miles by boat but about 40 miles by land. There's also a seasonal ferry service.

VISITOR INFORMATION

CONTACTS Eastport Area Chamber of Commerce. ⊠ *141 Water St., in Port Authority lobby, Eastport* ☎ *207/853–4644* ⊕ *www. eastportchamber.net.*

◉ Sights

National Historic Waterfront District

NEIGHBORHOOD | Anchoring downtown Eastport, this waterfront district extends from the Customs House down Water Street to Bank Square and the Peavey Memorial Library. Spanning such architectural styles as Federal, Victorian, Queen Anne, and Greek Revival, the district was largely built in the 19th century. A cannon sits on the lawn at the Romanesque Revival library, one of the many interesting structures. Benches are beside an iron drinking trough-turned-fountain in front of a bank-turned-museum, the Tides Institute & Museum of Art. ✉ *Eastport.*

Coffee and Quick Bites

Bocephus

$ | **AMERICAN** | Modern takes on sandwich fare and salads at this convenient takeout at the north end of downtown are so beautifully prepared that you almost hate to take a bite. One popular offering is the Bocephus Banh Mi (slow-cooked, Vietnamese-style pork loin served on a baguette with lightly pickled veggies, lettuce, cilantro, maple mayo, and house fish sauce for dipping). **Known for:** lobster sandwich on a brioche bun; local craft brews and wine from small-scale producers; crab sandwiches on a brioche bun. [$] *Average main: $16* ✉ *104 Water St., Eastport* ☎ *207/853–0600* 🌐 *www.facebook.com/biteintobocephus* 🕒 *Closed late Oct.–mid-June and Sun. and Thurs. from mid-Sept.–late Oct.*

Dastardly Dick's Wicked Good Coffee

$ | **CAFÉ** | **FAMILY** | The coffee isn't the only thing that's wicked good at this local café; homemade pastries, rich soups, and tasty sandwiches are all prepared daily, and the hot chocolate and chai are worth writing home about. There are nice murals on the walls, too. **Known for:** local gathering spot; daily soup specials; wicked good baked goods. [$] *Average main: $6* ✉ *62 Water St., Eastport* ☎ *207/853–2090* 🕒 *No lunch Sat. Closed Sun. and Mon. May–mid-Sept and Sat.–Mon. mid-Sept.–May.*

Hotels

The Kilby House Inn B&B

$ | **B&B/INN** | In this 1887 Queen Anne residence built by seaman Herbert Kilby, creamy white walls offset fine antique furnishings, for a brightening effect that evokes an old-fashioned summer home, especially as sea breezes blow through the large windows on a summer day; a carriage house can be booked for an extended stay. **Pros:** master bedroom has four-poster bed; rates adjusted for single occupancy; innkeeper goes all out to help guests plan outings, often to hidden gems beyond Eastport. **Cons:** carriage house only available weekly or longer; some small bathrooms; not on the water. [$] *Rooms from: $130* ✉ *122 Water St., Eastport* ☎ *207/214–6455, 207/853–0989* 🌐 *www.kilbyhouseinn.com* 🛏 *4 rooms* 🍴 *Free Breakfast.*

Chapter 8

ACADIA NATIONAL PARK

Updated by
Mary Ruoff

🏕 **Camping**
★★★★☆

🛏 **Hotels**
★★★★☆

🏃 **Activities**
★★★★★

👁 **Scenery**
★★★★★

👥 **Crowds**
★★★★☆

WELCOME TO ACADIA NATIONAL PARK

TOP REASONS TO GO

★ **Looping the park:** Get oriented along the 27-mile Park Loop Road, leaving plenty of time to stop at acclaimed locales like Sand Beach, Thunder Hole, and Otter Point.

★ **Unique roadways:** Acadia's 45 miles of crushed-stone carriage roads built and gifted by a famed philanthropic family can be enjoyed via two feet, two wheels, or horse-drawn carriage.

★ **A choice of flavors:** Many of the park's most popular attractions are on the east side of Mount Desert Island, including Park Loop Road, the carriage roads, and Cadillac Mountain. But Acadia's grand seascapes, forested lakes, and hiking trails also await on the "quiet" west side.

★ **Powerful popovers.** At the park's only restaurant, Jordan Pond House, gigantic popovers filled with strawberry jam have delighted visitors for more than 100 years.

★ **The parting sea:** Low tide exposes a land bridge between Bar Harbor and Bar Island—and an Acadia hike unlike any other.

Acadia National Park sprawls on both sides of Mount Desert Island.

1 East Side of Mount Desert Island. The busiest and largest part of Acadia National Park is near the amenities hub of Bar Harbor and home to many of its best-known attractions, including the carriage roads, Park Loop Road, Jordan Pond House, Cadillac Mountain, and Sieur de Monts. Hulls Cove Visitor Center is off Route 3, 3 miles from downtown Bar Harbor.

2 West Side of Mount Desert Island. Acadia also offers stunning scenery and great recreational opportunities on the island's "quiet side," where Southwest Harbor is a lower-key tourist hub and Bass Harbor lower yet. You can swim at the park's popular Echo Lake Beach, visit iconic Bass Harbor Head Light, and hike to the landmark Beech Mountain fire lookout tower.

3 Schoodic District. Visitors enjoy grand seascapes with a more secluded feel at the park's only mainland section at the bottom of this peninsula across Frenchman Bay from the east side of Mount Desert. Highlights include a loop road, bike paths, hiking trails, and the Schoodic Institute, an educational facility on the grounds of a former Navy base.

4 Isle au Haut. Acadia occupies half of this island out in the ocean 15 miles southwest of Mount Desert. It's accessible by ferry from Stonington on Deer Isle, itself reachable by bridge from the mainland west of Mount Desert. There's a small primitive campground, gravel roads for mountain biking, and hiking trails. Island amenities are meager.

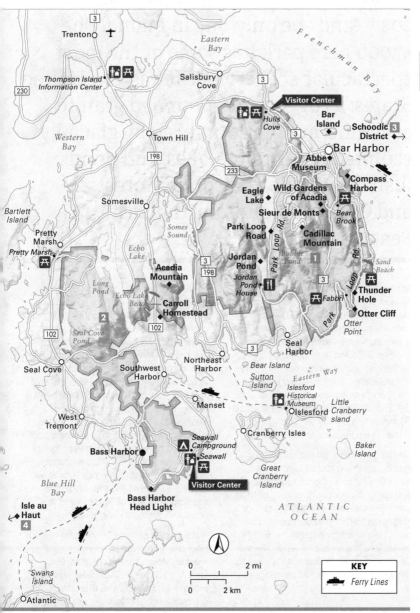

Trenton

3

230

Eastern Bay

Thompson Island
Information Center

Salisbury
Cove

3

Visitor Center

Hulls
Cove

Bar
Island

Frenchman Bay

Schoodic
District →

3

Western Bay

Town Hill

198

Somesville

Bartlett Island

Pretty
Marsh

Pretty Marsh

233

Abbe
Museum

Bar Harbor

Compass
Harbor

Eagle
Lake

Wild Gardens
of Acadia

Sieur de Monts

Bear Brook

Somes Sound

Echo Lake

Park Loop
Road

Cadillac
Mountain

Long Pond

Acadia
Mountain

Echo Lake Beach

Carroll
Homestead

Jordan
Pond

Jordan Pond House

Bubble Pond

1

3

Sand Beach

Thunder
Hole

2

102

Seal Cove Pond

102

3
198

Fabbri

Otter Cliff

Otter Point

Seal Cove

Southwest
Harbor

Northeast
Harbor

3

Seal
Harbor

Bear Island

Sutton Island

Eastern Way

Manset

Islesford
Historical
Museum

Islesford

Little Cranberry Island

West
Tremont

Cranberry Isles

Baker Island

Bass Harbor

Seawall Campground

Seawall

Visitor Center

Great Cranberry Island

Blue Hill Bay

Isle au
Haut

4

Bass Harbor
Head Light

ATLANTIC
OCEAN

Swans Island

Atlantic

0   2 mi

0   2 km

KEY
Ferry Lines

Mostly on Mount Desert Island, Acadia is among the nation's most popular national parks—4.07 million visits in 2021—and the only one in Maine. The 47,000-acre park has some of the most spectacular scenery in the eastern United States: a rugged surf-pounded granite coastline; an interior graced by glacially sculpted mountains, lakes, and ponds; lush deciduous and conifer forests; and Cadillac Mountain, the Eastern Seaboard's highest point.

Acadia has more than 150 miles of hiking trails and 45 miles of finely crafted crushed-stone carriage roads—used by walkers, runners, bikers, and horse-drawn carriages—with elegant stone bridges. Built and later gifted by late philanthropist and part-time resident John D. Rockefeller Jr., the network wends on the island's busier eastern side, as does the 27-mile Park Loop Road. Sand Beach, Thunder Hole, and Otter Cliff, along its Ocean Drive section, are must-sees.

On the island's northeast corner, Bar Harbor, the main tourist hub located, has a few hamlets beyond the village. Bordering Bar Harbor, the Town of Mount Desert has several villages, including Northeast Harbor and Somesville. Southwest Harbor encompasses the village center and the smaller seaside Manset. On the "quiet side," Trenton is home to Bass Harbor and other small villages.

To truly appreciate the park you must experience it by walking, hiking, biking, rock climbing, paddling, boating, or carriage ride. Making that easier, and helping protect Acadia's environment, are seasonal free Island Explorer buses serving the park and nearby towns. Acadia also encompasses all or parts of 19 other islands. Most are uninhabited, but only one is closed to the public. There are ranger-led boat tours to two, Little Cranberry and Baker off the bottom of Mount Desert. Inhabited year-round and accessible by ferry, Little Cranberry is home to a small park museum about island life. Almost the entirety of the seasonally inhabited Baker Island is in Acadia, including its namesake light.

Acadia extends to half of remote Isle au Haut, out in the ocean 15 miles southwest of Mount Desert. Reachable by ferry from Stonington on Deer Isle (don't worry, a bridge gets you there from the mainland), it offers rugged trails,

AVERAGE HIGH/LOW TEMPERATURES					
Jan.	Feb.	Mar.	Apr.	May	June
32/17	34/19	40/27	50/36	59/44	67/52
July	Aug.	Sept.	Oct.	Nov.	Dec.
73/57	72/57	65/51	56/43	46/34	37/24

primitive camping, and unpaved roads. On the Schoodic Peninsula east of Mount Desert, Acadia's only mainland district has bike paths, hiking, camping, ranger programs, and a loop drive all its own, with views of Mount Desert—Maine's largest island.

Planning

When to Go

During the summer season, days are usually warm and nights cool—bring a jacket. July tops the charts with a comfortable average daily high of 73°F. But there are hot and humid spells, more so in recent years. Peak visitation is late spring through October. July and August are the busiest months, but September—when the heat and humidity of summer begin to taper off—is one of the most enjoyable, and also busy. The foliage season in the first few weeks of October bustles, too. While Memorial Day and Labor Day mark the traditional beginning and end of high season, nowadays many seasonal establishments stay open through Indigenous Peoples Day/ Columbus Day and some longer.

Consider coming in mid-spring when temperatures start to rise but crowds haven't yet formed. Be sure to check for seasonal closures due to ice, snow, or mud on Acadia's carriage roads, unpaved roads, and trails. For hardy souls, winter can be a wonderful time to visit. While many dining and lodging facilities are hibernating, you can still find good options. Just know that from December

through mid-April, paved park roads are closed to vehicles except for two short sections of Park Loop Road. For unpaved roads, it's mid-November to mid-May. When enough snow flies, folks head to the park to snowshoe and cross-country ski—many carriage roads are groomed. Snowmobilers take to Park Loop Road, drive up Cadillac Mountain, and hit unpaved roads.

Regardless of when you decide to go, it's best to book your accommodations in advance, especially if you have a particular type of lodging in mind or will be visiting on a holiday weekend. Visitors are advised not to travel to the Acadia area in peak season without a reservation.

Getting Here and Around

AIR

Bangor International Airport (BGR) in Bangor is the closest major airport to Acadia National Park. The driving distance from Bangor to Mount Desert Island is approximately 50 miles. Car rentals, taxi, bus, and shuttle service are available.

Farther south, Portland International Airport (PWM) is approximately three hours to the Mount Desert Island area. Renting a car is your best bet for getting to Acadia National Park from here.

The small regional Hancock County–Bar Harbor Airport (BHB) is in Trenton just minutes from the causeway to Mount Desert Island. Cape Air/JetBlue have flights to and from Boston's Logan International Airport (BOS). Car rentals and taxi service are available, and the airport is a stop for the free seasonal Island

Explorer buses that serve Acadia and nearby towns.

CONTACTS Bangor–Bar Harbor Express Shuttle. ☒ *Bangor* ☎ *207/944–8429* ⊕ *www.bangorbarharborexpressshuttle. com.* **Bangor International Airport.** (*BGR*) ☒ *287 Godfrey Blvd., Bangor* ☎ *207/992– 4600* ⊕ *www.flybangor.com.* **Hancock County–Bar Harbor Airport.** (*BHB*) ☒ *143 Caruso Dr., Trenton* ☎ *207/667–7329* ⊕ *www.bhbairport.com.*

BUS

Operating seasonally, Island Explorer buses serve Acadia and communities throughout Mount Desert Island as well as neighboring Trenton. Though touted as free, donations are requested to support the service. Island Explorer also serves the mainland district of Acadia and nearby villages, including Winter Harbor, on the Schoodic Peninsula. You can get to the park's Schoodic District from the seasonal Bar Harbor–Winter Harbor Ferry via an Island Explorer bus.

Bus service starts in late May on the Schoodic Peninsula and late June in the Mount Desert area and runs through Indigenous Peoples Day/Columbus Day. A reduced fall schedule starts in late August. Island Explorer's designated stops include many campgrounds and hotels. The buses also pick up and drop off passengers anywhere along the route where it's safe to stop.

Buses have bike racks, but they only hold four or six bicycles. During the peak summer season, the Island Explorer Bicycle Express takes bikes and passengers by van from downtown Bar Harbor to Acadia's Eagle Lake Carriage Road. These vans can take tag-along bikes and small children's bikes but not tandem, fat-tire, or electric bikes; Island Explorer buses can't transport any specialty bikes.

CONTACTS Island Explorer. ☒ *Acadia National Park* ☎ *207/667–5796* ⊕ *www. exploreacadia.com.*

CAR

Route 3 leads to Mount Desert Island and Bar Harbor from Ellsworth and circles the eastern part of the island. Route 102 is the major road on the west side. Acadia National Park's Hulls Cove Visitor Center is off Route 3, 3 miles from downtown Bar Harbor. Acadia's main thoroughfare, 27-mile Park Loop Road, is accessible from the visitor center as well as park entrances (Cadillac Mountain) near downtown Bar Harbor on Route 233, south of Bar Harbor proper on Route 3 (Sieur de Monts), and in Seal Harbor on Route 3 (Stanley Brook Road). Much of the road is one-way.

Shaped like an upside-down "U" (some liken it to a pair of lobster claws), Mount Desert is relatively easy to navigate, though it may take longer than expected to reach some points. Somes Sound, a fjard (less steep-sided than a fjord) that runs up the middle of Mount Desert Island, requires drivers at the ends of the "U" to travel quite a distance to get to a town that is close as the crow flies. Beyond the geographical barriers, summer traffic can slow your progress and make finding a parking space, especially in Bar Harbor or Acadia, difficult to nearly impossible. Avoid the problem by hopping on one of the seasonal free Island Explorer buses that serve the park and nearby towns.

Park Essentials

ACCESSIBILITY

Many Acadia National Park sights and amenities are at least partly accessible to those with accessibility challenges. Island Explorer buses (but not all bus stops), park visitor and information centers, and many picnic areas and camping sites are wheelchair accessible. Accessibility varies for scenic overlooks, trails, and carriage roads. Echo Lake Beach has wheelchair-accessible changing rooms; stairs to the water prevent wheelchair access at Sand Beach. The Sieur de Monts area of the park has a Nature Center with exhibits and an information desk at wheelchair height; a trailhead for the mostly wheelchair-accessible 1.5-mile Jesup Path and Hemlock Path Loop; a level if narrow path through Wild Gardens of Acadia; and a wheelchair-accessible water fountain and water bottle-filling station. Check the park website for information on accessibility.

PARK FEES AND PERMITS

A National Parks pass is required to enter Acadia year-round; display it on your dashboard when parking at trailheads or parking areas. An annual national park's pass ($80) and the Acadia weekly pass ($30 per vehicle) can be purchased online at ⊕ www.Recreation.gov.

Within the park, passes can be purchased at the Hulls Cove Visitor Center, the Sand Beach Entrance Station on Park Loop Road, and park campgrounds (except Isle au Haut). Automated fee machines in the Hulls Cove Visitor Center parking lot pavilion and at Acadia's mainland Schoodic District (inside the gatehouse at the entrance to Schoodic Institute) sell Acadia's weekly pass. Third-party sellers like local chambers of commerce and park concessionaires also sell Acadia weekly passes.

The park is free on Martin Luther King Jr. Day (third Monday in January); Great American Outdoors Day (August 4); first Monday of National Park Week in mid-April; National Public Lands Day (fourth Saturday in September); and Veterans Day, November 11.

PARK HOURS

The park is open 24 hours a day year-round, but paved roads within the park on Mount Desert Island close December–mid-April except for two small sections of Park Look Road: Ocean Drive and the section providing access to Jordan Pond. Unpaved roads are closed from mid-November–mid-May. Paved roads are open year-round at Acadia's mainland section on Schoodic Peninsula.

CELL PHONE RECEPTION

Depending on your cell phone carrier, you may not always be able to rely on your cell phone while visiting Mount Desert Island.

Hotels

Lodging is not available within Acadia National Park. Bar Harbor has the greatest variety and number of lodging facilities, but they are also found in other Mount Desert Island towns and villages. Northeast Harbor and Southwest Harbor having the largest concentration outside Bar Harbor. With short notice in high season the Ellsworth area might be your best bet. Visiting the Acadia area in peak season without a reservation is not advised.

Restaurants

The Jordan Pond House Restaurant is the only dining option within the park, serving lunch, tea, and dinner late May to late October; it also has a takeout place. There are a number of restaurants serving a variety of cuisines in Bar Harbor, while smaller coastal communities typically have at least one or two small eateries. Northeast Harbor and Southwest Harbor have the largest concentration outside the main tourist hub of Bar Harbor.

PRICES

Restaurant prices in the reviews are the average cost of a main course at dinner, or if dinner is not served, at lunch. Restaurant reviews have been shortened. For full information, visit Fodors.com.

8

Acadia National Park PLANNING

What It Costs In U.S. Dollars			
$	$$	$$$	$$$$
RESTAURANTS			
under $18	$18–$24	$25–$35	over $35

Visitor Information

Mount Desert Chamber of Commerce isn't an island-wide chamber; it serves the Town of Mount Desert (Northeast Harbor, Somesville, and a few other villages). The two other island chambers are Bar Harbor Chamber of Commerce and Southwest Harbor & Tremont Chamber of Commerce.

CONTACTS Acadia National Park. ⊠ *Acadia National Park* ☎ *207/288–3338* ⊕ *www. nps.gov/acad.* **Bar Harbor Chamber of Commerce.** ⊠ *2 Cottage St., Bar Harbor* ☎ *207/288–5103* ⊕ *www.visitbarharbor. com.* **Mount Desert Chamber of Commerce.** ⊠ *41 Harbor Dr., Northeast Harbor* ☎ *207/276–5040* ⊕ *www.mtdesertchamber.org.* **Southwest Harbor & Tremont Chamber of Commerce.** ⊠ *329 Main St., Southwest Harbor* ☎ *207/244–9264* ⊕ *www.acadiachamber.com.* **Thompson Island Information Center.** ⊠ *1319 Bar Harbor Rd., Bar Harbor* ☎ *207/288–3338* ⊕ *www.nps.gov/acad/planyourvisit/hours. htm.*

East Side of Mount Desert Island

10 miles south of Ellsworth via Rte. 3.

Many of Acadia National Park's best-loved features, including all of its carriage roads, Sand Beach, and Cadillac Mountain, are on this side of Mount Desert Island. So, too, is Bar Harbor, the island's largest town and your best bet for finding lodging and dining.

◉ Sights

BEACHES
Sand Beach

BEACH | FAMILY | At this 290-yard-long pocket beach, hugged by picturesque rocky outcroppings, the combination of crashing waves and chilly water (normal range is 50–60°F) keeps most people on the beach. You'll find some swimmers at the height of summer, when lifeguards may be on duty, but the rest of the year this is a place for strolling and snapping photos. In fact, when the official swimming season (mid-June to early September) ends, more activities are allowed, from fishing and surfing to dog walking and boat launching/landing. **Amenities:** parking; toilets. **Best for:** solitude; sunrise; walking. ⊠ *Ocean Dr. section of Park Loop Rd., Acadia National Park* ☎ *207/288–3338* ⊕ *nps.gov/acad.*

GEOLOGICAL FORMATIONS
Thunder Hole

CAVE | When conditions are just so at this popular visitor attraction, the force of pounding surf being squeezed into a narrow slot of cliffside pink granite causes a boom that sounds like thunder and often sends ocean spray up to 40 feet into the air—soaking observers standing nearby behind safety railings. Time your visit within an hour or two of high tide for the best chance to observe the phenomenon; at low tide, take the stairway down to a viewing platform for a peak at the water-carved walls of the tiny inlet. ⊠ *Ocean Dr. section of Park Loop Rd., Acadia National Park* ✛ *About 1 mile south of Sand Beach* ☎ *207/288–3338* ⊕ *nps.gov/acad.*

SCENIC DRIVES
★ Park Loop Road

SCENIC DRIVE | FAMILY | This 27-mile road provides a perfect introduction to the park. You can drive it in an hour, but allow at least half a day, so that you can explore the many sites along the way, including Thunder Hole, Sand Beach, and Otter

Cliff. The route is also served by the free Island Explorer buses. Traffic is one-way from near the Route 233 entrance to the Stanley Brook Road entrance south of the Jordan Pond House. The 2-mile section known as Ocean Drive is open year-round, as is a small section that provides access to Jordan Pond from Seal Harbor. ✉ *Acadia National Park* ☎ *207/288–3338* ⊕ *nps.gov/acad.*

SCENIC STOPS
Bar Island
ISLAND | FAMILY | Offering one of Acadia National Park's more unique experiences, Bar Island is only accessible by foot and during a three-hour window when low tide exposes a ½-mile gravel bar connecting Bar Island to Bar Harbor. The entire Bar Island trail offers an easy 1.9-mile round-trip hike; once on the island you can enjoy views of Bar Harbor and Frenchman Bay. Make sure to check the tide charts before setting out, because once covered by rising tidal waters it'll be another nine hours before the land bridge is once again exposed. ✉ *Bar Harbor* ⊹ *Access via West St. then Bridge St.* ☎ *207/288–3338* ⊕ *nps.gov/acad.*

★ Cadillac Mountain
MOUNTAIN | FAMILY | One of Acadia's premier attractions, 1,530-foot Cadillac Mountain is the Eastern Seaboard's tallest mountain. Stunning panoramic views sweep across bays, islands, and mountains on and off Mount Desert Island. You can see Bar Harbor below on the northeast side and Eagle Lake to the west. Low-lying vegetation like pitch pine and wild blueberry plants accent granite slabs in the "subalpine-like" environment. There's a paved summit loop trail and several hiking trails up Cadillac, named for a Frenchman who explored here in the late 1600s and later founded Detroit. From mid-May–mid-October, a vehicle reservation (done through ⊕ www.recreation.gov) is needed to drive to the summit. Sunrise slots are in high demand, as this is one of the first places

in the country to see first light, not to mention the perfect spot to watch the sunset or stargaze in the spring and fall—Bar Harbor's light ordinance helps with that. ✉ *Cadillac Summit Rd., Acadia National Park* ☎ *207/288–3338* ⊕ *www.nps.gov/acad* ✉ *$6 per car in addition to park entrance fee (via www.recreation.gov)* ⊙ *Access road closes at 10 pm in season and Dec.–mid-Apr.*

Compass Harbor
TRAIL | FAMILY | Just beyond Bar Harbor proper, this easy 0.8-mile round-trip trail through woods to the shore passes through land that belonged to George B. Dorr—Acadia National Park's first superintendent and a key player in its creation. Views extend to Ironbound Island across Frenchman Bay, and you can check out remnants of Dorr's estate, including the manor house's foundation, remains of a saltwater pool, stone steps to the ocean, and old gardens and apple trees. *Easy.* ✉ *399 Main St., trailhead parking, Bar Harbor* ☎ *207/288–3338* ⊕ *nps.gov/acad.*

Eagle Lake
MARINA/PIER | Located just east of Acadia National Park headquarters, 436-acre Eagle Lake is the largest freshwater lake on Mountain Desert Island. Swimming is not allowed, but kayaking, canoeing, boating, and fishing are, and the encircling 6.1-mile carriage road invites walkers and cyclists. ✉ *Rte. 233, Bar Harbor* ⊹ *½ mile east of Acadia National Park headquarters* ☎ *207/288–3338* ⊕ *nps.gov/acad.*

★ Jordan Pond
BODY OF WATER | FAMILY | Soak up the mountain scenery, listen for the call of loons, and watch for cliff-nesting peregrine falcons along the 3.3-mile trail around this 187-acre tarn—a mountain lake formed by retreating glaciers—on Park Loop Road's two-way portion. Several carriage roads converge here, one marked by a fanciful gatehouse, one of two on the road network. Visitors kayak and canoe on the deep water (no

swimming) and gaze down on Great Pond after hiking up nearby mountains. A popular choice is The Bubbles, with twin peaks whose distinct shape makes up for what they lack in size. They rise across the water from Jordan Pond House Restaurant, where folks come for popovers served with strawberry jam and tea, hoping for a table on the expansive lawn—a tradition started in the 1890s in the original Jordan Pond House, which burned in 1979. The rebuild has a two-story gift shop and, on the upper level, an observation deck and Carriage Road Carry Out, with to-go items like sandwiches and salads—or try the popover sundae. Parking lots here fill fast in high season; consider biking or taking the free Island Explorer bus. ✉ *2928 Park Loop Rd. Seal Harbor* ☎ *207/288–3338* ⊕ *nps.gov/acad.*

Otter Cliff

NATURE SIGHT | Looming 110 feet above the crashing surf of the North Atlantic, Otter Cliff is the terminus of the popular Ocean Path walking trail, which starts 2 miles north at the Sand Beach parking lot. Don't fret if you're not up for the walk: you can still enjoy the view from the overlook just beyond the cliff, where you can often watch rock climbers on the cliff face. Nearby on the shore are thousands of round boulders of various sizes that have been smoothed into shape by many thousands of years of wave action. ✉ *Park Loop Rd., Bar Harbor* ✛ *About ¾ mile south of Thunder Hole on Park Loop Rd.* ☎ *207/288–3338* ⊕ *nps.gov/acad.*

★ Sieur de Monts

NATURE SIGHT | **FAMILY** | The seasonal ranger-staffed Nature Center is the first major stop along the Park Loop Road. There are exhibits about the park's conservation efforts, as well as a park information center. The area is known as the "Heart of Acadia," which memorializes George Dorr, Acadia National Park's

The Early Bird Gets the Sun ◉

Many people believe the top of Cadillac Mountain is the first place in the United States to see the sunrise. It is, though only from early October to early March. To experience first light atop Cadillac's granite summit, plan to get up *very* early. A timed reservation ($6 per car in addition to the park entrance fee via ⊕ *www.recreation. gov*) is required to drive up the mountain from mid-May through mid-October; sunrise slots are especially popular.

first superintendent, and includes walking trails, Sieur de Monts Spring, Wild Gardens of Acadia, and Abbe Museum (its main location is in downtown Bar Harbor), which honors the area's Native American heritage. ✉ *Park Loop Rd., Bar Harbor* ✛ *Also accessible from Rte. 3* ☎ *207/288–3338* ⊕ *nps.gov/acad* ◷ *Nature Center closed mid-Oct.–mid-May.*

TRAILS

Cadillac Mountain North Ridge Trail

TRAIL | The mostly exposed 4.4-mile round-trip summit hike rewards with expansive views of Bar Harbor, Frenchman Bay, and the Schoodic Peninsula for much of the way. The trail is worth undertaking at either sunrise or sunset (or both!). Parking can be limited, especially in high season, so park officials recommend taking the Island Explorer bus for access via a 0.1-mile section of the Kebo Brook Trail. *Moderate.* ✉ *Park Loop Rd., Bar Harbor* ✛ *Trailhead: Access is via Park Loop Rd. near where one-way travel to Sand Beach starts* ☎ *207/288–3338* ⊕ *nps.gov/acad.*

★ Ocean Path Trail

TRAIL | This easily accessible 4.4-mile round-trip trail runs parallel to the Ocean Drive section of the Park Loop Road from Sand Beach to Otter Point. It has some of the best scenery in Maine: cliffs and boulders of pink granite at the ocean's edge, twisted branches of dwarf jack pines, and ocean views that stretch to the horizon. Be sure to save time to stop at Thunder Hole, named for the sound the waves make as they thrash through a narrow opening in the granite cliffs, into a sea cave, and whoosh up and out. It's roughly halfway between Sand Beach and Otter Cliff, with steps leading down to the water to watch the wave action close up. Use caution as you descend (access may be limited due to storms), and also if you venture onto the outer cliffs along this walk. *Easy.* ✉ *Ocean Dr. section of Park Loop Rd., Acadia National Park* ✣ *Trailhead: Upper parking lot of Sand Beach* ☎ *207/288–3338* 🌐 *nps.gov/acad.*

VISITOR CENTERS

Hulls Cove Visitor Center

VISITOR CENTER | **FAMILY** | This is a great spot to get your bearings. A large 3D relief map of Mount Desert Island gives you the lay of the land, and there are free park and carriage road maps. The gift shop sells hiking maps, guidebooks, and a CD for a self-driving park tour and is well-stocked with books about Acadia. Ranger-led programs include guided hikes and other interpretive events, and there are Junior Ranger programs for kids, family-friendly campfire talks at campground amphitheaters (open to all visitors), and night sky talks at Sand Beach. ✉ *25 Visitor Center Rd., Bar Harbor* ☎ *207/288–3338* 🌐 *www.nps.gov/acad.*

🍴 Restaurants

Jordan Pond House Restaurant

$$ | **AMERICAN** | The only dining option within Acadia serves lunch, tea, and dinner as well as to-go items like sandwiches and salads. Most folks come for tea and popovers with strawberry jam on the lawn—a tradition started in the 1890s in the original Jordan Pond House—but the menu also includes chowders and entrees like a lobster dinner or the fresh catch of the day. **Known for:** popover sundae; lawn seating; popovers and strawberry jam. [$] *Average main: $20* ✉ *2928 Park Loop Rd., Acadia National Park* ☎ *207/276–3610* 🌐 *jordanpondhouse.com* 🕒 *Closed Nov.–late May.*

West Side of Mount Desert Island

8 miles east of Bar Harbor via Rte. 233 and Rte. 3.

On Acadia National Park's "quiet side" west of Somes Sounds, there's plenty to explore including Echo Lake Beach, which is the park's swimming beach with the warmest water, and Bass Harbor Head Light. Popular hiking trails adorn Acadia and Beech mountains.

👁 Sights

BEACHES

Echo Lake Beach

BEACH | **FAMILY** | A quiet lake surrounded by woods in the shadow of Beech Mountain, Echo Lake is one of Acadia's few swimming beaches. The water is considerably warmer, if muckier, than nearby ocean beaches, and dogs are allowed in the off-season. The surrounding trail network skirts the lake and ascends the mountain. A boat ramp is north of here along Route 102 at Ikes Point. **Amenities:** lifeguards (at times); parking; toilets. **Best for:** sunset;

swimming; solitude. ⊠ *Echo Lake Beach Rd., off Rte. 102 between Somesville and Southwest Harbor, Acadia National Park* ☎ *207/288–3338* ⊕ *nps.gov/acad.*

HISTORIC SIGHTS

★ Bass Harbor Head Light

LIGHTHOUSE | FAMILY | Built in 1858, this is one of Maine's most photographed lighthouses; it's been a part of Acadia National Park since 2020. Now automated, it marks the entrance to Bass Harbor and Blue Hill Bay at the island's southernmost point nearly 2 miles below Bass Harbor village. You can't go inside, but a walkway brings you to a seaside viewing area with placards about its history. The small parking lot typically fills for sunset viewing in high season and parking isn't allowed on the entrance road or on Route 102A. The free Island Explorer bus doesn't serve the lighthouse. ⊠ *116 Lighthouse Rd., off Rte. 102A, Bass Harbor* ☎ *207/288–3338* ⊕ *www.nps.gov/acad* ☒ *A National Parks pass is required.*

Carroll Homestead

FARM/RANCH | FAMILY | For almost 100 years beginning in the early 1800s, three generations of the Carroll family homesteaded at this small-scale farm that was donated to the park in 1982. A few miles north of the village of Southwest Harbor, the weathered farmhouse still stands and is occasionally opened for ranger-led tours during the summer; check the park website for details. ⊠ *Acadia National Park* ✛ *Turn off Rte. 102* ☎ *207/288–3338* ⊕ *nps.gov/acad.*

TRAILS

Beech Mountain

TRAIL | FAMILY | A unique payoff awaits on this 1.2-mile round-trip hike: a fire lookout tower where you can enjoy views of Somes Sound, Echo Lake, Acadia Mountain, and beyond from its platform. The forested and rocky trail is popular with sunset seekers, who are reminded to carry appropriate clothing and headlamps

for the descent. *Moderate.* ⊠ *Beech Hill Rd., Southwest Harbor* ✛ *Trailhead: 4 miles south of Somesville on Beech Hill Rd. off Rte. 102* ☎ *207/288–3338* ⊕ *nps. gov/acad.*

Ship Harbor Trail

TRAIL | FAMILY | Popular with families and birders, this 1.3-mile figure-8 trail loops through woods and follows a sheltered cove where you may spot great blue herons feeding in the mudflats during low tide. *Easy* ⊠ *Rte. 102A, Acadia National Park* ✛ *Trailhead: 1.2 miles west of Seawall picnic area on Rte. 102A* ☎ *207/288–3338* ⊕ *nps.gov/acad.*

★ St. Sauveur and Acadia Mountain Loop

TRAIL | If you're up for a challenge, this is one of the area's best hikes. The 3.9-mile round-trip loop summits both St. Sauveur and Acadia mountains. Ascents and descents are steep and strenuous, but the views of Somes Sound and beyond are grand. The hike begins at the Acadia Mountain trailhead. For a shorter excursion, follow the fire road that connects with the Acadia Mountain Trail section of the loop. *Difficult.* ⊠ *Rte. 102, Mount Desert* ✛ *Trailhead (Acadia Mountain): Rte. 102 just after Ikes Pt. on Echo Lake (opposite side of road)* ☎ *207/288–3338* ⊕ *www.nps.gov/acad.*

VISITOR CENTER

Seawall Ranger Station

VISITOR CENTER | This small information center is located at the park's Seawall Campground along Route 102A near the island's southernmost point. Stop here for park information and to purchase park passes. ⊠ *664 Seawall Rd., Southwest Harbor* ✛ *Off Rte. 102A* ☎ *207/288–3338* ⊕ *www.nps.gov/acad* ☽ *Closed mid-Oct.–mid-May.*

Schoodic District

25 miles east of Ellsworth via U.S. 1 and Rte. 186.

Acadia National Park's 3,900-acre Schoodic District sits at the bottom of Schoodic Peninsula, east of Mount Desert Island and mostly in Winter Harbor. The landscape of craggy coastline, towering evergreens, and views over Frenchman Bay is breathtaking—and less crowded than over at the park on Mount Desert. A scenic loop road spurs to Schoodic Point, the experiential pinnacle. Schoodic Head, the literal one, also has spectacular views—of ocean as well as forested peninsula. Biking is popular on the loop road and 8.3 miles of wide, interconnected packed-gravel bike paths (*no Class 2 or Class 3 e-bikes*). Also used by walkers, they were added in 2015 along with the campground and additional hiking trails. Ranging from easy coastal treks to difficult ascents, most trails are part of a network that links with the bike path system, which has some challenging climbs. The Schoodic District has education programs for visitors, including Junior Ranger activities for the kiddos. A seasonal passenger ferry links Bar Harbor and Winter Harbor, where it connects with free seasonal Island Explorer buses serving the park and peninsular villages (*see the Getting Here and Around section of the Chapter Planner for more information*).

 Sights

HISTORIC SIGHTS

Schoodic Institute

COLLEGE | FAMILY | Formerly apartments and offices for the U.S. Navy base that operated here for decades, this massive 1934 French Eclectic-style structure is on the National Registry of Historic Places. Today, the building is known as Rockefeller Hall, and its home to the Schoodic Institute, which is home base for many ranger-led programs and family-friendly activities at the park's Schoodic District, including public programs of its own (*some have fees and require overnight stays; check the institute's website for more information*); it's the largest facility of its kind at a national park. The Rockefeller Welcome Center is on the first floor. ⊠ *1 Atterbury Circle, Winter Harbor* ☎ *207/288–1310* ⊕ *www.schoodicinstitute.org.*

SCENIC DRIVES

Schoodic Loop Road

SCENIC DRIVE | FAMILY | Less than a mile from the entrance to Schoodic Woods Campground and Ranger Station, and just beyond Frazer Point Picnic Area, the only road into the park becomes one-way and continues for about 6 miles to the park exit (no RVs are allowed on the road after the campground entrance). Edging the coast and sprinkled with pullouts, the first few miles yield views of Grindstone Neck, Winter Harbor, Winter Harbor Lighthouse, and, across the water, Cadillac Mountain. After a few miles, a two-way spur, Arey Cove Road, passes Schoodic Institute en route to Schoodic Point. Here, huge slabs of pink granite lie jumbled along the shore, thrashed unmercifully by the crashing surf, and jack pines cling to life amid the rocks. Continuing on the loop road, stop at Blueberry Hill parking area to look out on near-shore islands. The Anvil and Alder trailheads are near here. From the park exit, continue two miles to Route 186 in Birch Harbor. There's a biking path trailhead with parking at the exit and another one about midway to Route 186, both on your left. ⊠ *Schoodic Loop Rd., Winter Harbor* ☎ *207/288–3338* ⊕ *nps.gov/acad.*

SCENIC STOPS

Blueberry Hill

SCENIC DRIVE | About a half mile beyond the Schoodic Point spur on the scenic one-way loop drive, this spot looks out on nearby Little Moose and Schoodic islands and the ocean beyond. It's also where to

Did You Know?

The Somesville Bridge, found on the West Side of Mount Desert Island, is a popular stop for a photo op.

park if you're planning to hike a loop consisting of the Alder and Anvil trails across the road from the parking lot. ⊠ *Schoodic Loop Rd., Winter Harbor* ✛ *About 1 mile east of Schoodic Point* ☎ *207/288–3338* ⊕ *nps.gov/acad.*

★ Schoodic Point

NATURE SIGHT | FAMILY | Massed granite ledges meet crashing waves at Schoodic Peninsula's tip, off the loop road at the end of Arey Cove Road. Dark basalt rock slices through pink granite, to dramatic effect. Look east for a close view of Little Moose Island; a bit farther away to the west is a sidelong view of Mount Desert Island; and to the south, an inspiring open ocean view. There are bathrooms and a good-size parking area. ⊠ *Arey Cove Rd., Winter Harbor* ☎ *207/288–3338* ⊕ *nps.gov/acad.*

TRAILS

Alder and Anvil Trails

TRAIL | Popular with birders, the Alder trail heads inland, passing fruit trees and alder bushes on an easy 1.2-mile out-and-back hike, but many hit the grassy path as part of a near-loop with the challenging 1.1-mile Anvil Trail, since trailheads for both are near the Blueberry Hill parking area on the loop road (you must cross the road to get to them). Steep and heavily rooted in sections as it climbs Schoodic Head, Anvil requires lots of rock climbing but rewards with wonderful water and island views from the rock knob overlook (side trail) for which it's named. After connecting with Schoodic Head Trail from Alder or Anvil, it's not far to the top of Schoodic Head, where expansive views of the surrounding seascape and landscape await. ⊠ *Schoodic Loop Rd., Winter Harbor* ✛ *Beyond turn for Schoodic Point* ☎ *207/288–3338* ⊕ *nps.gov/acad.*

Schoodic Head Ascents

TRAIL | FAMILY | You can drive up or walk up to the 440-foot summit —the highest point in these Acadia lands—along a narrow 1-mile gravel road. It's unmarked, so watch for it 2½ miles from the start of the one-way portion of Schoodic Loop

Road. Prefer an actual hiking trail? You've got options: plot your course for an easier or longer way up, or down. Starting at Schoodic Woods Campground, Buck Cove Mountain Trail—Schoodic's longest at 3.2 miles—summits its namesake before climbing Schoodic Head's north face. On the southeastern side, the challenging 1.1-mile Anvil trail links with 0.6-mile Schoodic Head Trail to the summit, as does the easy 0.6-mile Alder Trail. Trailheads for both are along the loop drive near the Blueberry Hill parking area; hikers often combine them. A bit farther is a terminus for the ½-mile East Trail; this challenging, steep climb up Schoodic Head's east face connects, near the summit, with Schoodic Head Trail. Regardless of your route, on a clear day atop Schoodic Head, spectacular views flow across the forested peninsula and island-dotted Frenchman Bay to Cadillac Mountain. ⊠ *Schoodic Loop Rd.* ☎ *207/288–3338* ⊕ *nps.gov/acad.*

VISITOR CENTERS

Rockefeller Welcome Center

VISITOR CENTER | FAMILY | This impressive 1934 structure resembles a mansion but was built as housing for personnel at the U.S. Navy base that operated on Schoodic Peninsula for decades. Now part of Schoodic Institute, an Acadia-affiliated research and education nonprofit, the first floor houses a seasonal park welcome center. You can get information, watch a video about Schoodic, and check out kid-friendly exhibits about this neck of Acadia and the navy base. There's a small gift shop area. An automated fee machine inside the gatehouse at the complex's entrance sells Acadia weekly park passes. ⊠ *1 Atterbury Circle, Winter Harbor* ✛ *Off Arey Cove Rd.* ☎ *207/288–3338* ⊕ *nps.gov/acad.*

Schoodic Woods Ranger Station

VISITOR CENTER | FAMILY | Built with materials from the surrounding region and opened in 2015 along with the campground here, this striking post-and-beam structure serves double duty as campground host and information center—Acadia passes and Federal Lands passes are sold. Inside, a large Schoodic District relief map centers the room, which has a gift shop area and exhibits, some hands-on, about the park. Comfy chairs flank a fireplace, inviting visitors to relax, pamphlet in hand, after chatting with a ranger or park volunteer. Outside, the setting is village-like, with walkways and handsome signage for bike paths that converge here, a stop for the free Island Explorer buses, and restrooms in a cabin-like building. Trailheads for 3.2-mile Buck Cove Mountain and 1.5-mile Lower Harbor trails are nearby. A campground amphitheater hosts ranger programs for park visitors and campers. ⊠ *54 Farview Dr., Winter Harbor* ✛ *Off Schoodic Loop Rd.* ☎ *207/288–3338* ⊕ *nps.gov/acad* ⊗ *Closed late Oct.–mid-May.*

Isle Au Haut

6 miles south of Stonington via ferry.

French explorer Samuel D. Champlain discovered Isle au Haut—or "High Island"—in 1604, but native populations left heaps of oyster shells here prior to his arrival. The only ferry is a passenger-only "mail boat" out of Stonington, but the 45-minute journey is well worth the effort. Acadia National Park covers about half of the island, with miles of rugged trails, and the boat will drop visitors off in the park at Duck Harbor in peak season. The park ranger station (restroom) is a quarter mile from the Town Landing, and from there it's about 4 miles to Duck Harbor. To get there, hit the trail or walk (or bike) the unpaved road, a slightly longer but faster route. Isle au Haut has a small general store and a gift shop but no restaurants or inns, though there are vacation rentals. There's one main road: partly paved and partly unpaved, it circles the island and goes through the park.

Book a Carriage Ride 👁

Riding down one of the park's scenic carriage roads in a horse-drawn carriage is a classic way to experience Acadia. Carriages of Acadia (⊕ *www.acadiahorses. com,* ☎ *877/276–3622*) offers rides out of Wildwood Stables in the park from late May to mid-October. Reservations are strongly recommended and can only be made by phone. There is a wheelchair-accessible carriage as well as a step stool to assist with boarding.

👁 Sights

SCENIC STOPS

Duck Harbor

MARINA/PIER | Acadia National Park's most primitive (and therefore secluded) campground is here, as is a dock for the passenger-only ferry that serves Isle au Haut from Stonington. Duck Harbor (there's a composting toilet) is the best jumping off point for the 18 miles of trails in the park, which lead through woods and to rocky shoreline, marshes, bogs, and a freshwater lake. Note that the ferry only stops at Duck Harbor from early June through early October. Off-season or if you miss the boat, you'll be hoofing it about 4 miles to the Isle au Haut Town Landing. Bring your bike or kayak for an extra fee or rent a bike from the ferry service. *Note: Kayaks and bikes are dropped off and picked up at the Town Landing only, not at Duck Harbor.* ⊠ *Duck Harbor, Isle Au Haut* ☎ *207/288–3338* ⊕ *nps.gov/acad.*

Western Head

TRAIL | Located at the southern tip of remote Isle au Haut, Western Head is accessible by foot or bicycle from the Town Landing. There are no amenities, so be sure to pack plenty of water and snacks.

Western Head Trail is most often hiked as a loop that includes Western Head Road and Cliff Trail (*bicycles are not allowed on trails*). Starting from Duck Harbor (*the ferry doesn't drop bikes off here, only at the Town Landing*) on the unpaved road, it's approximately 4 miles round-trip. Once off the wooded road, the trail alternates between forest and volcanic rock clifftop, with opportunities to go off-course and explore the rocky shoreline. Dramatic coastal cliff views are your reward for visiting perhaps the most remote corner of Acadia National Park. ⊠ *Isle Au Haut* ☏ *207/288–3338* ⊕ *nps.gov/acad.*

🏃 Activities

The best way to see Acadia National Park is to get out of your vehicle and explore on foot or by bicycle or boat. There are 45 miles of carriage roads that are perfect for walking and biking in the warmer months and for cross-country skiing and snowshoeing in winter. There are more than 150 miles of trails for hiking; numerous ponds and lakes for canoeing, kayaking, standup paddle boarding, fishing, and boating; a handful of beaches for swimming; and steep cliffs for rock climbing.

BIKING
Exploring Acadia National Park on a bike can be heavenly, and there are a variety of surfaces from paved to gravel, inland to seaside; always check ahead of time for trail closures. A park pass is required to ride anywhere within park boundaries; be sure to carry your pass or leave it in view in your parked car. On carriage roads, bicyclists must yield to everyone, including horses, and not exceed 20 mph; in winter, bikes are not permitted on carriage roads groomed for cross-country skiing. Bikes are allowed on carriage roads; biking Park Loop Road during peak season is discouraged as it's narrow, often congested, and lacks shoulders. Cyclists must ride with the flow of traffic where the road is one-way.

Seasonal Island Explorer buses that have four or six bike racks operate between Bar Harbor and Eagle Lake carriage road. Pick up a free carriage road map at the park's Hulls Cove Visitor Center or Nature Center, or download it from the website.

BIRD-WATCHING
Acadia National Park is for the birds—much to the enjoyment of birders of a feather from all corners. Famed ornithologist and avian illustrator Roger Tory Peterson is known to have deemed Mount Desert Island as "the warbler capital of the world." More than 20 species of the energetic and colorful songbirds breed here, while 300-plus bird species have been "encountered in or around the park," according to the National Park Service. The park's website outlines a dozen areas rich in birdwatching opportunities. Come fall, park rangers lead hawk watches from the summit of Cadillac Mountain, counting hundreds and even thousands of migrating raptors. In addition to its namesake tours, Bar Harbor Whale Watch Co. offers cruises that seek out the comically colorful seabird known as the puffin.

EDUCATIONAL PROGRAMS
The National Park Service offers a variety of ranger-led programming and tours, including the popular Junior Ranger Program for kids and, unique to Acadia National Park, citizen science opportunities at the Schoodic Institute, based at the mainland section on Schoodic Peninsula. Two ranger-led boat tours depart from Mount Desert Island. Out of Northeast Harbor, Islesford Historic and Scenic Cruise travels Somes Sounds and stops at Islesford on Little Cranberry Island to tour the park's Islesford Historic Museum. Departing from Bar Harbor, Baker Island Cruise follows the shoreline en route to Baker Island nine miles away. Passengers explore the island and check out its namesake light and an old homestead. Virtually all of Baker Island, including the lighthouse, is part of

Acadia. Baker Island doesn't have a year-round population and like Little Cranberry is part of the Cranberry Isles. *Visit the park website for more information.*

FLIGHTSEEING

Viewing the Acadia National Park region from above is a great way to get your bearings for your on-the-ground (and on-the-water) explorations, and perhaps the easiest way to wrap your arms around the sheer variety of scenery and attractions.

★ Scenic Flights of Acadia

AIR EXCURSIONS | For $144 per person, Scenic Flights of Acadia offers a 35-minute tour around the shoreline of Mount Desert Island, plus three other tours and fall foliage trips that fly over some of the island but head inland for the best color. Trips are out of Hancock County–Bar Harbor Airport. You can make reservations online or by phone; in Bar Harbor tickets are sold at Acadia Stand Up Paddle Boarding (*200 Main Street*). ✉ *1044 Bar Harbor Rd., Rte. 3, Trenton* ☎ *207/667–6527* ⊕ *www.scenicflightsofacadia.com.*

HIKING

Acadia National Park maintains more than 150 miles of hiking trails. Generally rocky and rooted, many are steep and require scrambling: most visitors find hiking here harder than expected. Even trails that aren't that difficult may take longer than you think. But there is a range of options, from easier strolls around lakes and mostly level paths to rigorous treks with climbs up rock faces and scrambles along cliffs. Whatever you have in mind, park rangers can help you plan hikes and walks that fit your abilities and time frame. Although trails are concentrated on the east side of the island, where they often connect with the park's carriage roads, the west side has plenty of scenic ones, too. For those wishing for a longer trek, try hiking up Cadillac Mountain or Dorr Mountain; Parkman, Sargeant, and Penobscot mountains are also good options. Most hiking is done mid-May–mid-November. In winter, cross-country skiing and snowshoeing replace hiking, assuming enough snow flies. Melting snow and ice can create precarious conditions in early to mid-spring.

■ TIP→ **Every so often folks die in Acadia National Park, from falling off trails or cliffs or being swept out to sea. The rocky shore can be gravelly and slippery—so watch your step. In springtime, conditions may seem fine for hiking until you get on a trail where shade has kept ice and snow intact or mud lingers from snowmelt.**

MULTISPORT OUTFITTERS

Name just about any popular sporting activity—kayaking, cycling, rock climbing, cross-country skiing, and snowshoeing, to say nothing of hiking—and chances are you can do it at Acadia National Park. Cadillac Mountain Sports (⊕ *www.cadillacsports.com*), with locations in Bar Harbor and Ellsworth, sells what you need to do all of them, and their staff will be happy to answer your questions and offer advice for where to go to exert yourself.

SWIMMING

The park has three swimming beaches. Sand Beach on Park Loop Road and Echo Lake Beach off Route 102 are the largest and most popular, with changing rooms and sometimes lifeguards on duty. Neither are found at Lake Wood, but its small, secluded beach is near Hulls Cove Visitor Center (the access road to the beach doesn't open until June 1).

Index

Photo Credits

Front Cover: Ron and Patty Thomas/ GettyImages [**Description:** Autumn country side in the Green Mountains, Vermont / New England autumn; charming autumn country side; rustic barn with autumn color]. **Back cover, from left to right:** Sean Pavone/Shutterstock. Boudewijn Sluijk/Shutterstock. Sean Pavone/Shutterstock. **Spine:** Cdrin/Shutterstock. **Interior, from left to right:** Kirkikis/iStockphoto (1). LorenzattoPhotos/iStockphoto (2-3). Bill Florence/Shutterstock (5). **Chapter 1: Experience Maine,Vermont and New Hampshire:** Doug Lemke/Shutterstock (6-7). James Kirkikis/Shutterstock (8-9). Nick Cote/Maine Office of Tourism (9). Vermont Elm/Shutterstock (9). QualityHD/Shutterstock (10). Calvin Henderson/Shutterstock (10). Courtesy of NH Tourism Board (10). DonLand/Shutterstock (10). Flashbacknyc/Shutterstock (11). Jejim/Shutterstock (11). Courtesy of Maine Office of Tourism (12). TJ Muzeni Photography (12). Kelsey Neukum/Shutterstock (12). Cindy Creighton/Shutterstock (12). Jon Bilous/ Shutterstock (13). Jiawangkun/Shutterstock (13). Mathew Trogner/Allagash Brewing Company (16). Shannonís Unshelled/Shack (16). Ron Gay/Flickr (16). Jenniffer Bakos Photography2015 (16). LS First Light LH (16). Mia & Steve Mestdagh/Flickr (17). Daryl Getman/DAGphotog.com (17). The Highroller Lobster Co (17). Due Mele/Wikimedia Commons (17). Kelsey Gayle (17). Agnes Kantaruk/Shutterstock (18). Punkbarby0/Shutterstock (18). Bogdanhoda/Dreamstime (18). TravnikovStudio/Shutterstock (18). Bhofack2/Dreamstime (18). Alexander Sviridov/ Shutterstock (19). Viiviien/Shutterstock (19). Dennis W Donohue/Shutterstock (19). E.J.Johnson Photography/Shutterstock (19). Daniel Rossi Limpi/Shutterstock (19). Snehit/Shutterstock (20). Leo W Kowal/Shutterstock (20). Adam Nixon Photography/Shutterstock (20). E.J.Johnson Photography/Shutterstock (21). Kate Sfeir/Shutterstock (21). TonyBaldasaro/Shutterstock (22). Due_mele/Roque Bluffs State Park, ME/Wikimedia Commons (22). Christine Anuszewski/ Adirondack Chairs (22). Eric Cote/Shutterstock (23). Anthony Dolan/Shutterstock (23). Lucky-photographer/Shutterstock (24). Courtesy of Maine Maritime Museum (24). Jiawangkun/ Shutterstock (24). Zack Frank/Shutterstock (25). Andy Duback Photography (25). SamaraHeisz5/Shutterstock (26). Xiaolin Zhang/Shutterstock (26). Sojourn Bicycling & Active Vacations (26). Songquan Deng/Shutterstock (27). Ricky Batista/Shutterstock (27). **Chapter 3: Best Fall Foliage Drives and Road Trips:** Aivoges/Dreamstime (51). Rabbit75_ist/iStockphoto (52-53). Michał Krakowiak/iStockphoto (55). Liliboas/iStockphoto (55). Adventure_Photo/ iStockphoto (55). Steffen Foerster Photography/Shutterstock (55). Magdasmith/iStockphoto (55). Michał Krakowiak/iStockphoto (55). Denis Jr. Tangney/pixels (56). Kevin Davidson/ iStockphoto (56). Kindra Clineff Photography (57). DonLand/iStockphoto (58). Donland/ Dreamstime (59). Sharan Singh/iStockphoto (60). Leesniderphotoimages/Dreamstime (61). Denis Tangney Jr./iStockphoto (62). Jill_InspiredByDesign/iStockphoto (63). DrPospisil/ Shutterstock (64). The Wilhelm Reich Infant Trust (65). **Chapter 4: Vermont:** Sean Pavone/iStockphoto (67). Alizada Studios/Shutterstock (79). Vtphotos/Dreamstime (86). Simon Pearce (99). DaleBHalbur/iStockphoto (102). Jonathan A. Mauer/Shutterstock (115). Don Landwehrle/Shutterstock (123). Skye Chalmers Photography (124). FashionStock.com/ Shutterstock (125). Hubert Schriebl (125). Marcio Silva/Shutterstock (126). Hubert Schriebl (126). Smugglers Notch Resort/Ski Vermont (127). Okemo Mountain Resort (128). Sean Pavone/iStockphoto (143). Sean Pavone/shutterstock (149). Meg M/Shutterstock (152). **Chapter 5: New Hampshire:** Sepavo/Dreamstime (155). Edella/Dreamstime (166). DenisTangneyJr/iStockphoto (170). Denis Tangney Jr./iStockphoto (178). Zack Frank/ Shutterstock (181). Kindra Clineff/Lake Winnipesaukee (183). Appalachianviews/ Dreamstime (198). BlacklistMauer/Dreamstime (209). Liz Van Steenburgh/Shutterstock (209). Jim Lozouski/Shutterstock (210). REI/Mike Kautz, Courtesy of AMC (211). Nialat/Shutterstock (212). RestonImages/Shutterstock (212). Nialat/Shutterstock (212). Jadimages/Shutterstock (213). Rebvt/Shutterstock (213). Ansgar Walk/wikipedia (213). J. Carmichael/wikipedia (213). Matty Symons/Shutterstock (215). Danita Delimont/Alamy (216). MRicart_Photography/Shutterstock (217). Jet Lowe/Wikimedia Commons (228). George Carmichael (234). **Chapter 6: Inland Maine:** E.J.Johnson Photography/Shutterstock (243). Mountinez/iStockphoto (258). Kazela/ Shutterstock (273). **Chapter 7: The Maine Coast:** Visit Maine (277). Kirkikisphoto/Dreamstime (290). Lewis Directed Films/Shutterstock (297). James Mattil/Shutterstock (304). Flashbacknyc/Shutterstock (324). Sean Pavone/Shutterstock (325). Maine State Museum (326). Allan Wood Photography/Shutterstock (326). Paul D. Lemke/iStockphoto (327). Bill Florence/Shutterstock (328). Robert Campbell (329). Casey Jordan (329). Dave Johnston (329). Paul Dionne/iStockphoto (330). Doug Lemke/Shutterstock (330). Imel9000/iStockphoto (330). Spwidoff/Shutterstock (335). Kindra Clineff/Desert Island,Southwest Harbor (355). Kindra Clineff Photography/Down East,Jonesport,Wild Blueberry Harvest (363). **Chapter 8: Acadia National Park:** Try Media/ iStockphoto (371). f11photo/Shutterstock (384). **About Our Writers:** All photos are courtesy of the writers.

*Every effort has been made to trace the copyright holders, and we apologize in advance for any accidental errors. We would be happy to apply the corrections in the following edition of this publication.

Notes

Fodor's MAINE, VERMONT, AND NEW HAMPSHIRE

Publisher: Stephen Horowitz, *General Manager*

Editorial: Douglas Stallings, *Editorial Director;* Jill Fergus, Amanda Sadlowski, *Senior Editors;* Brian Eschrich, Alexis Kelly, *Editors;* Angelique Kennedy-Chavannes, *Assistant Editor*

Design: Tina Malaney, *Director of Design and Production;* Jessica Gonzalez, *Senior Designer;* Erin Caceres, *Graphic Design Associate*

Production: Jennifer DePrima, *Editorial Production Manager;* Elyse Rozelle, *Senior Production Editor;* Monica White, *Production Editor*

Maps: Rebecca Baer, *Senior Map Editor;* Mark Stroud (Moon Street Cartography) and David Lindroth, *Cartographers*

Photography: Viviane Teles, *Senior Photo Editor;* Namrata Aggarwal, Neha Gupta, Payal Gupta, Ashok Kumar, *Photo Editors;* Eddie Aldrete, *Photo Production Intern;* Kadeem McPherson, *Photo Production Associate Intern*

Business and Operations: Chuck Hoover, *Chief Marketing Officer;* Robert Ames, *Group General Manager*

Public Relations and Marketing: Joe Ewaskiw, *Senior Director of Communications and Public Relations*

Fodors.com: Jeremy Tarr, *Editorial Director;* Rachael Levitt, *Managing Editor*

Technology: Jon Atkinson, *Director of Technology;* Rudresh Teotia, *Associate Director of Technology;* Alison Lieu, *Project Manager*

Writers: Jordan Barry, Andrew Collins, Alexandra Hall, Jessica Kelly, Annie Quigley, Christine Burns Rudalevige, Mary Ruoff, Mimi Steadman

Editor: Alexis Kelly, Douglas Stallings

Production Editor: Monica White

18th Edition

ISBN 9-781-64097-604-7

ISSN 1073-6581

All details in this book are based on information supplied to us at press time. Always confirm information when it matters, especially if you're making a detour to visit a specific place. Fodor's expressly disclaims any liability, loss, or risk, personal or otherwise, that is incurred as a consequence of the use of any of the contents of this book.

SPECIAL SALES
This book is available at special discounts for bulk purchases for sales promotions or premiums. For more information, e-mail SpecialMarkets@fodors.com.

PRINTED IN CANADA

10 9 8 7 6 5 4 3 2 1

MIX
Paper from responsible sources
FSC® C016245

About Our Writers

 Jordan Barry is a food writer for *Seven Days,* an alt-weekly newspaper based in Burlington, Vermont. She previously produced podcasts for Heritage Radio Network and Food52, and researched language development in the American cider industry as part of a master's degree in food studies at New York University. Barry grew up in Norman Rockwell's Arlington and now lives in Vergennes, Vermont's smallest city. You can follow her on Instagram @jordankbarry. She updated the Vermont chapter.

 Former Fodor's staff editor **Andrew Collins** is based in Mexico City, but spends much of his time in a small village in New Hampshire's Lake Sunapee region. A long-time contributor to more than 200 Fodor's guidebooks, he's also written for dozens of mainstream and LGBTQ+ publications including *Travel + Leisure, New Mexico Magazine, AAA Living,* and *The Advocate.* In addition, Collins teaches travel writing and food writing for New York City's Gotham Writers Workshop. Follow him on Instagram @TravelAndrew or at ⊕ *AndrewsTraveling.com.* He updated the Experience and Travel Smart chapters.

 Freelance writer and former newspaper reporter **Mary Ruoff** has written travel articles about her adopted state for the *Portland Press Herald* and other publications. During her career, she's covered many other subjects too, including shoe retailing, veterans, and locally grown foods. A St. Louis native, Mary has several journalism awards and a bachelor of journalism from Missouri School of Journalism. Her go-to Mainer is her husband, Michael Hodsdon, a mariner and grandson of a Down East fisherman. They live in Belfast. She updated Inland Maine, Acadia National Park, and parts of Maine Coast.

 Jessica Kelly is a food and travel journalist and photographer living in New York. Her work has appeared in *Condé Nast Traveler, Global Traveler, Elite Traveler, Insider, Wine Enthusiast, Kitchn, AAA World Magazine, Cosmopolitan, Food52, Eater, Food & Wine,* Thrillist, *Bon Appétit,* Matador Network, *Hemispheres,* Lonely Planet, and more. You can follow her on Instagram @Adventures.Are.Waiting. She updated parts of the Vermont chapter.

The Maine Coast chapter was updated by **Andrew Collins, Alexandra Hall, Annie Quigley, Christine Burns Rudalevige, Mary Ruoff,** and **Mimi Steadman.**